Baseball Playbook

by
RON POLK

foreword by
John Grisham

Visit TheBaseballPlaybook.com for more information!

DEDICATED TO . . .

All baseball coaches and players who have an interest in teaching and learning this great game.

ACKNOWLEDGMENTS

I wish to thank the following individuals who have made significant contributions to this Playbook. Luis Brande, Bo Carter, Mark Johnson, Straton Karatassos, Pat McMahon, Charles Scoggins and David Yukelson.

Along with those who have made a contribution to this Playbook, I can never forget all the coaches and players I have had the pleasure to work with in my coaching career who indirectly have made the biggest contribution in providing me with the incentive to put this Playbook together.

TABLE OF CONTENTS

Foreword – by John Grisham

I was a student at Mississippi State in 1976 when Ron Polk was hired to revive a declining program. This was before he was a published author. He quickly proved that he knew how to coach, but like many of us who sooner or later secretly put pen to paper, he showed no signs of literary potential.

There comes a time in the life of every author when inspiration spills forth, when the ideas cannot be contained any longer, when words have to be arranged in some fashion on paper so they can be saved forever.

Same with baseball coaches, or at least some of them. Ron Polk's knowledge of the game became so vast that he had to write this book just to store everything. His playbook is the most comprehensive collection of baseball basics, planning and strategies you'll find anywhere.

In 1993, Coach Polk came to dinner, but before we ate there was a little league game to be played. Coaching kids is nerve-wracking enough, but with a legendary college coach sitting in the bleachers watching every move, I, well, I choked. Didn't bunt. Didn't change pitchers. Didn't do this or that or a dozen other basic strategies covered in great detail in the following pages. After dinner, Coach Polk gave me a copy of his *Baseball Playbook*. I read it for hours one weekend. I pored over the diagrams, studied charts, read and re-read things I should've already known. After three days with this book, I was a new coach.

We lost our next six games, and, with the parents in open revolt, I put Polk away for awhile. I'd like to say we rallied and won the city championship, but fiction can only take me so far.

After my coaching career came mercifully to a close, I began reading his book for pleasure. No kidding. Coaching made me realize how little I knew about the game, but my love for baseball still drives me to a deeper understanding. I collect and read baseball books of all varieties – biography, humor, rules, how-to, strategy, even fiction, but when I want the final word on why a player did this or if he should have done that, I always go back to Ron Polk.

Baseball is a wonderfully complicated game. *The Baseball Playbook* is a superb manual in trying to understand it.

BASEBALL POLICIES AND REGULATIONS

It is very important as one begins the new season that both player and coach come to some common agreement as to the policies and regulations that will be in effect for the entire academic and athletic year.

These policies and regulations should be given and explained to each of the players at the first meeting of the squad so that there is no misunderstanding as to what the players can expect from the coaching staff and the baseball program itself.

It is quite beneficial that each player have an opportunity to individually discuss these policies and regulations with the head coach sometime during the year. In this way the coach might receive positive or negative feedback from each of the players in assisting him in formulating the succeeding year's policies and regulations.

Of course, they must be strictly adhered to throughout the course of the year so that both player and coach have a firm understanding of their importance to the program and that everyone always knows what is expected of them.

On the following pages you will find an example of the policies and regulations that might be in effect during the course of a season so that you might have a better understanding as to what might be entailed in drawing up this information.

NAME OF SCHOOL
BASEBALL POLICIES AND REGULATIONS

1. GENERAL PURPOSE FOR YOUR BEING AT _____:
        NAME OF SCHOOL

    A. To get an education, and to graduate from this school, and hopefully, to go on and get an advanced degree.

    B. To participate in the baseball program, and to assist your team in winning the conference championship. At the same time, with a little determination and ability, an opportunity to play professional baseball.

    C. To develop life long friends in an atmosphere of cordiality and purpose, both on and off the baseball field.

2. AS BASEBALL COACHES, IT IS OUR RESPONSIBILITY TO ASSIST YOU IN THE ABOVE. WE WILL DO THIS BY:

    A. Monitoring your courses and grades to insure that you are faithfully attending class and doing the work necessary to achieve graduation.

    B. Giving you the best possible baseball education to assure that you respond properly on the playing field so that your team may achieve the goal of winning the conference championship, and to allow you the opportunity to develop your skills to make you more attractive to professional baseball scouts.

    C. Placing you in a proper environment, both on and off the field, so that you may be allowed every opportunity to enjoy your stay at _____.
        NAME OF SCHOOL

3. TEAM POLICIES TO INSURE THE ABOVE:

    A. Appearance:

        1. You will be REQUESTED to dress properly around the campus as you represent yourself and the baseball program.

        2. During the Fall practice season and the entire Spring season, you will be REQUIRED to follow the below standards in regard to appearance:

            a. There will be no beards, nor facial hair. Mustaches will be allowed but they must be neatly trimmed at all times. You must have a clean shave each day.

            b. Sideburns may come down to the bottom of the earlobe and must be neatly trimmed.

            c. Hair may come down over the top of the ear, but no lower than one-quarter way down on the ear itself. Hair must be neatly tapered on the back.

        3. Your practice and game uniform will be laundered for you, but you will be REQUIRED to wear it properly.

        4. Your shoes for practice sessions will be BRUSHED.

        5. Your shoes for game days will be SHINED.

    B. Class Attendance:

        1. You will attend classes REGULARLY and ON TIME.

        2. You will not use as an excuse to miss practice any class assignment nor exam preparation unless that class assignment or exam is in direct conflict with the practice session. You will prepare yourself for assignments and exams over the entire semester, not on the last day.

2

3. No tutors or assistance will be provided any baseball player if it is found that academic difficulties are the result of poor attendance. This prohibition on assistance will be re-evaluated each semester.

4. No coach will intercede on your behalf with any instructor to allow you to circumvent any assignment due to the fact that you are a member of the baseball team, unless such assignment was missed due to the fact that the team was involved with games on the road.

5. Your first responsibility will be your classes. Your second responsibility will be the baseball team. They are both very important to you and the coaches.

C. Conduct On and Off the Field:

1. You will be expected to conduct yourself in a first class manner around campus and in the community.

2. You will be allowed to participate in any campus sponsored activity as long as it does not interfere with your classes and/or baseball.

3. Smoking:

a. If any baseball player is a cigarette or cigar smoker, he will declare himself as such to the coaching staff. This will mean that if a member of the coaching staff observes a declared smoker off campus smoking, then he will not be suspended. We are hoping that no one is a declared smoker. If so, we further hope that he will make every attempt to kick the habit. A declared smoker is not allowed to smoke on campus or on any baseball road trip.

b. If a player does not declare himself as a smoker, and is found smoking at any time, then he will be suspended for the duration of the year. This holds true also for a declared smoker who is found smoking on campus or on a road trip.

4. Chewing Tobacco:

a. We will allow any player to chew tobacco on or off the playing field as long as it does not show grotesquely.

b. You will refrain from spitting inside the dugout without using a container, in the locker room, or any area of the baseball stadium that the tobacco juice will not blend into the ground.

5. Drinking:

a. There will not be any declared drinkers.

b. You will be REQUIRED to refrain from any drinking of alcoholic beverages both on and off the campus. Off campus means anywhere in the county. This also includes the refraining from drinking on any road trips.

c. If caught drinking by any member of the coaching staff while in the county or on a road trip then you will be immediately suspended for the duration of the year.

6. Drugs:

a. You will be REQUIRED to refrain from partaking of drugs that are not prescribed by a physician.

b. If caught by any member of the coaching staff, you will be immediately suspended for the duration of the year, and possibly suspended from any future participation in the baseball program.

7. Swearing:

a. We are going to ask you to completely refrain from using any swear words. We will allow a short period of adjustment for those who have built up any bad habits.

D. Practice and Game Schedules:

1. All practice and pre-game schedules will be posted in the dormitory and locker room by 10:30 a.m. each day. You will be REQUIRED to read this schedule and know exactly what your responsibilities are before you get on the field.

2. Practice and pre-game schedules will be individually adjusted in order to insure that everyone has ample time to be present.

3. If for some reason you will be absent or late for practice, you will personally talk by phone or in person with one of the coaches prior to the scheduled time of practice, preferably well in advance so that adjustments can be made in the schedule.

4. You will allow yourself ample opportunity to perform all the prescribed stretching exercises in the outfield prior to the scheduled time of practice.

5. There will be NO excuses accepted for being late unless we are notified in advance. If you must use the training room for treatment, this will be done prior to practice and it will not interfere with your being on the field on time. Exceptions to this can be made if notified well in advance.

6. Anyone late for practice will be required to run a mile under 6:15 the next morning before they are eligible for practice or a game the next day.

7. No one will leave a practice session or game without prior approval of one of the coaches.

E. Injuries and Sickness:

1. All injuries and sickness will be reported immediately to the coaches and trainers so that treatment can be initiated as promptly as possible.

2. The team trainers and physicians will prescribe the limitations on practice and game performance.

F. Locker Room Procedure:

1. You will be EXPECTED to assist the team managers in keeping the locker room in first class condition. All trash will be properly disposed of in the trash containers located in the locker room.

2. No spikes will be worn in any part of the fieldhouse or locker room. All shoes will be cleaned off on the grass area next to the baseball field.

3. There will be absolutely NO horseplay in the locker room.

G. Equipment Room Procedure:

1. No one except the coaches and managers will be allowed in the equipment room. All equipment will be issued by the managers and coaches.

2. You will be responsible for any equipment issued. If you take it from the locker room you are responsible for it, so would advise you to leave all your equipment in the locker room so it will be safe.

3. You will be REQUIRED to take care of your equipment in a first class manner.

FIRST MEETING

In addition to the explanation of the policies and regulations at the first meeting of the players, it is very important that other matters and items of interest to the players should be detailed. An example of these items would be:

1. Introduction of the coaches
2. Introduction of the managers
3. Introduction of the trainers
4. Explanation of eligibility rules for participation
5. Registration procedure to insure proper class scheduling
6. Uniform requirements for first practice sessions
7. Physical examination information
8. Health and medical insurance information
9. Pre-season weight training and conditioning schedule
10. Field maintenance schedules
11. Laundry information
12. Review stretching exercises that will be used at practice
13. Discuss practice procedure
14. Discuss evaluation criteria used by coaches
15. First practice session - date and time
16. Coaches office hours
17. Game schedule information

At this first meeting each player should complete an information sheet similar to the one on the next page along with a class schedule on the following page.

PLAYER INFORMATION SHEET

Note: This information sheet can be used for a high school or college team.

1. NAME _____ / _____ / _____ / _____
          (Last)   (First)   (Middle)   (Nickname)

2. LOCAL ADDRESS _____ / _____ / _____
        (Street Address or PO #)   (City, State)   (Zip)

3. PARENTS' NAME _____ / _____
          (Father)   (Mother)

4. PARENT'S ADDRESS _____ / _____ / _____
        (Street Address or PO #)   (City, State)   (Zip)

5. BIRTH DATE _____ / _____ / _____ / _____ / _____
        (Month) (Day) (Year)   (City)   (State)

6. AGE _____   7. MAJOR IN SCHOOL _____

8. YEAR IN SCHOOL _____   9. TELEPHONE # (SCHOOL) _____

10. TELEPHONE # (PARENTS) (____) _____

11. SOCIAL SECURITY NUMBER _____

12. PRIMARY POSITION PLAYED _____ SECONDARY POSITION _____

13. LIST ALL HIGH SCHOOLS, JUNIOR COLLEGES OR FOUR YEAR COLLEGES ATTENDED:

NAME OF SCHOOL	YEAR(S) ATTENDED	PLAYED BASEBALL	
_____	_____	YES ( )	NO ( )
_____	_____	YES ( )	NO ( )
_____	_____	YES ( )	NO ( )
_____	_____	YES ( )	NO ( )

14. HAVE YOU EVER BEEN DRAFTED BY A PROFESSIONAL TEAM: YES ( )   NO ( )

15. NAME OF CLUB DRAFTED BY _____ YEAR DRAFTED _____

16. CAP SIZE _____   17. WAIST SIZE _____

18. SHOE SIZE _____   19. SHIRT SIZE _____

20. DO YOU RECEIVE ANY GOVERNMENT AID WHILE ATTENDING SCHOOL: YES ( ) NO ( ).
    IF YES, LIST NAME OF GRANT AND AMOUNT.

    1. _____ _____

    2. _____ _____

    3. _____ _____

CLASS SCHEDULE

TERM _____ 19_____

NAME _____

DORM/APT. NAME _____

RM/APT. # _____ PHONE _____

HOME ADDRESS _____

SPORT _____

YEAR IN SCHOOL _____

SOCIAL SECURITY # _____

PARENTS' NAMES _____

HOME PHONE NUMBER (___) _____

MONDAY — WEDNESDAY — FRIDAY CLASSES							TUESDAY — THURSDAY CLASSES						
COURSE # & NAME	SEC	CRS	CLASS BEGINS	CLASS ENDS	ROOM	PROFESSOR	COURSE # & NAME	SEC	CRS	CLASS BEGINS	CLASS ENDS	ROOM	PROFESSOR

COMMENTS:

BASEBALL SIGNS

After the policies and regulations in each player's Playbook should come a complete summary of the signs which will be used during the course of the season.

By having this information in the hands of each player and coach it saves valuable practice time which can be devoted to other areas of concern. It also enables the player who has a tough time grasping signs an opportunity to spend additional time studying and comprehending them.

It is very important that the coach not only list the signs that will be used, but also, to explain what the objective of each sign is. Since signs might change from year to year it might be best to leave a blank space in the player's Playbook for the actual signs and have each player fill them in when you go over this area in the Playbook.

By having this information in each player's hand there should be very little reason for an offensive or defensive sign being missed during the course of the season.

Following you will find an example of how the signs can be incorporated into the Playbook.

proper reaction can be made to a batted ball. With no strikes on the hitter the runner does not have to look in for the batter will not be hitting the ball.

4. With a 3-2 or 3-1 count on the batter, all baserunners must be sure that they do not get picked off and should steal unless they get a terrible jump. This will just about be an automatic steal when runners are forced to advance if the batter walks, especially with the 3-2 count.

5. If the steal sign is flashed and the runner does not get a good jump the coach will have to give you the steal sign again. If the coach does not give the runner the steal sign on the next pitch, then the steal is off until it is put on again.

6. There will never be any stealing when we are well ahead in the score. Well ahead would generally be about eight or nine runs from the first through the sixth inning, seven runs in the sixth, six runs in the seventh, and five runs in the eighth or ninth. This policy can change when taking into consideration the caliber of the team we are playing.

STEALING THIRD BASE

1. The steal sign for stealing thirdbase will be the same for stealing second base.

2. Each baserunner should know his proper lead at second base as he should at all bases.

3. The leads that we can use from second base are:

   A. **Standard lead**—This lead is generally one step and a dive from second base (approximately 15 feet). Can be a little wider for the quick runner. This lead should be two feet back from the direct line from second to third base when there is no force at third base. With a force at third base the runner should be in the path between the two bases. The standard lead is a stationary lead with movement toward third base when the pitcher commits himself to home plate. Movement back to second base should only occur on a pick-off attempt by the pitcher. No verbal help is needed from the third base coach in this lead.

   B. **Aggressive lead**—Starting from the standard lead off position the baserunner at second base allows the third base coach to increase his lead by verbal commands. These verbal commands are: ''right there'', or no sound indicating that the runner stays in that spot; ''okay one'' means to increase the lead by one complete shuffle step; ''back one'' means to decrease your lead by one complete shuffle step; a loud command of ''back'' means a quick cross-over step and return to the base as quickly as possible using a head first dive if there is a throw from the pitcher. The third base coach can bring the runner further off the base or back to the base by using the verbal command ''okay one'' or ''back one'' two or more times, one for each step he wants the runner to take.

   C. **Two out lead**—With two outs the baserunner positions himself in a short lead position (approximately 12' down the line and 10' directly back toward left field). This lead can be wider or closer depending on the ability of the runner. As the pitcher commits himself to the plate, the runner starts his walking lead toward third base. It is important that the baserunner remain in a straight line from his initial spot as he walks toward third base. This type of lead is used to eliminate having to take a wide turn at third base when attempting to score. There will be no commands from the third base coach on the two out lead unless the steal sign is on and the coach wishes to get the runner a little further off the base.

HIT AND RUN SIGN

1. The sign for the hit and run is:_____.

2. The batter will swing at any pitch that the catcher can reasonably handle. The batter must make contact on a hittable pitch, hopefully on the ground. If the pitch is well outside the strike zone and one that the catcher cannot handle without great effort, the batter will not swing. Preferably, we are looking for a ball hit to the opposite field especially with a righthanded hitter up.

3. At no time should a baserunner be picked off base when the hit and run sign is flashed. The runner must go even if he does not get a good jump for the batter will be swinging the bat to make contact. As on the steal, the runner must look into the plate area at the time the ball reaches the hitter.

4. We can hit and run with a runner at: first base only; first and third base; and first and second base.

RUN AND HIT SIGN

1. Many times the third base coach will not want the batter to know we are stealing so he will give the hit sign to the batter (clap his hands so the hitter turns to face the pitcher) and then quickly gives the steal sign to the runner. For this reason, we always want the runners to check the third base coach right after he finishes clapping his hands to the batter for he might follow with a quick set of signs for the baserunner(s).

FIRST AND THIRD DOUBLE STEAL SIGNS

With runners on first and third base, the baserunners need to be aware of various things that we might be able to do without the batter making contact with the ball. It is very important that both runners are looking at the third base coach once you return to your respective base. The following double steal plays can be run:

1. **Straight steal of second base**—The regular steal sign is given. The runner at third base will stay at third base unless the ball is misplayed at second base allowing him to score. The runner at third base on a straight steal will finish up his secondary lead two steps short of his normal lead and at least one foot on the inside of the baseline. As the catcher catches the ball and looks the runner back, fake a break towards the plate by pumping your arms and legs hard staying in place. If the catcher throws to the third baseman, dive back to the base. If the catcher throws through to second base, break for the plate a hard three or four steps, and again, pump your arms and legs hard in place. If the shortstop or second baseman cuts the ball off in front of the bag break quickly back to third base. If the throw goes through, hold your position. We are attempting to distract the catcher on his throw and the middle men on their tag hoping to allow the runner the opportunity to steal the base.

2. **Steal and stop prior to reaching second base**—The regular steal sign is given by the third base coach along with: _____. If this is not flashed, then it is a straight steal as above. If the sign is given the runner on first base will straight steal, stopping short of second base forcing the shortstop or the second baseman to make a play on you long enough to allow the runner on third an opportunity to score. The runner must pull up short enough that the middle man receiving the throw feels like he has a play, but far enough away so that he cannot make the tag. The runner at third base will break for the plate from the secondary lead once the ball leaves the catcher's hand. Be careful of the fake throw by the catcher. If the pitcher cuts the ball off, get in a rundown.

3. **Forced pick-off at first base**—The regular steal sign is given by the third base coach along with:_____ _____. The baserunner at first base must get a lead that would practically force the pitcher to throw to first base (about two steps farther than normal lead off base). If the pitcher does not throw over and the sign is flashed again take an additional step. Once the pitcher throws to first, break hard for second base attempting to draw an immediate throw from the first baseman. With less than two outs, the runner must go all the way into second base allowing the defense to make a play on you sliding head first into the base. With two outs, stop short of being tagged and try to stay in the rundown for as long as possible allowing the runner at third base to score. The baserunner at third base will get his regular lead on the stretch. When the pitcher turns to throw to first base take an additional three to four shuffle steps and be leaning toward the plate. If the first baseman throws the ball to second, the runner at third base will break for the plate. If the first baseman throws to third base, the runner will break for the plate. If the first baseman fakes the throw to either second or third base, the runner will go back to third base.

4. **Steal on the stretch**—The regular steal sign is given by the third base coach along with:_____ _____. The baserunner at first base breaks for second base when the pitcher starts his hands up on the stretch. Hopefully, the runner breaking from first base will force the pitcher to either balk or throw the ball to second base. With less than two outs, the baserunner goes all the way into the bag sliding. With two outs, stop prior to being tagged and get in a rundown long enough to allow the runner from third base a chance to score. The baserunner at third base will get his normal lead and once the pitcher turns to throw to first base, take a large shuffle step and lean toward the plate. If the pitcher throws to first base, then do exactly like we would do on the forced pickoff (3). If the pitcher steps off and looks the runner back to third base, then the runner at third base will freeze. When he throws the ball to second base, break for the plate. If the pitcher leaves the mound area and starts running at the runner going to second base, the runner at third base starts increasing his lead still enabling himself the chance to get back if the pitcher turns and throws to third base. Once the ball leaves his hand, break for the plate. The runner going to second base must make the pitcher throw the ball. If he doesn't then we have a runner at second base and the runner remains at third. The runner at third base needs to be aware of a possible fake throw by the pitcher. If so, get back to third base on the dive.

5. **Delayed steal on the catcher**—The regular steal sign is given by the third base coach along with:_____ _____. The baserunner at first base will take three large shuffle

hops toward second base as the pitcher delivers to the plate. On the last hop, he breaks for second base full speed. Hopefully, this will catch the catcher in a position where he does not react like he would on a straight steal. The baserunner at third base will take his normal walking lead. When the catcher releases the ball to second base, he will break for the plate. If the ball is cut-off by the pitcher, the runner tries to get back to third base, or stay in a rundown as long as possible. If the catcher fakes the throw to second base, he must again try to get back to third base or get in a rundown.

VISUAL SIGNS WITH RUNNER(S) ON BASE

Listed are the visual signs that the third base coach can use in communicating with the baserunner(s). This will eliminate the necessity to have to verbalize these reminders from the third base coach to the baserunner(s). The runner(s) must nod their head when the sign is flashed to reinforce in the third base coach's mind that the signal has been received and is understood.

1. **Pointing toward the ground**—This is a reminder to the baserunner(s) to make sure that the ball is hit on the ground before they advance. This is generally given when the bunt sign is on to be sure that the baserunner(s) do not break toward the next base until they read the down angle on the ball off the bat.

2. **Rolling of the hands in front of the chest**—Given to a baserunner at first base to remind him that he is responsible to get a good jump on the ground ball and to take the pivot man out at second base. Generally given to the runner when there is an important run at third base with one out.

3. **Closing hands in front of the chest**—The third base coach wants the baserunner(s) to shorten their lead. This will generally be given when the take sign is on and the coach feels like the lead is too long.

4. **Widening hands in front of the chest**—The third base coach wants the baserunner(s) to widen their lead. Each motion of the hands equals one normal step. Can be given when the third base coach wants the runner to take a large one-way lead back to first base to make the pitcher throw over.

5. **Horizontal motion with the hand in front of the chest**—The third base coach is reminding all runners to freeze on a line drive. Do not move toward the next base until the ball gets through the infield when a line drive is hit.

6. **Pointing at the shortstop**—Given to the baserunner at second base to remind him to check where the shortstop is playing with either no outs or one out with no force on. Also given to remind the runner to be sure that the ball gets through the infield on the left side of the diamond before advancing to third base.

7. **Pointing at second base**—Given to the baserunner at second base with no outs. Reminds him that on any long fly ball we want him to be tagging up at second base and advancing on the catch in the outfield.

8. **Crossing hands in front of the chest**—Given to the baserunner at second base with one out. Reminds him that on most fly balls we want him to come as far away from second base as he can and still return on the catch. However, on a long fly ball that will be caught we want him to be tagging up at second base.

9. **Holding hands out in front of chest**—Take no chances on the bases. This sign would be given when we are down in the score late in the game.

10. **Pointing at third base**—This is to remind the baserunner at first base not to make the first or third out at third base.

SIGNS FOR THE INFIELDERS FROM THE DUGOUT

1. **Two hands to the chest**—All infielders will play in on the edge of the grass. Make the play at the plate on all ground balls if the runner at third base breaks for the plate. There will be no attempted double play up the middle unless the ball carries either the shortstop or second baseman in the direction of second base.

2. **Two hands to the chest followed by punching motion with the right hand**—All infielders will start in on the grass line as above. As the pitcher delivers the ball to the plate quickly move back three steps. Be sure that you are set when the ball reaches the plate with your weight over the balls of your feet. In this position the shortstop and second baseman may have double play opportunities up the middle. If in doubt, go to the plate if the runner from third base is breaking for the plate. This

15

would be used to make the runner at third base think we will be in on the pitch when actually we are a few steps off the grass when the ball reaches the plate. This play would generally only be used for one or two pitches.

3. **One arm extended, other arm touching the chest**—The corners will be in for the force play at the plate if the bases are loaded or a quick double play at second base (depends on how well the ball is hit, and how many outs). The shortstop and second baseman will be in shallow double play depth. If the ball is hit on the ground hard, get the double play. If the ball is hit so that there is little chance for the double play, look the runner back to third base (if not forced) and get either the force out at second base or the out at first base.

4. **Arms crossed out in front of chest**—All infielders will play half way. Infielders can get either the double play or the force out at the plate, if the runner is forced. Much depends on the speed of the ball and where the ball takes the infielder.

5. **Arms crossed out in front of chest followed by the flashing of two fingers**—This means that the infielders will position themselves half way, plus two large steps back. This would be the deep half way position.

6. **Both arms extended in front of chest**—All the infielders will play regular depth.

7. **Pull side back, non-pull side in**—This will be communicated orally from the dugout. In this situation we would want the pull side at regular depth and the non-pull side half way or in on the grass.

8. Each motion of the hands from the dugout in a certain direction means for an infielder to move two steps.

SIGNS FOR THE OUTFIELDERS FROM THE DUGOUT

1. Each motion of the hands from the dugout in a certain direction means for an outfielder to move four steps.

SIGNS FOR THE FIRST BASEMAN FROM THE DUGOUT

1. **Pointing at first base**—Hold the baserunner on the base.

2. **Circling of right hand**—Play behind the runner four or five steps on the next pitch. Let the pitcher know before he gets on the rubber that you are playing behind the runner.

3. **Circling right hand and grabbing wrist**—Play behind the runner but be able to touch him from behind. As the pitch is delivered to the plate take two steps backward, especially with a lefthanded hitter at the plate. Again, let the pitcher know that you will not be holding the runner on.

4. **Flashing a two with the right hand**—Reminder to the first baseman with runners at first and third base that he is to follow the runner down to second base if he breaks. Only done with two outs.

5. **Pointing at the pitcher**—The first baseman is to call timeout and talk with the pitcher on the mound. This is a stalling technique to give the relief pitcher a little longer to warm up.

SIGNS FOR THE CATCHER FROM THE DUGOUT

1. Throw a pitchout on the next pitch. The catcher can call a pitchout on his own also. The sign from the dugout is:
_____.

2. Throw a fast ball. The sign from the dugout is:_____.

3. Throw the pitcher's best breaking pitch. The sign from the dugout is:_____.

4. Throw a change-up. The sign from the dugout is:_____.

5. Call the location of the pitch from the dugout. Signs needed are: up and inside; up and away; down and inside; down and away.

16

6. Intentionally walk the next batter or the batter currently at the plate. The sign from the dugout is:_____

7. Call timeout and talk to the pitcher. This is a stalling technique to give relief pitcher more time to warmup. The sign from the dugout is:_____.

SIGNS FOR THE PITCHER FROM THE DUGOUT

1. **Circling of right hand**—Do not take so much time between pitches. Speed up for you are working too slow.

2. **Holding up both hands in front of chest**—Take more time between pitches. Slow down for you are working too fast.

3. **Holding elbow up**—You are starting to drop your elbow. Get your elbow up during the delivery.

4. **Pointing at eyes**—Concentrate more on what you are doing. Watch the target.

5. **Pointing at a base**—Hold the runner a little closer. A steal threat. Taking too big of a lead.

SIGNALS BETWEEN CATCHER AND PITCHER

1. With no baserunner at second base we will always use the first sign. Generally, one will be the fast ball, two the curve ball, three the slider, and four the pitcher's speciality pitch or change-up. If the pitcher does not throw the curve, the slider will become the two pitch. The pitcher may change-up on the fast ball without letting the catcher know. If the catcher wants a change-up off any one of these pitches, he will flash the number for the pitch and then open and close his hand, indicating the change-up. In most cases, the pitcher will throw just the straight change-up for most pitchers cannot effectively change speeds on the breaking ball.

2. With a baserunner at second base, we will generally go with the second sign. The catcher needs to remind the pitcher that we are changing signs with a runner at second base by telling him, "runner at second base". Some pitchers need not be reminded, so use your own judgement. If someone observes the baserunner at second base flashing the signs to the hitter, the catcher will call timeout. Change the sign sequence with the pitcher. The catcher must always give at least three signs with a runner at second base. With no runner at second base you should only give the one sign.

3. **Location of pitches**—Once the sign is flashed for the type of pitch, the catcher can inform the pitcher where he would like the ball thrown:

    (A) Want the ball down and inside to the righthanded hitter, down and outside to the lefthanded hitter. Working for the strike. The sign is:_____.

    (B) Want the ball down and inside to the lefthanded hitter, down and outside to the righthanded hitter. Working for the strike. The sign is:_____.

    (C) Want the ball up and in to the lefthanded hitter, outside and up to the righthanded hitter. Working for the strike. The sign is:_____.

    (D) Want the ball up and in to the righthanded hitter, outside and up to the lefthanded hitter. Working for the strike. The sign is:_____.

    If the catcher wants the ball away from the strike zone with these locations, he will motion with the right hand in that direction after the direction sign is given.

4. **Shakeoff sign**—When the pitcher wants a new set of signs he will give the following sign to the catcher:_____
_____. The catcher will begin the series all over again.

5. **False shakeoff sign**—The false shakeoff sign is _____ from the pitcher to the catcher. The sign from the catcher to the pitcher is:_____. When the sign is given by the catcher the pitcher will flash his sign and then throw the pitch that was called for. When the sign is flashed by the pitcher the catcher just

stays with the original sign. If the coach has given the catcher a pitch to throw and the pitcher shakes him off, the catcher will call timeout and go out and talk with the pitcher. Stay with the sign the coach gave.

6. **Pitchout sign**—If the catcher wants to throw a pitchout the sign is:_____.

7. **Knockdown pitch**—If the catcher wants to throw a knockdown pitch, the sign is:_____
_____. We are not trying to hit the batter, we are just trying to get him off the plate. All knockdown pitches are to be thrown well up and in, not at the head or behind it.

OFFENSIVE SIGN STRUCTURE

Two criteria for the selection of offensive signs for a baseball team should be: (1) they are simple enough that all players can understand them and interpret from the sign what his responsibility is; and (2) they are disguised enough that the opposition is unable to pick them up and prepare the defense for what the offense will do. Thus, the coach must develop readable-undetectable signs. Readable signs for his club, undetectable signs for the opposition.

The higher the level of baseball, the more complex the signs should be for three reasons: (1) there are more offensive plays in the team's playbook; (2) the players at a higher level should have the experience necessary to understand a more complex sign structure; and (3) the opposition should have more experience in "stealing" signs.

Whenever signs are transmitted from the dugout to the third base coach and then to the batter and baserunner(s) you compound the problem in your sign communication. That is the reason why it is best in most levels of baseball to have the coach originating the signs to be the third base coach. If the third base coach is not the head coach, then a system of signs need to be developed from the head coach in the dugout to the third base coach. These signs must be flashed quickly to the third base coach so that there is no delay in getting the proper information to the players involved.

It might be best to allow the third base coach, even if he is not the head coach, the responsibility of originating the signs at most levels. The head coach and the third base coach can "set-up" the inning in the dugout before the coach goes out to the coaching box. In this way, they have some agreement of what they might want to do in an inning if certain situations arise.

Whichever way the signs are transmitted the most important fact of sign structure is the simplicity of the signs to those involved. At most levels, very few opposition players and coaches really make a great effort at "stealing" signs except when obvious steal or bunt situations arise.

When giving signs it is important that no more than six or seven touch points are given each time. All touch points should be clear with the coach facing all players involved so that everyone has a clear sight line to the coach. This might necessitate the coach moving around in the coaching box so that the pitcher is not in the way of the runner at first base. If the third base coach is wearing a jacket on a cold day he might need to slow down a little in giving his touch points, especially in those areas of the body that are covered by the jacket.

The hitter and baserunner(s) need to know when the signs are completed so that they do not have to hold their looks for any additional signs. This can be done by clapping the hands once when all the signs are completed. All players must hold their looks at the third base coach until the completion sign is given.

Types of Signs

There are numerous types of offensive signs that can be used:

1. **Missed touch system**—This system of signs allows the offensive team to construct their signs around what the coach does not touch rather than what he touches. As an example, the bunt sign can be keyed into the sign system by the fact that the third base coach will touch the bill of the cap all the time during his signs. When he fails to touch the bill of the cap, the bunt is on. The steal sign could be keyed on the missed belt. The coach will touch the belt during each sign sequence. When he fails to do so, the steal is on.

Thus, the hitter and baserunner(s) can clue in on the cap and the belt. When both are touched no sign is on. If you want to bunt and steal at the same time, both the cap and belt are missed. If you want to hit and run, you miss the belt and give the hit sign to the hitter. All the other signs can be incorporated into the missed touch system.

It is an excellent system to use if a coach is concerned that his signs might be "stolen" by the opposition. Anytime one wants to confuse the opposition for a game, or just an inning, all the coach has to do is to put an indicator in for the first sign which will indicate that a sign might be forthcoming. If no indicator sign is given, then no sign is on no matter what the coach misses in his sign system. Below is a complete sign system that can be used:

Sacrifice Bunt—Missed bill of the cap.
Drag Bunt—Missed bill of the cap followed by verbal command.

Squeeze Bunt—Missed bill of the cap plus finishing the signs with two claps of the hands rather than one.
Straight Steal—Missed belt.
Fake Bunt and Slash—Missed bill of cap—giving hitting motion with hands before clapping hands to finish signs.
Fake Bunt Slash Hit and Run—Missed bill of the cap, missed belt—giving hitting motion with hands before clapping the hands to finish signs.
Delayed Steal—Missed belt—pointing at the catcher before clapping the hands.
Double Steal—Missed belt—flashing a number before clapping the hands. The number flashed reflects the type of steal play.
Hit and Run—Missed belt—touching lip (hit sign) before clapping the hands.
Bunt and Steal—Missed cap and belt.
Take Sign—Start sign system with a clap of the hands.
Wipe Off Sign—Wiping right hand across the chest.
Indicator Sign (if needed)—Right hand wipe down the right leg. If done on the first sign there is a **chance** that a sign is forthcoming. If not done on the first sign then there will be no sign for that sequence.

2. **Regular touch system**—This is the most common type of sign system used in baseball. The coach will indicate the sign by touching the part of his body or uniform that reflects what he wishes to do. As long as the coach does not flash his signs too quickly it is an excellent system of using signs for it is easy for the players to pick up. If one does not use an indicator in the touch system they might be picked up by an excellent sign "stealer", especially in situations where the steal or bunt is an obvious offensive play. Below is an example of a complete sign system that might be used in the touch system with some combination signs:

Sacrifice Bunt—Touch bill of the cap.
Drag Bunt—Wipe bill of the cap.
Squeeze Bunt—Touch bill of the cap followed by touching lip.
Straight Steal—Right hand wipe of letters (chest area).
Delayed Steal—Right hand wipe of letters two times in succession.
Double Steal—Right hand wipe of letters - flashing a number before clapping the hands. The number flashed reflects the type of steal play.
Hit and Run—Right hand wipe of letters followed by right hand wipe of right thigh.
Bunt and Steal—Touch bill of the cap followed by right hand wipe of letters.
Take Sign—Touch belt with both hands at the same time.
Wipe Off Sign—Right hand wipe completely down right side of chest.
Fake Bunt and Slash—Touch bill of cap twice in succession.
Fake Bunt Slash Hit and Run—Touch bill of cap twice in succession followed by hitting motion with hands.

3. **Hold sign system**—The easiest sign system for players to read is the holding signs. Since they are the easiest to pick up for the players on offense, they are also the easiest for the other team to "steal".

Examples of holding signs would be:

Sacrifice Bunt—Clenched fist of right hand.
Straight Steal—Standing in a certain part of the coaching box.
Hit and Run—Coach bent over with both hands on knees.

The holding sign system is the best system to use if the signs are coming from the coach in the dugout to the batter and baserunner(s). In order to confuse the opposition a player in the dugout could give the holding signs. These are the best signs to use in lower levels of baseball to insure that there are no signs missed.

4. **Sequence and combination sign system**—This type of sign system is often used by professional baseball teams to assist in disguising the signs. Many times though, these signs become so confusing that many signs are missed by the players on offense.

The key to this system is that the third base coach must touch two or more parts of the body or clothing before a sign is in effect. In the sequence sign system there can be no intervening sign between the two signs. If there is, the sign is not on. An example of a complete sequence and combination sign system would be:

Sacrifice Bunt—Touch bill of cap, touch right cheek.

Drag Bunt—Touch bill of cap, right cheek, left cheek.
Squeeze Bunt—Touch bill of cap two times in succession, touch right cheek.
Straight Steal—Touch belt, wipe down right thigh.
Delayed Steal—Touch belt, wipe down right thigh, wipe down left thigh.
Double Steal—Touch belt two times in succession.
Hit and Run—Touch belt followed by hitting motion with hands.
Bunt and Steal—Touch bill of cap, touch belt.
Fake Bunt and Slash—Touch bill of cap, touch right ear.
Fake Bunt Slash Hit and Run—Touch bill of cap, touch belt, wipe down right thigh.
Take Sign—Touch right elbow, touch left elbow.
Wipe Off Sign—Wipe right hand across chest two times in succession.

As you can see these types of signs can get very confusing so quite a bit of time is needed in preparing a team to use sequence and combination signs.

5. **Repeat sign system**—This is an excellent sign system whereby the sign is not on unless the coach returns to the sign. For instance, if the bunt sign is the coach touching his belt, he would have to touch the belt for the first sign. If at anytime during the sign sequence he returns to the belt the sign is on. If he does not return to the belt then no sign is on. This sign system will enable the player to really concentrate on what the coach starts the sign system with. If he touches an area of his body or clothing first that a sign revolves around all he has to do is look for him to touch it again before the sign is on.

6. **Indicator sign system**—This is another popular sign system used in all levels of baseball. In this system a coach may flash any signal he wishes, but nothing is on unless he has given an indicator sign. When the indicator sign is given, then the next sign flashed is the actual sign. If no indicator is given there would be no sign. If the indicator sign is flashed and the next sign has no significance, again nothing is on. As an example, let's make the belt the indicator sign and the bill of the cap is the bunt. A coach might flash the following:

A. Wipe chest, touch belt, touch bill of cap, wipe down right thigh—Bunt is on.

B. Touch belt, wipe chest, touch bill of cap, wipe down right thigh—No sign on.

C. Touch bill of cap, touch belt, wipe down right thigh, wipe chest—No sign.

D. Wipe chest, touch bill of cap, wipe down right thigh, touch belt, touch bill of cap—Bunt is on.

The indicator sign will get the batter and baserunner(s) attention to be alert for a possible sign coming next. The indicator sign system is excellent in deceiving the opposition.

There are numerous other ways to flash signs, but these are the most popular ones used in baseball today. The most important thing in regard to signs is to be sure that you spend enough time with them in practice sessions so that everyone feels comfortable with them.

There is no worse feeling for a coach to have during a game then to flash a series of signs and wonder if a player or players might be confused. That is why it is recommended to practice the sign system during numerous intersquad games before the first regular season game. Another excellent time to work on signs is during batting practice sessions. The third base coach should stand in the coaching box during batting practice and flash signs to the hitter at the plate. The hitter will then run to first after his last cut and now the coach can coordinate some signs with the next batter along with the runner.

If enough time is spent on the signs there should be no trouble with these signs during a game. The system that some teams use to have the players flash back to the coach that they have received and understand the sign certainly should not be necessary and only leads to more confusion.

STRUCTURED BASEBALL PRACTICE SESSIONS

In most high school and college athletic programs, baseball has traditionally taken a back seat to football and basketball when it comes to the developing of highly structured and organized practice sessions. This is very unfortunate for with a little more effort in practice organization, a baseball coach can develop in his players a deeper appreciation for practice and the game of baseball.

One of the reasons for this fact is that in many baseball programs there are only one or two coaches involved, whereby in football and basketball they generally have a much larger staff. Even though a baseball coaching staff is limited to one or two coaches it should not mean that practice sessions become unorganized and unstructured. With a small coaching staff it does mean that it will take a little more time to organize these practice sessions so that everyone stays busy and the team accomplishes what needs to be done to prepare for the season.

In this section, we will attempt to detail what needs to be done in practice sessions to accomplish specific objectives. The basic objective of practice is to provide each player the opportunity to better himself as an individual in coordination with the preparation of a team for maximum performance.

The purpose of practice should also revolve around the concept of the presentation of fundamentals in a way that the learning process is not only complete but enjoyable. Generally speaking, those teams that have well organized and enjoyable practices have a better chance of success on game day.

Preparation of Daily Practice Schedules

Every baseball coach must take into account what he has to work with before he can properly organize individual practice sessions. This means that the coach must coordinate his practice schedule around the following:

1. Facilities available
2. Number of coaches on the staff
3. Number of athletes on the team
4. Practice time restrictions
5. Number of managers available
6. Availability of equipment
7. Availability of protective screens
8. Availability of batting tunnel(s) and batting cage

It may take a coach anywhere from 30 minutes to one hour to draw up his daily practice schedule depending on how detailed and comprehensive he wishes his practice schedule to be. Some coaches feel more comfortable with a less rigid time schedule at practice, while others deem it important to follow a strict time schedule where every minute of the practice day is planned. The head coach and his assistants must feel comfortable with whatever type of practice plan employed.

Whenever possible it is highly recommended to have the daily practice schedule typed up and run off on a ditto or xerox machine so that numerous copies can be distributed and posted. Copies of the schedule should be in the hands of all the coaches, the manager(s) and trainer(s). In addition, a practice schedule should be posted as early as possible where the players can observe it so that they may know exactly what the schedule for the day will be.

A practice schedule should be posted in the locker room, in the dugout, and on a board attached to the batting cage so that the players can refer to it whenever a question might arise. If any extra practice schedules are available, they might be passed out by the managers to any spectators who come out to the field to observe a practice session.

Along with the actual practice schedule, any announcements that need to be made can be done so on the schedule. This would include also a listing of those players who might be late to practice, injured players, etc. Athletes always appreciate organization, especially when it deals with their practice sessions.

Even though a coach might plan a highly organized and structured practice schedule he still should have the feeling that changes can be made during the practice if he feels that more time needs to be spent in a certain area. However, changes should be kept down to a minimum.

It might be best to plan the next day to come back to an area that enough time was not spent on the previous day rather than to elongate the practice schedule previously planned. A coach should never let his practice plan tie him and his coaches down to the point that the schedule takes away from the effectiveness of a practice. On the next three pages you will find an example of a daily practice schedule along with a blank batting practice outline.

Thursday—February 17th

1. Late today: **Whitfield** (on the field at 3:30).

2. Out for today: **Powers** (knee); **Carter** (shoulder). Attend practice in regular clothes. Can leave when batting practice begins.

3. Bring your class schedules with you to the locker room today so that we can put them on the master class schedule.

Pre-Practice

1:40 - 2:00 **Infielders**—Completing double plays. Stopwatch. **McMahon** (Fungo); **Purnell** (Catcher); **Polk** (Stopwatch). Coach **Brown**

Klipstein and **Jones**—Report to Coach **Osborne** in right field. Angle drills.

Open Hitting in left field off machine—10 cuts each. **Moorehead** (feeder). Coach **Johnson**

Practice

2:00 - 2:05 Meeting.

2:05 - 2:30 Fundamental Drill Series Number 1. Four minute stations today.

2:30 - 2:45 Bunt Defense Play Number 2 and 3. **Polk** (bunter); **Pitchers** feed from first baseline (3 plays each); **Catchers** (3 plays each).

2:45 - 2:55 Batting practice preparation. **Outfielders** and **catchers** on screens and cages.

2:55 - 4:35 Batting practice. Page 2.

4:35 - 4:55 **Pitchers**—Conditioning in outfield. Coach **Roth** and **McMahon**

Hitters—Baserunning. Coach **Polk** and **Johnson**
1. 5 minutes of double steal offense.
2. 4 1st to 3rd using third base coach, 3 not using third base coach.
3. Delayed steals—3 times each, 3 at a time.
4. Two out leads at second base, 3 times to the plate using third base coach.
5. 5 breaks from home plate to first base.

24

BATTING PRACTICE SCHEDULE

	Group I - 25	Group II - 25	Group III - 25	Group IV - 25
Pitchers	Smithson (15)-Ross Moses (10)-Porter	Moses (5) Taylor (15)-Bryan Kemp (5)-Knight	Kemp (10) Johnson (15)-Smith	Coach McMahon (25)
Catchers	Porter (15) Knight (10)	Smithson	Bryan	Ross
Hitters	Bullard Sottile Castoria Klipstein	Ross Murray Loe Gage	Fox Porter Willoughby Smith	Walker Bryan Knight Martz
Back up	Mundie	Susce	Smithson	Moses
1B Fungo **3B Fungo**	Kemp Susce	Mundie Wright	Fields Weathersby	Smithson Hardwick
First base	Knight	Martz	Castoria	Porter
Batting Range #1	Walker Bryan	Fox Porter	Knight Sottile	Murray Loe
Batting Range #2	Martz Smith	Willoughby Bullard	Klipstein Ross	Castoria Gage

Hitters—One sacrifice bunt and 6 cuts with contact first two rounds. Full speed to first base half way down. At first base, react to sacrifice bunt. First pitch after sacrifice bunt, steal second base. At second base, two secondary leads with one out and no force. React on third lead to batted ball. At third base, react to one out situation, infield in.

Pitchers—Those pitchers throwing in batting practice today, 7 foul poles around assignments. Those not throwing, 10 foul poles. Pitchers throwing: 1/3rd breaking pitches letting hitters know. Pitch from stretch with runners at first or second base. Runner at third base from windup. Throw no harder than 7/8's speed.

| **Coaches Stations:** | Brown
McMahon
Osborne
Johnson | 1-4-3-2
4-2-1-1
3-1-2-3
2-3-4-4 | #1 - CAGE
#2 - BR #1
#3 - BR #2
#4 - BULLPEN | **Other**—Catchers dividing time behind plate by thirds: no one on base; runner at first base; regular batting practice. |

BATTING PRACTICE SCHEDULE

	Group I - ___	Group II - ___	Group III - ___	Group IV - ___
Pitchers				
Catchers				
Hitters				
Back up				
1B Fungo **3B Fungo**				
First base				
Batting Range #1				
Batting Range #2				

Hitters—
Pitchers—

Coaches Stations—	**Other—**

Pre-Practice Schedule

Every practice session should provide the head coach and his staff the opportunity to work with individual players before the entire team arrives for practice. Players can be brought out by defensive positions, or for individual offense and defensive instruction in these pre-practice sessions.

The fewer the coaches on the staff would probably mean more numerous and longer pre-practice sessions in order to work with individual players. Post-practice time can also be used for individual work, but since the player might be a little tired after a practice, it is not nearly as effective as the pre-practice time.

A coach should never discourage players from coming out to practice early or staying late, but they should not be in a position to interfere with these pre- and post-practice sessions with designated individuals. It is also not wise to have a certain player involved in both the pre- and post-practice schedule on the same day since you would then be working with a fatigued athlete.

Meeting Prior To Practice

After the pre-practice session, the entire team is on the field at the designated time. A short meeting should take place where the head coach can go over information with the club that was not covered on the practice schedule or emphasize some points on the schedule itself.

Coming Onto The Field And Stretching Program

The tone for practice sessions can be established just by the way the players come onto the baseball field. They should be required to run at least three-quarters speed to the stretching area before they pick up a baseball. It is highly recommended that absolutely no activity take place on the field until the player undergoes a complete stretching program. An example of a stretching program is on the next page.

It does little good for players to come on the field, start throwing and working out, and then have a mass stretching program for the entire team at the same time. By requiring the players to stretch as soon as they come on the field it insures that they are physically ready for any activity they take part in. At the first practice session these stretching exercises must be presented and demonstrated so that they are always done in the proper sequence and manner.

Supervision of these stretching exercises is a must for at least the first week to be sure that all the players are doing them properly. After that time they should have no problem. The coaches might need to do a spot check on these stretching exercises to be sure that all the players maintain the same intensity.

After they finish their stretching, which should take no longer than 4-5 minutes, they should run back to their gloves at three-quarters speed and begin warming up their arm.

Warming Up

There is nothing in baseball that will set a player back any more than a sore arm. That is why adequate time must be spent with the players teaching them how to warmup their arms properly. During the early part of training, the arm must be protected from stress that would slow down a boy's progress. Players must be discouraged from throwing full speed without a graduate build up program.

It is natural for a baseball player to show off a good arm, many times before the arm is properly conditioned. Early season defensive drills should not require a boy to throw full speed unless the player has built up his arm to stand this possible stress.

Players should be encouraged to spend at least 7-8 minutes every practice day warming up their arms prior to any type of defensive work. They should plan their arrival time on the field to allow them enough time for stretching and throwing before they are involved in the practice session.

During these throwing sessions players should be encouraged to work on good throwing mechanics. It is so important that a baseball coach impress upon his players that these warmup sessions can be used to help themselves not only strengthen their arms, but also, to work on their mechanics and throwing accuracy. The players should be encouraged to throw with players who play the same defensive position. In this way the players can warm up at distances that reflect the position they play.

STRETCHING EXERCISES

As soon as you come onto the field you will run three-quarters speed to the left field foul line. You will put your glove down on the line and then run three-quarters speed to deep center field to begin your stretching exercises. Do not get in the way of any pre-practice session underway. Once you complete your stretching exercises, you will run three-quarters speed back to the left field foul line, pick up your glove, and begin warming up with a ball that you will get out of the ball bag on the line.

Exercises For All Players (in this order)

1. 10 rolling of arms backward and forward.
2. 10 fingertip pushups (hitters only)
3. 20 regular pushups (hitters only)
4. 10 toe touches with full stretching overhead.
5. 5 toe side touches each toe.
6. 5 toe to back ground touches.
7. 5 groin stretches each way.
8. *2 sit down toe touches—holding five seconds.
9. *5 hurdle stretches both legs.
10. *1 backward flip, open legs touch to ground and hold for 5 seconds.

  *Will be done in the locker room on any day that the field is wet but we are still practicing.

Exercises For Pitchers Prior To Throwing In Bullpen (in this order)

1. 10 rolling of arms backward and forward.
2. 10 toe touches and full stretching overhead.
3. 5 toe touches each toe.
4. 5 toe to back ground touches.
5. Series of arm pulling techniques (10 pulls each)
    1. Across chest
    2. Behind back
    3. Over head
    4. Pulling thumb
6. Medi-ball exercises (10 each)—To be done before and immediately after throwing.
    1. Circle leaning over
    2. Forward and backward leaning over
    3. Sideways leaning over
    4. Forward and back standing up

Availability Of Equipment

The managers must be organized to the point that the proper equipment is out by the time the players arrive for practice. All practice stations must have the needed equipment in place at the time the station is used for a drill.

It behooves the head coach to meet with the managers before a detailed practice session to answer any questions they might have about what equipment is needed at each station. Later in the Playbook the manager(s) responsibilities for practices and games is outlined.

Batting Practice

The batting practice phase of practice should take up about 60 to 70 per cent of a practice day. If organized properly many things can be accomplished during batting practice to keep everyone busy along with getting additional fundamental skills refined. Detailed below is what can be done in a batting practice session:

1. **Batting cage**—The batting cage is practically a necessity in order to have an organized and highly structured batting practice session. Not only does the cage keep most foul balls from leaving the field of play, but also, it enables the fungo hitters to hit ground balls to the infielders without having to worry about getting hit by a baseball off the bat.

2. **Pitchers**—It is vital to a good batting practice session that the pitchers throw strikes to the hitters for two reasons: (1) it allows the hitters to get the maximum number of cuts in the time segment allowed: (2) it builds confidence in the hitters at the plate for they do not have to fear for their lives.

This is an excellent time for the pitchers to work on their various pitches, but at the same time, it is the most important time for them to work on their control. On the batting practice schedule each pitcher is informed on when they are going to throw along with how long they will be throwing. The name of the catcher warming them up in the bullpen is listed next to their name.

The manager responsible for the time schedule in batting practice will inform the pitcher in the bullpen when he has five minutes to go before he starts throwing to the hitters on the main field. He will then be informed when he has one minute to go. At that time he will leave the bullpen running one-half speed to an area outside the third baseline (if he is warming up in the left field bullpen—outside the first baseline if warming up in the right field bullpen). In this way when the pitcher on the mound throws his last pitch, the next pitcher can jog to the mound and he is ready to go without having to throw any warmup pitches. There should be no delay in batting practice to change pitchers on the mound.

On the batting practice schedule the pitchers should be informed on how hard they are to throw that particular day, when and how much to pitch from the stretch, and when to throw from the windup. The amount of throwing for each pitcher is dictated by the physical conditioning of his arm at that point. Prior to the opening of the season each pitcher should be able to throw at least 15 minutes of batting practice every other day. Again, this is strictly individual for some pitchers might be able to throw longer and some might not be able to handle that much throwing every other day.

In most batting practice sessions the pitcher should let the hitter know what type of pitch he is throwing. This is also for the catcher's benefit. Some batting practice sessions can include time where the pitcher and catcher will communicate game signs not letting the hitters know what pitch is being thrown.

At least one-third of the time the pitcher should throw from the stretch position. If there will be baserunning done in these sessions then the pitcher can throw from the stretch with runners at first or second base. This should give the pitcher enough time from the stretch. At least one-third of the time the pitcher should throw breaking pitches along with speciality pitches (change-ups, fork balls, palm balls, knuckle balls, etc.). He would only throw those speciality pitches that he plans to use in game situations.

Each pitcher who is throwing in a batting practice session must be sure to properly stretch before he picks up a baseball in the bullpen. He needs to give himself enough time in the bullpen to stretch and warmup properly before he pitches on the main field.

It is highly recommended that all pitchers use a protective screen when throwing batting practice. Since the pitcher is generally just trying to throw strikes and not throwing "game hard" there is going to be more well hit balls in batting practice than in a regular game. The screen should be constructed in such a way that the pitcher is fully protected, but at the same time, is not so high that the pitcher has to change his normal release point and delivery.

Pitchers must be cautioned when using a screen that they must pretend it is not there so that their follow through is not affected. Occasionally when the pitchers are told to throw hard in batting practice or mix the pitches up without letting the hitter know what is coming, the screen can be removed.

Pitchers should receive a lot of ground balls during practice sessions on the main mound but we certainly do not want to lose them during a batting practice session as a result of a "shot" back at them.

Before each pitcher leaves the mound we want them to field a thrown bunt by the catcher, just like fielding a bunt in the game, pretending that there is a play at second base. Since the pitcher is always quite loose after his stint on the mound this is the best time to have him make this long hard throw to an infielder covering second base. We want the infielder covering the base, not to break for the base until the ball hits the ground so that the pitcher sees a moving target rather than just having the shortstop or second baseman standing on the bag. Thus, the manager will always yell to the pitcher and catcher "last pitch". The batter will not try to hit the ball thrown and the catcher will roll out the bunt yelling "two". Once he completes the throw to second base he leaves the mound and the next pitcher is ready to throw.

3. **Hitters**—The main function of batting practice is to allow the hitters the opportunity to get a lot of cuts, whether it be on the

main field or in the batting range(s). That is why it is so important to have pitchers throwing batting practice who can not only show the hitters a variety of pitches, but also, throw a high percentage of strikes.

In order to give all the hitters on your squad a maximum number of cuts it helps to have one or two batting ranges so that you can have a lot of hitting at various stations. If no batting ranges are available then you have to coordinate batting practice sessions around just one group hitting on the main field. If that is the case, then it behooves a coach to have a short toss, side toss, soft toss or batting tee station in operation somewhere away from the main field. These stations are detailed in the Playbook in the hitting section.

At no time should one hitter take more than 10-12 cuts with contact in a row at any of the hitting stations. This is to eliminate the hitters getting fatigued which may cause a hitter to change his mechanics. As long as the hitter gets a few minutes rest he should be able to get back in the cage or range and take additional cuts.

It is not wise to take too many cuts early in the practice season for the hitter's hands might start blistering which could set him back for a few days. If a coach builds up the number of cuts in practice sessions it will allow the hands to get stronger without any soft spots developing.

One of the keys to successful batting practice sessions is to have the hitters swing only at strikes even if the pitcher is having a difficult time finding the strike zone. If you encourage the hitters to swing at all pitches, or even those a little out of the strike zone, it takes away from the effectiveness of batting practice. We want the hitters to develop a keen awareness of the strike zone so that it carries over into the game hitting experience. The catchers are required to call balls and strikes for the hitters on the main field. In the batting range, the coach in charge of that station or another player can help the hitter out. Whenever a hitter swings at a pitch that is not a strike all the catcher has to say is "ball". If he does not swing at a pitch that is in the strike zone all the catcher has to say is "strike". If the pitch could go either way he just says "close". If the hitters are taking two strike swings then the catcher should call the close pitches strikes to encourage the hitter to protect the plate with two strikes on him.

It is best to divide your batting practice sessions into three or four groups (sample practice schedule is divided into four groups). If you want your starters and top reserves to get more cuts, then you can either have them hitting in groups with fewer hitters, or better yet, put them in the groups that will be allowed to hit a little longer.

On the bottom of the batting practice schedule you can inform the hitters what they are to do when they are hitting on the main field. They should always hit in the order listed on the schedule. It is very important to be sure that all the hitters in each group get the same amount of cuts. If the pitcher(s) are throwing strikes, each hitter should be able to get a number of swings. After the first two rounds are finished, then whatever time is left in their hitting group should be divided equally among the hitters in that group. It may only be one cut per person.

There are numerous things that you can have the batter work on during batting practice rather than having them just "swinging away". At least during the first two rounds there should be some purpose swings. You can also work on the players' sacrifice bunts, drag bunts and suicide squeeze bunts during these first two rounds.

The number of cuts that each hitter takes should be counted by the catcher predetermined by the coach as to whether the number of cuts taken are with contact or not. It is best that early in the practice season when tryouts are taking place that the coach have the number of cuts counted by the number of full swings. Otherwise, you may get a player or two who are trying out and you quickly find that there is little or no contact being made at the plate. This would really slow the batting practice session to a crawl. Once most of the early cuts are made, then the number of swings should be determined by contact swings.

During those rounds when the hitter will be running out of the box on the last cut, the catcher needs to tell the batter "last cut", followed by "coming out". This is to let the fungo hitter on the first base side know that the hitter will be running to first base on the next swing with contact and he should not fungo a baseball until the hitter passes him on the way to first base.

Whenever the hitters are to do any type of bunting at the plate, the catcher should come out from behind the plate and stand 15-20 feet away from the batter on the first or third base side. This is done for two reasons: (1) to retrieve the bunted ball if it is bunted close enough to the catcher without delaying the next pitch; and (2) to prevent the catcher from being injured by a foul tip since there is more chance of a foul tip hitting the catcher on a bunt attempt then when the batter is swinging. The catcher needs to hustle back behind the plate after the bunt so that there is no delay in the next pitch.

On those days when bunting will take place in the batting practice session, it would seriously delay things if the coach forced all the hitters to properly lay the bunt down before he can hit. The best approach for sacrifice bunts is to force the hitter to get the first one down by subtracting one of his cuts for each poor sacrifice bunt. A poor sacrifice bunt would be determined by the coach at the batting cage, and can include bunting a non-strike even if the ball is perfectly bunted. The determining factor is whether or not the bunt would have advanced an average runner. If it is bunted foul, bunted too hard, bunted too close to the catcher, or bunted at a poor angle away from the pitcher's mound then a cut is subtracted. This practice makes for much greater concentration on the hitter's part, and those who have a difficult time bunting learn how to bunt quickly.

It is not a good practice to allow everyone on the team to drag bunt for it would be a waste of valuable batting practice time. As soon as possible, the coaches need to designate what players will be drag bunters so that they can be worked with individually and have the opportunity to practice their drag bunting in these batting practice sessions when it is allowed. The best time to drag bunt is when the batter is running out of the box to first base. The drag bunters should not have a cut subtracted from their swings for a poor drag bunt. They just continue on to first base when they make contact with the ball.

Switch hitters should not be allowed any extra cuts in batting practice on the main field, but should be allowed a few more cuts in the batting range. Generally in the batting range the hitters will take quite a few more cuts then they would on the main field, especially if hitting off the machine or working a short toss station.

Listed below are some examples of what type of swings and bunts can be incorporated into batting practice sessions. This is what is listed next to the hitters section on the bottom of the batting practice schedule:

First two rounds—One sacrifice bunt and six cuts with contact. Subtract one cut for each poor bunt. Last cut first two rounds is a two strike swing. Drag bunters - first round only after two strike swing.

First two rounds—One fake bunt slash (must be a strike). Two hit and runs. Three cuts with contact. Drag bunters - first two rounds after last cut.

First three rounds—Two cuts with contact, one protect the baserunner on a steal, one hit and run, one fake bunt slash hit and run, two cuts with contact. No drag bunting.

First two rounds— One sacrifice bunt. Subtract one cut for each poor bunt. Six cuts with contact. When there is a baserunner at second base, no out swing. When there is a baserunner at third base suicide squeeze on the second pitch. No drag bunting.

First two rounds— Two-two strike swings, one hit and run, and four cuts with contact. Drag bunters - first two rounds.

First two rounds—One sacrifice bunt. Subtract one cut for each poor bunt. One fake bunt slash hit and run, one fake bunt slash, one hit and run, four cuts with contact.

Much of the hitting in batting practice can be coordinated with the baserunners so that it takes on, as much as possible, game situations.

4. **Baserunners**—Even though the coach should have a lot of baserunning practice towards the end of practice, a team can work on a lot of their baserunning during these batting practice sessions. Designated on the bottom of the batting practice schedule, a coach can detail for the players what baserunning will be done on that day. This is in conjunction with what the hitters are doing at the plate to give it a realistic flavor. It is best to restrict the baserunning to the first two rounds since after these rounds the hitters will be taking fewer cuts as their hitting group's time draws to a close.

The players should work on getting out of the batter's box as quick as possible on the last cut, for at least the first two rounds. They should go full speed until they reach the half way mark to first base and then go three-quarters speed into first base.

The coach responsible for the batting cage station should make sure that every player coming out of the box gets a good jump. If the player does not get a good jump, then he should be called back to take another cut and a cut is subtracted in the next round. Getting out of the box is such an important aspect of baserunning that much time needs to be spent on this technique, not only in the batting practice session, but in the baserunning part of practice.

Once the baserunner gets to first base, he needs to pretend that he is in a regular game. The pitcher will be pitching from the stretch anytime there is a runner at first base. On the batting practice schedule, the runner should be informed what he will be doing on the bases. It is always best, especially early in the practice season, for the runners to work on their primary and secondary lead. The primary lead being where they want to be when the pitcher is in the set position, and the secondary lead where they want to be when the catcher receives the ball or the batter makes contact.

The leads have got to be game-like so that if the batter hits a ground ball the runner at first base responds to the ball as he would in a game. The same holds true if the batter hits a line drive, pops the ball up, hits a fly ball, swings and misses or takes the pitch. So that the runner is ready for the next pitch, he needs to get back to his primary lead as fast as possible so that there is no delay. For instance, if the runner is working on his secondary lead and the hitter hits a ground ball, the runner should run full speed for about five or six steps, stop, and then get back to his lead at first base for the next pitch.

On the batting practice schedule it might say for all the baserunners at first base to take three game leads (primary and secondary) and then react to the ball. On the fourth pitch steal second base. On another day, he might take two leads reacting to the bunt at the plate first. On the first pitch after a successful bunt by the batter, he will hit and run with the batter. Another time he might delay steal. Whatever is done should be coordinated with the hitter at the plate which is detailed for all the players on the batting practice schedule.

Once he gets to second base, he will again be facing a pitcher who is throwing from the stretch position. On the schedule he should be informed on how many outs there are; whether he is in a force or non-force lead at second base; and how many times he will work on his primary and secondary lead. As an example, it might say on the schedule: No outs, no force, three proper leads. After the third pitch, react to the batted ball with the no out, no force lead. The hitter will be informed by the runner or the coach that the runner at second base will be responding to his swing. Thus, he must get him over to third base. The runner at second base will not break for third base until the ball enables him to do so. That means that the hitter must continue to try to get him over to third base before he can take his regular cuts. Of course, every swing with contact that does not get the job done counts as a cut. Another day the coach might have the runners work on two out leads; no out or one out lead with a force play at third base, etc.

Now the runner is at third base, and again will follow the schedule for the day for what he is to do at this base. The schedule might say: At third base, react to a one out situation with the infielders in on the grass, tie game, eighth inning. The runner will then respond to the ball off the bat as he would in a regular game. Since leading off third base is so important, a coach might want him to respond to two balls each time he is at third base. That means if a team is running the bases for the first two rounds of batting practice that each player will get to work on four leads at third base reacting to the ball as the situation describes.

Another day the team can work on the suicide squeeze with the runner at third base and the hitter responding. It is always best to allow the runner a couple of leads off third base before you require him to respond to the batted or bunted ball. In most cases, with a runner at third base the pitcher will be throwing from the windup working on looking the runner back to the base before he delivers to the plate. If there is also a baserunner at first base, then of course, the pitcher will have to throw from the stretch. When the runner at third base responds to the batted ball and heads full speed for the plate he must veer off once he gets near the batting cage so that he does not delay the next pitch. Now he is ready to get in line and hit again.

If enough coaches are available on a staff it is helpful to have a coach assigned to the baserunners during batting practice. He can assist them in finding their primary and secondary leads at all three bases and can correct any baserunning mistakes as they happen. If no coach is available for the baserunners, then the coach responsible for the batting cage will have to also watch the runners.

The coordination between the hitter and baserunners(s) during these batting practice sessions should be easy to define since it is detailed on the schedule for them each day. All hitters need to review their baserunning responsibility before they step in to hit so there is no confusion when they get on base. That is why it is very helpful to have a copy of the batting practice schedule on the batting cage.

5. **Catchers**—Hopefully, each squad a coach works with will have an adequate number of catchers to handle the pitchers on the main field and in the bullpen. If not, then some non-catchers will have to be used to warmup the pitchers in the bullpen. It is certainly not a good practice to ask a player to catch batting practice if he is not designated as a catcher, for obvious reasons.

It is necessary to have a regular catcher behind the plate whenever a regular pitcher is throwing. If a coach or another position player is throwing batting practice then it is not a necessity, although it really helps with the batting practice sequence.

The catcher working on the main field serves numerous functions. First and most important, is his responsibility to handle the pitcher throwing. Most of the time the pitchers will determine what pitches they will be throwing and will communicate this to the hitter and catcher. At other times the catcher and pitcher will use their game signs and will not tell the batter what pitch is coming.

Rather than having the catcher just sitting behind the plate catching batting practice, it is best to give him the opportunity to work on his fundamentals. This can be done by requiring each catcher to divide his time behind the plate into thirds. Thus, if he is catching 30 minutes of batting practice that day, he will divide his time segments into 10 minute blocks. The first third he should pretend that he is catching in a regular game with no runner on base with the umpire working behind him. The second segment he will pretend that there is a runner at first base, and the last part he will catch regular batting practice.

This type of work is much better then to require the catcher to work his full time behind the plate in game conditions, or worse yet, just catch regular batting practice. During these segments he can really concentrate on what he needs to work on in helping the pitcher, working with the umpire, and positioning himself to block low balls with runner(s) on base. He can also work on his mechanics to receive the ball with a possible steal situation in effect. A manager can be responsible to let the catcher know when to change.

In addition to working on his catching fundamentals, the catcher will call balls and strikes for each hitter as explained previously in this section. He must also keep the fungo hitter informed as to when the hitter will be coming out of the batter's box to run to first base. Each time the hitter is bunting, the catcher should come out from behind the plate to field the bunt. This also protects him from being possibly struck by a foul tip on the bunt attempt. Finally, he must throw a bunt to the pitcher on his last pitch as explained also in this section.

When there is a change of catchers in batting practice there should be no delay. The manager or coach in charge of batting practice needs to inform the next catcher at least five minutes before he is to catch on the main field, so that he has plenty of time to get the gear on.

6. **Fungo Hitters**—One of the keys to successful infield play is the work that the infielders receive during batting practice from the fungo hitters. That is why it is so important to give them a number of ground balls at this time. Since most of the coaches will be involved in other stations, it generally falls on the shoulders of the pitching staff to hit these fungos.

If you have a batting cage around home plate then there is no problem having a fungo hitter on both the first base and third base side of the plate area. If you do not have a batting cage it would not be wise to employ fungo hitters unless they can be protected from the batted balls.

It certainly does little good for the infielders to receive ground balls from poor fungo hitters. You will have some pitchers who can not handle a fungo bat at all. If so, it would be wise not to let them in the fungo circle unless you can train them quickly to become somewhat proficient at this skill. A pitcher who can swing a good fungo bat is a definite asset to the team.

On the sample practice schedule are listed the pitchers who will hit ground balls to the infielders during each of the hitting groups. The fungo hitter on the first base side will hit to any third baseman and second baseman wishing to take ground balls. The fungo hitter on the third base side will hit to any shortstop or first baseman. If there are no infielders wanting ground balls at that time, then the fungo hitter goes out in the outfield to shag balls or gets his running in on the warning track. The fungo hitter never leaves the fungo circle before he is sure that he will have no one interested in taking ground balls. Infielders wishing to take ground balls need to let the pitcher know at the beginning of each hitting group.

If there is more than one player at a position wanting ground balls it is best to have them alternate. If the pitcher is hitting ground balls to two different positions it is also better to alternate for it gives the fielder a chance to recover and get back into the proper ready position.

There is no need for a player to have to catch in for the fungo hitter for it just leads to more congestion around the batting cage. All infielders should throw the ball into the fungo hitter on one bounce so that it can be easily fielded in the bare hand.

The fungo hitter must time the ground balls so that the infielder is not fielding a ground ball off the fungo at the same time the hitter in the batter's box is swinging away. If timed properly, all infielders can concentrate solely on the fungoed baseball without having to keep one eye on the hitter at the plate. Once the catcher receives a pitched ball, or once a batted ball clears the infield the fungo hitter can hit a ground ball to an infielder. If the fungo hitter is not prepared to hit a ball at that time then he

33

should wait for the next pitch. When a hitter is bunting, the fungo hitter can hit a ball to an infielder being sure that he keeps the ball well away from the catcher fielding the bunt.

The fungo hitter on the first base side must be sure that he is not hitting a ball when the batter is coming out of the box full speed for first base. As explained previously in this section, it is the catcher's responsibility to let the first base fungo hitter know that the batter is coming out of the box on the last cut.

The third base fungo hitter should not hit a ground ball to the first baseman when there is a baserunner leading off first base or hit a ground ball to the shortstop when there is a runner leading off second base. All fungo hitters need to be aware of when the baserunners are stealing a base so that they are not dodging ground balls as they advance to the next base. This also holds true for the runners who are advancing to the next base when the hitter makes contact at the plate.

It is not the fungo hitter's responsibility to see how hard he can hit the ball at an infielder. A good fungo hitter will mix up the variety of balls hit in regard to velocity, angle to the infielder and texture of the bounces. He attempts to hit the types of ground balls that an infielder can expect to receive in a game. It is very important that he not get in the habit of just hitting the balls right at the infielder, for working him to his left and right is just as important as the ball right at him.

It takes a lot of practice to be a good fungo hitter, but those who become accomplished at this skill will have a lot of friends among the infielders. Those that are not proficient will find very few infielders requesting ground balls when it is their turn in the fungo circle.

7. **Back up**—Another responsibility the pitchers should have during batting practice is to serve the role as the back up man. This person should position himself behind second base about 10 feet on the outfield grass. This will keep him out of the way of the infielders taking ground balls along with protecting him somewhat from the batted ball. He should be protected by a screen so that if he has his back to the hitter he can avoid being injured by a batted ball. If he has no protective screen, then he needs to position himself another 10-15 feet away from the plate.

The back up man should have a large bag or bucket that he can use to put the baseballs in that come to his position from the shaggers. The pitcher on the main mound should yell "baseballs", when he has only four or five balls left to throw. The back up man should then run at least one-half speed to the mound and put all the baseballs into the container on the mound, and then run back to his position. It is certainly helpful to the pitcher on the main mound to have a ball container that is high enough off the ground that he does not have to bend down too far to get a baseball. This also saves valuable batting practice time.

Since there might be ground balls being hit by the fungo hitter(s) in addition to some throws being made to first base by the infielder(s), the back up man needs to keep alert as he runs to and from the mound. Also, he should never turn his back on the hitter at the plate when he is returning to the back up position.

With no exceptions, all baseballs hit by the hitter on the main field should go to the back up man. This also includes balls fielded by the infielders. It is a poor practice to have an infielder throw a ball back to the pitcher on the mound. The reason being that the pitcher might not be looking at the infielder when he throws the ball. Thus, just have **all** batted balls go to the back up man except those that the catcher fields on the bunt when he is out in front of the plate.

If no catcher is being used to catch batting practice on the main field, another bag or bucket needs to be next to the batting cage to put the balls in that go to the backstop. When enough baseballs gather in this area the next hitter, along with the hitter at the plate, need to gather the balls and run them out to the pitcher.

All baseballs coming to the back up man should be thrown on the ground so that there is no chance of injury due to an unsuspected throw. There is never any need to have more than one pitcher at the back up position.

8. **Infielders**—During batting practice all infielders should be required to receive some ground balls from the fungo hitters as long as the infield dirt is in playable condition. If the infield is not in good condition, ground balls will have a detrimental effect on the proper mechanics of an infielder.

The most important aspect for infielders taking ground balls during these batting practice sessions is that they take them under game conditions. That means that they should go full speed pretending that there is a baserunner who has just hit them a ground ball. It does absolutely no good to take a ground ball and not go full speed as in a game. In fact, it would be

34

better that a boy not take one ground ball unless he is able to give it a full effort. If he is not required to take the proper approach and angle to the ball in practice then he will have a difficult time properly doing so in a game.

This means that an infielder should take as many ground balls as he can going 100%. When he gets tired then he can either go in the outfield and shag balls, or stay in the infield and just take ground balls off the batted ball coming from the hitter at the plate. A boy might just want ten ground balls off a good fungo hitter in one group. Once he gets these balls he can then take a break and come back later for some more. Other infielders might just want to take the balls off the hitter at the plate. Thus, ground ball work in batting practice is something that a boy can use to improve his skills defensively. Going less than full speed will not get him ready properly for the regular season.

If an infielder is getting ground balls from a fungo hitter he should not field ground balls off the hitter at the plate unless they are close to his position. All balls that he fields from the hitter at the plate will go to the back up man on the ground. The balls he receives from the fungo hitter should be returned back to the fungo hitter on one bounce.

If the hitter at the plate hits a fly ball in the infield, the closest infielder needs to call for the ball and make the catch. The pitcher should not throw another pitch until the ball has been caught and the infielder has a chance to get back onto the dirt area. Those infielders taking ground balls from fungo hitters should not go a great distance to catch the fly ball.

All infielders during batting practice should have the opportunity to throw some baseballs to first base. A first baseman is assigned to each group for that purpose. Only ground balls off the fungo hitter's bat are ever thrown to first base for obvious safety reasons. The infielder should tell the first baseman that he will be throwing to him on all ground balls. Once he is finished another infielder can throw. Only one position should throw to first base at a time so that the first baseman can devote his full attention to them. That means that if there are two shortstops taking ground balls, both will alternate throwing to first base. A second baseman and shortstop would not alternate throwing to first base for obvious safety reasons. If another infielder wishes to throw, he will wait until the other infielder is finished. If he is going game speed he will not be too far from getting tired.

The infielders may also work on game speed double plays during batting practice, informing the first baseman what will transpire. The fungo hitter needs to be sure he hits the ball hard enough to get a double play for two reasons: (1) to simulate a double play type ground ball in a game; and (2) the pivot man will have to keep an eye out for the hitter at the plate if the batting practice pitcher is working quickly and the ball is not hit hard enough. If another protective screen is available, it can be placed in front of second base to protect the pivot man.

9. **First basemen**—All the first basemen should get a number of groundballs during batting practice, if the infield is in proper shape. As was mentioned for the infielders, a first baseman should go full speed on these ground balls simulating a game experience.

When he is taking ground balls from the third base side fungo hitter he will not be able to take any throws from the infielders. Once he is finished with his ground balls he needs to check with the infielders in his group to see if any want to throw to the base. If no infielder wishes to throw, he can either stay around first base and take ground balls off the hitter at the plate, or go in the outfield and become a shagger.

The first baseman must have a protective screen in front of the bag that is large enough to protect him from the batted ball. If no protective screen is available, then it would be best to pass on any throwing to first base. With the protective screen up, the first baseman can work on his shifting and taking bad throws without having to worry about the hitter at the plate.

10. **Outfielders**—There is no better time for an outfielder to work on getting a jump on the ball than during batting practice. The use of the fungo bat in hitting balls to an outfielder is fine, but it does not replace the hitter at home plate duplicating the game type conditions. This is why all the outfielders need to spend some time during batting practice each day putting themselves in game conditions reacting to the batted ball.

Each outfielder needs to determine how long they can go full speed on the ground balls, fly balls and line drives in their area. They might wish to go about ten minutes, take a break for ten minutes, and then finish up with another ten minutes of hard work. There should be no problem for a coach to determine when an outfielder is working under game conditions or shagging.

All other shaggers in the outfield need to stay clear of the outfielder reacting full speed to the batted ball. The outfielders should mentally place a runner on a certain base on every pitch so that he can create the proper angle and approach to the ball for a play at the forward base. He can use the runners that are on the bases in batting practice. All baseballs fielded must be thrown into the back up man on the ground. At no time should an outfielder throw to a base during batting practice.

11. **Shaggers**—In most cases the pitchers will comprise the bulk of the shaggers for batting practice. A pitcher should never be allowed to field balls in the infield due to the chance of an injury. Thus, when they are not pitching on the main mound, warming up in the bullpen, hitting fungos, serving as a back up man, or running in the outfield, they are shaggers. If the batting practice plan has numerous stations to man, then there will be times that there will be very few shaggers available. At other times, there may be more than enough.

It is wise for the head coach to establish the fact that all shaggers man areas of the outfield well away from the next player, especially when there are a few shaggers available. This is to keep them from congregating in one area of the outfield. At times, this might be relaxed when there is an abundance of shaggers and the entire outfield is adequately covered.

Any outfielder reacting to the batted ball at game speed must be allowed the opportunity to field the ball. If he is not going game speed, then he becomes just another shagger. The practice of two or three players going after the same ball must be discouraged in order to prevent an unnecessary injury.

All balls fielded by the shaggers are to be thrown into the back up area on the ground. Any ball that goes over the fence must be retrieved by the shagger who is closest to the fence where the ball left the field. If a team's outfield fence distances are rather short, then it would be a good practice to assign one player on the batting practice schedule to position himself on the other side of the fence. If a batter hits a foul ball out of the field of play, it should be the hitter's responsibility to retrieve the ball if no shagger helps him out. The best time for him to get the ball is after he finishes running the bases during the first two rounds. If he hits one out foul after the first two rounds, then he should go after the ball when his group finishes hitting. The coach at the batting cage might have to remind certain players of this responsibility.

12. **Pitchers running**—In addition to an extensive conditioning program that needs to be set up for the pitchers toward the end of practice, they can also get some running in during batting practice. The best place to do this running is on the warning track in the outfield. If there is no warning track on the field, then they should run close to the outfield fence so that they do not get in the way of an outfielder reacting to the ball, or the shaggers.

Those pitchers that are not throwing in batting practice may be assigned more running than those who are throwing that particular day. One excellent running drill during batting practice is to have pitchers start from the left field foul pole, and then run 7/8's speed to a spot designated in right center field. He then walks briskly to the right field foul pole, and then runs 7/8's speed to a spot designated in left center field. He then walks to the left field foul pole. The pitchers repeat this as many times as the coach designates on the practice schedule. Much will depend on how much running the pitchers will be doing at the completion of practice. A good figure to use on an average day is seven foul poles for those pitchers throwing in batting practice that day, and ten foul poles for those pitchers not throwing. Count one foul pole each time the pitcher runs, so if it is eight foul poles that day, he will make four round trips on the warning track.

The pitchers must work their running in around their other responsibilities during batting practice. No pitcher should be running when the schedule calls for him to be assigned to another area (back up, fungo, etc.) The only exception would be for the fungo hitter who finds that there are no infielders wanting ground balls in his group. He can then go ahead and get his running in. Thus, no pitcher should be assigned a responsibility for every hitting group, which would not leave him any time to get his foul poles in. Those pitchers throwing in the last group should do their running earlier in batting practice for there will be no time to do it after batting practice when the pitchers' regular conditioning program generally begins.

13. **Hitters in batting range**—It certainly helps the hitters when there is a batting range or two available so that each hitter can get a maximum number of swings each day. On the batting practice schedule, the hitters are assigned to the range area(s). The hitters might either hit off a pitching machine, throw to each other from the full distance, throw to each other from a shorter distance (short toss), side toss, batting tee work, etc. If enough coaches are available these batting range(s) need to be supervised.

If two batting ranges are available, then the two groups need to switch ranges at the half way point in the respective hitting group. The manager or coach assigned to keeping the time for batting practice can let the hitters in the ranges know when to switch.

36

14. **Bullpens**—The bullpen is a very important area in the batting practice plan. All pitchers who are scheduled to throw batting practice on the main field need to be given an adequate amount of time to get stretched out, in addition to warming up properly to throw. A catcher should always be assigned to the pitcher in the bullpen. On the sample batting practice schedule the name of the catcher who is to warm the pitcher up is listed next to the pitcher's name in the pitching column. If there is not enough regular catchers available then other non-pitchers can be assigned this task.

All catchers in the bullpen should wear a mask when the pitcher starts heating up and the catcher gets into the "down" position. If the catcher desires, he can put on the full gear. This is especially helpful to the catcher who is warming up a pitcher that has some control problems, or one that keeps his breaking pitchers low and in the dirt.

Other pitchers may also work in the bullpen even if they are not throwing that particular day. They will have to find their own catcher for any work they might wish to do. The pitchers may work on their pick-offs or any pitching drills at this time also, hopefully under the supervision of the pitching coach.

The manager responsible for keeping the time in batting practice will inform the pitcher when he has five minutes to go before he is to throw on the main field. He will then let him know when he has one minute to go so that he can start down to the main field at one-half speed. He will then be in a position to run onto the mound when the pitcher he is to replace has thrown his last pitch.

As can be easily seen by looking at the sample batting practice schedule along with following the description of each segment of the batting practice plan, a lot of work can be accomplished during this segment of practice if organized properly. With a one or two coach program much of this work will have to go unsupervised. That is why it is imperative that the head coach impress upon his team the importance of concentration and dedication to what they are doing. Game oriented practice experiences should carry over into better performances during the game itself. The players will enjoy this segment of the practice for they will all stay busy and get accomplished what they need to in order to better prepare themselves for the game experience.

Defensive Work in Practice

It is best to get all defensive team work done prior to batting practice whenever possible. The reason being that the players are fresher mentally and physically at this time. This would include: bunt defense plays; double steal defense plays; fundamental drill series for all positions; cut-offs and relays; steal defense; outfield-infield practice; etc. All of these types of plays will be detailed later in the Playbook.

Conditioning Work in Practice

It is always a good practice to save the last segment of the practice schedule for any conditioning work for the squad. If done before the end of practice it would fatigue the players for any type of skill work. It is also wise for the head coach to detail on the practice schedule the type, amount and duration of the conditioning work to be done.

The pitchers and hitters should be divided up to do their conditioning so that the hitters might do their work on the bases. The pitchers can be assigned to a coach and get their running done in the outfield while the hitters are working in the infield area.

The type, amount and duration of the conditioning work for the pitchers in practice can be determined by the head coach or pitching coach. It is important that a variety of running drills be employed so that the pitchers do not get completely bored and turned off by repetitious running.

For the hitters on the bases there are numerous baserunning drills that can be used so that the players are not only getting their conditioning work in, but are learning baserunning skills that can be game oriented. Detailed in the following section would be examples of five days of baserunning drills for the hitters:

Day One

1. Home to first base full speed five times simulating hitting the baseball. This is done by the hitter assuming his normal stance, taking a full cut with his hands so that when simulated contact is made he slaps his hands hard, and then follows through. Full speed out of the box to first base.

2. One base on ball from home plate. Three-quarters minimum speed to first base.

3. One full speed out of the box to first base reacting to first baseman on the base (coach or manager). When the first baseman comes off the bag down the line, yell "slide". This would simulate the actual slide in a regular game.

4. At first base. Two steals of second base off a righthanded pitcher (manager or coach). Pitcher mixes up what he does (throwing to the plate or picking runner off first base—no ball needed). Three at a time.

5. At first base. Two steals of second base off a lefthanded pitcher (manager or coach). Pitcher mixes up what he does (throwing to the plate or picking runner off first base-no ball needed). Three at a time.

6. At first base. Two hit and runs off a right-handed pitcher. Same as #4 and #5.

7. At first base. Two hit and runs off a left-handed pitcher. Same as #4 and #5.

8. At second base. React to batted ball (fungo hitter at the plate). No outs, no force. Three at a time. Need a manager or a coach at third base, shortstop, and on the mound for defense. Three times each. A time counts when advanced to third base.

9. 4-3-2-1 one-half speed from home plate. Simulated full swing. coming out of the box full speed for at least five steps. Then one-half speed. Jog back to home plate. Four home to first base; three home to second base; two home to third base; and one home to home.

Day Two

1. Right field line. Diving back to first base on pick-off five times. Get primary lead with right field foul line being first base. Coach or manager (pitcher).

2. Five head first slides from 90 feet into the right field line. Five at a time. Right field line is first base.

3. At home plate. Two full speeds to first base off simulated swing. Pretend hitting ground ball back to the pitcher.

4. At home plate. Two full speeds to first base off simulated swing. Pretend hitting ball to the second baseman.

5. At home plate. Two full speeds to first base off simulated swing. Pretend hitting ground ball to the shortstop.

6. At home plate. Two doubles to right center field. Simulate ball in front of you, no first base coach needed.

7. At home plate. Two doubles down left field line. Use first base coach (coach in box giving signal).

8. At first base. Two first to third base not using the third base coach. Simulate ball hit to left center field.

9. At first base. Two first to third base using third base coach (coach in box giving signal). Simulate ball hit down right field line.

10. 6-3-1-1 one-half speed.

Day Three

1. At home plate. Simulate four pop-ups to the infield. Full speed to first base. Last five steps, chop steps and stand on base.

2. At home plate. Simulate two texas league type fly balls. Full speed to one-half point between first and second base. Pretend catch is made.

3. At home plate. One simulated hit by pitch. Three-quarters speed minimum to first base.

4. At home plate. One simulated passed ball-wild pitch that goes to the backstop with a simulated runner at second base. Full speed to second base using the first base coach (coach in box using signal).

38

5. At home plate. Simulated triple to left center field one time. Pick up first base coach (coach in box giving signal). No need to pick up the third base coach since the ball is in front of you.

6. At first base. Three delayed steals off right-handed pitcher (manager or coach on the mound). Pitcher can pick-off on occasion.

7. First and third base double steal plays. Three at a time at each base. Two outs at all times. Coach in third base box gives signal. Five minutes. Need a catcher, a pitcher, a first baseman, a second baseman, and a third baseman (managers or coaches).

8. At third base. Simulate one out tag up situation. Coach hits fly balls from home plate with fungo. Managers in outfield. Three times each. Three at a time.

9. 1-1-1-1 one-half speed.

Day Four

1. At home plate. Simulate two ground balls to the shortstop with an overthrow at first base. Break down past the base-full speed to second base.

2. At home plate. Simulate one ground ball to the shortstop with an overthrow at first base. Start break to second base, and then get back to first base.

3. At home plate. Simulate two doubles. One to left center field, one to right center field. No need for first base coach for ball is in front.

4. At home plate. Three simulated routine fly balls to the outfield. One to left field, one to center field, and one to right field. Full speed to coach standing between first and second base.

5. At home plate. Three simulated singles to the outfield. One to left field, one to center field, one to right field. Full speed to coach standing between first and second base. Break down at that point and go back to first base full speed. Veer off as you go back to first base for there will be another runner rounding the base.

6. At home plate. Same as #5 three times. React to simulated base hit with a bobble in the outfield. Full speed to second base after breaking down where coach is standing between first and second base.

7. At first base. Two first to third base. Ball hit behind you. Pick up third base coach who will be holding you up at second base. React to misplay in right field. Break down and go full speed to third base.

8. At second base with two outs. Two second base to home plate using the third base coach (coach in box giving signals).

9. 1-1-1-1 one-half speed.

Day Five

1. At second base. Leads at the base using the third base coach. Three at a time. React to pitcher on the mound (manager or coach). Five minutes.

2. At first and second base with one out. Three at a time reacting to fungoed baseball (coach at the plate hitting fungos). Managers in outfield on defense. Five minutes. Coach at third base giving signals.

3. At third base. Simulate one out situation with the infield back. Reacting to fungoed baseball. Coach hitting fungos at home plate. Three at a time. Five minutes. Managers on defense in infield. Coach on the mound.

4. At first base. Three fake steals each, three at a time. Manager or coach on the mound. Occasional pick-off move.

5. At all three bases. Tagging up on fly balls in the outfield. Coach fungo at home plate. Managers in the outfield catching fly balls. Five minutes. Full speed to the next base.

6. At home plate. One simulated triple to left center field. Head first slide into third base. No base coaches needed since ball is in front of you.

7. 4-3-2-1 one-half speed.

There are numerous other simulated baserunning drills that can be incorporated during this segment of practice. The coach needs to make all these drills as realistic as possible to duplicate the game experience on the bases. If you have a pitcher that might be called on to be a pinch runner, he needs to be involved in these drills on numerous occasions.

Simulated Situations

A very important part of practice at least once a week is the simulated defensive drill. Nine players are on defense with a coach at the plate with a fungo bat. The baserunners will be those hitters who are not on defense at the time. Pitchers should not be used as baserunners unless one of them might be involved in pinch running duties during the season.

The coach then precedes to hit the ball anywhere on the field making sure that he first informs the defense and baserunners how many outs there are, the inning and the score. This information is needed so that the defense and the runners know when to take chances and when to play conservative. After about five or ten minutes, another nine players go on defense and the team out in the field become baserunners. The pitchers should change a little more frequently on the mound. A coach can set up just about any situation that might confront a team in a game. If inside, all that needs to be done is cut the base distances down in half and have the players respond at a much slower pace than game speed. The coach can throw the baseball from home plate when inside.

Defensive Practice Check List

A coach might want to keep track of what is being accomplished at each practice session so that he might be sure that he covers every aspect of defensive play before the first scheduled game. The amount of sessions devoted to each fundamental and the time spent on each should be determined by the head coach along with his assistant coaches. This will depend entirely on the experience level of the team along with the individual position players.

This is a sample practice check list. The coach can put down whatever defensive skills he wants to cover with each position. Next to the defensive skill he will place the date and time spent on this particular item. Thus on the sample practice check list next to the shifting techniques for the catchers, the coach has placed the date and time spent on this skill. After every practice day the coach will complete this practice check list.

PRACTICE CHECK LIST

Catchers

DATE AND TIME

Proper Shifting Technique	2/8 -10	2/19 - 5	3/1 - 10	3/9 - 5	3/17 - 10			
Handling Low Balls in Dirt								
Handling Pop-ups								
Tag Plays at the Plate								
Force Plays at the Plate								
Fielding Bunts								
Backing up Bases								
Giving Signs to Pitcher								
Pitchouts								
Intentional Walks								
Framing the Ball								
Double Steal Plays								
Play Number 1								
Play Number 2								
Play Number 3								
Play Number 4								
Bunt Defense Plays								
First Base Only								
First and Second								
Suicide Squeeze Defense								
Pick-off Plays								
Play #23								
Play #24								
Play #25								
Play #26								
Decoying Runner at Plate								
Throwing to Second Base								
Throwing to Third Base								
Using Cut-off Man								
Rundowns								
Throwing Ball From Backstop								

First Basemen

DATE AND TIME

Fielding Low Throws								
Holding Runners on Base								
Breaking Off Base								
Cut-Off Responsibilities								

First Basemen (Continued)

Double Steal Plays
    Play Number 1
    Play Number 2
    Play Number 3
    Play Number 4
Bunt Defense Plays
    First Base Only
    First and Second
Pick-off Plays
    Play #13
    Play #23
Fielding Bunts With Throw
3-6-3 Double Play
Playing Fence on Fly Ball
Throwing to Pitcher — 1B
Following Up Runners
Back Up Responsibilities
Ground Ball Communication
Shifting on First Base

Second Basemen

Holding Runner on Base
Preventing Delayed Steal
Back Up Throws From Plate
Covering 2B on Steals
Cut-off Responsibilities
Double Steal Plays
    Play Number 1
    Play Number 2
    Play Number 3
    Play Number 4
Bunt Defense Plays
    First Base Only
    First and Second
Pick-off Plays
    Play #14
    Play #24
Double Play Situations
    4-6-3
    6-4-3
    5-4-3
    1-4-3
Making Tag Plays
Tandem Relays
Decoying Runners
Rundowns
Fly Ball Communication
Inside Pick-off
Throwing Behind Runner
Ground Ball Communication

Shortstops

Holding Runner on Base							
Preventing Delayed Steal							
Back Up Throws From Plate							
Covering 2B on Steals							
Cut-off Responsibilities							
Double Steal Plays							
Play Number 1							
Play Number 2							
Play Number 3							
Play Number 4							
Bunt Defense Plays							
First Base Only							
First and Second							
Pick-off Plays							
Play #16							
Play #26							
Double Play Situations							
4-6-3							
6-4-3							
5-6-3							
3-6-3							
1-6-3							
Making Tag Plays							
Tandem Relays							
Decoying Runners							
Rundowns							
Fly Ball Communication							
Inside Pick-off							
Daylight Pick-off							
Throwing Behind Runner							
Ground Ball Communication							

Third Basemen

Holding Runner on Base							
Back Up Throws From 1B							
Covering 3B on Steals							
Cut-off Responsibilities							
Double Steal Plays							
Play Number 1							
Play Number 2							
Play Number 3							
Play Number 4							
Bunt Defense Plays							
First Base Only							
First and Second							
Pick-off Plays							
Play #15							
Play #25							
Double Play Situations							
5-4-3							
5-6-3							
1-5-3							

Third Basemen (Continued)

DATE AND TIME

Making Tag Plays
Decoying Runners
Rundowns
Fly Ball Communication
Throwing Behind Runner
Ground Ball Communication
Tandem Communication

Outfielders

DATE AND TIME

Using Cut-off Men
Using Relay Men
Throwing to Bases
    Ground Balls
    Fly Balls
Throwing to Plate
    Ground Ball
    Fly Balls
Playing the Fence
Fence Communication
Fly Ball Communication
Fly Ball Responsibilities
Backing up Bases
Rundown Responsibilities
Pick-off Responsibilities
Bunt Responsibilities
Throwing Behind Runner
Ball at Fence
Using Sunglasses

Pitchers

DATE AND TIME

Bunt Defense Plays
    First Base Only
    First and Second
Suicide Squeeze Defense
Double Steal Plays
    Play Number 1
    Play Number 2
    Play Number 3
    Play Number 4
Pick-off Plays
    Play #13
    Play #14
    Play #15
    Play #16
Inside Pick-off
Daylight Pick-off

Pitchers (Continued)

Double Play Situations							
1-6-3							
1-4-3							
3-6-1							
1-2-3							
Holding Runners on Base							
Backing up Bases							
Backing up Plate							
Covering Home Plate							
Fielding Ground Balls							
Delayed Steal Defense							
Covering First Base							
Fly Ball Communication							
Ground Ball Communication							
Rundown Responsibilities							
Intentional Walks							
Pitchouts							

Scrimmage Game Practice

As the old saying goes, "there is nothing that replaces game experience". This is certainly true for baseball. No matter how interesting and enjoyable the coach makes his practice sessions, his athletes will still want to test their skills against one another in game scrimmages. It should also be an enjoyable experience, along with finding out exactly how players fare under game conditions.

It is not a good practice to play too many inter-squad games at the expense of the detailed fundamental work that can be done in a structured practice session. It is up to the head coach to come up with a good balanced pre-season schedule of practices and games. Understandably, the playing of games enables the coaching staff to better evaluate the individual players, and also allows them the opportunity to find any areas of weaknesses that might be worked on during future practice sessions.

On the next two pages you will find a sample practice schedule with an inter-squad game being played. The coach might wish to balance a practice day by having a short practice working on fundamentals in addition to playing a game. However, it is generally best to keep these pre-game segments of practice quite short so the players are not too mentally and physically fatigued for the game. If at all possible, a short round of batting practice should be arranged prior to the game, but it is certainly not a necessity.

An organized and functional outfield-infield drill should precede the game if at all possible so that all the players have their arms and legs properly stretched out for the game itself. An explanation of two types of outfield-infield drill are detailed later in the Playbook.

As in a regular practice schedule, there should be some type of pre-practice workout for selected individuals, followed by a meeting of the entire team. After the meeting the coach can elect to go over a team defense drill, take a round of batting practice, or go directly into the outfield-infield drill as the starting pitchers warmup for the game.

After the outfield-infield drill there should be about a five minute break before the start of the game. This gives the starting pitchers additional time to warmup, and allows the other players a chance to get organized and prepare for the game itself.

Friday - February 18th

1. Late today: **Martz** (on the field at 3:15)

2. Make sure that you take your spikes off before entering the locker room. Also, if there is mud or dirt on your cleats, clean them off before bringing them in.

3. **Murphy**—Need to see you about your class schedule sometime before practice in the office.

Pre-Practice

1:40 - 2:00   Open hitting in the ranges:

                Left Field Range (Machine)—Coach **Osborne**
                Right Field Range (Short-toss)—Coach **Johnson**

                Knight and **Fox**—Report to Coach **Polk.** Work on ground balls in the infield. **Purnell** (Catcher)

Practice

2:00 - 2:05   Meeting

2:05 - 2:30   Fundamental Drill Series Number 2. Three minute stations.

2:30 - 2:45   Multiple outfield-infield drill (**Polk**—Fungo)
                Starting pitchers get warmed up in the bullpen.
                Smith and **Bolek** (Catchers until assigned catchers are finished with infield drill).

2:40 - 2:45   Game preparation.

2:45   11 inning 2-1 count game with runner at second base. Last out in previous inning is the runner at second. First inning it will be the last hitter in the lineup. **Lineups on the next page.**

Post-Game

Game mistakes
50 plus pickups for the losing team

Pitchers—During game, seven foul poles for those throwing today, 10 for those not throwing.

Hitters—   Five minutes of first and third offense.
                Four triples not using base coaches.
                4-3-2-1 one-half speed.

GAME LINEUPS

AWAY TEAM		HOME TEAM	
RF	GILLASPIE	RF	GAGE (DARLINGTON 7TH)
CF	SWANN (SMITH 7TH)	CF	WINKLER
LF	SMITH (SWANN 7TH)	LF	KLIPSTEIN (BAIRLEY 8TH)
1B	WALKER (BOND 7TH)	1B	CASTORIA (MALONEY 8TH)
2B	WHITE (VAN CLEVE 7TH)	2B	ZELMER (MARTZ 7TH)
SS	D'ERCOLE	SS	MARTZ (ZELMER 7TH)
3B	SOTTILE	3B	MALONEY (KLIPSTEIN 8TH)
C	PORTER (LOE 7TH)	C	BAIRLEY (SHANNON 8TH)
DH	LOE (PORTER 7TH)	DH	SHANNON (CASTORIA 8TH)
DH	BOND (WALKER 7TH)	DH	DARLINGTON (GAGE 7TH)
DH	VAN CLEVE (WHITE 7TH)		
P	BOND — EMRHEIN	P	HARDWICK — ROTH
	FLOWERS (4TH) — LOE		BARTLEY (4TH) — SHANNON
	WEATHERSBY (7TH) — EMRHEIN		TAYLOR (7TH) — SHANNON
	MORLOCK (10TH) — PORTER		MORLOCK (10TH)

MORLOCK PITCHES FOR BOTH TEAMS THE 10TH AND 11TH INNING.
BALLS AND STRIKES — McMAHON — ROTH (6TH) — BOLEK (9TH)
BASE UMPIRE — MYLES — PRUSER (7TH)
1B SHAGGER — SUSCE — SHREWSBERRY (7TH)
3B SHAGGER — MUNDIE — HARDWICK (7TH)
SCOREKEEPER — MOOREHEAD
SCOREBOOK — PURNELL
PRODUCTION RATING CHART — BOLEK
CONTROL CHART — MORLOCK — BRYANT (7TH)

It is recommended that the head coach make the lineups as balanced as possible for most of these scrimmage games. The reason for this being that it keeps both teams quite competitive. However, later in the practice season it is best to allow what looks like the starting infield to play together a little more often. As an example, the coach might have the number one infield and the number two outfield and catcher on the same team. Once or twice he could allow what looks like the starting team play against the number two squad. It is certainly not a good practice for the head coach to set lineups early in the practice season on this basis without allowing the players an adequate time to play themselves on or off the number one team. This could easily be done after the first player-coach evaluation explained later in the Playbook.

At the same time, early in the practice season it is best to allow all the players an equal amount of playing time per game. Later in the practice season, and after one or two player-coach evaluations, the better players should play a little longer each game. No player should be allowed to play in a scrimmage game unless he is 100% healthy. Playing squadmen out of position should also be frowned upon unless there is no way around it due to injuries or a shortage of personnel.

Players that are being evaluated at two positions should be permitted the opportunity to play both positions. You can either allow him to play two positions in one game, or play one position one day and the other position the next day. A boy who is a pitcher and a position player can either pitch one day and then play his position another, or he can pitch early in the game and then play a position toward the end of the contest. It is best to have a young man who is pitching one day and also required to play a position that day to be the starting pitcher for one of the teams. This eliminates the problem of having him leave the game to have to warmup in the bullpen, and also enables him to have the opportunity to pitch before he might be fatigued from playing another position.

In the two lineups on the sample schedule you will see that there are a few situations in regard to the batting order that would not be allowed in a regular season game. This is done to allow players to enter and leave the game in order to balance the lineups, and to provide the players a chance to play the same amount of innings either offensively or defensively. If the coach has an abundance of players to fill two squads he can always add one or two additional designated hitting spots in the lineup.

On the sample schedule the names of the players next to the pitchers are the catchers who are assigned to warm them up in the bullpen. This does not have to be a regular catcher, but as in the batting practice schedule discussed previously, it is best to assign a regular catcher to this task. A catcher can be assigned to warmup the pitcher in the bullpen and still be a designated hitter at that time. When his time comes to hit in the game, the pitcher can grab another player to throw to until his catcher comes back to the bullpen. All catchers should be required to wear a mask when in the bullpen and the pitcher begins throwing hard.

If at all possible, regular umpires should be used occasionally to work these scrimmage games. Many times a coach will find umpires in his community who enjoy working some games for no fee, or a man who is interested in working in the local umpire's association who wishes to be evaluated. If funds are available, it would be wise to employ qualified umpires for a few of these pre-season scrimmage games.

If regular umpires are not used, then coaches should be used to call balls and strikes from behind the mound. Using players to perform this task should be discouraged due to the pressure it places on a player when dealing with his peers. An exception to this would be when a coach has a player or players on his squad who are very capable at this assignment. Players can be used on the bases with the pitchers not throwing that day generally assigned this task, or a player who might be injured but can still move around the infield. No player or coach should be assigned to umpire for more than one-half of the game. The players must be discouraged from any complaining on calls made by players or coaches.

It is very important that the pitchers occasionally throw to hitters in game conditions with an umpire situated behind the plate. This is to provide the pitcher with an opportunity to throw to his catcher with an umpire looking over the catcher's shoulder as he would see in a regular game.

All balls that leave the playing field should be returned to the field of play by the pitchers who are not throwing that day, or those pitchers who have already thrown and are available to shag. The first base side shagger returns all the balls that leave the field, fair or foul, on the first base side of the field. The third base side shagger then takes the other side. By dividing the playing field from the backstop to the center field fence it is very easy for the shaggers to know what ball is their responsibility to retrieve. Shaggers should be required to run at least one-half speed after the ball. They can then walk back to the field once they have found the ball.

The pitchers should be required to do some running during the game similar to what they do during batting practice on a regular practice day. All running should be done on the warning track in the outfield. If none available, then they should run close to the fence. In the sample scrimmage game schedule, the pitchers are assigned to run either seven or ten foul poles that particular day. Seven for those throwing that day, and ten for those not throwing. The pitchers can run these foul poles anytime they are not assigned responsibilities as umpires, shaggers or charters. Those pitchers throwing last in the game must get their seven foul poles done early in the game since there will not be any time upon the completion of the game. Seven foul poles certainly will not fatigue a pitcher to throw three to five innings. If he is to throw more than five innings he should not be required to run prior to the time on the mound. Those pitchers who play another position should not be required to run since they will probably be back in the game in another capacity.

A manager can be assigned the task of keeping the score during the game. If a scoreboard is available on the field, then it can be put into operation. A manager should also be assigned to keep the baseballs in play, along with rubbing up all the new balls that enter the game.

Below is a manner in which the game score can be kept which provides initiative for the offense to concentrate on getting runners into scoring position, along with getting the runs across the plate. One run is subtracted from the offense's team score when:

    1. A hitter takes a called third strike.

    2. There is a baserunner at second base only with no outs, and the batter fails to get him to third base via the batted ball. A walk to the batter is okay.

    3. There is a baserunner at third base with no outs or one out and the hitter fails to score him. Walk okay.

Thus, a team can actually receive five negative runs in an inning when: Three outs are made via the called third strike;

one of the called third strikes occurs when there is a runner at second base only with no outs; the other called third strike occurs with a runner on third base with one out. So a final score might be in the minus runs, with let's say a score of −7 to −10. Of course, the −7 is the winning score. This scoring concept really impresses upon the hitters the need to get the job done with runners in scoring position. It makes for a very interesting finish many times when a team can actually win the game on defense by forcing the hitting team to tally up some negative runs. That is why you always have to play the bottom of the last inning even though the home team might be ahead. If they are ahead by more than five runs, the bottom of the inning does not have to be played since there is no way they can accumulate more than five negative runs.

It is always helpful to the spirit of the game to have the losing team members participate in a non-enjoyable session of some type of exercise. The use of pickups is excellent for achieving this objective since a member of the winning team can be responsible to throw the pickups to a member of the losing squad. As noted in the sample schedule, 50 plus pickups are designated for the losing team members. This means that the losing team members are dealt a **minimum** of 50 pickups. For every run past the five run difference in the score between the two teams, five additional pickups are added to the count. For example, let's say the final score is 9 to −3. That is a 12 run difference in the score, which is 7 runs over the 5 run difference. 5 × 7 = 35. That means that each member of the losing team is dealt 85 pickups after the game. What this accomplishes is to provide incentive for the team behind to close the gap before the game is over. You can imagine the consternation for a losing squad member if the difference in a score is 20 runs, and he must do 125 pickups (50 plus 75). You arrive at the 75 figure since it was 15 runs over the 5 allowed (15 × 5 = 75).

Rather than play regular 0-0 count games each day it is best many times to play scrimmage games with different counts on the batter each time they step to the plate. For example, on the sample schedule it indicates to the club that the game will be an 11 inning 2-1 count game with a baserunner at second base to start each inning. That means that every batter coming to the plate for the entire game will have a 2 ball-1 strike count on them. In addition, there will be a baserunner at second base at the start of each inning with the last out in the previous inning being the runner. In the first inning, the last hitter in the lineup will be the runner at second base.

Other days you can play combination counts. For example, you play a 12 inning game with each pitcher throwing four innings. During each pitcher's first two innings the count on each batter will be 3 balls-1 strike. The next two innings could be a 1 ball-2 strike count on each batter. You can also have a day with each pitcher starting the inning with the bases already loaded, with the last three outs in the previous inning the runners on base.

The advantages of playing these various count games, along with having runners on the base(s) to start the inning, is to confront the pitchers, hitters, baserunners and the defense with a lot of situations that will come up in a regular game. The traditional 0-0 count scrimmage game can be quite boring for the players and will not always force the offense and defense to be confronted with numerous situations. At the same time, 0-0 count games should also be played so that the pitchers have the opportunity to set up hitters as they would in a regular game.

Playing various count games provide the coaching staff a chance to help the pitchers analyze exactly what type of pitch and location they need to think about with this count on the batter. If a pitcher is forced to start each hitter with a 2 ball-0 strike count he will quickly learn what he needs to do in order to have some success on this particular count with the batter. The hitters can also learn quite a bit about the art of hitting with various counts on them each time to the plate. A coach quickly finds out who can protect the plate with two strikes and who has the discipline to handle counts when ahead of the pitcher.

Thus, with various count games along with occasionally starting runners on the bases, you will have a more exciting scrimmage game. At the same time all players will be confronted with numerous situations that they would not be confronted with in a traditional 0-0 count ball game. The score of these type games is kept just like the other games. One can imagine the number of runs that might cross the plate if you are to play a 3-1 or 3-0 count game even though negative runs might prove to be a factor. Of course, as you increase the count on each batter, the number of innings in a ball game can be increased. On a 3-2 count day, one can easily play an 18 inning game in a couple of hours.

The head coach needs to establish some rules for the scrimmage games. Examples of such rules might be:

   1. The 3-0 count is an automatic take unless there are runners in scoring position (second or third base).

   2. No base coaches will be used in the game. This is to force the runners to be aware of where the ball is at all times.

   3. Players can bunt, steal, hit and run, etc. whenever they wish since no base coaches will be used and no signs flashed. Always remember what the score is and what you are trying to accomplish.

4. The defensive team should use the regular bunt defense and double steal defense during these scrimmage games. The defense will determine themselves how they wish to play the infield in regard to depth depending on the score, inning, etc.

5. Players will go on and off the field at seven-eighths speed minimum. Pitchers one-half speed minimum on and off the mound.

6. Each pitcher will be allowed eight warmup pitches the first inning on the mound, five warmup pitches every other inning.

7. All pitchers will throw their designated number of innings on the game schedule unless an injury occurs.

8. Each team is responsible for keeping the bats and helmets in the dugout area. Both teams can stay in the third base dugout.

9. Play the game to win.

At the completion of the game, if time remains, the head coach should sit the entire team down on the field or in the locker room and quickly review all game mistakes. This is the best time to review these mistakes while the game is fresh in their minds. It is best that the coach write the mistakes down as they occur in the game so that he can be sure to cover those that he feels he needs to present to the club. If time does not allow the coach to cover these mistakes after the game then he should do so the next day at practice.

It is certainly wise and proper for the head coach and his assistants to talk to a boy when a mistake is made in the game, but it should be done at a time that it does not interrupt the course of the game itself. A coach does not have to mention names of players making mistakes in the post-game meeting for the player will know who he is when it is discussed. It certainly does no harm for every position player to hear about a mistake made by another positon player. When someone makes a mental mistake it becomes a team mistake. The meeting should not last longer than ten minutes unless an unusual number of mistakes were made in a particular game. Physical mistakes should not be discussed as a rule.

Post-game conditioning should be very similar to the type of running done after a regular practice. However, if for example the scrimmage game is let's say an 18 inning, 3-2 count game, keep in mind that the players will already have done quite a bit of conditioning running to and from their position. It is always best to go in this order after the game: (1) game mistakes meeting; (2) pickups for the losing team; (3) conditioning.

Keeping a detailed scorebook during these scrimmage games is certainly not necessary unless the coach wishes to post game statistics periodically. Many times statistics can be quite misleading when there are a very few games being played. For example, a hitter's batting average is certainly not reflective of his hitting ability over the course of a few games. A fine hitter might hit numerous line drives right in the hands of the defense, while another hitter hits quite a few "chinks" that fall in for base hits.

Posting statistics such as: fielding average, on base percentage, slugging percentage, etc. could also be done, but again, might not be reflective of a player's true ability unless a team was to play a lot of pre-season scrimmage games. If you play different count games it would not be wise to keep the pitcher's earned run averages. One can imagine what a four inning stint on the mound with a 3-1 count would do for a pitcher's earned run average, especially if each inning started with the bases loaded.

There are a couple of statistics that are deemed important. One being the pitcher's control chart and the other being the hitters and pitchers production rating chart. By using some type of control chart the pitchers will have an opportunity to evaluate their control in these pre-season games and compare themselves with the other pitchers on the staff. An example of a very simple control chart is on the next page. Pitchers are assigned to keep the control chart during the game from a vantage point behind the backstop so that they can accurately chart each type of pitch thrown by every pitcher.

All this pitcher has to do is put the symbol of the pitch thrown in the ball or strike column. One of the coaches can then take this information and post the results on the board in the locker room at least every two weeks. An example of how this might be posted is on the next two pages following the control chart. There is no question that this will provide all the pitchers on the staff with an opportunity to evaluate themselves with the rest of the pitchers.

PITCHERS CONTROL CHART

PITCHER KEEPING CHART: 1. _____

                       2. _____

DATE: _____

PITCHER	STRIKES	BALLS
1.		
2.		
3.		
4.		
5.		
6.		
7.		
8.		
9.		
10.		

SYMBOLS

C . . . . CURVE BALL	CH . . . . CHANGE-UP OFF FAST BALL
S . . . . SLIDER	P . . . . PALM BALL
F . . . . FAST BALL	FK . . . . FORK BALL
K . . . . KNUCKLE BALL	SC . . . . SCREW BALL

PITCHER CONTROL CHART
FEBRUARY 23RD

BREAKING PITCHES (CURVES AND SLIDERS)

PITCHER	THROWN	STRIKES	PERCENTAGE
TAYLOR	78	51	65.4
HARDWICK	83	51	61.4
MUNDIE	120	72	60.0
BOND	52	31	59.6
MYLES	137	81	59.1
D'ERCOLE	74	42	56.7
FLOWERS	135	75	55.5
BARTLEY	118	64	54.2
MORLOCK	88	46	52.3
WEATHERSBY	29	15	51.7
SHREWSBERRY	92	46	50.0
SUSCE	58	19	32.8

FAST BALLS (CHANGE-UPS)

PITCHER	THROWN	STRIKES	PERCENTAGE
MORLOCK	214 (16ch)	155 (10ch)	72.4
SHREWSBERRY	182 (25ch)	130 (16ch)	71.4
TAYLOR	208 (20ch)	141 (17ch)	67.8
MUNDIE	176 (26ch)	119 (16ch)	67.6
BOND	183 (16ch)	122 (12ch)	66.7
MYLES	223 (21ch)	148 (14ch)	66.36
HARDWICK	107 (3ch)	71 (2ch)	66.35
D'ERCOLE	172 (22ch)	113 (18ch)	65.7
WEATHERSBY	161 (2ch)	105 (2ch)	65.2
FLOWERS	137 (2ch)	84 (1ch)	61.3
SUSCE	263 (21ch)	154 (13ch)	58.6
BARTLEY	201	108	53.7

CONTINUED ON NEXT PAGE

SPECIALITY PITCHES
KNUCKLE BALLS, FORK BALLS, PALM BALLS, SCREW BALLS

PITCHER	THROWN	STRIKES	PERCENTAGE
WEATHERSBY	45 (K)	31	68.9
FLOWERS	24 (FK)	16	66.7
SUSCE	59 (P)	34	57.6
D'ERCOLE	34 (FK)	16	47.0
HARDWICK	9 (SC)	3	33.3
MYLES	1 (K)	0	00.0

TOTAL PITCHES

PITCHER	THROWN	STRIKES	PERCENTAGE
TAYLOR	286	192	67.1
MORLOCK	302	201	66.6
BOND	235	153	65.1
MUNDIE	296	191	64.5
WEATHERSBY	235	151	64.3
SHREWSBERRY	274	176	64.2
MYLES	361	229	63.4
HARDWICK	199	125	62.8
D'ERCOLE	280	171	61.1
FLOWERS	296	175	59.1
SUSCE	380	207	54.5
BARTLEY	319	172	53.9

Along with the control chart, the other statistic that is recommended to be kept in these scrimmage games would be the production rating chart. It seems to have more reliability and validity for grading performances of both the hitters and the pitchers than other statistics when you play a limited number of games.

The basic premise behind the production rating is the determination of the degree that each batter and pitcher reaches in accordance with the basic bat-meets-ball principle. You are basically awarding the batter with a higher score when he hits a ball that generally enables him to achieve success as a hitter, such as: the home run ball, the line drive, the hard ground ball, etc. At the same time, he will receive a lower score when a swing of the bat does not produce a productive type ball in play, such as: the swing and miss, the foul ball, the pop-up, the routine fly ball, the routine big hop ground ball, etc. Vice versa, the pitcher achieves success as a pitcher when he does not allow the hitter to become productive with the same swing of the bat. Thus, the pitcher becomes non-productive when he allows the batter to hit a ball hard.

One of the coaches should have the responsibility during these scrimmage games for keeping the production rating chart. The same person should keep the chart for all the games so that what was a four type ground ball one day is a four type ground ball another day. There are always balls hit during a game that could be graded differently from one scorer to another.

There are seven categories that are established on the bat-meets-ball principle in accordance with distance, speed, location and trajectory. Whether the ball that is hit allows the batter to reach base is irrelevant for you only grade the type of ball hit.

Below you will find the numerical rating used. No bunts are recorded unless the batter bunts at the ball and misses.

RATING	PRODUCTIVITY
0	Batter swings and misses; takes a called **third** strike; foul tips the ball directly back to the catcher.
1	Batter swings and fouls the ball straight back to the backstop or the area from dugout to dugout on the ground or in the air.
2	Batter swings and fouls the ball off weakly beyond the area of the dugouts on the ground or in the air; hits a pop fly anywhere in the infield area fair or foul.
3	Batter swings and fouls the ball off sharply away from the foul line; hits a routine fly ball in the outfield that is fair.
4	Batter swings and hits a fair ground ball weakly; hits a hump back line drive anywhere in fair territory in front of the outfielders.
5	Batter swings and hits a ground ball fairly hard; hits a long fly ball fairly hard; hits a line drive foul ball that is close to the foul line.
6	Batter swings and hits a line drive either on the ground or in the air; hits a home run.

Now you can see why the same person needs to keep the production rating for there are numerous times in the course of the game where it is difficult to determine what the grading of a ball would be. As long as the grader stays somewhat consistent from day to day, the production rating is a valuable tool for evaluating the performances of the hitters and pitchers.

If you have a batter who after quite a few games has a production rating of let's say 3.98, you have a productive hitter in your hands. If another batter after the same number of games has a production rating of 1.76, he is not being very productive at the plate. A pitcher with a production rating of 1.76 is getting the job done, while a pitcher with a 3.98 production rating is getting hit quite hard.

A batter might have a batting average of .400, but still have a low production rating, which would indicate that he has been quite lucky and has probably hit some "seeing eye balls". Another hitter might have a low batting average for the same number of games with a high production rating, which means that he has had some hard hit balls caught.

Below you will find the type of chart that is used by the person responsible for keeping the production rating. A new chart is used for each scrimmage game. An example of one hitter's production and one pitcher's production is presented. For each rating for a hitter, the same rating point must be given to the pitcher. If a player hits a six type ball, then the pitcher giving up the hard hit ball also receives a six. By dividing the number of swings into the total points you have the daily production rating.

PRODUCTION RATING CHART

DATE: _____

HITTER		SWINGS	POINTS	TOTALS
BAIRLEY	3-1-0-6-5-0-4-2-0-0-2	11	23	2.09
BOND				
BULLARD				
CASTORIA				
EMRHEIN				
GAGE				
GILLASPIE				
KLIPSTEIN				
LOE				
MALONEY				
MARTZ				
PORTER				
SHANNON				
SMITH				
SOTTILE				
WHITE				
WINKLER				
VAN CLEVE				
ZELMER				

PITCHERS		SWINGS	POINTS	TOTALS
BARTLEY				
FLOWERS				
HARDWICK	4-2-0-1-6-6-5-4-0-0-0-1-6-4-3-6-0-1-2-4-5-6-1-0-0-2-6-4	28	79	2.82
MORLOCK				
MUNDIE				
MYLES				
SUSCE				
TAYLOR				

In order for the players to see how they rank with each other, the production rating totals should be posted every week. An example of how it would be posted is below.

PRODUCTION RATING

HITTERS	TOTAL SWINGS	TOTAL POINTS	PRODUCTION RATING
MARTZ	89	318	3.57
SMITH	63	216	3.42
MALONEY	92	299	3.25
KLIPSTEIN	97	313	3.23
SOTTILE	78	233	2.99
LOE	84	246	2.93
PORTER	96	265	2.76
WHITE	74	198	2.68
GILLASPIE	107	281	2.63
ZELMER	102	263	2.58
CASTORIA	105	268	2.55
BOND	105	264	2.51
WINKLER	128	311	2.43
BAIRLEY	91	219	2.41
VAN CLEVE	75	176	2.35
GAGE	107	237	2.21
EMRHEIN	98	216	2.20
SHANNON	80	173	2.16
BULLARD	96	181	1.89

PITCHERS	TOTAL SWINGS	TOTAL POINTS	PRODUCTION RATING
SUSCE	163	358	2.20
MUNDIE	163	376	2.31
BARTLEY	132	307	2.33
TAYLOR	154	381	2.47
MORLOCK	164	423	2.58
MYLES	171	487	2.85
HARDWICK	105	334	3.18
FLOWERS	121	478	3.95

OUTFIELD-INFIELD DRILL

There are various ways that a coach can handle his outfield-infield practice for both his practice sessions and for the pre-game routine. In this section we will isolate on two ways that it can be done.

The three basic reasons for conducting the outfield-infield routine are: (1) it serves to warmup the players physically for the game; (2) it requires the players to employ certain skills which they will have to perform during the course of the game; and (3) it provides a psychological lift to the players as they perform their pre-game drill as a unit.

In regular practice sessions the outfield-infield routine does not have to be done everyday for it is not totally designed for learning new skills or developing fundamentals. It should be done prior to all scrimmage games, if time allows. Anytime the condition of the field is poor where the players' traction is bad, or they will be handling a wet baseball, it is always best to forgo the drill.

One of the keys to a successful outfield-infield practice is the fungo hitter. A capable fungo hitter can make just about any fielder look good. A poor fungo hitter can do just the opposite. It is our feeling that this routine is not designed to force the fielders to run all over the park chasing down baseballs. You have probably seen coaches hitting baseballs to their outfielders in these drills where the fielders have to range all over the field. This is not the time to be working on these type of skills. The time for these skills to be developed is during drill stations in practice sessions.

It certainly does no harm to have the outfielders and infielders go to their left and right to field the ball, but they should not have to go too far to do so, especially in the pre-game routine. Again, all you should try to do is use this time to loosen up the players physically, have them employ basic skills, and make them look and feel good. If that means hitting mostly big hop ground balls to the infielders, so be it. There is nothing that looks any worse than a coach hitting baseballs that are well out of reach or too tough to handle.

If the wind is blowing quite hard on a practice day or before a game it would be proper to hit more fly balls to the outfielders than during a normal outfield-infield practice. At the same token, if one of the outfield positions will have a sun problem during the game, the players at that position should receive fly balls. Otherwise, allow the outfielders a chance to field a ball cleanly and make a throw to a base or home plate.

Basic One Ball Outfield-Infield Drill

The first outfield-infield drill is the basic drill where the coach hitting the ball with his fungo bat will have just one ball in play at a time. When hitting to the outfielders for throws into second and third base, he positions himself generally on the third base side of the mound with a first baseman or catcher next to him feeding him baseballs to hit.

Each of the outfielders receives a fly ball, a ground ball or a line drive and throws two times to second base and two times to third base. It is best to not have the same outfielder throw all four of these throws in succession, for this would cause a delay as the fungo hitter would have to wait for him to get back in his proper position after throwing. If you have, let's say, two outfielders at each position, the fungo hitter would hit all six outfielders a ball and they would all throw to second base. The second baseman or shortstop who fields the ball at the bag would then throw the ball to the feeder next to the fungo hitter. The coach would then hit another round of balls to all six outfielders, and they again would throw to second base. On the next two rounds, the outfielders would throw to third base, and the third baseman would then throw to the feeder next to the fungo hitter. The feeder should always have a few extra balls in his possession in case of an overthrow at second or third base.

The shortstop and second baseman should work their basic cut-off mechanics and communication as they would in a game when the throws are coming into second base. The same holds true for the third baseman and the shortstop on the throws to third base.

When the coach wants the outfielders to throw to the plate he should position himself on either side of the plate so that he is not in the way of the third baseman or first baseman in cut-off position. Each outfielder should alternate throwing two balls to the plate. After all the outfielders have thrown to the plate twice then another coach or a pitcher can continue to hit them balls while the infielders are taking infield practice. This fungo hitter should position himself down either the right field or left field foul line with the outfielders out in deep center field alternating taking the balls off the fungo hitter's bat. There should be a person assigned to the fungo hitter to catch the balls for him from the outfielders. Another person could serve as the cut-off man so that the outfielders do not have to throw all the way into the area where the fungo hitter is located.

Now the coach is ready to hit the infield phase of the drill. As a rule, each infielder should have two ground balls that he would field and throw to first base, two ground balls that he would field and go the second base route for the double play. In addition, each infielder should be required to field one slow roller with a play to first base, and finish up with a simulated force play or tag play at the plate, with the infielder on the infield grass line.

As with the outfielders, the balls should be hit so that the infielders alternate taking their ground balls. When the first basemen get their first two ground balls they should throw to third base. After each round of single outs and double plays, the catcher should field a bunt tossed by the fungo hitter. The first two rounds they would throw the ball to first base, the next two rounds they would throw to second base for the potential double play. Throwing the ball around the infield can be done, but should be discouraged, due to the time problem unless you have a very few infielders in the infield drill.

Any ball fielded that is not hit on the ground should be thrown back to the catcher at home plate, and the infielder would receive another ball from the fungo hitter. The same holds true if the infielder makes a bad throw to either first or second base. If the ball is booted by the infielders then the fungo hitter will get another ball from one of the catchers, and hit him another ball on the ground. If the ball is booted, but the infielder can still make the play, he should be encouraged to do so.

When hitting ground balls to the third baseman, shortstops and second basemen the fungo hitter should position himself on the first base side of home plate. When hitting to the first baseman he should swing around to the third base side for the proper angle. If the fungo hitter wishes to stay on just one side during the whole infield practice, then he should stay on the third base side being careful he is not hit by a ball being thrown by the third baseman to the catcher at home plate.

The catchers should alternate each round throwing the ball back to the base of the fielder who made the play. When the ball is thrown by the catcher to second base, either to the shortstop or the second baseman, this fielder should then throw the ball to the third baseman who in turn would throw the ball to the catcher at the plate. When the catcher throws the ball on the bunt to either first or second base there is no need for him to throw it around the infield when it returns to him. The infield drill can end with the fungo hitter hitting pop-ups at the plate to all the catchers.

The best order for the infield drill would be: two outs at first base;two double play balls; one slow roller; and one force play at the plate. There are all kinds of variations in the single ball outfield-infield drill, but this is the basic way it is done by most clubs.

Multiple Ball Outfield-Infield Drill

The multiple ball outfield-infield drill is a major variation from the previously described drill. It is designed to keep more than one ball in play, and thus, speed up the drill itself. The benefits of this system of taking outfield-infield practice is that it gets the same thing done as the single ball drill, but gets it done much quicker. It is also a more spirited type of drill, and when done properly, will make your team look and feel like a "million dollars". A capable fungo hitter with good timing is the key to the success of this drill. A team of quality players with good defensive skills is also a big help.

If done properly the multiple ball outfield-infield drill should take only about seven to eight minutes if you have two players at each defensive position, along with three catchers. It might sound a little complicated, but it really is easy to learn.

Outfield Portion of Drill—The players should assume the positions on the field as diagrammed on the next page. The diagram shows two outfielders at each position, but the drill can be done with any number of outfielders.

The fungo hitter positions himself on the third base side of the mound with the two first basemen next to him. One first baseman will bring a bucket of baseballs with him as the team takes the field. His job will be to keep the fungo hitter supplied with baseballs by flipping a ball to him when he turns around after hitting the previous ball. Only one shortstop is needed in the outfield portion of the drill. The other shortstop can sit in the dugout and wait until the infield portion of the drill begins. You need only two second basemen, with one at second base and the other positioned about 70 feet behind him backing up all throws from the left fielders. You need two third basemen, with one at third base and the other positioned about 50 feet behind third base backing up all throws coming to third base from the outfield. Three catchers are used in the drill, one at home plate and the other two in the fungo circles adjacent to home plate. The catcher in the third base side fungo circle should have a bucket with him to put the baseballs in that will be coming from the back up third baseman.

MULTIPLE OUTFIELD DRILL—POSITIONING

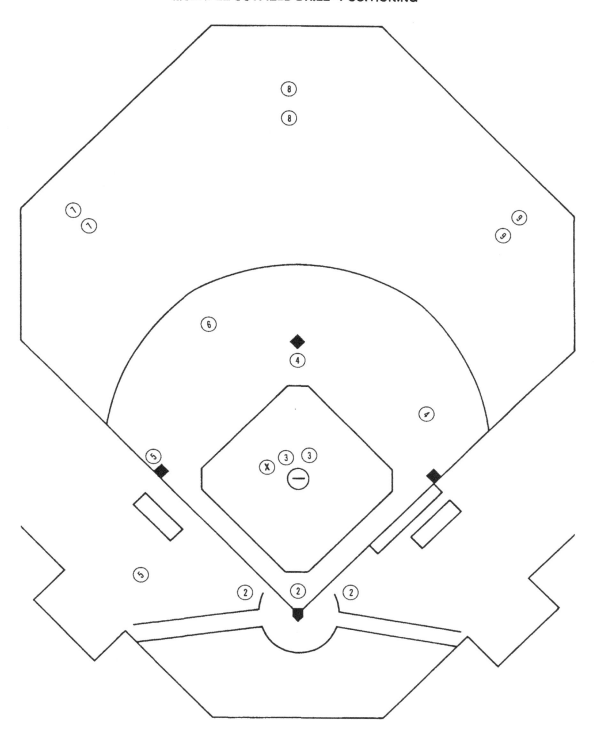

Once everyone is in position, the fungo hitter will proceed to hit baseballs to the outfielders as fast as he can without rushing himself or the first baseman feeding him baseballs. He must be careful not to hit the shortstop in front of him or the second baseman standing at second base since they will not be looking at him during the drill.

He will hit all the outfielders a ball starting with the left fielders. The whole idea behind the first portion of the drill is that the outfielders will alternate throwing the ball to second base and third base. So, the first left fielder will throw his ball to second base, and the second left fielder will throw his ball to third base. If you have a third left fielder he will throw now to second base. All the throws from the left fielders to both second and third base will be done without a cut-off man. The coach hitting with the fungo bat must be sure that he does not hit in the same direction when hitting to a specific position. Otherwise you would have your first left fielder fielding a ball and worried about being hit by another ball coming right at him. The coach must work each fielder slightly to his left or right away from the outfielder he hit the ball to previously.

The outfielders need to be sure to throw to the base that the outfielder throwing ahead of him did not throw to. After the first round the outfielders will switch so that no outfielder throws to second base or third base two times in a row. For example, this is the order for the outfielders with two at each position.

First Round

#1 Left fielder. . . . . .Second Base
#2 Left fielder. . . . . .Third Base
#1 Center fielder. . . . . .Second Base
#2 Center fielder. . . . . .Third Base
#1 Right fielder. . . . . .Second Base
#2 Right fielder. . . . . .Third Base

Second Round

#2 Left fielder. . . . . .Second Base
#1 Left fielder. . . . . .Third Base
#2 Center fielder. . . . . .Second Base
#1 Center fielder. . . . . .Third Base
#2 Right fielder. . . . . .Second Base
#1 Right fielder. . . . . .Third Base

Third Round—Same as First Round
Fourth Round—Same as Second Round

If you have an odd number of outfielders the alternating pattern stays the same. Let's say you have one left fielder, three center fielders and three right fielders. It would go like this:

First Round

#1 Left fielder. . . . . .Second Base
#1 Center fielder. . . . . .Third Base
#2 Center fielder. . . . . .Second Base
#3 Center fielder. . . . . .Third Base
#1 Right fielder. . . . . .Second Base
#2 Right fielder. . . . . .Third Base
#3 Right fielder. . . . . .Second Base

Second Round

#1 Left fielder. . . . . .Third Base
#1 Center fielder. . . . . .Second Base
#2 Center fielder. . . . . .Third Base
#3 Center fielder. . . . . .Second Base
#1 Right fielder. . . . . .Third Base
#2 Right fielder. . . . . .Second Base
#3 Right fielder. . . . . .Third Base

Third Round—Same as First Round
Fourth Round—Same as Second Round

As mentioned previously, the shortstop will not be the cut-off man for any balls thrown by the left fielders into second or third base. However, he will be the cut-off man for all balls thrown to third base by the center fielders and right fielders. After the last center fielder has thrown to third base he must hustle over into proper cut-off position for the balls being thrown by the right fielders into third base. Since every other ball is going to second base he will not be rushed each time he is the cut-off man. The proper cut-off communication should be used between the shortstop and the third baseman.

All the baseballs that come into second base will be fielded by the second baseman. Once fielded, he will immediately throw the ball to the back up second baseman positioned about 70 feet behind him. That second baseman will throw the ball to the first baseman next to the one feeding the fungo hitter. That first baseman will put the ball in the bucket so that the feeder has a continuous supply of baseballs for the fungo hitter.

All balls that come into third base will be fielded by the third baseman on the bag. Once fielded, he will throw the ball to the back up third baseman positioned about 70 feet behind him. The back up third baseman will then throw the ball to the catcher in the third base fungo circle, who will put the ball in the bucket that he brought with him onto the field.

As soon as the fungo hitter has hit a ball to the last right fielder in the fourth and final round, he will take the bucket of baseballs from the first baseman-feeder and hustle to the third base side fungo circle area. He will give the bucket to the catcher on that side who will now be his feeder while he hits the two rounds to the outfielders for their throws to the plate. The catcher in the first base fungo circle will now come over to the third base side and pick up the other bucket which should have a good supply of baseballs in it. He will take that bucket back to the first base side and prepare for the infield portion of the drill.

Each outfielder will throw two baseballs to home plate using the third baseman for the left fielders, and the two first basemen for the right fielders and center fielders as cut-off men. The original back up third baseman will now position himself at third base for any balls cut-off by the third baseman that he throws to third base. The original second baseman at second base will stay on the bag for any throws that the first baseman might throw to him that are cut-off. The shortstop has no responsibility at this time. The back up second baseman stays at the same spot and will receive any ball from the second basemen on the bag that was fielded by him on throws from the first baseman on the cut-off to second base. The back up second baseman will then throw the ball to the catcher in the first base side fungo circle, who will put the ball in the bucket. The third baseman at third base will throw any ball he receives from the third baseman in cut-off position to the catcher at home plate.

The catcher at home plate will use his cut-off men just as he would in the game, using the proper verbal commands to get them in the proper position and informing them on whether or not to cut the ball off. If the catcher wants any ball thrown by a left fielder cut-off by the third baseman, he will instruct him to cut the ball off and throw to third base. Any ball thrown by a center fielder that he wants cut-off by the first baseman, he will have him throw it to second base. All balls that are cut-off coming in from right field will be cut-off to the plate by the other first baseman. If there is no cut-off command by the catcher then the ball will be allowed to come to the plate area. The catcher needs to have his cut-off men cut all balls that will take him away from the plate area since there will be another ball coming in from the outfield right behind that ball.

One first baseman will position himself near the mound during the two rounds that the outfielders will be throwing to the plate. He will be in a position to cut-off any ball coming in from center field. The other first baseman will position himself to handle the cut-off responsibility on all balls coming in from right field.

The fungo hitter will have to slow down just a little from the pace he used hitting the balls to the outfielders for throws to second and third base since all balls are now coming to the same area, home plate. Just as one outfielder fields a ball in the outfield he can hit the next outfielder a ball. The catcher at home plate must be alert to the fact that as soon as he deals with one ball and cut-off man, there will be another ball coming in shortly. That is why he can never leave the area of home plate chasing down an errant throw.

The coach can develop his timing in the outfield drill through trial and error. He must also be very careful in this portion of the drill since both first basemen will have their back to him when he is hitting balls to the center fielders and right fielders.

As soon as the fungo hitter has hit a ball to the last right fielder, he will hustle over to the first base side fungo circle in preparation for the infield portion of the drill. There should be no delay in starting the infield drill unless one or two of the outfielders are also involved with the infield.

Infield Portion of the Drill—In the infield drill you can work with any number of infielders, but it is restricted to just three catchers. It certainly helps the effectiveness of the drill to have at least two infielders at every position, especially at first base. You will be dealing with quite a few balls in play at one time so the timing and accuracy of the fungo hitter is quite important.

Some of the ground rules that the infielders must follow in the multiple ball infield drill are:

1. Any ball that is hit to them in the air and caught should be treated just like a ground ball.

2. Any ball that goes over the head of an infielder or past him with no play, the fungo hitter will quickly give him another ball to work with.

3. Any ball booted by the infielder is a lost chance for that infielder unless he can recover the ball **very** quickly and can continue with the play. No infielder will chase down a ball that he misplays.

4. All throws must be accurate. All bad throws will not be replayed.

The fungo hitter must be sure to give the infielders good ground balls to work with. He can not afford to have them running all over the infield chasing down tough plays. The fungo hitter's purpose is to make all the infielders look good.

The three catchers are located in the following spots to begin the drill: one at home plate; one in the third base fungo circle area; one in the first base fungo circle area. The first base side catcher will feed baseballs to the fungo hitter from the bucket that he has next to him. He will feed the hitter balls when balls are being hit to the third basemen, the shortstops, and the second basemen. The third base side catcher will feed baseballs from his bucket to the fungo hitter when he is hitting ground balls to the first basemen. The catcher at home plate will be throwing to the bases as he would in a single ball drill, only in this drill, much quicker. If you do not have three catchers, then a pitcher or a manager can assume the task of feeding the fungo hitter in the first base side fungo circle area. Both buckets should have plenty of baseballs (minimum of ten in a bucket to start with).

The fungo hitter will serve up ground balls at a rapid pace depending on the experience of the group in working with the drill. When teaching the multiple drill the coach will have to go quite slow until they build up their confidence. Confidence in themselves, and also the others involved in the drill, so that they are not throwing a ball and looking out of the corner of their eye for a throw that they did not expect.

The drill begins with the fungo hitter delivering a ground ball to the first third baseman, who will field the ball and throw it to the first first baseman. The first baseman will throw the ball to the catcher at home plate, who will throw the ball to the first third baseman at the bag. The third baseman will now throw the ball to the catcher in the third base side fungo circle who will put the ball in the bucket. What gives the drill the multiple ball aspect is the fact that while the first third baseman is fielding his ground ball, the fungo hitter will be hitting another one to the second third baseman. Of course, the hitter must be sure to not hit the ball in the direct path of the first third baseman, as he is throwing to first base. Timing is also very important on the hitter's part.

The second third baseman fields his ground ball and the ball takes the same path: second third baseman, second first baseman, catcher at home plate, second third baseman, catcher on third base side, bucket. While the second third baseman is fielding his ground ball the fungo hitter will be hitting a ball to the first shortstop. He fields the ball and throws to the first first baseman, who throws it to the catcher at home plate. The catcher throws the ball to the first shortstop at second base, who throws it to the first third baseman. As before, the ball is then thrown to the catcher on the third base side and the ball is put in the bucket. The third baseman always throws the ball to the third base side catcher since the catcher at home plate is not prepared for the ball. He is busy enough throwing balls to the various bases.

While the first shortstop is fielding his ground ball, the fungo hitter will be hitting a ball to the second shortstop who will throw across the diamond to the second first baseman with the ball following the same path: second shortstop, second first baseman, catcher at home plate, second shortstop, second third baseman, catcher on third base side, bucket. If there is a third shortstop, the same path is followed with the first first baseman back on the bag receiving the throw.

While the second shortstop is fielding his ground ball, the fungo hitter will hit a ball to the first second baseman. He will throw the ball to the first first baseman and the ball takes the same type of path: first second baseman, first first baseman, catcher at home plate, first second baseman, first third baseman, catcher on the third base side, bucket. The second second baseman fields his ground ball and the ball follows the same path with the second first baseman and second third baseman involved.

After the fungo hitter hits a ground ball to the last second baseman, he will receive a ball from the catcher on the first base side and he hustles behind the home plate catcher to the third base side. He then hits a ground ball to the first first baseman who will throw his ground ball to the catcher at home plate. The catcher fields the ball and rolls himself an easy bunt on the first base side of the diamond. He fields the bunt and throws to the first first baseman at the bag. The first baseman will throw the ball to the catcher who fielded the bunt as he moves to the first base side fungo circle. As soon as the first first baseman has fielded his ground ball to throw to the catcher, the fungo hitter will hit a ball to the second first baseman that he received from the third base side catcher who is now feeding him baseballs. The second first baseman will field his ground ball and throw it to third base to the first third baseman, who in turn will throw the ball to the catcher at home plate who is now the catcher who was originally on the first side feeding the fungo hitter. This is the only time that the third basemen throws to the home plate catcher. The new catcher at home plate receives the throw from the third baseman and rolls himself an easy bunt on the third base side of the diamond. He will throw the ball to the second first baseman at the bag, who in turn will throw the ball to the catcher on the first base side and into the bucket it goes. As soon as the catcher throws his bunt to the first baseman he will move into the third base fungo circle, and the catcher that has been in that spot now becomes the home plate catcher. This movement on the bunted balls is how the catchers rotate in the drill. If you have more than two first basemen then all balls after the first two have been fielded are thrown to the new home plate catcher with no bunt involved.

It might sound a little confusing, but it is really quite simple once you get the catchers' rotation down pat. Thus, the path the ball takes on the first two rounds if you have two players at each position with three catchers is:

First Two Rounds

1st third baseman, 1st first baseman, Catcher, 1st third baseman, Catcher (3B side).

2nd third baseman, 2nd first baseman, Catcher, 2nd third baseman, Catcher (3B side).

1st Shortstop, 1st first baseman, Catcher, 1st Shortstop, 1st third baseman, Catcher (3B side).

2nd Shortstop, 2nd first baseman, Catcher, 2nd Shortstop, 2nd third baseman, Catcher (3B side).

1st second baseman, 1st first baseman, Catcher, 1st second baseman, 1st third baseman, Catcher (3B side).

2nd second baseman, 2nd first baseman, Catcher, 2nd second baseman, 2nd third baseman, Catcher (3B side).

1st first baseman, Catcher (throws bunt 1B side), 1st first baseman, Catcher (who threw bunt—now 1B side).

2nd first baseman, 1st third baseman, Catcher (who was on 1B side, throws bunt 3B side), 2nd first baseman, Catcher (1B side). Catcher who threw bunt rotates to 3B side, 3B side catcher now at plate.

The catcher at home plate has got to be very quick throwing the ball to the proper base each time, for as soon as he releases the ball, the first basemen are catching the next ball from an infielder to throw to the plate. The first baseman must give the catcher at home plate good throws to work with. The rotation of the catchers on the ground balls to the first baseman enable them all to handle the three spots during the infield drill (catcher at home plate, first base fungo side, third base fungo side). If you only have two catchers then they would just stay at the plate and the third base side. They would then rotate each time after a round. A pitcher or manager can feed the fungo hitter on the first base.

After the last ground ball has been hit to the last first baseman, the fungo hitter will get a ball from the feeder on the third base side and hustle back to the first base side to prepare for the double plays. It is best to just hit two rounds of single outs, two rounds of double plays, and one round of slow rollers with the play at first base. If you have less than two infielders at each position you can go with another round of single outs. If you have only one first baseman, he is going to stay **very** busy at first base.

You are going to have to assign a manager to switch buckets occasionally during the drill, especially if you did not start with many balls in each of the two buckets. Most of the balls will end up in the third base side bucket since most of the balls come to the third base side catcher.

If timed properly, there will be three or four balls in play most of the time. In the first round, the second shortstop is fielding his ground ball when the ball that the first third baseman fielded is now going in the bucket in the third base side.

With the fungo hitter back on the first base side, he is now ready to hit ground balls for the double plays. He must be sure to hit these ground balls hard enough that double plays could occur in a regular game situation. He also must be sure that the infielders do not have to range too far left and right to make the play.

The ball takes the exact same path as it did during the first two rounds, with the only exception being that a double play is made using the shortstops and second basemen as the pivot men. The other small exception would be that any time the shortstop or second baseman are to field the throw from the home plate catcher they will field it about 15 feet in front of the bag since there will be a double play being made back at the base at the time of this throw by the catcher. The catcher must be sure to throw accurately on his throw toward second base so that the ball does not get by the cut-off man and hit a shortstop or second baseman around the base.

The catchers' rotation is identical as it was on the first two rounds with the exception being that the bunt they throw for themselves will be fielded and thrown to second base rather than first base. Below is the path the ball takes for the two double play rounds with two infielders at each position along with the three catchers.

Double Play Rounds

1st third baseman, 1st second baseman, 1st first baseman, catcher, 1st third baseman, Catcher (3B side).

2nd third baseman, 2nd second baseman, 2nd first baseman, Catcher, 2nd third baseman, Catcher (3B side).

1st Shortstop, 1st second baseman, 1st first baseman, Catcher, 1st Shortstop in cut-off position, 1st third baseman, Catcher (3B side).

2nd Shortstop, 2nd second baseman, 2nd first baseman, Catcher, 2nd Shortstop in cut-off position, 2nd third baseman, Catcher (3B side).

1st second baseman, 1st Shortstop, 1st first baseman, Catcher, 1st second baseman in cut-off position, 1st third baseman, Catcher (3B side).

2nd second baseman, 2nd Shortstop, 2nd first baseman, Catcher, 2nd second baseman in cut-off position, 2nd third baseman, Catcher (3B side).

1st first baseman, 1st Shortstop, 1st first baseman, Catcher (throws bunt on 1B side, 1st Shortstop, 1st first baseman, Catcher (who threw bunt—now on 1B side).

2nd first baseman, 2nd Shortstop, 2nd first baseman, Catcher (who was on 1B side, throws bunt 3B side), 2nd Shortstop, 2nd first baseman, Catcher (1B side). Catcher who threw bunt rotates to 3B side, 3B side catcher now at plate.

If you have only two shortstops working the drill, the fungo hitter will have to wait for him to get back to second base before hitting the first second baseman his double play ball. The shortstop will be coming from the inside of the diamond after taking his throw from the catcher. The ground ball to the second first baseman will be delayed also for you must give the shortstop at second base a chance to field the double play bunt thrown by the catcher before the other shortstop can field the throw from the second first baseman. It just takes a little trial and error process before the fungo hitter and players get the drill down proper.

After the fungo hitter has hit the last first baseman his double play ground ball, he will get a ball from the third base side catcher and hustle back over to the first base side. The third base side catcher comes with him and positions himself on the first base side of the catcher there. He will now catch all throws coming from the first basemen who are fielding throws from the infielders. The first base side catcher will just feed balls to the fungo hitter not worrying about any throws coming from first base, since the other catcher will take these throws.

64

With the infielders in their regular depth position the fungo hitter will give each one of them a slow roller that will be thrown to first base. The first baseman will alternate taking these throws and will throw the ball to the catcher on the first base side of the feeder. The hitter will hit these slow rollers without any delay from one fielder to the next. After he hits the last second basemen his slow roller, he will get a ball from his feeder (first base side catcher) and hustle over to the third base side. He will then hit the first basemen their easy ground balls which they will throw to the catcher at home plate. The catcher at the plate will now feed the fungo hitter. After the last first baseman has thrown to the plate, the fungo hitter will hit a pop-up to the catcher at home plate.

Once the pop-up is caught by the catcher, that concludes the multiple ball outfield-infield drill. After looking over the mechanics of this pre-game drill, some coaches might consider it difficult to perform properly. Actually, the opposite is true. Players adapt quite easily to skills they enjoy and this drill provides the coach the means for bringing his team that much closer to an optimum level of performance. Not only will the players receive a boost by completing a snappy drill successfully, but a little bit is taken out of the opposing team when their players observe this action. Music played over the public address system while the drill is being conducted will add a little spice to the movement.

MANAGER(S) RESPONSIBILITIES—PRACTICE

It is quite helpful to the manager(s) for the baseball team to know exactly what their responsibilities are to the team for practice sessions. They can be an invaluable part of the practice schedule and should take an active part in all the activities. We have listed a sample selection of responsibilities for the manager(s) in practice.

1. Make sure that all players are measured and fitted outside of the equipment room. No player is allowed in the equipment room without the permission of one of the coaches.

2. Label all shelves in the equipment room so that every piece of equipment can be easily located.

3. Keep an accurate record of all equipment on inventory. Also, keep accurate records on all equipment given out to the players by: item; size; number; and player.

4. Keep an accurate inventory of Playbooks. Place tape inside each Playbook where the player may put his name, address and telephone number in the Playbook.

5. Keep the drawers in the equipment room free of junk. Keep only useful items in the drawers.

6. You are responsible for the name labels on each of the lockers. Keep a listing of the locker numbers and name of player assigned to each locker.

7. You will use Freshmen anytime you need assistance in carrying equipment both on and off the practice field.

8. Be sure that you lock the equipment door every time you leave the locker room. Also, be sure all doors are locked in locker room before you leave for practice. One of the managers should be the last person out of the locker room after practice is over.

9. We will issue towels at the completion of practice, not before.

10. No practice or game equipment is to be issued to anyone without my permission. We will try to issue all equipment at one time to eliminate any problem.

11. Notify me whenever a player loses a piece of his equipment.

12. Cordinate laundry procedure with personnel in the laundry service. Laundry must be in the locker room no later than 20 minutes before the first pre-practice session.

13. Want at least one manager on the field at least 20 minutes before the first pre-practice session to make sure that all the equipment needed is out, and in the proper area.

14. Responsible for posting the practice schedule on the batting cage and on the third base dugout. Any extra practice schedules available will go to spectators in the stands.

15. Coordinate with me when new baseballs are to be used in practice sessions. Will begin all inter-squad games with at least five new balls. Responsible for rubbing up all new baseballs for inter-squad games.

16. One manager will be designated as the time coordinator for practice sessions. Must have a stop watch. This manager will remain in the batting cage area throughout the entire batting practice schedule.

17. Responsible to repair all practice equipment. If not possible to repair, then to see that it gets to the right person for repair.

18. Need permission from me before you make any type of order for new equipment which is not on the equipment list for purchase.

19. Responsible for all equipment being put away at the completion of practice. Make sure that outside equipment shed is locked at the completion of practice.

20. Responsible for the pitching machine(s). Make sure they are up in the batting range(s) throwing strikes. Put away at the completion of practice.

21. You will have no field maintanence responsibilities unless informed by me.

22. Coordinate with the trainer any liquid refreshment needed on the field.

23. You will be asked to keep some charts during inter-squad games along with keeping the baseballs in play.

24. Clean off blackboard in locker room anytime we will be having a meeting.

25. Responsible for putting the lights on and turning them off when we have a night practice.

26. Responsible for transporting equipment to the indoor complex whenever we are forced to workout inside.

27. Will have assigned stations during fundamental drill series to assist the coaches at these stations.

FUNDAMENTAL DRILL SERIES

The preparation of a baseball team to handle defensive fundamentals in practice should correspond with their ability to deal with these fundamentals in a regular season game. Baseball coaches are always looking for ways in practice to better prepare their teams to handle defensive responsibilities.

The fundamental drill series provides a coach with the means and methods to cover practically every aspect of defensive play in an organized, structured and practical manner. Coaches in all sports will agree that repetitive drills done frequently, offer a better means of retention than those drills done with longer periods of time intervening between the drills. For example, working on rundown plays for a small amount of time every other day is better than working on them for a long period of time once every two weeks.

On the following pages, you will find a complete set of fundamental drill series that cover practically every aspect of defensive play. The drills are broken down into two series: drill series number one; and drill series number two. The drill series are designed to be done every other day, if time allows. Thus, drill series number one can be done on Monday, Wednesday and Friday; drill series number two can be done on Tuesday, Thursday and Saturday.

Those players who play more than one position would alternate at which position they work at for a series. For example, a player who is a pitcher and first baseman would go with the pitchers during fundamental drill series number one on one day, and the next time it is run he would work at first base. The same would hold true for fundamental drill series number two.

The number of coaches on a baseball staff will determine how many drills can be run at any one time. If there are only two coaches on a staff, the head coach can divide the drill stations so that there are only two drills going on at any one time. However, it is better to try to get quite a bit done during these drill stations, so the assigning of a manager or a senior to handle and supervise a drill station or two is much preferred.

The group in each drill station would spend about 15 minutes in the early part of the practice season with one of the coaches going over the purpose of the drill and all the mechanics. As you can imagine, this will take quite a few days. After all the drills are presented in fundamental drill series number one, then it is time to do all nine in one day's time, with each drill station lasting five minutes. With nine drill stations in fundamental drill series one, you will have a 45 minute practice segment. These drill segments are designated five minute stations, but after a few times with the five minute routine, you can drop down to four or three minutes. You should never go below three minutes for it would not allow enough time to give everyone a chance to get set up and get some work accomplished.

After the complete series number one has been presented and you have gone through a five minute segment, then the coaching staff can present all the drill stations in fundamental drill series number two (eight stations). Once they are all presented (15 minutes per drill), then the second drill series can be done in five minute segments, which would take 40 minutes of practice time. If you have enough coaches you can present at least two of the drill series each day, and since there are a total of 17 drill series (nine in the first, eight in the second), it would take you about nine days to present it all. If you have just one or two coaches on the staff then it will take quite a bit longer.

All the players should run at least one-half speed between stations so that no longer than 15 seconds are taken up from the time one drill segment is over and the next one begins. A manager would be assigned to keep accurate track of the time with a stop watch, and whistle when it is time to rotate. You should find that the players really enjoy the moving from one drill segment to the next rather than just working on one specific drill for an extended period of time. Again, you will find that their retention of fundamentals from day to day is much better due to the frequency of work at all the drills. So much time is wasted in many practice sessions where fundamental drills are presented to a club, and then you practice them so infrequently, that you must spend valuable practice time presenting them practically all over again. In the fundamental drill series presented here in the Playbook, once you spend the 15 minutes to present the mechanics and teaching points of a particular drill, you should not have to spend much time explaining it again.

During the abbreviated time allowed for each segment, every player at the position should have an opportunity to perform the drill. The person responsible for that drill station can correct any mistakes made with everyone involved listening. The more they work on each drill the fewer mistakes they should make. Since they generally work with a particular drill every other day, you will find this to be the case in the fundamental drill concept.

By running five minute segments of each drill series, in just two practice days you will confront your team with practically every defensive aspect of the game. This is the exciting and practical aspect of the fundamental drill series. Even though it takes awhile to present each of the segments, it will pay rich dividends when your club gets a small dose of repetitive game type responses every day.

In order to make the drills more game-like, you must require the players to go full speed during the drills using the same types of defensive signs that will be used in the game. This gives the drill series a little conditioning aspect to it also. You should find that the players do not get mentally fatigued during the drills since they will be going from station to station.

The players, managers and coaches should quickly learn the order of drill stations so that there is little time wasted going from station to station. The proper equipment needed at each station should be readily available, and since the only equipment needed is baseballs and possibly a fungo bat, this should cause no major problem.

All the fundamental drills presented on the following pages will be briefly explained so that you will understand what the drill entails. Since all the fundamental skills are explained in detail in the defensive sections of the Playbook, it is not necessary to discuss all the mechanics of each fundamental at this time.

FUNDAMENTAL DRILL SERIES NUMBER 1
DRILL #1

1. Infielders and Catchers

Force plays and tag play situations at the plate. Coach with fungo bat at home plate setting up the simulated situations and hitting all types of ground balls to the infielders. Examples of situations that might be set up: runner at third base only, one out, infield in on grass, late in game, important run at third base; bases loaded, no outs, infield half way, early in game; runners at first and third base, one out, middle inning of a game, corners in, shortstop and second baseman in double play depth. Coach can set up every possible situation that can arise with a runner at third base. Coach can hit to any infielder. Catchers working on force play and tag play mechanics at the plate.

2. Pitchers

Pitchers in left field working on ground ball mechanics. Pitchers are 60 feet apart facing their partner. One pitcher throws from the windup or the stretch to the other pitcher 60 feet away. He catches the ball and throws a ground ball back to the pitcher. Pitcher fields the ball properly and fakes the throw to first base using the proper footwork. The pitcher now becomes the catcher, and the catcher now is the pitcher. Will keep alternating for duration of drill. Space the pitchers far enough away from each other so the ground balls can move the pitcher left and right occasionally. Once good mechanics are established a coach may incorporate the use of a fungo in the drill.

3. Outfielders

In right field working on fence communication and going back on a fly ball. Outfielders will alternate with one in right center field yelling "fence" at the proper time when the outfielder is five to six full strides away from fence. Other outfielders will be lined up about 90 feet in front of the fence. Coach or manager will throw a high fly ball near the fence with the outfielders alternating going after the ball properly, listening to the communicating outfielder. The coach or manager throwing the ball will position himself about 90 feet in front of the outfielder who is in ready position to go back to the fence.

FUNDAMENTAL DRILL SERIES NUMBER 1
DRILL #1

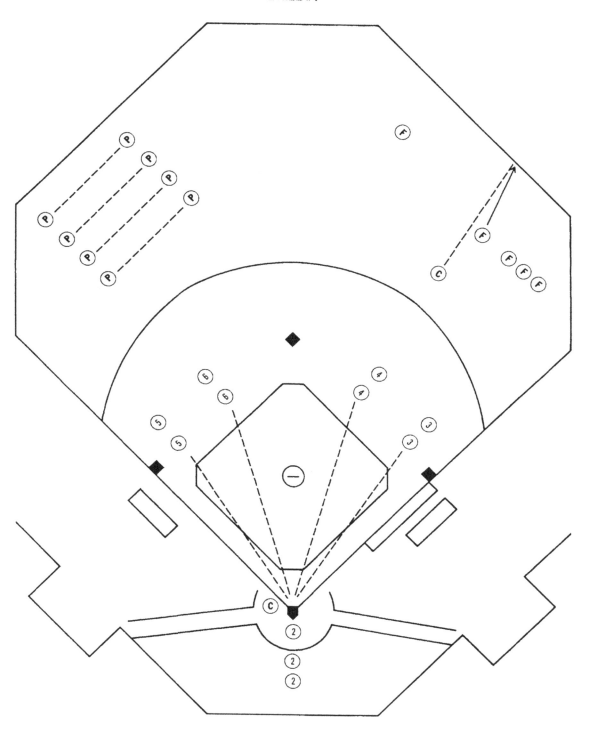

FUNDAMENTAL DRILL SERIES NUMBER 1
DRILL #2

1. Catchers and First Basemen

Catchers alternate fielding bunted balls with masks on. Bunt is thrown from behind the catcher. Catchers working on mechanics of fielding all types of bunts and throwing to first base. First basemen alternate taking the throw properly from the catcher, communicating whether he wants the ball thrown to the inside or outside ("inside"—"outside"). The first baseman should simulate bunt situation by charging toward home plate until he reads catcher's ball, and then retreat back to cover first base.

2. Shortstops and Second Basemen

Shortstops and second basemen communicating on ground balls hit around second base. Coach hits balls from a position about 20 feet from home plate so as to not interfere with the catchers fielding their bunts. Coach can hit to either the shortstop or second baseman alternating taking the ground balls. There will be no throws to first base. Fake the throw. If shortstop or second baseman wish to make an unassisted double play he will yell "I've got it". If he says nothing he will flip the ball to the pivot man on the base.

3. Third Basemen

Working on mechanics of fielding fly balls around the dugout and fence area. Thrower of these fly balls will position himself near the area of home plate. Third basemen will alternate.

4. Outfielders

In right center field working on mechanics of going back on fly balls. Outfielders will alternate. Person throwing over the outfielders head will position himself 90-120 feet from outfielders.

5. Pitchers

In left field reacting to all types of steals and trick plays with simulated runners at first and third base. Dealing with: regular steals; delayed steals; forced balk with runner at first base breaking on the stretch; and forced pick-off at first base with runner taking wide lead. All pitchers will be lined up in a straight line, throwing from the stretch. Coach will inform the pitchers what the runner at first and the runner at third base is going to do on the play. Pitchers will then react to the situation. As other mechanics in the fundamental drill series, this is discussed in detail in a later section of Playbook.

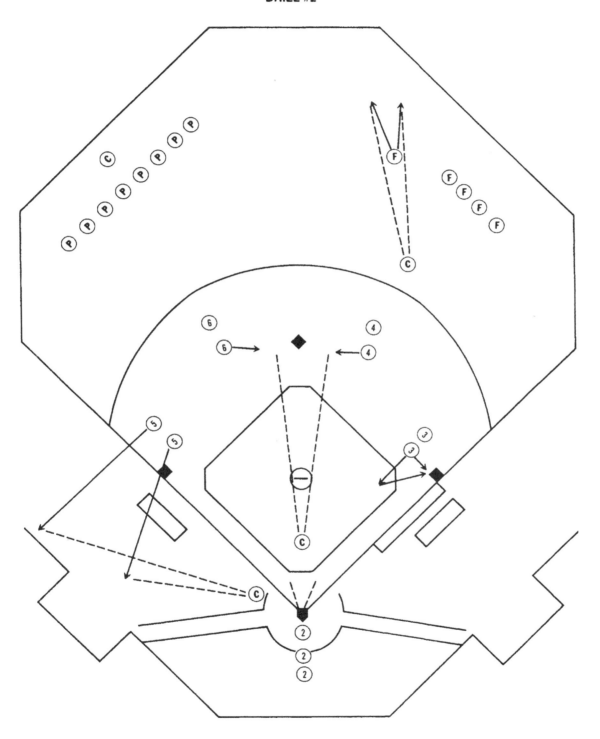

FUNDAMENTAL DRILL SERIES NUMBER 1
DRILL #3

1. Pitchers and First Basemen

Coach will hit ground balls to the first basemen from about five feet on the first base side of home plate so as to not interfere with the catchers fielding bunts on the third base side. Pitchers will fake the pitch to the plate either from the windup or the stretch and break to cover first base once the ball leaves the fungo hitter's bat. The first basemen will alternate taking ground balls from various depths on the infield. The fungo hitter needs to make the first basemen field all kinds of ground balls within their fielding range.

2. Catchers and Third Basemen

The catchers will alternate fielding bunted balls with their masks on. Bunt is thrown from behind the catcher so that the bunts go on the third base side of the diamond. Will be working on bunt communication between the third basemen and the catchers, along with the mechanics of fielding a bunted ball. If catcher takes the bunt, the third baseman retreats back to third base for a possible throw from the catcher. If the catcher reads no possible play at third base, he will fake the throw to first base. If the third baseman, who has priority on the bunted ball over the catcher, calls for the ball ("I've got it") he will fake the throw to first base. If in early break bunt defense with shortstop covering third base, then the catcher will yell "three" to the third baseman fielding bunt. Third baseman will then throw to the base, with the other third baseman covering (would be the shortstop on play).

3. Outfielders, Shortstops and Second Basemen

Fly ball communication with the coach throwing all types of fly balls from behind the mound. Outfielders working on coming in on fly balls, while the shortstops and second basemen will be working on going back on same fly balls. Main concentration in this drill is the communication between the fielders. The thrower will attempt to throw fly balls in the areas of the outfield where you would have a play on the ball by two or three fielders (designated by large X's on the diagram). The outfielders, shortstops and second basemen will alternate.

FUNDAMENTAL DRILL SERIES NUMBER 1
DRILL #3

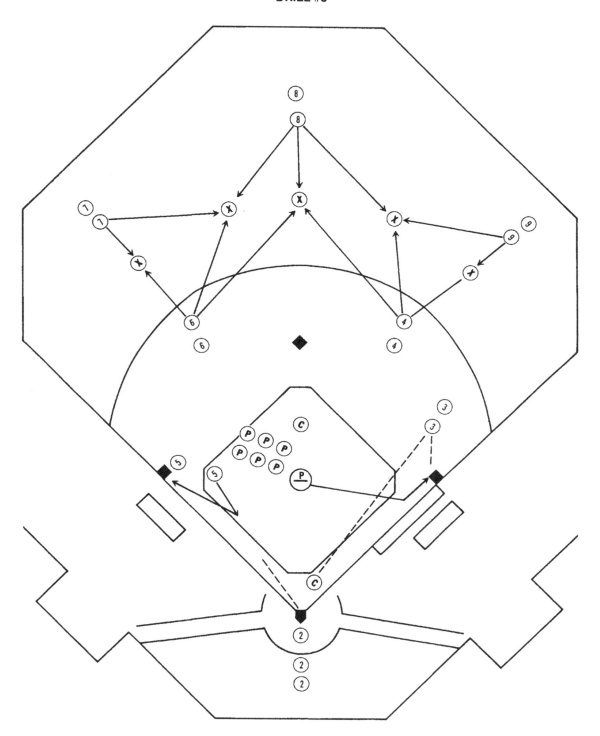

75

FUNDAMENTAL DRILL SERIES NUMBER 1
DRILL #4

1. Pitchers, First Basemen, Second Basemen and Catchers

Coach hits ground balls from the first base side of home plate to the right side of the infield. Pitchers, second basemen, first basemen working on ground ball communication. Catchers will alternate backing up the play at first base yelling to the pitcher "Get over there". Coach will hit all types of ground balls to the right side forcing the players to make all kinds of plays. Pitcher must let the first baseman know quickly when he can field the ball by saying "I've got it". Second baseman must let the first baseman know quickly when he can make the play by saying "I've got it". Pitchers working on covering first base when the first baseman fields the ball away from the base, or when the second baseman makes the play and the first baseman can not recover to get back to the bag. Second baseman and first baseman are instructed on what type of hitter at the plate: left or righthanded hitter; pull; regular or opposite field hitter. First basemen will alternate playing on and off the bag. The first baseman may occasionally miss the ball so the catcher can check himself on back up location.

2. Shortstops and Third Basemen

Coach hitting ground balls from the third base side of home plate to the left side of the infield. Fungo hitter will set up the situation: (1) baserunner at first and second base with possible force play at third base; (2) baserunner at second base not forced to advance. Fungo hitter tries to hit balls that will take the third basemen to their left and the shortstops to their right. Shortstop must let the third baseman know quickly when he can make the play "I've got it". Third baseman must make all the plays he can going to his left unless the shortstop can make the play much easier. If the third baseman fields a double play type ground ball, he will fake the throw to second base. If his only play is to first base, he will fake the throw to first base. If the shortstop fields the ball and has a force play at third base he will throw to the retreating third baseman if he can get back to the bag. If not, then he will fake the throw to second base or first base depending on the situation at hand. With no force play at third base, the shortstop fields the ball and simulates always that the runner at second base is breaking for third base. Shortstop must read whether third baseman can get back for tag play at third base. If so, he throws to the third baseman who will make the simulated tag. If not, the shortstop fakes the throw to first.

3. Outfielders

In deep center field charging ground balls with possible play at third base or home plate. All do-or-die plays. Coach will hit balls from second base. Outfielders will fake the throw to either third base or home plate, and then throw the ball back to hitter.

76

FUNDAMENTAL DRILL SERIES NUMBER 1
DRILL #4

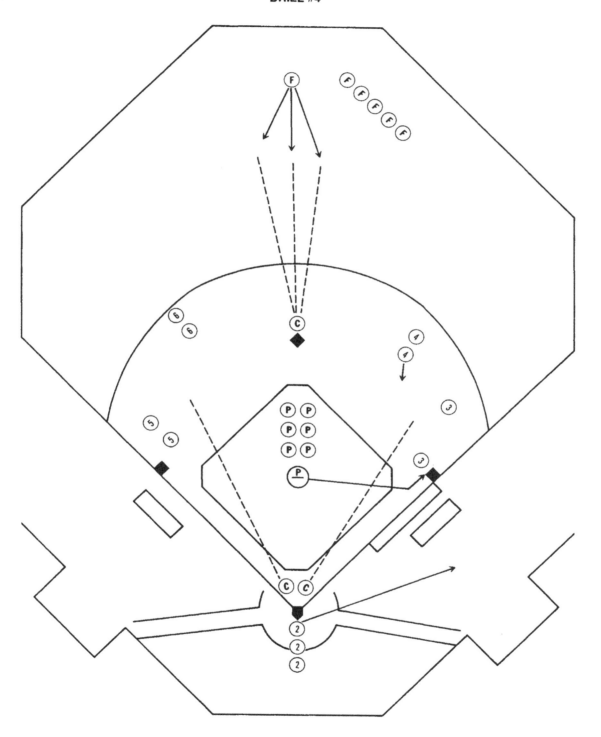

FUNDAMENTAL DRILL SERIES NUMBER 1
DRILL #5

1. **Pitchers, Third Basemen, Shortstops** and **Catchers**

Bunt communication on bunted balls to the third base side of the infield. Simulate baserunners at first and second base, with less than two outs. Coach will throw bunted balls from behind the catchers at home plate. Catchers will have masks on. Coach will tell the players which bunt defense play is in effect, and whether it is early in the game or late in the game (gamble). Catchers will call the play for the pitcher and third baseman when one of them fields the ball. If he wants fielder to throw to third base he yells "three-three". If he wants him to throw to first base he yells "one-one". If there is no play he yells "no play". If instructed to throw to third base, either the third baseman or shortstop will be at the bag depending on the bunt play in effect. If the throw is to be made to first base, the fielder fakes the throw simulating the throw in a game. If no play, fielder will fake the throw to first base and then look to third base for possible play on runner rounding bag. Players converging on bunted ball use proper communication and priority system as explained in bunt plays later in Playbook. Pitcher will initiate drill by simulating a pitch to home plate from the stretch position after the shortstop has completed his mechanics of holding the runner at second base.

2. **First Basemen** and **Second Basemen**

Coach will hit ground balls to the right side of the infield from the first base side of home plate so as to not interfere with the catchers fielding bunted balls on the third base side. Fungo hitter attempts to force the second basemen to their left, and the first basemen to their right as they alternate taking ground balls. Coach will tell fielders what type of hitter at the plate: left or righthanded hitter; pull; regular or opposite field hitter. Will also tell first basemen to play on or off the bag. Second basemen need to let the first basemen know when they can field the ball "I've got it". If the first baseman on a ground ball fields it away from the bag, he will fake the flip or throw to the pitcher who would be covering bag. If a second baseman fields the ball and the first baseman can not recover to get back to the bag, he will fake the throw to the pitcher who would be covering bag.

3. **Outfielders**

In outfield working on communication on balls in the gaps that can be caught. Also working on outfielders paths to the ball so that the center fielder catches the ball below the waist, and the adjacent outfielder well above the waist creating space between the two on the play. Coach will throw baseballs from shortstop position when throwing to left center field, and from second base when throwing to right center field. Outfielders will move from position to position. Outfielders will have to position themselves closer than normal to each other to take into consideration the ball is being thrown from the infield and not coming off the batted ball from the plate.

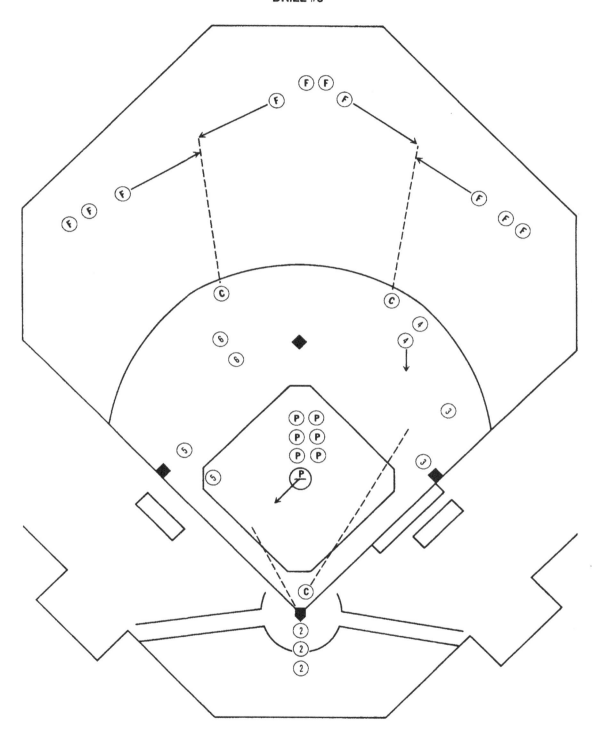

FUNDAMENTAL DRILL SERIES NUMBER 1
DRILL #6

1. Shortstops, Second Basemen and Pitchers

Working on regular pick-off play at second base involving the shortstops, second basemen and pitchers. A manager is the baserunner leading off second base. Pitchers alternate on mound picking up the pick-off sign from either the shortstop or second baseman. The sign can be given by either one of them before the pitcher gets on the rubber, or when he comes to the set position off the stretch. If the sign is given before he gets on the rubber, the pitcher must give the acknowledgment sign or else the pick-off play is not on. If given by the shortstop or the second baseman when he comes to the set in the stretch, no acknowledgment sign can be given. Pitchers can initiate the sign off the rubber to the shortstop or second baseman, but he must receive the acknowledgment sign back from the shortstop or second baseman in order to have the pick-off play on. This is a timed pick-off play which is discussed later in the Playbook. Pick-off plays #14 and #16.

2. Catchers, First Basemen and Third Basemen

Working on pick-offs from the catcher to the third basemen and first basemen. One catcher is in front of the mound throwing to the catcher at home plate who will have his mask on. Another catcher will simulate the hitter at the plate in either the right or left batter's box. The first baseman or third baseman can initiate the sign to the catcher, or the catcher can initiate the sign to the first baseman or third baseman. There must be an acknowledgment sign from the other party or the play is not on. When the sign is initiated and acknowledged, then on the first swing and miss or bunt and miss on the batter's part, the pick-off play is on. If the batter does not swing and miss, or bunt and miss then the pick-off is not on. The sign will remain on until the batter misses a pitch unless one of the parties involved wipes off the sign. The catchers will alternate after three throws each to first or third base. Simulate baserunner at first and third base. Pick-off plays #23 and #25 discussed later in Playbook.

3. Outfielders

Outfielders in right center field working on going to their right and left for ground balls being hit by the coach who is standing in deep second base position. The manager positions himself next to the fungo hitter. Outfielders working on correct angles, fielding the balls properly, setting up to throw, and throwing the ball to a relay or cut-off man.

FUNDAMENTAL DRILL SERIES NUMBER 1
DRILL #6

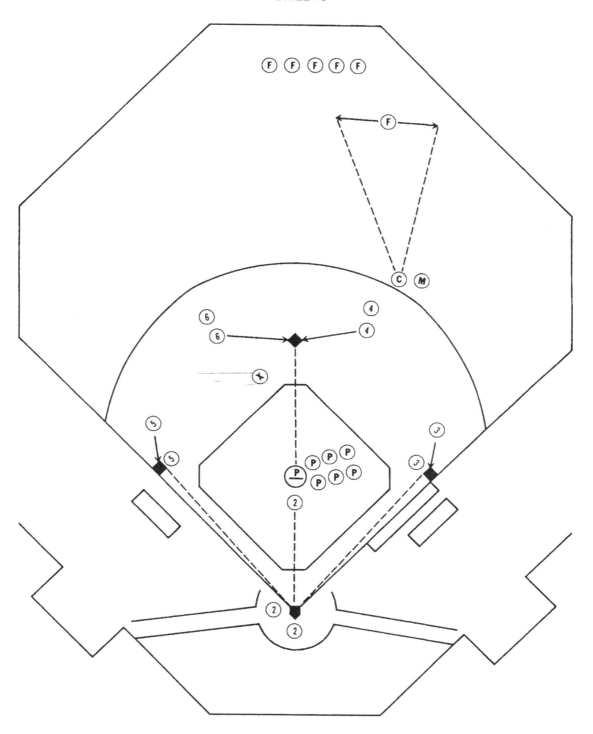

FUNDAMENTAL DRILL SERIES NUMBER 1
DRILL #7

1. Pitchers and First Basemen

Working on pick-off play at first base with baserunners at first and second base, (Pick-off Play #13). A manager will be the runner at first base. Players will simulate that there is also a runner at second base. Pitchers and first basemen will alternate working the pick-off. The sign can be given by the first baseman to the pitcher before he gets on the rubber. If so, the pitcher must give the acknowledgment sign back to him or the pick-off is not on. The pitcher can give the sign to the first baseman off the rubber, but in order for the play to be on, the first baseman must give it back to him. The first baseman can give the pick-off sign to a lefthanded pitcher when he is in the set position on the stretch. For a righthanded pitcher, it must be given when he is off the rubber. When the play is on, the righthanded pitcher will go to the set position. He will look to the runner at second base but be able to see the first baseman playing behind the runner at first base. When the first baseman breaks for the bag, the pitcher throws to the first baseman on the bag for the tag. The lefthanded pitcher will also come to the set position on the stretch when the play is on. When the pitcher lifts up his lead leg (right leg), the first baseman breaks for the bag to make the tag play on the runner.

2. Outfielders, Second Basemen and Shortstops

Working on the outfielders throwing behind the runner rounding second base on a well hit ball. The outfielders will go to their respective positions and alternate making the play. The shortstops and second basemen will also alternate covering second base depending on where the ball is hit in the outfield. You can use a manager or an extra player to simulate a baserunner at first base rounding second base on a well hit ball to the outfield. If no runners are available, then the defense will simulate a runner rounding the bag. Anytime the ball is not hit well, then the outfielder will field it properly and fake the throw to third base with the shortstop being in the proper cut-off position. On a well hit ball to the left fielder, the second baseman will approach the bag from behind the runner preparing himself for a throw to second base from left field. On a well hit ball to the center fielder, the second baseman will break to the mound side of second base and move into the bag when the ball leaves the center fielder's hand. The left fielder and center fielder need to eye fake the throw to third base, and then step and throw to second base when throwing behind the runner. On a well hit ball to the right fielder, where there is little chance for the runner to advance to third base, the shortstop will break from the cut-off position to second base when the ball leaves the right fielder's hand. When the outfielders are in doubt about the status of the runner, then they would throw to third base. In this drill, that would be a fake to third. Coach hits hard line drives right at the outfielders from behind the mound with a manager catching in at his side.

3. Catchers and Third Basemen

Alternate working on fly ball communication on balls thrown by the coach from home plate. Balls will be thrown to the general problem areas as designated by X's on the diagram. Proper fly ball communication used by the third basemen and catchers. Catchers have masks on.

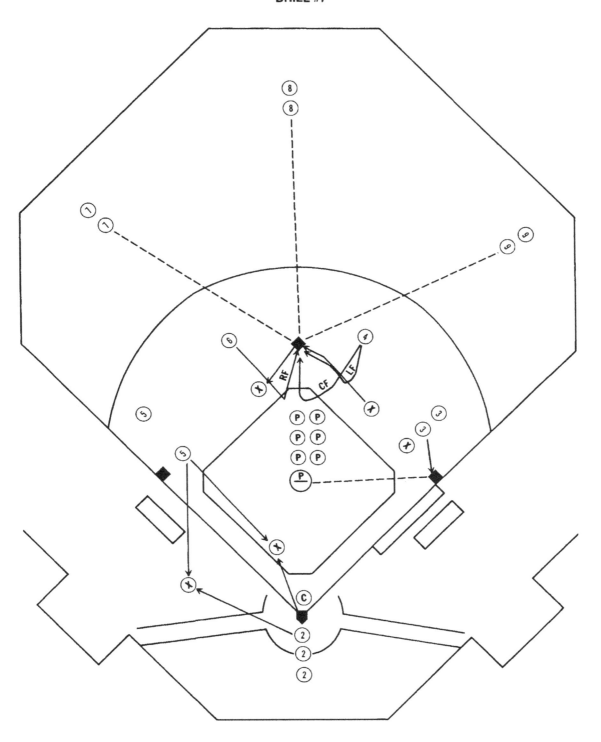

FUNDAMENTAL DRILL SERIES NUMBER 1
DRILL #8

1. Catchers, Shortstops and Second Basemen

This drill will follow the same mechanics as drill number six in the fundamental drill series number one where the catchers, first basemen and third basemen are involved. The only difference would be that either the shortstop or second baseman is now involved in the pick-off from the catcher on the first swing and miss or bunt and miss. Pick-off plays #24 and #26.

2. First Basemen and Third Basemen

Working on the first basemen and third basemen properly fielding bunted balls and throwing to either first base or third base. Coach will either fungo or throw out the bunts to either side from the right side of the batter's box. The coach can coordinate his bunt with the catcher throwing to the plate from the mound to make the play more realistic for the players involved. The coach will call out what bunt defense they are in with simulated runners at first and second base with less than two outs. The coach will either yell out: "one-one"; "three-three"; or "hold" depending on the nature of the bunt. Any time he yells out "hold", the fielder will fake the throw to first base and then look to third for a possible play on a runner rounding the bag too aggressively. He will yell out this command once the ball is on the ground. If the first baseman fields the ball and "one" is called, he will throw the bunted ball to first base where the other first baseman would be simulating the second baseman covering the bag. If the coach yells out "three", then the first baseman would field the bunt and throw the ball to third base where the third baseman would be in the standard bunt defense if the ball was bunted to the right side of the diamond. With the early break bunt defense called, the shortstop would be covering third base, so the other third baseman will simulate the shortstop being at the bag for the throw from the first baseman. If the third baseman fields the ball the coach will yell only "one" or "hold" on the standard bunt defense, and either "three", "one" or "hold" on the early break defense. The other first baseman not involved in the play will be at first base simulating the second baseman covering the base. The other third baseman not involved in the play will be at third base simulating the shortstop covering the bag on the early break.

3. Outfielders

In right field working on going back to the fence and picking up a ball properly that is on the ground, and throwing to the relay man (manager next to fungo hitter). The fungo hitter can either fungo or throw the ball to the fence. Outfielders alternate.

4. Pitchers

The pitchers are in left field working on their mechanics for the inside pick-off play at second base where the pitcher lifts up his lead leg from the stretch position and throws to either the shortstop or second baseman on the bag. The pitchers will pair up and throw inside pick-off moves to each other.

84

FUNDAMENTAL DRILL SERIES NUMBER 1
DRILL #8

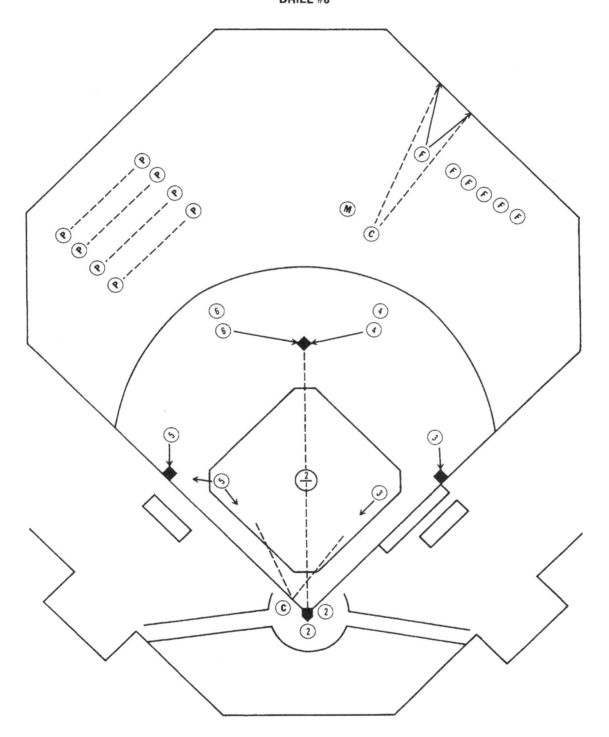

FUNDAMENTAL DRILL SERIES NUMBER 1
DRILL #9

1. Right Fielders, Second Basemen and First Basemen

Working on fly ball communication on balls down the right field line where all three players converge on the ball. The coach will throw fly balls from the right side of the home plate area to the area near the X as indicated on the diagram. Right fielders, second basemen and first basemen alternate.

2. Pitchers, Shortstops and Second Basemen

Working on the mechanics and timing involved on the inside pick-off move at second base. It can be either a verbal or visual sign from either the shortstop or second baseman to the pitcher. The pitcher can put on the sign by a visual sign to either the shortstop or second basemen. The acknowledgment sign must be given back unless the sign is given when the pitcher is on the rubber in the set position from the stretch. A manager will be the runner at second base. The pitchers will alternate on the mound working from the stretch position. Either the pitcher or the player receiving the throw at second base can originate the sign. When the play is on, either the shortstop or second baseman will break for second base when the pitcher picks up his lead leg. The second basemen will also be involved in station number 1, so they will have to alternate going out on the fly ball and handling the inside pick-off at the bag.

3. Third Basemen and Catchers

The catchers and third basemen will be working on rundown mechanics between third base and home plate. The outfielders not involved in station number 1 will be the runners in the rundown feeding the line from foul territory. The coach will position himself on the third base side of the mound, throwing the ball to either the third baseman or catcher to start the rundown. Rundown mechanics are discussed in detail later in the Playbook.

4. Left Fielders and Center Fielders

Involved as runners in the rundown between the third basemen and catchers as detailed in station 3. Will feed into the rundown from foul territory on the third base side. All outfielders who might be called on to play right field should be involved in station 1.

In the fundamental drill series number two, we have not detailed the mechanics of the bunt defense plays and pick-off plays as much as we did in the fundamental drill series number one since the pages directly following this drill series detail each of the plays involved.

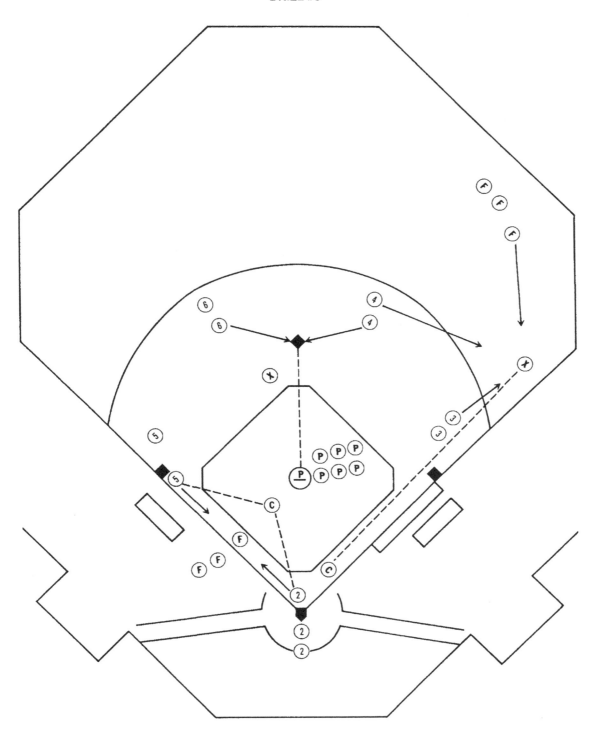

FUNDAMENTAL DRILL SERIES NUMBER 2
DRILL #1

1. **Pitchers** and **Third Basemen**

Working on pick-off play #15, which is detailed later in the Playbook. The pitchers and third basemen will alternate giving the pick-off sign and executing the play at third base. The outfielders not involved as baserunners at first base will serve as runners at third base. When pick-off play is made at third base, they fake getting back to the bag.

2. **Catchers, First Basemen, Shortstops** and **Second Basemen**

Working on the mechanics of the early break pitchout bunt defense which is detailed later in the Playbook. The outfielders not involved with being a runner leading off third base will be the runners at first base in this drill. The runners should occasionally break for second base when the catcher throws down to first base on the pitchout. At other times, they fake the fact that they will be attempting to get back to first base. All the defensive players involved will alternate on each play. One catcher will position himself in front of the mound serving as the pitcher who is throwing the pitchout to the plate. Another catcher will be in either the right or left batter's box with bat in hand, so that the catchers can work on their pitchout mechanics with both a righthanded and lefthanded hitter.

3. **Outfielders**

Will serve as baserunners at either first or third base.

FUNDAMENTAL DRILL SERIES NUMBER 2
DRILL #1

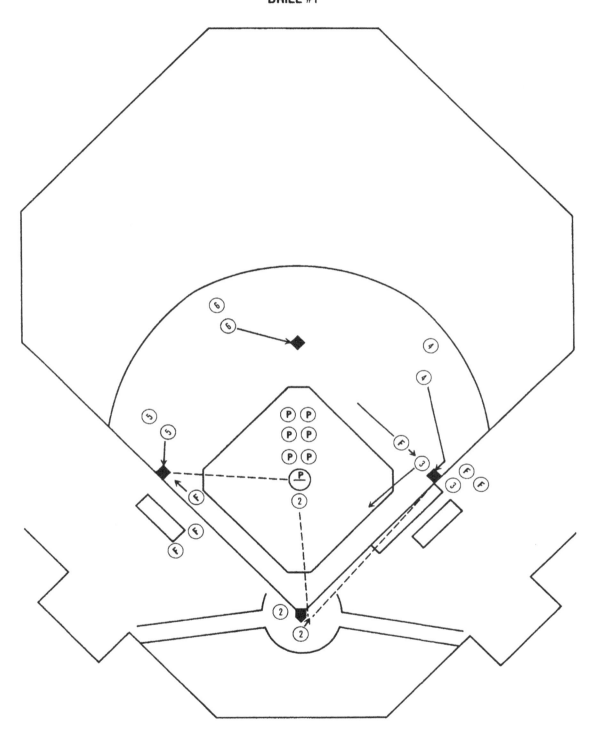

FUNDAMENTAL DRILL SERIES NUMBER 2
DRILL #2

1. **Pitchers, First Basemen, Second Basemen** and **Shortstops**

Pick-off play #13 with baserunners at first and second base. The same drill as in fundamental drill series number 1—drill number 7—station 1. The only difference is that an outfielder will be the baserunner at first base and will get in a rundown between first and second base. The pitcher will cover first base as the rundown begins. All defensive players will alternate.

2. **Third Baseman** and **Catchers**

Pick-off play #25 with a baserunner at third base. The same drill as in fundamental drill series number 1—drill number 6—station 2. The only difference is that an outfielder will be the baserunner at third base and will get in a rundown between third base and home plate. One catcher will throw to the plate from in front of the mound. Another catcher will simulate the hitter in either the right or left side of the batter's box. The other catcher, with mask on, will pick-off the runner at third base on the first swing or bunt and miss.

3. **Outfielders**

Will serve as baserunners at either first or third base.

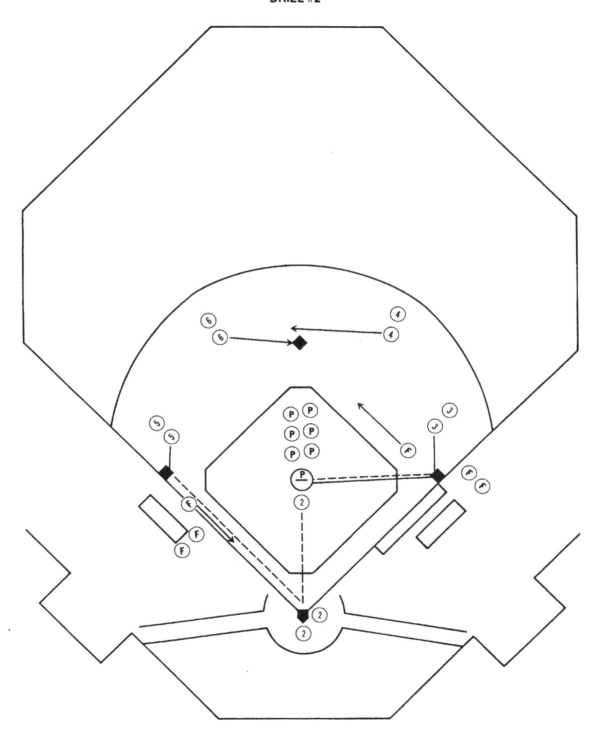

FUNDAMENTAL DRILL SERIES NUMBER 2
DRILL #3

1. First Basemen and Catchers

First basemen and catchers working on fly ball communication on balls thrown by coach from home plate area. The balls will be thrown to the general problem areas as designated by X's on the diagram. Proper fly ball communication used with the first basemen and catchers alternating. The catchers will have their masks on.

2. Pitchers

Working on getting to the proper back up position on balls hit to the outfield. Each pitcher will alternate on the mound faking the pitch to the plate and then reacting to the situation as presented by the coach standing behind him on the mound. Before the pitcher fakes the pitch, the coach will inform him as to what the simulated situation is in regard to baserunners, outs, and where the ball will be hit. After the pitch the pitcher will break full speed to the proper back up spot. For example: one out, baserunner at first base, base hit to center field. The pitcher should break to the back up position well behind third base. The coach should have a card of every back up situation the pitchers would be confronted with in a game so that he can be sure to cover as many as time permits each time the pitchers are involved in this drill.

3. Outfielders, Third Basemen, Second Basemen and Shortstops

Working on fly ball communication with the coach throwing fly balls to the general problem areas as designated by X's on the diagram. All defensive players will alternate on the fly balls using proper communication. Coach throws balls from behind the mound with a manager at his side receiving the throws from the fielders.

FUNDAMENTAL DRILL SERIES NUMBER 2
DRILL #3

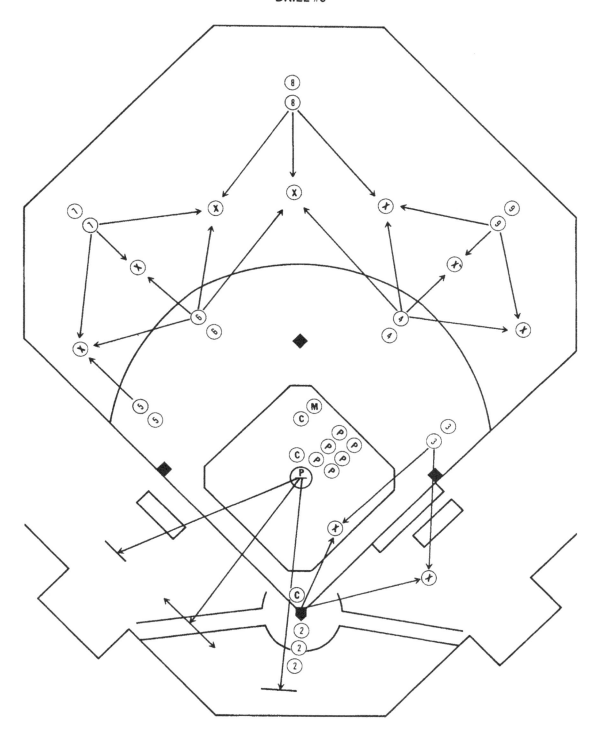

FUNDAMENTAL DRILL SERIES NUMBER 2
DRILL #4

1. Infielders, Catchers and Pitchers

Working on rundowns between all bases and home plate. The pitchers will feed from well outside the third baseline in foul territory so that they are not in the way of any rundown play that develops between third base and home plate. As each pitcher comes to the mound he will quickly assume the set position. The coach will set up right behind him on the mound and will determine which base the rundown will start at by either: throwing to the first baseman at first base; throwing to the second baseman or shortstop at second base; throwing to the third baseman at third base; or throwing to the catcher at the plate on a simulated unsuccessful squeeze bunt. The outfielders will serve as the baserunners at each base getting in a rundown as the play develops and attempting to get out of the rundown as best they can. The coach can have the runner at first base break for second base on the stretch to set up a rundown from the shortstop back to the first baseman. He can also have the runner at second base break for third base on the stretch to set up a rundown from the third baseman back to the second baseman. All others would originate on the runner at a base getting picked off that base. If the coach throws the ball to first base, the pitcher will cover first base on the rundown. If the ball is thrown to either the shortstop or second baseman at second base, the pitcher would break to back up the third baseman at third base. If the coach throws the ball to third base the pitcher will break for the plate to back up the catcher on the rundown. Finally, if the throw goes to the catcher at the plate on an unsuccessful squeeze bunt attempt, the pitcher will cover home plate. On plays at home plate where the pitcher is backing up the catcher the first baseman will come in and, if time allows, take the pitcher's spot. The complete mechanics of the rundown play are detailed in the infield section of the Playbook. All defensive players will alternate once involved in a rundown play, including the pitcher.

2. Outfielders

Will serve as the runners at first base, second base, and third base. The coach on the mound will motion to you for what he wishes you to do when the pitcher is at the set position.

FUNDAMENTAL DRILL SERIES NUMBER 2
DRILL #4

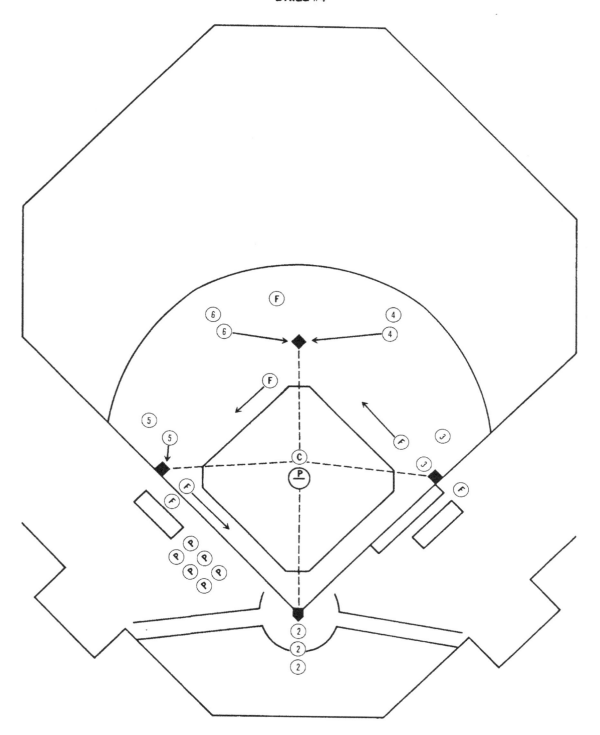

FUNDAMENTAL DRILL SERIES NUMBER 2
DRILL #5

1. Pitchers and Catchers

Working on the mechanics of the pitcher covering home plate on a wild pitch or passed ball with a simulated baserunner coming in from third base to score. A coach or manager will set up behind the catcher. The pitcher will fake a pitch to home plate. As the fake pitch is made the coach or manager will roll a ball somewhere behind the catcher. The pitcher will charge toward the plate and must point and verbally direct the catcher to the location of the ball ("back", for ball directly behind the catcher; "first base side", for ball to the catcher's right; and "third base side" for the ball to the catcher's left). Each catcher will alternate retrieving the ball, setting up properly and throwing accurately to the pitcher covering the plate. The pitcher will make the tag on the simulated runner coming in from third base. The pitcher must set up properly at the plate to allow the runner part of the plate to slide into, but at the same time, be in a position to make the proper tag.

2. First Basemen

The first basemen will alternate taking bad throws at first base from the coach standing between the mound and second base. The first basemen will break for the bag and set up properly, and then attempt to field: short hop throws; in-between hop throws; high throws; and throws that will take them either left or right off the bag. A manager will position himself behind the first basemen retrieving all balls that get by the first basemen and throw them back to the coach.

3. Outfielders, Second Basemen, Shortstops and Third Basemen

Working on the mechanics of the tandom relay play on a ball that gets by an outfielder to the fence. The coach will fungo the balls from behind second base to all areas of the field forcing the outfielders to go to all areas and angles of the fence. Once the ball is hit, and a sure double is in affect, both the shortstop and second basemen will go out for the tandom relay. The shortstops and second basemen will alternate. The mechanics of the tandom relay are detailed in the infield section of the Playbook. The third basemen in this drill will communicate where to throw the baseball. If he wants the throw to be made to third base he will yell "three-three", and the relay man will throw the ball to third base. If he wants the throw to be made to home plate he will yell "four-four", and the relay men will fake the throw to the plate. If he yells "hold", then the relay man will catch the ball and start running it back into the infield. The back man on the tandom relay will also communicate to the front man where to throw the ball listening to the third baseman. A manager will be at the fungo hitter's side catching the balls from the third basemen or tandom relay man back to the fungo hitter.

FUNDAMENTAL DRILL SERIES NUMBER 2
DRILL #5

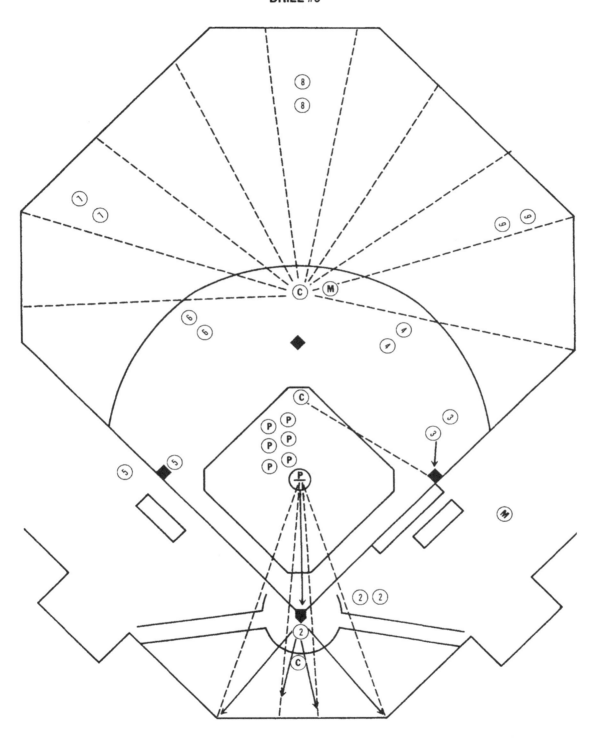

FUNDAMENTAL DRILL SERIES NUMBER 2
DRILL #6

1. Pitchers, Shortstops and Second Basemen

Working on the daylight pick-off play at second base between the pitchers and shortstops, with the second basemen backing up the throw to the bag. No sign is needed since the shortstop will break full speed for second base when the pitcher is in the set position on his stretch. A manager will be the runner at second base. When the pitcher sees daylight between the runner and the shortstop, he will turn and pick at the bag. The pitcher does not have to throw the ball to the shortstop, nor does he even have to turn towards second base if he feels that there would be no chance to retire the runner. If so, all he would do is step off the rubber and give the shortstop time to get back to his position before he goes back onto the rubber for the pitch to the plate. The shortstop can never break full speed to second base, break daylight between himself and the runner and then not continue on to the bag. All defensive players will alternate.

2. First Basemen, Catchers and Third Basemen

Working on fly ball communication between the third basemen, first basemen and catchers on balls thrown by the coach from home plate. The coach will throw the fly balls to the general problem areas as designated by the X's in the diagram. All defensive players will alternate. The catchers will have their masks on.

3. Outfielders

In center field throwing fly balls to each other from about 150 feet away. They will be working on getting into the proper position to throw to a base or the plate.

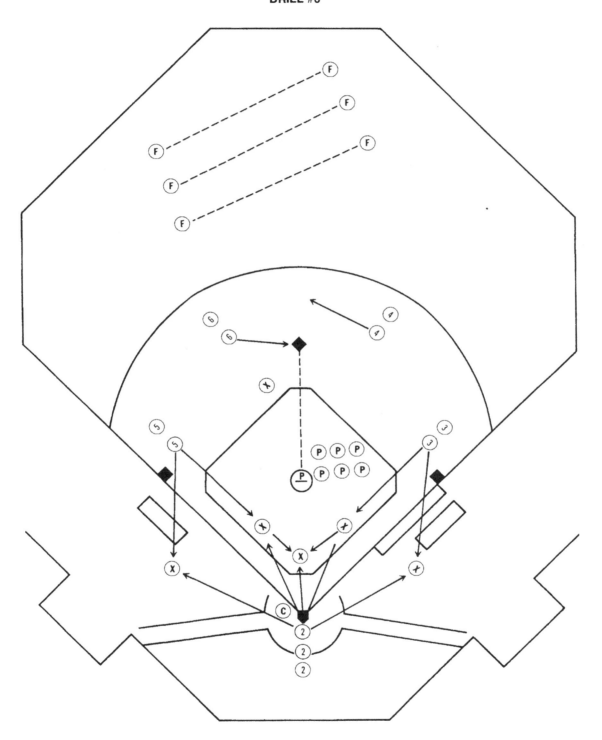

FUNDAMENTAL DRILL SERIES NUMBER 2
DRILL #7

1. Pitchers, Catchers, Shortstops and Second Basemen

Working on the bases loaded pick-off at second base from the pitcher to the shortstop. When the sign is on between the shortstop, pitcher and catcher, the pitcher will assume his normal position on the rubber as if to go into his windup for his delivery to the plate. The catcher will flash a sign to the pitcher as he would in a normal pitch, and then put his glove up for the target. Right after the catcher puts the glove up, the shortstop will break for second base. As soon as the catcher sees the shortstop break for the bag, he will drop his glove down and the pitcher will throw to the shortstop at second base for the attempted pick-off. A manager will be the runner at second base varying the distance of his lead on each play. If either the shortstop or the catcher sees that the runner at second base is not taking a wide enough lead, one or both of them would yell to the pitcher "step off". The play is then off until it is put back on by one of the three players involved. All pitchers, shortstops and catchers will alternate. Second basemen back up the play.

2. Third Basemen and First Basemen

The third basemen will field slow rollers from the coach hitting the ball from the first base side of home plate. The coach will hit all types of slowly hit balls to the third basemen so that they will have to come in and field the ball on the run. The coach will inform both the third basemen and first basemen as to whether there are runners on base or not. If there are runners on base, the third baseman fielding the ball must be sure that he throws an accurate throw to first base. The first basemen must be sure that he knocks down all bad throws to keep the runners from advancing. Both the third baseman and first baseman can gamble a little more if there are no runners on base at the time the ball is hit. The coach will position the third basemen at various depths and angles away from the line. This drill can also be used to help the third basemen read the path of a ball down the third baseline as to whether it will be fair or foul on the roll. A manager will position himself next to the coach to receive the throws back from either the first basemen or third basemen.

3. Outfielders

In center field throwing ground balls to each other from about 150 feet away. They will be working on getting to the ball at the proper angle, and fielding the ball properly to throw to a base or the plate.

FUNDAMENTAL DRILL SERIES NUMBER 2
DRILL #7

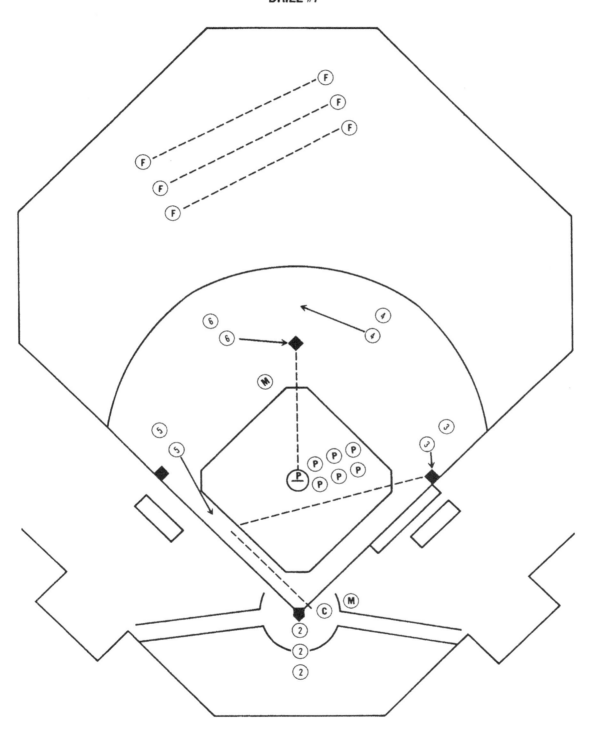

FUNDAMENTAL DRILL SERIES NUMBER 2
DRILL #8

1. **Pitchers, Shortstops, Second Basemen** and **Third Basemen**

Working on the pick-off play at second base off the early break bunt defense with runners at first and second base. This bunt defense and pick-off play is detailed in the next section of the Playbook. A manager will be the baserunner at second base varying the distance of his lead from play to play. Each pitcher will assume the set position on the stretch, working the pick-off with the second baseman at the proper time. If no pick-off sign is given on the play, the pitcher will fake the pitch to the plate.

2. **First Basemen**

Working on the proper mechanics of fielding fly balls at the fence thrown by a coach from the first base side of home plate. The first basemen will alternate.

3. **Outfielders**

In center field receiving fly balls from a fungo hitter positioned on the left field line. A manager will be in the cut-off position about half way between the outfielders and the fungo hitter. The outfielders will be working on the proper mechanics for fielding fly balls with a throw to a base or the plate.

4. **Catchers**

At home plate fielding all types of bunted balls rolled out by the coach standing behind the catcher at the plate. The catchers will alternate fielding the bunted balls properly and faking the throw to first base.

FUNDAMENTAL DRILL SERIES NUMBER 2
DRILL #8

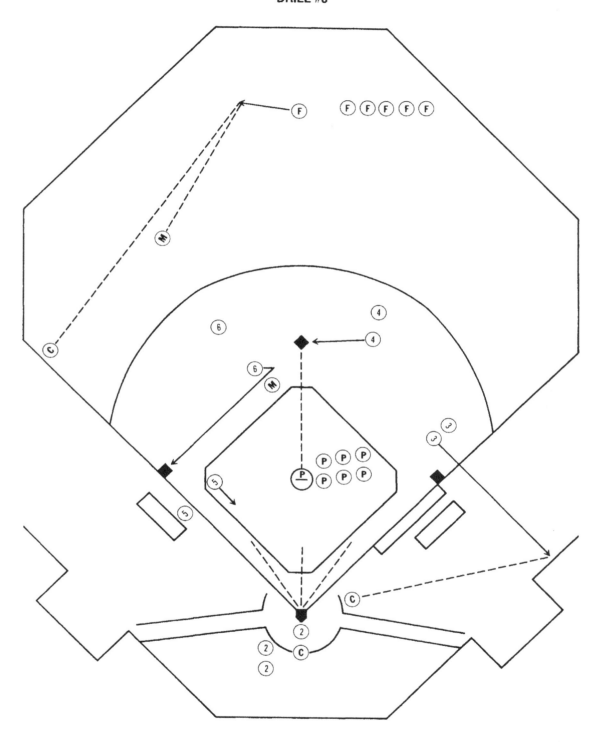

BUNT DEFENSE

One of the keys to successful team defense is the proper execution of the fundamentals of bunt defense. Many times in baseball the winner of a close game is the team that can handle this play properly, due to the fact that the sacrifice bunt play by the offense is generally attempted in the last few innings of a close game that will be decided by a run or two.

So that the players will feel comfortable with the plays that they run when the offensive team attempts the sacrifice bunt, a coach should never confuse his club by having too many bunt defense plays in the team playbook. Some of the important aspects of bunt defense that need to be covered are:

1. **Coach-team communication**—Anytime there is a possibility of a sacrifice bunt, all players must look to the dugout for the play to be called by the head coach. The plays can be called by flashing a number or by another visual sign by the coach to the defense. If no sign is given, the defense will not change from their normal position on defense but must still be prepared for a possible bunt. The coach will make the decision on what bunt defense play to call by analyzing what the offense might do taking into consideration: the score; the inning; the batter's offensive capabilities; the runners on base; and the opposing coach's offensive tendencies in past situations that call for a bunt. After making the decision that a bunt defense will be called, the coach must then decide what type of defense to run: one that honors the possibility of the hitter swinging away; an early break bunt defense where the defense is prepared to handle only the bunt; or a pick-off on a bunt defense to try to get a baserunner on the play.

2. **Throwing the ball to the hitter**—Whenever the likelihood of a sacrifice bunt is high, and a bunt defense play has been called by the coach, the catcher should call for a fast ball. The pitcher should attempt to throw a high fast ball in the strike zone since this is the toughest pitch to bunt and put on the ground. If there is doubt as to whether the hitter will bunt, the pitcher should throw a pitch down in the strike zone. If the first pitch is a ball, and the batter has squared around to bunt, then the next pitch should again be a fast ball belt high in the strike zone. You never want a pitcher throwing a fat high fast ball for the hitter to drive past the infielders if he gets the hit sign from his coach. When the pitcher gets behind in the count, there is more of a chance that the batter will get the "green light" to swing away at the next pitch.

3. **Priority system**—It is very important that a priority system be set up so that if two or more defensive players have a chance to field a bunted ball, the fielders know who has priority on the ball. Whenever a player on defense can make the play on the bunted ball he will yell loudly, "I've got it". If two or more players yell for the ball then the priority system will come into effect. An example of a priority system would be:

Position	Priority Over
Pitcher	First Baseman Only
First Baseman	No One
Catcher	Pitcher and First Baseman
Third Baseman	All Players
Second Baseman (early break)	No One

4. **Catcher calling play**—Since the catcher has the entire play in front of him, he should have the responsibility of making the decision as to what base the ball will be thrown too. He would do this by yelling loudly one of the following four commands: "three-three" (third base); "two-two" (second base); "one-one" (first base); "hold-hold" (don't throw to any base). If any player is instructed by the catcher to throw to the forward base (third base if there are runners at first and second base; second base if there is a runner at first base only), and then the player fumbles the ball, he should then throw the ball to the first baseman or second baseman to retire the hitter at first base. If the catcher fields the bunted ball, he should yell out which base he is throwing to so that the fielder at that base is prepared for the throw. If a defensive player is instructed by the catcher to not throw the ball to any base "hold-hold", he should always fake the throw to first base in hopes that a runner might take a wide turn at a base and a play can be made on him.

The catcher must take into effect many things before deciding where the play should be made, and this decision must be vocalized when the ball is on the ground and before the defensive player is actually fielding the ball. If done too early it could cause a problem in making a bad decision. If done too late it would make for a very difficult play for a player fielding the bunted ball and trying to position himself for the throw to a particular base. In the early part of a game (first through the sixth inning of a nine inning game; first through the fourth inning of a seven inning game), the catcher does not want to gamble on the forward runner unless he is sure that the out can be made. The catcher has got to allow the defense to get a sure out in this situation. Late in the game he can gamble on getting the out at the forward base as long as there is a play at that base.

5. **React to the batted ball**—All defensive players must react first to the batted ball and then to the bunted ball unless an early break bunt defense has been called. If a batter squares around to bunt when the pitcher begins to go into the stretch position, there is a good chance that a fake bunt slash, fake bunt slash hit and run, or a push bunt might be attempted. Unless the early break bunt defense is on, no defensive player should ever make any break toward a base until he reads the down angle of the ball off the bat on a bunt. Any movement by a defensive player prior to the actual bunt must be toward the plate, ready to move left or right if the hitter swings away. On an early break bunt defense, the defensive players involved must be sure to get themselves under control when the batter makes contact with the ball so that they can make a play on a hard bunt or push bunt.

6. **Fielding the throw at a base**—Whenever a throw is made to a base to retire a runner on a bunt attempt, the fielder must be sure he looks first for the bad throw from the player fielding the bunted ball. There is always a tendency on a player's part to rush the throw to retire a runner on a bunt attempt, especially if a play is being made on the forward runner. Many times the ball will be thrown off balance or rushed so badly that the thrower drops his arm slot causing the ball to tail away from the player trying to make the play at a base. Once the ball is in the air, and the fielder at the base has control of the base with his feet, he can stretch for the throw if he feels it is necessary to get the out on a close play. If it will not be a close play, then there is no need to stretch for the throw. All fielders need to be cautioned to not stretch for a thrown ball until it is in the air to prevent the poorly thrown ball from getting past the fielder due to his inability to make an adjustment from the stretch position. Once stretched out to field a thrown ball, the fielder severely restricts his ability to range right or left for a ball. It also makes it impossible to field a thrown ball that sails high. Once the ball is caught, the fielder needs to keep his head up for a possible play at another base. If the ball is poorly bunted, there is always a chance for a double play. If the bunt defense play is properly executed and the communication done quick enough, there should never be a situation where a fielder is not set at a base to field a thrown ball. Throwing to a moving target on a bunt play is a very difficult play for the thrower and receiver.

7. **Fielding the bunted ball and making the throw**—The coach must impress upon his players the importance of getting at least one out practically every time on a sacrifice bunt attempt. The only exception would be those times late in the game when the defense has to gamble on a forward runner. All other times an out has got to be made to prevent the offense from having a big inning. A defensive player must get to the bunted ball as quick as possible so that he does not have to rush himself through the actual fielding of the ball. He must look the ball into his glove making sure that he does not start moving his feet to make the throw to a base until the ball is in his glove. Once he fields the ball, he must pivot quickly and step in the direction of the throw that is to be made to a base. The only time a fielder should ever throw off-balance in a bunt play is when there is not time to set up and throw, and he is gambling on a runner at a forward base late in the game. A wild throw to a base must be prevented in a bunt defense situation. When throwing to a base where there is quite a bit of distance involved (generally second base), the fielder needs to possibly take an extra step (crow-hop) to assure some velocity and accuracy on the throw. A fielder should always sacrifice quickness for control and velocity on the throw to a base making sure that he keeps his elbow up on the throw in order to prevent the ball from sailing away from the fielder at a base. When the fielder feels that there might be a play on the lead runner, he should approach the bunted ball anticipating that play. He can then adjust if the catcher does not call that play.

On the following pages you will find various bunt defense plays for runners at first only, and runners at first and second base. There are numerous ways to defense the bunt, but the ones detailed in the Playbook are the ones that are basic and easy to learn. A coach can incorporate them into his practice schedule by sitting in the dugout, flashing the bunt defense sign and then follow the execution. The outfielders can be the baserunners on base, reacting full speed to the forward base when they read down angle on the bunted ball. One of the coaches can stand behind the catcher as the pitcher delivers to the plate and roll out all types of bunts forcing the defensive players to make all types of plays. He must inform the defense whether they are early in the game or late in the game, so that the catcher can make the decision as to whether or not to gamble on the forward runner or not. All defensive players will alternate on each bunt play.

STANDARD BUNT DEFENSE, RUNNER AT FIRST BASE
SIGN FROM COACH IS: _____

PITCHER—First concern is to hold the runner close to first base. Throws a high fast ball for a strike and then breaks for the plate if the batter squares around to bunt. Has front and slight right side responsibility. Has priority on the bunted ball over the first baseman only.

CATCHER—Calls for a fast ball. On the bunt, has front of the plate responsibility and calls the play for the third baseman, first baseman or pitcher. Has priority over all fielders on the bunt except the third baseman. If the third baseman fields the bunt, the catcher must cover third base until relieved by the third baseman.

FIRST BASEMAN—Holds the runner on base prepared for a pick-off attempt by the pitcher. Will break for the plate when the pitcher delivers to the plate. Has right side responsibility. Has priority over no one on the bunted ball. If the ball is bunted on the third base side, he should retreat quickly to first base. If the second baseman is covering the bag, he will allow the second baseman to receive the throw from the catcher, pitcher or third baseman.

SECOND BASEMAN—Must cheat slightly to first base and be aware of the possibility of a push bunt, slash or full swing by the hitter. When he reads the bunt, he must break full speed for first base coming in from the right field side of first base so that he is moving into the bag as the ball is thrown to first base by the fielder of the bunt. If the first baseman is retreating to the bag, he will have priority over the first baseman. Yell loudly "I've got it" to the first baseman so that he does not interfere with the play at the base.

THIRD BASEMAN—Positions himself 20 feet in on the grass from third base. Has complete left side responsibility. As he reads the bunt he will move to the plate under control being conscious of a push bunt, slash or swing. Has priority over all fielders on the bunted ball. If another fielder fields the bunt, retreats quickly to third base.

SHORTSTOP—Plays regular double play depth being alert for the push bunt, slash or full swing by the batter. When he reads the bunt, he will break full speed for second base and prepare for a possible throw from the fielder of the bunted ball.

LEFT FIELDER—As the ball is bunted breaks for a position to back up a possible play at third base from the first base area.

CENTER FIELDER—As the ball is bunted backs up the throw to second base.

RIGHT FIELDER—As the ball is bunted backs up the throw to first base.

STANDARD BUNT DEFENSE, RUNNER ON FIRST BASE

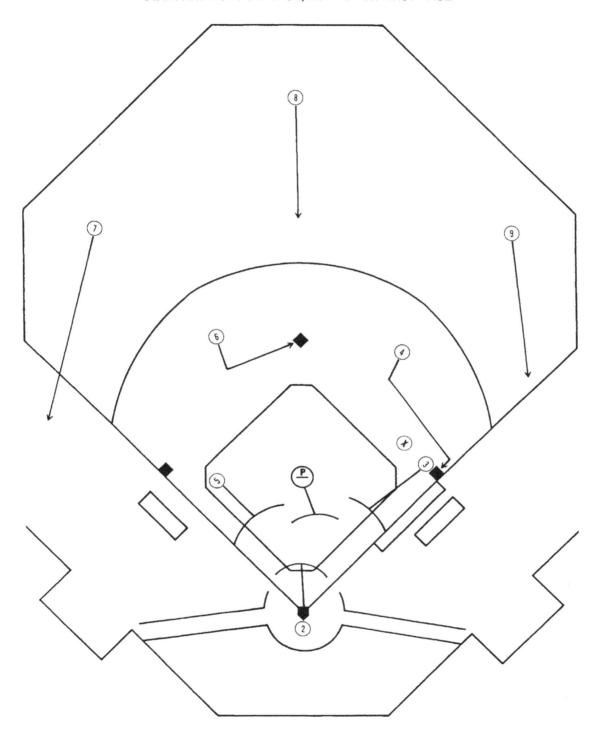

BUNT DEFENSE, RUNNER AT FIRST BASE—SECOND BASEMAN EARLY BREAK
SIGN FROM COACH IS:_____

PITCHER—First concern is to hold the runner close to first base. Throws a high fast ball for a strike and then breaks for the plate if the batter squares around to bunt. The pitcher will deliver the ball to the plate when: **Lefthanded pitcher**—When the second baseman passes the sight line between the pitcher and the runner at first base; **Righthanded pitcher**—When the pitcher sees the second baseman charging to the plate out of the corner of his eye as he looks to first base. Has front of the mound responsibility. Has priority on the bunted ball over the second baseman only.

CATCHER—Calls for a fast ball. On the bunt, has front of the plate responsibility and calls the play for the third baseman, second baseman or pitcher. Has priority over all fielders on the bunt except the third baseman. If the third baseman fields the bunt, the catcher must cover third base until relieved by the third baseman.

FIRST BASEMAN—Holds the runner on base prepared for a pick-off attempt by the pitcher. Does not break for the plate on the bunt attempt. Prepared to field the throw from the fielder of the bunted ball.

SECOND BASEMAN—Positions himself four steps off the infield grass. As the pitcher starts his stretch, breaks full speed to the plate and covers right side of the infield area in front of the plate. Breaks down as he approaches the plate being aware of a possible push bunt, slash or full swing. Has priority over no one on the bunted ball.

THIRD BASEMAN—Positions himself 20 feet in on the grass from third base. Has complete left side responsibility. As he reads the bunt he will move to the plate under control being conscious of a push bunt, slash or swing. Has priority over all fielders on the bunted ball. If another fielder fields the bunt, retreats quickly to third base.

SHORTSTOP—Plays regular double play depth being alert for the push bunt, slash or full swing by the batter. When he reads the bunt, he will break full speed for second base and prepare for a possible throw from the fielder of the bunt.

LEFT FIELDER—As the ball is bunted breaks for a position to back up a possible play at third base from the first base area.

CENTER FIELDER—As the ball is bunted backs up the throw to second base.

RIGHT FIELDER—As the ball is bunted backs up the throw to first base.

BUNT DEFENSE, RUNNER AT FIRST BASE
SECOND BASEMAN EARLY BREAK

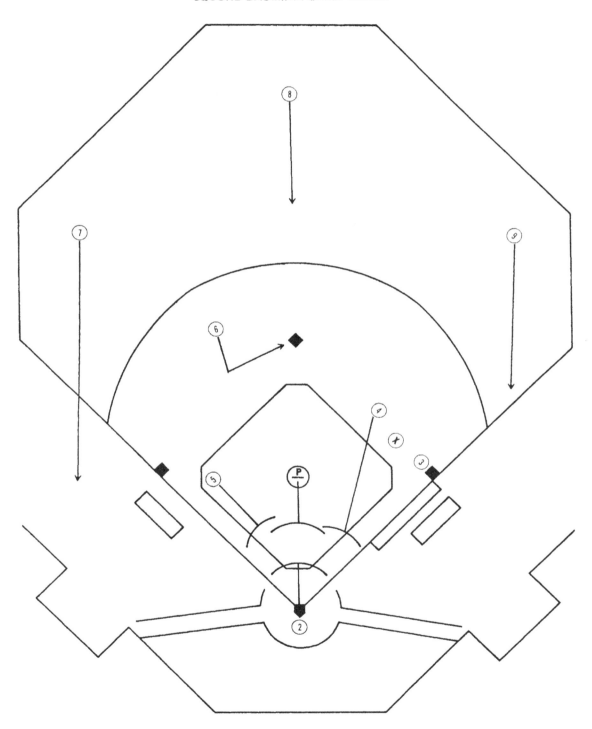

BUNT DEFENSE, RUNNER AT FIRST BASE—FIRST BASEMAN EARLY BREAK
SIGN FROM COACH IS: _____

PITCHER—Goes into the stretch position. When he comes to the set in the stretch, he will immediately deliver the ball to the plate. He should just come to a momentary pause so as to not balk. Throws a high fast ball for a strike. Has front of the mound responsibility. Has priority on the bunted ball over the first baseman only.

CATCHER—Calls for a fast ball. On the bunt, has front of the plate responsibility and calls the play for the third baseman, first baseman or pitcher. Has priority over all fielders on the bunt except the third baseman. If the third baseman fields the bunt, the catcher must cover third base until relieved by the third baseman.

FIRST BASEMAN—As soon as the pitcher reaches the top of the stretch going to the set position, he will break from first base full speed for the plate. Covers right side of the infield area in front of the plate. Breaks down as he approaches the plate being aware of a possible push bunt, slash or full swing. Has priority over no one on the bunted ball.

SECOND BASEMAN—Must cheat towards first base and be aware of the possibility of a push bunt, slash or full swing by the hitter. When he reads the bunt, he must break full speed for first base coming in from the right field side of first base so that he is moving into the bag as the ball is thrown to first base by the fielder of the bunt. The first baseman will not be able to get back to the bag if someone else fields the ball, so the second baseman would be the only one covering the bag for the throw.

THIRD BASEMAN—Positions himself 20 feet in on the grass from third base. Has complete left side responsibility. As he reads the bunt he will move to the plate under control being conscious of a push bunt, slash or swing. Has priority over all fielders on the bunted ball. If another fielder fields the bunt, retreats quickly to third base.

SHORTSTOP—Plays regular double play depth being alert for the push bunt, slash or full swing by the batter. When he reads the bunt, he will break full speed for second base and prepare for a possible throw from the fielder of the bunted ball.

LEFT FIELDER—As the ball is bunted breaks for a position to back up a possible play at third base from the first base area.

CENTER FIELDER—As the ball is bunted backs up the throw to second base.

RIGHT FIELDER—As the ball is bunted backs up the throw at first base.

110

BUNT DEFENSE, RUNNER AT FIRST BASE
FIRST BASEMAN EARLY BREAK

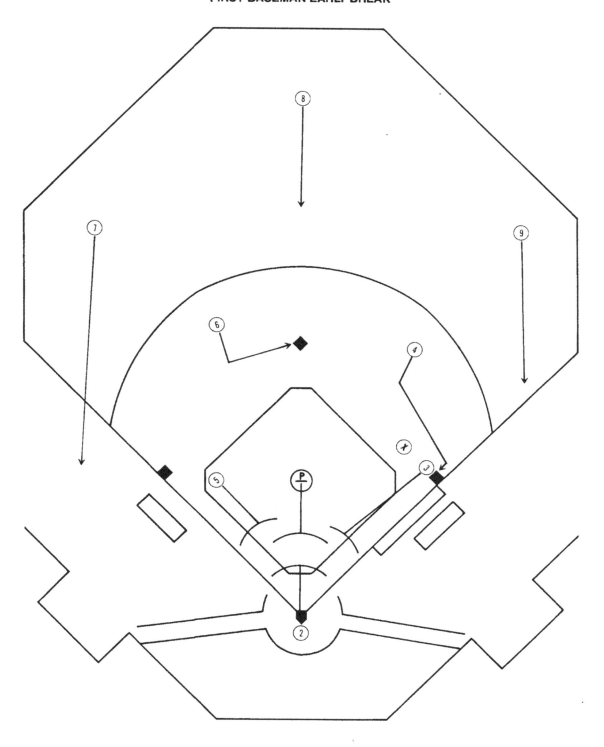

PICK-OFF EARLY BREAK BUNT DEFENSE - RUNNER AT FIRST BASE
SIGN FROM COACH IS:_____

PITCHER—Goes into the stretch position. When he comes to the set in the stretch, he will immediately throw a pitchout to the catcher at home plate. If the runner is picked off first base, he breaks for first base to serve as the back up on the rundown until the first baseman relieves him. If he throws a poor pitchout, he must be prepared to cover the area in front of the mound for the bunt.

CATCHER—Gives the pitchout sign to the pitcher. On the pitchout, will throw the ball to the second baseman covering first base if there is a play on the runner. If no play, he will not throw. If the runner is hung up between first and second base, he will run at the runner forcing him to break towards second or back to first base. Give up the ball when he breaks to either base. Be prepared to field the bunted ball and call the play if the pitcher throws a poor pitchout and the batter bunts the ball.

FIRST BASEMAN—As soon as the pitcher reaches the top of the stretch going to the set position, he will break from first base full speed for the plate. If the catcher throws the ball to the second baseman at first base, he retreats quickly back to first base to relieve the pitcher as the back up man on the rundown play. Must be prepared to field the bunted ball if the pitcher throws a poor pitchout and the batter bunts the ball. Be sure and charge well on the infield grass if there is a lefthanded batter as the catcher will be throwing to first base from the inside of the first baseline.

SECOND BASEMAN—Must cheat towards first base another four steps from the regular early break bunt defense position. As soon as the pitcher begins his move into the set position, he walks another two steps toward first base. When the pitcher reaches the set position, he breaks full speed for first base coming in from the right field side of the base prepared for the throw from the catcher.

THIRD BASEMAN—Positions himself 20 feet in on the grass from third base. Breaks for the plate as he would on the early break bunt defense. Retreat back to third base on the throw to first base by the catcher. Be prepared to field the bunted ball if the pitcher throws a poor pitchout and the batter bunts the ball.

SHORTSTOP—Plays regular double play depth. Will break for second base when the catcher throws the ball to the second baseman at first base.

LEFT FIELDER—As the ball is thrown to the second baseman at first base, backs up second base for a possible bad throw from the second baseman to the shortstop at second base. If the ball is bunted, he will back up a possible play at third base from the first base area.

CENTER FIELDER—If ball is thrown to first base breaks for second base to serve as the back up man on the possible rundown between first and second base. If ball is bunted, backs up the possible throw to second base.

RIGHT FIELDER—As soon as the pitcher comes to the set position, breaks for the right field line to back up the possible throw from the catcher to the second baseman at first base.

PICK-OFF EARLY BREAK BUNT DEFENSE
RUNNER AT FIRST BASE

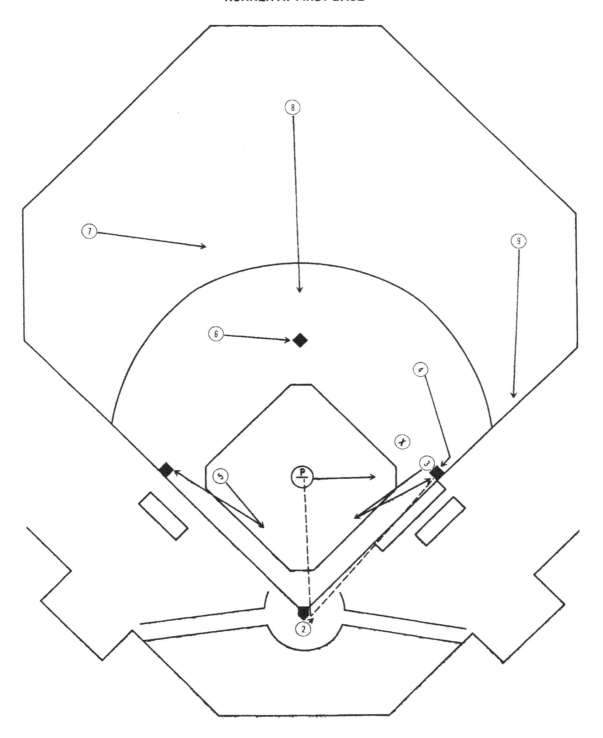

PICK-OFF FROM PITCHER TO FIRST BASEMAN OFF EARLY BREAK BUNT DEFENSE - RUNNER AT FIRST BASE

SIGN FROM COACH IS:_____

PITCHER—Watches first baseman as he goes into the stretch position. When the first baseman's left foot hits the ground will throw the ball to the first baseman at the bag.

FIRST BASEMAN—Want to make the runner at first base think that the early break bunt defense is on. As the pitcher gets to the top of the stretch position, he will take a hard right-left step as though going to the plate. Breaks hard back for the bag when his left foot hits the ground. Receives throw from the pitcher at the bag.

All the other positions will assume the spot that they would be at in the early break bunt defense at the time of the pitch.

PICK-OFF FROM PITCHER TO FIRST BASEMAN OFF EARLY BREAK BUNT
DEFENSE—RUNNER AT FIRST BASE

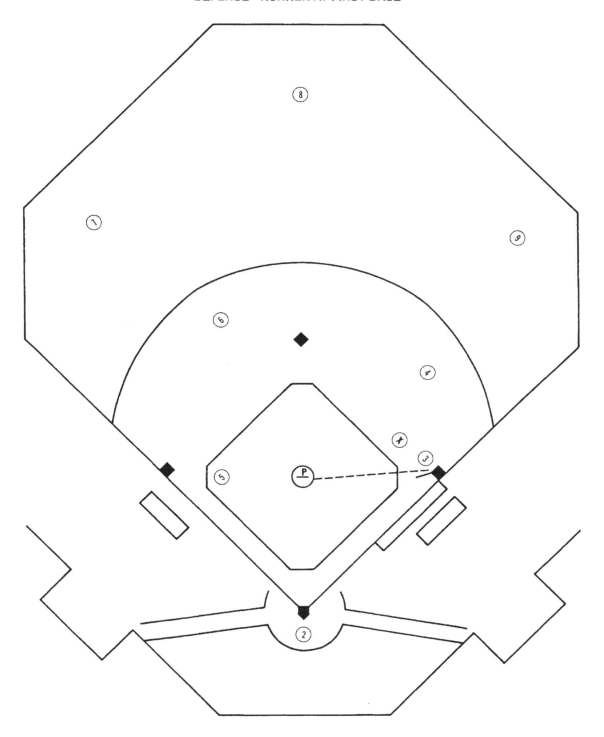

STANDARD BUNT DEFENSE, RUNNERS ON FIRST AND SECOND BASE
SIGN FROM COACH IS:_____

PITCHER—First concern is to hold the runner close to second base. Will throw a high fast ball for a strike when the shortstop steps toward second base with left foot and slaps glove. If the shortstop shows the pitcher the open glove, he will turn and pick at the bag. After releasing the ball, takes one step forward and then has left side responsibility. Has priority over the first baseman only on the bunted ball. If the third baseman fields the ball, covers third base.

CATCHER—Calls for a fast ball. On the bunt, has front of the plate responsibility and calls the play. Has priority over all fielders on the bunted ball except the third baseman. Covers home plate after the ball has been thrown to either third base or first base.

FIRST BASEMAN—Positions himself 20 feet in on the grass from first base. When the batter squares around to bunt, he breaks for the plate under control being conscious of the push bunt, slash or full swing. Must cover the complete right side of the infield. Has priority over no one on the bunted ball.

SECOND BASEMAN—Must cheat towards first base being aware of the possibility of a push bunt, slash or full swing by the batter. When he reads the bunt, he must break full speed for first base coming in from the right field side of first base so that he is moving into the bag as the ball is thrown to first base by the fielder of the bunt.

THIRD BASEMAN—Plays 10 feet in front of third base on the grass line facing the pitcher, with a good periphial view of the runner at second base, the pitcher and the batter. As the pitcher delivers the ball to the plate, he must check the runner at second base. If he is not stealing, he will take two steps toward the plate always conscious of a possible steal. The shortstop will let him know if the runner is breaking. As the ball is bunted, he must now read the bunted ball. If he reads that the pitcher, first baseman or catcher will make the play, reinforced when one of them yells "I've got it", he retreats quickly back to third base prepared for a possible throw from the fielder of the bunted ball. If he reads that he will have the best or only play on the bunted ball, he will break to the ball and make the play at first base to the second baseman covering. He has priority over all fielders on the bunted ball.

SHORTSTOP—Stands one yard behind the runner at second base. As the pitcher reaches the set position in the stretch, he jabs hard with the left foot towards the bag and slaps his glove hard in the same direction at the same time. The pitcher will deliver the ball to the plate on this movement. If the shortstop feels that the runner is too far from second base, he will show the pitcher the open glove rather than the slap of the glove and the pitcher will pick at the bag. As the ball is delivered to the plate, he backs up two steps prepared for a possible push bunt, slash or full swing. He must let the third baseman know if the runner is stealing third base ("there he goes").

LEFT FIELDER—Backs up possible throw to third base from the plate and from the first base area as the ball is bunted.

CENTER FIELDER—As the ball is bunted backs up the throw to second base even though there should not be any throw in that direction.

RIGHT FIELDER—As the ball is bunted backs up the throw to first base.

STANDARD BUNT DEFENSE, RUNNERS ON FIRST AND SECOND BASE

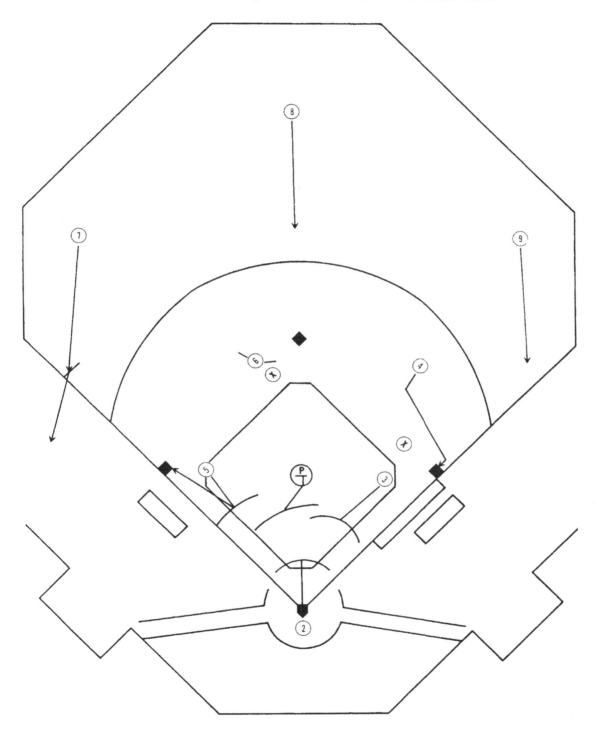

BUNT DEFENSE, RUNNERS ON FIRST AND SECOND BASE
SHORTSTOP EARLY BREAK
SIGN FROM COACH IS:_____

PITCHER—First concern is to hold the runner close to second base. When he reaches the set position in the stretch, the shortstop will step towards second base with his left foot and slaps the glove hard. The shortstop will then break full speed toward third base. When the shortstop clears the runner at second base by at least two steps, the pitcher will throw a high fast ball for a strike to the plate. If the runner at second base starts moving toward third base with the shortstop, the pitcher will step back off the rubber. If the shortstop shows the open glove on his move toward second base, the pitcher will pick at the bag. When the pitcher throws to the plate, he will have front of the mound responsibility on the bunted ball since the third baseman will cover the left side of the infield on his early break. The pitcher has priority over only the first baseman on the bunted ball.

CATCHER—Has the same responsibility as in the standard bunt defense with runners on first and second base.

FIRST BASEMAN—Has the same responsibility as in the standard bunt defense with runners on first and second base.

SECOND BASEMAN—Has the same responsibility as in the standard bunt defense with runners on first and second base.

THIRD BASEMAN—Plays 10 feet in front of third base on the grass line positioning himself the same as he did in the standard bunt defense with runners on first and second base. The only difference in responsibility is that he will break towards the plate once the pitcher delivers to the plate. If the pitcher steps off the rubber, then the runner at second base is coming down the line with the shortstop. If so, the third baseman retreats back to the bag for a possible throw from the pitcher. On the bunted ball, has left side responsibility and has priority over all fielders.

SHORTSTOP—Starts from the same position as he did on the standard bunt defense with runners on first and second base. As the pitcher reaches the set position in the stretch, he jabs hard with the left foot towards the bag and slaps his glove hard in the same direction. As soon as the left foot lands and he slaps the glove, he will pivot and break full speed toward third base. If he sees the runner coming with him towards third base on his break he will yell "step off" to the pitcher. If the shortstop feels that the runner is too far from second base, he will show the open glove to the pitcher rather than slapping his glove, and the pitcher will throw the ball to the bag on the pick-off attempt. If the pitcher throws to the plate, the shortstop continues on towards third base setting up at the base for a possible throw by the fielder of the bunted ball. Must be conscious always for the push bunt, slash or full swing as he is running towards third base.

OUTFIELDERS—All the outfielders have the same back up responsibility as they had with the standard bunt defense with runners at first and second base.

BUNT DEFENSE, RUNNERS ON FIRST AND SECOND BASE
SHORTSTOP EARLY BREAK

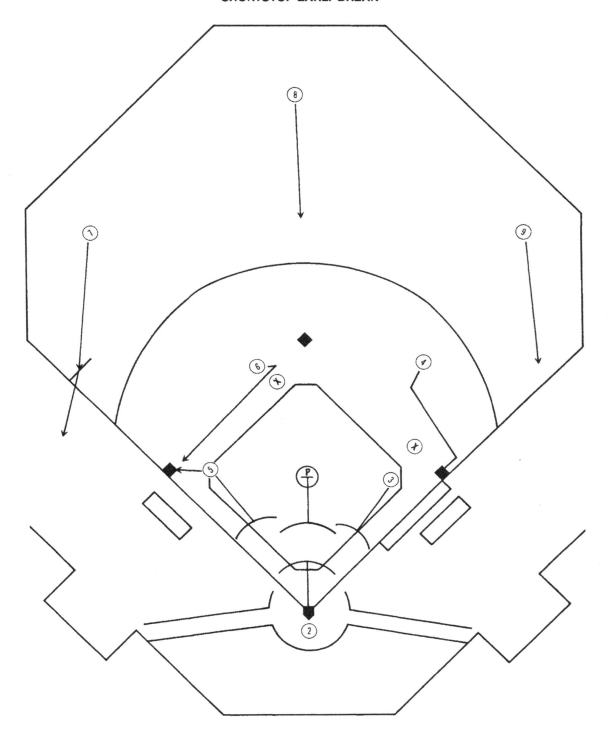

PICK-OFF EARLY BREAK BUNT DEFENSE WITH RUNNERS AT FIRST AND SECOND BASE

SIGN FROM COACH IS:_____

PITCHER—As the shortstop jab steps toward second base and slaps his glove, the pitcher will turn his head back towards the plate and count 1001. He will then throw the ball to second base where the second baseman will be covering the bag for a possible pick-off on the runner. If the runner makes a full break towards third base with the shortstop he will yell to the pitcher "step off". The pitcher will then step off and throw the ball to the third baseman, or if the runner has stopped between second and third base, he will run at the runner forcing him in either direction. Once he has forced him in either direction he will throw the ball to the third baseman or the second baseman depending upon which direction the runner has made his move.

CATCHER—Other than flashing the sign to the pitcher as if the pitcher will throw to the plate, the catcher has no responsibility on this pick-off play. Covers home plate.

FIRST BASEMAN—Has the same responsibility as in the early break bunt defense play. Will retreat back to first base as the play develops at second base.

SECOND BASEMAN—Assumes a position about four steps closer to second base than on the early break bunt defense with runners on first and second base. As the shortstop slaps his glove and jab steps toward second base, the second baseman will break full speed for the bag for the pick-off throw from the pitcher.

THIRD BASEMAN—Assumes the same position as he does in the early break bunt defense with runners on first and second base. As soon as the pitcher throws the ball to the second baseman at second base, he will retreat quickly to third base to field any possible throw to retire the runner coming from second base.

SHORTSTOP—Has the same responsibility as in the early break bunt defense with runners at first and second base. He will be hoping to draw the runner towards third base as he breaks after his movement toward second base. The shortstop will not show the open glove for the pick-off if the runner is too far away from the bag. If on his movement toward third base he sees that the runner is breaking also, he will yell to the pitcher "step off". He will then proceed to third base to back up the third baseman on the rundown play that might develop between second and third base.

LEFT FIELDER—Backs up any possible throw from second base to third base.

CENTER FIELDER—Backs up second base on the pick-off throw by the pitcher to the second baseman. If rundown develops, he will be the back up man for the second baseman.

RIGHT FIELDER—Backs up second base on any possible play there from third base if the runner is in a rundown.

PICK-OFF EARLY BREAK BUNT DEFENSE WITH RUNNERS AT
FIRST AND SECOND BASE

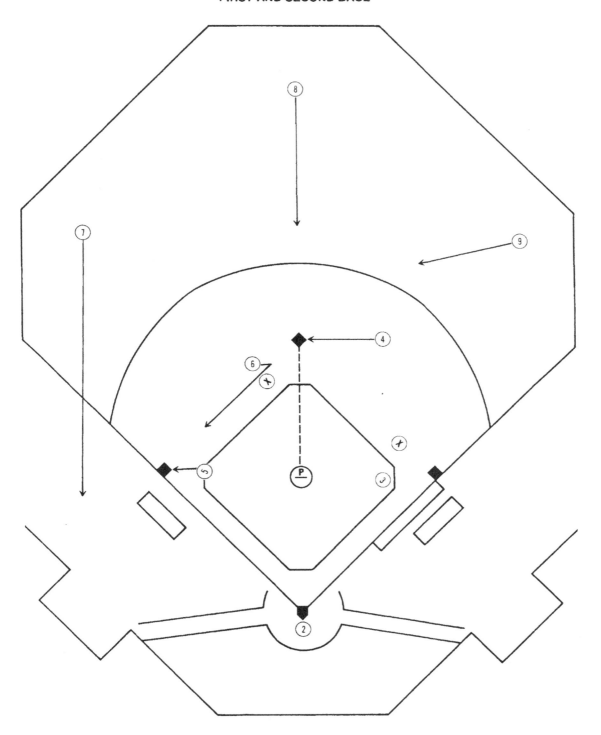

DOUBLE STEAL DEFENSE

A very important aspect of defensive play in baseball is the ability to properly defense the opponent's double steal offense with baserunners at first and third base.

If a team possesses a catcher with a quick release time along with a strong accurate arm there should be very little for the defense to worry about on this play. However, if a club does not have a catcher with this type of arm and their shortstop and second baseman are not able to make strong accurate throws, then they can expect to be challenged occasionally by the double steal. This is especially true of those clubs that have outstanding speed but very little offensive punch at the plate.

In most cases if a defense executes this play well, then the other team shuts down this part of their offense. The team that shows that they can not handle the pressure in this type of play can expect the double steal on numerous occasions. One generally finds that the higher the caliber and level of baseball played, the fewer times a team will attempt a double steal.

As in team bunt defense, a coach never wants to burden his club with too many defenses to control the double steal. If he does, he will find that the execution level on each separate play will go down with the number of plays added to the team's playbook.

It is the responsibility of the coach in the dugout to determine which one of the double steal plays will be in effect. He can communicate this information to the defense by flashing a sign from the dugout. As in the bunt defense plays, the type of play run can be changed from pitch to pitch so the defense needs to check with the coach after every pitch. The coach will take into consideration numerous items before selecting the type of play he wishes the defense to execute if the double steal occurs. These items would include:

1. **Number of outs**—The best time for an offense to run a double steal type play is with two outs, hoping to draw some type of throw on the runner going to second base in hopes that they can score the run from third. Since with no outs or one out, most teams will allow the batter the opportunity to score the runner from third base, the two out situation many times necessitates a different strategy both offensively and defensively.

2. **Inning**—The likelihood of a double steal play generally increases later in the game when the offense hopes to score a run at the expense of an out at second base. Early in the game most teams will try to play for the big inning. Thus, early in the game the defense should make the play on the runner going to second base while later in the game, with an important runner at third base, the defensive play called might place more emphasis on not allowing the runner at third base to advance.

3. **Score of the Game**—In almost all cases an opponent would not attempt a double steal if they are down by quite a few runs early in the game or down by more than one run in the last two innings. Of course, there are always exceptions to the rule. Throwing the ball through to second base is always preferred in situations where the runner at third base is not of paramount importance at the time of the double steal. When ahead in the score the defense should always get an out, even at the expense of a possible run scoring from third base. If the double steal defense is done properly a team should be able to make a play on the runner at second base, and at the same time, keep the runner at third base from scoring.

4. **Strength of Catcher's Arm**—If the catcher's arm is such that he has proven he can throw to second base accurately with velocity, then the coach should have him throw through to second base in most cases. If the catcher has a good arm there is more likelihood that the offense will try to take advantage of the pitcher by a forced balk or forced pick-off play at first base. If the catcher has a weak and inaccurate arm the coach should not allow a throw through to second base that might allow an important run to score from third base late in the game.

5. **Strength of Shortstop and Second Baseman's Arm**—Along with the ability of the catcher to throw through to second base, the strength of the arms with the pivot men handling the throw to second base must also be taken into consideration. If neither the shortstop or second baseman possess the ability to throw well, then the coach might be hesitant to throw through to second base when an important run is at third base late in the game.

6. **Hitter at the Plate**—Generally with a good hitter at the plate the offense will be hesitant to take the bat out of his hands by running any type of double steal play. A weak hitter will generally prompt the opposing coach to attempt some type of double steal play, especially with two strikes. This might even be the case knowing that if they are not successful then their weak hitter will have to lead off the next inning.

7. **Strength and Experience of Pitcher**—The pitcher who has a difficult time getting hitters out does not have to worry too much about trick double steal plays, and in many cases, even the straight double steal. The opposing coach would probably just rely on the hitter's ability to drive the runner in from third base unless there are less than two outs and he is trying to keep them out of a double play situation by running the straight steal. If the pitcher is dominating the opposing team's hitters, there would be more of a tendency on the opposing coach's part to try to get a run scored from third base, or advancing the runner to second base to get into scoring position without the batter swinging the bat. The defense can look for a possible trick double steal play at this time.

8. **Count on the Batter**—The best time to run a double steal play would be when the batter has two strikes on him with two outs. This is especially true if there is a poor hitter at the plate. With less than two outs, the offense would have more of a tendency to run with no strikes on the batter so that he might protect the runner by swinging and missing or faking the bunt. The 3-2 count with one out is always an ideal time to start the runner at first base on the straight steal.

9. **Ability of the Runner at First Base**—The better the baserunner at first base the more chance that the opposing coach will employ the straight steal. The weaker the runner at first base the more chance that there would be a variation from the straight steal by the offense. If there is little chance of retiring the runner at second base on the steal, it is advisable to refrain from throwing through to second base. With a slow runner at first base the defense should throw the ball through to second base.

10. **Ability of the Runner at Third Base**—The better the baserunner is at third base the greater the chance is that he will break for the plate on the throw through to second base. The weaker the runner is, the less of a chance. With an excellent runner at third base the defense should consider another defense other than the throw to second base. With a poor runner at third base the defense should throw to second base in most cases.

11. **Opposing Team's Double Steal Tendencies**—When teams play each other numerous times during the season each coach will know a little more about the other coach's philosophy and tendencies in regard to the double steal play. This is also the case when teams play each other every year as long as the same coach is still employed. A baseball coach generally falls into certain patterns in regard to their offensive and defensive tendencies, and this holds true for the double steal plays as well. Of course, changes in personnel from year to year can change this philosophy quickly. By knowing what these tendencies might be in certain situations, the coach can make a better decision on the type of double steal defense to employ.

As you can see, there are numerous variables involved in making the decision as to what double steal defense to use. Listed on the following pages are four plays that can be included in a team's Playbook.

DOUBLE STEAL DEFENSE, RUNNERS ON FIRST AND THIRD BASE
PLAY NUMBER ONE
SIGN FROM COACH IS: _____

PITCHER—After throwing the ball to the plate, the pitcher will receive the throw from the catcher at cap level or above if the runner breaks from first base. After he catches the baseball, he will check the runner at third base. If the runner is moving toward the plate hard, he will immediately throw to the catcher at the plate. He would then break for the plate to back up the catcher on the possible rundown play until the first baseman relieves him. If the runner is well off third base and then starts heading back toward the bag, he will immediately throw to the third baseman and break for the plate to back up the catcher on the possible rundown. If the runner has stopped between the plate and third base, the pitcher will run under control directly at the runner trying to make him go toward the plate or back to third base. If possible, it is best to have him go back toward third base. If the runner breaks for the plate, the pitcher will throw to the catcher at the plate. If he breaks for third base he will throw to the third baseman at the bag. If the runner does not break either way, the pitcher will make the tag in the baseline. If the runner at third base stays close to the bag when the pitcher receives the ball from the catcher, the pitcher will turn toward second base and fake the throw to the second baseman. He will then look back at the runner at third base. If he is breaking for the plate, he will throw the ball to the catcher at the plate. If the runner still is close to third base and the runner who started at first base has stopped between first and second base, he will immediately throw to the second baseman and then cover first base to back up the first baseman on the rundown.

CATCHER—Receives the pitch from the pitcher and using the same motion he would use in throwing to second base on the steal throws the ball back to the pitcher cap level or above if the runner at first base breaks toward second base. He will not look the runner back toward third base before throwing to the pitcher. He will cover the plate preparing for a possible throw from the pitcher if the runner breaks for the plate.

FIRST BASEMAN—When the pitcher receives the ball back from the catcher and a play is being made on the runner from third base, he will break for the plate relieving the pitcher on the possible rundown between the catcher and the third baseman. If no play is made on that runner, he will stay at first base for a possible play on the runner who started out at first base.

SECOND BASEMAN—As soon as the catcher receives the pitch from the pitcher, he will break for second base if the runner is stealing. He should be prepared for a possible overthrow of the pitcher by the catcher. He will cover second base if the pitcher makes the play on the runner who started at first base.

THIRD BASEMAN—As soon as the catcher receives the ball from the pitcher on the pitch he will break for third base if the runner at first is stealing. Will cover third base for any possible play.

SHORTSTOP—As soon as the catcher receives the pitch and the runner is stealing second base, he will break for third base to back up the third baseman on the possible rundown between third base and the plate.

LEFT FIELDER—Backs up all throws that might be made to third base.

CENTER FIELDER—Backs up all throws that might be made to second base.

RIGHT FIELDER—Breaks for first base as soon as the catcher receives the pitch and the runner breaks for second base. Will relieve the pitcher on the rundown that might develop between first and second base.

124

DOUBLE STEAL DEFENSE, RUNNERS ON FIRST AND THIRD BASE
PLAY NUMBER ONE

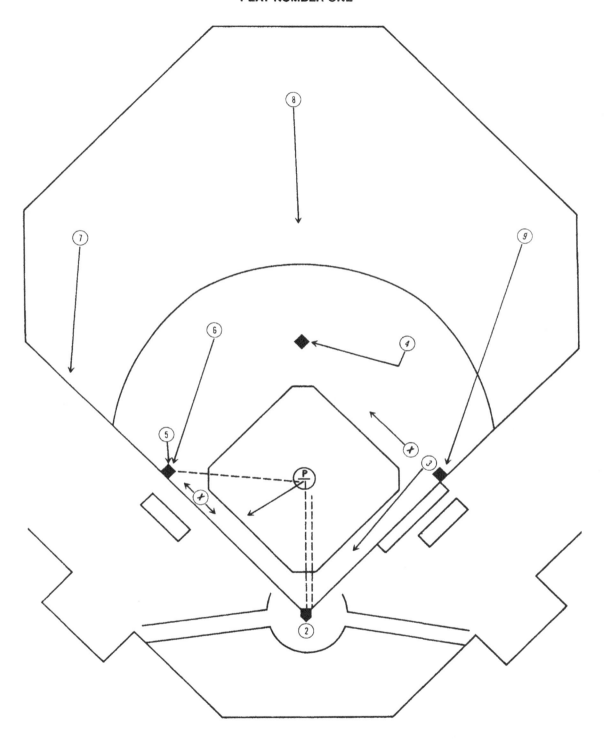

DOUBLE STEAL DEFENSE, RUNNERS ON FIRST AND THIRD BASE
PLAY NUMBER TWO
SIGN FROM COACH IS:_____

PITCHER—If the catcher throws the ball to third base after his fake throw to second base, the pitcher will break for the plate for back up coverage on a possible rundown play until relieved by the first baseman. If the catcher starts moving toward the runner stopped between first and second base, the pitcher will also be responsible for the plate.

CATCHER—If the runner at first base breaks for second base on the pitch, the catcher will make a full arm fake to second base hoping to draw the runner down the third baseline toward the plate. After the full arm fake, he will look to third base. If the third baseman has both arms in the air, he will throw to the base from the inside of the diamond. If the runner at third base starts down the line hard on the full arm fake, the catcher will run at him and get him into a rundown between the plate and third base. If the runner at third base stays near the bag and the runner who broke for second base has stopped between first and second base, the catcher will run toward the runner at a brisk jog completely under control. He will listen for the third baseman to let him know if the runner at third base breaks for the plate. If so, he will turn and throw to the pitcher covering the plate. Otherwise he will make the attempt at tagging the runner between first and second base using the first baseman and second baseman on a possible rundown.

FIRST BASEMAN—Will stay at first base in case the runner at first base stops between first and second base. If a rundown develops between the plate and third base, he will break for the plate and relieve the pitcher on the rundown.

SECOND BASEMAN—Will break for second base in case the runner stops between first and second base. Responsible for second base all the way.

THIRD BASEMAN—Will break for third base after the catcher receives the ball. If he feels that the runner at third base can be picked off by the catcher's throw, he will throw both hands in the air while setting up on the inside of third base. If there is no play on the runner, he would not throw his hands in the air. If the catcher runs at the runner stopped between first and second base, he will let him know if the runner breaks for the plate by yelling "four-four".

SHORTSTOP—As the catcher fakes the throw to second base he will start moving toward third base to back up the third baseman on a possible rundown play. If a rundown develops between first and second base he will break for second base to back up the second baseman on the rundown play.

LEFT FIELDER—As the catcher receives the ball, he will break to back up a possible throw to third base.

CENTER FIELDER—As the catcher receives the ball, he will back up any throws made to second base.

RIGHT FIELDER—As the catcher receives the ball, he will break for first base backing up the first baseman or pitcher on any possible rundown play.

DOUBLE STEAL DEFENSE, RUNNERS ON FIRST AND THIRD BASE
PLAY NUMBER TWO

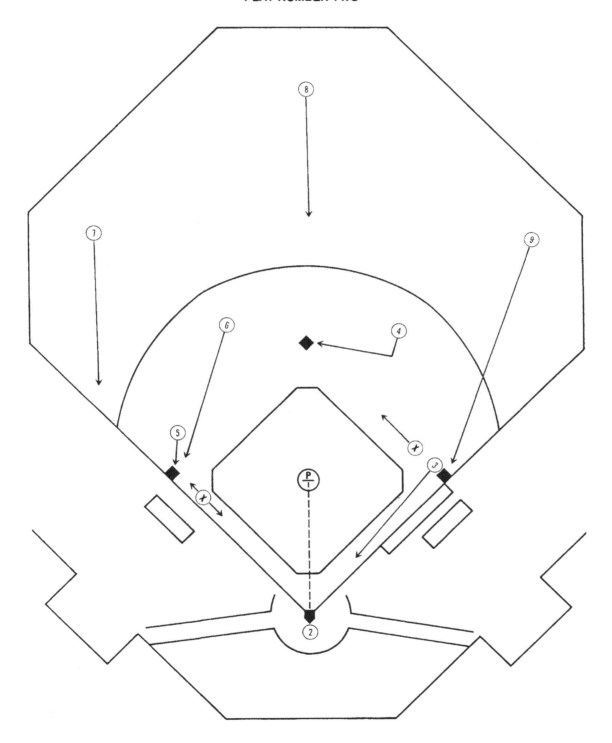

DOUBLE STEAL DEFENSE, RUNNERS AT FIRST AND THIRD BASE, RIGHTHANDED BATTER, NO OUTS OR ONE OUT, PLAY NUMBER THREE SIGN FROM COACH IS: _____

PITCHER—Fake the catch of the catcher's throw to second base in hopes that it will hold the runner at third base if he is breaking on the catcher's release. Be prepared to cover home plate if the catcher has to leave the plate area.

CATCHER—If the runner at first base breaks for second base on the pitch, he will throw the ball through to second base. He must be sure to look the runner back to third base while setting up to throw to second base. If the catcher sees the third baseman raise both arms in the air, he can either throw directly to the third baseman from the inside of the diamond, or he can full arm fake (play number two) if the runner is not that far away from the bag. After the full arm fake, he will throw to the third baseman covering the bag. If the ball goes through to second base, he needs to be prepared for a throw back to the plate for a possible play on the runner breaking from third base.

FIRST BASEMAN—After letting the catcher know that the runner is breaking for second base "there he goes", he will stay around the bag for any play that might develop on the runner that broke for second base. He will break for the plate if any rundown takes place between home and third base. He will relieve the pitcher at the plate on the rundown.

SECOND BASEMAN—As he sees the runner break for second base on the pitch, he will move towards the plate (right, left, right, left foot work). Once the ball passes the batter, he will break for a position about five steps in front of second base. He will be in a position to cut the ball off if the runner at third base breaks for the plate. He should be able to watch the ball in flight from the catcher, and out of the corner of his eye watch the runner at third base. The third baseman will yell "four-four" if the runner at third base breaks for the plate. If the runner at third base does not break for the plate, he will let the ball go through to the shortstop at second base. He must be sure that he drops his glove so he will not obstruct the shortstop's view of the ball.

THIRD BASEMAN—Will break for third base after the catcher receives the ball. If he feels that the runner at third base can be picked off by the catcher's throw, he will throw both hands in the air while setting up on the inside of third base. If there is no play on the runner, he would not throw his hands in the air. Once the ball is thrown by the catcher, he will yell immediately "four-four" if the runner at third base breaks for the plate.

SHORTSTOP—As he sees the runner break for second base on the pitch, he will move towards the plate (left, right, left, right foot work). Once the ball passes the batter, he will break for second base and prepare for the throw by the catcher. He will make the tag on the sliding runner if the ball is not cut-off by the second baseman. He must be sure to keep the ball in front of him so that it does not go into the outfield. If the runner stops before sliding, he will go after him getting the runner in a rundown between himself and the first baseman. He will listen for the third baseman for he will not be able to look at the runner while running the rundown play. If the third baseman yells "four-four", he will step and throw the ball to the catcher at home plate.

LEFT FIELDER—Backs up any possible throw to third base.

CENTER FIELDER—Backs up the throw from the catcher to second base.

RIGHT FIELDER—Backs up any throw to first base and is responsible for first base if a rundown develops between first and second base.

DOUBLE STEAL DEFENSE, RUNNERS AT FIRST AND THIRD BASE, RIGHTHANDED BATTER, NO OUTS OR ONE OUT, PLAY NUMBER THREE

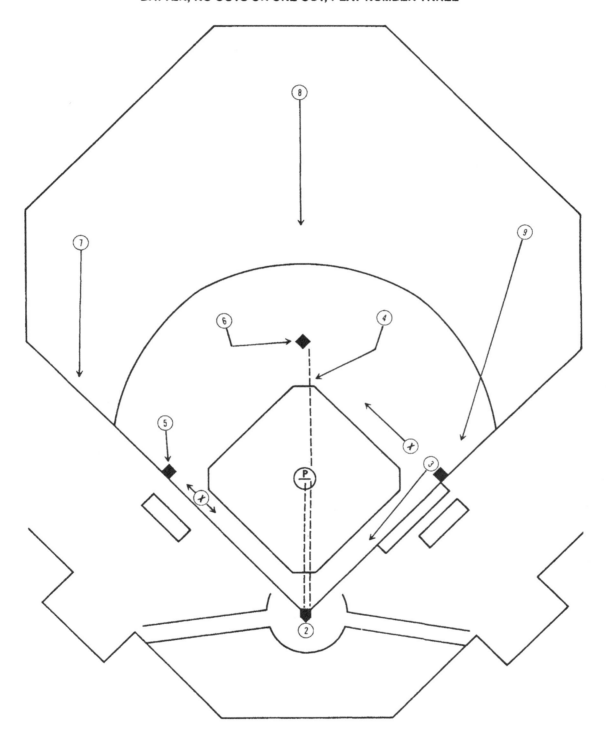

DOUBLE STEAL DEFENSE, RUNNERS AT FIRST AND THIRD BASE, LEFTHANDED BATTER, NO OUTS OR ONE OUT, PLAY NUMBER THREE

SIGN FROM COACH IS: _____

PITCHER—Fake the catch of the catcher's throw to second base in hopes that it will hold the runner at third base if he is breaking on the catcher's release. Be prepared to cover home plate if the catcher has to leave the plate area.

CATCHER—If the runner at first base breaks for second base on the pitch, he will throw through to second base. He must be sure to look the runner back to third base while setting up to throw to second base. If the catcher sees the third baseman raise both arms in the air, he can either throw directly to the third baseman from the inside of the diamond, or he can full arm fake (play number two) if the runner is not that far away from the bag. After the full arm fake, he will throw to the third baseman covering the bag. If the ball goes through to the shortstop at second base, he needs to be prepared for a throw back to the plate for a possible play on the runner breaking from third base.

FIRST BASEMAN—After letting the catcher know that the runner is breaking for second base "there he goes", he will stay around the bag for any play that might develop on the runner that broke for second base. He will break for the plate if any rundown takes place between home and third base. He will relieve the pitcher at the plate on the rundown.

SECOND BASEMAN—As he sees the runner break for second base on the pitch, he will hold until the ball passes the batter. He will then break to back up the throw from the catcher to the shortstop at second base. If he sees the runner at third base break for the plate on the throw by the catcher, he will yell "four-four" to the shortstop letting him know that he has a play at the plate. If the runner from first base stops between first and second base he will be the back up man on the rundown. He will let the shortstop and first baseman involved in the rundown know if the runner at third base breaks for the plate.

THIRD BASEMAN—Will break for third base after the catcher receives the ball. If he feels that the runner at third base can be picked off by the catcher's throw, he will throw both hands in the air while setting up on the inside of third base. If there is no play on the runner, he would not throw his hands in the air. Once the ball is thrown by the catcher, he will yell immediately "four-four" if the runner at third base breaks for the plate.

SHORTSTOP—As he sees the runner break for second base on the pitch, he will move towards the plate (left, right, left, right foot work). Once the ball passes the batter, he will break for second base and prepare for the throw by the catcher. He will make the tag on the sliding runner. If he hears the third baseman and second baseman yell "four-four", he will move towards the ball coming from the catcher and throw the ball back to the plate. If the runner happens to break late for the plate, he should make the quick tag on the runner and then come up throwing to the plate. If the runner stops before sliding, he will go after him getting the runner in a rundown between himself and the first baseman. He will listen for the second baseman and third baseman for a possible play at the plate during the rundown.

LEFT FIELDER—Backs up any possible throw to third base.

CENTER FIELDER—Backs up the throw from the catcher to second base.

RIGHT FIELDER—Backs up any throw to first base and is responsible for first base if a rundown develops between first and second base.

DOUBLE STEAL DEFENSE, RUNNERS AT FIRST AND THIRD BASE, LEFTHANDED BATTER, NO OUTS OR ONE OUT, PLAY NUMBER THREE

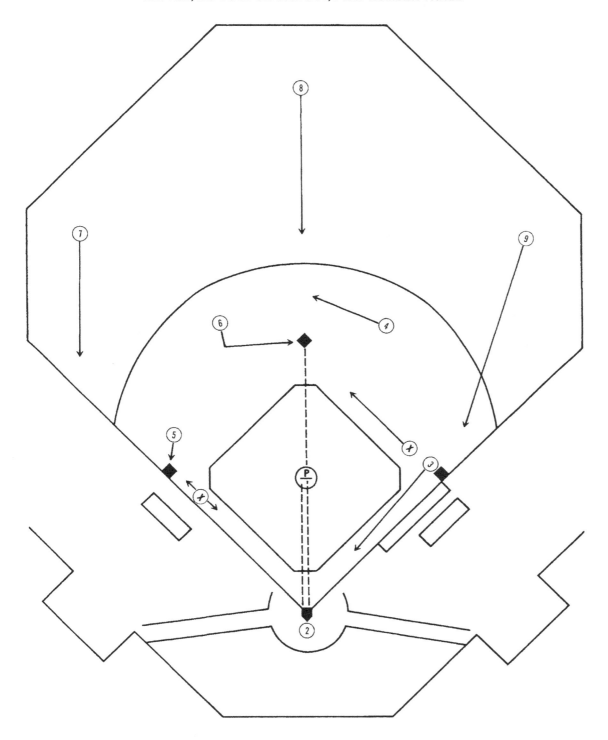

DOUBLE STEAL DEFENSE, RUNNERS AT FIRST AND THIRD BASE
TWO OUTS—PLAY NUMBER THREE
SIGN FROM COACH IS: _____

PITCHER—Fake the catch of the catcher's throw to second base in hopes that it will hold the runner at third base if he is breaking on the catcher's release. As soon as the ball passes his head, he will break for first base to cover the bag if the runner gets by the first baseman.

CATCHER—If the runner at first base breaks for second base on the pitch, he will throw the ball through to second base. He must be sure to look the runner back to third base while setting up to throw to second base. If the catcher sees the third baseman raise both arms in the air, he can either throw directly to the third baseman from the inside of the diamond, or he can full arm fake (play number two) if the runner is not that far away from the bag. After the full arm fake, he will throw to the third baseman covering the bag. If the ball goes through to second base, he needs to be prepared for a throw back to the plate for a possible play on the runner breaking from third base.

FIRST BASEMAN—After letting the catcher know that the runner is breaking for second base "there he goes", he will follow the runner down to second base staying about four to five steps behind him on the inside of the diamond. He will not break for second base until after the ball passes the batter. If the runner stops between first and second base, he will be in a position to receive the throw from the shortstop or second baseman depending on who has coverage at the bag. If he receives the throw he will attempt to make the tag on the runner before the baserunner at third base can cross the plate.

SECOND BASEMAN—If the second baseman is responsible for the bag (depends on the hitter at the plate), he will do the proper footwork so that he is not breaking for the bag until the ball passes the batter if the runner steals from first base. If he is not responsible for the bag he will back up the throw from the catcher to the shortstop. There will be no communication from the third baseman if the runner breaks from third base since the play will be made on the runner stealing second base. If the tag is late, then he will look to the plate for a possible play. If the runner stops between first and second base, he will step inside the diamond and throw the ball immediately to the first baseman trailing the runner.

SHORTSTOP—If the shortstop is responsible for the bag, he will do the proper footwork so that he is not breaking for the bag until the ball passes the batter if the runner steals from first base. If he is not responsible for the bag he will back up the throw from the catcher to the second baseman. There will be no communication from the third baseman if the runner breaks from third base since the play will be made on the runner stealing second base. If the tag is late, then he will look to the plate for a possible play. If the runner stops between first and second base, he will step inside the diamond and throw the ball immediately to the first baseman trailing the runner.

THIRD BASEMAN—Will break for third base after the catcher receives the ball. If he feels that the runner at third base can be picked off by the catcher's throw, he will throw both hands in the air while setting up on the inside of third base. He will not communicate to the shortstop and second baseman if the runner breaks for the plate.

LEFT FIELDER—Backs up any possible throw to third base.

CENTER FIELDER—Backs up the throw from the catcher to second base.

RIGHT FIELDER—Backs up any throw to first base and is responsible for first base if a rundown develops between first and second base.

DOUBLE STEAL DEFENSE, RUNNERS AT FIRST AND THIRD BASE
TWO OUTS—PLAY NUMBER THREE

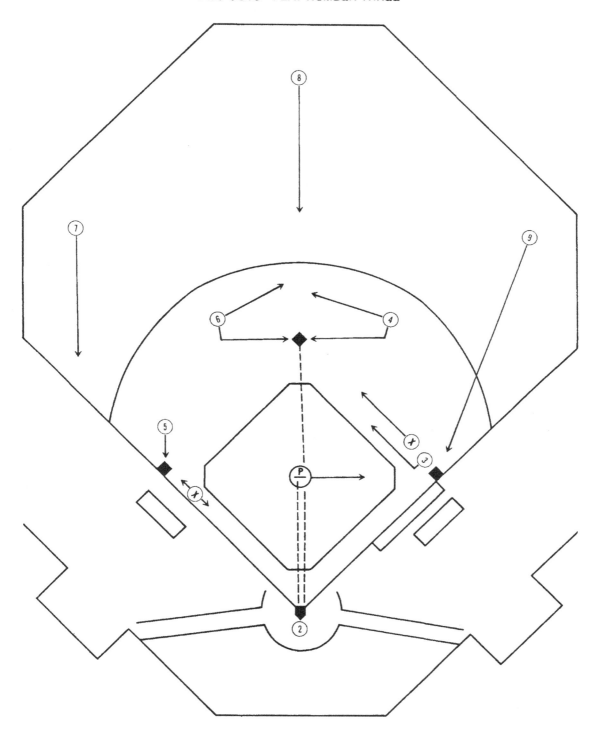

133

DOUBLE STEAL DEFENSE, RUNNERS ON FIRST AND THIRD BASE
PLAY NUMBER FOUR
SIGN FROM COACH IS: _____

PITCHER—Be prepared to cover home plate if the catcher gets involved in a rundown play between third base and the plate.

CATCHER—If the runner at first base breaks for second base on the pitch, he will throw the ball to the shortstop breaking toward the plate. He will not look the runner back to third base prior to the throw. However, if out of the corner of his eye he sees the runner breaking for the plate prior to his release, he will full arm fake. He will cover the plate for a possible return throw from the shortstop.

FIRST BASEMAN—After letting the catcher know that the runner is breaking for second base "there he goes", he will follow the runner down to second base after the ball passes the batter. If the runner stops between first and second base, he will be in a position to receive the throw from the shortstop if there is no play at the plate. If a rundown develops between the plate and third base, he will break for the plate and relieve the pitcher in the rundown play.

SECOND BASEMAN—As soon as the ball passes the batter he will break for second base to be in a position to field a possible throw from the shortstop if he has no play at the plate and the runner has slowed down on his approach to second base. He would also be in a position to field the throw from the catcher if he mistakingly throws through to the bag.

THIRD BASEMAN—As soon as the ball passes the batter, he will break for third base. If the throw goes through to the shortstop, he will let him know if the runner at third base breaks for the plate by yelling "four-four". He should be prepared for a possible throw from the shortstop. Also prepared for a throw from the catcher if the runner breaks for the plate prior to his release on the throw to the shortstop.

SHORTSTOP—If the runner at first base breaks for second base, he will wait for the ball to pass the batter. When it does, he will take two steps toward second base and then break for the plate under control. The catcher will be throwing the ball directly to him in hopes that it will cause the runner at third base to break for the plate. If the runner breaks, the shortstop will throw the ball immediately back to the catcher at the plate. He should field the throw from the catcher a couple of steps off the infield grass. If the runner from third base does not break for the plate, he will look to second base and see if there is any play on the runner coming from first base. If so, he will throw the ball to the second baseman at the bag. If the runner stops between first and second base, he will throw the ball to the first baseman trailing the runner and then back up the second baseman on the possible rundown play.

LEFT FIELDER—Backs up all throws that might be made to third base.

CENTER FIELDER—After the ball passes the batter he will break so that he is in a position to back up the throw from the catcher to the shortstop.

RIGHT FIELDER—After the ball passes the batter, he will break for first base to back up the first baseman on the possible rundown play between first and second base.

DOUBLE STEAL DEFENSE, RUNNERS AT FIRST AND THIRD BASE
PLAY NUMBER FOUR

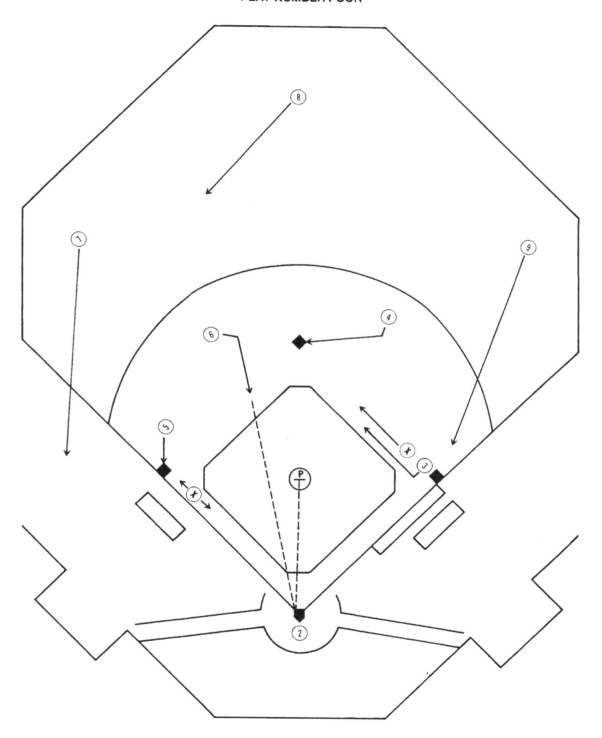

DOUBLE STEAL DEFENSE, RUNNERS ON FIRST AND THIRD BASE, RUNNER AT FIRST BASE STEALS ON THE STRETCH

PITCHER—Once the runner at first base breaks for second base on the stretch, the pitcher must calmly step back off the pitching rubber and look at the runner at third base. If the runner at third base is coming down the line hard toward the plate, he will throw the ball immediately to the catcher at the plate. If the runner at third base is off the base a considerable distance, he will immediately throw the ball to the third baseman at third base if he feels that a play can be made on the runner. In either case, when he throws the ball to either third base or the plate he will break for the plate to back up the catcher on the possible rundown. If the runner at third base has come well down the line between third base and the plate, the pitcher will run directly toward him under control. Once he gets him moving in either direction he will throw the ball to the third baseman or the catcher. If he can make the tag on the runner himself, he should do so and then look to see if there might be a play on the runner who broke from first base. If the runner at third base is close to the bag with no play on him, the pitcher should immediately turn toward second base and full arm fake the ball to the shortstop at the bag. Once he full arm fakes to second base, he will immediately turn and look at the runner at third base. He would then react the same way as before: if the runner is breaking toward the plate he will throw to the catcher; if the runner is off the bag and there is a play on him at third base he will throw to the third baseman at the bag; and if the runner is well down the line and moving in neither direction, he will run at him. If the runner who started at third base is still not far enough off the bag for a play to be made on him, the pitcher will again turn toward second base. If there is still a play on the runner going into second base, he will throw to the shortstop at second base. If the runner is now heading back to first base, he will throw to the first baseman at first base if there is a possible play. If the runner is caught between first and second base, he will throw the ball to the shortstop and then break for first base to back up the first baseman on the possible rundown play. If the runner is now at second base, he will again full arm fake to second base in hopes that it might draw the runner at third base off the bag. In all these reactions, the pitcher will not leave the area of the mound until he has thrown the ball to the proper base. Generally, when the runner at first base breaks on the stretch, a play is on with the runner at third base. A good full arm fake should cause the runner to break away from third base.

CATCHER—Will stay at home plate prepared for a possible throw from the pitcher. If a rundown occurs between first and second base he would prepare for a possible throw if the runner at third base breaks for the plate.

FIRST BASEMAN—Will stay at first base with no outs or one out and be prepared for a possible throw by the pitcher to first base if the runner turns around and heads back toward first base. With two outs, he will follow the runner down to second base so that he can receive the throw from the shortstop if the runner has stopped between first and second base and the pitcher has thrown the ball to second base. The tag on the runner must be made before the runner at third base can cross the plate.

SECOND BASEMAN—Responsible to back up the shortstop if the pitcher throws to the shortstop at second base. If a rundown occurs between first and second base he will back up the shortstop on the rundown. If a rundown occurs between third base and home plate, the shortstop will be breaking for third base to back up the third baseman which makes the second baseman now responsible for second base.

THIRD BASEMAN—Will cover third base for a possible throw from the pitcher. If the ball is thrown to the shortstop at second base, or the first baseman at first base, he will let them know if the runner breaks for the plate by yelling "four-four". With two outs he will say nothing for the rundown should be completed before the runner from third base crosses the plate.

SHORTSTOP—Is responsible for second base unless a rundown occurs between third base and the plate. If so, he will break for third base and back up the third baseman on the rundown. If he receives the ball from the pitcher at second base he will attempt to tag the runner. If a rundown occurs with no outs or one out, he will listen for the third baseman to let him and the first baseman know if the runner at third base breaks for the plate. With two outs the first baseman will follow the runner down toward second base so he should immediately throw the ball to the first baseman trailing the runner in hopes that he can make the tag before the runner at third base can cross the plate.

LEFT FIELDER—Backs up any possible throw to third base.

CENTER FIELDER—Backs up any possible throw to second base.

RIGHT FIELDER—Backs up any possible throw to first base. If a rundown occurs between first and second base he will break for first base and relieve the pitcher on the rundown play.

DOUBLE STEAL DEFENSE, RUNNERS AT FIRST AND THIRD BASE, RUNNER AT FIRST BASE GETS INTENTIONALLY PICKED OFF

PITCHER—If the pitcher sees that the runner at first base has an unusually wide lead at first base he should step off the rubber quickly and fake the throw to the first baseman at the bag. After the full arm fake to first base he should turn and check the runner at third base. Many times there is a set offensive play where the runner at third base will break for the plate when the pitcher throws to first base. By full arm faking to first base the pitcher might have a play on the runner at third base. If the pitcher thinks that he has a shot at the runner at first base from the set position, and the lead is not an abnormal one, then he should go ahead and pick at first base. If after the full arm fake the pitcher finds the runner at third base breaking for the plate he will immediately throw to the catcher at the plate and follow his throw backing up the catcher on a possible rundown play. If he has a play at third base after the full arm fake, he would throw to the third baseman and break for the plate for a possible rundown play. If the runner is well down the line and moving in neither direction hard, then the pitcher would run at him under control forcing him to third base or the plate before throwing to the third baseman or the catcher. If he can make the tag himself, he should do so. If the pitcher has thrown to the first baseman on the pick-off attempt, he should follow his throw to first base and serve as the back up man on the possible rundown. If after the full arm fake to first base he finds that there is no play on the runner at third base, he will look back to the runner who started at first base. If the runner is breaking for second base, he will throw the ball immediately to the shortstop at second base. If the runner has stopped between first and second base he should also throw the ball to the shortstop at second base as long as the runner is well away from the bag at first. If the runner is closer to first base when he stops, then he should throw the ball to the first baseman at first base. The pitcher should never leave the mound area unless it is to run at the runner between third base and the plate, or to back up the catcher or first baseman on a rundown play after he has thrown the ball.

CATCHER—Will stay at the plate prepared for a possible throw from the pitcher. If a rundown occurs between first and second base he would prepare for a possible throw if the runner at third base breaks for the plate.

FIRST BASEMAN—If the pitcher throws to first base on the pick-off attempt, he will attempt to tag the runner. If the runner has taken off full speed toward second base, he will look the runner back to third base quickly and then throw the ball to the shortstop at second base. If he sees the runner at third base moving down the line he will full arm fake the throw to second base. After the full arm fake he will look back to the runner at third base. If the runner is heading toward the plate he will throw to the plate and follow his throw to back up the catcher on a possible rundown. If the runner is well off third base he will throw to the third baseman for a play at the bag making sure that the runner is not moving toward the plate on his throw to third base. If the runner is well down the line and not moving hard in any direction, the first baseman will run at the runner under control forcing him back to third base. If so, he will throw to the third baseman for the tag. If the runner breaks for the plate he will throw to the catcher. If the first baseman can make the tag on the runner without a throw, he will do so. If the first baseman fields the pick-off throw from the pitcher and sees the runner well away from first base and not moving hard toward second base, he will full arm fake the throw to second base and check the runner at third base. If the runner at third base is close to the bag with no play on him, the first baseman will run at the runner between first and second base and get him in a rundown. With no outs or one out, he will listen for the third baseman to let him know if the runner at third base is breaking for the plate. With two outs the first baseman and shortstop will execute the rundown quickly and make the tag before the runner at third base can cross the plate.

SECOND BASEMAN—Responsible for backing up the shortstop at second base on the rundown play. If the shortstop is playing the hitter well in the hole, then the second baseman will be responsible for the bag on the pick-off at first base. If so, then the second baseman will take on the responsibilities listed for the shortstop.

THIRD BASEMAN—Will cover third base for a possible throw from the pitcher or first baseman. If there are no outs or one out and a rundown takes place between first and second base he will let the defensive players involved know if the runner at third base is breaking for the plate by yelling "four - four". If there are two outs he will say nothing.

SHORTSTOP—Is responsible for second base unless a rundown takes place between third base and the plate. If so, he will break for third base and back up the third baseman on the rundown. If playing in the hole and the second baseman has the throw from the first baseman on the pick-off, he will back up the second baseman on the possible rundown play.

LEFT FIELDER—Will back up third base for any possible throw from the pitcher or first baseman.

CENTER FIELDER—Will back up second base for any possible throw from the pitcher or first baseman.

RIGHT FIELDER—Will back up first base for any possible throw by the pitcher. If a rundown takes place between first and second base, he will cover first base relieving the pitcher on the rundown play.

DEFENSIVE SITUATIONS

Every baseball coach would love to think that when his team is on defense that all nine players will be in the proper position performing their prescribed task every time a ball is hit. Since there are so many different situations that can arise during the course of a baseball game, it is practically impossible for all nine players to react in the proper manner every time.

However, with a lot of practice in defensive situation work, along with individual study time in a player's playbook, the coach can feel somewhat comfortable that his club will react in the proper manner most of the time. It behooves a coach to spend ample time on defensive situation work because many times it does make the difference in a win or a loss.

On the following pages the Playbook has detailed for each position player where they are supposed to be and the task they are responsible to perform in that situation. As in all areas of baseball, each coach has his own way of defensing situations. Whichever way a coach wants his players to react, it needs to be detailed in their playbook and then practiced to the point that the players and coaches feel comfortable that the proper reaction will take place during the course of a game.

Practice in defensive situation work must be game-like whenever possible with runners placed on the bases and at the plate. A fungo hitter at the plate can force the defense to react in all the situations detailed. The runners must go full speed on contact so that all relays, cut-offs, mechanics and communication are performed as they are in an actual game.

If forced to work inside, the coach can continue to work on defensive situations by throwing the baseball from home plate simulating the hitter putting the ball in play. The distance between bases can be cut down to 45 feet. All defensive players and baserunners will run one-half speed. When the fielder comes up with the baseball, all defensive players will stop where they are at so that the coaching staff can check to be sure that each is in the proper spot.

The best time to evaluate a club's ability to handle defensive situations is in actual game scrimmages. It can become more beneficial when innings are started with players already on the bases so that the defense is confronted with various situations. The more times a coach can confront his defense with instantaneous situations the better they should react when these situations occur during an actual game.

SINGLE TO LEFT FIELD WITH NO RUNNER ON BASE OR A RUNNER AT THIRD BASE

PITCHER—Will break for first base on the single to left field. This is done to allow the first baseman to back up the throw from left field to second base and to prevent the runner from taking an aggressive turn at first base. Will watch the runner touch first base.

CATCHER—After he reads the base hit to left field, he will break for the area behind first base to back up any possible throw from the shortstop, second baseman or left fielder to first base.

FIRST BASEMAN—After he reads a definite base hit with no play at first base, he will move to a position to back up the throw to second base from the left fielder or shortstop. He will watch the runner round first base and if he makes a break for second base he will yell "there he goes". He will say nothing if the runner is not making a break for second base.

SECOND BASEMAN—Will cover second base on the single to left field preparing for a possible play at the base if the runner attempts to advance to second base. Will help the shortstop get into the proper cut-off position if the left fielder fields the ball well away from second base. If the first baseman yells "there he goes" he will use the shortstop for his cut-off man. If he says nothing to the shortstop the ball will come through to the base.

THIRD BASEMAN—After the ball passes him into left field he will cover third base always prepared to move toward second base on a deflected ball.

SHORTSTOP—After the ball goes past him into left field, he will break for the proper cut-off position for the throw to second base. If the first baseman lets him and the second baseman know that the runner is heading toward second base, he will listen for the second baseman for a possible cut-off and throw to second base. If he hears nothing from the second baseman he will let the ball go through to the base. If he hears nothing from the first baseman he will cut-off all throws he can handle without waiting for the second baseman to have him cut the ball off. Once he catches the baseball, he should quickly turn and check the runner rounding first base. If there is a possible play on him at first base, he will throw to the pitcher covering.

LEFT FIELDER—Fields the ball under control and throws to second base. If he hears the first baseman letting the defense know that the runner is heading toward second base he will immediately throw the ball to the base using the cut-off man (shortstop). He will never throw behind the runner rounding first base unless he has come to a complete stop near first base or is heading back toward the bag.

CENTER FIELDER—Backs up the left fielder.

RIGHT FIELDER—Breaks as soon as the ball is hit to back up the first baseman on any possible throw to second base.

SINGLE TO LEFT FIELD WITH NO RUNNER ON BASE OR A RUNNER
AT THIRD BASE

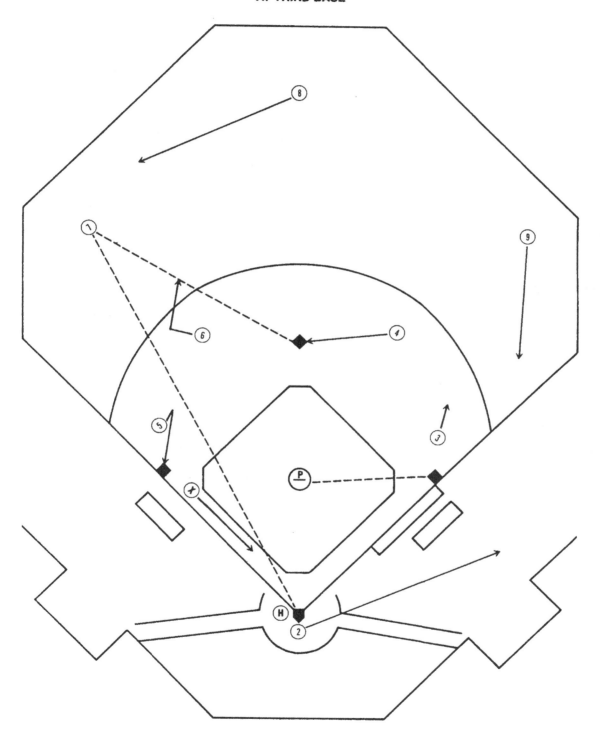

SINGLE TO CENTER FIELD WITH NO RUNNER ON BASE OR A RUNNER AT THIRD BASE

PITCHER—Will back up the throw from the center fielder to second base from the area of the mound. If both the shortstop and second baseman both go out for a possible play on the ball, he will have responsibility for second base.

CATCHER—After he reads the base hit to center field, he will break for the area behind first base to back up any possible throw from the center fielder, shortstop or second baseman.

FIRST BASEMAN—Will break for first base on the base hit to center field. Once he sees that there will be no play at the base, he will come to the inside and watch the runner touch the base. Will be responsible for first base if a play is made on the runner by the center fielder, shortstop or second baseman. If the runner makes a break for second base, he will yell "there he goes". He will say nothing if the runner is not making a break for second base.

SECOND BASEMAN—If the shortstop goes out for the cut-off to second base, he will cover second base. If he goes out for the cut-off, the shortstop will have the base. If both go out the shortstop has priority over the second baseman, who will return to the base. The pitcher will cover second base if both the shortstop and second baseman have a play on the ball away from the bag. If responsible for the base, he will help the shortstop get into proper cut-off position. If the first baseman yells "there he goes" he will use the shortstop for his cut-off man. If he says nothing to the shortstop the ball will come through to the base.

THIRD BASEMAN—On the base hit to center field he will start moving toward second base to cover the base if the shortstop or second baseman go out for a play on the ball. If the pitcher is covering the base, he will move to the mound area to back up the throw to second base. If the pitcher is not covering second base then the third baseman must do so listening for the first baseman to let him know if the runner is breaking toward the base.

SHORTSTOP—If the second baseman goes out for the cut-off to second base, he will cover second base. If he goes out for the cut-off, the second baseman will cover the base. He will have priority over the second baseman if both go out. If responsible for the base, he will help the second baseman get into proper cut-off position listening for the first baseman to let him know if the runner is breaking for second base.

LEFT FIELDER—Backs up the center fielder.

CENTER FIELDER—Fields the ball under control and throws to second base. If he hears the first baseman letting the defense know that the runner is heading toward second base he will immediately throw the ball to the base using the cut-off man if necessary. He will never throw behind the runner rounding first base unless he has come to a complete stop near first base or is heading back toward the bag.

RIGHT FIELDER—Backs up the center fielder.

SINGLE TO CENTER FIELD WITH NO RUNNER ON BASE OR A RUNNER
AT THIRD BASE

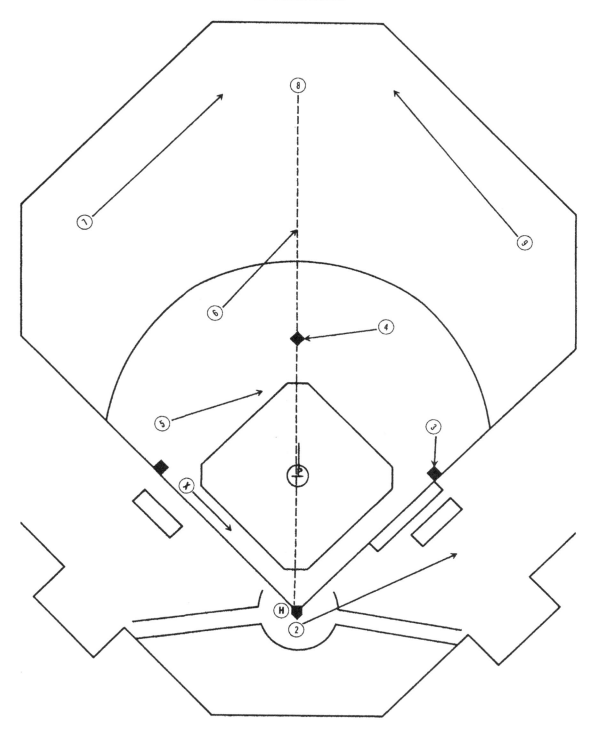

SINGLE TO RIGHT FIELD WITH NO RUNNER ON BASE OR A RUNNER AT THIRD BASE

PITCHER—Will break for first base on ball hit to the right side of the field. When he reads that there will be no play on the hitter at first base, he will break to an area well behind first base, lining himself up with the right fielder and catcher at first base. Will back up the possible throw from the right fielder to the catcher at the bag.

CATCHER—After he reads the base hit to right field, he will break down the first baseline trailing the hitter. He will set up at first base preparing for a possible throw from the right fielder to first base if the runner takes a big turn.

FIRST BASEMAN—After he reads the base hit to right field, he will start walking away from first base to decoy the runner into taking a wide turn around first base.

SECOND BASEMAN—Will go out and become the cut-off man for the right fielder's throw to second base. He will listen for the first baseman to let him know if the runner is breaking for second base. If he hears nothing from the first baseman, he will cut-off all throws he can handle without waiting for the shortstop to have him cut the ball off. Once he fields the ball, he should quickly turn toward first base and check the runner for a possible play to the catcher on the bag.

THIRD BASEMAN—Will back up the throw from the right fielder or second baseman to the shortstop at second base.

SHORTSTOP—Will cover second base on the base hit to right field preparing for a possible play at the base if the runner attempts to advance. He will help the second baseman get into proper cut-off position. If the first baseman yells "there he goes" he will use the second baseman for his cut-off man.

LEFT FIELDER—Breaks as soon as the ball is hit to back up second base on any throw from the right fielder or second baseman to the shortstop at the base.

CENTER FIELDER—Backs up the right fielder.

RIGHT FIELDER—Fields the ball under control. He will glance toward first base after fielding the ball. If the hitter has taken a wide turn and is either stopped or starting to return to first base, he can throw to the catcher covering the base. He must have eye contact toward second base just prior to releasing the ball. On release of the ball he will look and step toward first base. If there is no play on the hitter rounding first base, or the hitter breaks toward the next base, the right fielder will throw to second base using the second baseman as his cut-off man.

144

SINGLE TO RIGHT FIELD WITH NO RUNNER ON BASE OR A RUNNER
AT THIRD BASE

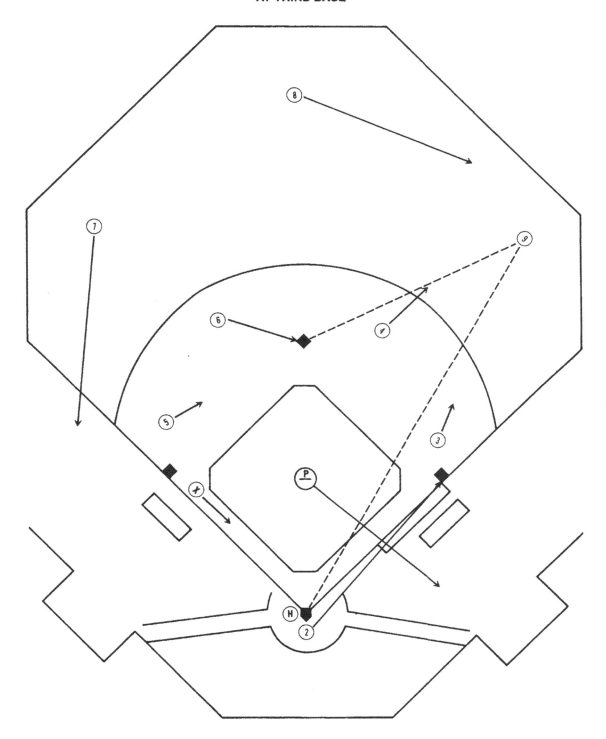

SINGLE TO LEFT FIELD WITH A RUNNER AT FIRST BASE OR RUNNERS AT FIRST AND THIRD BASE

PITCHER—Will break for an area behind third base to back up the possible throw to third base from the left fielder.

CATCHER—After he reads the base hit to left field with no play at the plate, he will move to a position in foul territory on the third base side to back up a wild throw to third base. His primary responsibility is to cover the plate if the runner advances on a bad throw to third base.

FIRST BASEMAN—After he reads the base hit to left field with no play at first base, he will move to the outside of the baseline watching the hitter touch first base. If the ball is thrown by the left fielder to second base he will back up the throw from the infield side while the right fielder backs up the throw from the outfield side. He will let the defense know if runner breaks for second base.

SECOND BASEMAN—As soon as he reads the base hit to left field with no force play at second base on the runner from first base, he will come in from the first base side of second base preparing for a possible throw from the left fielder. This play would be on the runner rounding second base when the left fielder feels that he has a chance to make the play at second base. If the runner heads for third base, the second baseman will set up at second base for a possible throw from the shortstop or third baseman on the batter-runner. Is responsible to watch the runner touch second base. He will let the third baseman know if the runner breaks for third base.

THIRD BASEMAN—As soon as he reads the base hit to left field he will set up at third base for a possible throw from the left fielder to third base. He will help the shortstop get into the proper cut-off position. If the ball comes through to third base he will look to second base for a possible play at the base on the batter-runner.

SHORTSTOP—Will serve as the cut-off man for the possible throw from the left fielder to third base. Will listen to the third baseman for a possible cut-off to third base or to second base. If no play at third base, he needs to check the runner rounding second base for a possible play to the second baseman.

LEFT FIELDER—Fields the ball so that he can make a play at third base if the runner attempts to advance. Will use the shortstop for his cut-off man. If the runner from first base takes a wide turn at second base he can throw to the second baseman at the bag coming in from the first base side of the base. He must be sure that the runner can not advance to third base on his throw behind the runner at second. If there is no play at second base and the runner is not advancing to third base, he will throw the ball immediately to the shortstop in cut-off position.

CENTER FIELDER—Backs up the left fielder.

RIGHT FIELDER—Breaks as soon as the ball is hit to back up the possible throw from the left fielder, shortstop or third baseman to second base. If ball goes through to third base he must quickly get to the position in line with the third baseman's possible throw to second base.

SINGLE TO LEFT FIELD WITH A RUNNER AT FIRST BASE OR RUNNERS AT FIRST AND THIRD BASE

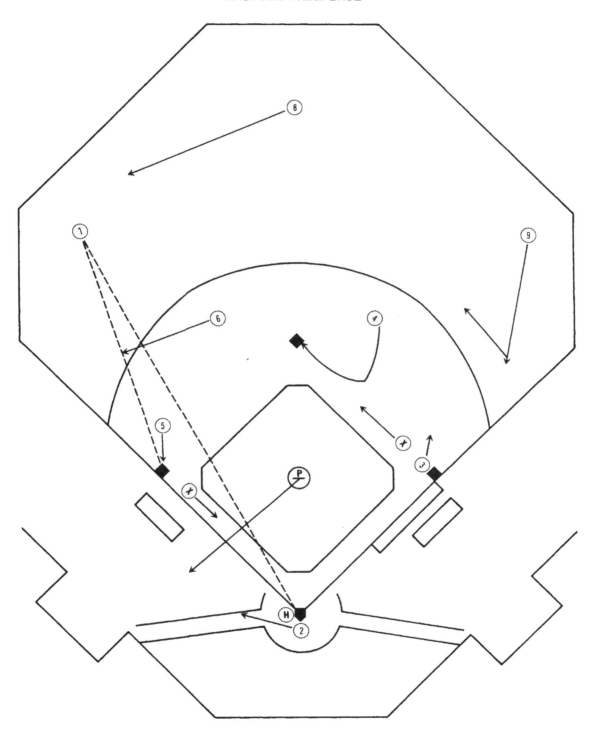

SINGLE TO CENTER FIELD WITH A RUNNER AT FIRST BASE OR RUNNERS AT FIRST AND THIRD BASE

PITCHER—Will break for an area behind third base to back up the possible throw to third base from the center fielder.

CATCHER—After he reads the base hit to center field with no play at the plate, he will move to the infield side of the plate to back up the possible throw from the center fielder to the second baseman at second base. He must be in a position to get back to the plate if the throw goes through to third base.

FIRST BASEMAN—After he reads the base hit to center field with no play at first base, he will move to the inside of the diamond watching the runner touch first base. He will let the defense know if the runner breaks for second base. Is responsible for first base if a play is made on the batter-runner at first base. If he sees both the shortstop and second baseman going out for a short fly ball, he is responsible to cover second base.

SECOND BASEMAN—As soon as he reads the base hit to center field with no force play at second base, he will move to the inside of the diamond and cover second base preparing for a possible throw from the center fielder. This play would be on the runner rounding second base when the center fielder throws behind the runner. If the runner heads for third base with the center fielder throwing to third base, the second baseman will set up at second base for a possible throw from the shortstop or third baseman on the batter-runner. He is responsible to watch the runner touch second base.

THIRD BASEMAN—As soon as he reads the base hit to center field, he will set up at third base for a possible throw from the center fielder to third base. He will help the shortstop get into proper cut-off position. If the ball comes through to third base he will look to second base for a possible play at the base on the batter-runner.

SHORTSTOP—Will serve as the cut-off man for a possible throw from the center fielder to third base. Will listen for the third baseman for a possible cut-off to third base or to second base. If no play at third base, he needs to check the runner rounding second base for a possible play to the second baseman.

LEFT FIELDER—Backs up the center fielder.

CENTER FIELDER—Fields the ball so that he can make a play at third base if the runner attempts to advance. Will use the shortstop for his cut-off man. If the runner from first base takes a wide turn at second base he can throw to the second baseman at the bag. The second baseman will be covering second base coming from the inside of the diamond. He must be sure that the runner can not advance to third base on his throw behind the runner at second. If there is no play at second base and the runner is not advancing to third base, he will throw the ball immediately to the shortstop in cut-off position.

RIGHT FIELDER—As soon as the ball is hit to center field he will break to back up the center fielder. When the center fielder fields the ball, he will break for a position behind second base backing up any possible overthrow to second base from the shortstop or third baseman.

SINGLE TO CENTER FIELD WITH A RUNNER AT FIRST BASE OR RUNNERS AT FIRST AND THIRD BASE

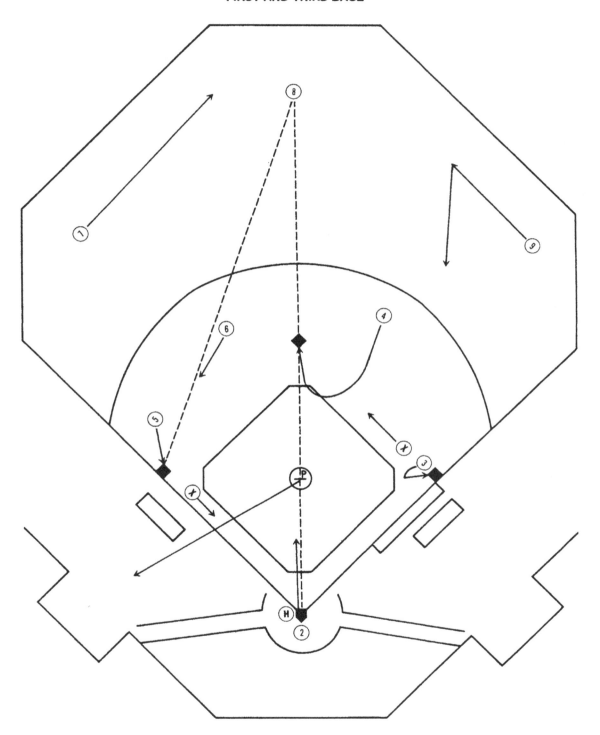

SINGLE TO RIGHT FIELD WITH A RUNNER AT FIRST BASE OR RUNNERS AT FIRST AND THIRD BASE

PITCHER—Will break for an area behind third base to back up the possible throw to third base from the right fielder.

CATCHER—After he reads the base hit to right field with no play at the plate, he will move down the outside of the third baseline to be in a position to recover a deflected ball that the third baseman can not handle. He must be in a position to get back to the plate if a possible play at the plate develops.

FIRST BASEMAN—After he reads the base hit to right field with no play at first base, he will move to the inside of the diamond watching the runner touch first base. He will let the defense know if the runner breaks for second base. He is responsible for first base if a play is made on the batter-runner at first base.

SECOND BASEMAN—As soon as he reads the base hit to right field he will move out a few steps toward the right fielder in case the ball gets by him and he becomes the front man on the tandom relay. As soon as the right fielder comes up with the ball, which will be thrown to the shortstop, the second baseman will immediately break for second base preparing for a possible throw from the shortstop or third baseman on the batter-runner. If the base hit to right field is one in which the runner from first base will not advance to third base, the right fielder will be throwing directly to the shortstop at second base. Once the second baseman sees the shortstop moving toward the bag, he will not be responsible for second base. Will watch the runner touch second base if the right fielder comes up with the ball.

THIRD BASEMAN—As soon as he reads the base hit to right field, he will set up at third base for a possible throw from the right fielder to third base. He will help the shortstop get into proper cut-off position. If the ball comes through to third base he will look to second base for a possible play at the base on the batter-runner.

SHORTSTOP—Will serve as the cut-off man for a possible throw from the right fielder to third base. Will listen for the third baseman for a possible cut-off to third base or to second base. If the base hit to right field is one in which the runner from first base will not advance to third base, the right fielder will be throwing to the shortstop at second base hoping to have a play on the runner rounding the base too far. The shortstop would break for second base on this play just as the right fielder's arm starts forward.

LEFT FIELDER—As soon as the ball is hit to right field he will break to a position backing up the throw from the right fielder to either the shortstop or second baseman at second base.

CENTER FIELDER—Backs up the right fielder. When the ball is fielded by the right fielder he will break for a position behind second base to back up a possible throw at that base from the shortstop or third baseman.

RIGHT FIELDER—Fields the ball so that he can make a play at third base if the runner attempts to advance. He will use the shortstop for his cut-off man. If the base hit to right field is one in which the runner from first base will not advance to third base, he will throw to the shortstop at second base for a possible play on the runner rounding the bag. If in doubt about the runner's intention to advance or not, he will throw the ball to third base even if the shortstop is moving toward second base. He will not have a cut-off man in this situation.

150

SINGLE TO RIGHT FIELD WITH A RUNNER AT FIRST BASE OR RUNNERS AT FIRST AND THIRD BASE

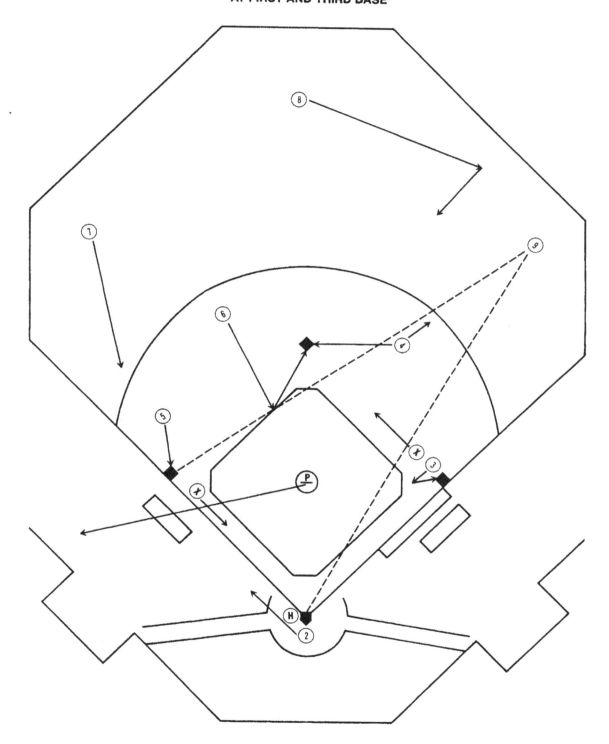

SINGLE TO LEFT FIELD IN HOLE WITH NO RUNNER ON BASE OR A RUNNER AT THIRD BASE

This is just one example of a situation where the shortstop and third baseman might switch responsibilities due to their cross cutting in the infield to make a play on a batted ball. In this case, the third baseman would take on the responsibilities of the shortstop and the shortstop would be responsible for third base. If done otherwise, both players might not be able to get to their proper positions on time.

With a runner at second base or runners at first and second base, the shortstop might become the cut-off man on the throw to the plate from the left fielder. The third baseman would have to recover quickly and get back to third base for a possible play at that base.

Both players must communicate when this situation occurs so that their switching of responsibilities does not cause any confusion on their part, and both players are of assistance to the other players on defense. Whenever possible, the shortstop and third basemen must try to recover so that they can assume their natural responsibilities. There are times when this is not possible, and that is the reasoning for their switching positions of responsibility. If a switch of responsibility is needed, the communication between the two would be "switch".

SINGLE TO LEFT FIELD IN HOLE WITH NO RUNNER ON BASE OR A RUNNER
AT THIRD BASE

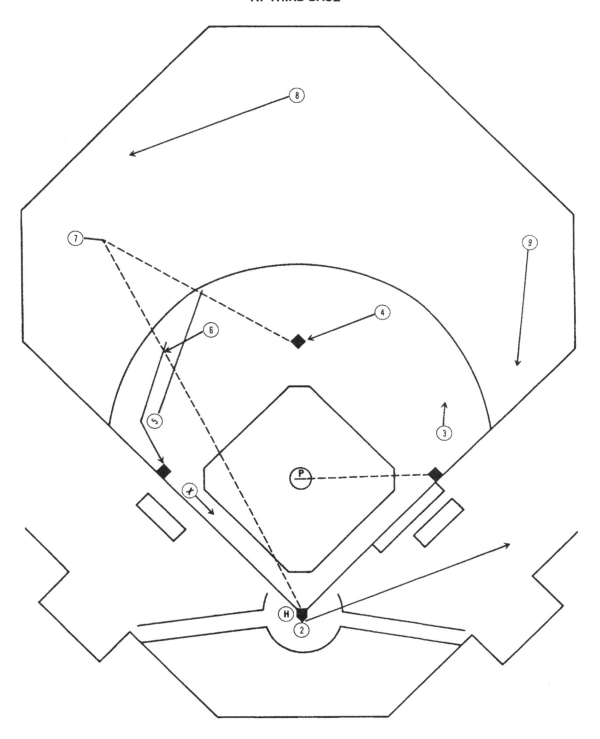

SINGLE TO CENTER FIELD IN HOLE WITH A RUNNER AT FIRST BASE OR RUNNERS AT FIRST AND THIRD BASE

This is just one example of a situation where the shortstop and second baseman might switch responsibilities due to their cross cutting in the infield to make a play on a batted ball. In this case, the second baseman would take on the responsibilities of the shortstop by being the cut-off man on the possible throw by the center fielder to third base. The shortstop would then be responsible for second base. If done otherwise, both players might not be able to get to their proper positions on time.

Both players must communicate when this situation occurs so that their switching of responsibilities does not cause any confusion on their part, and both players are of assistance to the other players on defense. Whenever possible, the shortstop and second baseman must try to recover so that they can assume their natural responsibilities. There are times when this is not possible, and that is the reasoning for their switching positions of responsibility. If a switch of responsibility is needed, the communication between the two would be "switch".

**SINGLE TO CENTER FIELD IN HOLE WITH A RUNNER AT FIRST BASE OR
RUNNERS AT FIRST AND THIRD BASE**

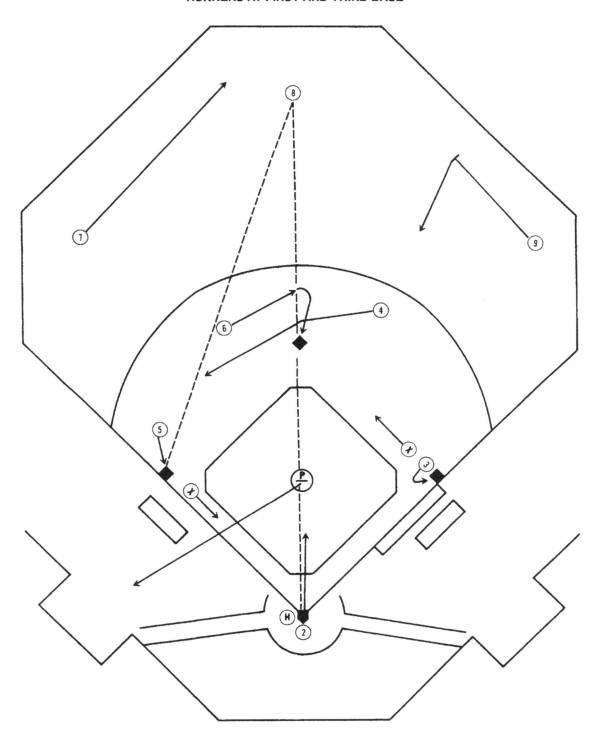

SINGLE TO RIGHT FIELD IN HOLE WITH NO RUNNER ON BASE OR A RUNNER AT THIRD BASE

This is just one example of a situation where the first baseman and the second baseman might switch responsibilities due to their cross cutting in the infield to make a play on a batted ball. In this case, the first baseman would take on the responsibilities of the second baseman by being the cut-off man on the right fielder's throw to the shortstop at second base. The second baseman would move in the direction of first base and cover the base if the catcher is not covering the base properly.

Another situation where the first baseman and the second baseman might switch responsibilities on the ball hit to right field in the hole would be when there was a runner at first base. If they have to cross cut, the first baseman would cover second base and the second baseman would be responsible for first base. The second baseman might also be in a better position to handle the cut-off from the right fielder to the plate with a runner at second base on a ball hit to the right fielder in the hole.

Both players must communicate when these situations occur so that their switching of responsibilities does not cause any confusion on their part, and both players are of assistance to the other players on defense. Whenever possible, the second baseman and the first baseman must try to recover so that they can assume their natural responsibilities. There are times when this is not possible, and that is the reasoning for their switching positions of responsibility. If a switch of responsibilities is needed, the communication between the two would be "switch".

156

SINGLE TO RIGHT FIELD IN HOLE WITH NO RUNNER ON BASE OR
A RUNNER AT THIRD BASE

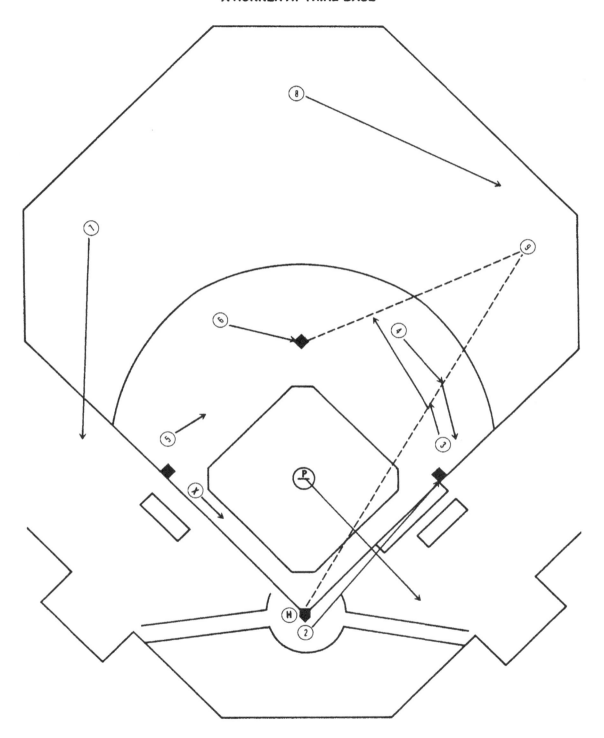

SINGLE TO LEFT FIELD WITH A RUNNER AT SECOND BASE OR RUNNERS AT SECOND AND THIRD BASE

PITCHER—Will break for an area behind home plate to back up the possible throw from the left fielder to the catcher.

CATCHER—Will be responsible for the plate, setting up for a possible throw from the left fielder. He will help the third baseman get into the proper cut-off position.

FIRST BASEMAN—Will be responsible for first base watching the batter-runner touch the base. He will let the defense know if the batter-runner breaks for second base. Is responsible to back up the throw from the left fielder to the second baseman at second base. He should always be prepared to move into cut-off position for the throw from the left fielder to the plate if he sees that the third baseman will be unable to get there.

SECOND BASEMAN—Will be responsible for second base preparing for a possible throw to the base from the left fielder if he has no play at the plate. He will listen for the first baseman to let him know if the batter-runner is breaking for second base. If the ball is thrown by the left fielder to the plate, he will prepare for a possible throw to second base by the third baseman or the catcher.

THIRD BASEMAN—Once he reads the base hit to left field he will immediately break for the cut-off position for the left fielder's possible throw to the plate. The catcher will assist him in getting into the proper cut-off position. Will listen to the catcher for the possible cut-off throw to the plate or to second base.

SHORTSTOP—If he reads that the base hit to left field is hit well enough that there will be a definite play at the plate, he will break for third base. He will be responsible for third base in case the runner rounds the base and returns. If the shortstop reads that there will be no play at the plate, he will move into the proper cut-off position for the left fielder's throw to second base.

LEFT FIELDER—Fields the ball so that he can make a possible play at the plate on the runner who started at second base. If he feels that he has a definite play on that runner he will throw to the plate through the third baseman serving as the cut-off man. If there is no chance for a play at the plate, he will throw the ball to the second baseman at second base to prevent the batter-runner from advancing.

CENTER FIELDER—Backs up the left fielder.

RIGHT FIELDER—As soon as the ball is hit he will break for a position behind second base to back up the throw to second base from the third baseman or the catcher.

SINGLE TO LEFT FIELD WITH A RUNNER AT SECOND BASE OR RUNNERS AT SECOND AND THIRD BASE

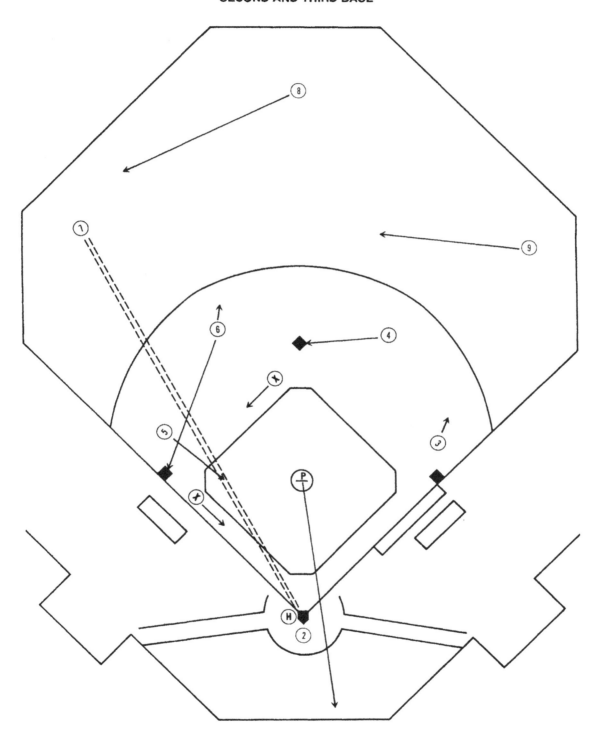

SINGLE TO CENTER FIELD WITH A RUNNER AT SECOND BASE OR RUNNERS AT SECOND AND THIRD BASE

PITCHER—Will break for an area behind home plate to back up the possible throw from the center fielder to the catcher.

CATCHER—Will be responsible for the plate, setting up for a possible throw from the center fielder. He will help the first baseman get into the proper cut-off position.

FIRST BASEMAN—Once he reads the base hit to center field, he will immediately break for the cut-off position for the center fielder's possible throw to the plate. The catcher will assist him in getting into the proper cut-off position. He will listen to the catcher for the possible cut-off throw to the plate or to second base. If the ball is thrown by the center fielder to the shortstop at second base, he will back up that throw.

SECOND BASEMAN—Once he reads the base hit to center field, he will immediately break for first base. He will be responsible for that base hoping to keep the batter-runner from taking a wide turn. Will set up at the base for a possible throw from the first baseman or the catcher. He will let the defense know if the batter-runner breaks toward second base.

THIRD BASEMAN—Will be responsible for third base along with watching the runner touch the base. He must be in a position to break toward the mound area if a ball deflects off the first baseman in cut-off position. As soon as he sees that there will be a play at the plate, he will start moving toward the cut-off man. He must be in a position to return to the base for a possible play on the batter-runner.

SHORTSTOP—Will be responsible for second base, preparing for a possible throw to the base from the center fielder if he has no play at the plate. He will listen for the second baseman to let him know if the batter-runner is breaking for second base. If the ball is thrown by the center fielder to the plate, he will prepare for a possible throw to second base by the first baseman or the catcher.

LEFT FIELDER—Backs up the center fielder. When the center fielder cleanly fields the ball, the left fielder will break immediately toward the left field line to back up a possible throw to third base.

CENTER FIELDER—Fields the ball so that he can make a possible play at the plate on the runner who started at second base. If he feels that he has a definite play on that runner, he will throw to the plate through the first baseman serving as the cut-off man. If there is no chance for a play at the plate, he will throw the ball to the shortstop at second base to prevent the batter-runner from advancing. He will be responsible for backing up any throw by the first baseman or catcher to the shortstop at second base.

RIGHT FIELDER—Backs up the center fielder.

SINGLE TO CENTER FIELD WITH A RUNNER AT SECOND BASE OR RUNNERS AT SECOND AND THIRD BASE

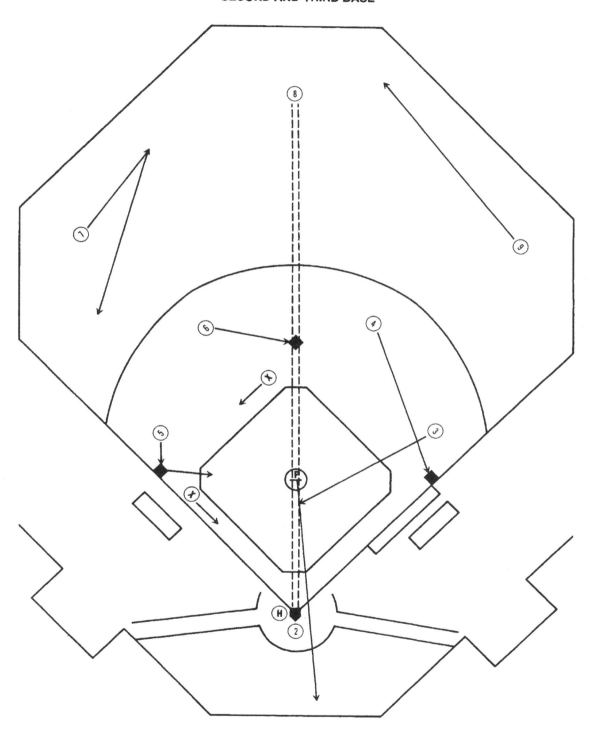

SINGLE TO RIGHT FIELD WITH A RUNNER AT SECOND BASE OR RUNNERS AT SECOND AND THIRD BASE

PITCHER—Will break for an area behind home plate to back up the possible throw from the right fielder to the catcher.

CATCHER—Will be responsible for the plate, setting up for a possible throw from the right fielder. He will help the first baseman get into the proper cut-off position.

FIRST BASEMAN—Once he reads the base hit to right field, he will immediately break for the cut-off position for the right fielder's possible throw to the plate. The catcher will assist him in getting into the proper cut-off position. He will listen to the catcher for the possible cut-off throw to the plate or to second base.

SECOND BASEMAN—Once he reads the base hit to right field, he will break immediately for first base. He will be responsible for that base hoping to keep the batter-runner from taking a wide turn. Will set up at the base for a possible throw from the first baseman or the catcher. He will let the defense know if the batter-runner breaks for second base.

THIRD BASEMAN—Will be responsible for third base along with watching the runner touch the base. He must be in a position to break toward the first baseman in cut-off position if a ball deflects off him. As soon as he sees that there will be a play at the plate, he will start moving toward the cut-off man. He must be in a position to return to the base for a possible play on the batter-runner.

SHORTSTOP—Will be responsible for second base, preparing for a possible throw to the base from the right fielder if he has no play at the plate. He will listen for the second baseman to let him know if the batter-runner is breaking for second base even though he should be able to see the runner while facing the right fielder. If the ball is thrown by the right fielder to the plate, he will prepare for a possible throw to second base by the first baseman or the catcher.

LEFT FIELDER—As soon as he reads the base hit to right field, he will immediately break for an area behind third base to back up that base on any possible play that might develop where a throw is made to third base. Also in a position to back up the right fielder's throw to second base.

CENTER FIELDER—Backs up the right fielder. When the right fielder cleanly fields the ball, he will immediately break for an area behind second base to back up any throw made at that base by the first baseman or the catcher.

RIGHT FIELDER—Fields the ball so that he can make a possible play at the plate on the runner who started at second base. If he feels that he has a definite play on that runner, he will throw to the plate through the first baseman serving as the cut-off man. If there is no chance for a play at the plate he will throw the ball to the shortstop at second base to prevent the batter-runner from advancing. He must be aware of backing up first base if a play is made on the batter-runner taking a wide turn.

162

SINGLE TO RIGHT FIELD WITH A RUNNER AT SECOND BASE OR RUNNERS AT SECOND AND THIRD BASE

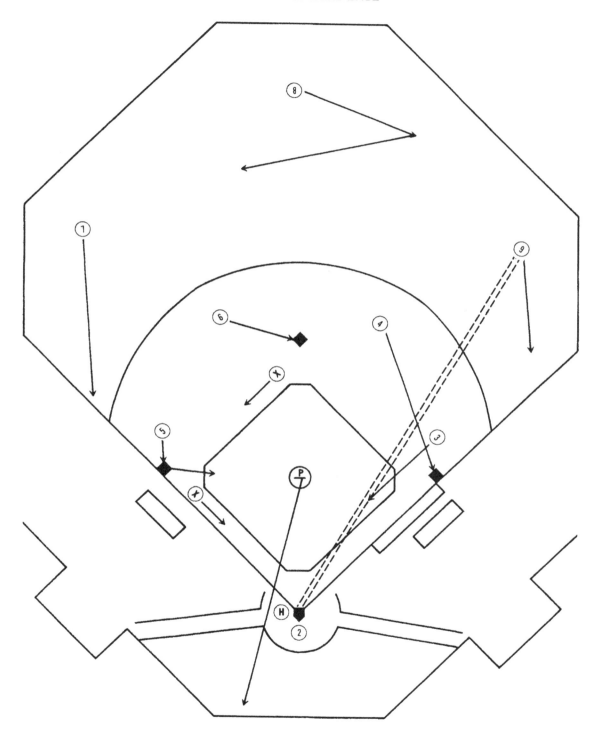

SINGLE TO LEFT FIELD WITH RUNNERS AT FIRST AND SECOND BASE OR THE BASES LOADED

PITCHER—Will break for an area behind home plate to back up the possible throw by the left fielder to third base or the plate. He must get to the spot which would be an equal distance away from where he needs to be on each directional throw. Once the ball is released to either third base or the plate, he will break for the proper back up position.

CATCHER—Will be responsible for the plate, setting up for a possible throw from the left fielder. He will help the third baseman get into the proper cut-off position.

FIRST BASEMAN—Will be responsible for first base unless he reads that the third baseman is unable to get to the cut-off position for the possible throw to the plate by the left fielder. If so, he will be the cut-off man on this throw. If he stays at first base he will let the defense know if the batter-runner breaks for second base. He will back up the possible throw to second base by the left fielder.

SECOND BASEMAN—Will be responsible for second base preparing for a possible throw to the base by the left fielder if he has no play at the plate or third base. He will listen for the first baseman to let him know if the batter-runner is breaking for second base. If the ball is thrown by the left fielder to the plate or third base, he will prepare for a possible throw to second base from the catcher, third baseman or the shortstop. He will watch the runner touch second base.

THIRD BASEMAN—Once he reads the base hit to left field he will immediately break for the cut-off position for the left fielder's possible throw to the plate. The catcher will assist him in getting into the proper cut-off position. He will listen for the catcher for the possible cut-off throw to the plate, to third base, or to second base. If the first baseman has moved into the cut-off position to the plate, the third baseman would return to third base. The first baseman should only be there if there is doubt whether the third baseman can get there in time.

SHORTSTOP—Once he reads the base hit to left field he will immediately break to third base to cover that base on any possible play that might develop. If he sees that the third baseman is close to the base and the first baseman is serving as the cut-off man on the left fielder's possible throw to the plate, then he will become the cut-off man for the left fielder's possible throw to third base. He will watch the runner touch third base.

LEFT FIELDER—Fields the ball so that he can make a possible play at the plate on the runner who started at second base. If he feels that he has a definite play on that runner he will throw to the plate through the third baseman serving as the cut-off man. If he has no play at the plate he might have a play to the shortstop at third base on the runner who started at first base. If the runner from second base will score without a play and the runner from first base will make third base without a play, he will throw the ball immediately to the second baseman at second base. He must be sure that the throw to second base will not allow the runner at third base to score on the throw. After throwing to the plate, he will back up third base for a possible play at that base.

CENTER FIELDER—Backs up the left fielder.

RIGHT FIELDER—As soon as he reads the base hit to left field he will break for an area behind second base to back up the possible throw by the third baseman, the catcher or the shortstop to second base.

SINGLE TO LEFT FIELD WITH RUNNERS AT FIRST AND SECOND BASE OR THE BASES LOADED

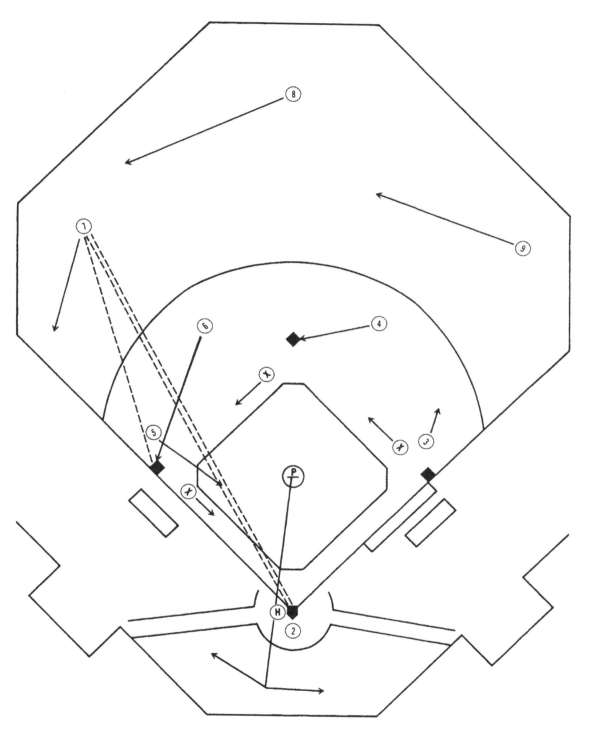

SINGLE TO CENTER FIELD WITH RUNNERS AT FIRST AND SECOND BASE OR THE BASES LOADED

PITCHER—Will break for an area in foul territory so that he is an equal distance between where he needs to be to back up the possible throw to third base or the possible throw to the plate. Once the ball is released by the center fielder, he will break immediately to back up the throw to either third base or the plate.

CATCHER—Will be responsible for the plate, setting up for a possible throw from the center fielder. He will help the first baseman get into the proper cut-off position.

FIRST BASEMAN—Once he reads the base hit to center field, he will immediately break for the cut-off position for the center fielder's possible throw to the plate. The catcher will assist him in getting into the proper cut-off position. He will listen for the catcher for the possible cut-off throw to the plate, to third base, or to second base.

SECOND BASEMAN—Will be responsible for second base preparing for a possible throw to the base by the center fielder if he has no play at the plate or third base. If the ball is thrown by the center fielder to the plate or third base, he will prepare for a possible throw to second base by the catcher, first baseman, third baseman or shortstop. He will watch the runner touch second base.

THIRD BASEMAN—Will be responsible for third base along with watching the runner touch the base. If the center fielder has no play at the plate, he will prepare for a possible throw to third base. He will help the shortstop get into the proper cut-off position. If the ball is thrown to the plate, he will prepare for a possible throw to third base from the catcher or first baseman.

SHORTSTOP—Once he reads the base hit to center field he will immediately break for the cut-off position for the center fielder's possible throw to third base. The third baseman will assist him in getting into the proper cut-off position. He will listen for the third baseman for the possible cut-off to third base or to the second baseman at second base.

LEFT FIELDER—Backs up the center fielder. When the center fielder cleanly fields the ball, he will break immediately toward the left field line to back up a possible throw to third base.

CENTER FIELDER—Fields the ball so that he can make a possible play at the plate on the runner who started at second base. If he feels that he has a definite play on that runner he will throw to the plate through the first baseman serving as the cut-off man. If he has no play at the plate he might have a play at third base on the runner who started at first base. In this case, he would throw to the third baseman through the shortstop serving as the cut-off man for the third baseman. If the runner from second base will score without a play and the runner from first base will make third base without a play, he will throw the ball immediately to the second baseman at second base. He must be sure that the throw to second base will not allow the runner at third base to score on the throw. After throwing to the plate, he will back up second base for a possible play at that base.

RIGHT FIELDER—Backs up the center fielder. When the center fielder cleanly fields the ball, the right fielder will break immediately toward the area behind second base backing up the possible throw to that base from the shortstop or third baseman.

SINGLE TO CENTER FIELD WITH RUNNERS AT FIRST AND SECOND BASE OR THE BASES LOADED

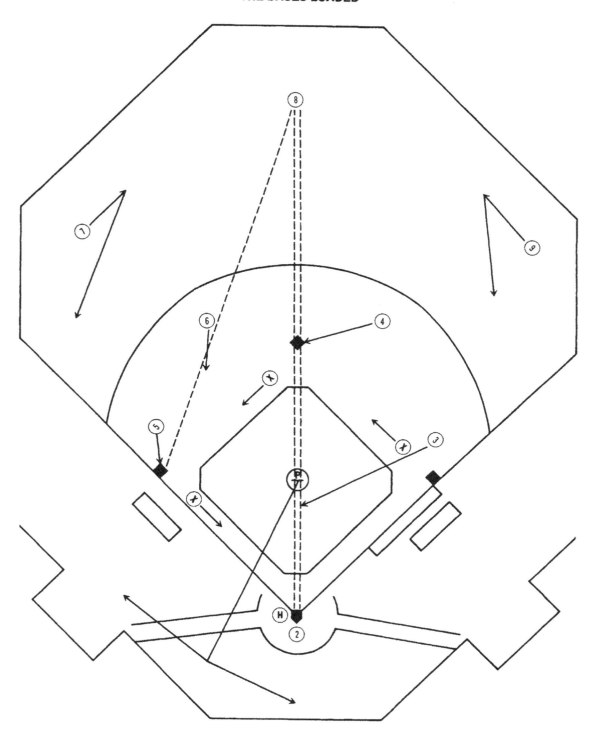

SINGLE TO RIGHT FIELD WITH RUNNERS AT FIRST AND SECOND BASE OR THE BASES LOADED

PITCHER—Will break for an area in foul territory so that he is an equal distance between where he needs to be to back up the possible throw to third base or the possible throw to the plate. Once the ball is released by the right fielder, he will break immediately to back up the throw to either third base or the plate.

CATCHER—Will be responsible for the plate, setting up for a possible throw from the right fielder. He will help the first baseman get into the proper cut-off position.

FIRST BASEMAN—Once he reads the base hit to right field he will immediately break for the cut-off position for the right fielder's possible throw to the plate. The catcher will assist him in getting into the proper cut-off position. He will listen for the catcher for the possible cut-off throw to the plate, to third base, or to second base.

SECOND BASEMAN—Will be responsible for second base preparing for a possible throw to the base by the right fielder if he has no play at the plate or third base. If the ball is thrown by the right fielder to the plate or third base, he will prepare for a possible throw to second base by the catcher, first baseman, third baseman or shortstop. He will watch the runner touch second base.

THIRD BASEMAN—Will be responsible for third base along with watching the runner touch the base. If the right fielder has no play at the plate, he will prepare for a possible throw to third base. He will help the shortstop get into the proper cut-off position. If the ball is thrown to the plate, he will prepare for a possible throw to third base from the catcher or first baseman.

SHORTSTOP—Once he reads the base hit to right field he will immediately break for the cut-off position for the right fielder's possible throw to third base. The third baseman will assist him in getting into the proper cut-off position. He will listen for the third baseman for the possible cut-off to third base or to the second baseman at second base.

LEFT FIELDER—As soon as he reads the base hit to right field, he will immediately break for an area behind third base to back up that base on any possible play that might develop where a throw is made to third base.

CENTER FIELDER—Backs up the right fielder. When the right fielder cleanly fields the ball, he will immediately break for an area behind second base to back up any throw made at that base.

RIGHT FIELDER—Fields the ball so that he can make a possible play at the plate on the runner who started at second base. If he feels that he has a definite play on that runner he will throw to the plate through the first baseman serving as the cut-off man. If he has no play at the plate he might have a play at third base on the runner who started at first base. In this case, he would throw to the third baseman through the shortstop serving as the cut-off man for the third baseman. If the runner from second base will score without a play and the runner from first base will make third base without a play, he will throw the ball immediately to the second baseman at second base. He must be sure that the throw to second base will not allow the runner at third base to score on the throw. After throwing the ball to the plate or to third base, he will back up second base for a possible throw to that base.

168

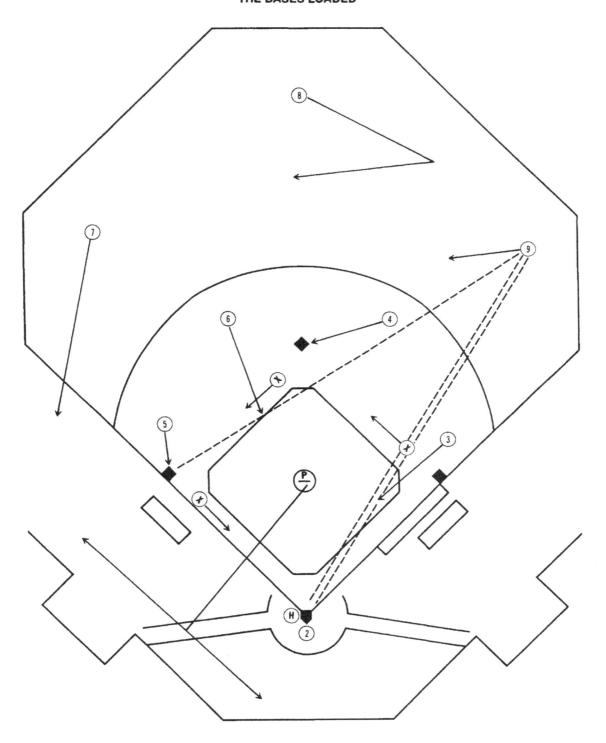

SINGLE TO LEFT FIELD CAUSING THE THIRD BASEMAN TO DIVE FOR THE BALL. RUNNER AT SECOND BASE, RUNNERS AT SECOND AND THIRD BASE, RUNNERS AT FIRST AND SECOND BASE, OR THE BASES LOADED.

PITCHER—Will break for an area behind home plate to back up the possible throw by the left fielder to third base or the plate. He must get to the spot which would be an equal distance away from where he needs to be on each directional throw. Once the ball is released to either third base or the plate, he will break for the proper back up position.

CATCHER—Will be responsible for the plate, setting up for a possible throw from the left fielder. He will help the first baseman get into the proper cut-off position.

FIRST BASEMAN—When he sees the base hit to left field and that the third baseman will be unable to get to the cut-off position for the left fielder's possible throw to the plate, he will immediately break for the cut-off position. The catcher will assist him in getting into the proper cut-off position. He will listen for the catcher for the possible cut-off throw to the plate, to third base, or to second base.

SECOND BASEMAN—Will be responsible for second base preparing for a possible throw to the base by the left fielder if he has no play at the plate or third base. If the ball is thrown by the left fielder to the plate or third base, he will prepare for a possible throw to second base from the catcher, first baseman, third baseman or shortstop. He will have to watch the batter-runner so that he can let the defense know if he is advancing to second base. Will watch the runner touch second base.

THIRD BASEMAN—If the base hit to left field causes him to leave his feet or his momentum takes him well away from getting to the proper cut-off position for the left fielder's possible throw to the plate, he will attempt to recover quickly and cover third base. If the shortstop is in better position to cover third base, he will then be the cut-off man for the left fielder's possible throw to third base.

SHORTSTOP—Once he reads the base hit to left field, he will immediately break for third base if he sees that the third baseman is not able to recover. If the third baseman can get back to third base then he will become the cut-off man for the left fielder's possible throw to third base. If he sees that the first baseman is not moving to the cut-off position for the left fielder's possible throw to the plate, he will immediately break for the cut-off position.

LEFT FIELDER—Fields the ball so that he can make a possible play at the plate on the runner who started at second base. If he feels that he has a definite play on that runner he will throw to the plate through the first baseman serving as the cut-off man. If he has no play at the plate he might have a play to the third baseman or shortstop at third base on the runner who started at first base. If the runner from second base will score without a play and the runner from first base will make third base without a play, he will throw the ball immediately to the second baseman at second base. He must be sure that the throw to second base will not allow the runner at third base to score on the throw. After throwing to the plate, he will back up third base for a possible play at that base.

CENTER FIELDER—Backs up the left fielder.

RIGHT FIELDER—As soon as he reads the base hit to left field he will break for an area behind second base to back up the possible throw by the third baseman, shortstop, catcher or first baseman to second base.

SINGLE TO LEFT FIELD-CAUSING THE THIRD BASEMAN TO DIVE FOR THE BALL. RUNNER AT SECOND BASE, RUNNERS AT SECOND AND THIRD BASE, RUNNERS AT FIRST AND SECOND BASE, OR THE BASES LOADED

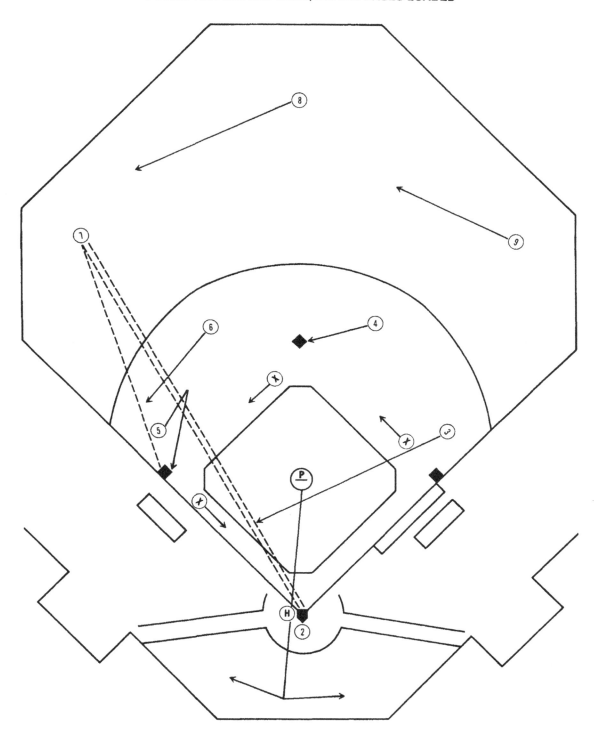

SINGLE TO RIGHT FIELD CAUSING THE FIRST BASEMAN TO DIVE FOR THE BALL. RUNNER AT SECOND BASE OR RUNNERS AT SECOND AND THIRD BASE.

PITCHER—Will break for an area behind home plate to back up the possible throw from the right fielder to the catcher.

CATCHER—Will be responsible for the plate, setting up for a possible throw from the right fielder. He will help the third baseman get into the proper cut-off position.

FIRST BASEMAN—If the base hit to right field causes him to leave his feet or his momentum takes him well away from getting to the proper cut-off position for the right fielder's possible throw to the plate, he will attempt to recover and cover first base. He will let the defense know if the batter-runner breaks for second base.

SECOND BASEMAN—Will be responsible for second base preparing for a possible throw to the base by the right fielder if he has no play at the plate. If the ball is thrown by the right fielder to the plate, he will prepare for a possible throw to second base from the catcher or third baseman.

THIRD BASEMAN—When he sees the base hit to right field and that the first baseman will be unable to get to the cut-off position for the right fielder's possible throw to the plate, he will immediately break for the cut-off position. The catcher will assist him in getting into the proper cut-off position. He will listen for the catcher for the possible cut-off throw to the plate or to second base.

SHORTSTOP—Once he reads the base hit to right field he will break for second base. When he sees that the second baseman will be able to recover to cover second base, he will break for third base to cover that base in case the batter-runner attempts to advance past second base. If he sees that the second baseman will not be able to recover, he will be responsible for second base preparing for a possible throw to that base by the right fielder.

LEFT FIELDER—As soon as he reads the base hit to right field, he will immediately break for an area behind third base to back up that base on any possible play that might develop where a throw is made to third base. Also in a position to back up the right fielder's throw to second base.

CENTER FIELDER—Backs up the right fielder. When the right fielder cleanly fields the ball, he will immediately break for an area behind second base to back up any throw made at that base by the third baseman or the catcher.

RIGHT FIELDER—Fields the ball so that he can make a possible play at the plate on the runner who started at second base. If he feels that he has a definite play on that runner, he will throw to the plate through the third baseman serving as the cut-off man. If there is no chance for a play at the plate, he will throw the ball to the second baseman at second base to prevent the batter-runner from advancing.

SINGLE TO RIGHT FIELD CAUSING THE FIRST BASEMAN TO DIVE FOR THE BALL.
RUNNER AT SECOND BASE OR RUNNER AT SECOND AND THIRD BASE

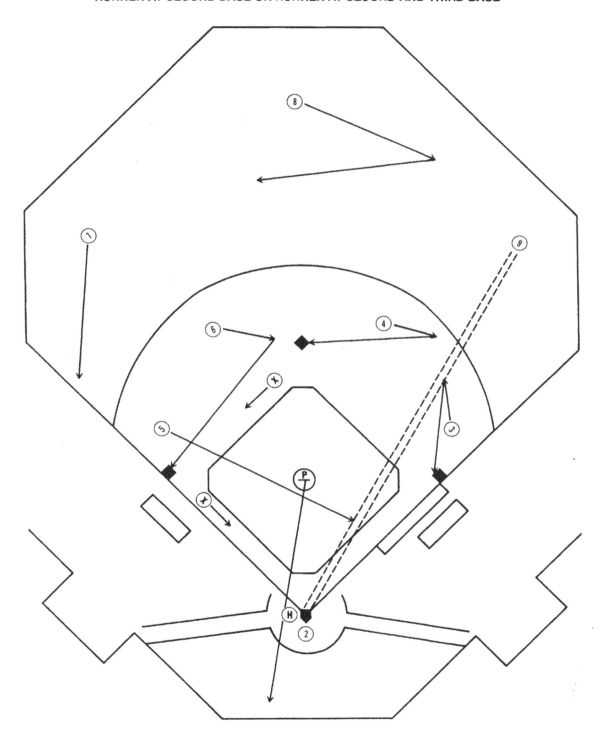

SINGLE TO RIGHT FIELD CAUSING THE FIRST BASEMAN TO DIVE FOR THE BALL. RUNNERS AT FIRST AND SECOND BASE OR THE BASES LOADED.

PITCHER—When he sees the base hit to right field and that the first baseman will be unable to get to the cut-off position for the right fielder's possible throw to the plate, he will immediately break for the cut-off position. The catcher will assist him in getting into the proper cut-off position. He will listen for the catcher for the possible cut-off throw to the plate, to third base, or to second base.

CATCHER—Will be responsible for the plate, setting up for a possible throw from the right fielder. He will help the pitcher get into the proper cut-off position.

FIRST BASEMAN—If the base hit to right field causes him to leave his feet or his momentum takes him well away from getting to the proper cut-off position for the right fielder's possible throw to the plate, he will attempt to recover and cover first base. He will let the defense know if the batter-runner breaks for second base.

SECOND BASEMAN—Will be responsible for second base, preparing for a possible throw to the base by the right fielder if he has no play at the plate or third base. If the ball is thrown by the right fielder to the plate or third base, he will prepare for a possible throw to second base by the catcher, pitcher, third baseman or shortstop. He will watch the runner touch second base.

THIRD BASEMAN—Will be responsible for third base along with watching the runner touch the base. If the right fielder has no play at the plate, he will prepare for a possible throw to third base. He will help the shortstop get into the proper cut-off position. If the ball is thrown to the plate, he will prepare for a possible throw to third base from the catcher or pitcher.

SHORTSTOP—Once he reads the base hit to right field he will immediately break for the cut-off position for the right fielder's possible throw to third base. The third baseman will assist him in getting into the proper cut-off position. He will listen for the third baseman for the possible cut-off to third base or to the second baseman at second base. If the right fielder throws the ball to second base, he will back up the throw.

LEFT FIELDER—As soon as he reads the base hit to right field, he will immediately break for an area behind third base to back up that base on the possible throw from the right fielder to third base. If he sees that the throw will be made to second base, he will move to a position to back up that throw.

CENTER FIELDER—Backs up the right fielder. When the right fielder cleanly fields the ball, he will immediately break for an area behind second base to back up any throw made at that base from the pitcher or catcher.

RIGHT FIELDER—Fields the ball so that he can make a possible play at the plate on the runner who started at second base. If he feels that he has a definite play on that runner he will throw to the plate through the pitcher serving as the cut-off man. He must be sure to keep the throw low since there will be no one backing up the plate. If he has no play at the plate he might have a play at third base on the runner who started at first base. In this case, he would throw to the third baseman through the shortstop serving as the cut-off man for the third baseman. If the runner from second base will score without a play and the runner from first base will make third base without a play, he will throw the ball immediately to the second baseman at second base.

SINGLE TO RIGHT FIELD CAUSING THE FIRST BASEMAN TO DIVE FOR THE BALL.
RUNNERS AT FIRST AND SECOND BASE OR THE BASES LOADED

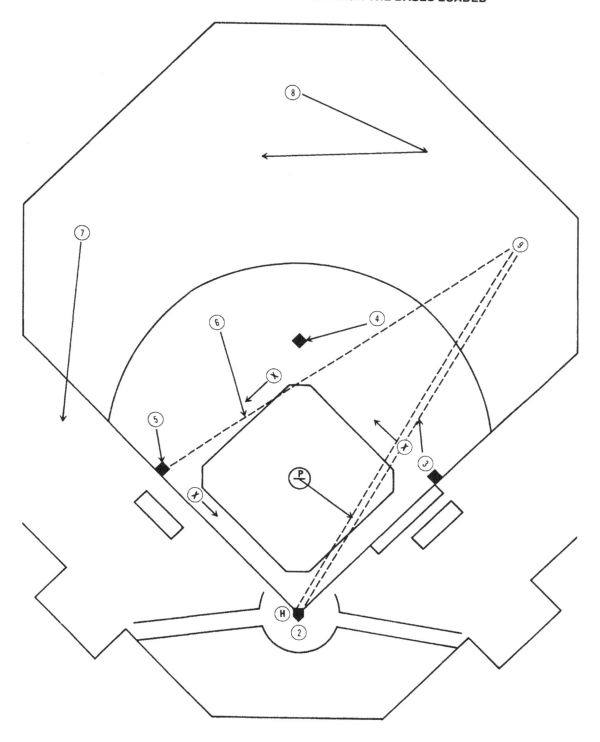

SURE DOUBLE DOWN THE LEFT FIELD LINE WITH NO RUNNERS ON BASE

PITCHER—Once he reads the extra base hit down the left field line he will break for an area behind third base to back up the base on a possible throw by the left fielder, shortstop or second baseman.

CATCHER—Once he reads the extra base hit down the left field line he will be in a position to help the pitcher back up the possible throw to third base. Will be responsible for the plate if a play develops there on the batter-runner.

FIRST BASEMAN—Will be responsible for watching the batter-runner touch first base. He will follow the runner down to second base being in a position at the base to field a possible throw from the shortstop, second baseman or third baseman.

SECOND BASEMAN—Once he reads the sure double down the left field line, he will be the back up man for the shortstop on the tandom relay. If there is any possible play on the batter-runner at second base, he will remain at second base positioning himself for a possible throw from the shortstop. In the tandom relay, he will be responsible to communicate with the shortstop as to where the ball is to be thrown, if at all.

SHORTSTOP—As soon as he reads the extra base hit down the left field line, he will become the front man on the tandom relay. He will be instructed by the second baseman as to where the ball is to be thrown, if at all. The play will either be to the third baseman at third base, to the first baseman at second base, or there will be no play at all where the shortstop will run the ball back to the infield area. The shortstop will set up at an angle away from the left field line so that the second baseman can get into the proper back up position on the tandom relay. If the distance to the left field fence is quite short, the shortstop will be the cut-off man for the left fielder's throw to third base. In this case, the second baseman will remain at second base.

THIRD BASEMAN—Will be responsible for third base communicating to the shortstop and second baseman if there is a possible play at third base or second base. The communication used by the third baseman and second baseman would be: "three-three" (throw to third base); "two-two" (throw to second base); "cut and hold" (no play at third base or second base— run the ball back to the infield area). The second baseman, who is the back man on the tandom relay, will have the final determination as to where the ball will be thrown, if at all.

LEFT FIELDER—Fields the ball down the left field line and throws to the shortstop, who is the front man on the tandom relay. If the distance to left field is quite short, he will throw the ball to third base through the shortstop serving as the cut-off man. This will also depend on the left fielder's arm strength.

CENTER FIELDER—As soon as he reads the extra base hit down the left field line, he will immediately break for a position behind second base to back up any possible throw from the third baseman to second base.

RIGHT FIELDER—As soon as he reads the extra base hit down the left field line, he will immediately break for a position behind second base to back up any possible throw from the shortstop or second baseman to the first baseman covering second base.

SURE DOUBLE DOWN THE LEFT FIELD LINE WITH NO RUNNERS ON BASE

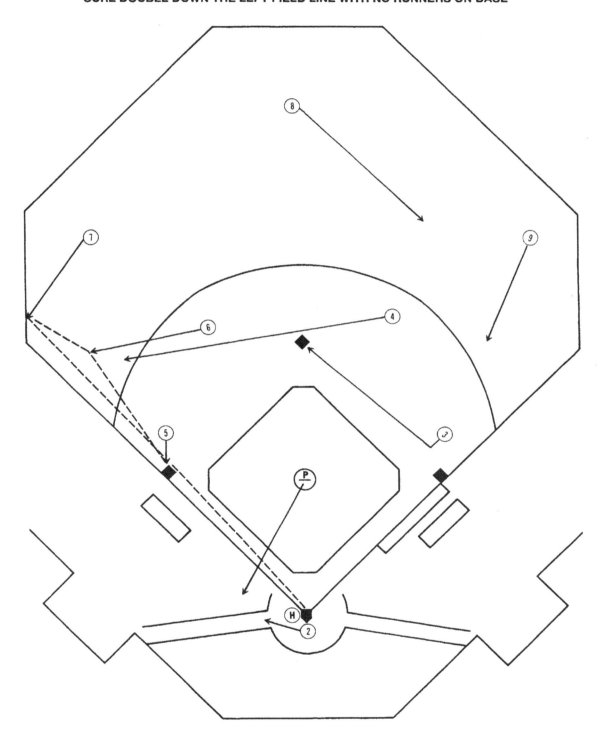

SURE DOUBLE DOWN THE RIGHT FIELD LINE WITH NO RUNNERS ON BASE

PITCHER—Once he reads the extra base hit down the right field line he will break for an area behind third base to back up the base on a possible throw by the second baseman or shortstop from the tandom relay.

CATCHER—Will be responsible for the plate if a play develops there on the batter-runner.

FIRST BASEMAN—Will be responsible for watching the batter-runner touch first base. He will follow the runner down to second base being in a position at the base to field a possible throw from the second baseman, shortstop, or third baseman.

SECOND BASEMAN—As soon as he reads the extra base hit down the right field line, he will become the front man on the tandom relay. He will be instructed by the shortstop as to where the ball is to be thrown, if at all. The play will either be to the third baseman at third base, to the first baseman at second base, or there will be no play at all where the second baseman will run the ball back to the infield area. The second baseman will set up at an angle away from the right field line so that the shortstop can get into proper back up position on the tandom relay.

SHORTSTOP—Once he reads the sure double down the right field line, he will be the back up man for the second baseman on the tandom relay. If there is any possible play on the batter-runner at second base, he will remain at second base positioning himself for a possible throw from the second baseman in cut-off position. In the tandom relay, he will be responsible to communicate with the second baseman as to where the ball is to be thrown, if at all.

THIRD BASEMAN—Will be responsible for third base communicating to the second baseman and shortstop if there is a possible play at third base. The communication used by the third baseman and shortstop would be: "three-three" (throw to third base); "two-two" (throw to second base); "cut and hold" (no play at third base or second base—run the ball back to the infield area). The shortstop, who is the back man on the tandom relay, will have the final determination as to where the ball will be thrown, if at all.

LEFT FIELDER—As soon as he reads the extra base hit down the right field line, he will immediately break for an area behind second base to back up that base on a possible throw by the second baseman or shortstop to the first baseman at second base.

CENTER FIELDER—As soon as he reads the extra base hit down the right field line, he will immediately break for a position behind second base to back up that base on a possible throw from the third baseman to the first baseman at second base.

RIGHT FIELDER—Fields the ball down the right field line and throws to the second baseman, who is the front man on the tandom relay.

SURE DOUBLE DOWN THE RIGHT FIELD LINE WITH NO RUNNERS ON BASE

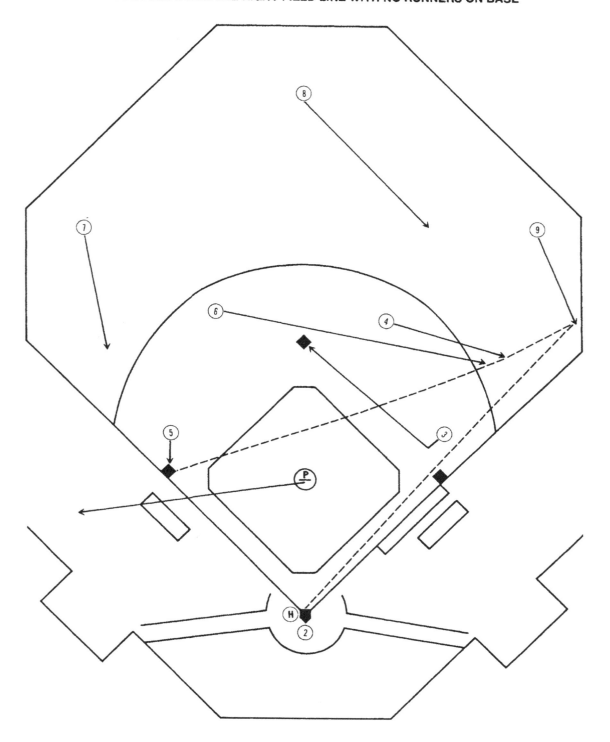

SURE DOUBLE DOWN THE LEFT FIELD LINE WITH A RUNNER AT FIRST BASE

PITCHER—Will break for an area behind home plate to back up a possible throw to either third base or the plate. He must get to the spot which would be an equal distance away from where he needs to be on each directional throw. Once the ball is released to either third base or the plate, he will break for the proper back up position.

CATCHER—Will be responsible for the plate, setting up for a possible play on the runner who started at first base. He will help the first baseman get into the proper cut-off position.

FIRST BASEMAN—When he sees the extra base hit down the left field line, he will break immediately for the cut-off position on a possible throw to the plate. The catcher will assist him in getting into the proper cut-off position. He will listen for the catcher for the possible cut-off throw to the plate, to third base or to second base.

SECOND BASEMAN—Once he reads the sure double down the left field line, he will be the back man for the shortstop on the tandom relay. In the tandom relay, he will be responsible to communicate with the shortstop as to where the ball is to be thrown, if at all.

SHORTSTOP—As soon as he reads the extra base hit down the left field line, he will become the front man on the tandom relay. He will be instructed by the second baseman as to where the ball is to be thrown, if at all. The play will either be to the third baseman at third base, to the right fielder at second base, to the catcher at the plate through the first baseman serving as the cut-off man, or no play at all where the shortstop will run the ball back to the infield area. The shortstop will set up at an angle away from the left field line so that the second baseman can get into the proper back up position on the tandom relay.

THIRD BASEMAN—Will be responsible for third base communicating to the shortstop and second baseman if there is a possible play at third base, to the plate, to second base, or no play on any runner. The communication used by the third baseman and second baseman would be: "four-four" (throw to the plate); "three-three" (throw to third base); "two-two" (throw to second base); "cut and hold" (no play on any runner—run the ball back to the infield area). The second baseman, who is the back man on the tandom relay, will have the final determination as to where the ball will be thrown, if at all.

LEFT FIELDER—Fields the ball down the left field line and throws to the shortstop, who is the front man on the tandom relay. As soon as he releases the ball, he will break for a position behind third base to back up the possible throw from the first baseman to the third baseman at third base.

CENTER FIELDER—As soon as he reads the extra base hit down the left field line, he will immediately break for a position behind second base to back up any possible throw from the third baseman to the right fielder at second base. Also backs up the possible throw by the first baseman to the right fielder at second base.

RIGHT FIELDER—As soon as he reads the extra base hit down the left field line, he will immediately break for second base. He will cover that base for a possible throw from the tandom relay players, the third baseman, the first baseman, or the catcher. If the throw comes from the shortstop or second baseman, he must be sure to knock the ball down since there will be no one backing up the play from that angle. He will watch the runner touch second base.

SURE DOUBLE DOWN THE LEFT FIELD LINE WITH A RUNNER AT FIRST BASE

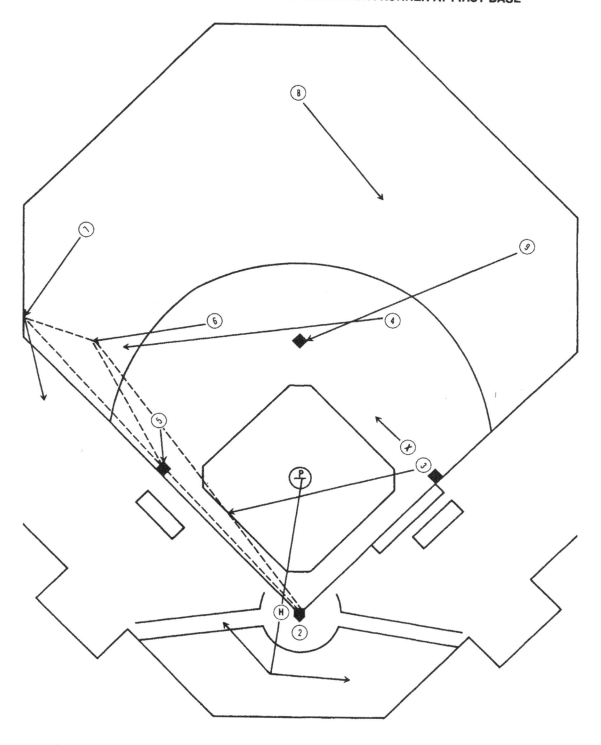

SURE DOUBLE TO LEFT CENTER FIELD WITH A RUNNER AT FIRST BASE

PITCHER—Will break for an area behind home plate to back up a possible throw to either third base or the plate. He must get to the spot which would be an equal distance away from where he needs to be on each directional throw. Once the ball is released to either third base or the plate, he will break for the proper back up position.

CATCHER—Will be responsible for the plate, setting up for a possible play on the runner who started at first base. He will help the first baseman get into the proper cut-off position.

FIRST BASEMAN—When he sees the extra base hit to left center field, he will break immediately for the cut-off position on a possible throw to the plate. The catcher will assist him in getting into the proper cut-off position. He will listen for the catcher for the possible cut-off throw to the plate, to third base or to second base. If he throws to the right fielder covering second base, he must be sure to throw accurately for there will be no one backing up the throw.

SECOND BASEMAN—Once he reads the sure extra base hit to left center field, he will be the back man for the shortstop on the tandom relay. In the tandom relay, he will be responsible to communicate with the shortstop as to where the ball is to be thrown, if at all.

SHORTSTOP—As soon as he reads the extra base hit to left center field, he will become the front man on the tandom relay. He will be instructed by the second baseman as to where the ball is to be thrown, if at all. The play will either be to the third baseman at third base, to the right fielder at second base, to the catcher at the plate through the first baseman serving as the cut-off man, or no play at all where the shortstop will run the ball back to the infield area. If the throw is made to the right fielder at second base, he must be sure to throw accurately for there will be no one backing up the throw.

THIRD BASEMAN—Will be responsible for third base communicating to the shortstop and second baseman if there is a possible play at third base, to the plate, to second base, or no play on any runner. The communication used by the third baseman and second baseman would be: "four-four" (throw to the plate); "three-three" (throw to third base); "two-two" (throw to second base); "cut and hold" (no play on any runner—run the ball back to the infield area). The second baseman, who is the back man on the tandom relay, will have the final determination as to where the ball will be thrown, if at all. Will watch the runner touch third base.

LEFT FIELDER—If he fields the ball, he will throw the ball to the shortstop serving as the front man on the tandom relay.

CENTER FIELDER—If he fields the ball, he will throw the ball to the shortstop serving as the front man on the tandom relay.

RIGHT FIELDER—As soon as he reads the extra base hit to left center field, he will immediately break for second base. He will cover that base for a possible throw from the tandom relay players, the third baseman, the first baseman, or the catcher. On any throw to second base, he must be sure to knock the ball down since there will be no one in a position to back up the throw. Will watch the runner who started at first base touch second base.

SURE DOUBLE TO LEFT CENTER FIELD WITH A RUNNER AT FIRST BASE

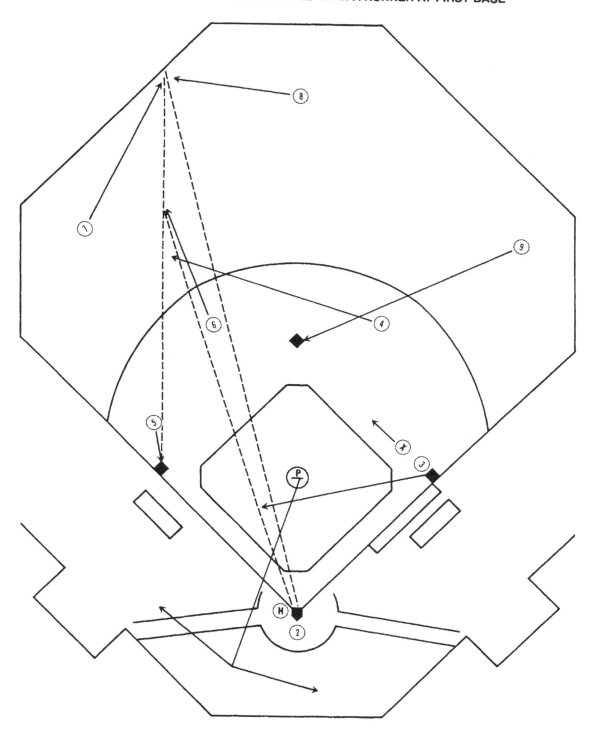

SURE DOUBLE TO RIGHT CENTER FIELD WITH A RUNNER AT FIRST BASE

PITCHER—Will break for an area behind home plate to back up a possible throw to either third base or the plate. He must get to the spot which would be an equal distance away from where he needs to be on each directional throw. Once the ball is released to either third base or the plate, he will break for the proper back up position.

CATCHER—Will be responsible for the plate, setting up for a possible play on the runner who started at first base. He will help the first baseman get into the proper cut-off position.

FIRST BASEMAN—When he sees the extra base hit to right center field, he will break immediately for the cut-off position on a possible throw to the plate. The catcher will assist him in getting into the proper cut-off position. He will listen for the catcher for the possible cut-off throw to the plate, or to third base.

SECOND BASEMAN—As soon as he reads the extra base hit to right center field, he will become the front man on the tandom relay. He will be instructed by the shortstop as to where the ball is to be thrown, if at all. The play will either be to the third baseman at third base, to the catcher at the plate through the first baseman serving as the cut-off man, or no play at all where the second baseman will run the ball back to the infield area.

SHORTSTOP—Once he reads the sure extra base hit to right center field, he will be the back man for the second baseman on the tandom relay. In the tandom relay, he will be responsible to communicate with the second baseman as to where the ball is to be thrown. As soon as the ball is thrown to either third base or the plate, he will break for second base to keep the batter-runner from taking a wide turn at that base.

THIRD BASEMAN—Will be responsible for third base communicating to the second baseman and shortstop if there is a possible play at third base, to the plate, or no play on any runner. The communication used by the third baseman and shortstop would be: "four-four" (throw to the plate); "three-three"(throw to third base); "cut and hold" (no play on any runner—run the ball back to the infield area). The shortstop, who is the back man on the tandom relay will have the final determination as to where the ball will be thrown, if at all. He will watch the runner who started at first base touch both second and third base.

LEFT FIELDER—As soon as he reads the extra base hit to right center field, he will immediately break for a position behind third base to back up that base on a possible throw from the first baseman.

CENTER FIELDER—If he fields the ball, he will throw the ball to the second baseman serving as the front man on the tandom relay.

RIGHT FIELDER—If he fields the ball, he will throw the ball to the second baseman serving as the front man on the tandom relay.

SURE DOUBLE TO RIGHT CENTER FIELD WITH A RUNNER AT FIRST BASE

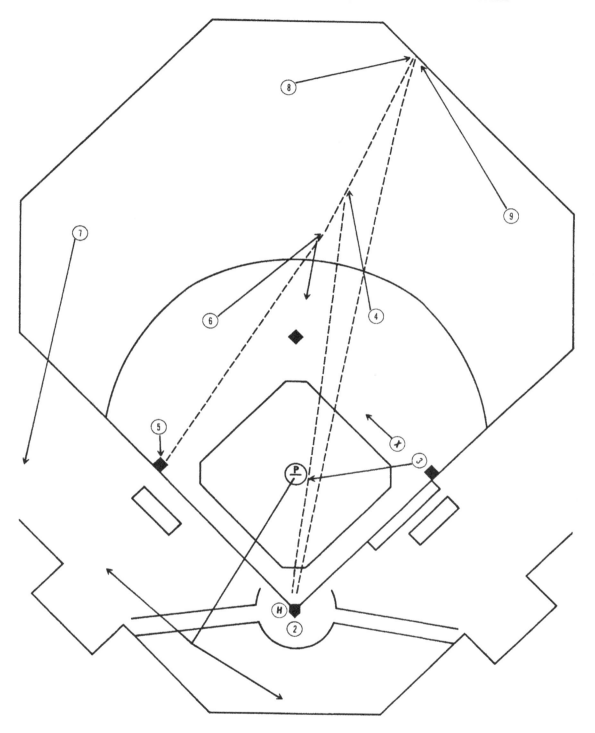

SURE DOUBLE DOWN THE RIGHT FIELD LINE WITH A RUNNER AT FIRST BASE

PITCHER—Will break for an area behind home plate to back up a possible throw to the plate.

CATCHER—Will be responsible for the plate, setting up for a possible play on the runner who started at first base. He will help the first baseman get into the proper cut-off position.

FIRST BASEMAN—When he sees the extra base hit down the right field line, he will break immediately for the cut-off position on a possible throw to the plate. The catcher will assist him in getting into the proper cut-off position. He will listen for the catcher for the possible cut-off throw to the plate, to third base or to second base.

SECOND BASEMAN—As soon as he reads the extra base hit down the right field line, he will become the front man on the tandom relay. He will be instructed by the shortstop as to where the ball is to be thrown, if at all. The play will either be to the third baseman at third base, to the center fielder at second base, to the catcher at the plate through the first baseman serving as the cut-off man, or no play at all where the second baseman will run the ball back to the infield area. If he throws the ball to the center fielder at second base, he must be sure to throw accurately since there will be no one in the back up position. The second baseman will set up at an angle away from the right field line so that the shortstop can get into the proper back up position on the tandom relay.

SHORTSTOP—Once he reads the sure double down the right field line, he will be the back up man for the second baseman on the tandom relay. In the tandom relay, he will be responsible to communicate with the second baseman as to where the ball is to be thrown.

THIRD BASEMAN—Will be responsible for third base communicating to the second baseman and shortstop if there is a possible play at third base, to the plate, to second base, or no play on any runner. The communication used by the third baseman and shortstop would be: "four-four" (throw to the plate); "three-three" (throw to third base); "two-two" (throw to second base); "cut and hold" (no play on any runner—run the ball back to the infield area). The shortstop, who is the back man on the tandom relay will have the final determination as to where the ball will be thrown, if at all. He will watch the runner who started at first base touch third base.

LEFT FIELDER—As soon as he reads the extra base hit down the right field line, he will break for an area behind third base to back up that base on any play made by the tandom relay players. If the throw is made to the plate he will move into back up position behind third base for any throw made to that base by the first baseman or the catcher.

CENTER FIELDER—As soon as he reads the extra base hit down the right field line, he will break for second base to cover that base to prevent the batter-runner from taking a wide turn. Will set up at the base for a possible throw from any of the defensive players. Will watch the runner who started at first base touch second base.

RIGHT FIELDER—Fields the ball down the right field line and throws to the second baseman, who is the front man on the tandom relay.

186

SURE DOUBLE DOWN THE RIGHT FIELD LINE WITH A RUNNER AT FIRST BASE

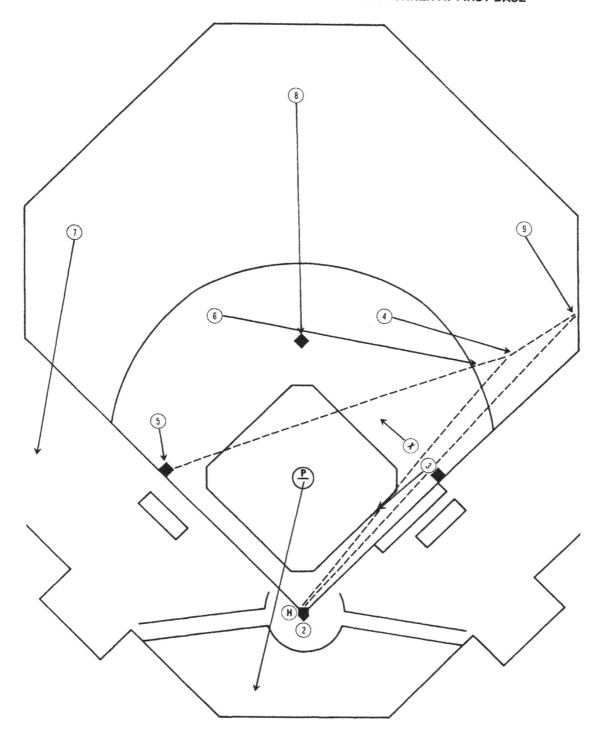

POP FLY BALL BETWEEN HOME PLATE AND FIRST BASE IN FOUL TERRITORY. RUNNERS ON FIRST AND THIRD BASE

PITCHER—Will be responsible for covering home plate preparing for a possible play at the plate on the runner tagging up at third base.

CATCHER—Will attempt to field the fly ball. Upon catching the ball, he will check the runner at third base. If the runner is breaking for the plate, he will throw the ball to the pitcher covering home plate. If the runner at third base is not breaking for the plate, but the runner at first base is breaking for second base, he will immediately throw the ball to the second baseman in cut-off position. If neither runner attempts to advance, he will run the ball back to the plate area.

FIRST BASEMAN—Same responsibility as the catcher. He has priority over the catcher on the fly ball. Will break for first base after the ball is thrown to either the pitcher or second baseman.

SECOND BASEMAN—As soon as he reads the pop fly ball between home plate and first base in foul territory, he will immediately break to the cut-off position between the fielder of the fly ball and the shortstop at second base. If the ball is thrown to him by the catcher or first baseman, he will check the runner at third base. If that runner is breaking for the plate, he will throw the ball to the pitcher covering home plate. If the runner at third base is not breaking for the plate, but the runner from first base is breaking for second base, he will throw the ball to the shortstop covering second base.

SHORTSTOP—Will be responsible for second base preparing for a throw from the second baseman in cut-off position if the runner from first base is breaking for second base.

THIRD BASEMAN—Will be responsible for third base communicating to the defense if the runner at third base tags up and breaks for the plate. If so, he will yell "four-four".

LEFT FIELDER—Will back up any possible throw made to third base.

CENTER FIELDER—Will back up any possible throw made to second base.

RIGHT FIELDER—Will back up first base. Will cover first base if the first baseman is not able to get there.

**POP FLY BALL BETWEEN HOME PLATE AND FIRST BASE IN FOUL TERRITORY.
RUNNERS ON FIRST AND THIRD BASE**

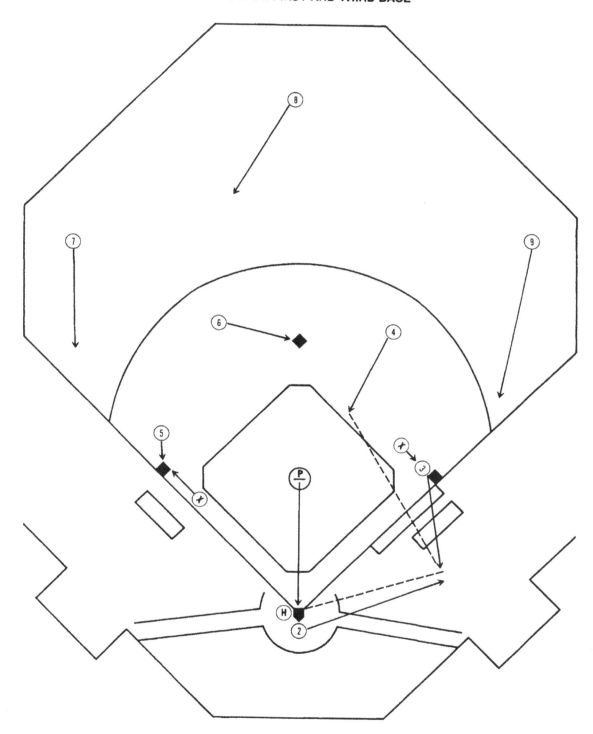

POP FLY BALL BETWEEN HOME PLATE AND THIRD BASE IN FOUL TERRITORY. RUNNERS ON FIRST AND THIRD BASE

PITCHER—Will be responsible for covering home plate preparing for a possible play at the plate on the runner tagging up at third base.

CATCHER—Will attempt to field the fly ball. Upon catching the ball, he will check the runner at third base. If the runner is breaking for the plate, he will throw the ball to the pitcher covering home plate. If the runner at third base is not breaking for the plate, but the runner at first base is breaking for second base, he will immediately throw the ball to the shortstop in cut-off position. If neither runner attempts to advance, he will run the ball back to the plate area.

FIRST BASEMAN—Will be responsible for first base. If there are two outs he will trail the runner down to second base.

SECOND BASEMAN—Will be responsible for second base preparing for a throw from the shortstop in cut-off position if the runner from first base is breaking for second base.

SHORTSTOP—As soon as he reads the pop fly ball between home plate and third base in foul territory, he will immediately break to the cut-off position between the fielder of the fly ball and the second baseman at second base. If the ball is thrown to him by the catcher or third baseman, he will check the runner at third base. If that runner is breaking for the plate, he will throw the ball to the pitcher covering home plate. If the runner at third base is not breaking for the plate, but the runner from first base is breaking for second base, he will throw the ball to the second baseman covering second base.

THIRD BASEMAN—Same responsibility as the catcher. He has priority over the catcher on the fly ball. Will break for third base after the ball is thrown to either the pitcher or the shortstop.

LEFT FIELDER—Will back up any possible throw made to third base.

CENTER FIELDER—Will back up any possible throw made to second base.

RIGHT FIELDER—Will back up any possible throw made to first base.

POP FLY BALL BETWEEN HOME PLATE AND THIRD BASE IN FOUL TERRITORY. RUNNERS ON FIRST AND THIRD BASE

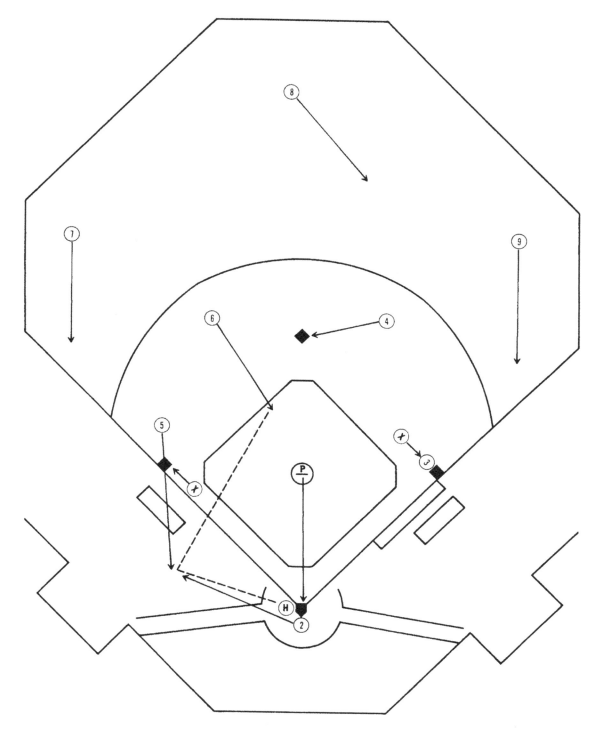

POP FLY BALL BEHIND FIRST BASE WITH RUNNERS ON FIRST AND THIRD BASE

PITCHER—Will move to a position on the first base side of the mound preparing for a throw from the fielder who catches the fly ball. If he receives that ball from the fielder, he will check the runner at third base. If that runner is breaking toward the plate, he will throw the ball to the catcher at home plate. If the runner at third base is not breaking toward the plate, but the runner from first base is continuing onto second base, he will throw the ball to the shortstop at second base.

CATCHER—Will be responsible for the plate preparing for a possible play if the runner from third base breaks for the plate.

FIRST BASEMAN—Will attempt to field the fly ball behind first base. Upon catching the ball, he will check the runner at third base. If he is breaking for the plate, he will throw the ball to the catcher at home plate. If the runner at third base is not breaking for the plate, he will check the runner at first base. If there are two outs, and the runner is breaking for second base, he will throw the ball to the shortstop at second base. If there are less than two outs, and the runner breaks for second base, he will throw the ball to the pitcher in the cut-off position. If neither runner is breaking for the forward base, he can either run the ball back into the infield, or he can throw the ball to the pitcher in cut-off position. He will break for first base after the ball is thrown by the fielder of the fly ball.

SECOND BASEMAN—Same responsibility as the first baseman with the exception that he will break for second base after the ball has been thrown by the fielder of the fly ball. He has priority over the first baseman on the fly ball.

SHORTSTOP—Will be responsible for second base preparing for a possible throw from the fielder of the fly ball or from the pitcher in cut-off position.

THIRD BASEMAN—Will be responsible for third base communicating to the defense if the runner at third base tags up and breaks for the plate. If so, he will yell "four-four".

LEFT FIELDER—Will back up any possible throw made to third base after backing up the throw to second base by the fielder of the fly ball.

CENTER FIELDER—Will back up any possible throw made to second base.

RIGHT FIELDER—Same responsibility as the first baseman and second baseman with the exception that he will back up first base for any possible play at that base after the ball has been thrown by the fielder of the fly ball. Has priority over both the first baseman and second baseman on the fly ball.

POP FLY BALL BEHIND FIRST BASE WITH RUNNERS ON FIRST AND THIRD BASE

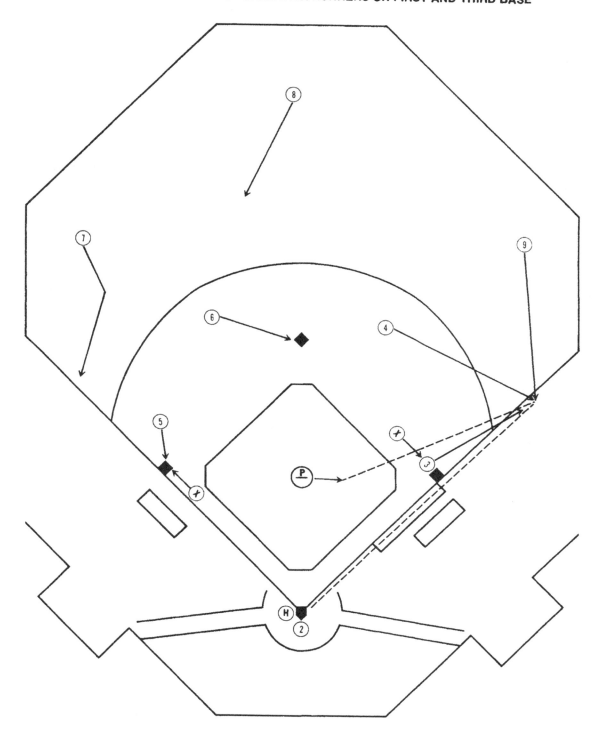

POP FLY BALL BEHIND THIRD BASE WITH RUNNERS ON FIRST AND THIRD BASE

PITCHER—Will move to a position on the third base side of the mound preparing for a throw from the fielder who catches the fly ball. If he receives the ball from the fielder, he will check the runner at third base. If that runner is breaking toward home plate, he will throw the ball to the catcher at home plate. If the runner at third base is not breaking toward the plate, but the runner from first base is continuing onto second base, he will throw the ball to the second baseman covering second base.

CATCHER—Will be responsible for the plate preparing for a possible play if the runner from third base breaks for the plate.

FIRST BASEMAN—Will be responsible for first base. If the runner at first base breaks for second base with two outs, he will follow the runner down to second base preparing for a possible throw from the second baseman if the runner stops prior to reaching the base.

SECOND BASEMAN—Will be responsible for second base preparing for a possible throw from the fielder of the fly ball or from the pitcher in cut-off position. If there are two outs and he receives the ball, he will throw the ball to the first baseman trailing the runner if the runner stops prior to reaching second base.

SHORTSTOP—Will attempt to field the fly ball behind third base. Upon catching the ball, he will check the runner at third base. If he is breaking for the plate, he will throw the ball to the catcher at home plate. If the runner at third base is not breaking for the plate, he will check the runner at first base. If there are two outs, and the runner is breaking for second base, he will throw the ball to the second baseman at second base. If there are less than two outs, and the runner breaks for second base, he will throw the ball to the pitcher in the cut-off position. If neither runner is breaking for the forward base, he can either run the ball back into the infield, or he can throw the ball to the pitcher in cut-off position. He will break for second base after the ball has been thrown by the fielder of the fly ball. He has priority over the third baseman on the fly ball.

THIRD BASEMAN—Same responsibility as the shortstop with the exception that he will break for third base after the ball has been thrown by the fielder of the fly ball.

LEFT FIELDER—Same responsibility as the shortstop and third baseman with the exception that he will back up third base for any possible play at that base after the ball has been thrown by the fielder of the fly ball. Has priority over the shortstop and third baseman on the fly ball.

CENTER FIELDER—Will back up any possible throw made to second base.

RIGHT FIELDER—Will back up any possible play made to first base after backing up the throw to second base from the fielder of the fly ball.

POP FLY BALL BEHIND THIRD BASE WITH RUNNERS ON FIRST AND THIRD BASE

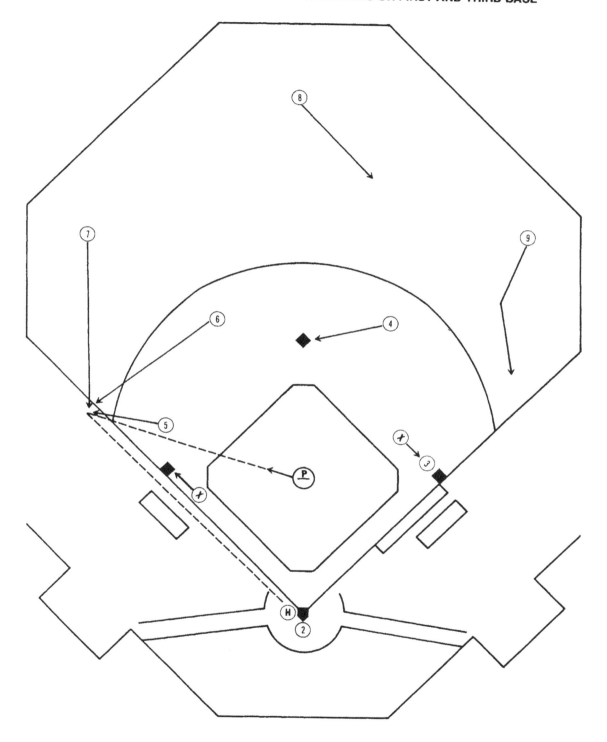

195

PASS BALL OR WILD PITCH WITH RUNNERS AT SECOND AND THIRD BASE, FIRST AND SECOND BASE, OR THE BASES LOADED

PITCHER—Will break for the plate preparing for a throw from the catcher on a runner attempting to score.

CATCHER—Will retrieve the ball to the backstop and throw to the pitcher if a runner is attempting to score.

FIRST BASEMAN—Once he reads the pass ball or wild pitch, he will break toward the mound to help the shortstop back up the catcher's throw to the pitcher at home plate.

SECOND BASEMAN—Will be responsible for second base.

SHORTSTOP—Once he reads the pass ball or wild pitch, he will break toward the mound to help the first baseman back up the catcher's throw to the pitcher at home plate.

THIRD BASEMAN—Will be responsible for third base.

LEFT FIELDER—Will back up third base for any possible play at that base.

CENTER FIELDER—Will back up second base for any possible play at that base.

RIGHT FIELDER—Will assist the center fielder in backing up second base on any possible play made at that base.

If the pass ball or wild pitch were to deflect off the catcher to the first base or third base side of the plate, then the infielders would assume the following responsibilities.

Ball goes to the third base side:

Catcher and **third baseman** retrieve the ball and throw to the **pitcher** covering home plate. **First baseman** backs up the throw from the catcher or third baseman to the pitcher at the plate. Will back up the throw from foul territory in line with the throw to the plate. **Second baseman** covers second base. **Shortstop** covers third base.

Ball goes to the first base side:

Catcher and **first baseman** retrieve the ball and throw to the **pitcher** covering home plate. **Third baseman** backs up the throw from the catcher or third baseman to the pitcher at the plate. Will back up the throw from foul territory in line with the throw to the plate. **Second baseman** covers second base. **Shortstop** covers third base.

**PASS BALL OR WILD PITCH WITH RUNNERS AT SECOND AND THIRD BASE,
FIRST AND SECOND BASE, OR THE BASES LOADED**

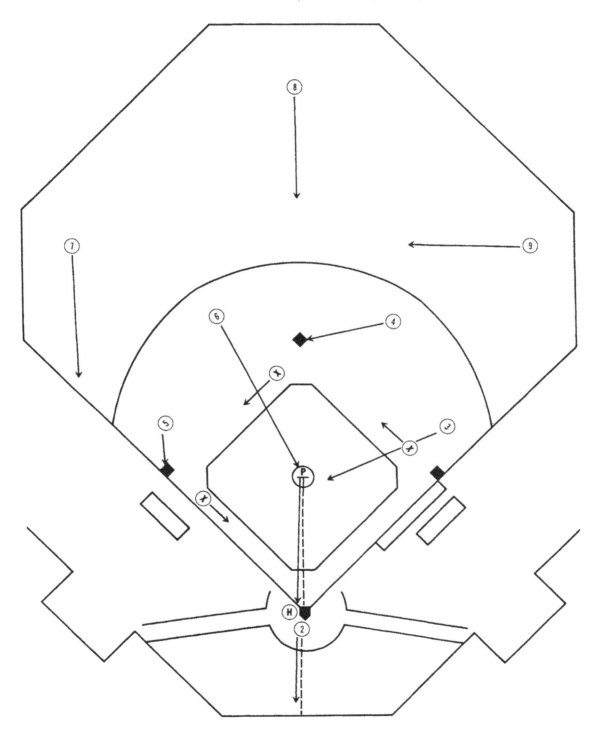

BALL FOUR OR STRIKE THREE TO THE BATTER WITH THE BALL GETTING BY THE CATCHER. RUNNERS AT SECOND AND THIRD BASE OR A RUNNER AT SECOND BASE

PITCHER—Will break for the plate preparing for a possible throw from the catcher if the runner rounding third base attempts to score. He will listen for the third baseman to let him know if the runner is breaking for the plate. If the catcher throws the ball to the shortstop in cut-off position on the mound, the pitcher will prepare for a possible throw from the shortstop to the plate if the runner at third base attempts to score.

CATCHER—Will retrieve the ball to the backstop. If the runner who started at second base attempts to score, he will throw the ball to the pitcher covering home plate. If he is not attempting to score, he will throw the ball to the shortstop in cut-off position on the mound. He will back up any return throw to the pitcher at the plate.

FIRST BASEMAN—Will watch the batter-runner touch first base. He will let the defense know if the runner is breaking for second base by yelling "two-two". If the batter-runner breaks for second base with two outs, he will follow him down to second base preparing for a possible throw from the second baseman if the runner stops prior to reaching second base. With less than two outs he will stay near first base preparing for a possible rundown play on the runner.

SECOND BASEMAN—Will be responsible for second base, preparing for a possible throw from the shortstop from his cut-off position on the mound. If he receives the ball from the shortstop with two outs, he will throw the ball to the trailing first baseman if the runner stops prior to reaching second base. With less than two outs, he will get the runner in a rundown between first and second base listening for the third baseman to let him know if the runner from third base breaks for the plate.

SHORTSTOP—Once he reads the ball getting by the catcher, he will break toward the mound to prepare for a possible throw by the catcher. If the catcher throws the ball to him on the mound, he will check the runner at third base. If the runner is breaking for the plate, he will throw the ball to the pitcher covering home plate. If the runner at third base is not advancing toward the plate, he will check the batter-runner. If he is advancing toward second base, he will throw the ball to the second baseman at second base, and then follow his throw to second base. If the runner is stopped between first and second base, he will run at the runner listening for the third baseman to let him know if the runner at third base is breaking for the plate. If the ball rolls to the first base or third base side of the plate, he will position himself so that he is in a direct line with the catcher and second base.

THIRD BASEMAN—Will be responsible for third base. He will let the defense know if the runner at third base is breaking for the plate by yelling "four-four"

LEFT FIELDER—Will back up any possible throw made by a defensive player to third base.

CENTER FIELDER—Will back up any possible throw made by a defensive player to second base.

RIGHT FIELDER—Will be responsible for covering first base if the first baseman is involved in a rundown on the batter-runner between first and second base.

BALL FOUR OR STRIKE THREE TO THE BATTER WITH THE BALL GETTING BY THE CATCHER. RUNNERS AT SECOND AND THIRD BASE OR A RUNNER AT SECOND BASE

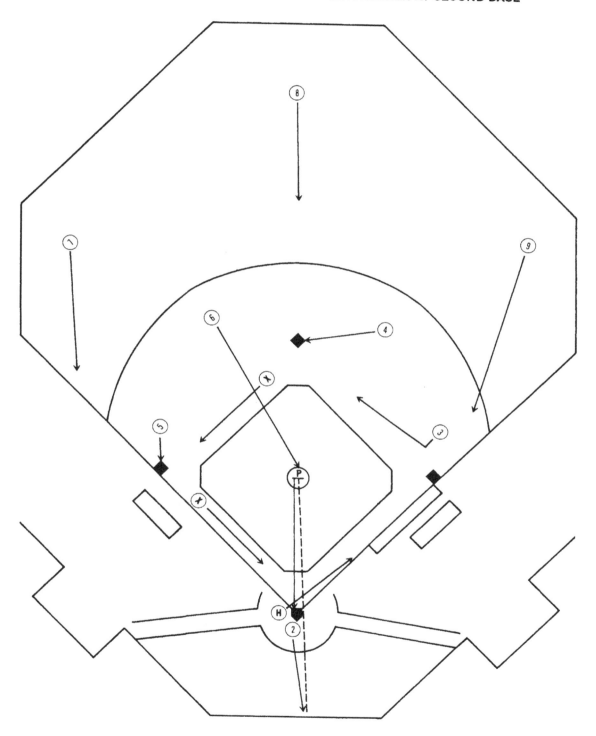

PICK-OFF PLAYS

There is probably no play in baseball that can change the momentum of a game more than a successful pick-off play on a runner. Vice-versa, an unsuccessful pick-off play where the ball is thrown away can change the momentum of the game in the favor of the offense.

This is the reason why it behooves a coach to develop a sound pick-off system so that the defense can keep the baserunners on the offensive team honest. It is important that the coach stress to his team that a pick-off play is successful even if there is no out made on the runner. The primary area of concern is for the defense to be able to control the baserunner's movement while the pitcher is in the set position, or when the catcher has received the ball on the pitch.

It is not practical for a team to have a large number of pick-off plays, for the larger the number of plays the more chance for poor execution and confusion. By establishing a simple sign and execution system the coaching staff can build a great deal of confidence in the team's ability to execute a sound pick-off play.

It is also very important that the players have the ability and confidence to put on a pick-off play without having to wait for the coach in the dugout to signal for a play. However, there should be a system established whereby the coach in the dugout can call a pick-off play if he desires.

In practice sessions, the coaching staff must prepare the defense to read when a pick-off play is in order. The signal system and execution techniques must be drilled to the point that the recognition of the pick-off play is apparent to all concerned. The fundamental drill series as already detailed in the Playbook, provides the opportunity for a team to work on all the pick-off plays on a daily basis.

The primary area of concern is the status of the runner at a respective base. By observing his primary and secondary lead techniques, the defense should be able to read what pick-off play might be most advantageous. A baserunner who takes a non-aggressive primary or secondary lead should not be bothered by the defense. It is best to save a pick-off play for that time when the chance of success is at the maximum level. Some baserunners will take very large primary leads, and then for some reason, take a very small secondary lead. Other runners take small primary leads, but then make a special effort to get a very large secondary lead on the catcher. The inexperienced aggressive baserunner is the type that is very susceptible to a pick-off.

The accuracy of the pick-off throw must be stressed as the team executes the pick-off plays in their fundamental drill work. Accuracy must be stressed more than the quickness of release and the velocity of the throw. As a player concentrates and works on his accuracy he can begin to develop his quickness of release and velocity. It certainly serves no purpose for a catcher or pitcher to rush a pick-off throw with great velocity only to find that the ball is thrown away and all runners advancing.

The target for all pick-off throws should be from the knees to the waist of the player receiving the throw. By concentrating between these two areas of the body, there can be a margin of error both with a high or low throw. If the pitcher or catcher attempts to throw to the ankle area of the receiver, any throw below that point could result in a ball getting by the fielder. A low throw also leads to the problem of the fielder trying to field the ball as the runner slides back into the base at the same level the ball is arriving at the base. Once a pitcher or catcher finds that he can throw accurately on his pick-off throws he can begin to place the ball on the side of the base that the runner is sliding.

The development of quickness and accuracy on pick-off throws should come about through technique work and constant practice. A coach will find that he will have some pitchers and catchers that can greatly improve their pick-off capabilities. He will find others who will have a difficult time mastering the proper technique. Hopefully, a coach can develop in his pitchers and catchers a respectable degree of confidence in their pick-off mechanics. A complete discussion of pick-off techniques for pitchers and catchers can be found in the Playbook in the pitching and catching section.

On the following pages, we will present some of the more popular pick-off plays used in baseball today.

SIGNAL SYSTEM

Whatever signal system is used by a team in their pick-off plays it must be one that is easily observed by the defensive players involved. At the same time, they must be the type of sign(s) that would not easily be picked up by the base coaches or the runner that the play will be made on. A complicated signal system might serve the purpose of keeping the sign a secret from the offensive team, but it might also cause confusion in the minds of the defensive players involved.

The only way players on defense will properly respond to a pick-off sign is when they have seen the sign flashed on numerous occasions. This is why it is important that when executing any pick-offs in the fundamental drill series, signs are used just as they would be in a regular game. The players on defense must develop a sound habit of anticipating pick-offs so when the sign is flashed by another player they can respond in the proper manner. There is nothing any more frustrating to a baseball coach than to have an infielder breaking toward a base anticipating a throw, only to find that the pitcher or catcher is not executing the play because the pick-off sign was missed.

The coach in the dugout must have the capability to flash a pick-off sign to a defensive player or to the entire team in the field. This is especially true when the pick-off play would be a part of a bunt defense play. When the bunt defense play sign is given from the dugout, the coach can indicate by sign if he wishes the defense to execute a pick-off play off the bunt defense. For example, if the sign for the early break bunt defense with runners at first and second base is for the coach to flash a clenched fist, then when he wipes his hand across his chest after the clenched fist, the pick-off play is on at second base off the early break bunt defense. Examples of pick-off plays off the bunt defense plays are detailed in an earlier section of the Playbook.

When the coach flashes a pick-off sign to an infielder or a catcher, the player receiving the sign will need to flash the sign to the other player involved, unless it is in conjunction with a bunt defense play. On bunt defense plays, all the defensive players will be looking at the coach in the dugout when the sign is flashed.

A coach should allow and encourage his players on defense to put on a pick-off play whenever he feels the situation warrants the attempt. It is not very practical to have the pitcher flash the sign to an infielder. However, if he is off the pitching rubber and he feels it is imperative to attempt a pick-off play, then he can flash the sign to an infielder. The pitcher must receive the sign back from the infielder in order for the play to be put into effect.

There are numerous ways that a signal can be flashed from an infielder to a pitcher for a pick-off attempt. Some examples of signs that could be used would be:

1. Wipe down the glove side leg with the glove.

2. Wipe down the free hand leg with the free hand.

3. From the hands on knee position, flexing the knees.

4. From the hands on knee position, standing up straight and then going back down to the hands on knee.

5. Jab step toward the base and then back to hands on knee position.

The sign must be obvious to the pitcher, but at the same time it can not be obvious to the base coaches. In most cases, the runner leading off a base will not be in a position to look at a fielder when he flashes the sign. However a base coach is not only in a position to pick up the sign but he can warn the runner if a sign is flashed. Anytime it is obvious that a pick-off sign has been noted by a base coach it can easily be changed when the defense comes back into the dugout.

If the infielder wants to give the sign to the pitcher when he is off the pitching rubber, he can do so by flashing the same sign he would flash to the pitcher when he is in the set position. If the sign is given to the pitcher off the rubber, the pitcher must flash a return sign back to the infielder. If he does not do so, the pick-off play is not on.

Infielders should never flash pick-off signs to the pitchers when they are on the rubber until their hands have come down to the set position on the stretch delivery. In this way, the infielders are assured that the pitchers have full concentration on the infielders. If the sign is flashed while a pitcher's hands are going into the set position, he may not be looking at the infielder while the sign is being flashed.

If the pitcher sees a pick-off sign flashed and he decides that he does not want to throw the pick-off, he should step off the rubber with his pivot foot. This would take the pick-off play off for the next pitch. It can be tried again the next time the pitcher comes to the set position. Anytime a pitcher steps off the rubber from the set position, he should do so with a quick motion of his pivot foot in hopes that it might cause the runner to break toward the next base.

All pick-off plays at first base with a righthanded pitcher must be flashed while the pitcher is off the rubber. This is due to the fact that the pitcher would be unable to see a sign flashed by the first baseman from the set position. The same holds true for the lefthanded pitcher with a runner leading off third base since it would be practically impossible for him to be able to see the third baseman. With a righthanded pitcher at the set position, it is often more difficult for him to see the second baseman flash a pick-off sign. With a lefthanded pitcher in this situation, the shortstop flashing a pick-off sign might be difficult to observe from the mound. This does not mean that these infielders can not call for the pick-off play at second base, but they need to understand that the sign flashed must be very clear to the pitcher in the set position.

Verbalizing pick-off signs can be used in certain situations, but it must be the type of verbal communication that the pitcher can easily hear and comprehend. It is wise to only have one or two verbal type pick-off plays for they are generally only effective one time in a game or series.

Signaling pick-off plays from an infielder to the catcher, or vice-versa, is a little more difficult than the signals from an infielder to a pitcher. The reason being that there is a greater distance involved between the two players responsible for the pick-off sign. This is why these pick-off signs need to be a little easier to pick up. A catcher who wishes to attempt a pick-off play on the next pitch with an infielder, must flash the sign, and the sign must be acknowledged by the infielder with a sign of his own. If no acknowledgement sign is flashed from the infielder back to the catcher, the play is not on. An infielder who flashes the pick-off sign to the catcher must also receive the acknowledgement sign from the catcher or the play is not on.

Some examples of the type of signals that can be used by the catcher and an infielder would be:

1. The catcher grabs his face mask as he looks at the infielder. The infielder tips the bill of his cap while looking at the catcher.

2. The catcher toes the dirt area in front of the plate. The infielder wipes his free hand across the chest area.

3. The catcher kicks his shin guard with the spikes. The infielder wipes down his leg with his glove.

It is very easy for the third baseman and the first baseman to know that the catcher is looking at him while he is flashing the pick-off sign. It is not so easy for the second baseman or the shortstop since it is sometimes difficult to determine the direction the catcher is looking. Because of this, the catcher must be sure he looks a little to the shortstop's right and to the second baseman's left when flashing the pick-off sign.

PICK-OFF PLAYS AT FIRST BASE FROM THE PITCHER

The basic pick-off play at first base with the first baseman holding the runner on base requires no signs being flashed. From the set position the pitcher must check the baserunner's primary lead. He must know the capability of the runner and his possible intentions in regard to a steal attempt. The primary concern as to whether he will throw over to the first baseman, is the nature of the runner's primary lead. He also will take into consideration the weight distribution of the runner and whether or not he is attempting to take a walking lead off first base. He does not have to show his best pick-off move unless he feels that he has an excellent chance to throw the runner out on the pick-off attempt.

When the first baseman is playing behind the runner at first base it allows for a timed pick-off play on the runner. Anytime the first baseman is going to play behind the runner at first base he must be sure to let the pitcher know before he gets onto the rubber. If he is on the pitching rubber, and he has not told him that he is playing behind the runner, he will remain at the base until after the pitch is made. Anytime there is a runner at second base he does not have to inform the pitcher that he is playing behind the runner.

If the first baseman observes that the runner at first base is taking an aggressive quick secondary lead on the pitch, he can put on a pick-off play when he is behind the runner. This is especially true with a lefthanded pitcher on the mound when the runner begins his secondary lead when the pitcher's lead leg comes up to deliver to the plate. With a 3-2 count on the batter and there are two outs, the runner will be breaking toward second base on the pitch to the plate. This is an excellent time to work a pick-off play at first base.

Once the signs have been flashed by both the first baseman and the pitcher, or by just the first baseman if the pitcher is toeing the rubber, the pick-off play is on unless the first baseman yells "step off" to the pitcher. This is the communication used by all infielders to the pitcher when a pick-off play is on and the infielder decides to take the play off. This is generally done when the runner leading off the base has adjusted his lead to the point that there will be no chance to pick him off.

202

With a righthanded pitcher on the mound, a pick-off play with the first baseman behind the runner must be put on before the pitcher gets on the rubber to get his sign from the catcher. With a lefthanded pitcher, the pick-off play can be signaled when the pitcher reaches the set position on the stretch.

Once the play has been signaled the following timing is involved on the pick-off. With a righthanded pitcher on the mound, he will pick up the first baseman out of the corner of his eye looking over his left shoulder. When the first baseman breaks for first base, the pitcher will throw to the base. If there is a runner at second base, the pitcher will look as though he is looking at the runner at second base. Out of the corner of his eye looking over his right shoulder he will watch the first baseman. When the first baseman breaks for first base he will throw to the base. It might seem very difficult for the pitcher to see the first baseman over his right shoulder, but with proper practice he can do so without letting the runner at first base know that he is watching the first baseman.

With a lefthanded pitcher on the mound, the first baseman will break full speed for first base when the pitcher lifts his lead leg as if to throw to the plate. The pitcher will then throw to first base using his best pick-off move.

With a righthanded pitcher on the mound, the defense can easily take advantage of a runner leading off first and third base with the 3-2 count, two out situation in effect with the runner from first base advancing toward second base on the pitch. The pitcher will come to the set position on the stretch. He will pick up his lead leg as if to deliver the ball to the plate. He will then step toward third base while faking the pick-off throw to third base, and then turn and check the runner at first base. Many times the runner at first base will take off for second base when the pitcher looks like he is delivering the ball to the plate only to find that the pitcher has just faked the throw to third base. The pitcher will then find that he has a play on the runner between first and second base.

Pick-off plays off the bunt defense plays at first base were discussed earlier in the Playbook in the bunt defense section.

PICK-OFF PLAYS AT SECOND BASE FROM THE PITCHER

There are numerous timed pick-off plays possible between the pitcher and the shortstop or second baseman at second base. We will discuss some of the more prominent ones used in the game today. In all these plays we are assuming that the signal for the pick-off has been flashed.

1. From the set position, the pitcher will check the runner leading off second base. When the pitcher turns his head toward the plate, the shortstop or second baseman (whichever player has signaled for the pick-off) will break full speed for second base. The pitcher will control his movement to second base on the pick-off by two factors: (1) how far the infielder is away from second base; and (2) how quick the infielder is who is covering the base. He will want to time his throw to second base so that the infielder covering the base can catch the ball under control and is set for the tag. On all timed pick-off plays we would rather have the ball arrive a little late to the infielder rather than a little early. If the pitcher's throw to the base is a little early, the defense chances having a ball get by the infielder allowing the runner to advance. It also causes problems when an infielder has to field the ball from the pitcher while moving into the tag position at the base. Thus, in this pick-off play the pitcher must control the timing involved to take into consideration the speed of the infielder and the distance he is way from the base. Another controlling aspect involved in the pitcher's pick-off on a timed play is his own quickness on the pick-off. This is why it is so important in all these timed pick-off plays that they are worked in practice with all the infielders so the pitching staff becomes familiar with the speed of the fielder to the base.

2. In this play the catcher will signal the pitcher when to throw the ball to second base on the pick-off play. The pitcher checks the runner at second base and then looks to the catcher. When the catcher drops his glove down from his regular target position, the pitcher will turn and throw the ball to either the shortstop or second baseman involved in the play. The shortstop or second baseman should break for the base when the pitcher has looked at the catcher for at least one full second. The catcher will drop his glove at the time he feels that the pitcher's throw will arrive at the base to be received by the infielder under control. Thus, if the infielder is close to the base he will drop his glove as soon as the infielder breaks for second base. If the infielder is a long way from the base, the catcher will wait to drop his glove until the infielder has started for the base a couple of steps.

3. The next type of pick-off play is a combination play involving both the shortstop and second baseman. When the pitcher comes to the set position in the stretch delivery he will check the runner at second base. The second baseman will then take two hard steps toward second base, and then stop. When the second baseman takes his first step back toward his regular position, the shortstop will break full speed for second base. The pitcher will turn and throw to second base when the

203

shortstop breaks for second base. The shortstop must set up close enough to second base to be able to get there in time to properly field the throw. This play can also be run with the shortstop faking toward the base and the second baseman covering on the pick-off attempt. Whichever infielder flashes the pick-off sign to the pitcher will be the fielder of the pick-off throw, and the other infielder will provide the fake on the runner.

4. One of the best pick-off plays at second base is the daylight play with the shortstop and pitcher involved. When the pitcher comes to the set position in the stretch delivery he will check the runner at second base. The shortstop will break full speed for the base if he feels that they have a good chance to retire the runner. When the pitcher sees daylight between the shortstop and the baserunner he will turn and throw the ball to second base. The shortstop must be sure that he does not ever break for second base full speed and then stop, unless he does not come close to breaking daylight between the pitcher and the runner at second base, This is the best pick-off play to run when the shortstop does not want to flash a pick-off sign to the pitcher, but he feels as though he has a good chance to pick the runner off base.

5. The inside pick-off play at second base is an excellent play to use when the runner at second base is found to be taking an aggressive quick secondary lead when the pitcher picks up his lead leg to deliver to the plate. The shortstop or second baseman (whichever one that flashes the sign) will break full speed for second base when the pitcher lifts up his lead leg from the set position. The pitcher will lift the lead leg up and come to his regular balance position. When he reaches the balance point, he will pivot on the rubber and throw the ball to the infielder covering second base in one continuous motion. A great time to put on the inside pick-off play is when there is a 3-2 count, two out situation with a runner at first base. The runner at second base will be breaking for third base when he thinks that the pitcher will be delivering the ball to the plate.

6. When the pitcher is throwing from the windup an excellent pick-off play can be attempted on the runner at second base. The pitcher will be on the pitching rubber looking as though he is receiving the sign from the catcher. After giving the sign for the pitch, the catcher will put his glove up to the target position. The shortstop will break full speed for second base a brief second after the catcher gives the target to the pitcher. The catcher will drop his glove down when he sees the shortstop break for second base. When the pitcher sees the catcher's glove drop, he will pivot and throw the ball to the shortstop covering the bag. Again, the catcher must allow for the distance the shortstop must cover in reaching second base.

Pick-off plays off the bunt defense plays at second base were discussed earlier in the Playbook in the bunt defense section.

PICK-OFF PLAYS AT THIRD BASE FROM THE PITCHER

The pitcher and third baseman must be very careful in attempting pick-off plays at third base. This is due to the fact that an errant throw will just about always result in the runner from third base scoring. As in all pick-off plays, it is important that the throw arrive late to the fielder rather than too early. This is even more important at third base.

If the third baseman observes that the runner at third base is taking a much too big primary lead, he can put on the pick-off play when the pitcher is in the set position. With a lefthanded pitcher on the mound, the third baseman must give the sign to the pitcher before he gets on the pitching rubber. With a righthanded pitcher on the mound, it can be put on before he gets on the pitching rubber or when the pitcher comes to the set position on the stretch delivery.

With a righthanded pitcher, the third baseman would break full speed to third base when the pitcher lifts up his lead leg as if to deliver the ball to the plate. The pitcher will then throw to third base using his best pick-off move making sure that he steps in the direction of the base.

With a lefthanded pitcher on the mound, he will pick up the third baseman out of the corner of his eye looking over his left shoulder if there is a runner at second base. With no runner at second base he will pick up the third baseman looking over his right shoulder. If there is a runner at second base, the pitcher will look as though he is checking the runner's lead at second base. Out of the corner of his eye he will pick up the third baseman so that when the infielder breaks for third base, the pitcher will turn and throw the ball to the base. With no runner at second base, the pitcher will also pivot and throw the pick-off when the third baseman breaks for the base as he sees the third baseman over his right shoulder.

The outfielders need to know all the pick-off signs so that they can break for their proper back up position when the pitcher throws to a base in an attempt to retire a runner. If an outfielder does not pick up the sign he must be alert for the possibility of a pick-off at anytime, and be breaking for the back up position whenever he observes the pitcher making an attempt at a base. This will also hold true for any pick-off play made by the catcher to an infielder.

204

PICK-OFF PLAYS FROM THE CATCHER TO THE INFIELDERS

The key as to whether or not a pick-off play should be attempted from the catcher to an infielder depends on the type of secondary lead that a runner is taking at a base. The secondary lead is the lead a runner has when the catcher receives the pitch. Each runner will have a different secondary lead, not only in regard to the distance he is away from a base, but in his weight distribution.

The quickness and baserunning skills of a runner will dictate how far he is able to get away from a base in both his primary and secondary lead. What is a good lead for one runner might be a poor lead for another runner. The catcher and the infielders need to determine whether a pick-off play is possible on a runner taking into consideration all the factors involved. If it is determined by both parties involved that a pick-off play should be attempted, the sign is flashed by one of them and then acknowledged by the other.

There are numerous factors involved other than just the distance of the secondary lead. A runner who has his weight leaning toward the forward base when the catcher receives the pitch, will have a very difficult time quickly returning to the base on a pick-off attempt. This especially is so if the runner's left foot lands in front of his right foot when the catcher receives the ball.

When a righthanded batter is at the plate, it makes for a more difficult pick-off throw on a runner leading off third base. With a lefthanded batter, the catcher will have a more difficult throw to first base. This does not mean that a pick-off can not be attempted in these situations but the catcher must be sure that he properly clears the batter when he is throwing to a base. Many times a baserunner is screened by the batter and does not see the catcher rise up to throw until it is too late to get back to the base.

The catchers need to understand that even though a pick-off sign has been flashed, they do not have to throw to the base. If the pitch received is one that makes it difficult to throw quickly and accurately to a base, then no throw should be made. Also, if the runner has made a quick recovery from his secondary lead, the catcher should not throw the ball. There must be a play on the runner before a pick-off throw is made.

It is also important that the catcher place a premium on accuracy on his throw anytime he is throwing to any base with a runner at third base. Too many baseball games are lost by an aggressive catcher attempting a pick-off play on a runner only to find the ball going into the outfield and a runner scoring from third base.

A team should never attempt a pick-off play at a base when there are two outs with a weak hitter at the plate who is behind in the count. Of course, if a runner takes a very large secondary lead and there is a great chance for an out to be made, a pick-off attempt could be made.

The catcher's arm must be taken into consideration in determining whether a pick-off attempt should be made. If a team has a catcher with a strong accurate arm they can attempt pick-off plays whenever a runner is taking advantage of the defense by taking an aggressive secondary lead. If the catcher's arm is weak and inaccurate the pick-off attempts should be kept to a minimum and only attempted whenever a runner can be easily picked off at a base. The defense must keep all runners honest in their secondary leads even if the catcher's arm is suspect.

There are four basic types of pick-off plays from the catcher to an infielder. Three of these plays would require the use of signs.

1. **Pick-off play on the next pitch received by the catcher**—Once the sign is flashed by the parties involved, the next pitch received by the catcher will be thrown to the base if there is a chance to retire the runner. This is an excellent pick-off to use on a runner who is observed taking a large secondary lead or one who is a potential steal threat. The infielder will break full speed for the base once the ball passes the batter. The infielder must position himself so that he is at the base ahead of the throw so that he is not fielding the ball on the run. The catcher will throw to the base if a play can be made on the runner.

2. **Pick-off play on the next pitch that the batter either swings and misses or attempts to bunt and misses**—Once the sign is flashed by the parties involved, the next pitch that the batter misses on a swing or bunt attempt will be thrown to the base if there is a chance to retire the runner. This is an excellent pick-off play to use on a runner who takes an extra step or leans toward the next base on his secondary lead whenever the batter swings or bunts at a pitch. It is also a good play when the batter is faced with a 3-2 count and there are less than two outs. Baserunners have a tendency to be overly aggressive in

this situation hoping that the batter will make contact if he starts his bat forward. In bunt situations this play will be perfect on a bunt and miss attempt by the batter. It takes an excellent baserunner to not take an extra step forward or lean in the direction of the forward base when the bunt sign has been flashed and the bat is positioned for a bunt attempt. Another time this play will work is when there is a runner at third base with the infield playing in on the grass with less than two outs. In this situation the runner at third base will be attempting to get a super jump on the batted ball to prevent being thrown out at the plate on a ground ball.

3. **Pick-off play on a pitchout**—If the infielder flashes a pick-off sign for the ball to be thrown on the next pitch, the catcher will have the right to call for a pitchout if the situation warrants it. This would be practical if the count is in the favor of the pitcher and there is a good hitter at the plate. The catcher does not want the hitter to have a chance of putting the ball in play and advancing the runner he wishes to possibly pick-off base. It also enables the catcher to have a better chance of clearing the batter on his pick-off attempt. The infielder should be able to read the pitchout sign which will allow him to get a better jump for the base, since he does not have to worry about a ball being hit by the batter.

4. **Pick-off play with no sign flashed**—The catcher should have the right to attempt a pick-off even though no sign has been flashed by an infielder. Anytime an infielder breaks for a base full speed after the ball has passed the hitter, the catcher can throw to the base. This is why an infielder can never break full speed for a base after the pitch and then stop short of the base. He must always go all the way to the base allowing the catcher the opportunity to make a throw if he feels as though a play can be made on the runner. Even if the catcher decides not to throw, it will make the runner a little more defensive in his next secondary lead if it looks like the defense is thinking about a pick-off play.

As mentioned previously, a team should not have too many pick-off plays in their playbook for it could lead to much confusion and poor timing. The team that perfects a couple of excellent pick-off plays at each base will keep the baserunners on the other club under control.

RULES FOR FORCE PLAYS IN THE INFIELD

Every baseball coach wants to establish various rules for his infielders and pitchers in regard to force play situations on ground balls. Even if general rules are discussed, the coach will still have to rely on the baseball instinct of the player fielding the ground ball. There are many variables involved when an infielder or pitcher must make the decision as to whether or not to go for the lead runner, go for the double play, or make the sure out on the batter-runner. These variables include: speed of the ball; angle of the ball to the fielder; directional momentum of the fielder; speed of the runner(s); score; outs; and inning.

There are some basic rules that the defense can follow in regard to these variables so that they are in a better position to make the proper play. The first rule is that they anticipate the ground ball before it is hit by the batter. Prior to the pitch, a fielder must review in his mind where he will go with a ground ball hit very hard (6 type ground ball); a ground ball hit with average velocity (5 type ground ball); or a ground ball hit quite slowly (4 type ground ball). Any indecision on the fielder's part could cost the defense a potential double play, or an out on the lead runner. Any major indecision on the fielder's part could mean that no out is made on any runner, including the batter-runner.

In a previous section of the Playbook, the production rating system is discussed whereby each ground ball is graded in regard to the speed of the ball off the bat. This system is very helpful in assisting infielders and pitchers on where the best play might be made on a ground ball when he has some options available to him. In practice sessions, the coach can hit various types of ground balls to the infielders and pitchers, and assist them in grading each ball (4, 5 or 6), so that they become familiar with the best options available in regard to the speed of the ball.

A general rule that is very helpful to the defense is that early in the game, outs must be made at the expense of gambling for an out on the lead runner. Early in the game is generally from the first inning through the sixth inning of a nine inning game. In a seven inning game, early in the game would be from the first through the fourth inning. Late in the game, the infielders and pitchers must give primary consideration to the runner at third base, especially if he is the tying or winning run in the last inning of the game.

Anytime the defense can make the double play early in the game, it should be attempted even if the runner at third base will score. Of course, if the double play can be started with the force out at the plate, then this is the best direction to go. Late in the game with an important run at third base, the double play via second base can be made only if the runner at third base is not able to cross the plate while the double play is being completed.

An infielder should never make an off-balance throw to a base or the plate unless it is the only way to make a play. This is especially true for the first baseman and third baseman who field ground balls on the second base side of the diamond and have a decision as to whether to throw to second base, or try to make the play at the plate. If the runner at third base is a very important run late in the game, then the play should be made at the plate. Otherwise, the play should be made at second base. Many times, the old baseball saying that you make the play "wherever the ball takes you" holds true.

On the following pages we will detail some rules to follow in regard to a fielder's options when there is a runner at third base. In practice sessions, various situations can be set up by the coach so that the defense has a chance to simulate game situations that might arise. By placing runners on the bases and having them run full speed, it will allow the defense ample opportunities to test their reactions. Prior to hitting various types of ground balls to the infielders and the pitcher on the mound, the coach needs to inform the defense as to what depth they will be playing, how many outs there are, the score of the game and the inning.

1. **Bases loaded with less than two outs—early innings.** The defense wants to get the double play the best way they can, especially with one out. With no outs they can gamble a little more on the double play via home plate. Again, the defense is looking for outs and when a double play type ground ball is hit, the defense needs to make the twin killing early in the game. Generally, the infield will not be playing in on the grass early in the ball game. Because of this, the double play via the pivot man at second base is generally the easiest route to go. Any ball hit to the second base side of the first baseman or the third baseman needs to go to second base. The same holds true for any ball hit to the second base side of the shortstop or second baseman. If the ball is hit to the first base side of the first baseman and he is close enough to touch first base, he should do so. From that point, he needs to decide which play can be made easier. Whatever direction he goes, to the plate or to second base he needs to communicate to the fielder that he must tag the runner by yelling out "tag". The same holds true for a ball hit to the third base side of the third baseman. Since the runner going to the plate might obstruct his view of the catcher, he might have an easier play at first base. Much will depend on where the runner heading for the plate is when the third baseman

makes the out at third base. The pitcher should always go the home plate route on any ground ball hit back to the mound unless the ball takes him well off the mound and he will have a very difficult throw to make to the plate. If that be the case, then he should make the play closest to where he fields the ball.

2. **Bases loaded with less than two outs—late innings.** In this case, the importance of the runner at third base will be of great importance as to where the throw will be made. If the runner at third base is an important run late in the game, the infield should be in on the grass. If the defensive team is ahead and the runner at third base is not the tying or winning run, the infield should be in double play depth. Anytime the defense is behind in the score in the later innings of the game, they will just about always have to play in on the grass to prevent the runner from third base from scoring. Anytime a coach can keep from playing the infield in on the grass he should do so. By playing the infield in, it gives the hitter the distinct advantage of hitting a ground ball past the infielders. If the infield is playing in on the grass, all ground balls fielded must be thrown to the plate in hopes that a double play might be made via the catcher to the first baseman. If no double play is possible, then they can at least get the force out at the plate. If the infield is in double play depth, the infielders will read the nature of the ground ball that they field and make the play accordingly. Anytime there is one out and a ground ball is fielded with a good chance for the double play via the pivot man at second base, it should be attempted. Again, the importance of the runner at third base must be considered. If the infield is in on the grass and the ball is hit to the first baseman or third baseman to the second base side of the diamond, they must give the pivot man at second base a chance to get back to the bag for the force out. A double play in this situation is generally not feasible so the play at the plate might be the best bet if the fielder can get a good throw off to the catcher. The pitcher will always throw to the plate on the ground ball back to him in this situation unless his momentum carries him well away from the mound and away from the plate.

3. **Runners at first and third base with less than two outs—early innings.** In almost all cases, in the early innings of a game the infield would be positioned in double play depth. As in the bases loaded situation, the defense will want to make the double play via the second base route even if it means that the runner from third base scores. If the defense is concerned about the runner at third base due to the nature of the game, they can play in shallow double play depth or play the corners in (third baseman and first baseman) and the middle (shortstop and second baseman) at regular double play depth. With one out, the infield would generally play a little shallower in their double play depth, so that they can have a better chance at completing the double play negating the runner at third base from scoring. The pitcher should always go the second base route for the double play type ground ball. If it is not a double play type ground ball, he can look the runner back to third base and go to either second base or first base for the out. Anytime the defense can keep the runner from first base off second base via the force out, it should be attempted. Again, in the early innings the defense must get an out, so this is not the time to gamble on a runner.

4. **Runners at first and third base with less than two outs—late innings.** The infield would need to play in on the grass if the runner at third base is an important run late in the game. This is especially true when there is one out. With no outs, the runner at third base will generally not break for the plate until the ground ball gets through the infield, so the infielders could play a few steps off the grass. Anytime the runner at third base is the tying or winning run late in the game, every ground ball fielded must be thrown to the plate if the runner is attempting to score. If the runner at third base is not breaking for the plate, then the pitcher or the infielder who fields the ball must get an out somewhere after checking the runner at third base. If the infield is playing in on the grass and the runner at third base does not break for the plate, the force out at second base should be made if possible. Again, the defense needs to be aware of the fact that the shortstop or second baseman will have a very difficult time covering second base for the force play. If so, the out should be made on the batter-runner at first base. If there is one out, the defense could play their corners in (third baseman and first baseman) and the middle (shortstop and second baseman) in double play depth. Since the first baseman will have to hold the runner on first base, he is already in the proper position when the pitch is made to the plate. By playing the defense in this manner, it will provide the opportunity to get the inning ending double play via the second base route. Again, the importance of the runner at third base must always be taken into consideration. If a 5 or 6 type ground ball is hit right at an infielder or the pitcher with one out, they should be able to get the double play ending the inning. With no outs, a ground ball of this type fielded would be played in accordance with the importance of the runner at third base. The defense would not want to complete the double play only to have the tying or winning run score. If the defense started the double play at second base with no outs, and the pivot man at second base saw that the runner at third base broke late for the plate, he can throw the ball to the catcher at home plate. The third baseman can yell "four-four", if the runner broke after the double play was started.

The signals that the coach in the dugout can use to control the depth of his infielders can be found in the signal section of the Playbook.

RULES FOR CUT-OFF PLAYS

Many baseball games are decided by the ability or inability of a team to properly execute the basic cut-off play. This is why it is very important that the baseball coach spend a considerable amount of time going over the rules for cut-off plays, and practicing their execution. In a previous section of the Playbook, the positioning of the infielders in regard to where they must be in relation to the ball and the baserunners was detailed and discussed.

Not only do the cut-off men need to be in the proper position on the field, but they need to be very much aware of the mechanics of the play itself. This not only pertains to the cut-off man, but also the player who is throwing the ball to a base or the plate in his attempt to retire a baserunner.

The cut-off play is initiated by an outfielder or a member of the tandom relay (shortstop or second baseman). The decision as to where to throw the ball will rest primarily with the person throwing the ball, even though he will receive some communication from other fielders as to where the best play might be made. We are again calling on baseball instinct to assist a fielder in making the final determination as to where the ball should be thrown if there are options available to him. Once the decision has been made as to where the ball will be thrown, it then boils down to the fielder's arm strength and accuracy.

There are some basic rules that the baseball coach can provide his players in regard to where the best throw might be made in a given situation. As the infielders must prepare themselves mentally for a ground ball to be hit to them, the outfielder must play the same game. This is to prevent him from having to think of the various options available to him while he is moving to the ball. One second of indecision will mean a few steps that the baserunner is closer to his destination. When there are some options available to the player fielding the ball in the outfield, the following criteria needs to be evaluated.

1. **Velocity of the ball hit**—We can again fall back on the production rating for grading the velocity of the ball hit to a fielder in helping him make his decision. If a 6 type ball is hit right at the outfielder, he would generally always have a play on the lead runner. The lead runner being either the runner who started at second base with a play at the plate; or the runner who started at first base with a play at third base. Of course, if the runner was stealing on the pitch, or he was moving on a 3-2 count two out situation, then this would not hold true to form. If a 5 type ball is hit right at the outfielder, then it is possible that a play can be made on the lead runner taking into consideration other criteria that will be discussed later. If it is a 4 type ball, there is generally no play on the lead runner even if the ball is hit right at the outfielder.

2. **Angle of the ball fielded**—A 6 type ground ball might not allow the outfielder the opportunity to make a play on the lead runner, if the fielder has to run at an extreme angle away from the base or the plate where the play on the lead runner would be made. Thus, the angle that the fielder must go in order to field the ball will be a major factor in his decision on where the play is to be made.

3. **Fielding the ball on the glove side or the throwing side**—If the fielder is able to cut the ball down at a good angle on his throwing side, he might have a play on the lead runner. If his angle of pursuit forces him to field the ball on his glove side, then his chances of being able to pivot and throw in time to retire the lead runner would be minimized.

4. **Depth the ball is fielded in the outfield**—Of course, the shallower an outfielder can play the better his chances of making a play on the lead runner at third base or the plate. His ability to charge the ground ball to shorten the throw to the base or the plate is a major consideration as to where the throw would be made.

5. **Condition of the ball**—The condition of the ball fielded would be a concern, especially on those days when the grass is wet and the fielder must concern himself with a long throw with a wet baseball.

6. **Arm strength and accuracy**—There is probably no greater consideration then the fielder's ability to throw the ball with great velocity and accuracy. A 6 type ground ball right at an outfielder with a weak arm still might not allow him the opportunity to retire a runner at third base or the plate. Vice-versa, a 5 type ground ball to an outfielder with a strong accurate arm could result in a play on the lead runner. Again, much would depend on the outfielder's depth and angle when the ball is fielded.

7. **Baserunner's speed**—Another major factor is the speed of the runner who the outfielder would attempt to retire at third base or the plate. Along with the baserunner's speed would be the jump he gets away from the base when the ball is hit. An outfielder should always know the general running speed of all the runners on base at the time of the pitch.

209

8. **Score**—The score of the game will dictate many times whether a play should be made on the lead runner, or a better play would be made to second base to keep the batter-runner from getting into scoring position, and also keep the double play in order. It would be foolish for an outfielder to make an attempt on a runner at the plate, when the tying run late in the game is represented by the batter-runner. If the chances of getting the out at the plate are excellent, then the throw should be made. If there is only an average chance to get the runner, then the play should be made to second base. This also holds true for plays being made at third base on the runner who started at first base. As a general rule, when the defense is two or more runs ahead, an outfielder or the throwing member of the tandom relay, should gamble on the lead runner if there is a legitimate chance of success. The same would hold true generally if the defense is behind in the score by two or more runs. Of course, if the lead runner is the tying or winning run late in the game, the defense has got to gamble on that runner in his attempt to score or get to third base.

9. **Inning of the game**—Early in the game a team can not afford to make a play on the lead runner unless the chance for success is high. By keeping the batter-runner off second base, especially with less than two outs, it provides the defense with the opportunity to get the double play with the next batter. Late in the game, the importance of the lead runner has got to take precedence over any other consideration. Early in the game, the defense is always looking for any chance to get an out to eliminate the big inning.

10. **Number of outs**—When there are two outs, the defense can afford to gamble a little more on the lead runner then when there are less than two outs. The offense will generally gamble more by sending a runner to the plate from second base with two outs, but will be very cautious of sending a runner to third base. If the attempt on the lead runner with two outs at the plate is unsuccessful, then the batter-runner will probably end up at second base. This however, will not give the offense many opportunities to score that runner. With no outs or one out, keeping the runner off second base provides the defense with a double play potential with the next batter coming to the plate. Generally, it takes two base hits to score a runner from first base and only one to score the runner from second base. Because of this, anytime the defense can keep the batter-runner off second base it gives the defensive team the decided edge.

As can be easily seen, the outfielder or the tandem relay man has numerous things to consider prior to making the final decision where the ball is to be thrown. Because of this, the defense must assist him by using the third baseman or the catcher to communicate their preference for where the throw should be made. Since both the third baseman and the catcher will have the play in front of them, they can offer great assistance to the fielder of the ball in making this important decision. This is especially true for the member of the tandem relay who fields the ball, since he will have his back completely turned to the infield.

As in all communication, it must be very loud so that every member of the defensive team can hear him. This is especially true for the fielder of the ball. Being that the third baseman is generally a little closer to the fielders, more than likely the communication will rest upon his shoulders. He will do so by yelling at least two times the following commands:

"Four-four"—Means throw the ball to the plate.
"Three-three"—Means throw the ball to third base.
"Two-two"—Means throw the ball to second base.
"Cut and hold" "cut and hold"—Means to run the ball in.

He should start yelling one of the above commands just prior to the ball reaching the glove of the fielder. This will give him plenty of time to observe the runners, and then make the decision as to what he would like the fielder to do with the baseball. As mentioned previously, even though the third baseman or the catcher communicates what play they feel would be the best, the player with the ball has still got to make the final decision. The communication the fielder receives from the third baseman or the catcher will certainly assist him in making the proper decision. The fielders need to understand that if their intention is to make a play on the lead runner, and then they misplay the ball, then the chances of continuing to make the play on that runner are quite minimal.

The back man on the tandem relay will also assist the front man in making the decision as to what the best play would be. As soon as the back man gets lined up properly behind the front man, and the fielder is just picking up the ball to throw to the front man in the tandem relay, the back man will turn and check out where the runners are. He will listen to the third baseman or the catcher communicating what play they think is best, and he in turn will offer his feelings to the front man by using the same commands as previously mentioned. Hopefully, the command given by the third baseman or the catcher would be the same as the back man on the tandem relay. If not, the back man's commands would take precedence over the other mainly since he is the closest to the fielder of the ball.

If the team does not have a "take charge" type of third baseman who is adept at communicating these commands, then this responsibility can fall on the catcher. What you do not want is for the third baseman to be yelling one command and the catcher another command. Again, the third baseman is the ideal person to issue the commands since he is closer to the fielder of the ball and might have a better feel for where the runners are than the catcher.

There will never be a cut-off man for the throw to third base from a member of the tandem relay. There will always be a cut-off man on any throw made to the plate by an outfielder or by the shortstop or second baseman on the tandem relay. Since there will be no cut-off man on the throw to third base, the third baseman must move to the ball anytime he is sure that the throw will not arrive in time to retire the runner. In this way he would have a better play on the batter-runner if he was to attempt to advance to second base on the throw to third base. In most cases, one of the outfielders will be covering second base on an extra base hit.

Anytime an outfielder or a member of the tandem relay is throwing the ball to a cut-off man, he should aim for his knees. Many coaches stress that they want the ball to hit the head of the cut-off man. By aiming for the knees, there will be less chance for the ball to be overthrown. It is better to have a low throw which can be fielded, than to have a high throw which sails over the cut-off man's head.

A cut-off man will be assisted into the proper position by the defensive player at a base or the plate. He will not control the depth of the cut-off man, but can help him get lined up with the fielder throwing the baseball. He will be instructed to move to his right or left by the commands "right" or "left". The cut-off man will start quickly moving in the direction of the command until he hears the fielder yell "okay". This alignment should all take place before the ball leaves the hand of the thrower. Occasionally, with a first baseman playing deep in the infield and a 6 type ball is hit right at the center fielder or the right fielder, he might have a little difficulty getting to the proper position before the ball leaves the thrower's hand. Other than this situation, there should never be any problem for a cut-off man being in the proper position when the ball is released.

The depth that the cut-off man assumes will be determined by various factors. The first being the depth of the fielder throwing the ball. The second being the strength of the fielder's arm. The closer that the ball is fielded toward the base or the plate where the throw will be made, the closer the cut-off man would be to the base or the plate. The stronger the arm of the fielder, the closer he would be also. The cut-off man needs to be in a position where the fielder can hit him in the knees with some ease.

It is always better to have the cut-off man as close to where the ball is being thrown for four reasons: (1) it will allow the defensive player at the base or the plate a better opportunity to make a decision on whether he wants the ball to be cut-off or not; (2) it allows the cut-off man more time to move to the poor throw at a better angle; (3) it is much easier for the cut-off man to move forward to the ball than to move backward; and (4) it will delay the batter-runner's or other baserunner's decision in taking an extra base as he waits to see if the throw is going to be cut. If the ball is to be cut-off and a play will be made at another base, he can move forward to the ball and be in a better position to cut the ball off and make the proper throw. Again, the distance the fielder is from the cut-off man and the strength of his arm must be taken into consideration.

The cut-off man should have both his arms in the air so that he is an easy target for the outfielder or the tandem relay infielder making the throw. As the ball is coming toward him he has got to anticipate somewhat what will be done with the ball. Out of the corner of his eye he should be able to see or sense where the runner(s) are. By anticipating where the play will be made, he will be able to better position himself so that the proper play can be made with a little more ease.

The defensive player at the plate or the base will inform the cut-off man if he wants the ball cut-off or not. This must be done well in advance of the ball getting to the cut-off man so that he can catch the ball if commanded without any major problem. If he is late with his cut-off command, it makes for a very difficult play for the cut-off man. A good rule for the defensive player making the command, is to have the ball cut any time he is in doubt.

There are various types of verbal commands that can be used. Many teams will have the player at the base or the plate say nothing if he wants the ball to come through the cut-off man. Others will have him say "go-go" or "let it go"-"let it go". These commands would be given as soon as he reads that the ball will be a good throw to his position. These commands are given as many times as possible before the ball passes through the cut-off man. If he wishes the ball to be cut by the cut-off man, he would yell "cut" as loud as he can. After communicating the cut, he must then tell the cut-off man what he wants him to do with the ball. It is best to use the numbering system for having the ball thrown to the plate or a certain base. A number is quicker to say and will not lead to any confusion on the part of the cut-off man. The commands would be:

"cut four"—Cut and throw the ball to the plate.
"cut three"—Cut and throw the ball to third base.
"cut two"—Cut and throw the ball to second base.
"cut hold"—Cut the ball with no play at the plate or a base.

Just because the command is for the cut-off man to throw to the plate or the base, does not mean that the cut-off man should make the throw unless there is a definite play on a runner. Again, when in doubt the ball should be cut-off. If possible, there should be a slight pause before the second command after the "cut" is made. This prevents the words from blending into each other and also gives the player yelling the command a better opportunity to decide what he wants the cut-off man to do with the ball.

The cut-off man needs to go after all bad throws just as if there is no defensive player behind him. If there is no play on the runner at the plate or the base, the defensive player behind the cut-off man needs to back up the bad throw since he will have a better angle on the ball. The cut-off man can assume that all poor throws will be cut-off, so he must get into a position to catch the ball. Even though the back man should always tell the cut-off man to cut-off a wide throw, if he hears nothing he must still attempt to catch the ball. This also pertains to a low throw that is rapidly losing velocity as it comes toward the cut-off man. This type of throw should be cut-off unless the infield is very hard and there is a chance that the ball will arrive at the base or the plate in one or two hops. The cut-off man should never get short hopped or in-between hopped on the throw. He will have ample opportunity to move forward and backward to prevent this from happening.
As a general rule, if the ball coming into the cut-off man is going to take the defensive player at the plate or the base two steps away from the tag area, he should have the ball cut by the cut-off man. Much will depend on where the runner is as the ball is coming into the area. On most throws the ball will get to the fielder quicker when it is not cut-off by the cut-off man.

The cut-off man should always fake the cut-off whenever he has not been instructed to catch the ball. This might keep all other runners from taking the extra base as the ball goes through the cut-off man. This is one reason why the saying of nothing if you want the ball to go through the cut-off man is more effective. By giving the comand "go-go" or "let it go" gives the baserunners the chance to take the extra base since they know that the ball will not be cut-off.

As the ball is coming toward the cut-off man and he anticipates that the throw will allow a definite play on the runner at the base or the plate, he will make sure that he keeps the ball lined up with his glove side. In this way, he is in a much better position to catch the ball if commanded and then throw the ball all in one motion. If he was to catch the ball on the non-glove side, he would have to pivot all the way around to the throwing side before making a proper throw to the base or the plate.

If the cut-off man anticipates that there will be no play at the base or the plate that he is lined up with, he should get lined up with the throw on his non-glove side. In this way he can catch the ball and make a throw to another base in one quick motion. Hopefully, the player commanding the cut-off man will give him ample time to make this type of adjustment. If in doubt as to what the play will be, the cut-off man should keep the throw slightly lined up with his glove side. This allows for a better chance of making the catch at the last possible moment. Anytime a cut-off man is throwing to a base or the plate, he must step and throw to the base whenever possible to prevent a poor throw. The closer he is to the receiver of his throw, the more he must be sure to make an accurate and easily seen throw.

The coach can set up situations in practice sessions where cut-off mechanics and communication can be worked on under game like conditions. Runners can be placed at various bases and instructed to run full speed when the ball is hit by the coach at the plate. There also needs to be a runner at the plate who will take off full speed once the ball leaves the bat of the fungo hitter. All types of balls can be hit to the outfield, including balls in the gap and down the foul lines so that the tandem relay men can be involved. The coach will need to make the defense aware of how many outs there are, what innning it is, and the score. This type of practice work also provides the coach the opportunity to evaluate the defense's ability to properly cover their various assignments. That is why a pitcher needs to be on the mound faking the pitch to the plate and then reacting once the ball is hit by the coach at the plate.

At this time also, the coach can set up fly ball communication situations with runners tagging up at various bases. This leads into the next section of the Playbook, which is fly ball communication from the infielders.

FLY BALL COMMUNICATION FROM THE INFIELDERS

Infielders involved as cut-off men will find they have much more time to get into their cut-off position on fly balls to the outfield. The exception would be if a 5 or 6 type ball is hit right at an outfielder. When this is the case, the cut-off man would have to really sprint in order to get to his proper position for the throw.

Whenever a fly ball is hit to the outfield with runner(s) on base, the outfielder will have two responsibilities: (1) catch the ball; and (2) throw the ball to the proper base or to the plate. As with ground balls, the outfielder will have the final decision as to where the ball will be thrown. However, since he will have his eyes in the sky as the ball starts coming down, he will not know the status of the runners on base in regard to whether or not they are tagging up. This is where the infielders come into the picture as they communicate to the outfielder what the runner(s) are doing on the base(s).

The defensive team should rely on the third baseman to communicate to the outfielders what the runners on base are doing in a fly ball situation. The reason that the third baseman should be responsible for this job is that he will have all the runners in front of him. He can even communicate on a fly ball to left field with a runner at third base, and he is the cut-off man on the throw to the plate. The shortstop or second baseman are also involved in the communication as they listen to the third baseman. Whichever one of them is going out into the outfield will be responsible to communicate with the outfielder. He will listen for the third baseman and then pass the same command onto the outfielder. With a runner tagging up at first base, the first baseman can also communicate the fact whether or not the runner is tagging at first base. The main item of concern is that the communication is the same so that there is no confusion on the part of the outfielder who is catching the ball.

The communication from the third baseman or other infielders involved should not begin until the ball starts its downward flight to the outfielder. This will allow the communicators ample time to evaluate the status of the baserunner(s). Of course, when a line drive is hit right at an outfielder the communication must be given as quickly as the third baseman can determine the status of the runner(s).

In the communication on the fly ball, the first command will give the outfielder the status of the runner, the second command would be where the ball should be thrown once caught. He should yell out each command twice so that there is no confusion as to what communication is being provided. The louder the infielders are, the better chance for the outfielder to hear them and position himself accordingly.

1. **Runner at third base only**—With the runner tagging up at third base, the communication would be: "tag-tag"—"four-four". If the runner is not tagging, the communication would be: "half way-half way". Anytime the outfielder hears the command of half way, he does not have to rush the catch and will then throw the ball into the cut-off man making sure that he makes an accurate throw.

2. **Runner at second base only**—With the runner tagging up at second base, the communication would be: "tag-tag"—"three-three". If the runner is not tagging, the communication would be: "half way-half way".

3. **Runner at first base only**—With the runner tagging up at first base, the communication would be: "tag-tag"—"two-two". If the runner is not tagging, the communication would be: "half way-half way".

4. **Runners at second and third base with a long fly ball and no play at the plate**—If the outfielder will not be able to make any play on the runner tagging at third base, then the defense will direct their attention to the runner at second base. If the runner at second base is tagging, the communication would be "tag-tag"—"three-three". If the runner at second base is not tagging it is important that the outfielder knows that this is the runner at second base. The communication would be: "half way at two"—"half way at two". The outfielder would throw the ball into the cut-off man at third base anytime the runner at second base is half way. It is important that the players understand that the term half way indicates that a runner is not tagging up, and it does not reflect the distance away from the base. The defense must be very careful of the runner who comes off the base a few steps on a long fly ball, and then goes back to the base and tags up when the ball is caught. The runner should be down the line at least a quarter of the way to the next base before it is assumed that he will not be tagging at the base.

5. **Runners at second and third base with a short fly ball with a play at the plate**—The communication in this situation would be the same as that with a runner at third base only. If the runner is tagging at third base, the communication would be: "tag-tag"—"four-four". If the runner is not tagging, the communication would be "half way at three"—"half way at three".

The only difference here is that the defense lets the outfielder know that they are referring to the runner at third base when he is half way.

6. **Runners at first and second base with a play at third base**—With the runner tagging at second base, the communication would be: "tag-tag"—"three-three". If the runner at second base is not tagging, the communication would be: "half way at two"—"half way at two". Again, the defense would have to let the outfielder know that it is the runner at second base not tagging up.

7. **Runners at first and second base with a long fly ball and no play at third base**—If the outfielder will not be able to make any play on the runner tagging up at second base, then the defense will direct their attention to the runner at first base. If the runner at first base is tagging, the communication would be: "tag-tag"—"two-two". If the runner at first base is not tagging, the communication would be: "half way at one"—"half way at one". The outfielder will then throw the ball quickly to the cut-off man at second base.

8. **Bases loaded with no play at the plate**—In this situation, the defense would center their attention on whatever runner they feel a play can be made on by the outfielder. If the runner at second base is tagging and there can be a play on him at third base, then the communication would be: "tag-tag"—"three-three". If he is not tagging at second base, the communication would be: "half way at two"—"half way at two". If the only play by the outfielder would be at second base with all the runners tagging, then the communication would be: "tag-tag"—"two-two". If the runner at first base is not tagging in this situation, the communication would be: "half way at one"—"half way at one". The outfielder must be sure to throw an accurate throw to the cut-off man any time the runner is half way so that there is no chance for the runners to advance if the ball gets by the cut-off man.

9. **Runners at first and third base with a long fly ball and no play at the plate**— If the runner at first base is tagging, the communication would be: "tag-tag"—"two-two". If the runner at first base is not tagging, the communication would be: "half way at one"—"half way at one".

It is important that the infielders work on this communication during scrimmage games or when fly balls are hit to the outfield with runners on base in a practice session. It might seem a little complex, but when the infielders understand that their attention is always directed to the base that a play can be made, then it becomes a very simple communication technique.

FLY BALL COMMUNICATION

A very important aspect of team defense in baseball is the communication techniques used by the fielders in catching fly balls. It is quite aggravating to a coaching staff when a catchable ball falls to the ground among two or more defensive players due to poor communication. Much time and effort must be spent in practice sessions working on fly ball communication so that all the players clearly understand what their responsibilities are, as well as the communicative techniques involved.

Once the players are comfortable with their fly ball communication, a coach will find his players become more aggressive going after fly balls. If there are continuous breakdowns in communication, the fielders will lose this aggressiveness due to their fear of running into each other.

In the fundamental drill series in practice sessions, the coach can throw fly balls to all the areas of the field where two or more players would converge. On the following page you will find a diagram of all these areas. In these practice sessions the players need to position themselves at their regular position and break for the ball full speed once it leaves the hand of the coach. By throwing the ball, the coach can better hit these target areas. A fungo hitter at home plate can be used on occasions when the coach wishes to involve all nine defensive players.

There are numerous ways a fielder can communicate his intentions of catching the fly ball. Some teams use the command "mine". Others use the command "I've got it". Whatever command that is used, it must be standard for the entire team. It also must be very loud so that everyone involved in the play can hear the command without any major difficulty. This is especially true when the game is being played in front of a large crowd, or on those days when there is a wind factor involved. In practice sessions a coach should require his players to communicate as loud as they would in a game, duplicating the atmosphere with a large crowd in attendance on a windy day.

There should not only be a command by the fielder who wishes to catch the ball, but a reply by all those other fielders in the area encouraging him to make the play. These replies could be: "take it"; "you got it"; or these commands followed by the first name of the fielder making the catch. Again, whatever command is used must be standard for the entire team.

In the following you will find a complete fly ball communication scheme that can be used quite effectively. We will also list the principles involved in this particular system.

1. A fielder should never be allowed to drift on any fly ball. If a coach allows his players to develop this habit, it will compound the difficulties in communication between the fielders. Once the ball is hit in the air, those players that have any chance to catch the ball must break full speed to the ball. Whenever possible, they should position themselves so that they are under control and in the proper fielding position. Drifting on the ball will also lead to poor positioning for a possible throw to a base or the plate.

2. A fielder should never call for the fly ball until it begins its downward flight. This will eliminate the problem of a fielder calling for the ball too quick, only to find that he is unable to make the play. By calling for the ball too early, other fielders who might have a chance to catch the ball often lose their aggressiveness. Once the fielders become accustomed to calling for the ball only when it starts downward, it will give all the fielders in the area the chance to move toward the ball at full speed.

3. When a player is absolutely sure that he can catch the fly ball, he will give the command of "I've got it", loud and clear. He should repeat this command over and over whenever he is moving into an area where other fielders might have a chance to make the play. Many times, two fielders could yell out "I've got it" at the same time, and both fielders would swear that they did not hear the other player's command. This is the reason for the multiple command, so that this problem would not occur. The only time a fielder would not need to yell for the ball is when the ball is hit right at him, and no other fielder could possibly make the play. There will be times when a fielder would have to delay his command for the ball due to the fact that he is not sure he can make the catch. In fact, sometimes he will have to wait until the last second due to the fact that he can not yell for the ball until he is sure he can make the play. Any ball that hits the ground should do so without any communication being heard.

4. Once a fielder has issued the command "I've got it", then all the other fielders in the immediate area will yell for him to take it, by issuing the command of "take it". This command must be given at least two times loud and clear. This will allow the fielder of the ball the opportunity to make the catch without having to worry about other fielders in the area attempting to catch

FLY BALL COMMUNICATION AREAS

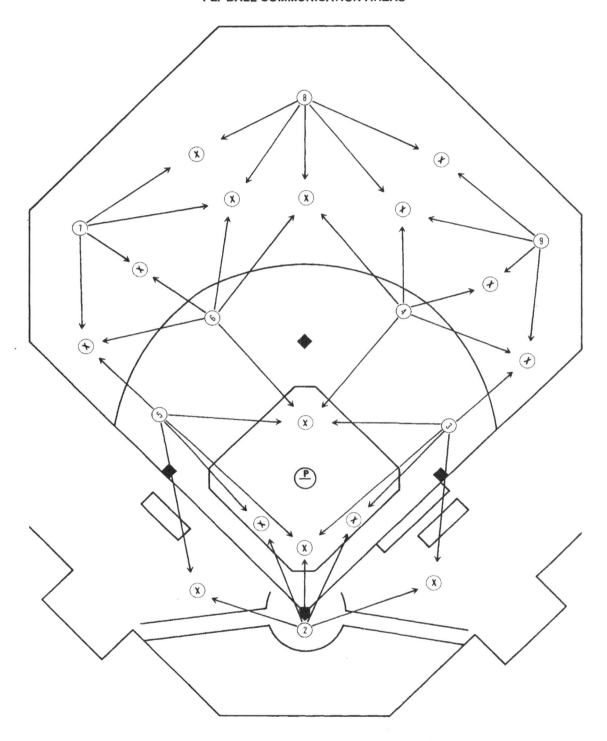

the ball also. There is nothing more uncomfortable for a fielder then when he hears footsteps as he is attempting to catch a fly ball. The priority system for fielding fly balls when two or more players issue the command of "I've got it" will be discussed later.

5. All the fielders in the immediate area of the player who is going to catch the fly ball should allow the fielder plenty of room to make the catch. If for some reason, the player who has called for the ball loses the sight of the ball (sun, etc.), he must yell immediately "I can't see it". The other fielders in the area would then make an attempt for the ball using the same communication as previously mentioned.

6. Fielders should never move to a fly ball with their eyes constantly checking out where the other fielders might be. This would slow down a player's movement to the ball, along with causing him to possibly misjudge the flight of the ball. One glance at the other fielder(s) as the ball is in its downward flight is all that is necessary.

7. At no time should a fielder command another fielder to "take it" without that fielder having already called for the ball. This will eliminate the confusion of having one fielder being commanded to take the ball, when that fielder might not be able to make the play. There should never be anyone directing traffic around a fly ball by calling out names. This just leads to more confusion.

8. A priority system has got to be established so that when two or more fielders call for the ball they understand which fielder has priority over the other. If no priority system is put into effect, then there could be serious communication problems. On the following page you will find a chart for the priority system used in this fly ball communication system. It lists each defensive position along with the positions that they have priority over on the fly ball, and the positions that would have priority over them.

9. Just because one fielder calls for the fly ball, it does not mean that he should be allowed to catch it. For instance, if an infielder is going into the outfield area for a fly ball and has called for the ball, an outfielder can call him off by yelling for the ball also. Anytime an outfielder can make the play coming toward the infield, he should do so. This is especially true if there is a runner tagging up at a base. If the infielder is under the ball and positioned properly, then the outfielder should not call him off. He should command the infielder to make the play by yelling "take it" at least two times. However, even if the infielder is under the ball and the outfielder calls for the ball, the outfielder must be allowed to make the play. They can never be in a situation where the player who yells the loudest takes the ball. Similar situations can take place in all the fly ball trouble areas where two or more fielders come together. An example of perfect fly ball communication would be:

A fly ball is hit to an area behind second base with the center fielder, the shortstop and the second baseman all going for the ball full speed. When the ball started its downward flight, both the shortstop and the second baseman started calling for the ball "I've got it". When the second baseman heard the shortstop call for the ball, he immediately started yelling "take it" to the shortstop. The center fielder seeing that he could make a better play on the ball than the shortstop or second baseman then started yelling "I've got it". As soon as the shortstop and second baseman heard the center fielder call for the ball, they both started yelling "take it" to the center fielder, allowing him the opportunity to make the play. If the center fielder had seen that he could not have made the play, or the shortstop was well under the ball he would have commanded the shortstop to "take it".

Once the fielder with priority issues the command "I've got it", it is his ball. He has got to make the play. This is why it is so important that the communication be loud and clear. A fielder should never be so aggressive that he calls for the ball only to find that he will have to make a tough catch, when another fielder has a much easier play.

10. When no communication is heard as the ball nears the ground, it merely means that no fielder thinks he can make the play on the ball. This still leaves the possibility of the dive play for one of the fielders. Just prior to his dive he should yell out "I've got it", so that the other fielders give him the opportunity to try to make the play. Once a player sees another player leave his feet for the dive play, he should avoid making contact with the player leaving his feet. If two players were to dive for the same ball, then there is a chance that an injury might occur if they were to make contact with each other. A coach must encourage the dive play on the part of his fielders when it is the only play they would have on a fly ball.

11. The major factor in a player being non-aggressive when going after a fly ball, is the chance of a collision with another fielder. This is why the proper communication system needs to be implemented in the fundamental drill series in practice sessions. Collisions will occur in a circumstance where two aggressive fielders both call for the ball at the last second, with their momentum carrying them into each other. The most common type of collision is when the outfielder is coming in on the

ball, and an infielder is going back on the ball. If the outfielder calls for the ball, it is the infielder's responsibility to get out of his way. If there is time, all he needs to do is check the path of the outfielder and then veer away from him. If the outfielder was to call for the ball at the last second and the infielder was unable to change his course, the infielder would hit the ground. This is the only way to prevent a dangerous head on collision. The outfielder must always stay on his feet even if he knows that there is going to be a collision. The worst thing that can happen now is that the outfielder is hit below the waist by the infielder.

12. Collisions between two outfielders going for a ball in the gap should happen infrequently. In the first place, there will be very few instances where a line drive type fly ball will cause both outfielders to be in a position to make the catch. Most of the time outfielders will come together for a fly ball at an angle toward the outfield fence. If the proper fly ball communication is used, there should be no problem in staying clear of one another. If both outfielders are going full speed for a ball in the gap with little angle to the fence, then you will have to create a gap between the fielders. This is done very easily by requiring the center fielder to catch the ball low (waist or below), and the adjacent outfielder (right fielder or left fielder) to catch the ball high (head or above). This will enable both fielders to attempt the catch, but keep them from following the same path to the ball. This needs to be worked on in the fundamental drill series in practice sessions so that the outfielders build up their confidence in one another. When you build their confidence in one another, it will make them more aggressive.

This system takes a little practice, but it has proved successful for many teams. When done properly, a ball hit in the air will be caught without any danger of losing a player due to a collision.

FLY BALL COMMUNICATION PRIORITY SYSTEM

DEFENSIVE POSITION	HAS PRIORITY OVER ON A FLY BALL	HAS NO PRIORITY OVER ON A FLY BALL
FIRST BASEMAN	CATCHER AND PITCHER	SECOND BASEMAN, THIRD BASEMAN, SHORTSTOP AND RIGHT FIELDER
SECOND BASEMAN	FIRST BASEMAN AND PITCHER	SHORTSTOP AND ALL OUTFIELDERS
SHORTSTOP	SECOND BASEMAN, THIRD BASEMAN, FIRST BASEMAN AND PITCHER	ALL OUTFIELDERS
THIRD BASEMAN	CATCHER, PITCHER AND FIRST BASEMAN	SHORTSTOP AND LEFT FIELDER
CATCHER	PITCHER	FIRST BASEMAN AND THIRD BASEMAN
PITCHER	NO FIELDER	CATCHER AND ALL INFIELDERS
LEFT FIELDER	ALL INFIELDERS	CENTER FIELDER
CENTER FIELDER	LEFT FIELDER, RIGHT FIELDER AND ALL INFIELDERS	—
RIGHT FIELDER	ALL INFIELDERS	CENTER FIELDER

Note: if the second baseman and third baseman were to ever be in a position to go after the same ball, the third baseman would take priority over the second baseman. We have just listed those positions that would ever have a chance to come together.

INFIELD COMMUNICATION

Many baseball coaches require their players on defense to chatter during the course of the game in order for them to stay "alive". This is especially true for the infielders. Let us present a contrary opinion to the concept of chatter. Meaningless chatter serves no useful purpose in the game of baseball. However, meaningful communication does serve a useful purpose.

The concept of chattering in baseball is due to the fact that there is a lot of time during the game when the ball is not in play. This so called "dead time" occurs when the pitcher receives the ball back from the catcher, and is preparing himself to throw the next pitch. We feel that this is not "dead time", but is "concentrating time". It is impossible to fully concentrate on all the things that could happen on the next pitch when one is required to chatter. Since we feel that senseless chatter serves no useful purpose to the game itself, we would recommend that defensive players say nothing unless they have something to say that has meaning to the game.

We feel that another reason for not chattering on defense is to provide the opportunity whereby when something is said by a member of the defensive team, everyone on defense is listening. If the defense has to wade through the "junk" communication to take out what is important, then information that is pertinent to the game might not be heard or comprehended. Thus, when something is said everyone is listening. This also enables the coach in the dugout to be better heard if he wishes to get the attention of members of the defense.

If there is any negative note to the "no chatter defense", it is generally in the eyes of the fans sitting in the stands wondering why everyone is relatively quiet while the pitcher is preparing to deliver the ball to the plate. This is due to the fact that baseball fans have become conditioned to hearing chatter, and feel that it is an integral part of the game. We would much rather have a team that is mentally relaxed and concentrating, than one who is spending all this time thinking up new things to say to please the coach and the fans.

The infielders need to communicate with each other, along with the other players on defense. This should be communication pertinent to the game. Examples of this type of communication follow.

1. **"Throw the ball across the infield"**—On full count situations with two outs, and the runners are forced to advance on the next pitch, the shortstop must communicate to the other members of the infield that they will not have a force play at second or third base. He can do this by just communicating the above since everyone in the infield will understand the meaning. With the same situation in effect, the center fielder might communicate to the right fielder and the left fielder this fact by saying "only a 6 right at you". He is basically saying to the other outfielders that they would only have a play on the lead runner if a 6 type ball was hit right at them.

2. **"I've got the base"**—The shortstop and second baseman must communicate with each other as to who will be covering second base on the following plays: sacrifice bunt; steal; ground ball back to the pitcher; and pick-off play at first base where the runner breaks and the first baseman throws to second base. Prior to the pitcher getting back on the rubber to get his sign from the catcher, this information must be given to him so that he knows who he will be throwing to at second base on a ground ball back to him. If there are two outs, the pitcher does not need to be told since his play will be at first base. In most cases whichever fielder has the responsibility for second base, he should have the base on all the plays just mentioned. This is to prevent confusion on the part of the shortstop and second baseman as to who covers the base. The only exception to this would be when a team would rather have the shortstop cover second base when a runner is picked off first base. This will give the first baseman an easier target to throw to since the shortstop will be coming in to the base at a better angle than the second baseman. It will also allow the second baseman a chance to move toward first base anytime a pick-off from the pitcher is made. This will allow him to be in a better position in case the ball deflects off the first baseman's glove. If this be the case, even when the second baseman has coverage of the bag the shortstop would still take the pick-off throw from the first baseman. If the shortstop is having to play the batter well to the third base side of the diamond and the second baseman has second base, then the communication would be that the second baseman will take the bag on every play including the pick-off at first base. Anytime the second baseman has the coverage at second base and the batter squares around to bunt, the shortstop automatically will cover second base allowing the second baseman to break for first base if the batter does bunt the ball. In most levels of baseball, it is not that important to disguise who has coverage for second base as most hitters do not have the ability to guide the ball into the area of the infielder covering on the hit and run. If the shortstop and second baseman use the proper footwork in covering second base on a steal or hit and run, they should never be that much out of position anyway. These mechanics will be discussed in detail in the infield section of the Playbook. If a team feels that it is important to

disguise who has coverage for second base, it can be easily done by a simple sign system. The problem is that the pitcher will not know who he will be throwing to when he gets a ground ball back to him for a force out at second base.

3. **"Ground ball you're going to second base"**—**"Ground ball you're going to the plate"**—The third baseman is responsible to remind the pitcher of what he will do with a ground ball hit directly back to the mound in the following situations: anytime there are runners at first and second base with less than two outs, he will say to the pitcher "ground ball you're going to second base"; anytime the bases are loaded with less than two outs, he will say to the pitcher "ground ball you're going to the plate". These reminders must be given to the pitcher before he gets on the rubber to get his sign from the catcher. The reason these reminders are so important is that many times a pitcher fails to think about what he will be doing with a ground ball back to him on the mound. This is due to the fact that his concentration is more on the batter, and the next pitch that he will be throwing. Any delay in the pitcher responding properly on a ground ball back to him on the mound, could result in a poor throw or a throw to the wrong base.

4. **"Two outs"**—This is a reminder from the second baseman to the first baseman anytime there are runners at first and third base with two outs. This is to remind the first baseman that he is responsible for following the runner down to second base if the runner breaks on the pitch to the plate. This double steal defense play was discussed in detail in the double steal defense section of the Playbook.

5. **"Five-six-three"**—The shortstop will communicate to the third baseman and the second baseman anytime he will be the pivot man at second base on a ball hit to the third baseman. This would be called if the hitter at the plate is a strict lefthanded pull hitter forcing the second baseman to move well to the first base side of second base. With the second baseman being so far away from the bag, it would be very difficult for him to get to second base for the force out at second base. Likewise, it would be practically impossible to complete a double play. So a "five-six-three" command to the infield will mean that the shortstop will cover second base if the third baseman fields the ball for the force out at second base, along with the double play attempt. The second baseman must break for second base anytime the ball is hit to the third base side of the field in case the ball is hit to the shortstop, or the ball forces the shortstop to break to his right. In this case, the second baseman would have to be at the bag for the force out attempt.

6. **"Let me know"**—Anytime the third baseman positions himself in front of third base with a runner at second base, he must tell the shortstop to let him know if the runner at second base breaks for third base on the pitch to the plate. Otherwise, it will be very difficult for the third baseman to see the runner from second base break on the steal or hit and run attempt. The shortstop would yell out "there he goes" for the benefit of not only the third baseman, but also the catcher.

7. **"Let him know"**—This would be the communication from the first baseman to the second baseman with a runner at first base and an open base at second base. In this situation the first baseman might be breaking early on a bunt play, or with runners at first and third base breaking early for a possible suicide squeeze attempt. The first baseman wants the second baseman to yell out "there he goes" if the runner at first base breaks on the pitch to the plate. This will let the defense know that the runner is stealing, and since the first baseman is breaking toward the plate on the pitch he will not be in a position to see the runner break.

8. **"I've got back up"**—The shortstop and second baseman must communicate with each other when there is a runner at second base or third base in regard to who will back up the catcher's throw back to the pitcher after each pitch. Generally, the second baseman will back up the throw with a righthanded hitter at the plate, with the shortstop backing up the throw with a lefthanded hitter. This could change depending on how the defense is playing a certain hitter. If there is a runner at second base, the shortstop or second baseman must be moving toward the bag as the ball is being thrown by the catcher. They should end up about four or five steps toward the base from their original position. If there is a runner at third base, the shortstop or second baseman must be two or three steps in front of second base when the ball reaches the pitcher. With the runner at third base, the catcher must be sure that he does not throw the ball to the pitcher until he sees the shortstop or second baseman moving toward the base. If the catcher is throwing the ball back to the pitcher too quick, all the shortstop or second baseman has to say to the catcher is "give me time".

9. **"Ground ball to my right, I'll let you know"**—With a runner at second base with less than two outs, the shortstop needs to let the third baseman know that on a ground ball to his right he will let the third baseman know if he can make the play. This communication must be done as soon as the shortstop reads the fact that he can field the ground ball. When the third baseman hears the shortstop yell "I've got it", he can then retreat quickly back to third base preparing for a possible throw from the shortstop for the force out or tag play. The third baseman must go to his left for every ground ball that he can field even if he hears the shortstop yell "I've got it". All the third baseman wants to know is that the shortstop can make the play, so

if he can not reach the ball he can get back to the base in time for a throw. If the shortstop reads that the third baseman will not be able to get back to third base in time, then he will have to make the throw to second base or first base. The throw to second base or first base will depend on where the runners were at the time of the pitch.

10. **"Keep moving"**—If an infielder or outfielder observes another member of the defensive team not moving with the count, this would be the communication used to remind him of the fact. Defensive movement with the count will be discussed in detail in the next section of the Playbook.

As one can easily see, there are numerous situations where the players on defense will need to communicate with each other. If a team's bunt defense plays, double steal defense plays, and pick-off plays are verbalized it will just add on to the communication system.

DEFENSIVE MOVEMENT BY THE COUNT

All outfielders and infielders must take numerous factors into consideration before they position themselves for each hitter. These factors will be discussed in detail in both the outfield and infield section of the Playbook. Once a defensive player, other than the catcher or pitcher, assumes their defensive position on each new hitter, then adjustments can be made after each pitch is thrown. These adjustments would primarily be caused by the ball and strike count on the batter.

A study was done quite a few years ago at Miami-Dade South Community College, to determine hitter tendencies in regard to pulled and non-pulled fair balls in accordance with the ball and strike count on all the hitters over the course of a season. It was concluded by the findings in this study that as the count built to the hitter's advantage, he would have more of a tendency to pull a fair ball. Vice-versa, when the count was to the pitcher's advantage, there was less chance of a ball being pulled fair. The study showed that close to 70% of all fair balls were pulled. The results of this study is below:

Ball-Strike Count	Pulled Fair Balls	Non-Pulled Fair Balls	Percentage Of All Fair Balls Pulled
2-0	52	12	.812
1-0	153	47	.765
3-2	85	28	.752
3-1	37	15	.711
0-2	48	21	.696
0-0	216	102	.679
2-2	97	48	.669
2-1	91	49	.650
1-1	118	68	.634
0-1	107	64	.626
1-2	106	71	.598

The 3-0 count was not included in the percentages for there were only seven balls hit fair on that count (5 pulled—2 non-pulled)

We are convinced that these percentages of pulled versus non-pulled balls would carry over into all levels of baseball. When a hitter has the count to his advantage (1-0; 2-0; 2-1; 3-1; and 3-0), he is generally looking for his pitch to hit. When he gets that pitch, he would have a tendency to get around on the ball a little quicker. The result being a ball that he would have more of a tendency to pull. When a hitter is faced with a ball-strike count to his disadvantage (0-1; 0-2; 1-2; and 2-2), he is generally attempting to make some type of contact with the ball, not necessarily his pitch. The result being a ball that might not be pulled as much as one when he was ahead in the count. The other counts (0-0; 1-1; 3-2), do not give any major advantage or disadvantage to the pitcher or the hitter.

Knowing these hitter tendencies, it would be unwise for a defensive player to remain at the same spot while the count builds on an individual batter. By requiring the players to move with the count, you are basically playing percentage baseball.

This movement on the count takes place after the catcher receives the pitch, and has thrown the ball back to the pitcher. This will give every fielder ample time to move the number of steps designated for their particular position.

Basically, all a player will be doing is moving to the pull side of the field when the hitter is ahead in the count, and move to the opposite field side when the pitcher is ahead in the count. It does no good at all to have one player moving with the count and an adjacent fielder not making any adjustments. All this will create is a gap between the two fielders which could cause a major problem.

If an infielder is responsible for coverage at a base, he will not be able to move with the count. For instance, if the first baseman is responsible for holding a runner on at first base, he will not move with the count. If a shortstop or second baseman has coverage of second base on the steal, the double play, etc., he will not be able to move with the count.

Defensive adjustments with the count can never take a player away from a base that he is responsible for if a play might develop at that base. The outfielders would never have to worry about this factor, so their movement with the count would be standard for each batter.

After each pitch to a hitter, the outfielders would make their adjustments so that they all take the same number of steps to the pull or the non-pull side. In a practice session, the coach will need to be sure that the size of their steps are somewhat the same so that unnatural gaps in the outfield do not occur. These steps should not be walking size steps, but are more sliding type steps. A sliding step would be about three-quarters the size of a regular walking step. Due to the fact that the percentages are favorable for a hitter ahead in the count to pull the ball a little more, these same percentages indicate that the ball would be hit a little deeper. Vice-versa, a hitter behind in the count generally would not take as an aggressive swing as he would when ahead in the count. Thus, when an outfielder is moving to the pull side he should move at a 45 degree angle away from the plate. When moving to the non-pull side, he would move at a 45 degree angle toward the hitter.

In order to standardize the number of steps for the outfielders to move, the coach can provide them with the below information:

Count On The Hitter	Steps To The Pull Side	Steps To The Non-Pull Side
0-0	—	—
1-0	3	—
2-0	6	—
2-1	3	—
3-0	9	—
3-1	6	—
3-2	2	—
1-1	—	—
2-2	—	1
0-1	—	2
0-2	—	4
1-2	—	2

An example of the above for the outfielders would be: A righthanded hitter is at the plate and all the outfielders have assumed their defensive position by taking into consideration: type of hitter; type of pitcher; score; inning; outs; fence distances; wind factor; outfielder's speed and ability to move forward, backward, left and right; and ability of the adjacent outfielder(s). Thus, his position is set for the 0-0 count. The first pitch is a ball and all the outfielders will move 3 steps to the pull side at a 45 degree angle away from the batter. The next pitch is a strike (1-1 count). All the outfielders will move back to the position they were for the 0-0 count. The next pitch is a strike (1-2 count). They all move 2 steps to the non-pull side at a 45 degree angle toward the hitter. The next pitch is a ball (2-2 count). They all move back one step toward their 0-0 count position. The next pitch is a ball (3-2 count). They move 3 steps to the pull side deep, which puts them 2 steps on the pull side from the 0-0 count position. It does not take a player very long before he gets all the steps down for this movement. On the 3-0 count, all the outfielders would be 9 steps away from the 0-0 count spot. In regular walking steps, this would be about 6-7 steps.

The infielders would not want to take the same number of steps as the outfielders for obvious reasons. Their number of steps would be less than the outfielders, and they would not move at an angle away from or toward the hitter as the outfielders do. The shortstop and second baseman would take more steps to the pull side and the non-pull side than the first baseman and third baseman. The reason being that the first baseman and the third baseman would be somewhat restricted due to their distance from the foul lines. As mentioned previously, any infielder who has coverage of a base would not be able to make an adjustment with the count. The shortstop and second baseman would move the below number of steps if no coverage of a base is in effect:

Count On The Hitter	Steps To The Pull Side	Steps To The Non-Pull Side
0-0	—	—
1-0	1	—
2-0	2	—
2-1	1	—
3-0	3	—
3-1	2	—
3-2	1	—
1-1	—	—
2-2	—	1
0-1	—	1
0-2	—	2
1-2	—	1

The first baseman and third baseman would move the below number of steps if no coverage of a base is in effect:

Count On The Hitter	Steps To The Pull Side	Steps To The Non-Pull Side
0-0	—	—
1-0	½	—
2-0	1	—
2-1	½	—
3-0	2	—
3-1	1	—
3-2	½	—
1-1	—	—
2-2	—	½
0-1	—	½
0-2	—	1
1-2	—	½

Movement with the count is certainly not difficult to teach and learn for the players on defense. It is just another factor in percentage baseball that can assist the defense to better position themselves to make the play.

BASERUNNING

Baserunning might be one of the most neglected areas of baseball taught on all levels, from youth leagues all the way up to major leagues. Since baseball games are won and lost many times on the base paths, a coach needs to spend plenty of time in practice perfecting baserunning skills.

This can be done during the batting practice segment of practice as detailed in the practice section of the Playbook. In addition, toward the end of practice, baserunning can be combined with conditioning work so that a concentrated effort can be assured in this important phase of the game.

A team that has an aggressive baserunning game plan can have a devastating effect on a defense, causing them to make errors on even routine plays. Baseball is a game of inches and seconds, and this certainly holds true in the art of baserunning. The coach who can prepare his players to run the bases effectively, will find that his club can take advantage of defensive mistakes much quicker.

We will break down the fundamentals of baserunning in detail, from the time the hitter becomes a baserunner (the crack of the bat):

1. **Baserunning starts with the crack of the bat**—The initial reaction of practically all baseball players is to watch the ball as it leaves the bat, rather than concentrating his efforts on getting a great jump out of the batter's box. Players need to be aware of the fact that for an average baserunner, for every tenth of second delay in getting to first base it will cost that runner two feet. Thus, if a player is a 4.5 runner to first base and he can decrease his time by two-tenths of a second, he will be four feet closer to the base. Many times, this distance is the factor in a runner being safe or out. Time must be spent in batting practice and in the baserunning segment of practice, working on just getting quicker out of the box.

2. **Good hitting mechanics allow a player to get a better jump out of the batter's box**—If a hitter has a tendency to hit off his heels or with his weight poorly distributed during the swing, it makes for a much more difficult break out of the batter's box. Those hitters that finish their swing with their weight on the balls of their feet, can get a much quicker jump out of the box. A batter that finishes his swing with practically all his weight on the rear foot would have a difficult time transferring that weight back forward to generate momentum toward first base. By perfecting hitting skills, a hitter should become a little better runner in regard to his quickness out of the box.

3. **First step out of the batter's box**—The righthanded hitter will take his first step to first base with his right foot, making sure that the step is such that he can generate power toward first base. If he overstrides on this initial first step, it would slow down his weight transfer so that his left foot can not be propelled quickly in the direction of first base. A lefthanded hitter would cross-over with his rear foot (left) by opening up his stride foot (right) after contact with the ball. The right foot would not leave the ground, but would be pivoted on the heel so that the hips are not locked preventing the accelerated cross-over step.

4. **First initial steps out of the batter's box**—Upon contact with the ball, the hitter should not concern himself with where the ball has been hit. The first four or five steps are so important in building up acceleration that his full concentration must be centered on getting out of the box. He should stay low out of the box very similar to a sprinter coming out of the blocks in track. He should stay low for the first four or five steps and then gradually raise up into proper running form toward first base. Only after raising up would he pick up the ball out of the corner of his eye.

5. **Picking up the flight of the ball**—Only after the fourth or fifth step should a batter pick up the flight of the ball. This should be done in a manner so that there is no chance of the runner slowing down in his attempt to reach first base. By angling his head slightly toward the infield, he would be able to pick up the flight of the ball, even if it has been hit down the third baseline. If a runner was to turn his upper part of his body to see the ball, it will take away from his speed to first base. Any ball hit to the second base side of the shortstop can easily be seen out of the corner of the eye without having to angle the head. After initial eye contact with the ball, the runner would then direct his attention to first base. He would know at that time where the ball is, and whether or not there will be a play on him at first base.

6. **Running in a straight line to first base**—It is very important that the runner comes out of the batter's box running in a straight line toward first base. After picking up the flight of the baseball off the bat, he would then direct his visual attention to the bag itself if there will be a play made at first base. We have all seen hitters stand in the front of the batter's box, and on their follow through on the swing, end up a couple of feet in front of the box. Instead of running in a straight line to first base from

this point, they angle toward the first baseline. Once they get to the first baseline, they then run in a straight path toward first base. This costs a runner valuable time. Wherever a runner finishes his swing in the batter's box is the point where he begins running in a straight line to first base.

7. **Stay on the baseline when the ball is fielded in front of the plate**—If a hitter was to hit or bunt the ball in front of the plate, he should stay right on the baseline as he runs to first base. This should be done so that the catcher will not have an unobstructed throw to the first baseman at first base. This also holds true when a hitter strikes out and the catcher drops the ball and must make the throw to first base. If the catcher was to drop the third strike and it goes into foul territory, the runner should stay on the outside of the restraining area on his way to first base. The batter-runner must stay in the restraining area if a play is being made on him from the area of home plate. The restraining area begins 45 feet down the line to first base.

8. **The baserunner should be responsible for himself if the ball is hit from the shortstop to the right field line**—There is no need for a baserunner to have to pick up the first base coach if the ball is hit to the shortstop on over to the right field line. The batter-runner would make the decision as to whether or not to go to second base. This is to prevent any problem with the visual communication between the first base coach and the runner. This means that the coaching staff will need to spend a great deal of time with the players going over baserunning philosophy. This policy of allowing the baserunners to determine their own destiny on the base paths might not be practical for lower levels of baseball. However, if a player is assigned the responsibility of being the first base coach, it is applicable to all levels of baseball. Since the ball is in front of the runner, there is no need for him to receive assistance from the base coach. Anytime you rely on one person to make a decision, and then communicate his decision to another person, you could have a problem. Any indecision or delay in communication can cost the runner a step or two. The runner knows his capabilities and the situation as well, if not better than the first base coach. Thus, it does not stand to reason why a runner can not react on his own.

9. **The baserunner will pick up the first base coach when the ball is hit to the third base side of the shortstop**—Due to the fact that a ball hit to the third base side of the shortstop would be a little more difficult for the batter-runner to locate, he should pick up the first base coach in the coaching box. The coach would then visually or vocally communicate to the runner whether he should run through the base, take a turn, or go for second base. In this situation, once the runner touches first base he will then make his own decisions on his baserunning status. Thus, if the first base coach informs the runner to take a turn at first base, the player can make his own decision on his status once he touches first base. The same holds true if the first base coach informs the runner that he wants him to go to second base. If the runner sees that he will not be able to get to second base ahead of the throw, he can put the brakes on and return to first base. Thus, the first base coach merely serves as a guide for the runner, but will not make his final decision.

10. **First base coach's signs to the batter-runner**—The first base coach must be sure that he gets to the back of the coaching box on the first baseline side whenever a ball is hit from the shortstop to the third baseline. On any other fair ball, he just needs to stay in the back of the coaching box. This is so the batter-runner can easily pick up the visual signs he will provide him as he approaches first base. On any other type of ball hit, the runner will not pick up the first base coach since he is responsible for the ball himself. When the baserunner is responsible to pick up the first base coach, the coach will want to give the runner his visual instructions at about the time he reaches the restraining area (45 feet down the first baseline from the plate). If given at this time, the runner will have ample opportunity to prepare for the possible turn at first base. If the sign is given after the runner enters this area, he will make it very difficult on the runner's part to make the proper turn. There are various types of visual signs that the first base coach can use to let the runner know what he wishes for him to do. For example, if there will be a play on the runner at first base, he can either point at first base or do nothing. This means that he wants the runner to run through the base. He could provide the runner with verbal encouragement, but this is certainly not necessary. If the first base coach wants the runner to take a turn at first base, he can hold both arms up in the air. Other first base coaches might point at first base with one hand and have the other hand in the air. If he wants the runner to go all the way to second base, he could wave one or both arms in a circular manner or just point to second base. As previously mentioned, once the runner touches first base, the first base coach can no longer be responsible for the runner's action. The first base coach should never give verbal or visual advice to the runner approaching first base when the ball is hit from the shortstop to the right field line. Once he starts doing this, the runners might get confused and a communication problem can arise. It is best to tell the runners that whenever they are in doubt as to whether to pick up the ball or pick up the first base coach, they are to pick up the ball. All the responsibilities of a first base coach are detailed in a later section of the Playbook.

11. **The batter-runner should never leap for first base**—Leaping for first base on a close play should be discouraged for two reasons: (1) the chance of an injury is much greater, due to the fact that the runner could pull a groin or hamstring muscle when he attempts to stretch out to reach the base; and (2) stretching for the base does not quicken a runner's time to the base, unless one has got to stride out just a few inches more than the normal running stride. On a wet day, a runner should

never attempt to over stride for first base. Not only is the ground in front of the base quite slick, but the base itself might be slippery causing a further chance for a serious injury. If it would take a longer stride than just a few inches, it is always best to take the extra step for both of the reasons mentioned.

12. **The runner should attempt to touch the front of the base**—It only stands to reason that the front of first base is closer to home plate than any other part of the base. The base should be hit so that the entire foot touches the front part of the base. If the runner was to hit the front of the base with just his toes, he could risk an ankle injury. This is especially so if the base is sitting high off the ground or is not tied down properly.

13. **The runner should touch first base every time**—Baserunners must get into the habit of touching first base when they are running through the bag, no matter if the throw might beat them to the base. If the first baseman drops the ball or it gets by him, the runner would be out when the base is touched by a defensive player with the ball in his possession. The runner should have eye contact with the base as he hits it to insure this fact.

14. **The runner must run full speed straight through first base**—It is surprising how some runners are observed slowing down just prior to touching first base, and others start angling off to the foul line side of the base on their approach. On a play at first base, the runner should pick out a spot five or six feet past the base and run full speed to that spot. This will assure that they run through the base full speed in a straight path down the line. The base should not be considered the end of the line for the runner attempting to beat the throw.

15. **The runner must watch the first baseman's feet as he approaches first base**—It should not be the responsibility of the first base coach to inform the runner that the first baseman is going to have to come off the base to catch a poor throw. As the runner approaches first base, he will watch the feet of the first baseman. If he sees the first baseman start moving down the first baseline with his feet, the runner will know that he will have to make an attempt to avoid the tag by sliding into the bag. If the first baseman is moving down the line on the infield side, the runner will prepare to slide to the foul side of first base. If he sees that the first baseman is moving to the foul side of the base, the runner will prepare to slide to the inside of first base. If the first baseman is moving toward the right field side of the base, the runner will run straight through the base. Even though the first base coach will be in a position to read the bad throw, the first baseman's feet will dictate much better what the runner needs to do to avoid the tag. Of course, the runner may overslide first base as long as he makes contact with the base on the slide.

16. **The runner should never slide into first base unless it is to avoid a tag**—There are two reasons why a runner should not slide into first base in his attempt to beat the throw: (1) it is not as quick as running straight through the base; and (2) there is a greater chance of injury on a slide. Numerous studies have proved that the head first slide or the feet first slide is not as quick as running through the base. The reason being that runners have got to slow themselves down in order to slide properly and safely into first base. The only time a runner should slide into first base is to avoid the first baseman's tag as previously mentioned. Anytime a player leaves his feet to slide, there is always a greater chance of sustaining an injury. This is more true at first base, since the player's sliding speed into the base is greater than at other bases. The reason being that at first base, the runner does not have to worry about oversliding the base.

17. **The runner should be responsible for any overthrow at first base**—As has been mentioned previously, once the baserunner touches first base, the first base coach should no longer be a factor in the runner's movements on the bases. This should also hold true for the runner who runs through first base and reacts to an overthrow. It should be the runner's responsibility to find the ball after crossing first base, not the first base coach. When the runner is two steps past first base, he must look to the right to see if there has been an overthrow. If so, he then will have to make the decision on whether to return to first base, or try to advance to second base. The runner is in a much better position to make this decision as he observes how far the ball has gone past first base, and who might be backing up the base. It is much easier for him to react to the situation rather than for the first base coach to react, make the decision, and then pass the decision on to the runner, who then must respond. A valuable step or two could be lost in this communication transfer. In baserunning practice sessions, the runners have got to build up the habit of looking to the right after crossing first base. With enough work, this practice of looking to the right will become a natural part of their home to first baserunning.

18. **The batter-runner must run full speed to first base on every play**—The baserunner must be aggressive enough that he treats every fair ball as a chance to take advantage of the defense. This means that the runner has got to make a full effort to first base no matter how much it looks like he will be out. Once the team on defense knows that every runner will be going full speed on every play, it could cause them to begin rushing through the fielding stage of the ball. Once a coach allows one player to go less than full speed to first base, this bad habit can become contagious throughout the entire team. The runner

can never assume that the defense will make even the most routine type of play. By going full speed at all times on the bases, a defensive mistake can be taken advantage of by an aggressive runner. A baseball team does not have to possess outstanding team speed to be a good baserunning team. Even on the routine infield fly ball a good baserunning team would have each of their players respond properly. A runner should run to first base full speed on the fly ball just as if there was a ground ball to the infield with a close play. The only difference being that on the infield fly ball, the runner will need to start slowing down about five or six steps in front of the bag so that he can respond if the ball is misplayed.

19. **Stretching a sure single into a possible double**—Every ball hit fair that the batter-runner reads as a sure single must be considered a possible double. If not, the runner will be unable to take maximum advantage of a mistake on the part of the defense. The runner must force the defense to stop him in his quest to get to second base. Only when the defense makes the play, would the runner go back to first base. When a runner gets thrown out at second base on a close play, he can generally look back and see where he could have picked up a step or two. Most of the time, this step or two could have been picked up at the time the runner asssumed that the ball was probably just a single.

20. **The runner must evaluate the entire situation before attempting to advance to second base**—As any baseball coach can readily understand, there are numerous advantages to having a runner at second base rather than having that same runner at first base. The main advantage being that he is potentially one base hit away from scoring when at second base. Another distinct advantage of being at second base is that it takes the defense away from the possible double play situation when there are less than two outs. At the same time, it would be foolish for a baserunner to get thrown our at second base in some situations. If a coach is to allow his players the opportunity to make most of their own base path decisions, he needs to spend quite a bit of time discussing baserunning philosophy with his players. The following are some rules and regulations in regard to when to gamble on advancing to second base. These rules will hold true for the following situations: (1) possibly stretching a single into a double; (2) advancing to second base on an infield overthrow; (3) advancing to second base on a pick-off overthrow; (4) advancing to second base on a passed ball or wild pitch; and (5) advancing to second base on a fly ball with the runner tagging up at first base.

A. **The runner's speed and texture of the infield**—The runner has got to take into consideration his speed along with the texture of the infield surface. A runner with great speed on a fast track can take advantage of a lot more opportunities to advance to second base than one with poor speed on a slow track.

B. **The score of the game and the inning**—When the runner's team is ahead in the game, he can gamble much more than if they are behind. This is especially true in the later innings of a game. A player never wants to be thrown out when behind in the score late in the game when his run will not be a factor.

C. **Number of outs**—As a general rule, the runner does not want to make the first out at second base. With one out, he can gamble a little more. With two outs he can gamble as much as the situation warrants him to do so.

D. **Hitter at the plate**—A runner at first base would not want to make the third out of an inning at second base with a very weak hitter at the plate. If so, the weak hitter would have to lead off the next inning. At the same time, with a power hitter coming up to the plate with two outs, it might be best to allow him the opportunity to hit a ball out of the park rather than to gamble on making the third out at second base. Many times the defense would just intentionally walk the power hitter with two outs and a runner at second base anyway. If the hitter at the plate is just a singles type hitter, and there are two outs, the runner at first base can afford to gamble on getting to second base.

E. **Ability of the defensive player throwing the ball to second base, and the distance of his throw**—The strength and accuracy of the thrower's arm is of great importance in determining wheher to go to second base. The distance of the throw is another important factor along with whether or not the player throwing the ball is fielding the ball on his glove side or his throwing side. For example, if a ball is hit down the right field line with a righthanded right fielder making the play on the ball, he would have to make a complete pivot before he could throw the ball to second base. If it was a lefthanded right fielder going to the line, he would not have to make this pivot. Thus, he would be in a better position to make a quicker throw to second base.

21. **The distance of the turn at first base**—Whenever the batter-runner makes a turn at first base, the distance of that turn will depend on the following: (1) runner's speed and texture of the infield dirt; (2) whether he is in a gamble situation or not; (3) arm strength and accuracy of the outfielder making the play on the ball; (4) distance the ball is away from second base; (5) whether the outfielder will make the play on the ball on his glove side or his throwing side; and (6) the outfielder's fielding ability. The runner must make as an aggressive turn at first base as the defense will allow him to make. If so, he can take

advantage of any mistake made on the part of the fielder. If he takes an aggressive turn, it will require him to come back to first base full speed.

22. Returning to first base on the turn—If the outfielder fields the ball cleanly on the base hit, the batter-runner will stop and return to first base. He will make the stop on the turn by bending low so that he can brace himself for an abrupt stop. The runner can not afford to stumble forward an extra step if he has gone the maximum distance on his turn. If the ball is fielded from the center field area to left field line, the runner will turn to the infield side on his way back to first base. In this way, he can observe the outfielder's throw to see whether the ball is being thrown to second base; to the cut-off man at another base; or to first base in an attempt to make a play on him returning to first base. If the ball is hit to the right field side of the outfield, the runner will turn to the outfield side on his way back to first base so that he can again watch the direction of the throw. Once the runner sees that the throw is being made to second base or to a cut-off man at another base, his next responsibility is to react to a possible overthrow at that base. It is not the first base coach's responsibility. This means that the runner must maintain eye contact with the ball as it comes into the infield area. The only exception would be if the outfielder throws the ball to first base behind the runner. If that be the case, the runner would break full speed for first base preparing for a play at that base.

23. Outfielder throwing behind the runner—If a runner takes an aggressive turn at any base, there is always the chance that an outfielder will choose to throw behind the runner. If so, the runner must make a very quick decision as to whether he will attempt to advance to the forward base, or return to the base that the ball is going to. This decision would have to be made taking into consideration all the factors that have been previously discussed. For example, if the batter-runner takes an aggressive turn at first base with a ball in the hands of the left fielder at medium depth in the outfield, the left fielder might decide to throw the ball to first base behind the runner. If so, the runner with any speed at all should be able to advance to second base on this long throw to first base. A ball fielded on the right field side of the outfield with a throw to first base, would have a shorter distance to travel. Along with this, the runner could not get as far down the line to second base with a ball hit to right field as he would with a ball in left field. The batter-runner must always be conscious of the catcher trailing him down to first base with a ball hit to right field. Whenever an outfielder trys to show his arm off by throwing behind the runner, an intelligent runner can take advantage of a great opportunity to advance to the next base.

24. Making the turn at first base—The coach needs to spend quite a bit of time with his players in baserunning practice on perfecting their turns at all the bases. The reason being that the better the turn, the quicker the runner will be to the forward base(s). It is not wise for the coach to demand that each player take the same path on the turn, for this is a very individual matter. What the coach wants to do is to assist each runner in perfecting the turn that is best for him. The ideal turn would be one in which the runner takes as an abbreviated turn as possible without losing too much speed on his approach to the base. It is strictly going to be a trial and error process in these baserunning practice sessions. We do not believe that any runner needs to start angling out on his turn to first base upon leaving the batter's box. Since the runner has 90 feet in front of him to make the turn, we want the runner to concentrate his full effort out of the box in generating maximum speed to first base. Once this has been achieved and he or the first base coach reads the fact that a turn at first base will be necessary, then his full concentration will be on the turn itself. If the turn is done properly, the runner will not have to slow down appreciably in order to complete the ideal turn at first base. For most runners, they would begin angling out for their turn at first base when they reach the 45 foot mark to first base (beginning of the restraining area). A boy who has a tough time angling out at this mark and maintaining good speed and body balance can start angling out a little ahead of this area. The key is to find the ideal spot in the baseline to begin the turn. Once the player starts angling out he should not have to decrease any of his speed. The distance that he angles away from the baseline will depend entirely on the runner's ability to maintain good body balance throughout the turn, along with maintaining as much quickness as possible. There should be no reason for any runner to have to angle out any farther than seven or eight feet from the first baseline. The only exception would be on those days when the field is wet or the ground in the area of the turn is loose. When that is the case, all runners should angle out two or three feet farther than they would on a regular surface. Once the runner has reached his ideal angle away from the baseline, he now must begin angling toward the base. This should again be a gradual angle in toward first base so that the runner can maintain as much speed as possible along with a proper body balance. Nothing looks any worse or takes away from an effective turn, than watching a runner stumble while he is angling away from the line or angling back into first base. If the runner maintains a gradual angle throughout his turn, there is no reason for him to lose control of his body. As the runner angles back toward first base, he will have to start slowing down gradually. When he is three or four steps away from making contact with the base, he will now concentrate his attention on the most important aspect of the turn which is touching the base and generating speed to second base. We feel that a runner should not have to reduce his speed by over 20% when approaching first base. If the coach finds a runner reducing his speed appreciably more than 20% when approaching first base, then the runner's angle has got to be widened.

25. Making contact with the base—The angle of the turn at first base should allow the runner complete ease in making proper contact with the base. If at all possible, it is best to hit the base with the left foot for two reasons: (1) hitting with the left foot will assist the runner in achieving the proper lean on his turn; and (2) it will enable him to push toward second base with his right foot, which is the contact foot with the ground. If he hits the base with his right foot, it is very difficult for the left foot to hit and steer the body in a direct path towards second base. The runner's entire body must lean slightly toward the infield side of first base on contact with the base. If the runner hits the base with no body lean to the inside, he will not be able to push off the base effectively in the direction of second base. Being straight up through first base will cause the body to angle away from this direct line. The runner can easily achieve the proper body lean by bending the left leg slightly on contact with the base. The bending of the left leg will also assist the runner in getting the proper push off the base toward second base. In addition to bending the leg, the runner should keep his left arm in tight to the body and drive his right elbow away from the body. This will allow the runner's left side to remain tight on the turn. There is never any reason for a runner to be more than three feet outside of the direct line between first and second base during the turn. If the runner is going out farther than three feet, he is not coming into the base at the proper angle or he is not achieving the proper body lean on contact with the base. The lean into the base should not be so extreme that the runner loses any body balance or speed through the bag. The proper body lean will enable the runner to accelerate off the base in almost a straight line toward second base. We do not want the runner to have to break stride in order to hit the base with his left foot. If he sees that his right foot will hit the base, then he will have to compensate for this fact with a greater lean to the inside of the diamond. Otherwise he will find that he will have the tendency to ride high on the base and his path will carry him toward the right field side of the base path between first and second base. With a lot of practice a baserunner should be able to hit all bases with his left foot practically every time without having to break stride. The runner must have complete eye contact with the base during the approach (three or four steps away from the base) and maintain eye contact with the base until his foot has left the base. By maintaining eye contact with the base, the runner will find that it will keep his head down and assist in the proper push off toward second base. The runner should attempt to hit the base in the same spot every time. The ideal contact spot is on the infield half side of the base with the ball of the foot pushing off on the second base side of the bag. By planting the foot in this manner, the runner will be able to push off the base in a direct line toward second base. If the runner hits the base high (right field side of the base) he will not be able to achieve the proper body lean, nor will he be able to use the base as effectively to generate maximum momentum toward second base. After contact with the base, the next step must also be with a bent leg achieving complete body control so that the runner can accelerate toward second base. At this time the runner will locate the baseball so that he can react to the situation at hand. Anytime the base is wet, the runner must be sure that he hits the base a little closer to the infield side so that there would be no chance for his foot to slip on the base. If he hits a wet base high on the bag, there is a good chance that his contact foot will slip. This is especially true if the runner leans in on his turn. This is the reason why a runner must angle out a little more when the field is wet so that he does not have to lean as much and this problem can be minimized. The turn at first base is very similar to the turns at second and third base. The only difference might be in the angle of approach at times, due to the fact that a runner might not be in a position to read what he will have to do at a base. If the runner is aware early enough that a turn at a base is evident, then the mechanics of the turn are the same for all bases.

26. **Fly ball to the outfield**—A baserunner must take tremendous pride in his reaction to a fly ball in the outfield, even if it looks like he will be a routine out. The runner's mechanics on his turn at first base should be the same for a fly ball as it would be if he was attempting to reach second base on an attempted double. A runner's time to first base on the turn should never be slower than three-tenths of a second from his time to the base when running straight through the base. If it is slower than this, either he is taking a poor turn at first base or he is not going at the speed necessary to qualify as an aggressive runner. The runner rounding first base needs to be cautious that he does not pass the runner who might have started at first base. On a fly ball, the runner at first base might be tagging up hoping to advance on the catch by the outfielder. If he is not tagging up, he will be advancing toward second base as far as possible so that he can return to first base if the ball is caught. If the batter-runner was to pass him between first and second base, and the outfielder misplays the ball, the batter-runner would be called out immediately by the umpire. The batter-runner must read the nature of any fly ball so that he would be in a position to advance to second base if the ball hits the ground. If the fly ball is hit to an area close to second base and dropped, he must be sure that he can reach second base before the ball arrives.

27. **Decoying infielder or catcher**—A runner should never be fooled by a decoying infielder or catcher as the runner approaches a base or the plate. An intelligent infielder or catcher will attempt to decoy a runner if there is a perfect throw coming into the base or the plate from behind the runner. He will do this by positioning himself two or three steps behind the base or the plate in line with the throw, making the runner think that there will be no play on him. He will do this hoping that the runner will slow down as he approaches the base or the plate, or he will not make an aggressive slide. The infielder or the catcher can also decoy a runner by standing erect on the base or the plate so that he does not give the runner the look that a play is imminent. At the last second he will assume the correct defensive position to catch the ball and make the tag. Thus, a runner must be aggressive at all times anticipating a decoy play by a defensive player. Three of the most common plays by a decoying infielder or catcher are:

230

A. The batter hits a ball down the right field line, and heads for second base. The shortstop will be receiving the ball from the right fielder which would be coming in from behind the runner as he approaches second base.

B. The runner at first base rounds second base on a base hit to center field or right field. The third baseman will be receiving the ball from the center fielder or right fielder coming in from behind the runner as he approaches third base.

C. The runner is attempting to score and the ball comes into the plate area from left field or center field. Generally a ball coming into the plate from right field will be seen by the runner as he approaches the plate.

28. Head first slide—In the section following the baserunning section, we will detail all the types of slides that can be made. This will include the head first slide, which is the best slide to make whenever there is going to be a close play at a base or the plate. There are numerous exceptions when a runner would not head first slide. This will all be presented in this next section.

29. The baserunner at first base—As soon as the runner reaches first base, he must quickly review in his mind the situation at hand (outs, inning, score, hitter at the plate, outfielders' arms, etc.). The first thing he must check is the outfielders' depths and location. As soon as this is done, he will pick up the third base coach for a possible sign. He will do this after every pitch as soon as he returns to first base. All signs must be taken with the runner on the base. The third base coach should flash the signs quickly so that the runner can devote his full attention to the pitcher as he begins the lead at first base. The following are the general rules for leading off first base:

A. **Using the first base coach**—The first base coach should not have to review the situation at hand with the runner when he gets to first base. This should be strictly the runner's responsibility. The only exception might be for a player who has proven his inability to concentrate on the bases. This is especially true if the runner is the tying or winning run late in the game. The more the first base coach has to review items of concern with the runners at first base, the more you will find the runners depending on the first base coach each time they are at first base. The same holds true when the runner assumes his primary lead at first base. If the runner is going to rely on the first base coach to yell "back" when the pitcher begins his pick-off move to first base, you will find that the runners will be a step slow reacting. When the runners know that they will receive no help from the first base coach on a pick-off attempt, you will find all the runners concentrating much more on the pitcher while they are leading off the base. The only exception to this rule would be when the first baseman is playing behind the runner. In this situation, the runner would probably take a little wider lead at first base and now the first base coach will have to let him know if the first baseman makes a break toward first base. You do not want your runner leading off first base to have to turn his head to check on the status of the first baseman. All the other responsibilities of the first base coach will be presented in a later section of the Playbook.

B. **Moving off the base**—Once the runner at first base has picked up the third base coach for the possible sign, he will devote his full attention to the pitcher as he begins moving off the base. He will not make any move off the base until he is absolutely sure that the ball is in the possession of the pitcher on the mound. We want the runners at all bases to achieve their full primary lead (final lead when the pitcher has come to the set position on the stretch) before the pitcher begins any movement into his stretch position. This will eliminate a pitcher's most effective pick-off move to a base, that being when he is going up or down with his hands to the set position. This means that the full primary lead must be achieved while the pitcher is receiving his sign from the catcher. The first steps away from the base can be easily achieved by pushing off the base with his left foot in front of his right foot. Then he would step with his right foot behind his left foot. Now he will take one large shuffle step with both feet putting him about 13 or 14 feet away from the base. The runner does not need to rush this footwork to the point that too much of his weight is moving toward second base too quickly. If this footwork is rushed, the runner could be susceptible to a pick-off from the pitcher prior to his moving into the set position. At this point the runner might wish to move off a little further away from the base. If so, he will step toward second base with his right foot, followed quickly by moving his left foot the same distance as he did his right foot. Neither foot should be off the ground in this movement so that the spikes clear the dirt. In this way, if the pitcher picks at first base, the runner can easily dive back to the base. Any movement from this point would be slight with the right foot moving just a few inches toward second base followed quickly the same distance by the left foot.

C. **The primary lead**—The length of a baserunner's primary lead will be determined by the following factors:

1. **Ability to get back to the base**—It stands to reason that the quicker the baserunner's ability to get back to first base on the dive, the farther from the base he can get in his primary lead.

2. **Condition of the infield surface**—If the infield area where the runner leads off the base is firm and in good

condition, the runner will be able to get back to first base with greater ease. If the dirt is loose or wet, it will be difficult to push off on a potential dive back to first base. Thus, the runner's lead will have to be shortened.

3. **Pitcher's pick-off move to first base**—The pitcher's quickness or deception on his pick-off move will help determine the length of the primary lead. The better the pitcher's move, the shorter the primary lead. The weaker the pitcher's pick-off move the longer the lead.

4. **The sign flashed by the coach**—The sign from the third base coach will be an important factor in the length of the runner's primary lead from first base. Examples of these signs would be:

a. **Take sign to the batter**—When the batter gets the take sign from the third base coach, the runner at first base must shorten his lead to insure the fact that he does not get picked off the base.

b. **Hit and run sign flashed**—The runner at first base can not afford to get picked off when the hit and run sign is on. Thus, if he needs to shorten his lead to insure this fact, he must do so.

c. **Fake steal sign flashed**—The runner can not afford to get picked off when he is to fake steal on the pitch. By shortening his lead at first base it will also help him fake steal a greater distance on the pitch.

d. **Steal sign flashed**—The distance of the primary lead will be affected by the type of steal called for by the third base coach. The mechanics of the various types of steals will be discussed later. If the count on the batter is 3-2 and the steal sign is flashed, the runner must be sure that he does not get picked off first base. He might have to shorten his lead in order to insure this fact.

e. **One way lead to first base flashed**—If the third base coach wants the runner at first base to take a long lead on the pitcher, he will lengthen his lead. This is to force the pitcher to show his pick-off move to first base.

D. **Depth of the lead**—When the first baseman is holding the runner on at first base, we want the runner to lead off the base so that the back of his heels are lined up with the inside of the bag. This is done so that the runner will be able to get another foot plus lead at first base on the pitcher. From the pitcher's view on the mound, it will appear to him that the runner is closer to first base as the runner gets closer to the pitcher on the rubber. If he leads off first base even with or behind the base he will not appear as close as he would from the inside, thus not allowing him another foot plus lead on the pitcher. With the first baseman playing behind the runner at first base, the runner should lead off even with the bag.

E. **Lead off stance of the baserunner**—Once the runner has established his primary lead, he must be in a stance so that he can properly react to a pick-off attempt. The feet should be slightly wider than shoulder width apart. This might vary from runner to runner due to anatomical differences. Generally, the taller the runner, the wider the stance must be. The weight must be on the balls of the feet with both arms hanging loosely in front of the body. He should never have his hands resting on his knees since it will cut down on his ability to react quickly on a pick-off attempt. The knees must be flexed slightly to insure that the runner can push off in either direction. When there is no steal sign on, the runner must be in a position to get back to first base if the pitcher picks at the base. Thus, both toes should be pointing straight ahead parallel to each other. If the steal sign is on, the right toe should be opened about two inches toward second base. This should not be noticeable enough to alert the pitcher or the first baseman. The pointing out of the right toe is done so that the runner can open up quicker on his first movement toward second base.

F. **Returning to first base on a pick-off attempt-dive play**—When the runner has his full primary lead at first base, the only way he will be able to get back to first base quickly is by diving back to the base. Since the runner will have his full primary lead prior to the pitcher moving into the stretch, the dive would be used practically on every pick-off attempt. The distance that the runner is away from first base will dictate whether or not he will use the cross-over dive or the lead leg dive. The cross-over dive should be used only if the runner has an extremely long lead from first base. This is the type of dive used when the runner has a one-way lead back to first base trying to draw a throw from the pitcher. The runner will cross-over with his right foot directly toward first base and then dive for the base. The lead leg dive would be used when the runner has his regular primary lead. The runner will lead with his left foot toward first base and then dive. The cross-over dive will take a split second longer, but the runner will be able to dive a greater distance. On both types of dives, the runner will stay low diving back to the base. His knees should not hit the ground on the dive. The blunt of the force with the ground should be taken on the chest area. He should reach for the base with his right hand only. This will allow him to get back to the base much quicker than if he was to dive back to the base with both arms extended. The one arm extended method will also allow the runner to reach further than with both arms extended. As soon as the runner touches the base, he should look up so that he can react to a possible overthrow at first base. The first base coach is not responsible for reacting to the overthrow. If the runner will be using the cross-over dive back to first base, then he will have more of his weight on his left side than his right. This is if there is no steal sign on. If the runner is using the lead leg dive back to first base, he should have more weight on his right side. This will just be a slight shifting of the weight onto the ball of the foot on either the left or right foot. If the steal sign is on, then the weight will be evenly distributed over the balls of both feet in both dive methods. A coach will find that some runners prefer one method to the other in diving back to the base. Whatever method is the best for that runner should be the one he uses. However, both methods should be presented and practiced. A coach can line his entire team down the right field line, using the right field line as first base. The coach can then stand where the second baseman normally positions himself and assume the stretch position. At this time, all the runners should have assumed their primary lead away from the base (right field line). The coach can tell them what sign is on, and then let them react. If the pitcher picks at first base, all the runners will dive back to the base (right field line). If the steal sign is on, and the pitcher fakes the pitch to the plate, all the runners will sprint toward an imaginary second base. This is the time that they can work on all their different leads as well as practice their dives. When they are diving on the grass, it makes for a much easier landing than if they were to practice their dives on the infield dirt. It is very important that the coach spend a lot of time with his runners on the mechanics of the dive play. When done properly, it means that the runner can get his maximum lead without fear of getting picked off the base.

G. **Returning to first base on a pick-off attempt—standing up**—If the full primary lead is established prior to the pitcher beginning his movement into the stretch, then the necessity for returning to first base standing up is minimized. However, there are times when the runner will have to return to the base standing up due to the fact that he is not far enough away from the base to dive back when the pick-off attempt occurs. These times would be:

1. The runner has not established his full primary lead and the pitcher picks at first base prior to his beginning the stretch. If there is a question in the runner's mind as to whether to dive back to the base or return standing up, he must dive.

2. The runner has an abbreviated one way lead back to first base. In this case the take sign is on, and the runner has shortened his lead to the point that a dive play is not possible or practical.

3. The runner has a shoulder, arm, hand or finger problem and risks further injury if he dives back to the base. Thus, the runner will have to take a conservative lead due to the fact that he can not dive back to the base.

If the runner takes his full lead with none of the above in effect, and he does not have to dive back to the base on a pick-off attempt, he does not have a big enough primary lead. We do not want a runner picked off first base, especially if no steal sign is on. However, he must be far enough away from the base in his primary lead that the dive play is the only way he can return to first base. Going back to first base standing up is only done when the dive play can not be done due to the reasons stated. When the runner takes his first step away from first base he must be prepared to return to the base at a moment's notice. This is why the runner can not be leading off a base without watching the pitcher at all times. He can not look back to the base at anytime. He will sense how far he is away from the base which is accomplished by constant practice. A smart pitcher will pick at first base when he observes a runner looking back to the base as he assumes his lead. If the runner is forced to return to first base standing up, it will be accomplished by a cross-over step with his right foot. Of course, if the runner is only a step away from the base when the pitcher picks, he should hit the base with whatever foot is closest. Many coaches teach the runner to return to the back of the base when forced to return standing up. This is done by hitting the back of the base with their left foot followed by swinging the right foot behind the base so as not to overrun the base. They practice this manner in order to be in a better position to avoid the tag by the first baseman. We do not consider this the ideal way to return to first base when forced to return standing up for the following reasons:

1. It is the slowest way to return to first base since the footwork is difficult to do quickly and a runner is returning to the back of the base. This is especially true if the runner is leading off first base with his heels lined up with the inside of the base.

2. It increases the chance of a runner coming off the base due to the momentum needed to hit the base in this manner. This is especially true when the runner must leap for the base with his left foot. If the infield surface is loose or the base wet, the chances of maintaining contact with the base are severely minimized.

3. It allows the first baseman to make a play on a poor throw by the pitcher on the second base side of the base. Since the runner is going into the back of the base, the first baseman can move easily to the second base side of the base to catch the poor throw.

4. If the ball does get by the first baseman, the runner will have his back to the ball. He must then turn and make a decision on whether to advance to second base or not.

We feel it is best to return to first base with the left foot hitting the inside corner of the base. With the cross-over step being used, the runner would cross-over toward the base with his right foot and then step on the base with his left foot. The right foot would then be placed firmly on the ground so that the runner's entire body is fully under control. In this manner the first baseman is not going to be able to come off the base on the second base side to catch a bad throw by the pitcher on that side of the base. The first baseman will be able to protect the runner standing firmly on the base from getting hit by the throw, but he will be unable to go after the throw on the other side of the runner. It is perfectly legal for a baserunner to position himself in this manner while returning to first base, as long as he does not push the first baseman on his return to the base. You will be surprised how many times the ball sails past first base when the runner handicaps the first baseman from fielding the throw on the second base side of first base. The runner must be sure that he does not cover his helmet with his hands, which is a natural reaction. He just needs to keep his arms to his side, for the first baseman will catch any ball that could hit the runner. If the runner is farther than the right-left cross-over step back to first base, he should be diving.

H. **Reading the pitcher's pick-off move to first base**—As mentioned previously, one of the prime considerations in determining the distance of the primary lead is the pitcher's ability to execute the pick-off play. By getting the entire primary lead prior to the pitcher going into the stretch, the righthanded pitcher's pick-off move accomplished going up or down with the hands is minimized a great deal. Thus, the runner will be dealing primarily with a pitcher who has assumed the set position. When there is no steal sign on for the runner at first base, he will have a one-way lead off the base. All of his concentration will be centered on the fact that as soon as he reads a pick-off attempt, he must return to first base as quickly as possible. There is never any reason for a runner to get picked off first base unless the steal sign is on when he would have either a two-way lead, or a one-way lead to second base. There are various ways that a pitcher can show the runner that he will be throwing the ball to first base. The following are some of these tell tale signs for both a righthanded and lefthanded pitcher:

1. **Righthanded pitcher**—From the set position, the righthanded pitcher's hands must come to a brief stop prior to delivering the ball to the plate. They do not have to come to a stop when throwing the ball to first base. As mentioned previously, a smart pitcher will pick at first base when his hands are moving into the set position hoping to find the runner at first base moving away from the base too quickly. When the runner has his full primary lead prior to the pitcher moving his hands to the set position, this will negate the effectiveness of this type of pick-off move. Since the runner will not receive any verbal assistance from the first base coach, all of his concentration is centered on the pitcher as soon as he takes that first step away from first base. A righthanded pitcher must do two things with his body in order to throw to first base from the set position: (1) clear the pitching rubber with his right foot; and (2) open up the front side of his body. With that being the case, the baserunner has just two areas of the body to center his full attention on: the right foot and the left side. If the pitcher comes to the set position with his left side opened toward first base, then his pick-off move to first base will be a little quicker. However, his quickness to the plate will be slower due to the fact that he will have to close the left side to deliver the ball effectively to the plate. The runner at first base must make a slight adjustment in his lead when he is facing a pitcher with an opened left side. From the set position, there is no way a righthanded pitcher can throw the ball to first base without lifting his right heel off the pitching rubber. Thus, with the runner at first base keying on the right foot, he will return to first base when he sees the right heel come off the pitching rubber. At the same time that the pitcher begins clearing the rubber with his right foot, the left side will be moving in the direction of first base. The runner who watches the head or upper part of the pitcher's body will definitely be a step slower in reacting to a pick-off attempt. If the steal sign is on, the runner will more than likely have a two-way lead which will allow him to return to first base or break for second base when the pitcher begins his motion to the plate. With the steal sign on, the runner can safely assume that the pitcher will be delivering the ball to the plate when he sees the right foot in full contact with the rubber while the left side moves. If so, the runner will break for second base. A word of caution in regard to this would be that a pitcher might execute a balk move so slight that it takes an observant umpire to pick it up. He will do this in either three ways: (1) he would bend his left knee slightly while his right foot is in full contact with the rubber, and then pick at first base; (2) he would bend his right knee while his right foot is in full contact with the rubber, and then pick at first base; and (3) he would bring his hands up from the set position just prior to picking at first base. The first two ways would definitely cause a problem for the runner who is stealing and concentrating on the right foot and left side. If this balk type of move occurs, the coach needs to present this fact to the umpires for their closer observation of the pitcher from the set position. The third type of balk move should not cause any major problem for the runner, unless the movement of the hands occurs while there is other movement of the lower extremities and the pitcher does not deliver to the plate. The runner who can center his attention on these two areas of the body on the righthanded pitcher should be able to get a good jump in either direction when the steal sign is on.

2. **Lefthanded pitcher**—From the set position, there is only one way that the lefthanded pitcher can throw the ball to first base, and that is to step off the rubber with his left foot. A lefthanded pitcher could throw to first base off this move when he finds a runner taking a very large primary lead while he is at the set position. If the baserunner is taking a large primary lead to force the pitcher to throw to first base when he breaks his hands from the set, then he must be very conscious of this type of pick-off move. While the lefthanded pitcher is holding at the set position, the runner must concentrate his full attention to the left foot. If he sees the foot move off the rubber, he must quickly dive back to first base. Once the pitcher breaks from the set position he can either deliver the ball to the plate or throw the ball to first base. As mentioned previously, if the steal is not on there is no reason for a runner to get picked off first base. This also holds true for a lefthanded pitcher with a great pick-off move. Against a lefthander on the mound, it is the responsibility of each runner to know his lead off capabilities as well as the ability of the pitcher to pick at first base. The pitcher must be observed from the dugout so that his pick-off move can be evaluated. It is especially important that the first runner or two who lead off first base, force the pitcher to execute his best move. They can do this by establishing a long one-way lead back to first base so that everyone on the team can observe his move. A lefthanded pitcher with a great pick-off move can severely hinder the offensive team's ability to steal second base. However, most lefthanded pitchers will give away the fact that they are throwing to first base. Some will give it away as soon as they break from the set position, while others will give it away sometime during their motion. The lefthander that does not show the pick-off to first base until the last moment will make it very difficult for a runner leading off first base with the steal sign on. There are numerous ways that the lefthanded pitcher can give away the fact that he will be throwing the ball to first base:

a. **Unnatural leg and toe kick**—Some pitchers will lift their lead leg (right) higher when going to first base than they would if delivering to the plate. They will also point their toe toward first base when going to first base, and keep the toe pointed more toward the ground when going to the plate. Of course, you will have some exceptions where a pitcher will lift his leg higher when going to the plate, along with having his toe pointed toward first base.

b. **Lead leg swing**—One of the easiest ways for a runner to get a big jump on the lefthanded pitcher when stealing second base, is when the pitcher swings his lead leg (right) past the rubber when delivering the ball to the plate. When he keeps his lead leg even with the pitching rubber when going to the plate or first base, it makes it that much tougher for the runner at first base. Once the lead leg passes the rubber, the pitcher is committed to throw the ball to the plate, or to second base if executing the inside pick-off move with a runner at second base.

c. **Head and eyes**—A tell tale give away for many lefthanded pitchers is what they do with their head and eyes when breaking from the set position. If there is one general rule that is followed by most lefthanders it is that they will keep their eyes on the runner at first base when they are delivering the ball to the plate. When they are going to pick at first base, their eyes are looking toward the plate. This eye contact is important when the pitcher reaches the balance point where the right leg is at its highest point for the drive to the plate or the step toward first base. The pitcher who can vary his looks going to the plate or to first base will make it extremely tough for a runner at first base. Another give away for a lefthanded pitcher is when he lifts his head and eyes toward the sky when bringing his hands up from the set position. This generally means that the pitcher is going to throw the ball to first base. When he is going to the plate, he keeps his head and eyes down to better keep his body in control for his drive to the plate.

d. **Pivot leg bend**—Most lefthanded pitchers will have to bend their pivot leg (left) in order to get some drive off the rubber when delivering the ball to the plate. The pitcher who bends the leg as soon as he breaks his hands from the set will have a very difficult time throwing the ball to first base. This is due to the fact that the bend in the pivot leg also will cause him to push off the rubber towards the plate. If the pitcher keeps his pivot leg straight during his motion, he is better able to throw the ball to first base.

e. **Hands**—A lefthander with an excellent move to first base will bring his hands up from the set position the same height when he is going to the plate, as when he is throwing the ball to first base. Other pitchers will either bring their hands higher or lower when going to first base than they would when going to the plate.

f. **Shoulders**—Some lefthanders will rotate their shoulders slightly toward second base when delivering the ball to the plate, but keep them squared to first base when going to that base for a pick-off attempt. The lefthander with the good move to first base will keep his shoulders square no matter in which direction he will go with the ball.

g. **Tempo of their movement**—Another general rule for many lefthanded pitchers is that when they are going to attempt the pick-off at first base there is a definite slowing down of their movement from the set position. Most pitchers establish a set rhythm in their delivery to the plate, and break the pace of their rhythm when going to first base. The pitcher who can keep his rhythm the same no matter which direction he is throwing the ball, will make it that much tougher for the runner at first base.

I. **Stealing second base**—Now that the runner reads that the pitcher will be delivering the ball to the plate, his concentration will be directed toward movement toward second base if the steal sign is on. The mechanics of stealing second base can basically be broken down into three areas of concern: (1) primary lead; (2) first steps toward second base; and (3) acceleration.

1. **Primary lead**—We have previously detailed information pertaining to the baserunner's primary lead while the pitcher is in the set position. Most of the attention was centered on the one-way lead back to first base when the steal sign was not on. Now with the steal sign on, we will discuss the primary lead that needs to be established by the runner. This will either be the two-way lead, the one-way lead to second base, or the walking lead.

a. **Two-way lead**—With the steal sign on, the runner wants to establish a primary lead that will enable him to be as far away from first base as possible, but still be in a position to get back to first base on a pick-off attempt by the pitcher. As mentioned previously, the distance of the lead will depend upon: (1) baserunner's ability to get back to first base; (2) pitcher's pick-off move to first base; and (3) condition of the infield surface. Once the lead has been established, the runner will attempt to position himself for maximum acceleration to second base when he reads that the pitcher will be delivering the ball to the plate. We advise that the right foot be placed so that the toes of the right foot are about two inches behind the toes of the left foot. At the same time, the toes of the right foot are pointing about two inches in the direction of second base. Some runners may need to bring the right foot back another one or two inches if they find that they are having a difficult time getting their weight transferred to second base on their initial movement in that direction. The more the runner points the right toe and drops back the right foot, the better his quickness should be in his initial movement toward second base. However, the more this is done the slower he will be in returning to first base on a pick-off attempt. This is why it is very important that the runners do not take such a big primary lead that they feel uncomfortable assuming this base stealing position. The longer the primary lead, the more the runner is thinking about getting back to first base and the less he is thinking about his movement toward second base. The runners need to work on their base stealing stance in practice sessions so that they find out what their capabilities are in regard to getting back to first base. With the steal sign on, it is important that the runner understands that he does not have to steal if he does not get a good jump. If he does not get a good jump he will establish his secondary lead as the pitch is on its way to the plate. He will then check with the third base coach to see if the steal sign is still on or not. By establishing the fact that the runner does not have to steal unless he gets a good jump, it will enable him to take a more comfortable lead. Of course, if the runner at first base is part of a double steal attempt with a runner at second base, he will have to break for second base even though he might not have gotten a good jump. If there is a runner at second base when the double steal sign is on, more then likely any play made by the catcher will be for the runner stealing third base. This will allow the runner at first base to take a comfortable lead. With a 3-2 or 3-1 count on the batter, the runner at first base should steal on the pitch unless he gets a very poor jump. On any other count he must get a perfect jump in order to continue on to second base. The runner needs to be very relaxed in his stealing stance so that he does not stiffen up while waiting for the pitcher to make a break from the set position. If the pitcher holds the ball too long at the set position (generally more than four seconds), the batter must protect the runner by calling for a timeout. This is especially true when the batter knows that the steal sign is on. The longer the pitcher holds the ball at the set position, the tougher it is for a runner to get a good jump on the steal attempt. We have found it helps many runners to bounce a little on the balls of their feet while the pitcher is holding at the set position. There should be no faking movements toward second base while the pitcher is holding at the set. This just creates body balance problems when the pitcher breaks from the set to deliver the ball to the plate or to first base on the pick-off attempt. Once the runner reads that the pitcher is going to deliver to the plate, the acceleration toward second base begins.

b. **One-way lead to second base**—This type of lead offers the baserunner the luxury of not having to worry about returning to first base. All of the runner's attention is centered on breaking toward second base on any movement from the set by the pitcher. Generally with a one-way lead to second base the runner will take a shorter lead from first base than he would take with a two-way lead with the steal sign on. This gives him the ability to get a great jump toward second base, and also provides him the feeling of some security since the pitcher's tendency to throw to first base will be minimized. The one-way primary lead on a steal attempt is primarily used against a lefthanded pitcher with an outstanding move to first base. With a righthanded pitcher it is generally best to execute the two-way lead unless the pitcher has an unusually great pick-off move to first base. The one-way stealing lead generally needs to be set up by both the third base coach and the runner at first base. If a lefthanded pitcher has a truly outstanding move to first base it would be foolish for the runner at first base to get a full two-way lead with the steal sign on. If he does take a big lead his chances of getting picked off first base will be high. Also, if the pitcher delivers the ball to the plate his chance of getting a great jump on the steal attempt will be small. The third base coach can assist the runner in varying the length of his lead at first base by a visual sign system. This is very important so that the coach and the runner attempt to "set" the lefthander up for that time when the steal sign is flashed. In practically all cases, a lefthanded pitcher will determine before he breaks from the set position whether he is going to throw the ball to first base or to the plate. It is very difficult for the pitcher to pick up his lead leg contemplating delivering the ball to the plate, only to change his mind at the last moment and throw the ball to first base. The pitcher is thinking pitch and location as he begins to deliver to the plate and has blocked out of his mind what he needs to do mechanically to throw the ball to first base. Thus, if the runner breaks for second base when the pitcher lifts his lead leg from the set for preparation to deliver the pitch, there is nothing that the pitcher can do to alter his motion. In this case, the runner will have a super jump toward second base on the steal attempt. For most lefthanded pitchers, the runner can break for second base when the lead foot begins its motion off the ground. If a pitcher has a very slow lead leg lift, then the runner may have to wait until the leg has come off the ground about a foot before breaking toward second base. Anytime a runner has a one-way lead to second base and the pitcher does throw the ball to first base, the runner should continue on to second base full speed. He will then attempt to beat the throw to second base from the first baseman who has received the ball from the pitcher. The runner needs to stay on the inside of the baseline to make it very difficult for the first baseman to have a clear throw to the shortstop or second baseman covering second base. A baserunner with excellent speed can beat this throw many times for it is going to take two quick and accurate throws to retire him at second base. Let us set up a situation for a baserunner leading off first base with a lefthander on the mound with an excellent pick-off move. The first lead the runner takes is a one-way lead back to first base. Thus, he would be a couple of feet past his regular primary two-way lead hoping to force the pitcher to throw to first base. If the pitcher does throw to first base, there will be no problem in getting back to the base in time. When the pitcher shows any motion with his lead leg, the runner crosses over with his right foot towards first base while watching the pitcher. If he sees that the pitcher is going to throw to first base, he will dive off the right foot for the base. If he sees that the pitcher is going to deliver the ball to the plate, he will take another step toward first base with his left foot after crossing over with his right foot. He will pivot off the left foot and move out quickly toward his secondary lead. If the pitcher does not pick at first base with this long one-way lead back to first base, it will make the runner look terrible. It will take on the appearance that the pitcher fooled the runner at first base to think he was throwing to first base. In all actuality, the runner is just working the lefthanded pitcher for that time when he is going to steal second base with great ease. Now with the steal sign on the runner can take his regular two-way primary lead in hopes that the pitcher will not throw the ball to first base. The runner might even be a couple of feet closer to first base than his normal two-way lead to insure even more that the pitcher will not pick at first base. From this lead the runner will take off for second base when the pitcher lifts his lead leg from the set position. If the pitcher does throw to first base, the runner continues on to second base in hopes that he might beat the throw from the first baseman to the player covering second base. The third base coach and the runner might want to take more than one one-way lead to first base to make the pitcher throw the ball to first base. All we are attempting to do is to steal second base when the chances for the pitcher throwing to first base are minimal. If the lefthanded pitcher has a poor move to first base, there is no reason to set up the steal with these type leads.

c. **Walking lead**—Another type of lead that can be done when the steal sign is on is the walking lead. The runner will take a short lead off first base, and will start walking toward second base as the pitcher holds at the set position. The walking lead is not an actual walk with the runner's body totally moving toward second base. It is a shuffling walk so that the runner can still get back to first base if he sees that the pitcher might pick. The runner can not afford to use a cross-over step once he gets a good distance away from first base. A smart pitcher will never deliver the ball to the plate when he sees the runner at first base moving toward second base. If the pitcher allows the runner to walk away from the base and then delivers to the plate, the runner should get a tremendous jump on the steal attempt. If the pitcher was to hold at the set position with the runner walking off the base, the runner must stop his movement once he gets to his full primary lead. If he continues past this point he will be easily picked off, especially if he is still moving in the direction of second base. The walking lead is only a good stealing lead when the runner finds that the pitcher is not concentrating on the runner at first base. The walking lead is usually only effective against a righthanded pitcher since the lefthanded pitcher will be able to see the runner moving toward second base from the set position.

2. **First steps toward second base**—The key to a runner being an effective base stealer is his ability to get a great jump when the pitcher delivers the ball to the plate. There are many players who have outstanding running speed but are unable to get a good jump. Vice-versa, there are many runners who have average running speed and are effective base

stealers due to the fact that they are able to get a good jump off their primary stealing lead. The first four or five steps are crucial toward achieving the proper acceleration toward second base. For this reason, the coach needs to spend a lot of time in baserunning practice working with his runners to get the maximum acceleration in these first four or five steps. The cross-over step is the best method to use in getting the proper movement from the primary lead stance. As previously mentioned, the runner's right foot needs to be slightly opened to enable his left side to cross-over without being hindered by a closed right side of the body. If the runner has his right foot pointing straight ahead, he would have to open up the right foot prior to crossing over with the left foot. When the runner reads that the pitcher is delivering the ball to the plate, various body parts must quickly be set in motion. The upper part of his body must turn toward second base so that the head does not raise up from the level it was at in the primary lead. Any motion of the head above this level will cause the upper part of the body to raise up, not enabling the runner to establish the proper momentum in the direction of second base. If the runner assumes a high stance on his primary lead, he would have to be sure that his head actually moves slightly downward to achieve this proper momentum. At the same time, he will pivot on the heel of his right foot so that the toes of that foot are pointing directly toward second base. His left arm will be thrown across the body directly toward second base to assist the upper part of the body to explode toward second base. His right arm needs to also assist in establishing the proper momentum. By driving the back of the right hand toward second base simultaneously when the left arm is driving across the body, it will initiate the proper momentum. Once the right hand and arm reach out toward second base, they are brought back to the side of the body preparing to pump hard as the runner begins his acceleration toward second base. The left foot must push off the ground for the cross-over step as all the other body parts are in motion. The runner must be sure that he does not push up off the ground, but pushes off the ground so that the left foot goes directly across the body toward second base. The push off of the left foot should not cause the body to rise, which if done would have a detrimental effect on the generation of momentum toward second base. The cross-over step toward second base can not be too long of a step. If the runner takes too big of a step with the left foot he will not be able to keep his body under proper balance. At the same time, it can not be too small of a step which would hinder the runner's acceleration. After the left foot hits the ground, the runner must begin his pumping motion with his arms as the first four or five steps are crucial toward achieving the proper acceleration.

3. **Acceleration**—During the first four or five steps the head and upper part of the body must continue to stay on the same plane as it was during the initial cross-over step. This is to insure that the body does not start rising too quickly in order to insure the proper body lean during the acceleration stage of the steal attempt. Once acceleration has been initiated, the runner can gradually elevate his body to achieve the ideal body lean for the duration of his run toward second base. The eyes should be focused directly at second base during this acceleration to insure that the runner is going in a straight line toward second base. Once acceleration has been completed the runner's next responsibility is to be in a position to locate the baseball as it enters the area of the plate. This is done so that he can properly react to a batted ball, a wild pitch, or a pass ball. He can not rely on the third base coach to inform him where the baseball has been hit, or if the ball has gotten by the catcher. If the runner practices the proper mechanics, his looking in toward the plate should not have any effect on his speed to second base. Through constant practice at looking in toward the plate on steal attempts, the runner will learn when the ball is about to reach the plate. He can not afford to look in too late for he will then not be in a position to see where the ball has gone. If he looks in a little too early, he will just remain looking in while running until he clearly knows the status of the ball. If the ball is hit in the air with less than two outs, the runner needs to respond to a possible catch. If the ball is a line drive with less than two outs the runner must be sure that the ball gets past the infield before continuing to advance. If the ball is on the ground he continues toward second base making sure that he does not get hit by the ground ball as he is advancing. If the ball gets by the catcher he will be in a position to make the proper turn at second base. If the ball is fielded cleanly by the catcher he can assume that there will be a play made on him at second base. When looking in toward the plate, the runner should not have to turn his head completely toward the plate. If he does, then he will definitely hinder his speed to second base. He will angle his head slightly in and down so that he can pick up the ball out of the corner of his left eye. He will continue to watch the ball until he knows the status of the ball. If the timing is proper, the runner should just have to look in toward the plate for one or two strides. If the hitter at the plate has no strikes on him, he will then be protecting the runner by swinging and missing or fake bunting, thus the runner does not have to look in toward the plate. This is due to the fact that there will be no contact by the hitter. The only problem that now could arise if the batter does not look in, is when the ball gets by the catcher. A good runner can develop his mechanics so that he would feel comfortable looking in toward the plate even in this situation.

J. **The secondary lead**—The secondary lead is just as important as the primary lead for the runner at first base. The secondary lead is the lead the runner will have off first base when the ball reaches the area of the plate. The distance of the secondary lead will depend on the following: (1) the runner's ability to get back to first base (speed and quickness); (2) the condition of the field surface; (3) the strength and accuracy of the catcher's arm; (4) whether there is a righthanded or lefthanded hitter at the plate (the catcher will have an easier throw on the pick-off attempt at first base with a righthanded

238

hitter at the plate); (5) if the first baseman is holding the runner on the base, or is playing behind the runner; (6) whether the runner is in a gambling or non-gambling situation; (7) the length and type of primary lead the runner has taken. When the ball reaches the plate, the runner must attempt to be as far away from the base as possible. Of course, the further the runner is away from first base, the closer he will be to second base. At the same time, the further he is away from first base, the better chance he will be picked off by the catcher's throw to the first baseman. Thus, the runner must find the perfect spot to be when he reaches his secondary lead. This can only be done through trial and error in scrimmage games. The first base coach should not be responsible to inform the runner that the catcher is throwing to first base for a pick-off attempt. If the first baseman is playing behind the runner at the time of the pitch, the runner will probably take a longer secondary lead. If that is the case, the first base coach will have to inform the runner if the first baseman breaks for the base as the ball reaches the plate. This communication would be a loud "get back". The first base coach must keep his eyes on the first baseman playing behind the runner, and out of the corner of his eye be in a position to pick up the ball as it reaches the plate. If he sees any movement of the first baseman toward the base, he must let the runner know to get back. If the first baseman is holding the runner on the base, then there is no need for any communication between the first base coach and the runner on a pick-off attempt. The mechanics of going from the primary lead to the secondary lead must be worked on in practice sessions so that the runners feel comfortable in moving from the primary lead at the time of the pitch. As soon as the runner reads that the pitcher is going to deliver the ball to the plate, he will begin moving toward his secondary lead. The distance of the primary lead has a major effect on how far the runner has got to go to achieve his secondary lead, along with the other factors previously mentioned. For instance, if the runner has a long one-way lead back to first base, then he will have very little distance to travel to the secondary lead. If the runner has a conservative one-way lead back to first base because of the pitcher having an exceptional pick-off move, then the distance for him to travel to his secondary lead will be great. It takes a pitcher between 1.2 and 2.0 seconds to break from the set position until the ball reaches the catcher's glove. The average time is about 1.5 seconds for most pitchers. This should allow the runner plenty of time to go from the primary lead to the secondary lead unless he has a very conservative lead off first base. The secondary lead is achieved by the runner taking shuffle steps toward second base. The length of the shuffle steps are an individual matter taking into consideration the distance that must be traveled. The runner should be facing the plate during the shuffle steps watching the ball leave the pitcher's hand. The final shuffle step should be completed as the ball leaves the pitcher's hand. At that time, the runner will turn his body so that his hips are pointing directly at the area where the shortstop normally stands on defense. He will have his body under complete control at this time for now he must perform the most important segment of the secondary lead. As he squares his body facing the area of the shortstop, he will bring his right foot into the air so that his right thigh is parallel to the ground. Just as the ball reaches the plate, his right foot starts toward the ground. If the runner reads that the nature of ball hit forces him to advance toward second base, he will drive off the right foot and head in that direction. If he reads that the ball will be caught by the catcher, he will pivot on the right foot and head back to first base. This is why it is so important that the runner have his hips lined up with the shortstop position in order that he can advance forward or return to first base. If he reaches the secondary lead with his hips and shoulders pointing toward the plate, he will be a step slow in breaking toward second base on the batted ball. If he lines his hips and shoulders directly toward second base, he will have a difficult time getting back to first base if the catcher receives the pitch. When the runner is leading off second base, he must point his hips and shoulders toward an area half way between third base and the plate so that he can react in either direction equally well. We recommend that the runner reach his secondary lead anticipating that the ball will be hit so that he can get a great jump toward second base. At the same time, the runner can not afford to be leaning toward second base anticipating contact only to find that the batter has swung and missed the pitch and now the catcher has a great opportunity to pick him off first base. This type of secondary lead takes a lot of practice during baserunning drills, batting practice, and scrimmage games. If done properly the runner will not be moving toward second base from a stationary position when he reaches his secondary lead. The runner must perfect the timing on the lead so that his right foot does not hit the ground too early. If it does hit the ground before the runner knows the status of the ball, then he will have to again generate momentum on his break toward second base. If the runner reads that the pitch is a slow curve or change-up, he will just slow down his movement of his right foot toward the ground. Another advantage of this type of secondary lead is that it gives the runner a tremendous jump toward second base when he reads that the pitch will be going into the dirt. Many teams have been very successful in giving their runners the "green light" anytime they read a pitch is going into the dirt and there is no runner at second base. Of course, the runner must always take into consideration whether or not his team is in a gambling or non-gambling situation at the time. This is especially effective if there is a runner at third base also, since the chance of the catcher throwing the ball to second base with a runner at third base is minimal. Most catchers will go to their knees to block the pitch in the dirt with runners on base. This makes it practically impossible for him to make a play on the runner breaking for second base even if he was to catch the ball off the dirt. This type of secondary lead is also effective when the batter is going to sacrifice bunt the runner to second base. If the runner reads the down angle of the ball off the bat as his right foot hits the ground, he should have a tremendous jump toward second base. He must be very conscious of the fact that the batter might take the pitch, or miss on the bunt attempt. If so, he will have to pivot on the right foot as it hits the ground and return quickly to first base. A runner can never allow his right foot to hit the ground, followed by a step toward the next base with his left foot, before knowing the status of the ball.

239

Once that left foot crosses over the right foot he must be absolutely sure that he is going to advance. Otherwise, he is a "dead duck" on a pick-off attempt. With two outs the runner will break for second base when the batter makes contact with the ball. With less than two outs he will break for second base on a ground ball; freeze and read the ball on a line drive; and move toward second base as far as possible on a fly ball. There is never any reason for a runner to be doubled off first base on a line drive in the infield unless he was stealing second base on the pitch; or the ball is hit right at the first baseman close to first base.

     K. **The fake steal**—The fake steal of second base can be very effective for the following reasons:

     1. It will enable the coaching staff of the team at bat to see how the second baseman and shortstop react when the runner makes a break toward second base. If they see that one or both of them are moving toward second base as the runner makes his break, then they will be very susceptible to the hit and run play during the course of the game. If they hold in their defensive positions until the ball passes the batter, then they will not be as susceptible to the hit and run play.

     2. It might open up a hole for the batter when the runner fakes the steal if the second baseman or shortstop (or both) move toward second base on the runner's break from first base.

     3. It might force the catcher to raise up as the pitch is coming to the plate, taking the close pitch away from the pitcher. In addition, the more a team fakes the steal the more the catcher might not respond as well mechanically when the runner actually does break for second base.

     4. The more a team fakes the steal one will find that the first baseman will not yell as loud to the catcher that the runner is breaking for second base by his command of "there he goes". One will also find that the first baseman will wait a little longer to communicate this fact to the catcher to see whether the runner is going all the way on the steal. The longer the first baseman waits to give this command to the catcher, the tougher it is for the catcher to be in a position to make a good throw to second base. This is especially true when there is a lefthanded hitter at the plate, whereby the catcher can not see the runner breaking for second base as early as he would with a righthanded hitter at the plate.

The negative aspect of the fake steal is that it puts the runner in a poor position to be completely under control when he reaches the secondary lead. However, with practice a runner should be able to get to the secondary lead under some control so that he can react to the ball as it reaches the plate. The runner's intentions are to make everyone on defense think that he is stealing second base. The mechanics of the fake steal are easily understood, but still difficult to perform. The runner will have to start from a primary lead that is about three or four feet shorter than his regular primary lead. He does this for two reasons: (1) he can not afford to get picked off on the fake steal; and (2) the closer he is to first base the further he can run close to full speed to his secondary lead. When he reads that the pitcher is definitely delivering the ball to the plate, he will cross-over with his left foot just as he would in stealing second base. All his mechanics are the same on this cross-over step along with the next step toward second base with his right foot. These first two steps should prompt the first baseman, second baseman, shortstop and catcher to think that the runner is stealing second base. After these two full speed steps, the runner will take another step toward second base with his left foot. However, this step would be about half the distance of his normal stride so that he can begin to slow down as he approaches his secondary lead. This abbreviated stride with the left foot is followed by the same short stride of the right foot. At this time the runner is now preparing to position himself so that he reaches the secondary lead under full control with his right foot in the air. This is done by the left foot being placed in front of the right foot so that the heel of the left foot is even with the toe of the right foot. Now the right foot is brought into the air so that the right thigh is parallel to the ground, and the runner is in a position to react to the ball as it reaches the area of the plate. The runner must be sure that his hips and shoulders are lined up with the area where the shortstop normally stands so that he does not have to completely turn around if the batter swings and misses or he takes the pitch. The tendency is for runners to go too far on the fake steal which puts them past their normal secondary lead position. Another tendency they will have is to start slowing down after the first cross-over step with the left foot. That next step with the right foot is the key to the effectiveness of the fake steal. It must also be a full quick stride toward second base. When done properly, it is a very effective aspect of a team's baserunning skills.

     L. **The delayed steal**—This type of steal is generally used when the runner at first base does not possess great speed, there is a lefthanded batter at the plate to assist in obstructing the catcher's view of the runner's lead, and the shortstop and second baseman are observed not moving toward second base after the ball passes the batter on previous pitches. The runner will take three large shuffle hops toward second base as the pitcher delivers the ball to the plate. On the last hop, he breaks for second base full speed.

30. **Reacting to a fly ball from first base**—The runner at first base must go as far as he can away from first base anytime

there is less than two outs and a ball is hit in the air. The distance that he would be away from first base will depend on all the same circumstances as previously discussed in regard to rounding first base on a base hit. If the runner goes far enough away from first base, he would have to return full speed back to the base if a play is made on him by the fielder of the ball. So many times we see baserunners not being aggressive enough on the distance they are away from first base. Then if the outfielder misplays or drops the ball they are not in good position to advance to third base. As in his turn at first base on a base hit, the runner must be able to see the ball at all times. If it is caught, he would continue to watch the ball as it is thrown into the infield so that he is in a position to advance on a very poor throw. Of course, the runner will have to go back to first base, tag up and then advance. If the outfielder was to make a play on him at first base, he would go back to the base full speed without watching the throw into first base. Any ball hit to the center fielder or on over to left field, he would return to first base by turning in toward the infield. Any ball hit to the right field side, he would return to first base by turning toward the outfield. This is done so that he can easily see the ball at all times as it is caught and thrown back into the infield. If the runner has rounded second base when the outfielder makes the catch, he must retouch second base before heading back to first base.

31. **Tagging up at first base**—There are numerous times when a runner would want to tag up at first base and advance to second base on a fly ball that is caught. At no time would a runner tag up at first base on a fair ball when there is any doubt in his mind that the ball will be a questionable catch. If the runner feels that there is any chance that the ball will not be caught on the fair ball, he must be as far away from first base as possible. The runner at first base must tag up on any foul ball. If there is any doubt as to whether a ball will be fair or foul, he should treat the ball as a fair ball. This is so that he is not caught tagging up at first base only to find that the ball drops near the line in fair territory. On a fair ball, the runner should never be tagging up at first base and then not advance to second base on the catch. Thus, he would be tagging up at first base when he knows for sure that he will be able to advance to second base on the catch. The following situations would prompt a runner to tag up at first base:

A. **On any foul ball hit in the air.** If the ball is caught, he will make the decision as to whether or not he will advance to second base. He will take into consideration where the fielder might throw the ball if there are runners on other bases. This is especially the case with a runner at third base also, since the throw would more than likely be to the plate to prevent the runner at third base from scoring.

B. **The ball is hit deep in the outfield**—If a ball is hit deep to the outfield in a large ball park, the runner should be tagging at first base and advancing on the catch. This is especially true with one out with the second out being made on the catch. If there is any doubt in the runner's mind that the ball might not be caught, then he would not be tagging at first base.

C. **The runner at second base is tagging up**—If there is a runner at second base with less than two outs, the runner at first base should be tagging at the base if the runner at second base is tagging. The runner at second base would never be tagging up unless he had intentions to advance to third base. Neither runner should be tagging if there is any chance that the catch will not be made. If the runner at first base sees the runner at second base is not tagging, then the runner at first base will go as far as he can away from first base. It would be foolish to have the runner at first base tagging, and the runner at second base off the base. If both runners are tagging and advancing on the catch, the runner at first base will advance to second base if the outfielder throws the ball to third base. If the runner at first base reads that the outfielder has no play at third base, he must be concerned about a possible throw by the outfielder to second base. If he does throw to second base, the runner can easily turn around and head back to first base unless he feels that he can beat the throw to second base. Anytime both runners are tagging at their respective base and the throw is going to third base, the runner from first base needs to be sure that the shortstop (cut-off man) can not cut the ball off and make an easy out at second base. This is especially true when the first out of the inning was made on the catch. With two outs, the runner can afford to gamble a little more.

D. **The runner at third base is tagging up**—On a routine fly ball that will be caught, both the runner at first base and the runner at third base will be tagging up. If the runner at third base attempts to score, the outfielder will be throwing the ball to the plate. If that be the case, the runner at first base would break for second base when the ball leaves the hand of the outfielder. He should be able to get to second base easily even though the third baseman or first baseman (cut-off men) might cut the ball off. On a long fly ball, the runner must be sure that the outfielder is going to throw to the plate before advancing to second base. If it is an extremely long fly ball he might be able to advance to second base even if the throw by the outfielder goes directly to second base.

E. **The bases are loaded and the runners at second and third base are tagging up**—Anytime the runner at first base sees the runners at second and third base tagging up at their respective bases, he must also tag up at first base. He will advance to second base if a play is made on the runner advancing to third base or the runner attempting to score from third base. As previously mentioned, the runner at first base can not afford to be thrown out at second base on a direct throw from the outfielder to second base, or from a cut-off man to the base.

F. The runners at first and third base tagging up on a short fly ball hit well away from second base—With runners at first and third base with less than two outs, the runners can put extreme pressure on the defense whenever a catchable short fly ball is hit well away from second base. This would be a fly ball hit behind first or third base in fair or foul territory, or a fly ball hit in foul territory between the plate and first base or the plate and third base. If both runners are tagging on the catch, the fielder with the ball must first be concerned about keeping the runner at third base from scoring. Because of this, the runner at first base can take off for second base hoping to draw the long throw to second base from the fielder of the fly ball. If the fielder does throw the ball to second base, the runner at third base should be able to score easily. If the fielder does not throw the ball to second base, then the runner from first base can continue onto second base. If the second out is made on the catch, the runner from first base must be sure that he does not run into the tag at second base before the runner from third base can score. If the runner at third base sees the throw coming to the plate when he breaks, he will stop and return back to third base.

32. **Mechanics of tagging up at a base**—It is very important that a runner tagging at any base use the proper mechanics so that he can achieve maximum acceleration as he breaks toward the next base or the plate. The timing is very important so that the runner does not leave the base too early. At the same time, he can not afford to leave the base too late if there will be a close play on him at the forward base or plate. Anytime a runner can easily advance on the catch to the forward base or the plate, he should pause momentarily in order to not chance an appeal play at the base. If it is going to be a close play, he must leave the base at the exact time the ball touches the glove of the fielder. The runner must be able to observe the catch himself, rather than relying on the first base or third base coach to tell him when to tag up. This will prevent any problem in the communication process between the player and coach. The coach might give him advice or a command while the ball is in the air as to what he wants him to do on the catch. This is especially true with a runner tagging up at third base. This would be one of three commands: (1) ''score''; (2) ''fake the break''; or (3) ''half way''. When the runner is going to tag up with no immediate thought of scoring from third base, he should break towards the plate attempting to draw a throw from the outfielder. If the outfielder happens to hold onto the baseball or makes a wild throw to the plate, the runner can then continue his break toward the plate. He should be able to do this without having to be commanded by the third base coach. As in most baserunning, this must be an instinctive move on the runner's part. The only way a runner can clearly see the ball while tagging up at a base is to have the foot on the base that will allow him full sight of the baseball as it is touched by the outfielder. For example, the runner tagging up at second base with a ball hit to right field would have his left foot on the base so he can easily see the outfielder. If he was to have his right foot on the base it would close his left side, making it practically impossible for him to observe the ball. With a runner at third base, and a ball is hit in foul territory on the left field side of the field, he would want to have his right foot on the base so that he can easily watch the ball. The runner should assume a straight up stance on the base with the foot not in contact with the base about a foot in front of the foot in contact with the bag. Just as the ball reaches the fielder's glove, he should drop and drive off the base so that he can use the base to achieve maximum acceleration. As he drops his weight down over the foot in contact with the base, he will step out with the front foot another foot and a half. He will then push off the base with the contact foot and begin running full speed to the forward base or the plate. It is wise for the coach to alert the umpires that this technique will be used by his club when tagging at a base. If an umpire is unaware of what is taking place, it will look to him that the runner began movement forward before the ball touches the fielder's glove. Since his contact foot will remain on the base while he drops his body and steps out with his front foot, this technique is perfectly legal. If the runner assumes the crouch position as he awaits the catch, he loses the rhythmical benefit of pushing off the base as he gets in the preferred technique mentioned.

33. **The runner avoiding the tag by the second baseman on the ground ball**—When the runner advances to second base on a ground ball to the right side of the infield, he must be alert to avoid a situation where the second baseman can field the ground ball and make an easy tag on him. This will prevent the easy double play with the second baseman making the tag, and then throwing the ball to first base for the second out. If the runner feels that he can get by the tag, he should attempt to do so. If there is any doubt in the runner's mind, he must stop and make the second baseman come after him. A smart second baseman will force the runner to stop and retreat back to first base if he can not make the quick tag. Once he has the runner moving back to first base, he will throw the ball to the first baseman. The first baseman can then throw the ball to the shortstop to make a tag on the runner breaking toward second base. The runner can not run out of the baseline to avoid the tag by the second baseman. Most umpires will give the benefit of the doubt to the second baseman when he attempts to tag the runner in front of him and there is doubt in his mind whether or not the runner went out of the baseline to avoid the tag.

34. **The runner should stay in the path of the ball on the bases**—Anytime a runner can legally interfere with the throw from one fielder to another when running on the bases, he should do so. At no time would the runner wish to appreciably reduce his time to the next base or the plate by changing his course in the base path. If the runner has a choice as to whether to run inside or outside the baseline, the path of the baseball coming into that base or the plate would be a factor in this determination. The runner can never interfere with the sight of the player fielding the ball by throwing up his arm or hands, or go out of the

baseline to allow the throw to hit him or obstruct the view of the fielder. There are numerous times that a situation comes up for a runner to take advantage of the path he would run to a base or the plate:

A. **Batter-runner heading for first base**—We have already presented in this section the opportunity a runner might have to legally interfere with the throw of the fielder of the ball in front of the plate. He can do this by staying on the inside edge of the foul line as he runs to first base. If the ball happens to get past the catcher on the third strike, the runner can stay on the outside of the restraining area if the ball is being thrown from foul territory on the first base side. If a runner is forced at the plate, the batter-runner should stay on the inside edge of the foul line when running to first base hoping to interfere with the catcher's throw to the first baseman.

B. **Runner at first base and a ball is hit to the first baseman on the home plate side of the baseline**—The runner should run on the inside of the base path so as to make it difficult for the first baseman and shortstop to complete the force out at second base. If the ball is fielded by the first baseman behind the baseline, the runner should run on the outside of the base path toward second base.

C. **Runner at first base and a ball is hit well to the second baseman's left**—With a ground ball hit well to the left of the second baseman, the runner needs to stay on the outside of the base path between first and second base. This is especially true if the second baseman is playing shallow when the batter makes contact with the ball.

D. **Runner at first base and a pick-off attempt by the pitcher or catcher gets by the first baseman**—If the runner knows that the throw will be coming to second base from the inside or the outside of the base path, he can run on the side the throw will be made from on a misplayed pick-off attempt at first base.

E. **Runner at second base and the shortstop fields the ball to his left**—If the runner at second base breaks toward third base on a ball to the shortstop's left, he should remain on the outside of the base path as he approaches third base. This will make it very difficult for the shortstop to make an unobstructed throw to the third baseman at third base.

F. **Runner at third base and the third baseman fields a ball going to his right close to the line**—The runner should stay in the inside of the base path as he runs toward the plate when the third baseman has gone toward the third baseline for the ground ball. It will make for a very difficult throw from the third baseman to the catcher to retire the runner. The same holds true for a sacrifice fly ball where the left fielder catches the ball near or on the left field line. If he catches the ball in foul territory, then the runner would stay on the outer side of the base path from third base to the plate.

35. **Runner heading for second base picking up the third base coach**—The runner leaving first base on the batted ball should be completely aware of the status of the baseball. As was the case with the runner rounding first base, we would want the runner to make his own decision as to whether or not to: (1) go to third base; (2) round second base; or (3) slide into second base. This is due to the fact that it is much easier for the baserunner to pick up the ball and make a decision, rather than having to pick up the third base coach who must make the decision and pass it along to the runner. We do want the runner to pick up the third base coach when the ball is hit where the runner can not easily see the ball in play. Some simple rules to follow in regard to when to pick up the third base coach would be:

A. **Any ball hit from the right fielder to the right field line**—If there is any doubt in the runner's mind if the ball was hit at the right fielder, he must pick up the ball.

B. **Any ball hit on the ground behind the runner heading for second base**—This also will necessitate the runner picking up the third base coach unless he knows that the ball will be fielded by the second baseman and a force out at second base might occur. If that be the case, then the runner will be sliding into second base without having to pick up the third base coach.

C. **On a steal or hit and run when the ball is hit behind the runner he will have to look at the third base coach**—This is even the case if the ball was hit to the center field side of the right fielder. This is due to the fact that the runner will have a very difficult time following the flight of the ball as he will be closing in on second base. In most cases, on a steal or hit and run with a base hit evident to the runner, he will be going to third base automatically.

The timing involved in picking up the third base coach is of extreme importance. This is so that the third base coach has ample opportunity to make a sound decision as to what he wants the runner to do, and to also allow the runner to make the proper turn at second base. If the runner picks up the third base coach too soon, two major problems can arise: (1) the third base coach has not had ample time to make a decision; and (2) the runner will have to hold his look for quite a few more strides which could take away from his maximum speed to second base. If the runner picks up the third base coach too late, three major problems can arise: (1) the runner might miss the visual sign given by the third base coach; (2) the closer the runner gets to second base, the further he will have to turn his head to pick up the third base coach which could affect his quickness; and (3) the runner's turn at second base could be affected if he is looking toward the third base coach as he approaches second base. The best time to pick up the third base coach is at approximately the 45 foot mark between first and second base (half way point). By that time the third base coach should be in a position to make a decision for the runner's behalf. If the coach has not made a decision at this time, the runner will continue toward second base preparing for the turn. Out of the corner of his eye he will continue to pick up the coach. He should not have to turn his head to do this unless the third base coach is very late in making a decision, and the runner is closing in on second base. If the runner starts closing in on second base and the coach has still not made a decision, then the runner must find the ball. This will be very difficult to do since the ball will be behind him as he approaches the base. That is why it is important for the third base coach to make the decision as quick as possible. If the runner is informed visually by the coach to come on to third base, the runner must again pick up the third base coach after he touches second base in case the coach has to change his mind, and now wants the runner to put "on the breaks" and return quickly to second base.

36. **The third base coach's signs to the runner approaching second base**—If the runner approaching second base needs assistance from the third base coach in determining what he should do, the third base coach's sign must be clear to the runner. It is very helpful to the runner to have the third base coach deep in the coach's box when he flashes the sign so that the runner will not have to turn his head completely to see the sign clearly. If the third base coach has a runner heading toward third base at the same time the runner is approaching second base, the coach will have to take care of the runner rounding third base first. This means that he will be moving out of the coach's box down toward home plate to help the runner as he rounds third base. If this is the case, the runner approaching second base will have to pick up the ball if the third base coach is not in any position to assist him. If the runner sees the third base coach holding up the runner rounding third base, then the runner approaching second base will realize that he will not be going to third base. A good third base coach will quickly take care of the runner coming into third base, and then immediately try to assist the runner approaching second base. There are times when this is not possible, since the third base coach might not be able to make a quick judgment on what he wants to do with the runner at third base. Thus, whenever the third base coach is not in a position to help the runner coming into the turn at second base, that runner will have to find the ball. This might mean that he will have to turn his head completely around to check the status of the ball, but this is a lot better than running out of control as he rounds second base. The runner must keep his head up as he leaves second base whenever there is a runner in front of him. If at the last minute the third base coach holds the runner up at third base, the runner leaving second base must stop quickly and return to second base. There are only three visual signs necessary for the runner looking at the third base coach as he approaches second base:

A. **Waving one or both arms in a circular motion**—This means that the third base coach wants the runner to round second base and head for third base. As previously mentioned, the runner must again pick up the third base coach after he hits the base, in case the coach has to change his mind. If that be the case, the runner will have to stop, and get back to second base quickly.

B. **Holding both arms high in the air**—The third base coach wants the runner to take an aggressive turn at second base, and then pick up the ball. The runner must have eye contact with the bag as he hits it; take two more aggressive steps toward third base; and then turn and find the ball as he shuffles toward third base. Once the runner touches second base after being instructed by the third base coach to take an aggressive turn and then pick up the ball, he is now completely responsible for his actions. If the outfielder happens to bobble the ball or makes a poor throw into the infield area, the baserunner will then be in a position to advance. Again, the runner must know the status of any runner ahead of him before he continues on to third base.

C. **Pointing at second base**—The third base coach wants the runner to take a turn at second base, but does not want him to take too many steps past the base. This would be the case if the ball is in the hands of an outfielder who could easily throw behind the runner if he takes too big of a turn. Again, once the runner hits the base and takes a couple of steps, he must find the ball himself and react.

The runner should approach second base with the intentions to continue on to third base. This is so that he does not start slowing down as he takes his turn at second base. The third base coach has to stop the runner by a visual sign. The third base coach should not have to inform a runner to slide at second base since this is the runner's responsibility. The runner must slide into second base anytime there is any chance for a force play being made on him at the base. He should be able to read this fact without any assistance.

37. **Making the turn at second base**—The actual turn at second base is very similar to the mechanics of the turn at first base with a few exceptions. There are times when the runner heading toward second base will have to angle out sharper than he would at first base. This is due to the fact that he might not always know quick enough whether he will be making a turn, or will have to go into second base on the slide due to a possible force play at the base. This should never be a problem when the ball is hit in front of him since the status of the ball will be known to the runner. With the ball hit behind him on the ground, it makes his decision a little more difficult. If the ball is fielded by the second baseman or the first baseman in the hole, the runner would look foolish being thrown out at second base while making a turn. This is why it is so important that the runner pick up the third base coach at the proper time so he will know early enough whether a turn at second base is necessary. As was the case rounding first base, a runner should never have to start his turn prior to the 45 foot mark (half way between first and second base) unless the infield surface is quite loose forcing the runner to make a little wider turn. Other than the fact that he will be picking up the third base coach in front of him after touching the base, the mechanics of the turn at second base is similar to the turn at first base.

38. **The runner must evaluate the entire situation before attempting to advance to third base**—As was the case rounding first base, the runner rounding second base must take into consideration numerous factors before deciding whether or not to advance to third base. If the ball is behind the runner approaching second base, the third base coach must weigh these same factors prior to making a decision for the runner. The following are some rules and regulations in regard to when to gamble on advancing to third base. These rules and regulations would hold true in the following situations: (1) possibly stretching a double into a triple; (2) possibly going from first to third base on a base hit by the batter; (3) advancing to third base after an overthrow by the catcher or infielder at second base; (4) advancing to third base after a errant pick-off attempt at first base; (5) advancing to third base on a pick-off overthrow at second base by the catcher or pitcher; and (6) advancing to third base on a fly ball to an outfielder.

   A. **The runner's speed and the texture of the infield**—The runner and the third base coach must take into consideration the speed of the runner along with the texture of the infield surface. A runner with great speed on a fast track can take advantage of a lot more opportunities to advance to third base than one with poor speed on a slow track.

   B. **The score of the game and the inning**—When the runner's team is ahead in the game, he can gamble much more than if they are behind. This is especially true in the later innnings of a game. A player never wants to be thrown out when behind in the score late in the game when his run will not be a factor.

   C. **The number of outs**—As a general rule, the runner or third base coach does not want to make the first or third out at third base. By making the first out at third base, it does not allow the runner to be at second base with no outs. The team on offense has got to feel that they can score a runner from second base with no outs most of the time. By making the third out at third base, it does not allow the runner to be at second base with two outs. With a runner at second base with two outs, a base hit should be able to score the runner since he will be breaking from second base at the crack of the bat. There are numerous ways a runner can score from third base with two outs where he can't from second base (balk, infield single, passed ball or wild pitch). However, to gamble on making it to third base with two outs is still not a good move taking into consideration the fact that he is almost as good at second base. With one out, the runner or coach can afford to gamble on making it to third base as long as they are not down in the score late in the game.

   D. **Hitter at the plate**—With a good hitter at the plate or a good hitter coming to the plate, the runner would certainly not want to make the third out at third base. The same holds true when a weak hitter is at the plate or coming to the plate. With the good hitter you would want him to have the opportunity to swing the bat, and with the weak hitter you do not want him leading off the next inning. With the ''meat of the batting order'' coming up, a runner would be foolish to make the first out at third base. A team that has a very difficult time hitting the ball would want to gamble a little more on the bases than a team that has a good hitting attack.

   E. **Ability of the defensive player throwing the ball to third base, and the distance of the throw**—The strength and accuracy of the thrower's arm is of great importance in determining whether to go to third base. The distance of the throw is another important factor along with whether or not the player throwing the ball is fielding the ball on his glove side or his throwing side. Anytime the outfield grass is wet and a ball is hit on the ground, more chances can be taken by the runner since the outfielder will have to make the throw to third base with a wet ball.

39. **The runner can not be decoyed by the shortstop or second baseman on a fly ball or line drive as he approaches second base**—With the runner stealing second base or running on a hit and run from first base, he must be conscious of the fact that the shortstop or second baseman might fake the fielding of a ground ball when the ball is hit in the air. They would do

this to make the runner think that a ground ball has been hit, making him continue his advancement to second base while the ball is being fielded in the air by a defensive player. If the runner looks in toward the plate on the steal or hit and run, he should never be decoyed by a shortstop or second baseman in this manner.

40. **Runner at second base—Ball four or strike three with the ball getting by the catcher**—With a runner at second base, and the batter-runner finds the ball gets by the catcher on the fourth ball or third strike, he must take off full speed to first base. He will pick up the first base coach as he advances to first base since the ball will be behind him. If the offensive team is in a gambling situation, the first base coach should send the runner toward second base. If they are in a non-gambling situation (down in the score late in the game) the first base coach should have the runner make an aggressive turn unless there will be an immediate play on the runner at first base. In the gambling situation the batter-runner wants to force the catcher near the backstop to make the long throw to second base. By the time the catcher fields the ball at the backstop, the runner who started at second base should be rounding third base. He will be in a position to react to the catcher's possible throw to second base. If he sees the ball leave the catcher's hand with no cut-off man near the mound, he will continue on to the plate. If the catcher throws to the pitcher covering the plate, he can easily stop and return to third base. If the catcher holds onto the baseball, he will remain at third base. If the catcher does not throw the ball, or throws the ball to the pitcher or the cut-off man, the batter-runner will continue on to second base. The batter-runner should never get himself tagged out at second base with two outs before the runner who started at second base has had a chance to score. He must stop before he reaches second base to prevent this possiblity, and stay in the rundown as long as he can. With less than two outs he will go into second base full speed. While the shortstop or second baseman is making the play on him, the runner will have an easy opportunity to cross the plate. Thus, the offense will be sacrificing the batter-runner to score a run from third base. Most of the time the catcher will hesitate throwing the ball all the way to second base, which should give the batter-runner a good chance of beating the throw, if made.

41. **The baseruner at second base**—As soon as the runner reaches second base, he must quickly review in his mind the situation at hand (outs, inning, score, hitter at the plate, outfielder's arms, etc.). As was the case at first base, he must check the outfielders' depths and locations. As soon as this is done, he will pick up the third base coach for a possible sign. He will pick up the third base coach as soon as he returns to second base after every pitch to the batter. The third base coach should flash the signs quickly so that the runner can devote his full attention to the pitcher as he begins his primary lead at second base. The following are the general rules for leading off second base.

A. **Using the third base coach**—As was the case with the runner leading off first base, the runner at second base should not need any major assistance from the third base coach as he establishes his primary lead. He should also not need any assistance from the third base coach in reviewing the situation at hand. This should be strictly the runner's responsibility. The only exception might be for a player who has proven his inability to concentrate on the bases. This is especially true if the runner is the tying or winning run late in the game. There will be times that the runner at second base will need assistance from the third base coach as will be explained in the discussion on the various types of leads.

B. **Leads at second base**—The movement away from second base to establish the primary lead is very similar to the manner which it is done at first base. With this being the case, we will not devote as much time to this movement as we did when discussing this facet of baserunning at first base. It is very important that the runner not make any move off second base until he is absolutely sure that the ball is in the possession of the pitcher on the mound. As was the case at first base, we want the runner to achieve his full primary lead before the pitcher begins any movement from the stretch position. The length of the primary lead will be determined by the following factors: (1) ability of the runner to get back to second base; (2) condition of the infield surface; (3) pitcher's pick-off move to second base; and (4) the nature of the sign flashed by the third base coach. The distance that the shortstop and second baseman are away from the base should not be a factor in the primary lead unless the runner has established the aggressive lead, which is one of the leads which will now be discussed.

1. **Standard lead**—This lead is generally one step and a dive from second base (approximately 15 feet). It can be a little longer for the quick runner. This lead should be two feet back from the direct line from second to third base when there is no force at third base. This will allow the runner to be in a little better position for his turn at third base. With a force at third base, the runner should be in the direct path between the two bases. This enables the runner to be in the best position to get to third base as quickly as possible in case the force play is made at that base. The runner does not need to lead off second base with the back of his heels lined up with the inside of the base as he did at first base. This type of lead is not as effective as it is at first base where the angle of the runner from the pitcher's view is greater than it is for the pitcher looking at the runner leading off second base. The standard lead is a stationary lead with movement toward third base when the pitcher commits himself to home plate. Movement back to second base should only occur on a pick-off attempt by the pitcher. No verbal help is needed from the third base coach on this type of lead. The runner should

not move back toward second base even though the shortstop or second baseman are moving toward the base. His full concentration is on the pitcher. When he begins the pick-off move, then he can begin his dive back into the base. The runner can never afford to look toward second base when his standard lead is established.

2. **Aggressive lead**—This lead is generally used when the runner at second base has the steal sign from the coach. It can also be used to force the shortstop and second baseman to move closer to second base in order to keep the runner from taking too big of a lead on the pitcher from the set position. The closer the shortstop or second baseman are to second base, the more holes the batter has on the ground ball. The runner will start from the standard lead off position and then allow the third base coach to increase his lead by verbal commands. These commands would be: "right there", or no sound indicates that the runner stays in the same spot; "okay one", means for the runner to increase his lead by one complete shuffle step; "back one", means for the runner to decrease his lead by one complete shuffle step; "back", is a loud command by the third base coach telling the runner to take a quick cross-over step and return to second base as quickly as possible using a head first slide if there is a throw to the base by the pitcher; "okay one" or "back one", can be used by the third base coach to bring the runner further off the base or back to the base. By using either of these verbal commands two or more times, the runner will take one step for each command by the coach.

3. **Two out lead**—With two outs the baserunner positions himself in a short lead position (approximately 12′ down the line and 10′ directly back toward left field). This lead can be wider or closer depending on the ability of the runner. As the pitcher commits himself to the plate, the runner starts his walking lead directly toward third base. It is important that the baserunner remain in a straight line from his initial spot as he walks toward third base. This type of lead is used to eliminate having to take a wide turn at third base when attempting to score. There would be no commands from the third base coach on the two out lead unless the steal sign is on and the coach wishes to get the runner a little further off the base. The coach would then use the commands as indicated in the aggressive lead.

C. **Reading the pitcher's pick-off move to second base**—There is never any reason for a runner to get picked off second base unless the steal sign is on. Thus, the runner will have a one-way lead back to second base as he assumes his primary lead. His full concentration is on the pitcher so that he can cross-over and dive back to second base when he detects that the pitcher is going to throw to the shortstop or second baseman at the base. The back heel will again be the visual key for the runner at second base as it was for the runner at first base. The pitcher must clear the pitching rubber in order to throw the ball to second base even though he might start movement of his body prior to the clearing. There is one exception to this rule, and that would be when the pitcher executes the inside pick-off move at second base. With the inside pick-off move, the pitcher would pick up the lead leg from the set position and then when the lead leg gets to the balance position, he would step with that leg toward second base. Thus, he would not start pivoting on the rubber with his pivot foot until the lead leg starts moving in the direction of second base. The runner must be sure that he does not rush to his secondary lead as soon as the pitcher picks up his lead leg. If the runner does rush toward the secondary lead on the first move of the pitcher with the lead leg, he would be very susceptible to the inside pick-off move. This is especially true when the count on the batter is three balls and two strikes, with two outs and a runner at first base or the bases are loaded. Since the runner at second base will be breaking toward third base on the pitch, this is the ideal time for the pitcher to throw to the shortstop or second baseman via the inside pick. The inside pick-off is a very difficult move to master for most pitchers as the tendency is to give the move away too early as the pitcher picks up the lead leg. Most pitchers will give the runner a different type of motion when he will be attempting this pick-off than the motion he uses when delivering the ball to the plate. Anytime a runner observes an unnatural motion by the pitcher when he breaks from the set, he should not make any move toward third base until the pitcher actually begins pushing off the rubber on his delivery to the plate. The runner would still have time to get to the secondary lead when the ball reaches the plate. Another pick-off move that the runner at second base must be conscious of is the pick-off from the windup position as the pitcher receives his sign from the catcher. This move is done with runners at second and third base or the bases are loaded. On a signal from the catcher, the pitcher will pivot on the rubber and throw the ball to the shortstop or second baseman who broke for the base prompting the catcher's signal to the pitcher. An observant baserunner should never be guilty of being picked off on the inside or windup pick. When the runner reads a pick at second base, his mechanics of diving back to second base are similar to the mechanics discussed with the runner at first base. The exception might be that on an aggressive lead the runner will not only have to cross-over with his right foot to prepare for the dive into the base, but he might have to take another step with his left foot prior to the actual dive. This is done so that the runner does not end up short of the target.

D. **Stealing third base**—Many coaches and players feel that it is easier to steal third base than it is to steal second base. There are many reasons why this might be the case, with the primary reason being that a runner can get a longer lead at second base than he can at first base. This is due to the fact that there is no fielder holding the runner on base as the first baseman does at first base. The runner can also get a little further away from second base than he could at first base since the pitcher's pick-off move will take a little longer than it does at first base. Another factor in the runner's favor at second base is that the pitcher many times does not concern himself with this runner as much as he did with the runner leading off first base. Due to this fact the pitcher can develop the habit of checking the runner casually prior to delivering to the plate. He might also get into a set rhythm whereby he gives the runner just one look and then delivers to the plate in the same time sequence on each pitch. As was the case at first base, the runner should never attempt to steal third base if he does not get a good jump. If he does not get the proper jump he will move out to his secondary lead, just as he did when at first base. When he returns to second base after the pitch, he will check with the third base coach for the possibility of the steal sign being flashed again. A coach can put a runner on his own in regard to stealing second base or third base, but this is strictly a matter for the coach to decide. Anytime a runner is put on his own to steal, it behooves the coach to spend a lot of time with the runner explaining the situations he will be confronted with as a possible base stealer. The runner at second base would have to attempt the steal of third base even if he does not get a good jump when there is also a runner at first base. This would be a double steal which is generally done when the count is three balls and two strikes on the batter with less than two outs. The stealing mechanics at second base are similar to the mechanics used at first base in regard to the cross-over step, etc. It is much easier for the runner stealing third base to look in toward the plate than it is for the runner stealing second base since the angle to the plate is much less. If it is found that the pitcher is a "one-looker" it makes the steal of third base that much easier. The coach can flash the regular steal sign to the runner at second base followed by another sign indicating that the "one-looker" steal is in affect. In this type of steal the runner will take his standard lead. When the pitcher comes to the set position and looks at the runner, he will remain in the standard lead. When the pitcher looks back to the plate the runner will take three large shuffle steps toward third base. The shuffle steps are the same type used in the delayed steal from first base. If the pitcher delivers the ball to the plate anytime during the shuffle steps, the runner will break for third base. If the pitcher does not throw to the plate when the three shuffle steps are completed, the runner will stop and start the shuffle steps back to his standard lead and then hold there for the pitcher to make his move. If the pitcher looks back the second time during the three shuffle steps, the runner will stop immediately and break back to second base preparing for a dive into the base if the pitcher picks at the base. The "one-looker" steal is a gambling type steal whereby the pitcher has set up a pattern on his looks to second base. If the pitcher happens to break the pattern there is a chance that the runner will be picked off second base. For a pitcher that does not set any type of pattern on his looks to second base, the aggressive type lead would be in effect. There is never any need to delay steal or fake the steal from second base since the catcher will have the full view of the runner at second base. If there are two outs and the steal sign is flashed, the runner will have to come back into the baseline to assume his lead. He would not want to position himself back of the baseline as he would with two outs and no steal in effect. The steal of third base with two outs is generally not a good strategic move on the offense's part.

E. **The secondary lead**—The secondary lead mechanics at second base are similar to the mechanics used by the runner at first base with a couple of exceptions. The runner's distance from second base when he completes his secondary lead will be further than the lead he would have at first base. This is due to the fact that the catcher has a longer throw to second base than he does at first base on a pick-off attempt. The other exception would be that the runner at second base would aim his shoulder and hips to an area half way between third base and the plate when he reaches his secondary lead. The runner at first base assumes the secondary lead with his hips and shoulder pointing at the shortstop position. This enables the runner at each base to either return to the base or move toward the next base equally well depending on the status of the baseball. The distance of the secondary lead at second base will depend on all the same factors as discussed for the secondary lead at first base.

42. **Reacting to a fly ball from second base**—A runner must quickly decide on whether or not to tag up at second base on a fly ball, for any delay in doing so might jeopardize his chances for successfully advancing to third base on the catch. Most of the time this decision will have to be made by the runner, for if he waits for the third base coach to make the decision and pass it along to him, valuable reaction time can be lost. The coach must spend time with his players giving them the general rules they should follow in tagging up at second base. These rules would be:

A. **A foul ball hit in the air**—The runner at second base must tag up on any foul ball hit in the air. If there is any doubt as to whether the ball will be fair or foul, he should treat the ball as a fair ball. This is so that he is not caught tagging up at second base on a short fly ball only to find that the ball drops near the foul line in fair territory. If the ball is caught in foul territory, the runner will make the decision as to whether or not he will advance to third base. If there is a runner at third base, the runner at second base must be sure that the runner at third will be breaking for the plate before advancing too far toward third base. Since the play will generally be made at the plate on any foul ball with a runner tagging at third base, the runner at second base should be able to advance to third base. With a foul ball hit well down the left field line, the runner at second base must be conscious of the throw to third base if there is no play for the left fielder at the plate.

B. **The ball is hit deep in the outfield**—With less than two outs, the runner at second base will want to tag at second

248

base on all catchable fly balls hit deep in the outfield. If there is doubt in the runner's mind that the ball might not be caught, the runner needs to be far enough away from the base so that if the catch is made he can return to second base. He can then tag at the base and advance toward third base. The runner should never be holding on second base when there is a chance that the ball will not be caught. The distance the runner will be away from second base is dictated by various factors in regard to the status of the ball. He must be in a position to return to the base on the catch, and still be able to advance to third base. It is foolish for a runner to be tagging at second base on a catchable long fly ball, for if the ball hits the ground he might have a very difficult time scoring from second base. If he is off the base, it makes it much easier for him to advance to the plate. A quick runner can also be off the base on a catchable long fly ball that is hit in an area of the outfield well away from third base.

C. **The ball is hit to an outfielder so that he would have a play on the runner advancing to third base on the tag**—A general rule for the runners to follow is that with no outs it is important that a runner make every effort to advance to third base on the catch. Of course, he will take into consideration the situation of the game and all the factors previously discussed. With one out the runner would be more conservative in advancing to third base on the catch, since he does not want to make the third out at third base. In either case, the runner should never be tagging at second base and not advance to third base unless there was a runner also tagging at third base. If the runner decides he can not tag and advance to third base, then he would get as far away from second base as he can and still be able to get back to second base on a possible throw by the outfielder to the base. If there is any doubt in the runner's mind that the ball might not be caught, he would never be tagging at the base.

D. **The runner at third base is tagging up at third base**—On a fly ball that will be caught in the outfield with less than two outs, both the runners at second and third base would be tagging if there is a chance for the runner at third base to score on the catch. The runner at second base needs to recognize the fact that the outfielder will be throwing to the plate as long as there is a play to be made there. If the throw will be to the plate, the runner at second base will tag and advance to third base on the throw to the plate. If the outfielder has no play at the plate, the runner at second base must make the decision as to whether he will be able to advance to third base on the catch. If he decides he will not be able to advance, then he would position himself away from the base so that he could possibly score if the ball is misplayed. If there is any chance that the outfielder will throw to the plate, the runner must be tagging at second base. Anytime the runner at second base sees that the runner at third base is not going to tag on a catch, he will come down the line to third base as far as he possibly can and still be able to return to second base if the outfielder makes the play at that base. If there is a chance that the outfielder will not be able to catch the ball, the runner at second base would not be tagging. He would be off the base far enough away to return for the tag and advance as discussed in the previous section.

43. **The runner at second base responding to a ground ball or line drive**—Upon reaching the secondary lead at second base, the runner must be in a position to respond properly to the batted ball. With two outs, the runner will break for third base at the "crack of the bat". With less than two outs, and the runner is forced on a ground ball to advance with a runner at first base also, he will break for third base when he reads the down angle of the ball off the hitter's bat. With less than two outs and the runner is not forced to advance, he must read quickly the status of the ball and the fielders in the immediate area of the ball. On a line drive, the runner at second base must freeze at his secondary lead (as the right foot hits the ground). If he reads that there is any chance that the ball will be caught in the infield, he must quickly head back to second base. If the ball does go through the infield, he can recover and make it easily to third base. There is never any reason for a runner to be doubled up at second base on a line drive in the infield unless it is a "shot" right at the shortstop or second baseman. If he takes an additional step away from his secondary lead or freezes too long, there is a good chance that he will be doubled up on a line drive back to the pitcher, the first baseman or third baseman as well. Anytime the runner at second base is not forced to advance, he must check out the shortstop after every pitch to see where he is playing the hitter. This is so he can better respond to a ground ball in the area of the shortstop when he is not forced to advance. Some general rules that the runner should follow in responding to a ground ball at second base with less than two outs, and not forced to advance are:

A. **Ball hit so that the third baseman moves toward the plate**—Anytime the runner at second base sees the batted ball force the third baseman to move toward the plate, the runner might be able to advance to third base. This depends a great deal on the third baseman's depth at the time of the pitch. If the third baseman is positioned even with third base or in front of the base and has to move forward on the ground ball, the runner at second base would have a good chance of advancing to third base. If the third baseman is behind the baseline, then the chances of advancing are diminished depending on the speed of the ball hit by the batter. On a bunted ball, there should be no problem for the runner to advance unless the pitcher breaks to the third base side and the third baseman is able to stay near the base.

B. **Ball hit to the pitcher**—The ground ball back to the pitcher is probably the toughest ball for the runner at second base to read as it comes off the bat, and this is why many runners are caught off second base on the ball fielded by the pitcher. The runner must make sure that the ball gets past the pitcher before he breaks toward third base. Since the runner at second base is instructed to break for third base on a ground ball up the middle or to the right side of the infield, one can easily see how susceptible the runner can be if the ball is fielded by the pitcher. Thus, the runner cannot afford to advance from his secondary lead on the ball hit up the middle until it has cleared the area of the mound. If the pitcher has to move off the mound to the first base side of the field on the ground ball, the runner should be able to advance to third base if he gets a good jump. More than likely, this type of ground ball will be slowly hit if the pitcher has to come off the mound to field it, allowing the runner ample time to get to third base. If the pitcher is forced by the ground ball to come off the mound toward the plate, the runner might also be able to make it to third base due to the nature of the ground ball hit by the batter. If the pitcher is forced to break from the mound to the third base side, the runner must hold unless the ground ball has also forced the third baseman to break towards the ball as well.

C. **Ball hit forces the shortstop to go to his left**—The location of the shortstop, the direction of the ground ball, and the speed of the ball are the determining factors in whether or not the runner at second base can advance on the ground ball that is hit in the area of the shortstop. For example, if the shortstop is playing a righthanded hitter to the pull side, the runner can advance to third base on any ground ball that forces the shortstop to go well to his left. The same type of ground ball would not cause the runner to advance if the shortstop was playing the hitter straight away or to the opposite field positioning himself closer to second base. This is why it is so important that the runner check out the position of the shortstop after every pitch. On a slow hit ground ball to the runner's left that gets by the pitcher, it should allow the runner to advance no matter where the shortstop positions himself. The runner's speed, the jump he gets from his secondary lead, the defensive ability of the shortstop, and the situation in the game (outs, inning, score, etc.) also must be taken into consideration on a ground ball hit to the area of the shortstop.

D. **Ball hit to the right side of the infield**—In most cases, the ball hit to the right side of the infield will allow the runner at second base to advance to third base. However, if the second baseman and first baseman are playing shallow and the ground ball is well hit, it could prompt the runner to hold at second base. As before, the situation in the game and the nature of the ground ball must always be taken into consideration by the runner.

E. **Ball hit with a runner at third base also**—At no time can the runner at second base break for third base without knowing what the runner at third base is going to do on the ground ball. The runner at second base who breaks for third base on a ground ball only to find that the runner at third base has stopped his movement to the plate, will cost his club an out on a runner who is in scoring position. This is why it is so important for the runner at second base to check the runner's movement at third base before advancing. It is very helpful to the runner at second base if he knows what the runner at third base will be doing on a ground ball. The third base coach can inform the runner at second base via a visual sign what the runner at third base is going to be doing on a ground ball. For example, if the runner at third base is going on any ground ball (down angle), the third base coach can point to the ground as he looks at the runner at second base. If the runner at third base will be holding unless the ground ball gets through the infield, the third base coach can hold up both hands in front of him as he looks at the runner at second base. This sign will inform the runner that the runner at third base is holding on the ground ball. The visual sign to the runner at second base must be provided him before he begins his movement off second base to obtain his primary lead on the pitcher. If the runner at third base is breaking for the plate on a ground ball (generally done with one out), the runner at second base should advance to third base on any ground ball that he would normally advance on with no runner at third base.

F. **Ball hit in the hole between the third baseman and the shortstop**—The runner at second base cannot move toward third base on a ground ball hit to his right until he sees that the ball will get through the infield. The runner should position himself as far away from second base as he can so he can react forward if a ball gets through the infield. At the same time, he can not get so far away from the base that the third baseman or shortstop can throw behind him to the second baseman at second base. If the third baseman or shortstop goes into the hole to field the ball, the runner with good speed might be able to advance to third base when the ball leaves the hand of the fielder for the long throw to first base. The runner must be sure that he does not break for third base until the ball leaves the hand of the infielder, for a smart infielder will fake the throw to first base if he feels that there will be no play on the batter-runner. After the fake, he will throw the ball to the second baseman covering second base. If the third baseman is playing deep, and the ground ball takes him well to his left into the hole, the runner at second base might be able to advance to third base. This is due to the fact that the third baseman's angle to the baseline would not enable him to field the ball and make the tag of the runner heading toward third base. Good baserunning instinct is very important for a runner to have, especially as he reacts to ground balls when at second base and not forced to advance.

44. **The runner heading for third base picking up the third base coach**—The runner leaving second base on the batted ball should be completely aware of the status of the baseball. He would be responsible for his actions until he picks up the

250

third base coach for visual instructions as he approaches third base. Hopefully, the third base coach is in a position to be easily seen by the runner. The third base coach should not hesitate to move out of the coach's box toward the plate for two reasons: (1) the runner will be able to maintain eye contact with the coach throughout the turn, except for that time he will be touching third base; and (2) it will give the third base coach a longer time to make a decision on what he wants the runner to do. Since the runner heading for third base will have the ball behind him when the ball is in the outfield, he must pick up the third base coach for his visual instructions. If the ball happens to be in front of the runner as he approaches third base, the third base coach would not be needed. For example, a runner at first base heads for third base on a base hit only to find that the ball is overthrown at third base. Since the ball and the play is in front of the runner, he will use his own judgment on whether to advance to the plate.

45. **The third base coach's signs to the runner approaching third base**—With the ball behind the runner as he approaches third base, the third base coach will be required to offer the runner assistance. The third base coach must be sure to provide the runner with a clear sign so that there is no confusion. It is very important that the runner always contemplates scoring as he heads for third base, and then he can make the adjustment if he is held up by the third base coach. Many times you see a runner break from his secondary lead at second base thinking that he will be held up by the third base coach due to the nature of the ball hit. This generally leads to a non-aggressive approach to third base as he prepares to be held up by the coach. The runner must remain aggressive throughout his approach to third base forcing the third base coach to stop him. There is nothing any more frustrating for a third base coach than to see a runner lose his aggressiveness on his turn at third base due to the fact that he thinks that he will not be scoring on the play. When the third base coach then wants the runner to score, valuable time and distance is lost and now the coach might have to change his initial decision to score on the play. The following are the visual signs that can be used by the third base coach for the runner approaching third base:

A. **No sign is flashed**—The runner must consider that he will be scoring on the play when the third base coach provides no sign to the runner. In this way, the coach can always hold the runner up at a later stage of the turn. If no sign is flashed as the runner approaches the third base coach after hitting the base, it must be interpreted that he is to score. This allows the third base coach the luxury of waiting to the last possible moment to make a decision on whether he wants to hold the runner on the turn. If the third base coach has come well down the line to make the decision, it provides him more time to stop the runner. Of course, there is always the point of no return when the runner gets past the coach.

B. **Waving one or both arms in a circular motion**—This signal means that the third base coach definitely wants the runner to score on the play. If the coach wishes to wait a little longer to make the decision on sending the runner to the plate, then he would not flash any sign for the runner. The runner must always interpret this signal as an indication by the third base coach that he will be scoring and that there will be a play made on him at the plate. This is especially the case when there are two outs with the possibility of another runner being tagged out at another base. Often a runner heading for the plate will slow down when he sees no play is going to be made on him, only to find that the play was made on another runner prior to his crossing the plate. This would mean that his run would not count.

C. **Holding both arms high in the air**—If the third base coach flashes this sign prior to the runner touching third base, it will imply to the runner that he will not attempt to score. Once the runner touches third base, he will aggressively round the base and then find the ball as he continues shuffling toward the plate. As soon as the runner makes contact with third base, the third base coach is no longer responsible for his actions in response to the ball in play. This is why the runner needs to locate the ball just after making contact with the base. This is to eliminate the communication problem between the coach and the runner if there was a misplay of the ball in the outfield by the fielder or by the relay man. If the runner waits for the coach to respond to the misplay and pass this information on to the runner, valuable time and distance will be lost. If this sign is flashed to the runner after touching third base, it is an indication from the coach that he does not want the runner to continue on toward the plate. Since the runner continues running full speed toward the plate until visually commanded to stop, this sign will force the runner to stop as quickly as possible. Once the runner gets his body under control, he will be responsible to pick up the ball and respond accordingly. This sign might be flashed when the runner is well past third base since the coach might have to delay his decision due to the fact that the status of the ball is still uncertain.

D. **Holding both hands in the air followed quickly by pointing both hands at third base along with a loud command of "get back"**—This sign would be used when the third base coach has held up the runner after he touched third base and is now advancing toward the plate. If there is urgency for the runner to return quickly to third base, this is the visual sign and vocal command used. The runner will stop as quickly as possible, pivot, and head back to third base. Since there is a chance that a play will be made on the runner back at third base, the runner must be prepared to dive back into the bag. The runner must realize that there are times when the third base coach has delayed his decision until the last possible second, and now has to stop the runner hoping that he can return to the base before the ball does.

E. **The third base coach on one knee bringing both arms down toward the ground**—Anytime there will be a play made on the runner approaching third base, the third base coach will want the runner to slide into the base. He can signal this fact to the runner by getting down on one knee and bringing both arms down toward the ground. In addition, the third base coach can yell "slide". If the throw is coming into the area of third base to either the infield side or the outfield side of the bag, the coach can motion with his hands for the runner to slide to the side of the base away from where the ball is heading. Once the runner slides into third base, the runner is then responsible to pick up the ball if it gets past the third baseman.

46. **The baserunner at third base**—As soon as the runner reaches third base, he must quickly review in his mind the situation at hand (outs, inning, score, etc.). The third base coach can review with the runner what he wishes him to do in various ground ball situations, taking into consideration how the infield is playing in regard to depth. It still will be the responsibility of the runner to react to the batted ball. The runner must check the third base coach each time he returns to third base for any possible sign that might be on.

A. **Leads at third base**—The movement away from third base is very similar to the movement away from both first and second base. There should never be any reason for a runner at third base to be picked off the base by the pitcher. The runner at first base and second base might get picked off on different types of stealing leads, but this should not be the case for the runner at third base. The offensive team can never afford to lose a runner at third base on a pick-off, since he is so close to scoring. The runner at third base will be faced with a pitcher either throwing from the stretch or from the windup:

1. **Pitcher stretching**—The runner must obtain his primary lead at third base very similar to the way he assumed the lead at first base and second base. The distance away from the base in the primary lead will depend on all the factors previously discussed at first base and second base. Another factor would be how far the third baseman is playing away from the bag. Of course, the farther the third baseman is away from third base, the farther the runner might get on his primary lead. The runner must assume his primary lead so that his toes are on the third baseline as he faces the pitcher. From this position he would have a one-way lead back to third base so that there is no chance he would be picked off if the third baseman breaks for the base as the pitcher throws to the bag. Once the pitcher shows that he will definitely be throwing to the plate, the runner will begin moving to the plate to establish his secondary lead. The runner must be sure that the righthanded pitcher does not disguise the fact that he will be throwing to the plate, and then throw to third base. This is similar to the situation with the lefthanded pitcher throwing to first base from the set position to attempt to pick-off the runner at first base. The runner must never commit himself to the plate until he is absolutely sure that the pitcher is going to the plate, even if the suicide squeeze play is in effect. Thus, there is no such thing as a one-way lead to the plate, or the two-way lead with a runner at third base and the pitcher throwing from the stretch. He would only have a one-way lead back to third base, and then make the adjustment toward the plate when he sees that the pitcher is actually going to deliver the ball to the hitter.

2. **Pitcher winding up**—Once the pitcher begins his motion to the plate via the windup, the runner at third base can begin walking to his secondary lead. He would start his walk to the plate only when the pitcher starts his windup since the pitcher could still throw to third base prior to his initial movement into the windup. The runner must be a comfortable distance away from the base taking this fact into account. Once the windup begins, he will start moving toward the plate to establish the proper secondary lead so that he is in the proper position in the base path when the ball reaches the hitter.

B. **The secondary lead**—The secondary lead at third base is probably the most important mechanic in baserunning. The reason is that the runner at third base is close to scoring and his ability or inability to generate momentum toward the plate off the secondary lead can mean the difference between a run or an out. The distance of the secondary lead at third base will depend on all the factors that have been previously mentioned for the runner's secondary lead at first and second base. The other factor involved with the secondary lead at third base is whether there is a righthanded or lefthanded hitter at the plate. The runner at third base can take about another step lead on his secondary lead with a righthander at the plate than he can with a lefthanded hitter in the batter's box. This is because the righthanded hitter will partially obstruct the catcher's view of the runner establishing his secondary lead. It is also quite difficult for the catcher to make a proper throw to the third baseman with the righthanded hitter between him and the third baseman if he attempts to pick him off third base. With a lefthanded hitter at the plate, the catcher has an unobstructed view of the runner at third base and does not have to throw over a hitter to reach his target. The runner must have his hips and shoulders facing home plate when he reaches his secondary lead so that he can generate maximum acceleration toward the plate. As was the case at first and second base on the secondary lead, the right foot is in the air (right thigh parallel to the ground) and heading toward the ground as the ball reaches the batter. If the runner is going to break toward the plate off the secondary lead, he will just continue down with his right foot and head for the plate at full speed. If he reads that the status of the ball will not allow him to move toward the plate (hitter does not make contact), he will land on the right foot and begin his movement back toward third base. The runner should be in foul territory while moving forward in his secondary lead. His left foot should be about two inches away from the foul line in foul territory as it hits on each step toward the plate. This will insure that his entire body is in foul territory throughout the secondary lead. It is important for the runner to be in foul territory at this time in case a batted ball was to hit him. If he was in fair territory at the time the ball makes contact with him, he will be called out by the umpire. At the same time, he should not be any farther than two inches in foul territory with his left foot during the entire secondary lead. The further he is in foul territory the longer the distance to the plate. There is an exception to this rule in the case of a bases loaded situation, with two outs and a 3 ball - 2 strike count on the batter. When this is the case and the runner is forced to advance, he would be much farther away from the foul line in order to insure his safety from being struck by a batted ball. The runner should never be more than one-third of the way down the line from third base when the ball reaches the hitter at the plate. He should be about 10 feet away from the foul line getting himself under control so that he can attempt to avoid a batted ball heading in his direction. The runners at first and second base will be heading full speed to the forward base as soon as they read that the pitcher is committed to throwing the ball to the plate. A smart pitcher will always pitch from the stretch position in this situation in order to keep the runners from getting a big jump. If the pitcher is throwing from the stretch, the runner at third base should achieve his normal secondary lead plus a few additional steps toward the plate while angling off into foul territory.

C. **The return to third base from the secondary lead**—Once the runner reads that the ball will be caught by the catcher, he must be in a position off his secondary lead to return to third base as quickly as possible. If the catcher attempts the pick-off at third base, the runner should be able to return to the base on the dive. The runner must always assume each time the catcher receives the pitch that there will be a play made on him by the catcher. If there is no play, the runner can then adjust the tempo of his return to third base. With a righthander hitter at the plate, the runner's view of the catcher might be blocked partially to the point the runner will not see the catcher rise up to throw to third base. This is why he must assume that a play will be made on him back at third base, and then adjust when it is evident that no play will be made. The mechanics of the return to third base requires that the runner hit the ground with his right foot, and then quickly pivot in order to allow the body to be heading back toward third base. As soon as the right foot hits the ground and the pivot begins, the runner will step with his left foot over the foul line so that the toes of the left foot are pointing in the direction of where the shortstop normally stands. The left foot would be about one foot in fair territory when it touches the ground. By this procedure, the runner has opened his hips properly in order to quickly return to third base. If the runner was to just step in the general direction of the mound with his left foot, it would lock his left hip and appreciably affect his quickness on the return. The right foot would then drive directly toward third base which should put the runner's entire body in fair territory on the return. The runner must remain low as he pivots and returns to third base if there is a play being made on him by the catcher. By returning to third base from the inside of the diamond it will severely restrict the catcher's ability to throw the ball effectively to the third baseman for two reasons: (1) the catcher will not have a clear view of the third baseman since the runner is in the direct path between the catcher and the third baseman who is setting up on the inside of the base; and (2) the catcher will be concerned about the possibility of hitting the runner with the throw. Just about the time the runner's left foot hits on the inside of the diamond, he will know whether or not the catcher is going to attempt the pick-off at third base. If he reads that the catcher is rising up to make the throw, the runner will set his sights on returning to third base as quickly as possible on the dive play. There should never be any reason for a runner to get picked off third base by the catcher. If he does, it is because his secondary lead was too long or his mechanics on the turn were not executed properly. The runner must be very careful anytime the batter swings and misses or bunts and misses that he does not lean toward the plate upon the completion of his secondary lead. This will make it practically impossible to pivot properly on the right foot causing the runner extreme problems in returning to third base. If the runner observes that the catcher is not going to throw to third base, then he can slow down his footwork on his return to third base. He must keep his eye on the catcher at all times, and then follow the ball back to the pitcher as he returns to third base. If the catcher happens to overthrow the pitcher, and the shortstop or second baseman is not backing up the pitcher, the runner at third base might be able to score.

D. **The runner responding from his secondary lead to a passed ball or wild pitch**—The runner at third base must respond at a moment's notice when the ball gets by the catcher due to a passed ball or wild pitch. When the runner reaches the secondary lead and the right foot starts toward the ground, he should be able to generate momentum forward if he sees the ball get by the catcher. At no time should he be returning to third base when the ball reaches the catcher, nor should he be in a position of reacting to the passed ball or wild pitch from a standing stop. As in all baserunning, there are times to gamble and there are times to be conservative. This holds true for the runner at third base on a passed ball or wild pitch. The following factors are taken into consideration by the runner when he makes his decision on whether to advance or hold: (1) runner's speed and the type of jump he can generate toward the plate; (2) distance the ball is away from the plate; (3) catcher's quickness and ability; (4) pitcher's quickness in covering home plate; (5) score of the game; (6) inning of the game; (7) number of outs; (8) texture of the dirt in the baseline; and (9) batter at the plate. After discussing gambling factors at other bases, there is no need for us to break down each of these factors with the exception of those that are unique to the runner at third base reacting to a passed ball or wild pitch. The distance that the ball is away from the plate is sometimes deceiving, especially when the ball rolls toward the first base side of home plate. The angle of the ball to the runner does not allow the runner a good view of the speed and distance of the ball. On all other balls that get by the catcher, the runner should be able to judge the speed and distance of the ball. If playing on a field with a backstop that has a hard surface, the runner must be sure that the ball will not rebound off the wall back to the area of home plate. The quickness of the catcher and the ability of the pitcher to cover the plate are very important considerations. A pitcher might be quick, but he might not get a great jump toward the plate. On a ball rolling to the third base side of the plate, the catcher will have a much more difficult time throwing the ball to the pitcher at the plate due to the fact that his angle to the plate will be away from his throwing side. If a runner decides not to advance on the play, he should follow the catcher's throw to the pitcher since an overthrow of the plate occurs quite frequently on this type of play. If the ball rolls to the first base or third base side, many times the first baseman or third baseman will not back up the throw from the catcher to the pitcher. The number of outs is a very important consideration on the runner's part when he makes the decision on whether he will gamble on scoring on the passed ball or wild pitch. With no outs, the runner cannot gamble on scoring unless his team is well ahead in the score. It is foolish for a runner to ever be thrown out at the plate with no outs since the offensive team should be able to score him from third base sometime during the remainder of the inning. With one out, a great chance can be taken. With two outs, a greater chance can be taken. Of course, all of the other items of consideration must be taken into consideration before the runner makes the attempt to score. The third base coach cannot assist the runner in responding to the passed ball or wild pitch. By the time the third base coach makes his decision and passes it along to the runner, valuable time and distance will be lost.

E. **The runner responding to a line drive at third base with less than two outs**—With two outs, the runner at third base will be breaking for the plate no matter what type of ball is hit by the batter. With less than two outs, the runner must respond to the nature of the ball hit. The runner at third base must freeze when he reads a line drive off the bat of the hitter. After freezing initially, he should begin his pivot work back to third base very similar to the catcher's attempt to pick him off the base. In this way he will be in a position to get back to third base if the line drive is caught by the pitcher or an infielder. Once the ball gets through the infield, he will have plenty of time to pivot back toward the plate and score. There is never any reason for a runner at third base getting doubled up on a line drive in the infield unless the ball is hit directly at the third baseman. If the runner was to take another step toward the plate off his secondary lead on the line drive, there is a good chance he will be doubled up on a ball caught by an infielder or the pitcher.

F. **The runner responding to a ground ball at third base with less than two outs**—On a ground ball, there are numerous factors that must be taken into consideration by the runner before he decides whether to advance toward the plate, return to third base, or freeze and react to the fielder handling the ground ball. These factors which will be discussed in detail are: (1) depth of the infielders; (2) speed and direction of the ground ball; (3) runners at other bases; and (4) factors associated with gambling on scoring.

1. **Depth of the infielders**—Once the runner reaches third base, the third base coach can provide assistance to the runner in analyzing the situation. Together they can check out the infielders in regard to their depth and the positions they will be assuming in regard to playing the hitter at the plate. The infielders would be either: (1) playing in on the grass; (2) playing a few steps off the grass; (3) playing half way; (4) playing half way plus a couple of steps deeper; (5) playing back at regular depth; (6) first baseman and third baseman playing even with the baselines and the shortstop and second baseman playing in double play depth; or (7) the pull side of the infield is playing back with the non-pull side of the infield playing in on the grass or half way. Thus, there are numerous ways that an infield can set up on defense with a runner at third base. In most cases, when the infield is playing back in regular depth the runner at third base can score on any ground ball that gets by the pitcher up the middle of the infield. A ball to the first baseman or third baseman would cause the runner to generally hold with no outs, and advance to the plate with one out. It is a good baserunning philosophy to attempt to score from third base with one out when the runner reads the down angle on the ball off the bat. This should be read as the right foot approaches the ground off the secondary lead. This is true as long as the offensive team is in a gambling situation. If the offensive team is behind in the score late in the game, the runner at third base must make the ground ball go through the infield with one out unless it is a double play type ground ball with a runner at first base. Anytime the runner at third base breaks for the plate in this one out situation, he should get in the rundown if the throw to the plate allows him the chance to stop prior to the tag by the catcher. He must stay in the rundown as long as possible to allow the batter-runner a chance to hopefully advance to second base. It should also allow all other runners to advance as far as they can. With two outs, no runner should advance to third base when the runner who started at third base is caught in the rundown. This will enable the runner in the rundown the opportunity to return to third base. With no outs or one out, all runners must advance to the forward base whenever a rundown occurs. If the tag on the runner in a rundown is imminent, no runner would advance risking the fact that he could be thrown out after the tag. By going on the down angle with one out, the runner at third base will force the infielder or pitcher to make a clean play on the ground ball.

It will also force the fielder to make a perfect throw to the catcher since the runner should have a tremendous jump on the ball off the bat. If the runner hesitates, valuable time and distance are affected. The third base coach should advise the runner in the one out situation whether he wants him to go on the down angle; make the ball go through the infield; or advance on the ground ball past the pitcher up the middle of the infield.

2. **Speed and direction of the ground ball**—Good baserunning instincts will allow a baserunner at third base to respond to various types of ground balls in regard to the speed and direction of the ball. Even with the infield playing in on the grass, a swinging bunt or a very slow ground ball might allow the runner at third base to score. With the infield playing half way to regular depth a runner with good speed can easily score on a slow ground ball even with no outs if he gets a good jump. Anytime the runner does not get a good jump on the ground ball he is probably better off holding at third base, unless he is going on down angle off the bat. With a ball hit down the third baseline with no outs, the runner must quickly return to third base from his secondary lead to avoid being tagged out by the third baseman if he was to field the ball near the base. With one out and the runner is going on down angle, he should break for the plate and stay on the inside of the baseline as he attempts to score. Anytime the third baseman is forced to move toward the plate to field a slow ground ball, the runner at third base can move off the base toward the plate as far as the third baseman is away from the base. Once the third baseman throws the ball to first base, the runner might be far enough down the line to score on the throw. The runner must be alert for a fake throw to first base by the third baseman, followed by his throwing the ball to the shortstop covering third base or to the catcher at home plate. With no outs, all ground balls must get by the pitcher before the runner at third base attempts to advance toward the plate. Any ball that forces the first baseman or third baseman to go to the second base side of their fielding position, should allow a runner to score, even with no outs. Much depends on the speed of the ball, the jump that the runner gets, and the fielding ability of the player making the play on the ball. These are just a few examples of situations that can come up where a runner is forced to respond to the direction and the speed of the ground ball. By going on down angle with one out when in a gambling situation, you take a lot of guesswork out of baserunning on the runner's part. With no outs, he must be sure that he can make the plate safely before advancing.

3. **Runners at other bases**—Of course, with the bases loaded the runner at third base will advance on all ground balls. A runner at second base should not directly affect the status of the runner at third base in regard to attempting to score or not on a ground ball. It is extremely helpful to the runner at second base to know if the runner is going on down angle. The third base coach can let him know through a set signal whether or not the runner at third base is going on the down angle to the plate. With a runner at first base, the status of the runner at third base can be very much affected on the ground ball with less than two outs. Anytime a double play type ground ball is hit to an infielder or the pitcher, the runner at third base must break for the plate with less than two outs. The only exception to this rule might be if the runner at third base is the tying or winning run in the last inning of the game with no outs. If that is the case, the runner should hold and then break for the plate once he reads that the ball will be thrown to the pivot man at second base. There is no need for the first out to be made at the plate if the runner at third is that important of a run. There is no greater baserunning mistake than to have a runner at third base with no outs remain at third base while the defense executes a double play via second base. The runner at third base should hope that the infielder or pitcher makes a play on him at the plate on a hard hit ball so that his team can stay out of a double play. Normally the defense will not concern themselves with the runner at third base unless he is a very important run late in the game. If the infielder or pitcher throws the ball to the plate and the runner is going to be out by a great distance, he must stop and remain in the rundown between third and home plate as long as possible. This is to allow the batter-runner and all other runners to advance to the forward bases. If the runner at third base is breaking on down angle it should make for a close play at the plate unless the ball was sharply hit at the pitcher or the infielder. Anytime the ball is hit in front of the plate, the runner at third base should hold assuming that the catcher can field the ball and make the tag if he attempts to score. If the ball hit is not a double play type ground ball with another runner at first base, the runner at third base must react to the ball as he would if there was no runner at first base. Thus, with one out he would break on down angle if in a gambling situation. If in a non-gambling situation, he would hold unless he sees the ball is hit by the pitcher up the middle of the diamond. If the ball is hit to the first baseman or third baseman, he would hold unless the ball carries the fielder toward the second base side of the diamond. With no outs and a ground ball is hit that could not be a double play type ball, he would hold unless he feels that he can easily beat the throw to the plate. If he holds, and then sees the fielder of the ball throw to second base, he can then break for the plate. If he does not get a good jump on this play he should hold, for he would risk having the pivot man at second base throw him out at the plate after making the force out at second base.

4. **Factors associated with gambling on scoring**—The number of outs, the inning, the score, the runner's speed, the texture of the baseline, the fielding ability and strength of fielder's arm, and the hitter coming up to the plate are all factors that must be taken into consideration by the runner at third base on whether he will advance to the plate on the

ground ball. This is in addition to the depth and location of all the infielders, the speed and direction of the ground ball, and the runners at other bases. Since there are so many factors involved, the third base coach must rely on the baserunning instinct of the runner at third base. There is no way that the third base coach can help the runner other than to discuss with him some of the basic strategy prior to the runner beginning his primary lead.

47. Reacting to a fly ball from third base—The runner at third base must quickly respond from his secondary lead to a ball that is hit in the air past the infielders. Any delay in doing so might jeopardize his chances for successfully advancing to the plate. As soon as he reads the fly ball, the runner must make the decision on whether he will go back to the base for the tag. The third base coach can help him in making this decision since there is time for this communication while the ball is in the air. The general rules that should be followed by the runner and third base coach in responding to a fly ball are:

A. A foul ball hit in the air—The runner at third base must tag up on any foul ball hit in the air. If there is any doubt as to whether the ball will be fair or foul, he should treat the ball as a fair ball. This is so that he is not caught tagging at third base on a short fly ball only to find that the ball drops near the foul line in fair territory. If the ball is caught in foul territory, the runner will make the decision as to whether or not he will advance to the plate. The third base coach can communicate what he wants the runner to do by one of three commands: (1) "score"—means for the runner to tag and break for the plate when the ball is caught; (2) "fake the break"—means for the runner to tag and break for the plate but do not attempt to score unless the ball is poorly thrown; or (3) "half-way"—move down the line. If the runner reads that the throw from the fielder will be well off the mark when faking the break, he can respond by attempting to score. He must be careful not to go so far down the line that the cut-off man or the catcher can field the ball and make a play on him back at third base. The runner should always force the fielder of the fly ball to make the throw to the plate, even if he is not attempting to score. The factors previously mentioned in regard to when to gamble and when to play conservative all come into play as the runner and third base coach make the decision on whether to score.

B. A fly ball hit deep in the outfield—As soon as the runner at third base reads from his secondary lead the ball in the air, he will return quickly to third base for the tag up and advance to the plate on the catch. If there is not going to be a play at the plate on the runner, he should pause for a brief second after the catch before leaving the base. This is to insure that he does not leave the base too early with no play at the plate. There is no reason for a runner to be called out by an umpire for leaving a base too early when there is little or no chance he will be thrown out at the forward base or the plate. This is especially true for the runner tagging up at third base. If there will be a play at the plate after the catch, the runner needs to leave the base at the exact time the ball touches the outfielder's glove. The third base coach should not be responsible to tell the runner when to break for the plate. The runner must watch the ball and break for the plate at the proper time. This is to eliminate any delay in transmission of a communication from the third base coach to the runner. If the second out is made on the catch in the outfield with a runner also tagging at another base, the runner from third base must be sure that he goes full speed to the plate. If the throw is made to another base and the out is made on another runner before the runner from third base crosses the plate, the run will not count. For this reason, a runner tagging at another base with the second out being made on the catch, must be sure that he is not thrown out at the forward base before the runner has an opportunity to cross the plate.

C. A short fly ball with a questionable catch—Anytime a short fly ball is hit that looks to the runner at third base that it will be a questionable catch by an outfielder or infielder, he should not be tagging at third base. If he was to be tagging at third base and the ball drops to the ground, he might have a very difficult time scoring. If he is off the base and the ball is not caught, then he should be able to score quite easily. The only exception to this rule would be when an infielder is going out in the outfield to make an over the shoulder catch, and there is no chance for an outfielder to make the play. If that be the case, the runner at third base can be tagging since the infielder making the catch would have to change directions before making the throw to the plate. This would be practically an impossible play for an infielder unless he has a very strong and accurate arm. If the runner at third base sees that the infielder is going to be able to get under the ball, then the strategy at third base would change. If the infielder catching the ball has a very weak and inaccurate arm, it is best for the runner to be tagging at the base if he is moving away from the infield at the time of the catch. If there is no question in the runner's mind that the infielder with a strong arm will catch the ball, he could be tagging at third base and break toward the plate hoping to draw the throw by the infielder. If he reads that the throw will be well away from home plate with no chance for the cut-off man to catch the ball, he can advance. If the throw is going to be cut-off or heading for an area near the plate, he can stop and return to third base. With two outs, the runner at third base can afford to gamble on this play as long as his team is in a gambling situation.

48. Reacting to the safety squeeze and the suicide squeeze bunt—There are times that the offensive team might deem it necessary to attempt to score the runner from third base on a safety squeeze or a suicide squeeze bunt. The runner at third base must execute the proper baserunning fundamentals in both of these type of plays:

A. **Safety squeeze**—Generally the sign flashed to the batter would be the regular sacrifice bunt sign. The runner at third base would treat this play as he would if he was breaking on the down angle on a batted ball. Since the batter does not have to bunt the ball, the runner cannot afford to advance farther than his regular secondary lead if the bunt is not laid down by the batter. Once he reads the bunted ball leaving the bat toward the ground, he would break full speed from his secondary lead. If the ball is bunted in the area near the plate, he should stop and quickly begin retreating back toward third base. While doing so, he would watch the catcher's throw to first base so that he might be able to react properly to an overthrow at first base. Any other type of bunted ball should allow the runner from third base the opportunity to score if he gets a good break toward the plate from his secondary lead.

B. **Suicide squeeze**—In this play the batter will be attempting to bunt any pitch that the catcher can get his glove on. It is very important that the baserunner at third base not break too early and give away the squeeze bunt. If he does break early, the pitcher might be able to pitch out on the batter, or in the case of a righthanded hitter, throw up and in on him so that he would have a difficult time of getting the bat on the ball. With a righthanded pitcher throwing from the windup, the runner at third base should start his walking lead when he begins motion into the windup. This walking lead should not give the pitcher or the defense any notion that the suicide squeeze play is on. When the pitcher's right hand passes his pivot leg (right leg), the runner should break full speed for the plate. At this point in the delivery, the pitcher is not going to be able to change the direction of his pitch to the plate. With a righthanded pitcher throwing from the set position, the runner will have to hold on his primary lead until the pitcher's right arm again passes his pivot leg. Once that occurs, the runner will break full speed for the plate. When executing the suicide squeeze with the pitcher throwing from the set position, the runner must be able to stop if he reads that the pitch is missed by the batter or he lays down a bunt near the plate. If he is unable to return to third base, he should get into a rundown and allow any baserunner(s) an opportunity to advance to a forward base. With a lefthanded pitcher throwing from the windup, the runner at third base should take a walking lead as he begins his windup similar to what he would do with a righthanded pitcher. As the pitcher lifts his lead leg (right leg) for his kick to the plate, the baserunner would break full speed for the plate. The runner can walk a little faster in his walking lead off a lefthanded pitcher than he can off a righthanded pitcher since the lefthanded pitcher will not be able to keep as good of eye contact with the runner during his walking lead. With a lefthanded pitcher throwing from the stretch, the runner should hold his break to the plate until the pitcher lifts his right leg to deliver the ball to the plate. As soon as the leg lifts off the ground he should break full speed to the plate. If the batter misses the bunt the baserunner must get into a rundown and let other runners who might be on base advance.

49. **Stealing of home plate**—The stealing of home plate by the runner at third base is not generally a high percentage play by the offensive team. All the right combinations must be in affect before it should be attempted. These combinations might be: (1) the runner at third base possesses great speed; (2) the batter at the plate is not a great hitter or is being overmatched by the pitcher; (3) there are two outs; (4) there are less than two strikes on the batter if there are two outs; (5) there is a righthanded hitter at the plate; (6) there is a lefthanded pitcher throwing from the windup who does not check the runner at third base, and he has a very slow and deliberate motion to the plate; (7) there is a righthanded pitcher throwing from the windup who does not check the runner at third base, and he has an unbelievable slow delivery to the plate; (8) the offensive team is in a gambling situation in terms of the score and inning of the game. The runner at third base would have to assume a large primary lead from third base and break full speed for the plate once the pitcher starts his first motion into the windup. The hitter must be informed by the third base coach via the steal sign that the runner will be attempting the steal of home plate. This is so that the batter does not swing the bat in an attempt to make contact with the ball. With no strikes on the batter, he should swing and miss late on the pitch to keep the catcher in back of the plate. With one strike he should not swing and miss, but stay in the batter's box until the runner starts his slide into the plate. The lefthanded batter's opportunity to help the runner stealing home plate is minimal. He should still swing and miss late with no strikes.

50. **The on deck hitter coaching the runner approaching home plate**—The on deck hitter will be the coach for the runner heading toward the plate at all times. As soon as the ball is hit, he must break for a position about 20 feet on the first base side of the plate so that he is in a direct line with the runner approaching the plate. His visual and verbal signs to the runner would be: (1) if he wants him to cross home plate without sliding he will put both arms high up in the air and yell "up-up"; (2) if he wants him to slide into home plate he will get down on one knee and motion both hands to the ground and yell "slide-slide". It is very important that the on deck hitter have the runner slide at anytime there is any chance of a play on the runner at the plate. Once he informs the runner to slide he must stay with the signal even though the play at the plate does not develop. This is to prevent the runner from starting his slide and then attempting to cross the plate trying to stand up at the last second. This could be a dangerous situation for the runner. The on deck hitter must get as close as he can to the plate when there is a runner at third base and less than two outs. This is so he will not have a great distance to run to be in a position to help the runner as he approaches the plate. With a runner at second base, he can assume his regular position in the on deck circle. The on deck hitter must be sure that he does not get so close to the plate that he is in danger of getting struck by a foul ball off

257

the hitter's bat. The on deck hitter should expect that the umpire or catcher will clear the sliding area to the plate of any equipment (bat, helmet, catcher's mask). If not, then the on deck hitter must assume this responsibility. This would not be possible if the runner sliding into the plate was at third base at the time of the pitch.

51. The runner sliding into home plate—If a runner approaching the plate observes that the catcher has the ball securely in his possession and he is in a position to make the easy tag, the runner should attempt to avoid the tag by stopping and getting in a rundown. If he cannot stop early enough, then he would try to run toward the plate on the catcher's glove side hoping the impact with the glove might dislodge the ball from the catcher's glove. If the catcher must come up the third base line to field the throw and make the tag on the runner, he should attempt to avoid the tag without running out of the baseline. The catcher is not allowed to position himself in the baseline without the ball unless he is in the act of fielding the ball. If the catcher is in the baseline without the ball and is not in the act of fielding the ball, the runner should avoid the collision with the catcher in order to prevent an injury. If contact happens to take place in this situation, the runner would be awarded home plate by the umpire. If the tag play is to be made in the area of the plate, the baserunner should attempt to slide to the inside or outside of the plate depending on the position of the catcher at the time of the tag. At no time should the runner slide head first into home plate if the catcher has the plate blocked. This is a very dangerous maneuver on the runner's part. The head first slide can be used by the runner in his attempt to avoid the tag at the plate when the catcher does not have the plate blocked. In this way he can attempt to hit the plate with a hand as he slides to the inside or the outside of the plate to avoid the tag. The hook slide into home plate is also a good type of slide to avoid the tag since it offers the catcher a smaller area of the body to tag. If the catcher has the plate blocked, the runner should feet first slide directly into the glove in hopes that the contact with the glove might dislodge the ball. If the runner happens to slide past the plate without touching the plate with any part of his body, he should attempt to return to the plate as soon as possible.

SLIDING

The ability to slide and the desire to slide are two very important ingredients in forming an aggressive baserunning ball club. When a player has not somewhat mastered the techniques of sliding and/or does not have a positive experience from sliding, his aggressiveness on the base paths will be severely hampered. Consequently, sliding practice becomes as much an important part of the coach's teaching plan as the many other facets of the game.

Sliding is often neglected because it is felt that sliding is something that comes "natural" or is "too dangerous" to teach. While sliding is a natural movement for some, as hitting is for some, for the most part it must be taught; taught so that it will be an asset in reaching the next base, and taught so that painful experiences and injuries will not result from poor techniques.

There are three basic reasons for sliding: (1) to reach a base going full speed without going by it; (2) to avoid a tag at a base; and (3) to break up a double play attempt. In all cases, once a decision has been made that a slide is in order, the runner can never change his mind. This is the area where more injuries occur than in any other area of the techniques of sliding. Once the runner decides to slide he must slide. If the runner has any doubt as to whether or not to slide, he must slide.

The proper sliding technique is an aggressive movement. A baserunner must approach the sliding moment with aggressiveness. In like manner, while being aggressive, he must be relaxed. A rigid, non-rhythmical sliding movement will certainly increase the chances of injuries occurring. Aggressiveness and relaxation are a result of confidence. This confidence is achieved when the runner knows the proper techniques, and has practiced his sliding on numerous occasions.

Sliding must be explained and mentally pictured as nothing more than a gradual lowering or controlled falling of the body. It is not a leap, a jump, or a dive. Rather it is simply a glide on the top portion of the ground.

Finally, injuries often occur in sliding from placing too much weight on one area of the body during the slide. Good sliding techniques will allow the friction to be placed throughout a large area of the body which decreases abrasions and jolting.

1. **Teaching area and dress**—Certainly there are many varied areas and dress to teach sliding. It is a fairly well accepted technique to teach sliding with pants or heavier material, long sleeve shirts, and in stocking feet. The heavier material and long sleeves help avoid abrasions while the stocking feet help avoid the catching of cleats in the ground. The areas used to teach sliding are much more varied. Sliding pits with sawdust or some other loose material have often been used but are not recommended as they tend to cause a leaping or jumping approach. Watered down areas in the grass outfield area as well as blankets on gym floors are areas used also. Perhaps one of the best techniques for learning the feet first approach to sliding is the use of long cardboard. These sheets of cardboard can be obtained from new refrigerator boxes or bed mattress boxes. A loose base toward the end of the cardboard should be used. The advantages here are numerous:

   A. The player can slide easily.

   B. The player does not need to slide full speed when the slide is first being learned.

   C. It is relatively safe from jarring and bruising.

   D. It is fun for the player.

   E. It can be used on any surface, inside or outside.

Perhaps the one hazard it can present is that floor burn type abrasions occur with direct skin contact with the cardboard. It becomes important immediately to the player to follow proper sliding techniques so that this will not happen on a regular basis.

2. **The bent leg slide**—The bent leg or straight in slide is the most popular slide, and most other slides with the exception of the head first slide are adaptations from this basic slide. The bent leg slide is one of two slides (head first being the other), which affords the slider the opportunity of reaching the bag at the earliest possible moment. The following are coaching points in teaching the bent leg slide using the cardboard and the proper dress mentioned previously:

   A. The players sit on the ground with their legs spread, arms to their side, and the weight of the upper body resting on the palms of the hand and buttocks.

259

1. The players should bend one leg under. They will find that one leg is more comfortable than the other in bent position.

2. The leg bent under should resemble a figure four (4) with the lower leg of the bent leg crossing just under the knee of the straight leg. The bent leg should remain parallel to the ground in the slide. If it does not, too much friction will be placed on either the knee or the ankle resulting in possible abrasions.

3. The cleats of the shoe of the foot which is under should be facing out away from the ground to prevent catching the cleats on the sliding surface.

4. The straight leg is extended forward with the knee slightly bent so as not to cause a jamming effect when it meets the bag. The foot should be approximately six to ten inches off the ground to avoid catching the cleats on the ground.

5. The buttocks should remain fully on the ground. Sliding on one side or the other results in the familiar term "strawberries".

6. The upper body is extended back to where both shoulder blades almost touch the ground.

7. The neck is arched with the head down toward the chest so the bag and area in front can be seen easily.

8. The arms are bent at the elbows with the hands up in the air. Placing grass or dirt in the hands will help avoid the normal reaction of trying to break the fall with the use of the hands.

9. As the players are still sitting on the ground after moving through these movements, a mental picture of the "glide" should be made:

    a. A controlled fall with final push-off made by the leg which is bent.

    b. Contact with the ground will be made first on the outside of the lower portion of the leg which is bent.

    c. The player will then hit on both sides of the buttocks.

    d. The player will then hit on the lower back area.

    e. The relaxed extended leg is lowered and the heel of the foot makes contact with the near edge of the base.

B. Upon completion of these "dry runs" while sitting on the ground, the players may now slide on the cardboard. They should start running approximately fifteen yards away and slide at three-quarter's speed until a good feel is established. The coach should place himself on both knees at the side of the cardboard toward the end and hold the loose base. A player on each side of the cardboard might be needed to secure the cardboard from moving. This will depend on the surface under the cardboard.

3. **Pop-up slide off the bent leg slide**—This slide is very similar to the bent leg slide except the runner finishes standing on the base and ready to advance if possible. It is used in various situations, but normally it is used at the following times: (1) when a tag will not be made in time but the runner cannot afford to over run the base; (2) when a possible bad throw is approaching the base and the runner needs to be ready to advance on the play; and (3) when a player wants to get to the bag quickly on a force play attempt. The same fundamentals are used in the pop-up slide as with the bent leg slide with the following exceptions:

A. The runner should start the slide a little closer to the bag (approximately eight feet rather than ten feet).

B. The upper body remains in a sit-up position with the body weight on the bent lower leg and extended back to the buttocks. The center of gravity of the body should remain between the knee and buttocks and not exceed past the waist.

C. The extended leg is slightly bent and raised three to four inches off the ground. The bag is contacted by the instep of the extended leg.

260

D. As contact is made with the bag the leg straightens and the upper body is thrust forward. Providing that the slide is aggressive, this should be enough to carry the body back to the upward position. If a runner has problems achieving this position, he can use his hands to give him a quick thrust upward, although this should rarely be needed.

4. **The hook slide**—The hook slide, or the "93 foot slide" as referred to by many coaches, is used to avoid a tag. The decision to use the hook slide is based usually on the premise that the ball will beat the runner to the sliding area, but it is off target slightly. It is not considered the fastest slide between two points as the tagging of the base is made by the leg further back than the front leg. Hence the reference to the "93 foot slide". The disadvantage of this slide, other than the fact it is the slowest way into a base, is that there is a greater chance for oversliding the base. It is also a dangerous way to slide unless the player has the proper mechanics and technique. The following are coaching points used in teaching the hook slide:

A. **When sliding to the right side:**

   1. The player will push off the left foot prior to starting his slide.

   2. Neither one of the player's legs should be in a "tucked" position. The outside of the right leg (calf and thigh) should make contact with the ground first. The leg should be bent slightly with the bottom of the foot pointed in so as not to catch the cleats.

   3. The left leg should be relatively straight with a slight bend in the knee. The inner part of the lower leg should contact the ground with the bottom of the foot pointed out while the toe is pointed forward in anticipation of contacting the bag with the "shoestring". The player should not bend the left knee any more than necessary to hook the base. The more he bends the knee, the longer it will take for him to make contact with the base.

   4. More of the player's weight should be distributed on the right part of the buttocks. The upper body should almost be in a flat position with the head up and eyes on the bag.

   5. The player should try to keep both his hands and elbows off the ground to prevent any jarring motion.

   6. In the final mental picture of the hook slide, the legs should be in a "scissor" type position with the body weight on the right side.

B. **When sliding to the left side**—For a hook slide to the left side, a player would simply reverse the procedure as described for hook sliding to the right side of the bag.

5. **Breaking up the double play**—This particular slide should also be taught as it is an integral part of the offensive game. This type of slide is one where there is a greater chance of injury due to the fact that contact is generally made with the pivot man at second base. There should never be any intention on the runner's part to hurt the pivot man as he attempts to complete the double play. The runner merely wishes to disrupt the pivot man's attempt to make an unobstructed throw to first base. The basic purpose of the slide is twofold: (1) to cause a disruption in the infielder's pivot and throw to another base; and (2) to discourage the infielder from trying the same movement in the future when a similar situation arises. The slide can be taught on the same cardboard using a blocking dummy rather than a loose base. All procedures used in the bent leg slide should be adhered to with the following exceptions:

A. After contact with the ground, the player should lean slightly to the bent leg side.

B. The player should bend the extended leg so it is now at approximately a 45 degree angle somewhat similar to the bent leg. The bottom of the foot of the extended leg should now be pointed out slightly.

C. With the "shoestrings" or the lower part of the extended foot, he should attempt to disrupt the infielder by driving into his lower legs and moving them out from under him when his weight moves upward.

D. Attention should be made to the opponent's pre-game infield drill to learn the preference the shortstop and second basemen have as to which side of the base they pivot on for their throw to first base.

The slider must be able to make some contact with the base with some part of his body. If not, it is an illegal slide and he will be called out along with the batter-runner. The slider must be on the ground when he makes contact with the pivot man in order to make a legal slide into the base.

6. **The head first slide**—The head first slide is becoming more and more a part of the game of baseball. Although few studies have been made, the theory certainly lends one to believe that if a ballplayer aggressively slides head first, he will get to the base quicker than with the conventional feet first slide. He will get to the base quicker since he does not have to move his center of gravity back as in the leg first approach. Along with being a quicker approach to a base, it also has other distinct advantages: (1) if done properly, it is a safer type of slide; (2) it allows the runner the opportunity to avoid a tag much easier by slipping his fingers around the tag; (3) the runner can see the ball come into the area of the bag easier than he can with the feet first slide, thus allowing him a better opportunity to avoid the tag; and (4) an aggressive head first slide might sway the umpire's call on a close play. The disadvantage of a head first slide is the fact that it is much more difficult to respond to a poor throw since the runner will have to come up to his feet to continue onto the next base or to the plate. The head first slide is not a desirable slide in the following two situations: (1) tag plays at home plate when the catcher is clearly blocking the entire plate since this could cause a severe injury; and (2) when breaking up a double play. Once the runner commits himself to the head first slide, he must continue through by going full speed. When the slide is taught properly and the techniques are mastered, the head first slide will become a positive part of the team's baserunning plan. The following are coaching points in teaching the head first slide. The area used should be a soft grass area in the outfield. If desired, the area can be watered prior to the drill. If you are fortunate enough to have a tarp to spare, water on top of a tarp will be sufficient. Spikes, long shirts, and pants should be worn when practicing the head first slide.

A. Begin by instructing your players as to the proper mental picture of the slide. It is simply a glide on top of the grass. It is not a dive or a leap.

B. The runner should begin lowering his upper body and placing his center of gravity further and further in front of his legs.

C. As his body lowers and the weight moves forward his final thrust forward should be made with only one leg.

D. On his final thrust forward his body must be low to the ground (as though he were running and gliding on top of water).

E. His arms should be stretched forward with only a slight bend in the elbows. The head should remain up so as to see the base and the ball entering the area of the base.

F. His chest, legs, and arms should all be in one plane—parallel to the ground.

G. Contact with the ground should be made simultaneously with the forearms, chest and thighs.

H. Problem areas to watch are: the elbows or hands breaking the fall; the chest caved in; or knees breaking the fall. The body should be kept straight on contact with the ground, but not rigid.

I. The player's hands should somewhat "catch" the base to avoid jamming fingers into the base.

In practicing the technique, dives back to first base on pick-off attempts can be used. Short runs with good, aggressive explosion on the final thrust can also be used. Once the feeling of the slide is accomplished, the faster and more aggressive the slide, the better it will be performed.

BASIC RUNNING FUNDAMENTALS

It certainly stands to reason that the quicker a player can run the better baserunner he should be on the base paths. A coach can assist his players in improving their quickness as a runner by spending practice time with them reviewing proper running fundamentals and technique.

If we observe a number of people running, it becomes clear that the ability to sprint efficiently is not completely natural. Various aspects of good sprinting are somewhat artificial, so they must be learned. Therefore, it requires special attention to eliminate faulty habits and to develop proper body lean, leg, knee, arm, and hip action as early as possible through continuous awareness of correct form and practice with intent to improve.

1. **Warmup for explosive action**—Prior to any type of sprint work, a player must prepare his body muscles for explosive action of the leg muscles. Not only should players be required to jog several laps prior to explosive running, but they should be required to follow the prescribed stretching exercises presented in a previous section of the Playbook.

2. **Body lean**—The first few steps of a sprint, the body should be low with a large body lean. At maximum speed the center of gravity should be in front of the feet (approximately 25 degree angle from heel of foot through the body). If a runner runs straight up in the air, he will detract from his ability to run effectively.

3. **The head**—The runner must relax his teeth and jaws when he is running. The jaws must be so relaxed that they might even flop while running. He must keep his eyes focused straight ahead to insure that he is running in a straight line. The head must be kept in natural alignment with the body. If a runner moves his head from side to side while running, it will detract from his running speed and also disorient him in the way of running in a straight line. The head should not be flopping up and down, but should remain steady throughout the sprint.

4. **The arms and shoulders**—The shoulders must remain square to the direction that the runner is going. The arms should be carried at a 90 degree angle at the elbow, and they should not cross the midline of the body. If the arms cross the midline of the body it will throw the body balance off. If one rides a bike and starts throwing the arms across the midline of the body, one will see vividly the effect that this has on maintaining body balance. The arms must be pumped vigorously moving alternately and parallel to each other while staying close to the body. The hands should come up no higher than the shoulders, and no lower than the hips. The forearms and hands should be relaxed. The fingers should be loose, so that the runner does not establish a tight fist while pumping his arms.

5. **The chest and back**—The back should remain straight as the chest is held out to establish the proper body lean. This position of the back and chest helps the pelvis to be in a proper position for maximum effectiveness.

6. **The legs**—The runner should lift his knees as he runs so that the knees are about parallel to the ground. The lower leg should extend after the peak height is reached by the knee.

7. **The feet**—The feet should hit the ground so most of the weight is on the ball of the feet.

8. **The toes**—The toes should be pointing straight ahead at all times.

9. **The stride**—The stride should be at least as long as the body is in height when the runner is running full speed. The stride should carry the runner low to the ground.

SPRINT FORM DRILLS

Once the coach has spent time with his players going over the basic running fundamentals, he will need to organize some practice time to run some sprint form drills. The players can go through each exercise two or three times with the coaching staff making comments and adjustments. The players will run approximately 20-30 yards each time through. The players need to concentrate on one exercise each time. The coach needs to use the building block effect so that at the conclusion of all the drills, all the parts come together in hopes that the players are running with perfect form. The movements in these drills are exaggerated in hopes that a happy medium will be attained when sprinting.

1. **High knee drill**—The players will run in place lifting their knees high. They will then run about 20-30 yards lifting their knees high as they run. The lifting of the knees should be a powerful, but relaxed movement. The high knee lift helps to lengthen the stride; adds to the force the pushing leg applies against the ground; and permits the lead foot to be moving faster when it hits the ground.

2. **Reach drill**—The players will run so that when their knees reach their peak height the lower leg straightens out and then whips downward. The stride length is increased on each sprint and the foreleg is placed in a position from which it can whip downward and backward. In actual sprinting, no such extreme reach of the foreleg would be used.

3. **Run tall with proper lean**—The players will now run raising high on their toes and leaning from the ankles. They will move out pushing high on their toes with full attention to their foot, ankle, knee and hip joints. The head will be in natural alignment with their chest out. This drill establishes the habit of making a fuller stride that is powerful, long and forward.

4. **Arm action drill**—The players will stand in place bending their arms to a 90 degree angle, and then pump their arms from a standing position. They need to be sure that their angle does not change and that their shoulders are relaxed. They will then run 20-30 yards stressing vigorous but correct arm action.

5. **Relaxation drill**—Relaxation is the key to sprinting. The players will run 20-30 yards stressing faster, but looser action. Relaxation does not require a special skill, but requires concentrated effort.

6. **Perfect form drill**—The players put all the parts together in a smooth working whole - high knees, foreleg reach, arm action, run tall and relaxation.

FIRST BASE COACH GUIDELINES

Before the head coach allows a player or assistant coach to assume the responsibilities of being the first base coach, he needs to spend ample time with him detailing guidelines that he needs to follow in that capacity. The following are guidelines for the first base coach including the principles of baserunning that were detailed in the baserunning section of the Playbook.

1. Hustle to and from the first base coaching box at all times.

2. Never say anything to a member of the other team if their dugout is on the first base side. This is especially true if they were to make comments to you that you feel are not proper. Just look like you do not hear a word they are saying.

3. Never say anything to the umpire in regard to a call that has been made that you might disagree with. This would not be applicable if the first base coach was a member of the coaching staff. If an argument does arise, allow the head coach the opportunity to represent the ball club in the dispute when he arrives on the scene.

4. You must know the arm strength of the left fielder since you will have the responsibility to assist the batter-runner when a ball is hit to the third base side of the shortstop. On any ball hit from the shortstop's position on over to the right field line, the batter-runner will be responsible for his actions.

5. Assume a position in the coaching box as deep as you can so that the batter-runner can easily pick you up as he approaches first base on a ball hit to left field. The closer you can get to the first baseline allows the runner that much better view of you as he approaches first base.

6. When you are going to assist the batter-runner due to the nature of the ball hit, the following visual signs are to be used: (1) when you provide no sign at all, you want the runner to run through the base for there will be a play made by an infielder at first base; (2) when you hold both arms up in the air, you want the runner to round the base aggressively and then find the ball; and (3) when you want the runner to attempt to reach second base on the batted ball, you will wave one or both arms in a circular manner. You will want to provide one of these three signs at about the time the runner enters the restraining area (45 feet down the first baseline from the plate). If the sign is flashed after the runner reaches this mark, it will make for a very difficult turn on the runner's part.

7. Make sure that you are aware of all the situations in our baserunning principles in regard to when we want to gamble advancing to second base and when we want to be somewhat conservative. Know the speed of all the runners on the team along with their ability to make the turn at first base.

8. You are not to assist the runner when there is an overthrow at first base either on the batted ball or when a pick-off attempt gets by the first baseman. This would be an errant pick-off attempt by the pitcher or by the catcher. The runner must react on his own to the ball.

9. You are not to assist the batter-runner in his reacting to a poor throw to first base where the first baseman has to come off the base. This is the batter-runner's responsibility.

10. Once the runner touches first base on his turn you are not to assist him in reacting to the batted ball. This is the batter-runner's responsibility.

11. When the runner arrives at first base, you do not need to review the situation in the ball game with the runner, unless the runner is one that has a difficult time concentrating. He should be aware himself of the number of outs; inning; score; other runners on base; outfielder's arms; etc. Make sure that the runner checks the depths and positions of the outfielder before he moves off the base. He should not have to be reminded to check with the third base coach for a possible sign, but if you observe him not looking at the third base coach he will need to be reminded of that fact.

12. Make sure that you know the signs as well as anyone on the baseball team, so that if the runner at first base is confused by a sign, he can call time out and consult with you in the coaching box.

13. When the runner is assuming his primary lead at first base you will never yell at him to "get back" if you observe the pitcher throwing over to first base on the pick-off attempt. This is the runner's responsibility. The same holds true if the catcher attempts to pick the runner off first base on his secondary lead. The only time you will assist the runner at first base

while in his primary or secondary lead is when the first baseman is playing behind the runner. In this situation, you will face the first baseman so that you can watch him at all times. You do not need to watch the pitcher. Once you see the runner begin his movement toward his secondary lead you will glance in toward the plate so that you are not hit by the batted ball. If you want the runner to take another step toward second base on his primary lead you will say "okay one". If you want the runner to take a step back toward first base on his primary lead you will say "back one". This all depends on the position of the first baseman and his possible movement toward or away from first base. If the first baseman makes a definite break toward first base you will yell "back, back, back".

14. Assist the runner at first base in being sure that the hidden ball trick would not be successful if tried.

15. If you are able to read the lefthanded pitcher's pick-off move to first base, pass along this information to the runner. Be aware of any special type of picks the pitcher has used in past games. This would also include catcher's pick-off attempts. Once this information is passed along to the runner, you will not assist him once he achieves his lead from first base.

16. Look for the first baseman's sign for the pick-off when playing behind the runner. This includes pick-offs from the pitcher and catcher.

17. If the pitcher has consistently thrown the ball in the dirt at the plate, remind the runner that he can break for second base when the catcher goes to his knees. This is especially true with two outs and in a gambling situation. With a runner at third base it should be an automatic reaction by the runner at first base.

18. Might let the baserunner at first base know which side of second base the second baseman and shortstop have pivoted on the double play.

19. Make sure that all runners at first base take the inside lead with their heels lined up with the inside of the base.

20. With a runner at second base, and the batter receives a walk or strikes out and the ball gets by the catcher, you should wave the batter-runner down to second base as long as we are in a gambling situation.

21. On a base hit with the play being made at the plate on another runner, the first base coach can yell at the batter-runner to "make the throw go through". This is so the runner does not get thrown out at second base when the ball is cut-off by the cut-off man.

22. Attempt to read the catcher's signs to the pitcher if he was to display the signs so that they can be seen by you. In like manner, observe the pitcher's particular characteristics as he may tip what pitch he is throwing. If so, you might be able to assist the batter in knowing what type of pitch the pitcher will be delivering.

23. When the third out is made at first base, be sure to get the runner's helmet and run it back to the dugout area.

THIRD BASE COACH GUIDELINES

It is the general feeling of most baseball people that a third base coach can win or lose a few games each year solely based on the judgment factor as to whether or not to send a runner to the plate. This section of the Playbook will not attempt to down play the judgment factor, but will concentrate mainly on guidelines that a third base coach should use in coordinating the offensive attack.

One of the more important considerations must be that an experienced coach should be in the third base coaching box, and one should never alternate coaches from game to game. Consistency is needed on a daily basis between the third base coach and the players so that there is no confusion on the timing involved in the signal system and in the signals used to assist the runners. Whenever possible the coach in the third base coaching box should be the one originating the signals to prevent any communication problem or delay that might occur in flashing signs from the dugout to the third base coach. In crucial late inning situations, the head coach in the dugout can take charge and communicate visually with the third base coach what he wishes to have done in the way of offensive game strategy. It is best in these situations for the head coach to meet with the third base coach prior to the start of the inning and communicate what he wishes to have done if certain situations were to arise. Whenever possible the head coach should be the third base coach in order to eliminate any problems in this area.

Listed are some guidelines for the third base coach to follow using the principles of baserunning that were detailed in the baserunning section of the Playbook:

1. Hustle to and from the third base coaching box at all times.

2. Never say anything to a member of the other team if their dugout is on the third base side. This is especially true if they were to make comments to you that you feel are not proper. Just look like you do not hear a word they are saying.

3. If the third base coach is not the head coach, any arguments with an umpire must be brief until the head coach arrives to represent the ball club. If the third base coach happens to be a player, he should not say anything to an umpire when a disputed call arises.

4. The third base coach must know the arm strength of every player on the defensive team so that he can better assist the runner in making decisions on the base paths. You will be involved in assisting the runner anytime the ball is in an area of the field that does not allow the baserunner the opportunity to clearly view the ball.

5. The position that the third base coach assumes in the coaching box will depend on where the runners are on base. Anytime there is a righthanded pull hitter at the plate, you should position yourself deep in the coaching box so that you will have more time to avoid a line drive hit your way. With a runner at first base, you must flash your signs to the runner at a position in the box so that the runner has a clear view of you. Make sure that the pitcher does not get in a direct line between you and the baserunner at first base. With a runner at first base only, position yourself as deep in the coaching box as possible so that the runner approaching second base can easily see you if he needs your assistance. With a runner at second base, position yourself in the middle to front part of the coaching box so you will have a clear view of the shortstop and second baseman if you are assisting the runner in his primary lead. This position in the coaching box will also enable you to quickly move toward home plate as you assist the runner on his turn at third base.

6. The sign system used by the third base coach was discussed in detail in the signal system of the Playbook so there is no need to review the sign structure in this section.

7. The visual signs used by the third base coach to assist the runner approaching second base and third base were detailed in the baserunning section of the Playbook. The third base coach must know the speed and baserunning ability of each runner on the team.

8. You must be completely aware of the situation in the game so that you can make the decision as to when to gamble with the runner, or when to play conservative with him. The runner will be making all his decisions for himself when the ball is within his peripheral vision as detailed in the baserunning section of the Playbook. Your timing in regard to making these decisions is crucial so that you give the runner enough time to react to your signal. At the same time, you cannot make the decision too quick or else you endanger the status of the runner. Being a good third base coach takes a lot of practice and game experience.

9. Do not assist a runner at second base or third base in their reacting to an errant pick-off throw by either the pitcher or the catcher. This is the baserunner's responsibility.

10. Once the runner has touched third base on the slide or when he is held up at the base by your signal, you are no longer responsible for his actions. He will quickly find the ball and make his own decision on whether or not to advance.

11. When the runner arrives at third base with less than two outs, you will need to review with him what you will want him to do on a ground ball in the infield. This information was presented in the baserunning section of the Playbook. Once you have presented this information to the runner at third base, you will need to let the runner at second base know what you will be doing via a visual sign. If there is a runner at first base, he will not need to know what the runner at third base will be doing on a ground ball. Once the ball is hit, you will not communicate to the runner what you want him to do. This is the runner's responsibility.

12. You may assist a runner at third base if he is not taking a big enough primary lead or secondary lead. At the same time, if his primary or secondary lead is too long, you will need to inform him of this fact.

13. You will not let the runner know if the catcher is going to attempt a pick-off at third base. This is the runner's responsibility.

14. Assist the runners at third base and second base in being sure that the hidden ball trick would not be successful if tried.

15. You can assist the runner at second base on a tag up situation, but hopefully, he can assume this responsibility himself. You can communicate this information when the ball is hit in the air by either the command of: "tag" or "halfway".

16. You can assist the runner at third base on a tag up situation by telling him to either: "score"; "fake the break"; or "halfway". All the criteria listed in the baserunning section of the Playbook must be taken into consideration before you give the runner one of these commands. The runner is responsible to time the tag by watching the fielder who is going to make the play on the fly ball.

17. You will be responsible to assist the runner at second base when the stealing lead is in affect. This information can be found in the baserunning section of the Playbook. With the standard lead, no communication is necessary.

18. You are not to assist the runner in reacting to a passed ball or wild pitch that gets away from the catcher. This is the runner's responsibility.

19. Attempt to read the catcher's signs to the pitcher if he was to display the signs so that they can be seen by you. In like manner, observe the pitcher's particular characteristics as he may tip what pitch he is throwing. If so, you might be able to assist the batter in knowing what type of pitch the pitcher will be delivering.

20. When the third out is made at second base or third base, be sure to get the runner(s) helmet(s) and run them back to the dugout.

HITTING

This section of the Playbook will deal with the various aspects of teaching the art of hitting. A baseball coaching staff has to spend a lot of time in practice sessions with this phase of the game, since hitting is a tough skill to learn. Every baseball coach has his own hitting philosophy and his own way to teach hitting. However, it should not be the intention of a coach to program all his hitters in a standard mold. What works for one hitter might not work for another hitter.

The good hitting coach is one who can analyze a hitter who is having a difficult time making solid contact, and then offer suggestions for correction in a way that the young man can understand and comprehend what adjustments need to be made. If a boy makes consistent solid contact with the ball, it is best to allow him the opportunity to stay with his swing even though his hitting mechanics do not fit the classic stereotype of proper hitting fundamentals. We have all seen examples of a good hitter getting confused by a coach who wants to make some mechanical changes in his swing. The general rule to follow is that when a hitter is having great success, leave him alone. When a hitter is not having good success swinging the bat, see if you can assist him to get the maximum out of his potential as a hitter. If a coach feels as though a good hitter might become a better hitter with one or two adjustments in his swing, you can have him experiment with these slight adjustments in a practice session. The key is to communicate with the boy so that these minor adjustments can be incorporated into his hitting fundamentals without any major difficulty on the boy's part.

This hitting section will deal first with the basic hitting fundamentals that will apply to almost all hitters. The Playbook will then discuss in detail common hitting faults and their corrections, followed by isolated hitting drills that the coach might use to help the hitters master the basic fundamentals. Since bat discipline is an important facet of hitting, time will be spent going over the basic thought patterns that a hitter must have in his mind while at the plate. Finally, we will discuss the means and methods that can be used by a coaching staff to enable the hitters to help evaluate themselves as hitters.

A player must have certain athletic skills before he can become a good hitter, since hitting is a very tough skill to master. A capable hitting coach can assist a young man in getting the maximum out of his potential as a hitter. It is hoped that this hitting section will help a coach to understand what fundamentals and training methods can be used to reach this objective.

BASIC HITTING FUNDAMENTALS

1. BAT SELECTION

It is important that each player find a bat that he can control throughout the entire swing. The coaching staff can assist the hitters in selecting the bat that best fits their swing ability. Generally, if a player has small hands it is best to have him use a bat with a small handle. The player with large hands can easily use a bat with a thicker handle. It is better to have a bat too light than one that is too heavy. A heavy bat must be started early on the swing which would not allow the hitter the luxury of being able to wait on the pitch. A hitter who continually check swings across the plate is probably using too heavy of a bat. The bat must feel comfortable to the hitter, and at the same time, provide him with the sensation that he possesses a high degree of bat quickness. It is not wise to allow a hitter to change bat sizes on a continuous basis during the season. The only exception might be if the boy is fatigued toward the end of the season and wishes to drop down a notch in his bat weight.

2. GRIP ON THE BAT

The shorter the lever, the more control a hitter will have of the bat, but less power. The longer the lever, the more power a hitter will have with his bat, but less control. The coaching staff can assist each hitter in determining how far his hands should be up the bat, if any. The strength of the hitter and his ability to generate bat speed through the strike zone are determining factors in this decision. The length and weight of the bat will also be factors that need to be taken into consideration by the coach and the player. Of course, with two strikes on the hitter, he must sacrifice a little power for more control of the bat. He must keep his hands loose on the bat in order to allow the hands to be quick to the ball when the swing is initiated. The hands will tighten with impact on the ball. A hitter who squeezes the bat as he prepares to read the pitch, will have a very difficult time initiating proper bat speed. Good wrist action into the pitch is assisted when a boy has a good firm grip on the bat that is not hindered by his squeezing the handle. The bat should be placed in the hands at approximately the base of the fingers. It cannot be jammed back in the palm of the hand as this will restrict good hand action. The hitter who has the bat back well in his hands will have a tendency to sweep the bat which retards bat speed.

3. KNUCKLE ALIGNMENT

It is the general consensus of hitting instructors that with the middle knuckles of the hands somewhat aligned, it is the easiest alignment in which to achieve the best swing. Many hitters find they have better control of their swing when they align the middle knuckle of the top hand somewhere between the middle and last knuckle of the bottom hand. Knuckle alignment depends to a great degree on the type of hitter a coach is working with. A hitter who has good wrists will want to align the middle knuckles of both hands as he grips the bat. It is never wise to allow a boy to have his middle knuckles of his top hand aligned with the first knuckles of his bottom hand for this will hinder him in generating any type of bat speed.

4. POSITION IN THE BATTERS' BOX

Proper plate coverage is an important item to consider. It is important that the hitter have good coverage of his strong areas of the strike zone. The further back he is in the batters' box, the more time he will have to read the pitch. The breaking pitch has a tendency to be harder to hit when the hitter is deep in the box as it can catch the corner of the plate and move out of the strike zone prior to contact with the ball. Obviously moving up in the box will help eliminate this problem but it will mean that you will have less time to read the pitch and then swing the bat. Many hitters feel that moving up in the box is advantageous when facing a control, breaking ball pitcher who does not throw hard. When facing a power pitcher, many hitters will move to the back of the box. Thus, the depth in the batters' box depends entirely on the nature of the hitter and the type of pitcher throwing. A player with tremendous bat speed can move up in the box since he will not take as long to initiate the swing. In this position he will be able to make contact with the breaking pitch before it has had a chance to "tie" him up either on the inside of the plate or on the outside of the plate. The hitter who does not possess great bat quickness might achieve more success by positioning himself further back in the box, especially when facing a power pitcher. The hitter who crowds the plate will find that he will have a very difficult time getting the barrel of the bat to the ball, unless he possesses good strength and bat quickness. It will also cause the hitter to have the sensation that he will have to open up his body early which will make him very susceptible to breaking pitches and off speed pitches over the outer half of the plate. At the same time, the batter who stands well away from the plate will have a high degree of difficulty handling the ball over the outer half of the plate. If he compensates for this fact by stepping into the pitch, he will find that he can be easily jammed by a power pitcher who throws the ball in the inner half of the strike zone. The best stance for the young hitter is one that provides maximum plate coverage so that he cannot be pitched to on the inner or outer half of the plate. If the hitter likes to go the other way with the pitch, he will need to back off the plate a little more than normal. If he considers himself a pull hitter, then he will move closer to the plate slightly. Again, the position in the batters' box is the individual hitter's personal preference which can be adjusted slightly depending on the type of pitcher throwing.

5. FEET

The feet should be set a little past shoulder width in length. The weight should be on the balls of the feet. The rear foot can be pointed in (toward the plate) slightly to aid in the quickness of the pivot as the swing begins. The front foot should be slightly opened toward the pitcher to enable the front hip to achieve flexibility through the swing. If the front foot is pointed in toward the plate, it makes it very difficult for the hitter's body to open up on the good inside half of the plate fast ball. If a hitter has a narrow stance he might have a tendency to over stride, while a wide stance has a tendency to produce a shorter stride. Since a short stride is necessary to achieve consistent bat contact, the wider stance is preferred to most hitters. The wide stance provides the hitter the feeling of stability as he awaits the pitch.

6. KNEES

Most hitters prefer to have their knees slightly bent in the stance. This helps relax the entire body as he awaits the pitch. If the hitter prefers to crouch in his stance, he will find that he will have a little tougher time seeing the ball out of the hand of the pitcher. If the hitter assumes a straight up stance with no bend at the knees, he will find that he will eventually have to bend the knees as he strides into the pitch. This is why it is best for most hitters to achieve this slight bend in the knees while they await the pitch.

7. WAIST

The same holds true for the waist as it does for the knees in the basic stance. A slight bend at the waist helps to avoid a too straight or rigid body position. The more the hitter bends at the waist over the plate, the tougher it is for him to see the ball and the more chance that the inside pitch will cause him severe problems. The hitter with the straight up stance will have a difficult time generating momentum into the pitch.

8. SHOULDERS

The shoulders should be level in the basic stance, or the front shoulder might be a little lower than the back shoulder. The back shoulder should not be lower than the front shoulder for it would cause a tendency to dip the back shoulder even more during the actual swing. Dipping the back shoulder during the swing will cause the hitter to uppercut the ball and increase the length of the swing itself. The chin should be at a higher plane than the front shoulder.

9. HEAD AND EYES

The head should be held at a straight up position for this provides the hitter with the best view of the pitched ball. A tilted head decreases the batter's optimum vision. The hitter should have his head turned toward the pitcher so that he can see the pitcher with both eyes. Many times hitters with closed stances or extreme inward rotation prior to the stride, will pick up the ball with only one eye.

10. ARMS, ELBOWS AND HANDS

There are numerous variations of hitting styles in regard to the bat position during the stance itself. The arms, elbows and hands must be positioned to hold the bat at the optimum position for the individual hitter so that his swing is not handicapped by improper mechanics. The hitting style of the individual hitter will affect the position of his arms, elbows and hands. However, there are some general basic mechanics for practically all hitters to follow in order to increase bat speed and contact:

A. The bat should be held at a position somewhere between the horizontal and vertical plane. The stronger the hitter the more vertical he might want to position his bat in the stance. The weaker the hitter physically, the more he should position his bat on the horizontal plane. A hitter who holds the bat straight up could find that it leads to two undesirable actions:

1. The bat will need to be moved to the horizontal position in order to make solid contact with the ball. Thus, it is time consuming when a hitter takes the bat from the vertical plane to the horizontal plane. He will have to start his bat a little earlier, which will not allow him to wait on the pitch. The longer the hitter can wait to read pitch and location, the better hitter he will be.

2. If the bat does not move down toward the horizontal position during the swing, the hitter will consequently have a "golf-like" bat arc. This will cause not only an improper approach to the ball, but it will almost eliminate any possibility of his being able to hit the pitch above the waist and in.

B. The hitter cannot afford to wrap his bat behind his head during the stance or when he inward rotates to position his hands for the actual swing. A "bat-wrapper" will find that he has a longer approach to the ball due to the fact that the barrel of the bat has a longer distance to travel. This is especially true for the hitter who does not possess great bat quickness. The physically strong hitter might get away with a little bat wrap which will enable him to build up bat speed as he makes contact with the pitch.

C. The hands should hold the bat directly out from the back arm pit. For most hitters, the bat should be held comfortably away from the body, but not more than six to eight inches. The further the hands get away from the body it lessens the hitter's leverage, force and balance advantage when the bat starts forward on the actual swing. If the hands are held real close to the body, it makes it very difficult for the hitter to generate any bat speed. This type of hitter can be easily jammed since he has a very difficult time getting the barrel of the bat through the contact area with the ball.

D. The hands should be held at the maximum heighth of the strike zone. This will allow the hitter to move in only one direction with his hands, and that is in the downward plane to the ball. If the hitter holds his bat at another level it would necessitate his moving his hands either high or low depending on the location of the pitch on the vertical plane.

E. The elbows should be comfortably held away from the body. They should remain in somewhat the same plane although the back elbow can be a little higher than the front elbow. A low back elbow usually results in initiating a dip type of approach to the ball. The front elbow should be bent and close to a 90 degree angle. The front elbow in the stance should not cross the midline of the body. If so, the hitter will not be able to generate explosive hand action to the ball since he will have a tendency to sweep at the ball with his hands.

11. INWARD ROTATION

Just prior to the release of the ball, the hitter should dip his front knee in slightly and let his body rotate as a unit back. This aids in "cocking the gun" and getting proper rhythmical motion initiated for a good, smooth, fluid swing. The hitter's hands must go back before they come forward. The inward rotation must be completed just prior to the stride.

12. STRIDE

The stride should be made directly toward the pitcher just after he releases the ball. It should be a soft glide onto the big toe completed without allowing the foot to leave the ground more than two inches. The stride length itself depends to a great deal on the nature of the hitter, but there should be no reason for it to be longer than eight to twelve inches. His hands, body weight and head should all remain back during the stride.

13. HIPS

The hips will initiate the swing. The back hip should be rotated forward when beginning the swing. The hips should be opened to a degree that the belly button will be facing toward the area that the ball will be hit. The hips should not start open until the batter has read the nature of the pitch in regard to the type of pitch and its location in the strike zone.

14. FRONT SHOULDER

The front shoulder should be the guide to the ball. It should always point to the ball until the swing actually occurs. This will mean that the front shoulder must remain pointed down and in slightly. If the front shoulder opens up too soon, the batter will lose valuable bat speed along with an inability to hit the pitch on the outer part of the plate.

15. HEAD AND EYES DURING SWING

A hitter's chin should be near his front shoulder prior to the swing. The chin should actually start somewhat over the front shoulder and finish somewhat over the back shoulder when the swing is completed. It is important that the hitter get a feeling that his head remains somewhat over the ball during the swing. The hitter should train his eyes to pick up the ball as soon as possible and not be distracted by particular movements from the pitcher. Holding the mouth opened just prior to and during the pitch and swing will decrease the chances of an involuntary blink occurring.

272

16. WEIGHT DISTRIBUTION

The hitter must keep his body weight on the balls of the feet. Approximately 60% of the body weight should be over the back foot. Upon the initial stride, a slight shift back of the weight should be made so that when the front foot completes the stride, approximately 70% of the body weight is over the inside of the rear foot. This weight will transfer as the bat comes forward through the ball. The hitter must be sure that he does not have a major bend at the knee on the stride leg which would cause his weight to come forward prior to the actual swing itself.

17. REAR FOOT

Power and stability come from hitting off the rear foot. As the hips begin to rotate, the rear foot heel must come up in order to aid the rotation of the foot. The pivot must be made in order for the hips to come open. The knee of the rear foot must bend slightly in order to help in this rotation.

18. BAT ARC

The barrel of the bat must be taken directly to the path of the ball. While approaching the ball, the hands should remain higher than the ball and the barrel of the bat should remain higher than the hands. While to some people this bat arc resembles a "chopping motion", it actually is simply taking a direct path to the flight of the ball. Upon contact and extension of the arms, the bat should be going through the ball at a level plane. Driving through the ball is the terminology that best describes this action. The arms should be extended on contact with all pitches. However prior to contact, the arms should not extend as this produces a sweeping motion. The hand action is important. The top hand should have the palm facing the ball upon contact (that is if the hand was opened). There is very little power and resistance to the contact with the ball if the top hand's palm is facing straight up or has rolled over the bat too early, and is facing straight down upon contact.

We have just described some of the basic hitting fundamentals that the coach needs to be aware of when he is teaching a young man how to hit the ball. The next section will explain in detail some of the more common hitting faults and what a coach and hitter can do in order to correct these faults.

HITTING: COMMON FAULTS AND CORRECTIONS

Prior to any comments concerning hitting faults and their corrections, a sound and basic philosophy must be determined as to what a coach wants his hitters to attempt to achieve at the plate. Along with this, a sound and basic philosophy must be established on how he will go about teaching them these methods.

While one hitting coach would like to have a power hitting ballclub, another may desire a punching-singles hitting attack. In like manner, one coach may prefer the "inside-out" approach to the ball when swinging; another may desire the "outside-in" approach of the hands to the ball. Consequently, what may be a hitting fault for one coach may not be for another coach.

Since there are numerous philosophies of hitting, it is important that we spend some time discussing a basic philosophy for hitting. This is with the knowledge that every hitter is different and what will work for one hitter might not work for another hitter. The coach must be able to adjust to the physical capabilities of each individual hitter on his team. The hitting coach who forces a rigid, narrow hitting philosophy on every member of the team will hinder the development of some hitters, while assisting others.

Basic Philosophy

We are basically attempting to achieve a swing which will be quick enough to allow us an adequate amount of time to "read" the pitch. The old adage that "the longer you can wait, the better hitter you will be" certainly holds importance to hitting the baseball.

The fact that line drives and ground balls produce more men on base is another basis for our particular philosophy. Studies have shown that three out of ten ground balls hit will fall in for base hits, and that the runners on base average will be approximately 40%. Out of ten line drives hit, almost eight of them will fall in for a base hit and will produce an on base average of over 80%. Fly balls will fall in for base hits only two out of ten times and will produce an on base average of a little over 20%. These statistics were drawn from some Division I NCAA universities and included all opponents as well as the home team being researched. It has been further supported by other studies. Thus, with these facts in mind, we can further project a hitting philosophy to include a strong desire to hit line drives and ground balls. This is certainly not to say that a coach should totally discourage a hitter from "power hitting" if his strengths lie in that area. Even for the power hitter though, importance needs to be stressed that his approach to the ball be relatively compact with a straight arc to the ball.

A hitting philosophy that would be based on the premise that inside pitches should be pulled and outside pitches should be driven to the opposite field is a sound one. In conjunction with this philosophy, the hitter's initial movement of the bat toward the ball should have the barrel of the bat higher than the hands. This is an attempt to bring the hitting area of the bat straight to the anticipated contact area with the ball. Upon contact, the arms should be extended and the bat should be traveling in a relatively level plane just prior to its follow through across the shoulder blades. This hitting approach is often referred to as "chopping" the ball or "swinging down" on the ball. Actually it is simply taking the straightest path between the two points and upon contact, the bat should be relatively level with the ground. By taking this approach, the hitter is allowed the opportunity to wait longer to read the pitch and is more apt to hit line drives and ground balls.

Basic Coaching/Teaching Approach

A simile can be drawn to a hitter and his handwriting, each having its own personality but following basic fundamentals in order to achieve its purpose. If the handwriting does not adhere to the basic structure of the letters in the alphabet, it becomes useless. In like manner, if the hitting skill does not adhere to the basic fundamentals of body mechanics, it becomes useless. The point to be made here is that each hitter is an individual with his very own strengths, weaknesses and uniqueness. He must be allowed to exhibit and improve upon these characteristics which he possesses. Placing every hitter in the same stance or with the exact same swing certainly would be an injustice to the hitter and to the team. Certain fundamentals, guidelines, and/or boundaries are needed, but it is equally as important to allow fluctuations within the basic philosophy of hitting if the coach is going to achieve the maximum from each of his hitters. There is an old poem that has been passed along that illustrates this point. The author is unknown, but the point is clear.

"There once was a .400 hitter named Krantz
Who had a most unusual stance.
But with the coach's correction
His form is now perfection,
But he can't hit the seat of his pants."

274

Mental Pictures

In working with any type of teaching, something must be mentioned concerning "mental pictures". It has been said that what the mind can perceive, the body can achieve. If a hitter's mind can "tune in" or "picture" what the body is supposed to accomplish, the skill is close to being accomplished. Three areas worth mentioning in teaching mental pictures would be the approach of: (1) visual/mental; (2) verbal/mental; and (3) physical/mental.

1. **Visual/Mental Approach**—The visual/mental approach can best be illustrated by simply watching two brothers or a father and son move about in some type of activity. It becomes apparent in a short amount of time that their physical movements or mannerisms are very similar. Perhaps their body make-ups or structures are similar, but the mannerisms are similar on the most part because the youngest has seen the older so many times that his mind has taught his body those movements. The mind has seen a physical movement, pictured it, and transferred it to the body. Thus, in this visual/mental approach to receiving "mental pictures", a coach may want to demonstrate or show films or pictures of the techniques he wishes to teach. Constantly seeing correct techniques can have a very positive result in learning a skill.

2. **Verbal/Mental Approach**—The verbal/mental approach to teaching mental pictures is very important also. This is the area perhaps used the most by coaches. Unfortunately, it is also the area which produces the poorest coaching techniques. A coach can verbally "feed" a mental picture to a hitter. To be successful at this approach, a coach needs to have a repertoire of different verbal statements which produce the same action. In other words, what statements produce a proper mental picture for one hitter may do nothing for the next. An illustration of the above comment would be as follows: a hitter may not be able to picture the comment, "keep your back shoulder up in your approach to the ball," but he may tune in to "aim your front shoulder at the ball." Or, one coach may say, "hit the ball hard," while another may say, "drive through the ball." Again, the point here is that if your hitter is listening, there is a verbal comment you can make which will help him receive a good mental picture. It may take the coach numerous different phrases or verbal mental pictures to say the same things, but it can be achieved.

In connection with the verbal/mental approach, a caution should be made. Teaching with negative verbal statements to help positive mental pictures will, in most cases, result in negative mental pictures. The statement, "don't drop your back shoulder" will leave in the mind a picture of a hitter dropping his back shoulder. It does not leave a mental picture of what is desired. In teaching mental pictures verbally, be specific and positive.

3. **Physical/Mental Approach**—The other area of the teaching approach to help receive mental pictures is the physical/mental approach. This can be accomplished by the hitter himself. In this particular approach, a hitter may gain the desired mental picture by simply concentrating on that area until he "feels" the picture. A coach can help the hitter achieve this by devising isolated hitting drills which give the hitter an opportunity to work on the one particular area of his swing. It may be simply swings in front of a mirror, swings off a tee, throwing the bat into a fence, hitting a tire, or chopping down a tree. Whatever the drill, it can be an asset in helping the hitter "feel" the proper mental picture.

Building Confidence

Little needs to be said concerning the importance confidence has in not only hitting but in all walks of life. Building confidence in a hitter while finding faults and working on corrections can be an awesome task. There are avenues which can be utilized that can help correct mistakes and also build confidence.

Certainly the first place confidence is going to be built is within the player's own self-image of himself. A coach can play a key role in this area. Helping the hitter to see himself as a totally good person is a beginning. This does not mean simply as a hitter or ballplayer, but as a person. If he has a good self-image of himself, if he likes himself, he is more likely to achieve confidence in specific areas. In breaking this self-image down to baseball, the coach might consider using the technique of "one to one". This simply means for every one area I find fault, I am going to also mention one area where I find achievement. All too often coaches spend the entire practice finding faults and working on correcting them. This certainly is an important part of coaching, but building confidence in a player is equally important. It may be a good technique to precede each "fault finding" statement with a positive statement concerning the hitter's skill. This obviously could not always be done, but should be considered more often.

Practice sessions are the best area to build confidence. Coaches need to be sure their practice sessions are designed to provide every player a reasonable opportunity for success. If this means shadow swinging with positive reinforcement from the coach, then it must be done. Hitting the balls off tees can provide this opportunity.

Practice sessions should utilize drill areas for isolating particular parts of the swing. It is extremely difficult to concentrate on parts of your swing when a wild young pitcher is throwing batting practice. If faults are going to be corrected, the practice area must be constructed to afford the hitter a good chance to concentrate on that correction.

And finally, if hitting is going to be improved, the hitter must realize it will take time. The difference between a .200 hitter and a .300 hitter is simply one more hit in ten trips to the plate. Noticeable differences do not always appear immediately. Perhaps a good approach to practice would be, "in some small way I can improve on yesterday, today." Trying to become a great hitter **today** will leave the hitter discouraged and disillusioned. Letting each day and each practice influence the following day and following practice in a positive fashion will help achieve team and individual goals. By improving on one part of the swing at a time, the entire swing will eventually come together. The hitter and the coach must be patient.

Common Faults and Corrections

There are an endless amount of faults or improper hitting mechanics concerned with the total hitting picture. The major and more common faults will be presented as well as some of the correctional techniques used to correct these faults. It is important again to emphasize that what is one person's fault may not be for another, and what is a correction for one may not help the other. Numerous basic correctional techniques will be presented for each fault. Certainly all the correctional techniques need not be presented to the hitter. Hopefully, there will be one correctional technique in the group that may help your hitter.

1. MENTAL

A. Fear of being hit by the ball

A hitter, in most cases subconsciously, lets the weight get on his heels or finds himself stepping "in the bucket" away from the pitch. Curve balls back him off the plate with ease.

Correction: Let the hitter know this is a normal fear, and all intelligent hitters should have this concern. However, that fear cannot dominate his approach to hitting. The fear must be surfaced and realized. The hitter must realize that he will not have sucess if fear is involved with his hitting. The question he needs to deal with is simply this: "Would I rather strike out or get hit by the ball?" If he would rather get hit, progress can be made. All physical corrections to this fault are useless unless he makes the mental commitment. Once this is made, corrections such as the following can be presented:

1. Stride toward the pitch.

2. Keep the weight off your heels and on the balls of your feet.

3. Build confidence by playing soft toss, short toss, hitting off the tee, or playing pepper.

4. Lengthen the pepper games gradually until he is hitting a pitch relatively close to the normal pitching distance.

5. Teach the hitters how to roll with the inside pitch by turning their shoulders in and letting the ball glance off the body. Tennis balls can be used for this drill.

6. Have the hitter stand in hitting box while pitchers throw to catchers in the bullpen.

B. Fear of failure

The hitter constantly comes to the plate with a fear that he will not succeed. In most cases if the fear persists, he will be correct.

Correction: Build as much confidence in this type of hitter as you can. Do not put undue pressure on him. He needs to relax and enjoy playing the game. He must be led to realize that his desire for success must override and diminish his fear of failure. Negative attitudes do not produce positive results. Positive pictures must be implanted in his mind.

C. Non-Aggressiveness

The hitter simply does not "get after it" when it is his turn to hit. He is too cautious and lets pitches go that he should be hitting.

Correction: Many areas of thought can contribute to this type of hitter. He must be taught to realize that aggressiveness can overcome many faults a hitter might have. Good hitters are not shy or timid at the plate. They simply "dare to be great". To get the hitter out of this fault:

1. Make him swing more—give him the hit and run sign.

2. Be less concerned with areas of the strike zone that are "his pitch" areas.

3. Challenge the pitcher. Realize it is a "one on one" battle and the pitcher is trying to embarrass you.

4. More than anything else, anticipate the next pitch will be a strike and then adjust. Thinking "maybe strike, maybe ball" produces non-aggressive hitters.

D. Lack of poise

The hitter becomes irritated at his early performance at the plate and presses himself to the point where he either loses confidence in himself or begins swinging harder and harder and forgets proper hitting mechanics.

Correction: Realize that three out of ten balls hit fall for base hits for the **good** hitter. Keep swinging properly, they will fall. Realize also that each moment of your life and, in particular, each time at the plate, influences the next moment and the next time at the plate. Positive pictures, adjustments, and approaches must be made prior to the next time to the plate.

2. PHYSICAL

A. Feet

1. **Stepping in the bucket**—The hitter strides away from the pitch. This results in weight getting on the heels; hips and shoulders opening too quickly; and the using of the body to help "drive" the ball becomes impossible.

Correction:

a. Place a bat directly behind the heels of the hitter so it is pointed at the pitcher. Instruct the hitter not to touch the bat in his stride.

b. Close the stance. In like manner, keep the shoulders, hips, and even the front foot rotated in slightly.

c. Keep the weight on the balls of the feet.

d. Practice hitting the outside pitch to the opposite field.

e. Practice striding in the bullpen when the pitcher is throwing to the catcher.

f. Put more weight on the front foot so that there will be less weight transfer during the stride. Consequently, a smaller stride will mean a shorter distance that the foot can go in the bucket.

2. **Stepping toward the plate**—Too much weight toward the toes of the feet. Hitter actually hits across his body and often gets jammed by inside pitches. The hips are unable to rotate and initiate the swing because they become locked or restricted in movement.

Correction:

    a. Open stance including hips, shoulders and front foot.

    b. Move closer to the plate with the back foot.

    c. Keep weight off the toes.

    3. **Overstriding**—The hitter strides too long causing weight to be shifted on the front foot and causing body imbalance. The hitter is left to hit with nothing but his arms and hands.

Correction:

    a. Lengthen the hitter's stance.

    b. Shorten the stride—place an object in front of the hitter's front foot and instruct him not to step on it.

    c. Practice with no stride in soft toss hitting area.

    d. Tie a rope from ankle to ankle with the rope's length being the maximum distance you want to stride.

    e. Practice striding soft on the front foot.

    f. Let front foot "glide" and land on the inside of the foot toward the big toe.

    g. Hit from the back side, not the front side. Concentrate on a "quiet front side and a loud back side". Thus, the rear hip and pivot will be stronger.

    h. Pivot around the hips not the front foot. Hit off the back leg more.

    i. Keep the head close to the same area it began at in the stance.

    j. Inward rotation of the front knee, hip, and shoulder can also help keep the weight back on the back leg.

    k. Place more weight on the front foot in the stance.

    4. **Locking feet**—Feet remain stationary and do not pivot body causing poor hip action and rhythm.

Correction:

    a. Place bat behind small of back and through the insides of the arms at the bend of the elbows. Practice rotating hips with the weight on the ball of the back foot and the heel of the front foot. Pivot back foot so hips do not lock and then "roll over" the front foot.

    b. Stride with open front foot.

    c. Open stance slightly.

    d. Start with back foot turned in slightly and heel off the ground.

B. **Legs**

    1. **Leg dipper**—Hitter bends legs too much during the swing. Swing is initiated by legs dipping down (particularly the back leg) to plane of the ball. This results in a longer bat arc and in most cases, an upper cut approach to the ball.

Correction:

    a. Stand tall on the back side.

b. Bat arc needs to be straight toward the ball by starting from a hands up position.

c. Keep front shoulder down.

d. Keep waist and hip rotation on a level plane.

2. **Leg jumper**—Hitter literally jumps at the ball causing poor body mechanics and an off balance swing. It is a combination of overstriding and lunging with the body.

Correction:

a. Quiet the body and let the hands hit. Focus attention on the hands and not the body.

b. No stride drills in practice (soft toss, short toss).

c. Inward rotation of front half of body.

d. Place more weight on the front foot in the stance.

e. Lengthen stance.

3. **Stiff front leg**—Hitter strides onto a stiff front leg prior to swing. Often results in lunging and hitter pulling off the pitch and not hitting through the ball.

Correction:

a. Stride soft onto big toe.

b. Concentrate on short stride with non-stiff leg.

c. Transfer weight "through the ball" rather than leaving it all on the back leg.

C. **Body**

1. **Lunger**—The hitter lets the upper half of his body drive forward ahead of the lower half. Consequently he can not rotate hips properly and there is body imbalance. Hitter becomes more of an arm swinger.

Correction:

a. Concentrate hitting from the back side.

b. Stand tall and keep the head still during the stride and swing.

c. Concentrate on pivoting off back foot.

d. Don't reach for the ball, let it come to you.

e. Inward rotation to help keep upper body back.

f. Widen stance.

2. **Body sitter**—Hitter lets hips "step in the bucket". The rear end drops and the buttocks sticks out. Causes poor hip rotation and weight gets on the heels.

Correction:

a. Stand tall during the stance and swing.

b. Keep weight on the balls of the feet.

c. Drive hips from back side.

d. Move slightly away from the plate which will force you to move into the pitch.

D. Hips

1. **Stiff hips**—Hitter swings the bat with all arms and no body as hips remain stationary.

Correction:

a. Practice with the bat behind the back between the inside of the elbows. Rotate hips thrusting the back hip forward.

b. Belly button and back leg knee should rotate and point toward the area the ball is hit.

c. Loosen the body so a rhythm can be employed. Relax hands on bat.

d. Inward rotation prior to stride so the hips will be cocked and ready to explode and initiate the upper body swing.

e. Be sure weight is on the ball of back foot so pivot can be accomplished.

2. **Imbalanced plane of hips**—Hitter's hips or waist do not rotate on a level plane. The back side of the hitter collapses and causes a long bat arc, a dip, and upper cut.

Correction:

a. Practice hip swing as mentioned in previous "stiff hip" correction.

b. Remain "tall" on back side.

c. Keep front shoulder down in the approach to the ball.

d. Bring barrel straight to ball.

3. **Back side drag**—Hitter attempts to hit by thrusting his front side forward and jerking it open. Causes poor body balance and improper body movement toward ball. Back side is not given a chance to explode and drags through the swing.

Correction:

a. Quiet front side of the body.

b. Lengthen stance.

c. Concentrate on hitting from back side. Back hip should drive forward and begin the rotation of the swing.

d. Keep weight back longer.

E. Shoulders

1. **Dipper**—Hitter's back shoulder drops down in its initial approach to the ball. Causes a longer bat arc and upper cut.

280

Correction:

a. Begin in a stance with the shoulders level or with the front shoulder down slightly.

b. Back elbow should be higher than front elbow.

c. In initial approach to the ball, keep the barrel above the hands, and hands above ball.

d. Aim front shoulder at the ball.

e. Keep back elbow away from the side.

f. Stand "tall" on the back side.

g. Keep chin higher than front shoulder.

h. Practice hitting while on one knee in side toss drill.

2. **Flying shoulder**—Hitter's front shoulder pulls out too early causing dragging or sweeping of the bat and forcing head to come out which results in poor eye contact. Hitter pulls off pitch and actually runs out of bat.

Correction:

a. Aim front shoulder at ball.

b. Inward rotation which cocks front shoulder in.

c. Drive toward ball with front shoulder.

d. Keep chin over shoulder as long as possible.

e. Concentrate on hitting from back side.

f. Work on hitting to opposite field.

F. Arms

1. **Straight front arm**—Hitter lets front arm get straight prior to and during his swing. Causes a sweeping of the bat and a long arc.

Correction:

a. In stance, be sure front arm is not straight.

b. Inward rotation prior to stride by simply moving hips and shoulders in and not moving arms back.

c. Keep front shoulder in longer.

d. Concentrate on hitting with hands with particular emphasis on top hand speed.

e. Short stroke the ball with arm extension only at contact.

f. Move hands in closer to body.

2. **Hitch**—Hitter drops his hands as pitch is delivered and then rushes them back up. Causes a delay in the swing (resulting in late swings) and rushes rhythm.

Correction:

    a. Start hands lower in stance and then bring them up as pitch is delivered.

    b. Keep front shoulder level or down.

    c. Raise back elbow in stance.

    d. Lay bat on shoulders in stance.

G. Hands

    1. **Poor bat control**—Hitter is unable to control the path of his bat. His body is thrown off balance and consequently his timing is poor.

Correction:

    a. Use a lighter bat.

    b. Short bat arc. Go straight to the ball with the hands.

    c. Stay compact with the swing. Don't overswing.

    d. Choke up on the bat for better bat control.

    e. Strengthen arms and hands through various strengthening programs.

    2. **Poor bat speed**—Hitter is unable to generate good bat speed in his swing causing poor drive into the ball and late, weak swings.

Correction:

    a. Swing with emphasis on quickness of muscles and not "muscling up" on swing.

    b. Be sure knuckles are aligned correctly—middle knuckles in relatively straight path to each other.

    c. Be sure bat is being held out toward the fingers and not jammed into the hands.

    d. Relax entire body. Let hips rotate and hands work.

    e. Strive for short bat arc.

    f. Shorten stride.

    g. Practice throwing bat into screen—exploding with the hands.

    h. Practice hitting the tip end of a stick held by a teammate. The teammate may move the stick when the bat starts to move.

    i. Strengthen hands and arms.

    j. Be sure extra movement of the bat is eliminated while pitch is coming.

    3. **Bat Wrapper**—Hitter allows the barrel of the bat to wrap around his head prior to the swing which causes a longer path for the barrel to travel to make contact with the ball.

282

Correction:

    a. Lay the bat on the shoulder and start from that position toward the ball.

    b. Simply have the bat pointed out over back side shoulder.

    c. When inward rotation occurs, be sure it simply consists of body rotation (front knee, hip, and shoulder tilting inward). Do not let hands or arms move outside the body turn. Often the hands "cock" the bat behind the head.

    4. **Riding top hand**—Hitter is constantly making contact with the ball with his top hand's palm facing directly up in the sky. Causes many pop-ups and poor bat speed.

Correction:

    a. Concentrate on throwing the barrel through the ball.

    b. Drive the top hand through the ball with palm of hand (if open) facing pitcher.

    c. Be sure middle knuckles are aligned.

    d. Practice hitting side or soft toss with top hand only using a shortened wooden bat. Hitter can be on knee.

H. Head

    1. **Head tilter**—Hitter allows head to tilt from the horizontal plane in either his stance or during his swing causing poor vision.

Correction:

    a. Realize first that as the head tilts, the vision becomes impaired.

    b. Start with head straight in stance and keep it that way during the swing.

    2. **Head traveler**—Hitter's head does one or more of three separate movements; (1) it travels forward too much during the stride; (2) it bounces and does not stay in relatively the same plane; and (3) it pulls out during the swing causing poor eye contact.

Correction:

    a. Keep head quiet.

    b. Concentrate on seeing the ball leave the bat.

    c. Shorten stride and stride soft.

    d. Hit more off back leg.

    e. Keep from "dropping and driving" the back leg in the stride forward.

    3. **One eye hitter**—Hitter either in his stance or during his inward rotation turns his head to the point that if he shuts his front eye, he no longer can see the pitcher. This means he is "reading" the pitch with but one eye.

Correction:

    a. Turn head so both eyes can see the pitcher.

b. Rotate only the front shoulder, hip and knee in inward rotation.

c. May need to open front side slightly.

I. Swing

1. **Sweep hitter**—Hitter has slow bat as a result of a long radius arc. Arms tend to get straight too early and hitter appears stiff with very little hand action.

Correction:

a. Bring hands in closer to body.

b. Concentrate on not letting the front arm get straight prior to swing.

c. Practice swing standing directly in front of a wall facing a pitcher as though he were throwing to spot on wall. If arc gets long early, hitter will hit wall.

d. Concentrate on hitting with good hand action. Be sure middle knuckles are aligned properly.

2. **Swings too early**—Hitter constantly hitting ball off end of bat pulling balls too much. Easily fooled by breaking pitches, off speed pitches, and pitches on outside part of plate.

Correction:

a. Establish a good inward rotation.

b. Stride soft and short.

c. Keep front side (particularly hip and shoulder) in longer.

d. Use lighter bat so hitter will not feel he has to start swing early.

e. Concentrate on driving ball more up the middle and to the opposite field.

f. May want to close stance slightly and turn front foot in.

g. The fear of being jammed is probably causing the mental problem. Remember, for as many times as the "timing" is off by being too early, it should also be off the same amount for being late. More outs are made on outside pitches than inside pitches.

3. **Long bat arc**—Hitter does not stay "within" himself. No longer does he have a compact swing. The bat arc starts behind the hitter's back shoulder in a wide, long arc taking extra time to get to the contact spot.

Correction:

a. Very similar to sweep hitter. Concentrate on throwing barrel toward ball with good hand speed.

b. Bring barrel straight toward ball.

4. **Swing too late**—Hitter simply does not get the "meat" of the bat in the contact zone quick enough.

Correction:

a. Be sure bat is not resting in palm of hands. Get out closer to fingers.

b. Inward rotation of front side will help get rhythm of swing started.

284

c. Concentrate on throwing the barrel of the bat at the ball.

d. Relax. Reflexes are hampered by tightening up.

e. Align middle knuckles.

f. Shorten the stride and take straight path to the ball.

g. Be sure hips are exploding.

h. Open stance slightly.

5. **Pusher**—Hitter leads too much with hands causing barrel to be behind hands. Lets his weight transfer too quickly to front side.

Correction:

a. Stay within self. Don't let hands get way in front of body.

b. Throw the barrel at the ball with good hand action. Throw the top hand.

c. Keep weight back. Stride soft.

d. Strive to "hurt" the ball with good hand drive through the ball.

6. **Uppercutter**—Hitter drops the back shoulder and/or knee as he begins swing. Results in poor contact and fly balls or pop-ups.

Correction:

a. Concentrate on keeping front shoulder down slightly. Aim the shoulder at the approaching ball.

b. Keep the back side (leg particularly) relatively straight or "tall".

c. Remember line drives and ground balls produce many more hits than do fly balls.

d. Bring the barrel straight toward the contact area.

e. Make sure palm of top hand is facing pitcher when contacting the ball.

f. Practice hitting on one knee in soft toss drill.

7. **Worm killer**—Hitter constantly drives ball into the ground resulting in big hop ground balls.

Correction:

a. Be sure the knob of the bat is going toward the pitcher in the initial approach to the ball.

b. Concentrate on stronger bottom hand action. Do not let the top hand do all the work. Be sure it (top hand) does not roll over the top of the bat during contact.

c. Drop back shoulder and elbow slightly in approaching the ball.

d. Drive through the ball.

e. Keep weight back.

f. Practice hitting on one knee with short wooden bat held in bottom hand only.

8. **Pulls off ball**—Hitter lets power area of swing come across his body rather than extending it through the ball.

Correction:

a. Drive through the ball. Proper bat arc should not be a perfect circle but should extend through the ball prior to coming across the body.

b. Keep front shoulder and hip in longer. Do not pull the swing away from the ball.

c. Close the front foot and shoulder slightly.

d. Close the stance slightly.

9. **Poor finish**—Upon contact, hitter quits with the thrust of the swing. The bat does not finish around the back and results in a poor rhythmical swing and poor bat velocity.

Correction:

a. Relax the swing. Let the bat go where it wants after contact.

b. Concentrate on driving through the ball with good hand speed.

c. Finish with the barrel around the shoulder blades.

d. Handle of barrel should end by resting on front upper arm.

J. **Hitting slumps**—Every hitter has his good days and bad days. Often the good days tend to influence further good days while bad days tend to influence bad days. Slumps usually develop first in the head. Confidence is slightly shattered but not lost. The normal reaction is to take a lot of extra swings to get "back in the groove". Sometimes this works, but more often than not, it results in two pitfalls: (1) the hands get tired from a lot of extra work; and (2) concentration is lost after a period of time and bad habits result. The next day to compensate for the tired hands, the hitter swings harder and harder and soon his proper mechanics are gone. Certainly this is not the only way slumps get started. It does, however, illustrate the point that slumps are both mental problems and physical problems, and that they tend to influence one another as the anxiety of the hitter increases. Some suggestions to correct the hitting slumps of hitters are as follows:

1. Remember that every time at bat is a new day.

2. Take a day off—get away from it all.

3. Play long pepper.

4. Review hitting mechanics—work off a tee.

5. Relax—don't overswing.

6. Place bat on shoulder, elbows down and hit with concentration on solid contact.

7. Use lighter bat or choke up. Control your swing.

8. Use good bat discipline.

9. Work on hitting ball up the middle or to the opposite side.

ISOLATED HITTING DRILLS

The importance of isolating concentration on one particular phase of the total hitting skill becomes paramount to the hitter who strives for improvement. During a hitting drill situation, concentration on numerous skills concerned with hitting dilutes each individual skill of its needed positive mental attention. The objective of the following hitting areas is to have each hitter concentrate solely on one area until the skill becomes comfortable, learned and established into the reaction of the hitter. This will allow clear and total concentration on the opposing pitcher and his particular unique characteristics and abilities.

The following are considered 14 extremely important phases of hitting. Hitting faults usually fall into one of these categories. Correcting an area of weakness within the total hitting skill can be readily and easily devised through these individual drills. It is imperative that the mental attitude and concentration of the hitter be the same during a hitting drill situation as in a game situation. If a hitter is unable to carry a learned reaction from within the hitting drill situation to the live hitting area, the problem may be his mental attitude toward hitting.

The coach should spend the first week of practice isolating hitting areas with all his hitters. Each day two new phases of the hitting skill should be introduced and time allowed for each drill to be executed by each hitter. In the following weeks of practice, particular drills should be designated for work each day as you rotate from live hitting, machine hitting, and to an area of supervised drill work in the daily practice.

During the season a coach should find the hitters constantly going to these drill areas to work on a particular phase of the hitting skill. In particular, you should find the drill of short toss popular and rewarding even to the extent of incorporating the drill in your pre-game batting practice.

1. Mental Approach

The coach should start first with the mental approach to hitting. This is a discussion with the players on the areas which are important in attaining a positive mental picture. The areas of discussion are as follows:

A. **Fear**—You must rather be hit than strike out. You can not hit with the weight on the heels. Bring this subconscious fear to the surface and defeat it.

B. **Confidence**—You must be able to answer yes to the question: Do I think I can hit? Get mental hits in the on-deck circle. Tell yourself I can and will hit the ball hard. False confidence belongs to has-beens. Practice breeds confidence and confidence breeds success. You will become a better hitter when you believe in yourself as a hitter.

C. **Compete**—Be aggressive—always anticipate a strike on each pitch. Accept the challenge that the pitcher is trying to embarrass you. Good hitters are not timid.

D. **Poise**—Realize that three out of ten balls hit fall in for good hitters. Hustle even when you fail—do not let the pitcher know who has won. Don't get mad—it averts concentration. Can you come back in the ninth inning after going 0-3 at the plate?

E. **Self-knowledge**—Do you as a hitter know your strengths and weaknesses? Do you know what needs to be done in the following situations: fly ball; bunt; hit to right side; infield in; two strike swing? Are you willing to give in?

F. **Knowledge of opponent**—Questions you must have answers for during the course of a game: What does the pitcher throw? When does he throw it? Where does he release it? What did he get me out on last time? Learn something from every pitch. Take educated guesses on counts favorable to you as a hitter (3-0; 3-1; 2-0; 1-0).

G. **Ability to concentrate**—This depends upon desire, pride, and maturity. Poor concentration reinforces bad habits. When this happens, it is better to stop the skill practice rather than to proceed further.

H. **Visualization**—Think positive. See in your mind success and then plan on it. Picture your performance in your mind. Practice thinking in pictures. You must have a mental picture before you can materially accomplish the skill.

2. Stance

Next you would work on the stance and this can be a mass drill or with partners.

A. **Be comfortable**—Check the stances out to see if the hitters look comfortable in their basic stance.

B. **Extremes in stance**—This means you must have extreme ability: (1) stance—open/closed; (2) bat position—straight/around head; (3) box position—can I cover the corner? What pitch am I asking for? (4) hands—in or out; (5) head—tilted.

C. **Recommendations**—(1) feet width—a little wider than shoulder width apart; (2) toe position—back toe facing slightly in; (3) head position—level head, two eye vision; (4) slight bend of body—too much will cause poor head position; (5) weight on the balls of the feet—60% on back foot; (6) bat toward the horizontal plane; (7) hand position—even with armpit approximately six inches from the body; (8) back elbow slightly out; (9) front elbow bent, not straight; (10) elbows at approximately the same plane.

3. Bat Arc

The next drill is for the bat arc and this should be practiced upon the command of the coach, in mass drill.

A. **Quickest path between two points is a straight line.** Go straight to the ball.

B. **Eliminate dips.**

C. **Upon extension of arms, bat should be level.** The idea is to get the bat to the line of flight of the ball as quickly as possible. At point of contact, bat arc should be level.

D. **Follow through around shoulder blades.**

4. One Knee Drill

The one knee drill or soft toss should be one of your more popular drills with the hitters.

A. **Proper position** (for righthanded batter). Right knee on towel, left knee bent.

B. **Proper grip.** Strive for middle knuckle alignment and bat held more in the fingers than in the palm of the hand.

C. **Soft toss partner.** Let partner get set and mentally ready prior to each pitch. Tosser kneels on one knee slightly forward and to the right of the righthanded hitter. Should be approximately five yards away and tossing underhand to hitter.

D. **Isolate the hands.** Choke up if you need to.

E. **Do not sweep.** Use the hands to drive through the ball.

5. Bat Speed

Bat speed drills are a very important part of the whole drill scheme.

A. **Rapid swing**—Merely get in stance and rapidly take swings back and forth: (1) good warmup and isolation of hands; (2) good practice on feel of grip; (3) can be done with bat or cable.

B. **Short bat or one-handed swing drill:** (1) bottom hand (use sawed-off bats). The bottom fingers are important or the batter will have a lazy bottom hand. Drive knob toward pitcher (don't pull off); (2) top hand (choke-up)—throw barrel through ball and explode for quickness.

C. **Bat/Barrel throw**—Actually throw the bat into a screen: (1) get the feel of throwing the barrel—the mental picture of thrusting the barrel at ball; (2) try throwing the bat with the weight completely on the front foot; (3) try throwing the bat with

288

the weight completely on the back foot; (4) try throwing without moving the hips; (5) and then throw with both hips and hands (the initiator and concluder) and with proper transfer of weight.

D. **Hitting sticks**—The partner holds stick out. Hitter tries to hit the tip of the stick before the partner can move it; (1) helps to isolate the hands and eliminate wasted motion; (2) stick should be held at different levels; (3) take barrel directly to the stick (no dips).

6. No Stride-Short Toss Drill

Performed by the tosser kneeling behind the pitching screen located approximately eight yards from the hitter. A backstop or hitting cage should be behind the tosser. The ball is tossed overhand to the hitter who is facing the tosser.

A. Excellent drill for a hitter when in a slump.

B. Helps isolate the importance of hands.

C. Turn toes in slightly toward the pitcher and take slightly wider stance.

D. Concentrate on waiting as long as possible and then explode. The longer a batter can wait, the better he will be as a hitter.

7. Inward Rotation and Stride Drill

These two areas can be drilled in mass group by simulating throwing the ball or faking a throw in the short toss area.

A. **Inward rotation**—(1) this is the cock of the gun—the backswing in golf; (2) a needed rhythm for timing (all one motion—no stop); (3) something to get going—a coil; (4) execution—the front knee should bend in slightly. The batter should rotate from the waist, not the arms or hands. A cock of the hips, and the front shoulder goes toward the chin. This is just prior and during the initial movement of the stride; (5) this is the place or time of many bad habits. This eliminates the bad habits and increases a needed physiological preliminary movement. The hands must go back before they go forward.

B. **Stride**—(1) prior to the stride, there is a 60/40 weight distribution; (2) the step forward should be low to the ground with the foot pointed open slightly. Stride on the big toe of the foot and step softly as though stepping on eggs. The stride should be eight to twelve inches toward the pitcher. The stride should not be with a stiff front leg. Keep the weight and hands back. The stride does not take added weight. Upon initial completion of the stride approximately 70% of the body weight should be on the inside of the back foot.

8. Hip Drill

Place the bat behind the back, interlocking both elbows. This drill can be done in mass group by simulating throwing the ball and telling the hitters where the pitch is located in the strike zone.

A. The hips are the initiator of the swing.

B. A correlation between slow hips and slow hands are evident.

C. The further the hips must rotate, the sooner they must explode: (1) for an inside pitch, the navel should be pointing at contact toward left field (if righthanded hitter)—hips must begin earlier here; (2) down middle—the navel should be pointing toward center field at contact; (3) outside pitch—the navel pointing toward opposite field at contact. Hips can wait longer since they do not have to rotate as far.

D. Pay close attention to the feet as they pivot. The hitter must get his back heel up in order to rotate off the back foot.

9. Hitting Through The Ball With Proper Weight Transfer

This drill is a good front shoulder guide to help the hitters drive through the ball.

A. **Hitting through the ball.** Hit through tires chained at different levels to a fence: (1) secure a mental picture of transfer of weight. This is the idea of chopping a tree (arm extension and proper wrist position). It is a controlled boxing punch; (2) transfer weight through the ball. Often the problem is hitting to the ball and this causes a pulling off motion; (3) bat arc is not a perfect circle. The proper arc goes through the ball before coming around.

B. **Front shoulder guide** (the striding guide). This drill can be done in short toss drill: (1) one of the most important parts of the swing; (2) aim the front shoulder toward the ball as the stride begins and until the hips have begun their rotation; (3) benefits—this is the technique of striding toward the ball. The hands will stay back. There is less chance of getting fooled as the batter has not opened up. It keeps the batter cocked and gives him full capacity for the swing. Also, it aids in proper transfer of weight. The batter takes the inside pitch with the front shoulder rotated in.

10. **Hitting Outside Pitch**

This skill can be isolated by playing short toss. The mental picture and decision prior to the pitch must be that the batter will get a strike, get a pitch down the middle, that he will drive it to center field. Adjustments can best be made for either inside or outside pitches with this mental thought.

A. More outs are made on outside pitches than on inside pitches. The batter must be equally conscious of both inside and outside pitches.

B. Know where you want to make contact with the ball in relation to the plate. This is in order to get maximum drive through the ball. The batter can wait until the ball is almost at the plate. He should not find himself reaching for the ball.

C. Three problems exist with the outside pitch: (1) trying to pull the pitch; (2) not waiting, which means that the front shoulder comes out too quickly; and (3) the weight transfers too early. These latter two are usually due to the fear of being jammed.

D. **Proper execution.** Stay back with both the weight and the hands. Aim the front shoulder at the ball. Do not let the top hand coast, drag, or slap through the swing. Do not aim the ball to the opposite side. Get a mental picture of driving through the ball. The navel should be facing the opposite field. It is critical that the batter does not overswing when hitting the outside pitch.

11. **Hitting Inside Pitch**

This skill can also be isolated by playing short toss.

A. This is the pitch that dictates the poor hitter's entire mental and physical approach to hitting.

B. Too much concern on the hitter's part that he will get jammed affects his ability to handle the pitch down the middle or outside as well as the curve ball or off speed pitch.

C. Timing should be off both ways equally. For as many times as the batter hits the ball on the end of the bat, he should also be hitting the ball on the handle.

D. **Common faults.** There is a subconscious quitting because the batter is late. Dipping and not extending the arms on contact and the weight remaining on the back foot are common faults. Another fault, a stiff front leg, results when the hitter gives in and determines that he cannot hit the ball on the meat of the bat.

E. **Proper execution.** The batter should know where he wants to make contact with the ball in relation to the plate in order to get maximum drive through the ball, out in front of the plate. The hips must explode and initiate a quick arc proper swing. It should be a straight line from bat to ball. This is not a power swing, but a quick swing. The power will be there if executed properly because of the longer rotary motion of the hips, trunk and arms. Drive through the ball with a good transfer of weight. The top hand must not be lazy but must throw the barrel so that the arms will be extended upon impact. The navel should be facing the strong side of the field. The batter should not muscle the swing, but should relax and the quickness will come naturally.

12. Hitting High Pitch

This skill can be isolated in the short toss or the soft toss drill.

A. Hands should be at the top of the strike zone when the pitch is delivered.

B. A conscious mental effort should be made to chop the high pitch. The barrel should be above the hands. If this is not done, a dip or dropping of the back shoulder will occur resulting in either a high fly ball, or hitting under the ball for an easy pop-up.

C. If proper techniques are followed from the previous day, the hitter should almost be on top of the pivoted back foot when making contact.

13. Hitting Low Pitch

This can also be isolated in the short toss or soft toss drill. In relation to the inside, outside, and high pitches, the low pitch often causes further problems because: (1) the hands must go further down; and (2) the eyes become further away from the visual path of the ball.

A. Chief problems concerning the low pitch are golfing at the ball, with the eyes too far away from the path of the ball. The bat becomes almost perpendicular to the path of the ball which increases greatly the difficulty of good contact with the ball.

B. **Important techniques:** These consist of not dropping the back knee when initiating the swing as this will result in a dip; the drive should be made straight to the ball with the front leg bent slightly more than on the other pitches; as the hips rotate, the back knee may bend so as to get down on the ball, but it should not be an extreme bend. Again the techniques already discussed are important: a good mental picture of aiming the front shoulder toward the ball is important as well as hitting through the ball. An upper cut is not necessary if contact is made at the moment of extension of the arms. The batter should take the hands to the ball.

14. Two Strike Swing

This can be isolated in the short toss drill or in live or machine hitting. Be sure that emphasis is placed on the two strike priority which is not to strike out. Make the opponents make a play on the batter.

A. Techniques are wide ranged here because it is important that the swing or stance is not a drastic change from the normal swing and stance. Some adjustments are as follows: move closer to the plate; move up in the box; choke up or split grip; open the stance slightly; concentrate on solid contact with quick hands; do not overswing or power the ball; and think of driving the ball back up the middle or to the opposite field.

B. A slight mental adjustment toward the size of the strike zone should be made. Widen the zone an inch and do not expect any sympathy on the cardinal sin of taking a called third strike.

C. Two strike swings should be practiced.

HITTERS EVALUATE THEMSELVES

In very simple terms, the hitters' evaluation of themselves is designed to insure that both the coach and the hitter are working toward the same end product. The evaluation should surface not only the individual's total picture of himself as a hitter, but also the coach's ideas as he sees the hitter.

The following is the hitter's own questionnaire. Find out if you are on the same "wave length" as your hitters in regard to their mental picture of themselves. This may open the door to the communication needed to increase the hitting production of your team.

QUESTION #1

1. **Pitch Selection**

   A. At which areas of the strike zone do you feel you can fairly consistently handle a pitch? (Circle those areas)

1. High Inside	2. High Middle	3. High Outside
4. Medium Inside	5. Medium Middle	6. Medium Outside
7. Low Inside	8. Low Middle	9. Low Outside

   B. Which one area of the strike zone do you feel can be considered "your pitch" area? (Circle one area)

1. High Inside	2. High Middle	3. High Outside
4. Medium Inside	5. Medium Middle	6. Medium Outside
7. Low Inside	8. Low Middle	9. Low Outside

   C. Which areas of the strike zone do you feel are your weak areas? These would be areas that you have poor success in handling a pitch. (Circle those areas)

1. High Inside	2. High Middle	3. High Outside
4. Medium Inside	5. Medium Middle	6. Medium Outside
7. Low Inside	8. Low Middle	9. Low Outside

Hitting coaches all too often find themselves trying to make each player perfect hitters. The results often fall into the old equation statement; "Try to make good great and you end up with average". A coach needs to realize that all hitters have their own strong spots and weak spots in the strike zone.

Against normal pitching, a good hitter should be able to handle approximately 70% of the strike zone with particular areas within that 70% area being stronger than others. The remaining 30%, the weak spots, are areas where a hitter should not swing until he gets two strikes.

Too often a coach changes the hitter's entire philosophy and hitting style to correct the 30% weak spot area and consequently hurts the 70% hitting strength area. Assuming the strength spot area is wider than the weak spot area, the job of the coach is to:

1. Insure that the individual's strength areas stays intact.

2. Attempt to gradually decrease the weak spot area of the strike zone without decreasing the original strength area.

292

Often the difference between a good hitter and an average hitter is not physical ability, but simply that the good hitter consistently swings and hits balls within his hitting area (strength zone), while the weak hitter swings and hits pitches in his weak area.

Once a strength zone is established, an area within that zone can be declared "my pitch" area. This should be the area where the hitter looks for his pitch on a 2-0; 3-0; or 3-1 count.

QUESTION #2

2. **Hitting Spray**

Where is your:

A. Power Area Spray

B. Solid Contact Area Spray

Simply darken the entire area you feel best explains your thoughts. See the example below:

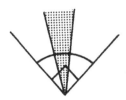

Another area where both the individual player and the coach should communicate is dealing with where the hitter should be hitting the ball.

Not every hitter is a spray hitter just as not every hitter is a power hitter. The basic hitting philosophy should be to work from the premise that the ball thrown down the middle of the plate should be hit back up the middle. Some hitters, in order to keep them aggressive and to maximize their hitting style, pull the pitch down the middle to their strong side power alley while others must go up the middle. Some hitters are strong and quick enough to place the outside pitch in the opposite side power alley while others must drive the ball directly to the opposite field.

The coach and hitter need to come to an understanding on what best suits the individual hitter's talents.

QUESTION #3

3. In what area of the field do the balls go that you hit poorly?

A. Ground balls _____

Why? _____

_____

_____

B. Fly balls _____

Why? _____

_____

_____

Again, here is an opportunity for both the hitter and the coach to surface and realize a particular area of difficulty in each hitter's individual make-up. The answer "why" gives both the hitter and the coach the opportunity to emphasize and work out the problems that must be solved.

QUESTION #4

4. Considering your individual talents, how do you feel you can best help this team at the plate? (Example: singles, singles and doubles, power, drag bunting, bat control, advancing runners, walks because of good idea of strike zone, etc.). **Be Specific**

_____

_____

_____

_____

_____

QUESTION #5

5. Of the total hitting skill (including mental as well as physical), which two areas will you improve on this week? How will you improve this skill? (Example: Keeping weight back longer or shortening stride and striding softer).

AREAS	HOW
1. _____	1. _____
_____	_____
2. _____	2. _____
_____	_____

This final question is one the coach may wish to ask on a weekly basis. This certainly will aid in isolating hitting problems and concentrating on improving that area.

PLAYER HITTING QUESTIONNAIRE

1. Pitch Selection

A. At which areas of the strike zone do you feel you can fairly consistently handle a pitch? (Circle these areas)

1. High Inside	2. High Middle	3. High Outside
4. Medium Inside	5. Medium Middle	6. Medium Outside
7. Low Inside	8. Low Middle	9. Low Outside

B. Which one area of the strike zone do you feel can be considered "your pitch" area? (Circle one area)

1. High Inside	2. High Middle	3. High Outside
4. Medium Inside	5. Medium Middle	6. Medium Outside
7. Low Inside	8. Low Middle	9. Low Outside

C. Which areas of the strike zone do you feel are your weak areas? These would be areas that you have poor success in handling a pitch. (Circle those areas)

1. High Inside	2. High Middle	3. High Outside
4. Medium Inside	5. Medium Middle	6. Medium Outside
7. Low Inside	8. Low Middle	9. Low Outside

---

2. Hitting Spray

Where is your:

A. Power Area Spray

B. Solid Contact Area Spray

Simply darken the entire area you feel best explains your thoughts. See the example below:

3. In what area of the field do the balls go that you hit poorly?

    A. Ground balls _____

       Why? _____

       _____

       _____

    B. Fly balls _____

       Why? _____

       _____

       _____

4. Considering your individual talents, how do you feel you can best help this team at the plate? (Example: singles, singles and doubles, power, drag bunting, bat control, advancing runners, walks because of good idea of strike zone, etc.). **Be Specific**

_____

_____

_____

_____

5. Of the total hitting skill (including mental as well as physical), which two areas will you improve on this week? How will you improve this skill? (Example: Keeping weight back longer or shortening stride and striding softer).

                              AREAS   **HOW**

    1. _____   1. _____

       _____   _____

    2. _____   2. _____

       _____   _____

BAT DISCIPLINE

Baseball coaches will all admit that the physical proficiency in hitting is keyed on meeting the ball squarely with good bat speed. They would further admit that this is a very difficult skill to master, and this is the reason why all coaches are interested in finding ways to enable their hitters to perform this feat with some degree of regular success. This is where the subject of bat discipline comes into play. This is one of those mental aspects of hitting that most coaches spend very little time on, but bat discipline may play one of the largest roles in bat productivity.

Bat discipline boils down to just one mental decision: yes, I will swing at this pitch; or no, I will not swing at this pitch. Doesn't it sound simple? Yes or no? Swing or don't swing? It may sound simple but all baseball coaches know how difficult this is due to the fact that this decision must be made while a baseball is coming into the plate area at a tremendous rate of speed, and in many cases with movement in the vertical and horizontal plane.

Good bat discipline can help a poor fundamental hitter more than it can help a good fundamental hitter. There are times that the good hitter can make contact off a pitcher's great pitch whereby the poor hitter could not have a high degree of success on the same pitch. The poor hitter is not able to have this success due to the fact that his hitting mechanics are not as finely structured as the good hitter. This is not to say that a good hitter can not become a better hitter with good bat discipline. It means merely that bat discipline is the crutch that the poor hitter needs in order to achieve some success while the good hitter can use it to achieve greater success.

When teaching bat discipline, the coach needs to stress the importance of maintaining aggressiveness at the plate. If a team continually hears from the coach that they are swinging at too many bad pitches, it could lead to their losing their aggressiveness as they start taking too many good pitches. The bat discipline philosophy has to center around the mental to physical concept of "yes, yes, yes, no" or "yes, yes, yes, yes". The former being when the hitter takes the pitch, and the latter being when the hitter swings at the pitch. A hitter must establish the fact that he will be swinging at the pitch, and then make the adjustment to hold back on the swing at the last possible instance. Once a hitter starts saying to himself that he would like to see where the pitch is before swinging, he will lose the ability to "pull the trigger". When a hitter loses his aggressiveness he hinders his ability to establish himself both mentally and physically as a good hitter.

For purposes of clarification and understanding, let's break bat discipline down to its simplest form. Your team is playing in a high school baseball game and the pitcher your team is facing is an average high school pitcher. Being that he is an average high school pitcher, he is able to get the ball over the plate with some degree of frequency and has a couple of different pitches that he can throw. If he throws seven pitches to a batter, he probably will be able to throw two pitches that would have the marks of a perfect pitch for him. This means that the velocity, movement and location were as good as he can achieve on a pitch. Two of the seven pitches thrown would be the type that the pitcher wishes he could retrieve before it reaches the batter. This is due to the fact that either the velocity, movement or location of the pitch is poor. The other three pitches from the average high school pitcher would be average pitches. This means that the velocity, movement and location are not perfect for him, but at the same time it is not a poor type of pitch. Thus, this pitcher is capable of throwing two perfect pitches, two poor pitches, and three average pitches in these seven deliveries to the plate.

If the pitcher throwing against your team is an above average high school pitcher, his pitch breakdown might be: three perfect pitches; three average pitches; and one poor pitch. The poor high school pitcher might have a pitch breakdown of: one perfect pitch; three average pitches; and three poor pitches.

If a hitter could know when the pitcher was going to throw his perfect pitch, his average pitch, or his poor pitch, hitting would be a lot simpler than it is. The batter would take all the pitcher's perfect pitches (except with two strikes), and swing at all his poor pitches that are in the strike zone. Of course, this is not the case since the batter never knows what type of pitch he will receive until he reads the ball as it leaves the pitcher's hand.

The degree of success a hitter would have on this average high school pitcher will depend on how many of his poor pitches he swings at and how many of his perfect pitches he takes. As mentioned previously, the good hitters on a team might have some degree of success with the pitcher's perfect pitches, but the poor hitter will get very little accomplished. However, if the good hitter would wait for the average or poor pitch, his degree of success as a hitter should rise. The poor hitter might be able to remain in the starting lineup with some degree of success if he can discipline himself to swing at just poor or average pitches. He can not afford to swing at a pitcher's perfect pitch unless he has two strikes on him.

The basic premise in bat discipline lies in the fact that there are very few pitchers in high school or college who are going to consistently throw perfect pitches. Even the best pitchers are going to make a mistake and that is when the hitter needs to respond by "pulling the trigger".

How does a coach teach bat discipline? Let's go back to the average high school pitcher to analyze what hitters need to do mentally and physically to respond to the pitched ball in a positive manner. By using the following situation as an example, the coach might be able to get across the idea to his club that bat discipline is a vital ingredient in becoming a good hitter.

The first hitter to the plate receives one of the pitcher's great pitches on the first pitch, and he swings at the ball. He subsequently hits a weak ground ball back to the pitcher for the first out of the inning. The reason that this was a great pitch for the pitcher was that he threw a good fast ball on the outside black of the plate. Now what did this batter just do? He swung at the first pitch merely because it looked like a strike even though it was a difficult pitch for him to hit well. If he would have taken that first pitch, the worst that he could be would be facing an 0-1 count. Let's say that the batter had good bat discipline and he took that perfect pitch for a strike. If we go strictly by percentages, this means that the average pitcher now has one great pitch left, three average pitches left, and two poor pitches left of the seven pitches he would throw. Thus, the chances of him throwing another perfect pitch are somewhat minimized. On the next pitch, the pitcher throws another perfect pitch (curve ball on the knees for a strike). The batter swings at this pitch and pops the ball up in the infield for an easy out. If he had taken this pitch for a strike, he would now have a 0-2 count on him. However, he would still have the opportunity to swing at another pitch. Since this average pitcher has already thrown two great pitches, his chances of throwing another great pitch would be further minimized. With two strikes the batter must now concentrate on making some contact at the plate and can not be concerned about the type of pitch that might be thrown, other than the fact that he must protect the plate. Hopefully, the pitcher does not throw another great pitch. If he does, the next batter certainly will have a better chance of seeing some average pitches or poor pitches unless the pitcher is having a great day on the mound.

A hitter who swings at one of a pitcher's great pitches when he (the hitter) is ahead in the count is committing a cardinal hitting sin. If he takes one of the pitcher's poor pitches when ahead in the count, he is committing the same type of hitting sin. A hitter must be in a position to respond to the challenge that each pitch thrown provides him taking into consideration the following: (1) the skill level of the pitcher; (2) his hitting skill level; (3) the ball-strike count; (4) the game situation; and (5) the plate umpire.

1. **The skill level of the pitcher**—The better the pitcher, the more the individual hitter must practice good bat discipline. For example, if a pitcher possesses an excellent slider, a hitter must lay off that pitch with less than two strikes unless the pitcher happens to throw the slider into his hitting zone. One of the reasons a particular pitcher might be having success is that he has the ability to throw his great pitches to areas of the strike zone that make it very difficult for the hitter to make good contact (up and in; low and away). Since the good pitcher will throw less mistake pitches than the average or poor pitcher, the hitter can not afford to take any mistake pitch. He must be thinking "swing, swing, swing, yes", or "swing, swing, swing, no". We have all heard many times hitters come back to the dugout saying that they should have jumped all over a certain pitch. Since a great pitcher will make few mistake pitches, the hitter must be ready to respond when he reads the pitch in his hitting zone. With a poor pitcher on the mound, the number of mistake pitches will increase so the hitter can be very selective. If the pitcher does not possess a "strikeout" pitch, the batter can afford to have two strikes on him. With a great pitcher on the mound, the hitter with two strikes is definitely "in the hole". Thus, the skill level of the pitcher will be a major factor in a hitter's bat discipline.

2. **His hitting skill level**—Every hitter has certain areas of the strike zone that he likes to have the ball thrown to. At the same time, there are certain areas of the strike zone that a hitter has a tough time making solid contact with the ball. Hitters need to realize that even the great hitters have a difficult time making good contact in certain areas of the strike zone. The reason they are great hitters is that they understand this fact and practice good bat discipline according to where the ball is in relation to their strike zone. Hitters need to also realize that some hitters can make good contact with balls outside the strike zone, while other hitters need to have the pitch in the confines of the strike zone in order to make solid contact. Thus, every hitter is different, and every hitter must fully understand his capabilities and limitations as a hitter. Those hitters who never make adjustments at the plate and have little or no understanding of their hitting zones, will have a very difficult time becoming established hitters. A hitter must read the type of pitch and the location of the pitch before he can swing at the ball. If he is a good fast ball hitter and likes the pitch on the inside part of the plate belt high, when he reads that pitch in that zone he must be ready to "pull the trigger". Hitters can improve their batting average by being selective at the plate, but still maintain their aggressiveness so that when the pitch they want "arrives" the bat "flies".

Many hitters have a very difficult time hitting good breaking pitches. If that is the case, they must discipline themselves to lay off the good breaking pitch unless they have two strikes on them. As a general rule, most pitchers will have a more difficult time throwing breaking pitches for strikes then they will their fast ball and change-up. Once the pitcher gets behind in the count, there is a better chance that the hitter will see more fast balls. Again, each hitter must determine what he is looking for from each pitcher by taking into consideration the location of the pitch in the strike zone and the type of pitch thrown. A hitter should never swing at a change-up with less than two strikes on him unless one of two things are in effect: (1) the hitter is guessing change-up; and (2) the change-up is in his hitting zone. The coach should be in a position to help each hitter evaluate his strength and weaknesses in regard to hitting zones and the type of pitches he should be looking for in certain situations. Guess hitting is highly recommended for most hitters who have good bat discipline when they are ahead in the count.

3. **The ball-strike count**—One of the major considerations a hitter must take into account in establishing good bat discipline is the ball-strike count. Every hitter would love to be in a position each time at bat to face the pitcher when he (the hitter) is ahead in the count (3-0; 3-1; 2-0; 1-0; 2-1). The pitcher would then have to throw a pitch over the plate, and this pitch would generally be his best control pitch. In most cases, the pitcher's best control pitch is the fast ball. The pitcher who can throw his breaking pitches or change-up over the plate in these ball-strike situations is going to be a very effective pitcher. The average high school or college pitcher is not able to get the breaking pitch and change-up over consistently, so the hitter is now in a position to guess fast ball. If the fast ball is thrown in his hitting zone, he needs to "jump all over this pitch". The hitter who practices good bat discipline should have a chance to face the average pitcher in these ball-strike counts a couple of times per game. It is important that the hitter know what type of pitch the pitcher he is facing generally throws when ahead in the count and when behind in the count. Pitchers generally establish some type of pitch pattern during the game, and the intelligent hitter would then be in a position to look for certain pitches in the various ball-strike counts. If a pitcher has a difficult time getting his breaking pitch over the plate, the hitter must be patient in hopes that the pitcher gets behind in the count. If that occurs, the hitter can "look fast ball".

4. **The game situation**—There are various game situations that arise during the course of a game when the hitter must practice good bat discipline. The following are some of these sitautions with a brief discussion in regard to what the hitter must do in practicing good bat discipline when these situations arise in a game:

A. **Lead off hitter in the game or in an inning**—It is very important that the first hitter each inning find a way to get on base. The old saying that if "the defense can get the first batter out in the inning—the inning is half over" has a lot of merit. In order to have a big inning, the first hitter needs to get on base. Of course, the easiest way to do this is via the base on balls. Thus, the first hitter must practice good bat discipline so that he might have a great chance of getting on base via the walk or hitting one of the pitcher's "mistake pitches". The pitcher's confidence receives a tremendous lift when he gets the lead off hitter out, especially if the out is made on one of his better pitches. If the lead off hitter is not a good breaking ball hitter, he must take this pitch unless he reads a poor breaking pitch in his hitting zone. The lead off hitter for a team must be a young man who has a knack for good bat discipline and has a high on base percentage.

B. **Baserunner at first base with no outs**—The number two hitter in the lineup should be a hitter who has the ability to hit the ball to the right side of the field. Thus, the righthanded number two hitter should have the ability to drive the ball to the right side, and the lefthanded number two hitter should have the ability to pull the ball. With the first baseman holding a runner on at first base, it generally opens up the hole on the right side of the infield. If the shortstop and second baseman are playing the lefthanded hitter well to the pull side of the infield, the hitter must be able to drive the ball to the opposite field if the pitch is out over the plate. This is especially true if the third baseman is playing shallow at third base to protect against the sacrifice or drag bunt. It is much more difficult for the defense to complete a double play on the right side of the infield than it is from the left side of the infield. With a runner at first base with no outs, the hitter must discipline himself to look for the pitch in his hitting zone that he can drive to that area of the infield that will provide him the better chance to stay out of the double play. If the hit and run is on, the hitter needs to have some idea whether the shortstop or second baseman is covering second base so that he can "take a shot" to the vacated hole.

C. **Baserunner at second base with no outs**—This game situation should force the hitter to practice great bat discipline. He must discipline himself to respond to a pitch that he can hit hard to the right side of the infield to get the runner from second base over to third base. This is especially true in a close game where the runner at second base is a very important run. The hitter should make every effort to accomplish this without denying himself a chance to get a base hit. The righthanded hitter should look for a pitch that he can handle from the middle of the plate to the outside corner of the plate. An intelligent pitcher will attempt to keep the ball in on the hands of the righthanded hitter in this situation, so the hitter must discipline himself to take the inside pitch. There are very few righthanded hitters who can drive the inside pitch to the right side of the infield. Once the hitter has two strikes on him, he must then attempt to make solid contact while protecting the plate no matter where the pitch might be within the strike zone. The lefthanded hitter in this situation must look for a pitch that he can pull when he has no or one strike on him. As with the righthanded hitter, with two strikes he must make contact without forcing himself to have to pull the pitch. The intelligent pitcher will try to keep the ball away from the lefthanded hitter with the runner at second base and no outs. For this reason, the lefthanded hitter must look for a ball from the middle of the plate to the inside corner of the plate when he has no or one strike on him. The hitter must get the runner over to third base so that he can score on a sacrifice fly ball or base hit. A coach hates to think that he would have to sacrifice bunt in this situation, but he may have to do just that if the hitter does not have the capability to get the important run over to third base with the swing of the bat.

D. **Baserunner at third base with less than two outs**—The coach finds out quickly who really has great bat discipline on his club when this situation arises in the game. The hitter must look for a pitch that he can hit hard somewhere. The hitter who attempts to hit a long fly ball in this situation might find that the swing predicated on this type of attempt might result in a fly ball in the infield. It is better that the hitter concentrate on getting a pitch that he can "drive" somewhere, rather than to attempt to hit a fly ball. With less than two strikes, the hitter must be looking for a pitcher's "mistake" pitch. With two strikes, the hitter should just concentrate on making contact with the ball. A hitter should never be called out on a third strike with a runner in scoring position, particularly at third base. When the infield is playing in on the grass, the hitter should make even more of an effort to get a good pitch to hit with less than two strikes, since a hard ground ball will have an excellent chance of getting through the infield. The offensive team can not afford a fly ball in the infield or a strikeout with a baserunner at third base with less than two outs. The hitter must take tremendous pride in getting the runner at third base across the plate with his time at the plate.

E. **Baserunners at first and third base with one out**—Every attempt must be made to stay out of an inning ending double play in this situation. This is especially the case late in the game with an important run at third base. If the head coach decides to start the runner from first base, the hitter must exercise good bat discipline so that he might take advantage of the movement of the infielders to cover the steal attempt. Since it is much more difficult for the defense to complete a double play on the right side of the infield, the hitter should make every effort to go to that side of the field if the pitch allows him to do so.

F. **No runners on base with two outs**—In this situation, the hitter should be looking for the type of pitch when ahead in the count that he might be able to hit for extra bases. By getting the batter-runner to second base with two outs, there is a good chance he can score on a single in the outfield. There would be no chance of his scoring from first base on the same single to the outfield.

5. **The plate umpire**—The home plate umpire certainly is a factor in bat discipline. The nature of his strike zone should dictate to a large degree what the batter can and can not do with the particular pitcher on the mound. For example, if the umpire is a low ball umpire, the hitter must take this into consideration when evaluating the pitch on the way to the plate. With two strikes, he needs to protect the low part of the strike zone. With less than two strikes, he does not want the umpire's low strike to affect his swing tendency since all it would do is force him to swing at a pitch that he might not be able to handle effectively. If the umpire has a "tight" strike zone, the hitter can practice much better bat discipline than he would if the umpire has a "loose" strike zone. Hopefully, the plate umpire will establish his strike zone early in the game, and maintain that strike zone throughout the contest. If the strike zone constantly shifts, then the hitter needs to be sure that he protects the plate a little more when he has two strikes.

Bat discipline can be developed in batting practice with the coach staying with the hitters in the batting cage area so that all swings taken have some purpose to them. Swinging at pitches outside the strike zone in these batting practice sessions will carry over into the game as a rule. If hitters do not practice some degree of bat discipline in batting practice, it makes for a tougher time for the discipline to be carried over into the game itself. Situation hitting in batting practice sessions provide an opportunity for the player and coach to evaluate the hitter's bat discipline.

Inter-squad games provide an excellent opportunity for the entire team to work on their bat discipline. This is the reason for the different count games that should be played on many inter-squad game days. By placing the hitter in a certain count each time he steps to the plate, the batter learns what he is looking for in regard to the ball-strike count.

You can always tell a team that has good bat discipline for they seem to always jump on mistake pitches, and take the pitcher's good deliveries to the plate. A pitcher who has control problems but has good movement on his pitches loves to face a team with poor bat discipline, for they will keep him in the game by swinging at anything he throws in the general area of the strike zone.

Since bat discipline is basically mental concentration combined with the integration of the mental thought patterns with the physical capabilities of the hitter, it is difficult to teach. However, the coach who will spend time with his hitters preparing them mentally for what they must do at the plate should be coaching a more disciplined explosive offensive baseball team.

BUNTING

No team has a complete offensive attack without the proper use of the bunt in their arsenal of offensive weapons. While in the past decade bunting has often been labeled by baseball knowledgeables as "the lost art", no coach can deny its main function and importance of advancing a baserunner to the following base.

The designated hitter, the re-entry rule, the speed-up rules, the aluminum bat, the astroturf fields, the emphasis on the power hitting attack, all have taken its toll on the degree of use of the bunt. Whether the bunt is or is not used more today is speculative; the important concept to gather is that the bunt will alter the outcome of many games each season. With this in mind, the following areas of the bunting game will be presented.

1. Sacrifice bunting
2. Drag bunting
3. Push bunting
4. Fake bunt-slash

A few general statements concerning bunting must proceed the presentation of these types of bunts.

1. The importance of the bunting game must be stressed to the entire team. The team needs to realize the coaches bunting philosophy prior to the first game. Too often the hitter reacts to the bunt signal with the apparent thought that the coach does not feel he can hit in this key situation. Consequently his mental approach is not as well concentrated on the task at hand as it might be if he were given the hitaway sign. Stressing the idea that a hitter would not be called on to bunt unless it was important can help. Often a correlation is drawn between a team that sacrifice bunts well and a team that is a "total" team and not a group of individuals. Good bunting can draw a "team" effort. A well-rounded team will take pride in their bunting game.

2. The team must realize that the sacrifice bunt means "total" sacrifice. The most important item to remember is to advance the runner. Trying to be too perfect, or waiting too long to show the bunt, or running before the ball is on the ground, often indicates the hitter is becoming overly conscious with reaching first base safely.

3. Just as it is with hitting, the degree of success in bunting is dependent on bunting a good pitch. Bunting at poor pitches will decrease the chances of success and will also decrease the chance of drawing a walk which is the best way to advance the runner. The importance of bunting at strikes that are not high in the strike zone must be stressed.

4. While it is important not to be too perfect in the placement of the bunted ball, the bunter should approach the task with the thought that a poorly placed bunted ball should go foul and not toward the pitcher. It is generally accepted that with a runner on first base, the bunt should most likely be placed down in the first base side of the infield. With a runner at first and second base, the ball should be placed down the third base side of the infield. Adjustments can be made depending on the defensive alignment and its personnel.

5. Obviously, the one result a coach does not want while bunting is the pop-up. It not only makes for an easy out, but can also strand the runner attempting to advance. Practicing with the idea of bunting the top half of the ball with the lower half of the bat can emphasize the importance of getting the ball on the ground.

6. Once the decision to bunt has been made, the hitter should get in the batter's box with a stance slightly closer up in the box toward the pitcher. "Cheating up in the box" will not only allow the hitter to bunt the ball before it breaks away from the meat of the plate, but it will also allow him a better chance of keeping the ball in fair territory. The further a hitter is back in the box, the greater chance for foul balls. Obviously, a too drastic change in the position in the box will cause a greater chance of alerting the defense to the intentions of the batter.

7. As in any other area of the game, bunting must be practiced. Bunting stations with lines drawn or targets established for emphasis in good bunts can be of enormous help. Charts kept on each individual's success can be done. A "Bunters Club" can be formed to add incentive to the practice effort. While these are areas of importance in teaching successful bunting, the best bunting practice is done during batting practice or in game-type situations with the pitcher throwing full speed from the stretch position. Batting practice is the area where bunting practice occurs the most. Remind the pitchers to not "let-up" when the bunt is being attempted. An important concept to also remember is that bunting, like a free throw in basketball, does not occur five or six times in a row. A hitter will be asked to bunt at any time during the course of the game. It might be

best to have the hitter swing away a couple of times, then bunt, then swing away and then bunt again. This is better than having the batter bunt two or three in a row prior to his normal batting practice.

In the baseball sign section of the Playbook, further explanations of bunting philosophy have already been presented.

1. Sacrifice Bunting—Fundamentals

A. As the pitcher strides forward with his lead leg from the stretch, the hitter should square around to bunt. It is better to be too early than too late. The caution here is to be sure that the hitter waits until the pitcher has committed himself to the plate. A quick pick-off move is often used by the pitcher to see if the batter squares around. If the batter does show his intentions to bunt, the defensive strategy can then be altered to decrease the chances of advancing the runner on the following pitch.

B. There are two basic methods used in squaring around to bunt:

    1. **Back foot shuffle**—The back foot is moved forward so that the toes are parallel to each other. This method is usually the easiest to learn.

    2. **Heal-toe-pivot**—The hitter pivots on the heels of his front foot and the toe of his back foot. This method allows a smoother transition back to a hitting position when using a fake bunt-slash.

Whichever method is used, it is important that the hips and shoulders be square to the pitcher.

C. Once the batter has completed the squaring around movement (hips and shoulders square to the pitcher), there are two basic sacrifice bunting methods that can be used:

    1. **Level bat approach**

        a. Knees slightly bent.

        b. 70% of body weight on the front foot (this helps avoid lunging at the ball).

        c. Slide top hand up the bat to approximately the trademark area. The bat should be held in the fingers in a "pinching-like" grasp so as to avoid the fingers being hit by the ball and to achieve a softer "give" when the ball strikes the bat. The fingers should be on the bottom with the thumb on the top.

        d. Extend the arms forward at the top height of the strike zone with the bat parallel with the ground.

        e. The back of the bottom hand should be visable to the hitter with the elbow slightly bent away from the body.

        f. Be sure the bat covers the entire plate (this helps avoid "punching" or "jabbing" at the ball). Test this by dropping the bat. The bat should lie on the ground **in front** of the plate and extend completely across the width of the plate.

        g. From this position the bunter should attempt to keep his eyes in the same plane as the ball by merely bending at the knees.

    2. **Bat angle approach**

        a. Knees slightly bent.

        b. 70% of body weight on the front foot (this helps avoid lunging at the ball).

        c. Slide top hand up the bat to approximately the trademark area. The bat should be held in the fingers in a "pinching-like" grasp so as to avoid the fingers being hit by the ball and to achieve a softer "give" when the ball strikes the bat. The fingers should be on the bottom with the thumb on the top.

d. Extend the arms forward with the top hand at the top of the strike zone and the bottom hand approximately one foot lower.

e. From this position the bunter should attempt to keep his eyes in the same plane as the ball by merely bending at the knees.

f. When contacting the ball, keep the bat at the established angle. Any balls which are deflected off the bat will not be popped up, but will deflect back or down. While this is an advantage, it is probably the hardest of the two methods to master.

D. When bunting down the first base line, the righthanded hitter merely points the knob of his bat toward third base (the lefthanded hitter points the barrel toward third base). When bunting down the third base line, the righthanded hitter points the barrel toward first base (the lefthanded hitter points the knob toward first base).

E. It is important to stress the idea of not "jabbing" at the ball. The bunter should attempt to "catch the ball" on the bat.

2. Drag Bunting—Fundamentals

The ability to drag bunt can surely add an additional 10 or 15 points on a hitter's batting average. Proper execution and deception are the key ingredients. Speed, contrary to popular belief, is not the key ingredient.

An average runner will have excellent success if his execution and deception are well learned. Defensive alignments to prevent the drag against the "speedsters" almost always exist. This is not to de-emphasize the good runners from drag bunting, but the point to be made here is that the average runner is the man who will catch the defense back.

While teaching the drag bunt, three points should be stressed. First, showing the defense that a hitter is a potential drag bunter will move the corners in slightly. This of course will increase the opportunity for ground ball hits to go through the infield. This in itself is certainly one of the hidden advantages of being a drag bunting threat.

Secondly, patience is needed if a hitter is going to be a drag bunter. A hitter with a .300 batting average will not succeed in getting a hit 70% of the time. A good drag bunter will drag at least at a .300 clip. However, unsuccessful drag bunts are very discouraging much more so than not getting a hit while swinging at the ball. The coach must continue to encourage the drag to his good drag bunters. Stress again that poor bunts, particularly drag bunts, should go foul.

Thirdly, 90% of drag bunt attempts occur on the first pitch. If no attempt is made, many corner infielders will drop back. Perhaps the best time to drag bunt is after the first pitch.

In the baseball sign section of the Playbook, further explanations of drag bunting philosophy have already been presented. The following are the fundamentals involved with drag bunting:

A. Righthanded hitters

1. "Cheat up" in the batter's box slightly.

2. As the ball is released by the pitcher, move the right foot back slightly (away from home plate).

3. As the left hand pulls the knob down to a position approximately six inches in front of the right hip, slide the right hand up to the trademark area grasping the bat with the same grip as used in the sacrifice bunt.

4. Approach the ball with a level bat.

5. Be cautious not to transfer the body weight over the left foot too early. This causes the bunter to start running prior to bunting the ball which is a crucial mistake. Sacrifice one step toward first base for accurate placement of the bunted ball.

A. Lefthanded hitters

1. "Cheat up" in the batter's box slightly.

2. As the ball is released by the pitcher, the right foot should be opened slightly.

3. As the right hand pulls the knob down to a position approximately six inches in front of the left hip, slide the left hand up to the trademark area grasping the bat with the same grip as used in the sacrifice bunt.

4. Approach the ball with a level bat.

5. As the ball approaches, the weight is shifted to the right foot and the left foot begins to come forward directly toward the pitcher. This cross-over type step should always be toward the pitcher and should not be completed until after the bat has made contact with the ball.

6. The lefthanded hitter should be particularly cautious not to move toward first base too early. The location of the bunt is much more important than the additional step that drag bunters try to achieve so often. See the ball down prior to running to first base.

3. Push Bunting—Fundamentals

The push bunt is employed when the first baseman is playing back. Incentive is added when the pitcher falls off to the third base side of the mound and/or is slow covering first base. The ball is directed at a target between the first baseman and the second baseman. The ball must force the first baseman to the second base side forcing either the first baseman or the second baseman to field the ball. It must be hard enough to get by the pitcher and yet soft enough that the second baseman can not successfully handle the ball and throw the push bunt to the first baseman covering the base. As the touch and location of placement of the ball are much easier to achieve for a righthanded hitter, lefthanded batters will rarely use the push bunt. If the lefthanded hitter does attempt this bunt, his mechanics will be the same as the drag bunt. He must get the barrel out firmly extending the bat toward the ball, and then push the ball toward a point between the first baseman and second baseman.

A. Righthanded hitters push bunts

1. Attempt to push bunt balls that are over the middle of the plate or toward the outside of the plate. Assuming a batting stance away from the plate will help the push bunter get a good pitch to push.

2. After the ball is released, the batter should move his right hand up toward the trademark area in a similar grip with other bunts. Holding the bat with more firmness is important in the push bunt.

3. The arms should not be extended. Bring the knob of the bat close to the left side of the chest. The right hand should be in toward the body holding the bat level with the ground.

4. The weight is shifted to the front foot prior to contact. The right foot starts forward at contact.

5. The arms and hands should firmly extend the bat toward the ball, pushing the ball toward a point between first base and second base.

4. Fake Bunt and Slash—Fundamentals

This particular offensive tactic is used primarily when the defense is either playing in very close in a bunt defense or the defensive men are moving early to cover particular areas of the infield to defense the possible bunt. If the corner men are stationed on the infield grass and are charging on the pitch, the fake bunt slash can be an excellent offensive tactic. Also, if the second baseman and shortstop are moving early to cover either third, second, or first base, chances for success in this tactic are excellent.

A. Fake bunt slash technique (for both righthanded and lefthanded hitters)

1. Square around (heel-toe pivot) after the pitcher has come to his set position and is starting to commit himself to home plate. Squaring around too early will alert the defense that possibly a fake bunt is in order. Most pitchers will have a fairly set pattern as to how long they remain in the set position. Squaring around just as the pitcher moves from his set position to throw to home plate is the ideal time.

2. As the body is shifted into the heel-toe pivot approach, slide the top hand up the bat but not as far as the trademark area which is normally used. Be sure not to transfer your weight to the front leg as is normally done in the sacrifice bunt. You must look like you are setting up to bunt the ball to make the defense react to the bunted ball.

3. Just as the pitcher is releasing the ball, slide the bottom hand up to the top hand and bring the bat back to its original hitting position. At the same time, the heel-toe pivot is simply reversed bringing the body back in the hitting position.

4. Obviously, little time is allowed for a full inward rotation or full swing. However, a good, short, compact stroke can be achieved. It is important to try to drive the ball on the ground as the infield will most likely be somewhat out of position. The pitch must be a strike before swinging.

The fake bunt slash can also be employed as a hit and run tactic. If this is employed, the hitter then must swing at the pitch whether it is a strike or not providing it is not in the dirt. The batter must again attempt to hit the ball on the ground. This is more important off the hit and run than off the fake bunt slash.

PITCHING

There is general agreement among baseball people that pitching is the most important facet of the game. A team's success in the won-loss column is generally reflected by the overall effectiveness of the pitching staff.

Due to the importance of pitching, the baseball coach needs to spend a great deal of time in the training and development of his pitching staff. It is recommended that a head coach fortunate enough to have an assistant coach, assign this coach with the task of working with the pitchers. If the assistant coach does not have the background to work with the pitchers, then the head coach should take on this responsibility. The pitchers need a great deal of attention in the area of training and fundamental development, and this takes the expertise of a knowledgeable coach.

This section of the Playbook will deal in detail with the basic fundamentals of pitching. Along with these fundamentals, various other aspects of pitching will be presented outside of the mechanical skills involved in pitching a baseball. As is the case with hitters, each individual pitcher has his own strengths and weaknesses and it is the responsibility of the coach assigned to the pitchers to help correct these weaknesses along with building on the individual pitcher's strength areas. The baseball coach needs to be aware that physical stature does not make or break a pitcher. A number of great pitchers have been young men of small stature. If a boy has a good arm along with innate athletic ability he can be developed into a quality pitcher. This may take a little time and effort on the coach's part, but it will certainly pay dividends in a team's success. There is a lot of truth in the statement "as the pitching staff goes the baseball team goes".

The first part of the pitching section will deal with the actual mechanics of pitching. In developing a pitcher's mechanics, the coach is attempting to eliminate those mechanical factors that would not allow the pitcher to generate the maximum speed, rotation and location on the pitched ball that his ability allows him. Every pitcher will not look the same as he throws the baseball, and the coach that attempts to develop his pitching staffs' basic fundamentals around a set pattern will find that what might work for one pitcher might not work with another pitcher. The coach needs to develop a pitcher around that young man's capabilities, not on the capabilities of any other pitcher on his staff.

In dealing with the mechanics of pitching, we will be referring to the mechanics as applied to a righthanded pitcher. The mechanics for the lefthanded pitcher would simply be the reverse of the righthander. We will deal first with the pitcher throwing from the windup followed by the mechanics for the stretch delivery.

WINDUP

1. Stance on the mound

A. The stance should be relaxed so that the pitcher uses as little energy as possible. He should further conserve energy by not walking around the mound unnecessarily. He must keep tension at a minimum by taking nice easy breaths between pitches.

B. The pitcher's stance should be square to the plate. The shoulders and hips should be facing the plate which will enable him to take a full turn on the rubber when he begins his actual pivot in the windup.

C. The feet should be a comfortable distance apart so that he can remain erect in taking his sign from the catcher. It is recommended that the feet be approximately six to twelve inches apart.

D. The throwing arm should be extended comfortably to his side to further reduce any tension in the arm and shoulder.

2. Pivot foot

A. Pitchers should be discouraged from moving around on the rubber with their pivot foot. It is not a good practice to move the pivot foot on the rubber to gain better control. It is recommended that the righthanded pitcher have his pivot foot near the right corner of the rubber, while the lefthanded pitcher should have his pivot foot near the left corner of the rubber. This provides the pitcher with the best angle to the outside half of the plate. It further allows him to throw his breaking pitch at the middle of the plate attempting to hit the outside corner of the plate with a little more frequency at a better angle. Pitching from near the corner of the rubber will reduce the pitcher's chances of throwing across his body, which will be discussed later in this section. The final advantage of pitching from near the end of the rubber is that it gives the hitter a more difficult angle from which to see the pitch and hides better the spin and rotation on the ball.

B. The pivot foot should be in contact with the rubber with the ball of the foot extending over the front edge. The pivot foot should point forward and a little toward the third base line.

C. The pitcher's weight should be primarily on the front pivot foot. This will enable him to transfer his weight back more easily as he begins the movement into the windup.

3. Beginning of the windup

A. The primary purpose of the windup is to transfer the body weight back to gather up the force and power to deliver the pitch to the plate.

B. During the initial movement into the windup, the pitcher's body should be relaxed and void of tension. This will allow the body to function to the maximum in delivering the pitch.

C. As the pitcher begins the windup he should have his head up with his eyes on the target. His eyes should remain on the target throughout the delivery.

D. The pitcher must not step too far back with his left foot (non-pivot foot) as he begins his motion into the windup. This could lead to rushing if the pitcher steps too far back with the left foot, for then he would have to generate additional force to move the left leg back forward. The distance back with the left foot should be no farther than six to eight inches in length from where the pitcher assumed his stance as he takes the sign from the catcher.

E. As the weight is shifted back to the rear foot the pitcher's arms will come up toward his head. It is important that the pitcher move his hands and arms in a direction that is toward the plate. If he was to move the hands and arms outward toward either first or third base it could cause an improper arm action as the pitcher continues with the windup delivery. Thus, arm action in the windup should always be vertical and not horizontal.

F. The preliminary motion of the rear foot and the movement of the hands and arms must be consistent on every pitch.

4. Hiding the ball

A. The pitcher must attempt to hide the ball from the hitter during the windup. This can be done by placing the hand deep in the glove which would easily cover the ball and wrist from the batter's view. The back of the glove should remain toward the plate. If the pitcher brings his hands back well over his head in the windup, it makes it much easier for the hitter to see the wrist and ball in the glove. This is one of the reasons why a pitcher should not bring his hands too far over or behind the head.

B. The ball should remain hidden behind the glove and body throughout the delivery. The first time the hitter should see the ball is when the arm is up and the ball is just about to be released from the hand.

5. No windup delivery

A. Many pitchers have gone to the no windup delivery whereby they do not bring their hands up over their head as they prepare to pivot on the rubber. This type of delivery can be used when a pitcher's windup is not consistent on every pitch, and he has a difficult time maintaining proper body balance with the conventional windup. The pitching coach might experiment with the no windup delivery if a pitcher's full windup is not allowing him to gather his body in the proper manner to deliver the ball to the plate.

B. The no windup delivery can also be used by the pitcher who might be having control problems pitching with the full windup. This is especially the case for the pitcher whose full windup is causing him problems in gaining the proper balance point as his pivots on the rubber.

C. The no windup delivery also might aid the pitcher who might have a difficult time hiding the ball from the batter.

6. Double pump windup

A. A variation of the conventional windup would be when the pitcher executes the double pump windup. The pitcher

307

would merely execute the preliminary motion of the windup by bringing his hands up to his head as he normally would. He would then drop his hands down and start the windup again as he rocks back with his non-pivot foot.

B. This is an excellent move for the pitcher to perform a few times in a game. Its purpose is to hinder the concentration and rhythm of the hitter.

7. Positioning of pivot foot on rubber during pivot

A. The actual pivot on the rubber should be executed without the pivot foot lifting off the rubber. When completed, the pivot foot toe is pointing toward third base with the entire outside portion of the foot in solid contact with the home plate side of the pitching rubber.

B. He should not be pivoting on top of the pitching rubber since this would not allow for an effective push off the rubber. This also puts the pivot foot in a very unstable position. It is also recommended that the pivot foot not be half on and half off the rubber while starting movement toward home plate as this provides for a poor base for needed balance.

8. First balance point

A. The pitcher can not afford to keep his hands near or behind his head in the windup for too long a period of time. If he does then he will have a tendency to begin lifting his stride leg before the hands reach the belt area where they need to be when he reaches the first balance point.

B. The pitcher needs to move his hands from near or behind his head down to the belt line area by the time the stride leg has been lifted off the ground.

C. The pivot leg should be slightly bent at the knee to afford the pitcher the proper balance as he prepares the body for the drive toward the plate.

D. As the hands reach the belt area, the lead leg is lifted off the ground so that the thigh is parallel to the ground. Thus, the pitcher has now reached the first balance point in his delivery. At this point the following is in effect: he is balanced on the rear pivot leg which is bent slightly at the knee; the stride leg is up so that the thigh is parallel to the ground; the hands are down in the area of the belt; and the shoulders and hips are closed so that they are facing the area near third base.

E. At this balance point, the pitcher's body should not be moving toward the plate. If so, he will find that he will be rushing his delivery which will cause problems in his mechanics as he releases from the first balance point.

9. Shoulder and hip pivot

A. At the time the pitcher reaches the first balance point he should have achieved a full pivot of the hips and shoulders so that the hitter should be able to see the left rear pocket of the pitcher, along with seeing some part of the number(s) on the pitcher's back. The hitter should not be able to clearly see the number(s). If that is the case, the pitcher has pivoted too far with his hips and shoulders past the 90 degree mark. Any pivot past the 90 degree mark serves no useful purpose in providing additional power on the delivery to the plate.

B. The pitcher must keep his left shoulder closed to the hitter to ensure that his weight is well balanced over the pivot foot. If the front shoulder is open as the pitcher pivots it will not allow him to be properly balanced as he leaves the first balance point in the delivery.

C. Very few pitchers are effective with a high leg kick, a larger degree of turn than 90 degrees with their hips and shoulders, and an unorthodox first balance point. However, if a pitcher is successful with an unusual type of delivery, leave him alone. If they are unsuccessful with an unconventional delivery in reaching the first balance point, they need to work on the mechanics mentioned.

10. Rushing

A. Rushing the delivery is one of the greatest problems for most pitchers. If the boy's body weight moves out too soon toward the plate, a rushing arm action will develop. This generally brings about control problems, loss of velocity, short-arming and arm soreness. Pitches will generally be high, the breaking pitch will be flat, and the pitcher will not be able to achieve a mechanically smooth delivery.

B. If the stride leg lands and the throwing arm is still back, the pitcher will have a pulling motion of the throwing arm instead of having the arm in full coordination with the body. The arm will attempt to "catch up" with the body.

C. When a pitcher is rushing it is practically impossible for him to "get on top of the ball". His arm will try to "catch up" with the body by taking a shorter arm arc which leads many times to him dropping his elbow and short-arming the pitch to the plate.

D. The pitcher who attempts to drive his body to the plate to achieve additional velocity and power in his delivery will find that this generally leads to rushing the delivery. He ends up throwing just with his arm as the body is so far ahead of the arm. This is the cause for numerous arm injuries.

E. In eliminating rushing, the pitcher needs to achieve the first balance point completely under control of his body. Prior to the drive of the back leg forward, the throwing arm must drop down, back and up. As this takes place, the front shoulder opens and the pitcher's weight transfers forward to the front side as the back leg drives toward the plate.

11. Taking the ball out of the glove

A. The proper arm action begins with the break of the hands from the first balance point. At the time the ball is taken from the glove, the palm of the throwing hand should be facing the ground. If the ball is taken out of the glove with the palm facing up, it will lead to an improper arm arc and cause a reduction in hand speed.

B. The wrist should be bent forward slightly as the ball leaves the glove at the area of the belt. The forward wrist and palm down action of the hand should be maintained throughout the down, back and up movement of the arm. The palm will turn up and the wrist will snap back and then forward only as the arm starts moving toward the plate.

12. Second balance point and power position

A. Before driving forward, several actions must take place first: the separation of the hands; the arm swing down, back and up; the upper body (shoulders and hips) properly pivoted; and the lead leg and pivot leg in the first balanced position.

B. At this point in the delivery, the arm is now up and preparing to accelerate forward to release the ball in the proper downward plane. The body should assist the arm in this process by staying closed until that time that the arm is up and ready to deliver the ball.

13. Short arming the ball

A. A pitcher who is classified as a short-armer is one who throws with a restricted full arm action. Instead of getting a full, free arm extension, the arm takes a much shorter path from the separation of the hands to the release point. Of course, the mechanical advantage of an arm is enhanced greatly by the long arm action. The longer the arm arc the greater will be the power generated in the pitch. Most good pitchers have a full, free arm extension from the breaking of the hands to the release point.

B. The full and free arm action can be severely hampered if the pitcher is a rusher with his body. When the pitcher's body moves toward the plate too quickly, the arm will have a tendency to shorten up in order to catch up with the body.

14. Arm hook

A. Any movement of the throwing arm out of the separation of the hands from the first balance point must be down and back toward second base. Many pitchers are guilty of arm hooking when they bring their throwing arm down and then hook the arm in the direction of first base. This movement of the throwing arm takes the arm out of the proper plane of arm action.

B. Arm hooking will result in a reduction of hand speed, can cause severe control problems and may cause arm fatigue and soreness.

C. Due to the irregular path, the arm will take a little longer getting to the release point. If the pitcher does not wait with his body for the arm to get to the proper release point after arm hooking, he will rush his delivery causing him to short arm the ball, drop his elbow, and push the ball to the plate.

15. **Opening up the body for the stride**

A. In the first balance point, the stride leg is up and the front shoulder and hip are closed. The throwing arm has now had the opportunity to swing down, back and up as the pitcher starts foward but has not exploded with his body toward the plate.

B. The lead leg should come up with the toe pointing down and it should not be swung backward past the rubber. Swinging the lead leg past the rubber serves no useful purpose in the delivery.

C. While the hips will open as the stride is made, the upper body should stay closed until the arm has reached the top of the backswing and is preparing to move toward the plate. The shoulders should open up as the arm and hand move toward the release area. The pitcher can not afford to open the front shoulder as he begins the stride for he will lose much of his power in the delivery.

16. **Stride**

A. The stride toward the plate is a very important aspect of the pitching delivery. The stride must be consistent in order to minimize variations in the release point of the ball.

B. It is important for the pitcher to step straight forward with his stride foot. The stride should be comfortable and natural for the pitching delivery of the individual pitcher.

C. The length of the stride would depend on the pitcher's height and his physical structure. Overstriding should be guarded against since it mechanically puts the pitcher's throwing arm at a disadvantage in achieving the downward plane on release. The pitcher who overstrides will generally pitch high and have very little break on the breaking pitch as a rule.

D. The pitcher should not stride so that his stride foot lands too far to the third base side of a line from his pivot foot to home plate. This is commonly referred to as throwing across the body. This will lock the pitcher's hips and cause him to throw against his front leg.

E. At the same time, the pitcher should not open too much with his stride foot. The pitcher who strides too far to the first base side will generally open up his hips and shoulders too fast, causing a loss of power. Since the hips and shoulders must stay closed as long as possible to provide the power to the delivery, opening up too far with the stride foot can cause the pitcher to become a "thrower" or "slinger" without proper body leverage.

F. Thus, the stride foot should land as close as possible near the imaginary line drawn from the pivot foot to the plate. Many pitchers find that stepping just a few inches toward the third base side of this line will keep their shoulders and hips closed slightly longer providing additional power to their delivery.

G. As the stride foot hits the ground, the shock should be absorbed on the ball of the foot. If a boy lands on his heels it would cause him to lock his front knee which in turn would jar the head and eyes causing an improper delivery and follow-through.

H. One of the key points in the stride is that the knee of the striding leg should remain bent when the foot lands. This bent knee should be flexible so that it will give with the pitch and enable the pitcher to have a smooth follow-through.

I. The pitcher's toe should be pointed toward the plate on contact with the ground. It is important that he step in the same spot on each pitch, although the pitcher would generally shorten his stride when throwing the breaking pitch.

J. The pitcher should not rush his stride by rushing out with the bottom half of his body. Many pitchers kick out too soon and too quick with their striding leg which compounds the problem with rushing through the delivery.

K. The pitcher should not kick out with his striding leg as he prepares to stride toward the plate. This will cause the boy to arch his back and prevent the thrust of his power from going directly toward the plate. This kick of the lead leg will also have a tendency to slow the arm action down, making it difficult to get the elbow up into the correct position.

310

17. Lead arm action

A. When the lead or glove hand comes forward, the hitter should only be able to see the back of the pitcher's glove. If the pitcher has his palm facing the ground, it may cause him to open up his lead shoulder too quick causing the pitcher to drop his throwing arm and elbow. The correct action of the lead arm will keep the lead shoulder closed that much longer.

B. Many coaches tell their pitchers to throw their lead arm at the hitter in hopes that it will hide the ball from the hitter that much longer. This is poor advice because in this case, both arms would be going in opposite directions at the same time. It is much easier if the pitcher's glove hand goes back with his throwing hand, and then forward with the throwing hand. As the throwing hand follows through, the glove should move toward the pitcher's body facing the chest.

C. The glove hand should be kept above the elbow of the lead arm. If the pitcher should drop the hand below the elbow, his lead elbow will be up, which could in turn force his lead shoulder up. This would in turn cause him to drop his back shoulder resulting in him not being able to get on top of the ball.

D. By the pitcher keeping the elbow of the glove hand next to his side, he is in a much better position to field a well hit ball back at him.

18. Throwing arm action

A. It is important for the coach to find the best angle of delivery for each of his pitchers. The arm action should be a smooth, free movement with as little muscular tension as possible.

B. To determine a boy's natural way of throwing, hit him some fungos in the outfield and watch him throw the ball back. That generally will be his natural way of throwing and the way he should pitch.

C. To find the best arm angle and release point that will produce the most power for the individual pitcher, you can experiment with your pitchers by standing in front of them and clasping their hand at different release points and angles and see from which point (straight-overhand, three-quarters, or sidearm) they can deliver the most force against your hand.

D. The greater the arm angle downward, the greater mechanical advantage the pitcher will have in his delivery to the plate. The farther the hand goes away from the head at the point of release, the less mechanical advantage the pitcher has. The elbow must be up, at shoulder level or above. If a pitch is made with a dropped elbow, the pitcher's hand will be traveling almost parallel to the ground and he can not pitch on a downward plane. Of course, there are successful pitchers who pitch three-quarters or sidearm so this can not be a hard and fast rule for all pitchers. These pitchers must have a lot of movement on their ball or else they will not be effective at these types of arm slots.

E. If a pitcher thinks in terms of breaking his hands quickly the right arm has an opportunity to swing down, back and up, with the weight still on the right pivot leg. Now, the pitcher is in a position to explode, releasing the ball on a downward plane.

F. A pitcher can not afford to be lazy with his pitching hand and arm. He should always reach out when throwing with the feeling that his arm is accelerating in front of the body.

G. Although the actual release point is above and somewhere in front of the head, the pitcher must think about releasing the ball well out in front of his body to achieve maximum effectiveness. In other words, he must think low when releasing the ball. After coming over the top, he must release the ball with his fingers on top of the ball, imparting strong wrist action.

H. When the pitcher's arm starts forward, the wrist should bend back. The elbow will lead first followed by the forward action of the arm and wrist. The forearm should be kept as perpendicular to the ground as possible.

19. Wrist action

A. The arm and wrist should be loose and relaxed as the ball is released with good wrist snap. When the arm moves toward the release point, the wrist will flip back and then snap forward as the ball is being released.

B. The index and middle fingers are pulled downward on the ball to insure that the proper spin is imparted on the ball.

20. **Release**

A. The final segment of the delivery is the release of the ball and follow-through. As previously mentioned, the movement should all be coordinated with the thrust of the legs, hips, shoulders and throwing arm.

B. The rear pivot leg should drive the weight onto the bent stride leg. Simultaneously with this action, the hips and shoulders should be opened. It is important that the lead shoulder be moved down and slightly toward the first baseline, which will keep the rear shoulder higher than the lead shoulder at release.

C. Upon release, the elbow must be at least as high as the shoulder to insure that the pitcher keeps the ball down and can establish an effective breaking pitch.

D. The eyes must remain on the catcher's target throughout the delivery and release. It is important that the head not be moved too far to the left at release. If that occurs, the pitcher will have a difficult time keeping his eye on the target. It will also cause the pitcher's upper body to open up too far causing him to lose power and having a difficult time keeping the ball down in the strike zone.

E. The pitcher must think about releasing the ball well out in front of the body even though the actual release point is above the head. He must think low when releasing the ball to achieve the downward plane of the ball from his hand.

F. The pitcher must develop a consistent point of release for control purposes. By throwing the ball over and over in the bullpen, in batting practice and in game situations, he should get the feeling of the proper release point for all his pitches.

21. **Follow-through**

A. A good follow-through is important for speed, control, and setting the pitcher up to be in a position to field the ball. The pitcher who falls to the glove side will generally not get the hip and shoulder rotation necessary to provide power in the pitch.

B. The weight should be over the stride foot on the follow-through. The pivot leg should continue to provide the force in the delivery by coming off the rubber with the heel up providing force for the right hip to drive toward the plate. If the pitcher does not explode with the back hip, he will lose power in his delivery.

C. The throwing arm should follow-through and finish to the first base side of the stride leg. A smooth follow-through will help eliminate strain on the pitcher's arm and add movement to all pitches. A pitching motion which stops abruptly upon release of the ball would retard the speed and control of the pitch.

D. The pivot leg foot should swing around to a position almost parallel to the stride foot. From this position the pitcher is in a proper position to become a fielder.

STRETCH DELIVERY—SET POSITION

1. The rules state that the pitcher in the stretch position must have his rear pivot foot in contact with the pitching rubber and the other foot forward. The ball must be held in both hands in front of the pitcher's body. In the preliminary stretch, the hands must come together with a pause before delivering to the plate.

2. It is recommended for all pitchers to have their toes parallel to each other in the set position with the feet about 12 to 18 inches apart. Most of the weight should be on the rear foot as he assumes the set position to check the runner(s).

3. The overhand pitcher should pitch from a squared away stance (toes parallel). The overhand pitcher starts his delivery with a slight dropping of the back shoulder as he bends his right pivot leg for the push off the rubber. The correct front shoulder action is up and down. The squared stance is an advantage to the pitcher because he simply will pick up the lead leg, drop the rear shoulder slightly, and then drive toward the plate.

4. The three-quarter or sidearm pitcher might want to assume a slightly open stance from the stretch with his left toe facing a few inches toward first base. The three-quarter or sidearm pitcher will want to rotate his shoulder slightly from left to right and the open stance will allow him better to roll into the delivery.

5. The front shoulder should be in a direct line with the plate. If the pitcher has his front shoulder toward first base the runner will get a good jump when he turns it back toward the plate for the pitch. If the righthanded pitcher has a difficult time seeing the runner at first base he can open the shoulder slightly. By tucking the chin down from the set, he should find that he will be in a better position to see the runner at first base.

6. There should be a slight flexion of the right leg in the set position. A pitcher should never stand with his legs straight and stiff from the stretch.

7. The pitching action in the set position is similar to the windup delivery except that the action is speeded up by using a lower leg kick, a lesser body turn of the shoulders and hips, and a hard push off the rubber.

8. The pitcher must develop his techniques from the stretch position so that he does not have an exaggerated leg kick which would give the runner(s) a tremendous jump on the steal or hit and run.

9. From the set position the pitcher's hands should be above the belt line. If they are below the belt the hands would have to come all the way up to the chest area before they break. This would cost the pitcher valuable time in his delivery to the plate. When the stride leg comes off the ground the hands should move up to the area where the hands would separate. The pitcher who brings his hands up without coordinating this movement with the lifting of the stride leg will lose valuable time in delivering the pitch to the plate.

10. The pitcher who breaks his hands without first lifting them slightly generally fails to keep his weight back, which would cause him to rush his delivery which would mean a serious loss of power in the pitch.

BASIC PITCHES

FAST BALL

The fast ball can not be taught by a coach to a pitcher as much as the breaking pitch and change-up might be taught. The fast ball must be developed over a long period of time from an early age until the necessary strength, coordination and force are in existence to allow the pitcher to deliver the ball at a high degree of velocity. While it might take a few weeks to develop a respectable curve ball or breaking pitch, it generally requires years to develop the good live fast ball.

Being an effective pitcher does not mean a boy must have an over-powering fast ball. Of course, the harder a young man can throw the ball the more effective he should be as a pitcher as long as he can control the pitch and establish some movement of the ball as it is delivered to the plate. A pitcher who throws a great fast ball with little control or movement will find that his effectiveness in getting hitters out will be diminished due to the fact that hitters can "groove" their swing to the boy's fast ball. By establishing a good breaking pitch and off-speed pitch, a pitcher will make his fast ball that much more effective.

Many baseball coaches believe that a boy is born to throw the fast ball just as some coaches believe that hitters are born to hit. We believe that this is partially true, but we have seen numerous examples of boys who can throw the good hard fast ball who were not gifted with the body structure that generally coincides with the ability to throw hard. The classic body structure for a pitcher that throws hard would be: (1) a tall and lean boy with long arms and big hands; (2) flexible arms and a strong loose wrist; and (3) well-coordinated athlete with long sinewy muscles.

If a pitcher is not fortunate enough to be anatomically structured to meet the requirements for a born fast ball pitcher, he should not give up all hope. He can still become a "hard thrower" by developing his talents around his own capabilities and limitations. This can be done in the way of a strength program, a lot of throwing under supervision of a knowledgeable pitching coach, and "fine tuning" of his mechanics to assist him in getting the maximum out of his ability. Since all pitchers are not six feet—four inches tall, weigh 195 pounds, have long arms and hands, long muscles, a live flexible arm and wrist, and are very well coordinated, a coach can still assist a pitcher in developing his fast ball skills without the benefit of these traits.

The fast ball can be improved by adhering to certain basic fundamentals. Following is a summary of these fundamentals that a pitcher must develop in order to have an effective fast ball.

313

1. **Grip**

   A. There are two basic types of grips used in throwing the fast ball: (1) across the seams; and (2) with the seams.

   1. **Across the seams**—Many pitchers grip the fast ball across the seams at the widest part in order to achieve the four seam rotation as the ball leaves the index and middle finger in a six-to-twelve rotation. Other pitchers grip the ball across the seams at the narrowest point. This is especially true for pitchers who have very short fingers. Gripping the ball across the wide seams allows the thumb to also grip a seam providing more of a feel to the ball. The across the seams grip is used by pitchers who are hard throwers and wish to have their fast ball "rise" as it is delivered to the plate. The ball does not actually "rise" but since it has the six-to-twelve rotation it does not have the tendency to drop or sink on its path to the plate. A pitcher can generally throw his fast ball a little harder with either of these across the seam grips, but will find that the ball has very little movement.

   2. **With the seams**—If a pitcher is having a difficult time getting his fast ball to move, he can grip the ball with the seams. He can do this along the narrowest point of the seams, or he can do this along the widest point of the seams. When throwing the fast ball with the seams, the pitcher will have a better chance of establishing some movement in the pitch on its way to the plate. This might be at the expense of control and velocity, but this is purely an individual matter for each pitcher. A pitcher needs to experiment with the various seam grips to find one that feels comfortable to him and allows him the chance to establish some movement on his ball. A fast ball thrown with very little movement can be quite hittable unless it is thrown with a great deal of velocity along with good location.

   B. It is very important that the ball be gripped firmly as far out toward the fingertips as possible. Holding the fast ball further back in the hand does not permit active finger action on the ball and takes away from the flexibility in the wrist and hand as the ball is released. The ball should not be gripped tight for it will lock the wrist and finger muscles, reducing their range of motion. A too-tight grip also induces advanced muscle fatigue that contributes to poorly timed ball releases and control problems. There should be space between the ball and the palm of the hand so that a finger can easily be moved in and out of the space when the pitcher has his fast ball grip.

   C. The index and middle fingers should not be too far apart when gripping the fast ball. When the fingers are too far apart it tends to lock the wrist and prevent good movement of the wrist as the fast ball is being released. At the same time, the index and middle finger should not be too close together. If so, it can cause severe control problems since the ball can easily slide off the fingers as the ball is being released. A recommended distance between the index and middle finger is about one inch.

   D. In order for a fast ball to achieve some movement on its way to the plate, the ball must be released in such a manner that the "true" six-to-twelve rotation is not in effect. There are various ways that this can be done:

   1. By holding the ball slightly off center with the index and middle fingers so that the ball leaves the pitcher's hand with the fingers not on top of the ball.

   2. By varying the thumb position on the ball it will have an affect on how the ball leaves the pitcher's hand. Remember that an unbalanced finger or thumb placement may allow the ball to move but it generally occurs at the expense of some velocity.

   3. By tilting the wrist slightly as the ball is being released it will cause the ball to leave the fingers so that movement should occur. This is due to the fact that the ball will leave the fingers at an angle away from the strict vertical plane.

   4. By dropping the arm slot away from the strict over-the-top delivery should assist in getting some movement on the fast ball. This does not mean that the pitcher has to drop down to a three-quarters or even sidearm delivery to get this movement.

   5. By changing the finger pressure on the ball so that there is an unequal amount of pressure applied by the index and middle finger as the ball leaves the hand.

2. **Arm and wrist action**

   A. Each individual pitcher has an angle of delivery from which his fast ball is most effective. The degree of effectiveness lies in the area of velocity, movement and control. The pitching coach should assist the young pitcher in finding what arm slot is best for him so that the pitcher might develop a high degree of consistency with his fast ball. It is not recommended that the pitcher change his arm slot from pitch to pitch for this would seriously affect his control. In pre-season workouts the pitcher might experiment with some different arm slots for his fast ball to see what feels comfortable. If a pitcher does not have a "live" arm he will probably have a little more success dropping down a little so that he might obtain some movement on his fast ball. If the pitcher has a good "live" arm he should pitch from over the top unless he finds that his fast ball is more effective with a different arm slot.

B. The arm and wrist must always be loose and relaxed from the time the pitcher breaks his hands. This will allow him to get maximum movement and velocity on his fast ball. A pitcher who attempts to throw his fast ball at maximum velocity will generally find that this action will tighten his arm and wrist muscles causing a loss of velocity and restricted movement on the ball. It will also severely hinder the control of the pitch since the pitcher generally will overthrow with the use of his body rather than just increasing arm speed. It is best for a pitcher to throw his fast ball at about 95% velocity to insure that he does not overthrow the ball. This will also aid the pitcher in throwing with the all important rhythm that is characteristic of successful pitchers.

3. Variations of the fast ball

There are numerous types of fast balls which can be thrown by the pitcher. It is important that the pitcher establish consistency with his basic fast ball before he starts experimenting with other ways to deliver the ball to the plate. If a pitcher can give the hitter a couple of different "looks" to his fast ball, it will make him that much more effective. Following are some variations of the fast ball:

A. Sinking fast ball

1. If thrown properly, the sinking fast ball is a very effective pitch since the ball will have a tendency to sink on its way to the plate. It is an ideal pitch to deliver in double play situations as it generally produces ground balls.

2. The sinking fast ball should be thrown with the seams. When the pitcher looks at the ball in his hand he should be able to see the wide seam to the right of his middle finger. The middle finger should be placed right next to the seam, not on top of it.

3. The sinker is thrown with a three-quarters to sidearm motion. This will automatically allow the wrist to be turned slightly as the ball is released.

4. The thumb plays an important role in the sinker. The ball can be off-centered by moving the thumb up slightly to the side of the little finger. The ball will literally turn over the thumb upon release.

5. It is important to exert pressure with the index finger as the ball is released. To get the idea of the sinker, the pitcher should hold the ball out away from him and slightly behind his right ear. The index and middle finger are behind the ball and the thumb in front. As he rotates the hand inward and downward he will be looking at the back of his hand as the ball turns over the thumb by exerting pressure with the index finger. This is why the sinker is commonly called "the turn over fast ball".

6. In throwing a good sinker, the pitcher must utilize a body action which will drive him toward the hitter in a lower position than his fast ball and other pitches. The drop and go movement will allow him to stay on top of the ball, cutting and releasing it at the last moment, well out in front of the body.

7. By bending the right pivot knee, the body drops down and then is pushed forward. The throwing arm is extended across the body with the follow-through carrying the arm completely across the body.

8. The turn of the arm is more important than the flip of the wrist, prior to the point of release. The arm movement sweeping across the body gives the sinker a downward rotation. The pitch is released off the right corner tip of the middle finger. The pitcher must stay on top of the ball until the actual point of release.

9. The sinker ball is a very difficult pitch to master because of the unorthodox motion of the release. However, the sinking fast ball when thrown properly is one of the best pitches that a pitcher can throw due to the fact that the ball will move downward as it approaches the plate.

315

B. **Rising fast ball**

    1. The rising fast ball is gripped across the wide seams to get four seam rotation. The fingers are slightly spread so that the middle and index fingers even up to provide for equal finger pressure (six-to-twelve rotation).

    2. The ring and little finger are bent and curled under the side of the ball. The ball can be thrown with a three-quarters to overhand release. If thrown three-quarters the ball will have a tendency to ride in on the righthanded hitter (from a righthanded pitcher). If thrown overhand the ball will have a tendency to "rise" due to the nature of the spin imparted to the ball on release.

C. **Running fast ball**

    1. The running fast ball is gripped along the narrow seams and released with a three-quarters delivery. The finger pressure is applied by the index finger and imparts an eight-to-two rotation on the ball.

    2. This is the type of pitch that a pitcher who has had trouble getting movement on the ball should attempt to throw. Rather than releasing the ball with equal pressure on the index and middle finger, he will exert more pressure on the index finger as the ball is released. The fast ball spin remains with the wrist still snapping forward as with the conventional fast ball.

D. **Tailing fast ball**

    1. The tailing fast ball is gripped just like the rising fast ball but is released somewhat sidearm off the ends of the fingers with a three-to-nine rotation.

    2. Just as in the conventional fast ball the finger pressure must remain equalized between the index and middle finger.

CURVE BALL

    The curve ball is a pitch that can "make or break the pitcher". If a pitcher does not have an effective breaking pitch, the hitters can "sit" on his fast ball. No matter how hard a pitcher can throw the fast ball, good hitters can eventually time the ball and start making good contact. The curve ball added to a pitcher's arsenal forces the batter to contend with the vertical and horizontal movement of the ball.

    Fundamentally, a curve ball is used to fool the hitter, to disrupt his timing, and to keep him off balance. If thrown properly, the pitch should not put a strain on the pitcher's arm. If thrown incorrectly the curve ball can cause severe arm problems due to the nature of the movement of the arm and shoulder in imparting spin on the ball. The pitching coach must be sure to teach the curve ball in the proper sequence and not allow the young pitcher to throw a hard curve ball until he masters the basic fundamentals.

    It is important to understand how a pitched baseball curves on its way to the plate. When a ball is in flight but not spinning, it is exposed to a uniform air flow in one direction, and it follows in a straight line. When the ball is made to rotate sideways, friction between the ball and the air around it forms a sort of whirlpool or eddy. When this happens, the air flow is no longer in one direction; the whirlpool brings another force into play. This double force on only one side of the ball produces a lateral force which drives it in the direction toward which it is spinning. Thus, the tighter and quicker the spin, the greater the movement of the ball in the direction of the spin.

    A pitched baseball will travel in a uniformly curved path from the time it leaves the pitcher's hand until it reaches the catcher's glove. There is no such thing as a sharp breaking curve, in the sense that a ball can be thrown so that it flies in a straight line and then suddenly veers off. To an observer at or behind the plate, it appears that the ball travels fairly straight most of the way and then breaks suddenly and sharply near the plate. Actually, the curve ball arcs toward or away from the plate throughout its flight. The quicker the pitch is thrown along with the tightness of the spin will dictate what the hitter actually sees of the ball as it breaks. The batter, because he views the flight of the ball at an angle, can not discern the gradual arc of the ball and believes at times that the ball actually curves right at the last second prior to reaching the plate.

    A curve ball breaks more on a damp day when the air is heavy, and at high altitudes a curve is little more than a "wrinkle"

316

due to the rarified atmosphere prevalent there. Along with that, a curve ball pitcher operates more effectively when throwing into the wind.

The following are the basic fundamentals for throwing the curve ball:

1. **Grip**

   A. There are basic principles for gripping the curve ball, although there are numerous variations from this grip. The ball should be gripped loosely but firmly. It should be held well out on the fingers in order to insure that the ball is not choked back in the palm of the hand. In relation to the fast ball, the curve ball is not gripped quite as far out in the fingers, but it should not be choked as this creates problems with obtaining a tight spin. The further back in the hand that the ball is held the less chance for the pitcher to impart the proper spin on the ball. If the pitcher grips the curve ball too tightly with his fingers, he will find that his wrist will automatically tighten up which will severely restrict the proper release of the curve ball.

   B. The middle finger needs to be resting against the seam at either the narrowest point of the seams on the baseball or at the widest point of the seams. Most pitchers prefer to grip the curve ball along the narrow seams. The index finger should be a little closer to the middle finger than in the fast ball grip, but this is an individual matter for the pitcher. The thumb should be opposite the index and middle finger with a loose grip as well.

   C. Firm pressure should be exerted between the thumb and the middle finger, with the index finger resting loosely on the ball.

2. **Arm and hand action**

   A. The initial arm action in throwing the curve ball should be identical with that for the fast ball. Many pitchers pull the ball out of the glove with the throwing hand already wrapped for the curve ball release which causes the arm to slow down as it is brought back and then up to release the ball. The pitcher must think fast ball out of the glove and not worry about imparting the curve ball rotation on the ball until just prior to release. Wrapping leads to a slow breaking curve ball.

   B. The pitcher's arm should be away from the body as his elbow starts forward first. The pitch really starts to take shape when the arm reaches a point behind the right ear (righthanded pitcher). The entire arm must be involved in the motion, which will be down and across the chest.

   C. The curve ball should be thrown with a raised bent elbow with the arm straightening out as the ball is released. Throwing the curve ball properly entails the extension of the elbow and an inward rotation of the wrist so that, on release of the ball, the palm is facing the pitcher and the back of the hand is toward the hitter.

   D. The elbow should always be above the shoulder when the curve ball is being thrown. It is also important that the throwing arm shoulder be above the lead shoulder when the ball is released so that the pitcher is releasing the ball down hill. If not, he will have a very difficult time getting on top of the pitch. When that happens, the ball will not break on the downward plane and he will be throwing a flat curve ball.

   E. The elbow precedes the hand and is kept away from the body to assure that the full arm snap pulls the ball through. The elbow remains up (at shoulder level) until the wrist begins to snap. This enables the pitcher to stay on top of the ball and also makes the pitch look more like the fast ball to the hitter at this stage of the motion.

3. **Finger and wrist action**

   A. The pitcher's wrist must be cocked back of the head. The arm is away from the body as the wrist is just starting to cock itself. Thus, the elbow starts forward first and then the wrist starts to flatten itself out. The more the pitcher's wrist is bent, the greater and slower the curve.

   B. As the elbow starts forward first the wrist should turn over and snap downward to put a rapid spin on the ball. The ball should be released over the first and second joints of the index finger.

   C. Only the thumb and first two fingers should be used in throwing the curve ball. The ring and little finger should be bent into the palm. Any gripping pressure by the ring or little finger will impair both speed and rotation of the ball.

D. A quick flip of the thumb upon release will help impart more rotation and thus add to the sharpness of the break.

4. Release of the curve ball and follow through

A. The pitcher should use a shorter stride when throwing the curve ball than he does with his other pitches. The shorter stride enables the pitcher to get more on top of the pitch and facilitates the bending of the back. It will also enable the pitcher to complete a better follow through as his arm sweeps across the body. The longer stride usually forces too much extension of the arm which restricts the pitcher from getting over the top of the ball to pull it down.

B. Many pitchers find it is helpful when throwing the curve ball to open up the stride leg a little further from the straight line to home plate than he does with his other pitches. This will assist the arm in swinging down across the left leg after the ball has been released.

C. The follow through adds nothing to the curve ball itself. After the ball leaves the hand, only air resistance and the force of gravity can have any effect upon the flight of the ball. The follow through is carried out for two reasons: (1) the momentum of the arm from the release point should remain in motion at the same velocity to insure that the pitcher does not "quit" on the ball during the actual release; and (2) the follow through also has a practical value in that it places the pitcher in position to field the ball should it be hit back at him.

D. The arm must make a full sweep to come along side and past the knee of the striding leg. The smooth follow through and finish insures that the throwing arm follows a full and consistent path from release point to finish.

5. Other teaching points in throwing the curve ball

A. It is important that the pitcher not try to throw the curve ball too hard. Pitchers who try for velocity usually have a stiff wrist. He might also lose the feel of the curve ball when he overthrows it due to the stress he places on imparting maximum spin along with maximum velocity. A good rule to follow is that you "throw" the fast ball and you "pitch" the curve ball.

B .The curve ball needs to be pulled down on release, not pushed down. He must have the feeling that the ball is being released out in front of the throwing shoulder.

C. A slow curve may be thrown by holding the ball very loosely and then, on release, permitting it to roll over the second joint of the index finger. The fingertips should not touch the ball. Generally, the looser the grip the slower the pitch.

D. If the pitcher wants to throw a faster curve ball, he may simply move his hand away from his head a little more. The closer the hand is to the head, the slower and bigger the curve ball will be to the plate.

E. If the curve ball is hanging, then the following mechanical problems could be in effect:

1. The pitcher is not pulling down on the ball enough. Again, it is a pulling motion, not a pushing motion.

2. He might be letting go of the ball too soon. The pitcher must have the feeling that he is releasing the curve ball out in front of his body, even though it is released well before his hand is in front of the throwing shoulder.

3. Poor wrist action will cause a curve ball to lose its proper rotation. He must establish the proper wrist action so that the curve ball spin can be imparted on the ball as it leaves the hand.

4. If the pitcher grips the ball too tight or too far back in the palm it will effect the spin of the curve ball. The fingers must be relaxed and loose on the ball.

5. Probably the main reason why a pitcher starts losing rotation on the curve ball is that he does not get on top of the ball. This might be due to his dropping his elbow, overstriding, on not keeping his index and middle finger on top of the ball as he enters the release area of his delivery. A prime reason is that he often opens up his front shoulder too early which does not allow for his throwing arm to get out in front of his body. This usually occurs when the pitcher overthrows the curve ball.

318

SLIDER

The slider has become a very popular pitch, so much so that it is not considered a speciality pitch anymore. The true slider will break faster and flatter than the good curve ball. The strength of the slider rests in the fact that it looks like a fast ball coming toward the plate, and then hopefully, looks to the hitter like it breaks at the last second. An astute hitter can usually pick up the curve ball rotation out of the hand, but has a much more difficult time picking up the slider rotation. One of the advantages of the slider over the curve ball is that it is much easier to throw for strikes since it does not break to the degree that the curve ball will break. However, a poor slider is a very hittable pitch since it does not break very much, and in most cases, is thrown slower than the fast ball. The true slider will rotate in a two-to-eight or three-to-nine clockwise rotation from the righthanded pitcher.

1. Grip

A. The grip on the slider will vary from pitcher to pitcher. Some pitchers grip the fast ball and slider the same way. Whatever grip is used, the slider must be held slightly off-center with the middle and index finger placed to the outside of the ball.

B. The index finger should be placed next to a seam with the thumb on a seam underneath the ball. The fingers and thumb should not grip the ball too tightly until right at the moment of release as this can spoil the wrist action which is vital in throwing a good slider with velocity and sharpness.

C. Throughout the windup, most of the pressure is on the middle finger since this is the finger that will exert the maximum pressure on the ball on release. The index finger should rest slightly on the ball during the windup.

2. Finger and wrist action

A. One of the keys to throwing an effective slider is the use of the fingers in achieving the tight slider spin. The wrist will snap down just like it would on the fast ball, with the middle finger generating the spin necessary to make the ball slide.

B. The fingers must remain on top of the ball (slightly off center) as the hand moves to the release point. If the fingers get to the side of the ball prior to the release point, it will cause a slower breaking pitch.

C. At release, the fingers must run down the side of the ball. As the fingers move down the side of the ball, the wrist is snapped down just as in the release of the fast ball.

D. As the ball is released, the pitcher should grip hard with both the index and middle finger to further insure the tightness of the spin as the fingers run down the side of the ball. The faster the spin, the more the break.

E. The ball will be released off the side of the index finger and off the inside tip of the middle finger. Again, the wrist is not turned on release as this would just flatten the pitch out along with putting extreme pressure on the elbow. As the fingers run down the side of the ball, the wrist is already turned outward slightly.

3. Arm action and follow through

A. The arm moves down and across the body during the follow through. This is a slightly different path than the arm takes on the fast ball where the arm goes straight down to achieve the six-to-twelve rotation on the ball.

B. The pitcher must concentrate on a full follow through so that upon release the arm has generated as much velocity as it would in throwing the fast ball. In all actuality, the good hard slider is just a "cut" fast ball where the ball leaves the fingers with the spin of a bullet.

CHANGE-UP

Many times we have seen a pitcher who had good mechanics and a good live fast ball fail miserably when he was sent to the mound for game action. This type of pitcher is struggling constantly with men on base. He seems to be continually behind in the count, and when he gets two strikes on the hitter, the batter manages to foul off pitch after pitch until the pitcher makes a mistake. After several innings during which he throws an excessive number of pitches, the pitcher begins to tire. It is improbable that a player who follows this pattern will be around in the latter stages of the game. This type of pitcher could solve his problems by adding one pitch to his repertoire, the change-up.

The change-up is one of the best pitches in baseball, but many pitchers are afraid to throw the pitch for they are afraid that the pitch will be hit hard since he is not throwing the ball hard. Thus, the coach needs to sell his pitching staff on the advantages of throwing a change-up. This is especially true for higher levels of baseball where the pitcher faces the good fast ball hitters.

The strength of the change-up lies in the fact that hitting a baseball requires fine timing. Thus, the change-up is the pitch that can disrupt a hitter's timing. The other advantage of the change-up is that it will make the pitcher's fast ball that much more effective when the hitter has to start looking for the off-speed pitch as well as the "heater". The change-up can easily be taught, but what is difficult to teach is confidence in the pitch. Once the pitcher knows he can get good hitters out with an off-speed pitch, it will make him that much more of an effective pitcher.

A low release point must be emphasized from the start because there is a tendency for the ball to go high, and the off-speed pitch must be thrown low in order to be effective. Some coaches tell their pitchers to bounce the ball off the plate in attempting to have them exaggerate the low release point which is imperative in keeping the ball low. The change-up thrown to the outer half of the plate is generally more effective than the one thrown to the inner half of the plate since the hitter will generally be well in front of the pitch if he swings at the ball.

The following is a summary of the fundamentals that a pitcher must develop in order to have an effective change-up:

1. Grip

There are several grips commonly used by pitchers to throw the change-up. The coach can assist the pitcher in experimenting with various grips until he finds the one grip that the pitcher feels most comfortable with in throwing his off-speed pitch.

A. **Choking the ball**—The pitcher would grip the ball back in the palm of his hand. The fingertips are raised slightly as the ball is released. In this grip there should be greater pressure on the second row of knuckles on the first two fingers. These fingers straighten out upon releasing the ball. On the release, the hand is behind the ball and not on top of the ball as it is for the fast ball.

B. **Three fingers and choke**—Some pitchers find it more effective for control purposes to place three fingers on top of the ball rather than the two fingers they use to grip the fast ball.

C. **Circle grip**—The pitcher holds the ball with the middle finger and ring finger on top of the ball. The thumb and index finger are held to the inside of the ball. The little finger is held to the outside of the ball. The thumb and index finger are held together in the shape of a circle.

2. Hand, wrist and arm action

A. The hitter should not be able to detect that a change-up is being thrown by observing a slowing down of hand or arm speed. All the actions of the hand, wrist and arm should be similar to the speed of the fast ball. The grip and release must assist in killing the velocity of the pitch.

B. The wrist must be "dead" at release so that the velocity of the pitch would be affected. By not snapping the wrist and fingers as he would in delivering the fast ball, the variance in velocity will be achieved.

C. The pitcher's stiff wrist action would simulate the same action he would use in pulling down a window shade. He should feel like his wrist is going to hit the dirt.

D. The elbow of the throwing arm must be kept higher than the throwing arm shoulder to prevent the change-up from being delivered high to the plate. The lowering of the elbow is a common occurrence when throwing the change-up, for very often when the pitcher loses arm speed, the elbow will drop.

320

3. Lower body action

A. Some pitchers find it more effective to lengthen the stride on the change-up which will happen naturally if they do not push off the rubber as they would do with their fast ball delivery.

B. Many pitchers throw an effective change-up without altering anything with their grip or arm speed. They do this by not getting the maximum push-off the pitching rubber. They use the "dead" leg approach whereby their pivot leg and foot drag off the rubber as they are about to release the ball. If done properly, the ball will not be thrown as hard as when they get the maximum push-off the rubber.

SCREW BALL

The screw ball is an excellent change-of-speed pitch, most effective if used by a righthanded pitcher against a left-handed hitter or by a lefthanded pitcher against a righthanded hitter. The screw ball is basically a backwards curve ball since it breaks the opposite way from the curve ball.

The ball may be gripped with the normal fast ball grip holding the ball loosely and near the end of the fingers. The pitcher attempts to impart a nine-to-three or clockwise rotation on the ball (righthanded pitcher).

The ball leaves the hand off the outside of the middle finger. As the arm is brought forward the forearm is rotated clockwise or inward so that the index and middle fingers are on the pitcher's side of the ball when it is released. The ball is pushed over the middle finger by the thumb. The index finger and the thumb play a major role in imparting the screwball rotation on the ball.

The clockwise or inward rotation of the arm can place a strain on the pitcher's arm if the ball is not delivered properly. By forcing the elbow higher in the delivery it will also force the shoulder to remain slightly inward rotated which in turn will allow the forearm to rotate to the inside much easier. The arm must be fully extended on release with no major snapping of the elbow.

FORK BALL

This is another one of those specialty pitches that is difficult to throw and control. If thrown properly it will provide a pitcher with an excellent off-speed pitch. The good fork ball will come up to the plate with very little rotation on the ball. The break on the fork ball is in the downward plane, thus serving as an excellent pitch for getting the hitter to hit the ball on the ground. Several relief pitchers have made the fork ball famous.

The ball is jammed between the index and middle finger which are bent on the sides of the ball. The thumb should be opposite exerting some pressure on the ball. The ball literally slides out of the hand between the spread fingers with little wrist action other than a slight snap downward right at release.

KNUCKLE BALL

The knuckle ball is probably the most famous of the specialty pitches. The knuckle ball takes the most erratic course to the plate with its movement being highly unpredictable. It might sink, swerve to either side, or appear to jump up and down on its way to the plate. This makes it a very difficult pitch for the pitcher to control, along with being a tough pitch for the catcher to get his glove on at times. The reason for the erratic movement of the pitch is that there is little or no rotation on the ball as it leaves the pitcher's hand.

There are several methods used for throwing the knuckle ball. The most popular method is the one in which the pitcher digs his fingernails into the seams. On release, the fingers are extended and push the ball to the plate. The ball can be thrown with one, two or three fingers. Most effective knuckleballs are thrown with two fingers. The wrist remains stiff making it an effective off-speed pitch that reacts to the various air currents on its way to the plate.

The other method of throwing the knuckle ball is where the pitcher places the first joints of the index and middle finger on the ball between the seams where they are the narrowest. The thumb and the other two fingers encircle the ball. Upon release, the pitcher extends the two bent fingers which gives the pitch a little more speed than with the fingertip method of delivering the knuckle ball. This method requires a good wrist snap and will often result in more rotation on the ball than in the other method.

321

TIPPING PITCHES

There are many ways that a pitcher can tip his pitches to the batter, base coaches, or the opposing bench. The pitching coach needs to carefully observe the pitcher to insure that his mechanics during the delivery do not enable any member of the opposing team to "read" the pitch prior to the ball being released. If it looks like a pitcher has excellent "stuff" yet the hitters look like they are digging in at the plate and making good contact, it might be an indication that they are picking up his pitches. This could be as result of a change in his delivery or that someone is picking up the signs from the catcher. Some of the ways that a pitcher can tip his pitches in the delivery would be the following:

1. **Changing arm angles**—A pitcher should throw all his pitches from just about the same arm angle in order to improve effectiveness along with disguising the pitch. If he was to throw his fast ball from a three-quarters arm slot and his curve ball from over the top, it would be very easy for this to be observed by the hitter at the plate. If the pitcher is able to throw both his fast ball and breaking pitches from various arm angles, then it would be impossible for him to give away the type of pitch that will be thrown. However, very few young pitchers can throw effectively from different arm angles so this practice needs to be discouraged in most cases.

2. **Change in pumping action**—If a pitcher was to pump higher during his windup when throwing one pitch and then not as high when throwing another pitch, this action can easily be observed by the opposition.

3. **Lead leg action**—Some pitchers are guilty of lifting their lead leg higher as they prepare to kick to the plate when throwing the fast ball. This is especially true for the "hard thrower" who attempts to get more body action into his delivery in order to achieve more velocity in the pitch.

4. **Hand action into the glove**—When throwing the breaking pitch, some pitchers will have their wrist turned inward as the pitching hand comes by their side during the backswing. If not during the backswing, the pitcher might turn the wrist in as the pitching hand enters the glove. Thus, an observant hitter would easily be able to see this action from the batter's box.

5. **Glove action**—Some pitchers are guilty of turning their gloves differently during the windup when throwing the breaking pitch versus the fast ball.

6. **Fingering the ball**—Pitchers who throw a specialty pitch like the knuckle ball or fork ball are sometimes guilty of fingering the ball prior to the delivery in such manner than an observant hitter or coach can read the type of pitch that will be thrown.

7. **Exposing the ball from the set position**—When the pitcher is getting the sign from the catcher he must not be guilty of exposing the ball to the first base or third base coach in such a way that they can pick up the type of pitch that will be thrown. This is especially true for those pitchers who hold the ball differently when throwing their fast ball versus the breaking pitch or specialty pitch. The pitcher should have plenty of time when he brings his hands to the set position to grip the ball in the manner he wishes to deliver the pitch.

CONTROL

One of the keys to being a successful pitcher at any level of baseball is the ability to throw the ball with a high degree of control. A pitcher might be able to throw his fast ball at over 90 miles per hour, and have a wicked break in his curve ball or slider, but if he can not throw these basic pitches for strikes he will never be a successful pitcher. There are many examples of highly successful pitchers who do not possess awesome velocity or movement in their pitches. The only reason that they are successful is that they are capable of throwing the ball wherever they want to on most occasions. The pitcher who possesses the awesome fast ball and the "major league" breaking pitch and can throw these pitches for strikes, will be a very effective pitcher.

Physically, poor control is usually caused by some "flaw" in the delivery. If that is the case, it is up to the pitching coach to assist the pitcher in correcting this "flaw". If poor control is caused by poor concentration or lack of confidence on the pitcher's part, then the coach has a much more difficult task at hand in helping the pitcher.

A pitcher with great control certainly has the ability to throw strikes and keep the number of bases on balls down to a minimum. This same pitcher should also have the ability to throw balls. In pitching strategy that will be discussed later, a pitcher will often want to throw a ball to set up the next pitch, or to be able to come up and in on a hitter without hitting him with the ball. When a pitcher wants to miss the outside corner of the plate with his fast ball, he can not afford to have the ball enter the strike zone enabling the hitter to possibly make good contact with the pitch.

The pitcher with good control is able to stay ahead in the count so that he can be in a better position to set up the hitter and make him swing at the pitcher's pitches. A pitcher with poor control will fall behind in the count consistently forcing him to come into the strike zone in order to prevent the hitter from walking.

Good control will allow the pitcher to pitch to spots, taking advantage of any weaknesses in the batter's hitting ability. The pitcher with poor control must throw to the center of the plate hoping that the ball hits a corner of the strike zone.

A pitcher with good control of one pitch and little control of another pitch will find that the disciplined hitter will lay off the pitch he can not control early in the count hoping to gain the advantage in the count. When that occurs, the hitter will be able to guess the control pitch which will give the hitter a decided advantage on the pitcher. It does little for a pitcher to have an awesome break on his curve ball, only to find that he has a nearly impossible job in getting it over the plate.

Thus, control on the pitcher's part is a vital aspect of pitching success. The two components of control are the physical and mental aspect:

1. **Physical aspect of control**—The pitcher must have a consistent delivery in order to have good control of all his pitches. If he has a consistent delivery, it will then be much easier for him to make adjustments when he is wild. The following are some basic physical causes of wildness:

   A. **Not picking up the target**—The pitcher must fix his gaze upon the target, whether it be the catcher's glove or a part of the catcher's equipment other than the glove (shinguards, etc.). The eyes must remain constantly on the target throughout the delivery. With men on base, the pitcher must remember to fix his eyes back on the target before going to the plate.

   B. **Pitching from various release points and arm angles**—It takes a special pitcher to be capable of throwing strikes consistently when he throws from various release points and arm angles. The pitcher must establish as much consistency as possible in his release point and arm angle in order to achieve the control necessary to be effective.

   C. **Landing on the heel**—If a pitcher lands on the heel of his striding foot it will jar the whole body which throws his control off. The stride should be made on the ball of the foot.

   D. **Throwing across the body**—Throwing across the body causes the pitcher to lock his front hip and impedes a smooth delivery and follow through. The pitcher must land with his stride foot near the center line in order to allow his front side to open up to obtain the smooth delivery necessary to achieve proper control.

   E. **Moving around the rubber**—Moving around the pitching rubber hurts control more than it helps it. The pitcher should become accustomed to pitching from the same spot on the rubber on each pitch. It is much easier to make adjustments for control problems when there is consistency on where the pitcher is on the rubber.

   F. **Over- and under-striding**—This is one of the major reasons that pitchers suffer control problems. The pitcher needs to establish consistency on where his pivot foot lands in order to achieve good control of his pitches.

   G. **Excessive body movements**—The pitcher should avoid excessive body movements in his delivery. He should pitch with a "quiet" body unless he has developed good control with these excessive bodily movements in his delivery. The no-windup delivery has proved to be quite successful for those pitchers who have had control problems with exaggerated and excessive body movements.

   H. **Rushing with the body**—The pitcher who finds that he is throwing the ball consistently high might be guilty of rushing with his body. This would cause the arm to lag behind the body causing the ball to be released too soon. Thus, the pitcher is not in a position to release the ball out in front of the body, causing the ball to come in high to the plate area.

   I. **Poor follow through**—Pitchers with poor control often do not have a consistent, smooth, and full follow through. The pitcher must learn to finish on every pitch he throws to the plate.

   J. **Poor physical condition**—Any pitcher who is in poor physical condition is going to have control problems, especially late in the game when fatigue starts to set in. When the legs get tired the pitcher loses his ability to establish the consistency necessary for a smooth delivery. He will also have a tendency to drop his elbow when his arm starts getting tired, which will cause the ball to be high in the strike zone.

2. **Mental aspect of control**—Physical problems with control can be easily observed by an astute pitching coach, and hopefully these problems can be corrected. Mental problems with control are also easily observed, but much more difficult to correct than physical problems. The following are some mental causes of wildness:

A. **Pitching too fine**—This is one of the leading causes of control problems whereby the pitcher wants to "fine tune" each pitch in hopes that he might nibble at the perimeters of the strike zone. Generally this is the result of the pitcher not having complete confidence in his ability to throw effective pitches within the strike zone. He feels that he does not have enough "stuff" to ever throw a pitch that will split the strike zone. This pitcher needs to understand that he must challenge even the good hitters with his best pitches, eliminating the fear that the ball might be well hit. Once a pitcher starts aiming the ball to the plate, he will lose the movement on the pitch and will find that his velocity is also affected. A pitcher can never afford to ease up when a seige of wildness starts to set in. He must go right after the hitter.

B. **Fear of failure**—This is where the pitcher takes the mound worried that he might have a bad performance rather than mentally charging the mound telling himself that he is going to have a super performance. The pitcher who fears failures will never successfully challenge hitters. This is the pitcher who should have better control of his pitches, but seems to be always behind in the count. This is especially true when there is a tough hitter at the plate. The coach needs to instill in this young man that he is the "king of the hill" and if he is going to get "ripped", then let it happen with his best pitches. All too often this type of pitcher would rather walk a hitter than let him hit, thus he will never have to face the thought that the hitter is better than him.

C. **Low confidence**—It is difficult for a pitcher to build confidence in himself as a pitcher when every time he takes the mound he has a poor performance. This is why it is so important that a young pitcher have the opportunity to taste some success before having to face a good hitting ballclub. The coach can pick his spots for the young pitcher to throw in until he gains maturity and confidence to face the challenge of a good hitting ballclub. Many times this is not possible and the young pitcher is "thrown out to the wolves". The pitcher with a low confidence level will pitch very cautiously, and this will generally mean that he will have a difficult time throwing the ball where he wants to.

D. **Lack of concentration**—A pitcher must be a great concentrator in order to be a successful pitcher. He must have the innate ability to "tune out" all distractions that might take away from his ability to concentrate on what he will be attempting to do on the next pitch to the plate. Examples of distractions that can hinder good concentration would be: (1) adverse weather conditions; (2) crowd noise; (3) a batter who constantly steps out of the batter's box; (4) a baserunner leading off first base who is a stealing threat; and (5) a mound which is not to his liking. Concentration can also be affected by an unsettling situation that has just occurred such as: (1) the plate umpire missing a pitch that should have been called a strike; (2) a fielder making a crucial error; (3) a bad pitch that just landed over the left field fence; or (4) awareness on the pitcher's part that the bullpen has just come alive. The good concentrater is one that can overcome these types of distractions and focus his complete attention on the matter in front of him, not on something that he has little control over. The pitcher's control will surely suffer when a pitcher loses his concentration.

E. **Lack of mound experience**—In establishing control, the pitcher who has a wealth of mound experience has a distinct advantage over the pitcher who has little mound experience. It stands to reason that control comes about through trial and error. Thus, the pitcher who has a lot of mound experience will have the mental capacity to battle a seige of poor control more so than the pitcher who has had little mound experience. The coach needs to understand this fact in dealing with a young inexperienced pitcher who is having a difficult time mastering his control.

The coach who has a young pitcher who has a good arm and a fairly good command of a couple of pitches, might find that the inability to throw strikes might be as a result of these mental factors. The coach must deal with these factors in a way that the pitcher understands that this is all a part of gaining mound maturity. When the pitcher learns to master his concentration and poise, he will become a better pitcher. If the pitcher allows these mental factors to affect his performance, then the inability to throw strikes will compound all the other problems he will have to deal with under game conditions.

THE THINKING PITCHER AND GAME STRATEGY

Once the pitcher has established the fact that he has command of his fast ball, one type of breaking pitch, and an

324

off-speed or speciality pitch, then the next aspect of pitching that must be dealt with by the coach is the pitcher's ability to pitch intelligently. Pitching intelligently will allow a pitcher to be somewhat effective even though he does not have an awesome arsenal of pitches.

All coaches have seen pitchers who have great "stuff' but still can not seem to establish themselves as winning pitchers. This is generally due to the fact that the pitcher is constantly throwing "mistake" pitches. This section will deal with the aspect of pitching from the neck on up, which means using one's head.

THE THINKING PITCHER

In using one's head to pitch there are many items that must be taken into consideration:

1. **Analysis of the Pitcher's Strengths and Weaknesses**—The pitcher who takes the mound unaware of his strengths and weaknesses as a pitcher will have a very difficult time mastering the fine art of pitching. Thus, the pitcher must be completely aware of what type of pitcher he is in order to be effective. Am I a power pitcher? Am I a control pitcher? Am I a breaking ball pitcher? The pitcher who can only throw his fast ball 80-81 miles per hour is certainly not going to be a power type pitcher. Thus, he will have to rely on pinpoint control, the development of a good breaking pitch, and establish the capability of changing speeds. A pitcher that can throw the fast ball in the 90-95 miles per hour range can utilize this capability in establishing his fast ball as his "out" pitch. This certainly does not mean that he should be unable to throw a breaking pitch or off-speed pitch. The hard thrower who has an effective breaking pitch and off-speed pitch will make his fast ball that much more effective. Hitting the baseball is a matter of timing the pitched ball. Thus, the more times that the pitcher can show the hitter a different type of pitch with various degrees of velocity, the better his chances of disrupting the hitter's timing.

2. **Analysis of the Strength and Weaknesses of the Hitter**—Pitching a baseball to a hitter is a one on one proposition. The pitcher is attempting to get the hitter to either strike out or force him to hit the type of ball that will enable his defense to make a routine play. The hitter is attempting to make solid contact at the plate so that the defense will have a difficult time getting him out. Thus, it stands to reason that the more the pitcher knows about the hitter the better chance he will have in retiring the hitter by throwing the types of pitches he has a difficult time making solid contact with when he swings the bat. The hitter will also attempt to quickly analyze the strengths and weaknesses of the pitcher so that he can take advantage of this information to become a more intelligent hitter. The following items need to be taken into consideration by the pitcher and catcher when throwing to an individual hitter:

A. **Depth of the stance in the batter's box**—As a general rule, the pitcher will want to throw more fast balls to a hitter who positions himself in the front part of the batter's box, and throw more breaking pitches to the hitter who stands toward the back of the box. The fast ball will get to the hitter quicker when he is in the front part of the box, and thus, he will have to possess a very quick bat in order to handle the good hard fast ball. However, some good fast ball hitters will move up in the batter's box to "set-up" the pitcher to throw more fast balls, but this is the exception to the rule. The hitter in the back of the box wants to have more time to see the fast ball, so he might not be a great fast ball hitter. This hitter will find that the good breaking pitch will be a most difficult pitch for him to hit due to the fact that the ball can "catch" the outside corner of the plate without the batter being in a position to get the "meat of the bat" on the ball. A poor breaking ball hitter will generally move up in the batter's box so that he can make contact with the pitch at a better angle as it enters the area of the strike zone. However, just because a hitter is in the front of the box does not mean that breaking balls can not be thrown. If he is a poor breaking ball hitter, he will still have a difficult time hitting this pitch no matter where he stands in the box.

B. **Distance away from the plate in the stance**—As a general rule, the hitter who stands well away from the plate is doing so because he has had a difficult time making solid contact with pitches on the inside half of the strike zone. This stance allows him the opportunity to now get his arms extended on this pitch. The batter who crowds the plate is generally a good fast ball hitter who feels as though he can get around on most pitches. If the batter really crowds the plate, the pitcher with the good live fast ball can still work inside unless he finds out quickly that the hitter possesses a very quick bat. If so, breaking pitches and off-speed pitches are now in order. The outer half of the plate should be the pitcher's target area on the batter who stands well away from the plate, especially with breaking pitches. If this hitter shows the pitcher and catcher that he is stepping in toward the plate when he strides, the good fast ball on the inner half of the plate could easily "tie him up good". The distance away from the plate along with the nature of the swing will dictate where the majority of the pitches need to be thrown. For instance, if the batter stands well away from the plate in his stance and he does not step towards the area of the plate in his stride, he will have an almost impossible task of covering the outside half of the plate with the "fat of his bat".

C. **Batter assumes an open stance**—The batter with an open stance generally likes the inside pitch due to the fact the open stance allows him to start his swing with the front hip already open. If on the stride, the stride foot continues to keep the

325

front foot open, this batter should have a very difficult time handling a pitch on the outer half of the plate. Breaking pitches on the outer half of the plate are called for with this type of hitter. Some hitters who assume an open stance at the plate do so because they have not been able to generate much bat speed from the conventional squared stance. Thus, the pitcher with a good live arm might be able to jam him with an inside fast ball on occasions. This pitch needs to be well in on the hands to be effective. Generally, a hitter with an open stance does not have great power.

D. **Batter assumes a closed stance**—The batter with a closed stance is interested in having good plate coverage at all times. Generally, the exaggerated closed stance hitter is one who does not possess a great deal of power due to the fact that he is more interested in making contact with all types of pitches rather than looking for pitches that he can explode on with his hips and hands leading the way. Unless the hitter with a closed stance possesses a real quick bat, the best pitch to him is the good fast ball on the inner half of the plate. This should result often in him getting jammed on the pitch if the placement of the pitch is good. Much depends on the distance the hitter positions himself from the plate in the closed stance. There are hitters who start with a closed stance, and then when they stride they have an open stance approach to the ball. Vice-versa, there are hitters who start with an open stance, and then they stride into the plate. The position of the body when the stride foot lands takes precedent over the position of the body in the stance when a pitcher and catcher are determining how to pitch to the batter.

E. **Batter takes a long stride**—As a general rule, the hitter who takes a long stride is a good low ball hitter and has a difficult time getting on top of the high pitch. This is due to the fact that the long stride forces the upper part of the body down dragging the hands down with the stride itself. This allows for the hitter's hands to approach the low pitch at a good angle. It does not allow the hands to approach the high pitch at a good angle for making solid contact. The long stride hitter can usually be thrown change-ups and breaking pitches as he will not have good body control and will have to commit himself early. If the long strider is still able to keep his hands back on the stride he might be less susceptible to change-ups and breaking pitches. As a rule, the long strider is an overly aggressive hitter so changing speeds on him can be effective.

F. **Batter assumes a crouch stance**—This is generally a low ball line drive type hitter who is intent on making contact at the plate. He is not generally a major home run threat from this crouch stance since the crouch does not allow him to mechanically generate a great amount of bat speed into the pitch. This type of batter should be worked high in the strike zone. If he is a pull hitter, pitch him high and away. If he is not a pull hitter, pitch him high and inside. If he starts from the crouch and then straightens up when he strides, he now becomes more susceptible to low pitches, breaking pitches and change-ups over the outer half of the plate.

G. **Batter assumes a straight-up stance**—This is more than likely a high ball hitter due to the fact that his hands will be generally high in the stance enabling him to get the proper angle of his bat on the high pitch. Thus, he should be pitched low in the strike zone until he can prove to the pitcher and catcher that he can handle the low pitch. If on the stride, the straight-up stance hitter moves his body down, then high pitches are in order since his body movement should cause the hands to be lowered as the pitch enters the area of the plate.

H. **Batter has an upper cut swing**—Once the pitcher and catcher note that a batter has an upper cut swing, they should be aware of the fact that he might have a very difficult time handling the high pitch. If he is not a pull hitter, he should be pitched up and in. If he is a pull hitter, he should be pitched up and away. More than likely, he will be a good low ball hitter since his bat barrel angle will be such that the low ball will be his contact pitch. The upper cut hitter is generally one who is a guess hitter and is more interested in hitting the long ball than making consistent contact.

I. **Batter lunges at the ball**—If the batter has a difficult time keeping his weight back on the stride, he will be susceptible to high and tight fast balls or change-ups on the outer half of the plate. In fact, the lunge hitter will have a very difficult time hitting any type of pitch well unless the ball happens to hit his bat on the swing. Mixing the types and speed of pitches will make the lunge hitter practically an "automatic out".

J. **Batter hitches his hands down prior to the swing**—If a batter drops his hands as the pitch is on the way to the plate, he will have a most difficult time handling the high pitch. Of course, much depends on the size of the hitch, the timing of the hitch, and where his hands were at the beginning and end of the hitch. The hitch hitter would have more success on the pitch low in the strike zone.

K. **Batter steps in the bucket**—If the batter's stride takes his front side away from the plate area, he is a classic "step in the bucket" hitter. The angle away from the plate and the distance of the stride will determine how he should be pitched to. If he pulls off the plate a great deal, the pitches away will be practically impossible for him to hit well. Breaking pitches moving

326

toward the outer part of the plate will prove very troublesome to this type of hitter. It is best not to throw him inside unless it is a waste pitch well up and in on his hands.

L. **Batter steps toward the plate**—You would pitch this type of batter the same way you would pitch a batter that was in a closed stance. Keep the ball in on his hands, for the stride in toward the plate should lock his front side up to the point that he will have a difficult time getting the barrel of the bat on the ball.

M. **Batter pulls off the ball on the swing**—This batter might stride straight toward the pitcher but still be guilty of pulling off the ball on the swing itself. He will do this by pulling his head, front shoulder and front hip away from the pitch just as the bat starts forward on the swing. This type of batter needs to have balls thrown to the outer half of the plate, preferably breaking pitches that move away from him. If the ball is properly spotted on the outer half of the plate, he should not have much success in making solid contact with the ball. This type of hitter can usually handle the high pitch much easier than he can the low pitch. Thus, keeping the ball down and away should get the job done.

N. **Batter chokes up on the bat**—The batter who chokes up on the bat is the toughest kind of hitter to pitch to. These hitters are usually only interested in establishing good bat control. This makes them tough to fool by changing speeds, and it is quite difficult to get the fast ball by them unless it is spotted well. The best plan is to work them in and out along with trying to jam them in on the hands with the good fast ball. As a rule, a hitter who chokes up on the bat does not possess great strength, and that is the reason why he might be jammed with the fast ball. This is especially so if the pitcher has been working him away, and he starts leaning over the plate to protect the outer half of the plate.

O. **Batter who holds the bat on the end**—This is generally the batting style of a hitter who is quite strong and feels as though he can get the bat around holding it down on the end. He is usually a pull hitter, or likes to think of himself as a pull hitter. If the pitcher and catcher observe that this type of hitter can not get the bat around with good bat speed, then the "book" on him would be to jam him for the out pitch. If he shows that he can get the bat around holding it on the end and wants to pull the ball, then he should be worked outside. This batter generally has poor bat control and changing speeds to keep him off-balance could be effective.

P. **Batter holds the bat straight up**—If the bat remains straight up on the hitter's stride, this bat position should not enable the hitter to get around on high hard fast balls. He is usually a low ball hitter who likes to golf the ball. Usually, this type of batter is a long ball hitter.

Q. **Batter holds the bat flat**—If the bat remains near the horizontal plane on the hitter's stride, this hitter should have success making contact with the high pitch. The pitcher needs to keep the ball down in the strike zone. Usually, this type of batter is a line drive hitter who wishes to make consistent contact.

R. **Batter takes a long swing (stiff arm or sweep hitter)**—This hitter is usually slow getting around on the ball and should be thrown fast balls on the inside part of the plate. Since this type of batter has to start his swing early, change-ups on the outer part of the plate should be effective.

If a pitcher has great control he can certainly take advantage of this in pitching to the hitters just described. However, it is more important to get ahead of the hitters than trying to pitch to spots unless the pitcher has super control. If a pitcher has little control but a lot of movement on his pitches, then he should pitch to the plate and not pitch to a certain type of hitter.

3. **Pitch selection strategy**—In addition to the pitcher knowing his and the batter's strengths and weaknesses, the pitcher and catcher should have basic pitch selection strategy.

A. **Fast balls**

1. The pitcher must be able to establish the fact that he can throw the fast ball low and away and up and in. If the pitcher does not possess good velocity with his fast ball, he must be careful throwing up and in, especially if the ball is in the strike zone. The pitcher with less velocity must work to keep the ball down and in the strike zone.

2. As a rule, low and in is a poor location for the fast ball unless the hitter has shown that he is unable to handle the fast ball in this spot.

3. The pitcher must keep the fast ball down in a double play situation hoping to force the hitter to hit the ball on the

ground. When the sacrifice bunt is in order, the pitcher must throw the batter a high fast ball hoping to get him to bunt the ball in the air. If unsure as to whether or not a hitter is going to bunt or not, keep the ball down.

4. When facing the good hitter, the pitcher will have to move the fast ball around in the strike zone. Just because a hitter has shown that he does not hit the fast ball on the inside part of the plate, this does not mean that the fast ball should be thrown to that spot everytime. Eventually a smart hitter will make an adjustment in his stance or swing to make some contact with this pitch. The dumb hitter who makes no adjustment should be dealt with by just continuing to throw to that part of the strike zone with the fast ball.

5. If the pitcher has excellent velocity and control of the fast ball, he needs to throw this pitch to the weaker hitters in the lineup. Make them establish the fact that they can hit the fast ball before relying on the breaking pitch or change-up as the out pitch. Otherwise, the pitcher might be doing a poor hitter a favor by giving him an off-speed pitch when he has not made any contact with the fast ball.

B. Curve balls

1. The pitcher who can get his curve ball over the plate with consistency will find that this will make his fast ball that much more effective since the hitters can not just "sit" on the fast ball. This is especially true when the pitcher is behind in the count. If he throws the fast ball practically every time he is behind in the count, he will start getting hit hard against a good hitting team.

2. The pitcher must never be afraid to lead off a hitter with the curve ball. He must continue to mix his pitches up so that the pitcher does not get into a set pattern. Of course, if the pitcher can not get his curve ball over the plate with some consistency this will affect his pitching strategy.

3. When the pitcher is behind in the count, he should not be throwing the curve ball for the corners. He should be throwing the strike curve ball. When he is ahead in the count, then he can start "nipping" the corners with his curve ball.

4. In most cases, the curve ball should be thrown low and away. A curve ball up in the strike zone is a hittable pitch. The righthander should keep the curve ball down and in on the lefthanded hitter and low and away on the right handed hitter. The lefthander should keep the curve ball down and away on the lefthanded hitter and down and in on the righthanded hitter.

5. The curve ball is an excellent pitch in the double play situation if the pitcher can keep the ball low in the strike zone.

6. Of course, the curve ball is a very effective pitch against a "pull conscious" hitter.

C. Sliders

1. The slider should be used in much the same way as the curve ball. If the pitcher's slider does not break down a little on its way to the plate, he must be sure to work the pitch down in the strike zone. Otherwise, the slider up in the strike zone with no movement down can be a very hittable pitch.

2. The slider may be less effective against the opposite handed hitter than the curve ball.

3. It is not easy for a pitcher to throw both a curve ball and a slider for many times the mechanics in the one pitch might take away from the mechanics in the other pitch. If a pitcher can master either the curve ball or the slider he should stick with one of the two pitches for his breaking pitch. If he can master both pitches, he will be that much more effective.

D. Change-ups

1. This is an excellent pitch to use when the pitcher and catcher feel that the hitter is looking for the fast ball or hard slider.

2. The good change-up can be the pitcher's out pitch when he is facing the over anxious hitter who takes the big stride. The lunging hitter who might hit off his front foot is very much susceptible to the change-up.

3. If the pitcher and catcher see that a certain hitter is pulling the fast ball, it is time to change speeds on him. The good change-up in the pitcher's arsenal of pitches will make his fast ball that much quicker in the eyes of the hitter. Once you have shown him the good change-up he might not get around on the fast ball as well as he would if he did not have to look for a possible off-speed pitch.

4. The change-up is especially effective against opposite handed hitters. The pitch should be thrown to the outer half of the plate so that the barrel of the bat is hopefully out in front of the ball on the swing.

5. The two strike change-up is generally not a good pitch, especially to a hitter who protects the plate and is trying to make contact to the opposite field. If the pitcher and catcher observe that a big strong hitter makes no adjustments in his swing with two strikes, then the pitcher who has an excellent change-up can use this pitch even with two strikes.

6. The change-up should not be thrown with a baserunner at third base and less than two outs since the change-up very often results in a fly ball.

7. The change-up to a lefthanded hitter with the first baseman holding a runner on at first base is generally not a good pitch because of the big hole on the right side of the infield.

8. The 1:0; 2-0; 2-1; and 3-1 counts are good counts to throw the change-up for these are the counts that the hitter might be looking fast ball.

E. Specialty pitches

1. If a pitcher has good command of another type of pitch (knuckle ball, fork ball, screw ball, etc.) he certainly will want to throw these pitches whenever he feels that they will be effective against the hitter at the plate. As a rule, specialty pitches are not as easy to control as the basic pitches previously discussed. Thus, the pitcher certainly does not want to fall behind a hitter by using his non-control specialty pitch. If the pitcher has control and great movement out of one of these pitches, then he certainly should use the pitch not only for a control pitch, but also for his out pitch.

2. It is very important that a pitcher does not allow himself to get beat at a critical point in the game by throwing a specialty pitch that might not have good movement or location. If a pitcher is going to get beat, it should be as a result of the batter hitting the pitcher's best pitch. If the specialty type pitch is the pitcher's best pitch, then that is the pitch he needs to use in this critical time of the game when he can not afford to give up a big hit.

4. **Situation pitching**—The pitcher and catcher must always take into consideration the situation in the game before making the final decision on the type of pitch to be thrown and the location for that pitch. The following are various situations that can confront the pitcher and catcher during a game, and the recommended pitch and/or location.

A. **Lefthanded hitter, runner at first base**—You do not want the lefthanded hitter to be able to pull the ball in the hole between the second baseman and first baseman if the first baseman is holding the runner on at first base. Thus, the hitter needs to be worked on the outer half of the plate, avoiding off-speed pitches if at all possible. If there is a righthanded opposite field hitter at the plate in the same situation, then he needs to be worked on the inner half of the plate. This does not mean that he still can not drive the ball to the opposite field, but it does make his job a little more difficult. The change-up can be thrown to this righthanded hitter in this situation even though this opposite field hitter is generally not susceptible to change-ups. Hopefully, he will pull the ball if he makes contact. Much depends on the location of the second baseman when throwing to the plate with the first baseman holding a runner on first base. If the second baseman is playing the hitter close to first base, then it would not be as important to completely avoid the hitter hitting the ball to the right side of the field.

B. **Lefthanded hitter, runner at second base with no outs**—The lefthanded hitter in this situation will be looking for a pitch that he can pull. This is especially true late in the game when the runner at second base is an important run in a close game. The pitcher must keep the ball on the outer half of the plate, avoiding change-ups and any other off-speed pitch (specialty pitch). If the batter does not "bite" at the pitch(s) and balls have been called, then the pitcher will need to challenge the hitter with the fast ball over the plate. Lefthanded pitchers can throw curve balls and sliders to the lefthanded hitter in this situation if these breaking pitches have good velocity to them.

C. **Righthanded hitter, runner at second base with no outs**—The righthanded hitter in this situation will be looking for a pitch that he can drive to the right side of the field. This is especially true late in the game when the runner at second base is an important run. The pitcher must keep the ball on the inner half of the plate. If the pitcher misses the inside corner on the first two pitches (2-0 count) then he will have to come in with a pitch over the plate. It is preferred that these pitches be breaking balls (especially from the lefthanded pitcher) or change-ups since these pitches have a better chance of being pulled than the fast ball. Much depends on the pitcher's ability to throw the breaking pitch or change-up over the plate.

D. **Runner at third base with less than two outs**—The pitcher is looking for the strikeout or pop-up in the infield in this situation. This is especially true if the runner at third base is an important run late in the game. He can not afford to give up a long fly ball or a ground ball (especially if the infield is in on the grass late in the game). Early in the game the pitcher and defense are more interested in getting outs to avoid the big inning. With the winning or tying run at third base late in the game, the pitcher must be at his best. He must go with his best stuff hoping to get ahead in the count. The pitcher must challenge the hitter for he can not afford to get behind in the count. He can not be afraid to come up and in on the batter, for this is the location of a pitch that would produce more chances for a pop-up or swing and miss. He must have the confidence to throw the breaking ball down even if behind in the count. He should avoid change-ups since this pitch often produces fly balls to the outfield. Once ahead in the count, go after the hitter with your best strikeout pitch.

E. **Double play possibility**—The double play is the great rally killer and the pitcher's best friend. Good pitchers have a knack for throwing the ground ball when it is in order. The pitcher and catcher must know which pitch has the greatest chance of producing a ground ball with this batter at the plate. All pitches must be down in the strike zone since the low pitch produces many more ground balls than the high pitch. Avoid throwing change-ups when looking for the double play.

F. **Sacrifice bunt situation**—The pitcher and catcher are going to be very much aware of the fact that a sacrifice bunt is in order due to the nature of the game, the situation at hand, and the type of batter at the plate. When the situation leads the pitcher and catcher to believe that a sacrifice bunt might be in order, the pitcher must throw the batter a high fast ball. It is preferred that the pitch be a couple of inches above the top of the batter's strike zone. This is a very tough pitch to bunt on the ground. If the first pitch is a ball and the batter has squared around to bunt, the next pitch should be another high fast ball, attempting to throw a strike at the top of the batter's strike zone. If the second pitch misses bringing the count to 2-0, then the pitcher should throw a fast ball for a strike, hopefully from the belt to the top of the strike zone of the hitter. There will be times that the coach might give his hitter the "green light" on this 2-0 pitch knowing that the pitcher must throw the pitch in the strike zone. Thus, the batter might have a great pitch to hit. This is why the pitcher must still throw a good fast ball with velocity on this 2-0 count. With runners at first and second base, the pitcher needs to recognize the fact that the hitter will generally be trying to bunt the ball to the third base side of the infield. In order to make this difficult to accomplish, the pitcher should work the pitch inside to the lefthanded hitter and outside to the righthanded hitter. If the defensive team's bunt defense calls for an early break toward the plate by one of the infielders, the pitcher should throw to the area of the plate that will allow the hitter to bunt the ball into the hands of the charging infielder.

G. **Squeeze bunt situation**—Anytime the pitcher suspects that a squeeze bunt might be attempted by the offense, the pitcher needs to pitch from the set position. This will force the runner at third base to hold until he reads that the pitcher is definitely going to deliver the ball to the plate. The defensive team may also want to signal for a pitchout if they suspect a suicide squeeze is on. If the runner at third base does not break too early on the suicide squeeze, there is nothing that the pitcher can do other than to break hard toward the plate once he sees the batter square around to bunt the ball. If the runner leaves third base too early, the pitcher can then make an adjustment in his pitch to the plate. With a lefthanded hitter, he should throw the ball well outside of the strike zone as he would when throwing a pitchout. The pitch would be such that the batter would have no opportunity to get the bat on the ball. With a righthanded hitter at the plate, there are two locations that the pitch can be thrown to: (1) well up and in; and (2) well low and in. Both of these locations would force the batter to get out of the way of the pitch, no matter how important it was for him to try to get the bunt down. The pitcher is not trying to hit the batter, but if he does, the runner is forced to go back to third base. The up and in pitch is preferred since it is easier for the catcher to handle than the low inside pitch. Generally the batter will hit the dirt on the up and in pitch which means that his chances of getting hit are minimized. It is also a more difficult pitch to bunt than the ball thrown low and inside.

H. **Tying or winnning run at second base late in the game**—With first base open and a better than average hitter at the plate, the pitcher must pitch extra fine to the batter when the tying or winning run is at second base late in the game. If the batter happens to walk, not much damage has been done. The pitcher certainly does not want to walk a below average hitter who might be the winning run with a better than average hitter in the on deck circle. Pitching extra fine means that the pitcher must throw his best control pitch so that he can pitch to spots just outside the strike zone. The pitcher can not afford to throw a pitch that he has little control of only to see it enter the heart of the strike zone, which is not the area of the plate he wanted the pitch to go. It is recommended many times for the coach to intentionally walk the batter with first base open, especially if the pitcher quickly falls behind in the count. Much depends on the type of hitter at the plate, the success the pitcher has had with the batter at the plate, and the situation in the game. If the pitcher gets ahead of the hitter in this situation, he can not afford to give the hitter anything good at all to hit.

I. **Tying or winning run at first base late in the game**—With the tying or winning run at first base late in the game, the pitcher does not want to walk the batter. This would put this very important runner at second base. Thus, the pitcher should challenge the hitter with strikes, especially if he gets behind in the count. Of course, with less than two outs he is looking for the ground ball so he needs to keep the ball down in the strike zone. With two outs, he wants to also keep the ball down to prevent the extra base hit that would score the runner from first base.

J. **Hit and run situation**—The pitcher needs to recognize the fact that the hit and run is generally used when the pitcher is in a vulnerable position in the ball and strike count with no outs. The common hit and run counts are: 1-0; 2-0; and 2-1. However, the hit and run can be run on any ball strike count when there is less than two strikes on the batter and less than two outs in the inning. If the hitter at the plate exhibits good bat control and the runner at first base has average to above average speed, then this is the excellent hit and run combination. The game situation (score and inning) is also an important consideration. Anytime the hit and run is suspected, the pitcher with good control needs to keep the ball on the inside part of the plate. This is to prevent the hitter from easily driving a pitch to the opposite field.

K. **Pitching around a great hitter**—There may be times in a season when a pitching staff can just not get a certain hitter on the opposing team out. Thus, in a critical situation a team does not want this great hitter to be the one who beats them. Of course, much depends on the ability level of the hitter batting behind this great hitter. Anytime the tying or winning run is in scoring position with first base open, a coach should either intentionally walk this hitter 'or make sure that he is pitched around. In pitching terminology, you would want the pitcher to make this batter hit his pitch or chase the bad ball. Breaking balls off the plate are good pitches, especially with the aggressive hitter at the plate. The most important thought is to keep everything out of his strong hitting zones, giving him absolutely nothing good to hit.

L. **Pitcher protecting a lead late in the game**—Anytime the pitcher has been afforded a lead by his team late in the game, the pitcher must think strikes to bring the "W" home. This is especially true if he has been given a big lead since the offensive team will probably be taking the first strike. The pitcher must throw in a manner that he will challenge the hitters to hit their way on base. With errorless defense, it still generally takes three singles to score one run. If a home run threat is at the plate with no one on and the pitcher protecting a two run or bigger lead, he must go right after him with strikes in the area of the strike zone he is most vulnerable. If he happens to hit a home run with a two run lead, the pitcher's team is still up by one run. It is generally agreed upon by coaches that a pitcher in this situaiton should stay with what got him this far with extra emphasis on throwing strikes.

5. **Other pitching strategy**—We have detailed already some basic pitching strategy in regard to the hitters' and pitchers' strengths and weaknesses, pitch selection strategy and situation pitching. We will now deal with other important areas of pitching strategy that the pitching staff needs to review.

A. **Pitcher using strength against strength**—If the hitter's strength are the same as the pitcher's strength, the pitcher must go after the hitter with his strength. For instance, a good fast ball pitcher facing a good fast ball hitter at a crucial time in the game should go after the hitter with his fast ball. It is foolish for the pitcher to go with his number two pitch in this situation if the game is on the line. This is why it is so important that a pitcher have great command of two pitches. If so, he will then have a distinct advantage over the hitter.

B. **Pitching to the anxious hitter**—The pitcher needs to make the anxious hitter wait at the plate whenever possible. This type of hitter is anxious to get going and is easily bothered when the pitcher takes his time between pitches. This is the hitter to double pump on occasionally from the windup, or hold a little longer at the set when pitching from the stretch. The anxious hitter many times is a first ball hitter so he can be prompted many times to swing at a bad ball on the first pitch.

C. **Pitching to the deliberate hitter**—A pitcher will face numerous hitters who are very deliberate in their approach to hitting. These hitters like to take their time at the plate and do not like to be rushed. The pitcher should work faster to this type of hitter, which will force the hitter to perform according to the pitcher's rate of speed rather than his own. Many times a good fast ball can be thrown by this hitter since it generally takes a pitch or two for him to get himself mentally and physically ready to hit.

D. **Pitching to a guess hitter**—The guess hitter is one who is always trying to guess what type of pitch the pitcher will throw on the next delivery to the plate. The good guess hitter will only do so when he is ahead in the count. Some guess hitters will attempt to guess the pitch being thrown no matter what the count, and subsequently can be easily fooled by the intelligent pitcher and catcher working together to out think the hitter. When facing a hitter that looks like a guess hitter (takes a great cut on the 2-0 fast ball as if he knew that the fast ball was coming), the pitcher and catcher should try to think as if they were the hitter. Thus, by mixing up the pitches on various ball-strike counts, the guess hitter will quickly lose his confidence in being able to guess what the pitcher will be throwing in certain situations. This is why it is so important that the pitcher have excellent command of at least two pitches, so the guess hitter can never "sit" on just one pitch in a given situation. Another device that works well against the guess hitter is the false shake-off sign by the pitcher.

E. **Breaking up the hitter's rhythm**—We have mentioned earlier that hitting involves a lot of concentration, timing and rhythm. Anything that the pitcher can do to disrupt the hitter's concentration, timing and rhythm will prove invaluable to the pitcher. This is especially true when facing a hitter that has proved to be a tough out, and one that looks like he has all the confidence in the world that he will hit the ball hard. There are numerous ways that a pitcher can disrupt a hitter of this kind:

1. **Varying the time between pitches**—Varying the time between pitches is particularly easy to do from the stretch as the pitcher can vary the amount of time he holds at the set position. One time he can break from the set immediately after the legal pause, and on the next pitch he can hold for two or three seconds. In the windup, it is not recommended that the pitcher change the pace of his windup dramatically. This may prove more of a hindrance to the pitcher than to the hitter. However, he can change the pace of the beginning of the windup after getting his sign from the catcher. A pitcher should never get into a set pattern on the pace of his delivery to the plate.

2. **Shake-off sign**—The pitcher and catcher can very often upset the batter by shaking the sign off (shaking the head or a glove wipe on the body) even if it means returning to the original sign called for. This is why it is important that the pitching staff have a shake-off sign and a false shake-off sign. Shaking pitches off occasionally will not only force the batter to wait, but will get him to thinking more about what the pitcher might throw. This is especially true when the pitcher shakes off two or three signs in succession. It is further helpful to follow the shake-off sign with a confident nod of the head to show the hitter that this is the pitch the pitcher has complete confidence in throwing.

3. **Double pumping from the windup**—There is probably nothing that a pitcher can do that is more distracting to a batter than to double pump from the windup. This is especially true with a two strike count on the hitter when he is already in a defensive position at the plate.

F. **In-out and up-down principle**—A pitcher can never afford to get into a set pattern of pitching to a hitter to just one basic area of the strike zone. This is true even if a certain hitter has shown very little ability to hit a pitch in one area of the strike zone. For instance, if the "book" on a certain hitter is that he has a difficult time hitting pitches on the outside corner of the plate, by continually throwing to this area, a hitter will eventually make some type of adjustment to handle this pitch a little better. Thus, the pitcher must also come in on this hitter to prevent him from making this type of adjustment. One good hard fast ball in on the fist should "do the trick". The "out" pitch will still be the pitch on the outer part of the plate. A pitcher with great control can pitch in-out and up-down with great effectiveness. This is more true for the pitcher who does not have super "stuff". The pitcher who has the great assortment of pitches does not need to concern himself as much with pitching in-out and up-down. Pitchers can never start pitching so fine to the point that they get behind a hitter by attempting to nip the corners, nip the knees, and work the letters. When he gets ahead in the count, this is the time to throw to the spots that he and the catcher feel the hitter is most vulnerable.

G. **Ball-strike count situation pitching**—One of the keys to being a successful pitcher is for the pitcher to completely understand his pitching strategy in relation to the ball-strike count on the hitter. When ahead of the hitter, the pitcher should have the distinct advantage over the hitter. When behind in the count, the advantage swings to the batter. This is why it is so important that the pitcher concentrate on getting ahead of the hitter as much as possible. The following are some thought patterns that the pitcher needs to comprehend in the various ball-strike counts that he will face.

1. **Pitcher behind in the count** (3-0; 3-1; 2-0; 3-2)—In these four ball-strike counts, the hitter is ahead in the count on the pitcher. Thus, the pitcher must get the ball over the plate for a strike. We would even consider the 3-2 count as a hitter's advantage count since the pitcher must throw a strike or risk walking the batter. The recommended way for the pitcher to pitch in these four ball-strike counts is for the pitcher to stay away from facing them. He must stay ahead of the hitter unless he happens to be pitching around a certain batter. When the pitcher is facing these counts he must throw a pitch that he has control of, and one that he can put a "little something on". If not, he is liable to get "ripped". If the pitcher has developed a good change-up that he can control, these are excellent counts to throw this pitch. This is especially true with an anxious hitter at the plate. A breaking pitch is also a good pitch to throw if it can be thrown for a

strike since the hitter is probably going to be guessing fast ball in most cases. When the pitcher throws the fast ball, he needs to be sure that the pitch has a little something extra on it so that the batter's ball-strike count advantage does not also allow him to get a "meat" fast ball to hit. This is especially true on the 3-0 count.

2. **Pitcher attempting to even the count or prevent getting behind in the count** (0-0; 1-0; 2-1; 2-2)—In these four ball-strike counts, the pitcher is trying to even the count or keep from throwing a ball which will put him behind the hitter on the count. The 0-0 count can also be placed in this category due to the fact that a ball thrown on the first pitch will quickly put the pitcher at a slight disadvantage. These are all excellent counts for the pitcher to throw his best control breaking pitch forcing the hitter to swing the bat. Hopefully, he will swing at this pitch and hit the ball for an out. There is no reason in these counts for a pitcher to ever "groove" a fast ball. This is where the in-out or up-down fast ball for a strike comes into the picture. A change-up is also an effective pitch in these counts if the pitcher has good control of this pitch and is facing a hitter that looks like a good fast ball hitter.

3. **Pitcher ahead in the count** (0-1; 1-1; 1-2)—The pitcher has a distinct advantage over the hitter in these three counts, so he can now pitch with a little more fineness. The pitcher can put a little extra on the pitch without a great fear that he will be at a major disadvantage if he happens to throw a ball. These are the counts that are good spots to try to get the batter to hit a bad pitch, or with a 1-2 count, to strike him out. This is the time to throw the strikeout breaking pitch rather than the control breaking pitch as the pitcher would throw when behind the batter in the count. In these counts, the batter should never get a good pitch to hit.

4. **Pitcher well ahead in the count** (0-2)—With the 0-2 count, the pitcher should have the batter in a position to literally "hit out of his hand". Pitchers who can consistently get hitters in the 0-2 ball-strike count are going to "win". Now is the time to get the batter to swing at a bad pitch since he is just trying to protect the plate, and is very subject to swinging at a pitch out of the strike zone. At no time should the 0-2 pitch enter the area of the strike zone so that the batter can make good contact with the ball. At the same time the pitch should not be a total waste pitch that the batter would never swing at due to the fact that the ball is so far out of the strike zone. The good control pitch is preferred in this situation so that the pitcher does not miss with the pitch only to find the pitch entering the "heart" of the hitter's strike zone. How many times has a baseball coach asked a pitcher why his 0-2 pitch to a certain hitter was hit hard due to the fact that it was a very hittable pitch? In most cases, the pitcher will respond to the coach, "I didn't mean for the ball to go there." Thus, the pitcher must throw a control pitch to a vulnerable area outside the strike zone with an 0-2 count on the batter. It is not wise to throw a change-up on the 0-2 pitch since the batter is in a defensive position at the plate, which does not lead to an aggressive type of swing as a rule. Basically, there are three areas of thought here and they can all be used depending on the situation: The 0-2 pitch can be used to: (1) move a hitter off the plate; (2) set-up the hitter for the 1-2 pitch; and (3) get him to go after a pitch he can not hit well.

6. **Pitchouts and intentional walks**—Prior to going into the section on the pitcher holding runners on base and proper pick-off mechanics, it is important that we present a brief discussion of the pitchout and intentional walk mechanics. The head coach will generally determine that he wants the batter at the plate to be intentionally walked. The pitcher will pitch from the stretch making sure that any runners on base do not get a big primary lead. The catcher will give the pitcher the target well outside of the plate with either his bare hand (righthanded batter) or with his glove (lefthanded batter). The catcher can not leave the catcher's box until the pitcher delivers the ball to the plate. The pitcher should throw the ball about three-quarters speed being careful that he does not aim the ball. This could cause for a very erratic throw which could get by the catcher. He should throw the ball chest high to the catcher. The pitchout will be thrown also to the chest high position of the catcher, but of course, the catcher will not be able to give the outside target as he does with the intentional walk. Some catchers prefer to have the ball thrown shoulder height to them on the pitchout, so the pitcher needs to be aware of the catcher's preference in regard to the height of the pitchout. The pitchout will be called by the catcher via a set sign that he will give the pitcher while in his crouch position behind the plate. A member of the coaching staff may flash the pitchout sign to the catcher if they suspect that a runner might be stealing on the next pitch or there is a chance for the hit and run play. When the pitchout sign is given to the pitcher, he should hold the runner a little longer from his set position than normal. This may take a little of the runner's edge off his movement on the pitcher's delivery to the plate. When the pitcher delivers the pitchout to the plate, he must deliver the ball quickly, eliminating any major leg kick that he might use in his normal delivery to the plate from the set position and yet still not "give away" the pitchout to the runner. He would throw his fast ball about two feet outside the outside edge of the plate between the chest and shoulders of the catcher. If he throws the ball any closer than two feet outside of the plate there is always the chance that a batter on the hit and run play might be able to get the bat on the ball. He should not aim the ball to this location, nor should he drop his arm to quicken his release of the ball. This could cause the ball to sail on him, thus putting the catcher in a poor position to catch the ball and throw to the base that the runner is attempting to steal.

HOLDING RUNNERS ON BASE AND PICK-OFF MECHANICS

The pitcher can certainly help himself and his team appreciably by developing sound mechanics for holding runners on their respective bases. In many cases when a runner successfully steals a base, much of the blame can be placed on the pitcher. This is due to the fact that he either allowed the runner to get too big of a primary lead, or took too long to deliver the ball to the plate. If the pitcher allows a runner to take a big primary lead followed by a slow delivery time of the ball to the plate, his catcher will have to possess an "accurate cannon" for an arm to ever have any chance of throwing a runner out stealing base. We will now detail what a pitcher must do in order to keep a runner close at all three bases, and the pick-off mechanics he must master at the three bases.

1. **Runner at first base**—The pitcher must recognize the fact that any runner on first base is a stealing threat. He should have some knowledge of each of the opposing runners' base stealing capabilities before he takes the mound. Armed with this information, he can better prepare himself for that time that he will be called on by the defense to keep this runner honest as he leads off first base. The runner might assist the pitcher by tipping off the fact that he is stealing second base by one of the following unnatural leads or body movements: (1) an exaggerated lean toward second base; (2) pointing his front foot (right foot) a little more toward second base; (3) bouncing on the balls of his feet while leading off base; (4) taking a bigger lead than normal; (5) taking an unusually short lead (one-way steal); and (6) taking a walking lead off first base. The pitcher must also be fully aware of the opponent's offensive philosophy and pattern of play. This can be picked up from scouting reports given to him by the coaching staff or personal observation of the team in past performances. Some teams like to run quite a bit and some teams are very conservative in regard to their stealing bases. The following are points of emphasis for the pitcher in holding a runner on at first base:

A. **Pitching from the stretch**—When the pitcher comes to the set position on the stretch delivery, his body must be in a position to allow him to easily see the runner leading off first base. Some righthanded pitchers because of their body structure have a very difficult time watching the runner lead off first base. This problem can be remedied by turning his shoulders slightly to the left, still keeping his front foot pointing toward the batter. He must not turn the shoulder too far toward first base due to the fact that the runner at first base would get a tremendous jump on his steal attempt when the pitcher has to rotate his shoulders away from first base to deliver the ball to the plate. The righthanded pitcher can tuck his chin down toward his left shoulder also if he is having a difficult time seeing the runner at first base. Since the pitcher will have to lift his head up to deliver the ball to the plate, this could also give the runner at first base a little edge when stealing second base. Of course, the lefthanded pitcher has no problem observing the runner leading off first base.

B. **Changing the pattern on the stretch**—It is important for the pitcher to never fall into a set pattern as he goes to the set position in his stretch delivery. At the same time, he can not afford to have one pattern when going to the plate, and one when attempting to pick the runner off first base. Upsetting the rhythm and timing of the runner at first base is his primary concern and this can be accomplished by changing the pace of the movement of the hands to the set position. He can also vary the number of looks to first base along with changing the time sequence from the set to the time the hands break to deliver the ball to the plate.

C. **Pick-off at first base**—When the pitcher throws the ball to first base from the stretch delivery, he should always have a definite purpose in mind. Of course, the main purpose would be the hope of retiring the runner on a successful pick-off play. Other times he might wish to just keep the runner honest so that he is aware that the pitcher cares about him. It is foolish for a pitcher to show the runner at first base and all his teammates in the dugout his best pick-off move early in the game. Many times the first runner who gets to first base is instructed by his coach to take a large one-way lead off the base in hopes that he can force the pitcher to show his best pick-off move. This is done more often when there is a lefthanded pitcher on the mound. There are five spots in the stretch delivery that the pitcher can throw the ball to first base in an attempt to pick-off the runner: (1) off the rubber; (2) going up in the stretch; (3) coming down in the stretch; (4) from the set position (RH); and (5) after leaving the set (LH).

1. **Off the rubber**—The pitcher might wish to throw to first base as soon as he gets the ball back from the catcher if he sees that the runner at first base happens to be off the base and not paying much attention to the pitcher. The pitcher can step back off the rubber with his pivot foot at any time during the stretch delivery, but he can not break his hands from the set position until the foot clearly leaves the pitching rubber. He can combine this movement with a quick throw to first base. Many times a quick movement off the rubber from the set position will prompt a runner to make an initial break toward second base if the steal sign is on.

2. **Going up in the stretch**—This is one of the best times for the righthanded pitcher to attempt a pick-off at first

base. The lefthanded pitcher would have to step back off the rubber if he wishes to throw to first base as his hands are going up in the stretch delivery. This is due to the fact that a pitcher has to step toward first base in order to throw there when his pivot foot is in contact with the rubber. This would be a difficult feat to accomplish with the pivot foot still on the rubber for the lefthanded pitcher. Many runners are still getting their lead away from first base as the righthanded pitcher's hands are going up in the stretch, and this is the reason why a pick-off at this time can be most effective. It is well to note that the pitcher will have his arm in the best position for a quick short throw to first base when his hands are at about the shoulder level either going up or coming down toward the set position.

3. **Coming down in the stretch**—For a runner who continues to work on a longer lead away from first base as the pitcher's hands start down toward the set position, this would be an ideal time for a pick-off attempt at first base. Anytime a runner is still establishing his lead at this time, he is bound to be in poor position to recover and return to first base when he reads the pick-off attempt. If the runner at first base has his full lead established before the pitcher goes up or down in the stretch delivery, he will not be that susceptible to being picked off at first base. Again, this is a very difficult time for the lefthanded pitcher to throw to first base unless he steps back off the rubber with his pivot foot.

4. **From the set position (righthanded pitcher)**—The righthanded pitcher will make most of his pick-off attempts when he reaches the set position in the stretch delivery. From the set, he can attempt to pick-off the runner at first base at anytime since he is not required to come to a stop with his hands when throwing to first base. However, he must come to a momentary stop with his hands before he can deliver the ball to the plate.

5. **After leaving the set position (lefthanded pitcher)**—After the lefthanded pitcher breaks from the set position in the stretch delivery, he can either deliver the ball to the plate or he can attempt the pick-off at first base. The righthanded pitcher can only attempt one type of pick-off at this point. This is when there is also a runner at third base, and he fakes the throw to third base. After stepping toward third base and faking the throw to that base, he turns and makes a quick throw to first base if he has a play on the runner. This type of pick-off is used when it is suspected that the runner at first base is going to be stealing second base on the pitch. It can also be used with runners at first and third base and a 3-2 count on the batter with two outs. Since the runner at first base will be breaking toward second base on the pitch, this movement by the pitcher from the set position may allow him the opportunity to retire the runner at first base without having to throw a pitch to the plate.

D. **Pick-off mechanics at first base (righthanded pitcher)**—The righthanded pitcher must practice his pick-off moves to first base from the different positions in the stretch delivery. While working on his various pick-off moves to first base, he must concentrate his efforts on being able to throw the ball accurately to the first baseman. It is great to have a real quick pick-off move to first base with a lot of velocity on the throw, but if the ball is not thrown accurately the pick-off attempt will not be successful. This could also cause the wild throw at first base allowing the runner to advance. The ideal location for pick-off attempts at all three bases is at the knees of the fielder on the baserunner's side of the base. The following are the basic pick-off mechanics at first base for the righthanded pitcher:

1. The key to a successful pick-off at first base for a righthanded pitcher is the quickness of his actions, the velocity he can generate on the throw, and the accuracy of the thrown ball to the first baseman at the bag. With a lefthanded pitcher, deception is one of the major keys to a successful pick-off at first base. There is very little deception available to the righthanded pitcher.

2. The basic mechanics for the jump pivot pick-off attempt at first base are identical from the various spots in the stretch delivery: going up with the hands; coming down with the hands; and at the set position. Any deception practiced by the righthanded pitcher would basically be from the standpoint of the runner not knowing at which spot in the delivery the ball may be thrown to first base.

3. The action of the pitcher's feet are the most critical mechanic for the pick-off at first base. The quicker the feet the better the pitcher gets his body in the proper position to assist his arm in quickly releasing the ball. It is important that the feet not be spread wide apart as this will cause balance problems as well as weight shifting problems. The jump pivot is not actually a jump off the ground since any movement in the air with either foot will slow the pitcher's delivery time of the ball to first base. Both spikes should just barely clear the ground as the pitcher positions his feet to enable his body to open up properly for the throw to first base. The jump pivot when completed places the right foot on the dirt area directly in front of the pitching rubber with the toe of the foot facing home plate. The left foot would end up about two to three inches to the left of a straight line from the edge of the pitching rubber to first base. The feet have got to be extremely quick in this action so that the feet are planted when the ball is about to be released. The left toe should be pointing toward first base when the foot lands.

4. As the jump pivot is in motion with the feet, the pitcher's left shoulder must open up quickly and fully in the direction of first base. If the shoulder or the feet do not open up fully enough, the pitcher will be throwing across his body increasing the possibility of a wild throw to first base.

5. The glove hand should stay close to the chest area to prevent the upper part of the body from moving too far to the left causing poor body balance for the throw to first base. Too much movement away from the body of the glove hand will also cause the elbow to drop on the throwing arm.

6. The throw must be made with a short arm action with the elbow up as the ball is about to be released. The jump pivot and shoulder rotation toward first base should provide the arm with enough momentum to generate power for the throw. The pitcher should never feel as though he has to reach back for something extra on this type of pivot. The hands should separate from the glove as the jump pivot and shoulder turn begins so that when the left foot lands, the right arm is up and the ball is being released to first base. There is no reason for the throwing hand to drop below the area of the chest no matter from which point in the stretch the hands break for the pick-off. The pitchers with great pick-off moves seldom allow the throwing hand to fall below the level of the shoulders. The shorter the arm arc out of the glove, the quicker the ball will be released to first base.

E. **Pick-off mechanics at first base (lefthanded pitcher)**—The lefthanded pitcher must diligently practice his pick-off move to first base in order that he can keep all the runners who reach first base completely stymied as to when he is going to throw the ball to first base when he breaks from the set position. The key to this success is the pitcher consistently breaking from the set position the same way each time, not allowing the runner to know whether he will be going to the plate or to first base until the last second. The following are the basic pick-off mechanics at first base for the lefthanded pitcher:

1. If the pitcher observes that the runner is taking too big of a primary lead while he is holding at the set, he can step back off the rubber with his left foot and snap throw the ball to first base without moving either foot in the direction of first base. This would be a sidearm or underhand type of a throw. This is a very difficult movement to master but can prove to be effective for the runner who is a long way from first base and not concerned about a pick-off throw at this point in the pitcher's stretch delivery.

2. Once the pitcher assumes the set position, he should know whether he will be delivering the ball to the plate or going to attempt a pick-off at first base with either an average move, a good move, or his best move. It is practically impossible for him to be thinking about the pitch to the plate as he breaks from the set, and then to change his mind when he sees the runner at first base make a movement toward second base. This change of direction is only possible for the pitcher who has a very slow leg lift with his right leg when he breaks from the set position. Thus, if the pitcher observes out of the corner of his eye that the runner at first base has taken off for second base, it is best that the pitcher just concentrate his full effort on the pitch itself. Otherwise, he will be more concerned about the runner's jump toward second base and the pitch to the plate will not be his major concern.

3. As the pitcher breaks from the set position, he must have the same "look" to the runner at first base each and everytime. As mentioned in the baserunning section of the Playbook, there are numerous keys that a runner can look for from the lefthanded pitcher to give away the fact that he is either going to throw the ball to the plate or a pick-off will be attempted at first base. For many lefthanded pitchers, the head and the eyes give him away to the runner. A pitcher with poor head and eye action will always be looking toward home plate when they are going to throw the ball to first base, and will be looking toward first base when they are going to throw the ball to the plate. The pitcher who can alternate his looks to first base and the plate each time will be that much more effective in holding the runner longer at first base on a steal attempt. It will also assist him in disguising better his pick-off move to first base. The ideal head and eye movement on a pick-off attempt at first base is to have the head and eyes looking toward first base from the set position. Just as the right foot lifts off the ground and the hands start moving from the set, the pitcher will look toward the plate followed quickly by a look back to first base. As the hands break in front of the pitcher's body and the right leg is at the balance point, he will look back to a spot about halfway between home plate and first base and throw the ball to first base for the pick-off attempt. Hopefully this type of head and eye action will freeze the runner off the base, especially if he has a two-way stealing lead. Other times he may wish to just keep his head and eyes pointing toward first base when throwing over to the base, and pointing toward home plate when throwing to the plate.

4. The pivot leg on the rubber (left leg) must be flexed slightly at the knee with the weight evenly distributed over the foot when the pitcher breaks from the set position. The leg must actually begin to drive toward the plate in order to freeze the runner off the base. At the last instant, as the momentum to first base is initiated, the weight must be shifted to the ball

of the foot. If the pitcher keeps his left knee straight when throwing to first base and bends it when going to the plate, the runner at first base would easily be able to pick this up after a couple of pitches and maybe one pick-off attempt at first base.

5. The lead leg (right leg) must be lifted the same height each time. If the pitcher's lead leg is lifted higher when going to first base than it is lifted when going to the plate, this will certainly give his intentions away to the runner at first base. The same holds true for the pitcher's lead leg toe. Some pitchers will point their toe toward first base when throwing to the base, and keep their toe pointed straight down when throwing to the plate. As mentioned previously, the lefthanded pitcher that can duplicate all his actions breaking from the set position no matter which direction he will be throwing the ball, will have a very effective move to first base.

6. The shoulders must remain square to first base throughout the move to first base or to the plate. The upper body should remain relatively static while the hands are breaking from the set position and the lead leg raises up to prepare for the pitch or the throw to first base. If the shoulders rotate toward second base it will generally mean that the pitcher is going to throw to the plate.

7. One of the easiest ways for the runner at first base to get a big jump on the lefthanded pitcher when stealing second base is when the pitcher swings his lead leg (right leg) past the rubber when delivering the ball to the plate. Thus, the pitcher needs to keep his lead leg even with the pitching rubber when going to the plate or to first base. Once the lead leg passes the rubber, the pitcher is committed to throw the ball to the plate, unless he is going to execute an inside pick-off play at second base. If he was to throw the ball to first base after the lead leg has gone back of the rubber, it is a balk if detected by the umpire. The closer the pitcher can keep the lead leg near the plane of the pitching rubber the more effective his pick-off move at first base will become.

8. As the pitcher starts his motion from the set position by raising his lead leg, his hands should also move up and slightly away from the body. This movement away from the body will serve a twofold purpose: (1) the arm action has a tendency to freeze or isolate the runner; and (2) it helps to free the pitcher's arm out and away from his body for good throwing action for the delivery to home plate or for the attempted pick-off at first base. The pitcher's hand and arm action out of the glove at this point in time should look identical for when he delivers the ball to the plate. Once the throwing hand breaks from the glove, the runner at first base must be making the decision on his status as a baserunner. If the pitcher's move is such that he has frozen the runner at this point, there is very little chance for the runner to get a great jump on an attempted steal of second base. If the pitcher has given away his intentions prior to or at the time the throwing hand breaks from the glove, the runner at first base should be able to get a good jump on a steal attempt. There is also an excellent chance that the runner could be picked off first base if at this point in time he has not started his motion back to first base. The successful pick-off at first base will now depend on how quickly and accurately the pitcher can throw the ball to the first baseman. His arm action and step toward first base must be such that there is no wasted motion or time delay.

9. The pitcher must step in the general direction of first base when throwing to the base for the pick-off attempt. This is interpreted as the right foot landing on the first base side of the 45 degree angle between first base and home plate. By pointing the right toe toward first base as it lands on the throw to first base, the pitcher may be able to step further toward home plate than the 45 degree angle without being called for a balk. By taking a step directly toward first base with the left foot after the ball leaves the pitcher's hand, it will assist in making the umpire feel that movement toward first base was accomplished.

10. The tempo of the pitcher's movement from the set position must be the same for when he throws to the plate as when he throws to first base on the pick-off attempt. Many pitchers will slow down or speed up the tempo of their movement from the set position when throwing to first base as contrasted by the tempo of their movement from the set position when delivering the ball to the plate. This would again be something that the opposing team could pick up as they attempt to ''read'' the lefthanded pitcher's move to first base.

2. **Runner at second base**—The pitching staff must fully recognize the fact that the runner at second base can steal third base just as easily as the runner at first base can steal second base. Since the runner can get a longer lead from second base than he can from first base, many base runners feel that third base is easier to steal than second base. The main reason why more runners do not attempt to steal third base is the fact that at second base they are already in scoring position. Thus, the coach and the runner do not want to gamble having a runner in scoring position thrown out at third base on a steal attempt. If the pitcher and his middle infielders do not do a good job of holding a quick runner on at second base, the steal of third base

can be a high percentage move on the runner's part. One of the main reasons that a runner can get a bigger lead at second base than he can at first base is that it takes a little longer for the pitcher to make a pick-off attempt at second base since he must make a 180 degree turn before delivering the ball to the shortstop or second baseman at the bag.

A. **Holding the runner on at second base**—The pitcher will expect a lot of help from one or both of his middle infielders in holding a runner close to second base. In the earlier pick-off section of the Playbook various types of pick-off plays were detailed that can be used to keep the runner at second base honest, and allow for a smoothly executed pick-off attempt. All of the basic strategy used by the pitcher in holding the runner on at first base can be used also with holding a runner on at second base. These items would include: (1) knowledge of the runner's capabilities and the offensive strategy of the opposing team taking into consideration the situation in the game; (2) reading any unnatural leads or body movements by the runner; (3) changing the timing pattern on the stretch delivery; and (4) alternating the number of looks at the runner leading off the base. The pitcher will not have any difficulty in seeing the runner at second base from the set position as the righthanded pitcher does with a runner leading off first base. Thus, there is never any reason for a pitcher to have any problem in evaluating the type of lead that the runner might be taking at second base. Alternating the number of looks at the runner at second base is a very important factor in properly dealing with the runner. If the pitcher was to fall into any set pattern on his looks to second base, the runner with the steal of third base in mind could get a major jump on the pitcher. This is especially true of the pitcher who can be classified as a "one-looker". After his one look at the runner at second base, he will turn his head back to the plate and then deliver the ball to the plate in a set time pattern. Thus, the runner can feel somewhat safe with this type of pitcher to begin his movement toward third base when the pitcher turns his head back toward the plate.

B. **Pick-off mechanics at second base**—The three basic types of pick-off mechanics used by a pitcher in making an attempt to retire the runner at second base would be: (1) the conventional jump pivot; (2) the inside pick-off move; and (3) the pick-off from the windup position on the rubber. All three moves can be effective deterrents in keeping a runner honest at second base along with the distinct possibility of an out deriving from one of these pick-off moves. The actual timing and signal system used in these three types of pick-off plays in conjunction with one of the middle infielders was previously detailed in the pick-off section of the Playbook. We will discuss in detail the mechanics for the pitcher in each of these three pick-off moves. The mechanics for both the righthanded and lefthanded pitcher are the same for each of these three basic plays.

1. **The conventional jump pivot**—The key to a successful jump pivot pick-off at second base is the quickness of the pitcher's feet in the actual pivot from the set position. Since the runner at second base will generally be keying on the pitcher's feet, the quickness of the feet will be the ultimate key to a successful attempt on the runner. The pitcher can attempt the pick-off at second base anytime during the stretch delivery, but it is normally done once the pitcher has assumed the set position. This is due to the fact that this is a basic timing play between the pitcher and one of the middle infielders breaking for the base. This is difficult to accomplish if the play develops prior to the pitcher coming to the set position. It is important that the pitching staff understand that the pitcher does not have to throw the ball to second base once he jump pivots, as he would have to do when dealing with the runner at first base. As long as he steps in the general direction of second base, he does not have to throw the ball if he sees that there is no chance for a play on the runner. The mechanics for the jump pivot to second base are somewhat identical with the mechanics for the righthanded pitcher's pick-off move to first base. The only major exception would be that the pitcher must make a 180 degree jump pivot in order to clear the rubber and allow for a proper throw to second base. This is accomplished by a quick jump pivot whereby his pivot foot which was in contact wtih the rubber ends up about six inches in front of the rubber, and his non-pivot foot pointing in the general direction of second base about four to six inches on the second base side of the rubber. As was the case with the righthander's pick-off move to first base, this is not a leap in the air type of pivot. The closer he can keep both feet to the ground as he pivots, the quicker he will be in delivering the ball to second base. The arm action is the same as it was for the move to first base (short arm arc-snap throw). At the time the feet are set on the jump pivot, the pitcher's arm should be up and the ball is just about to be released. The pitcher should always jump pivot to his glove side to second base. There are some pitchers that jump pivot in the other direction, but this will cause them to drop their arm which will take a little away from their velocity and accuracy on the throw. If they attempt to get the arm up on this type of pivot to second base, valuable time is wasted in releasing the ball.

2. **The inside pick-off move**—This pick-off move to second base is generally prompted when the runner at second base is observed taking a quick aggressive move to his secondary lead whenever the pitcher picks up his lead leg to throw to the plate. The key to the success of this move is the ability of the pitcher to lift the lead leg achieving a proper balance point, and then rotating on his pivot foot in contact with the rubber as he steps toward second base for the pick-off attempt. If the pitcher can freeze the runner at his primary lead or force him to move toward third base as he reaches this balance point, the chance for success on this type of pick-off is great. Thus, as the lead leg comes up and

reaches the balance point, the pitcher who can make the runner think that this is his normal motion for a delivery to the plate can get the out at second base most of the time. The pitcher must not lean backward toward second base as the move develops, nor can he start turning with the upper part of the body until the lead leg reaches its normal height for the delivery to the plate. Any unnatural motion associated with this move can quickly be detected by the runner. As the pitcher reaches the balance point, he would rotate on the rubber onto the toes of the pivot foot. If there happens to be a hole in front of the rubber, the pitcher must be sure to place his entire foot on the rubber itself, to expedite this pivot action. The hands coming up with the lead leg must remain parallel to the body right up until the point that the pivoting takes place on the rubber. Once the rotation of the body begins, the movement has got to be quick for the runner will be able to observe that there is going to be a pick-off attempt on him at second base. As the pitcher rotates on the rubber and quickly brings his stride leg down stepping directly toward second base, the arm should already be up and in a position to release the ball to the shortstop or second baseman at the base. Due to the fact that the rotation of the body is reverse to the glove side rotation as used in the jump pivot pick-off at second base, there is a natural inclination to drop the arm on the throw to second base. This is done to speed up the release of the ball from the hand. This is acceptable as long as the pitcher can still achieve the velocity and accuracy necessary for a good throw to the base. If at all possible, the pitcher should attempt to get the arm up prior to his releasing the ball. The use of video-tape is recommended in practice sessions in working with the pitching staff in developing their mechanics on the inside pick-off move. By placing the camera at the primary lead position of a baserunner at second base, the pitchers can easily see what they look like to the runner at second base. This move is a deception move with great quickness, so the pitchers need to work on this deception in practice sessions. The use of video-tape is highly recommended for evaluating the pick-off moves of the pitching staff at all three bases.

3. **The pick-off from the windup position on the rubber**—Many times the runner leading off second base is not fully concentrating on the pitcher when the pitcher is assuming the windup position on the rubber. This is in comparison to the times that the pitcher is at the set position when the runner is most concerned about a possible pick-off attempt. Thus, with the proper execution and timing the pitcher may be able to pick the runner off second base with the pick-off move initiated from the windup position on the rubber. As mentioned previously in the pick-off section of the Playbook, this is a basic timing play with the catcher signaling the pitcher when to throw to second base as the shortstop breaks toward the bag. As was the case with the other pick-off moves at second base, the runner at second base should not detect anything out of the ordinary on the pitcher's part prior to the actual movement of the body on the pick-off attempt. The pitcher who normally has his hands together in front of his body as he prepares for the windup will have a slight edge in quickness on this throw to second base, in comparison with the pitcher who has his throwing arm hanging from his side. This does not mean that the pitcher who normally has his arm hanging from his side should change his windup stance. This certainly will be evident to the runner at second base alerting him to the fact that there might be something out of the ordinary about to occur. The only thing different that the pitcher should do is to put a little more weight on his front pivot foot on the rubber. He should also make sure that the pivot foot is on top of the rubber so that the front spikes are on the rubber, not hanging over the front of the rubber. This is done to make the pivot on the rubber that much easier. It should not be noticeable to the runner at second base. As soon as the pitcher is signaled by the catcher to pick at second base, he will merely pivot on the rubber with his front foot and quickly step toward second base with his back foot. He must step directly toward second base with the non-pivot foot. As with all quick pick-off moves at any base, the arm should be brought up quickly to the throwing position so that there is no wasted motion with the arm. Since the pitcher is pivoting to the glove side on this move, there should be no reason for the pitcher's arm to drop when releasing the ball. As in all pick-off plays at second base, the pitcher does not have to throw the ball if he sees that he has no play on the runner.

3. **Runner at third base**—The pitcher and third baseman must always concern themselves with the runner leading off third base to be sure that he is not allowed the opportunity to take too big a lead off the base. Of course, the bigger the lead at third base the closer the runner is to the plate.

A. **Holding the runner on at third base**—Anytime the pitcher is concerned about the runner at third base because of a possible suicide squeeze attempt, a steal of home plate, or an important runner at third base is taking an aggressive secondary lead he should pitch from the stretch delivery. If none of these factors are evident, then he should pitch from the windup delivery. When the pitcher is throwing from the windup, he must always check the runner at third base as he begins his motion. This is so he might be in a better position to make an adjustment in his pitch to the plate if he was to observe the runner breaking full speed for the plate. If the runner is merely taking his regular walking lead, the pitcher can look back toward the plate to pick up his target. Once the pitcher's lead leg lifts off the ground for the delivery to the plate from the windup, he should begin focusing all his attention on the pitch to the plate. Checking the runner at third base from the windup is most important for the lefthanded pitcher since the runner could get a tremendous jump towards the plate if he is not checked on his initial movement toward the plate. The righthanded pitcher can easily check the runner's status from the set position, and can hold his gaze on the runner as his lead leg comes off the ground. This can not be done by the lefthanded pitcher breaking from the set position since he will have his back completely to the runner at third base. The pitcher can never allow the runner at third base to break his concentration on the pitch by feinting motions toward the plate. Anytime the pitcher and third baseman feel that a runner at third base is taking too big of a primary lead, or the runner's secondary lead is a little too aggressive, then a timed pick-off play can be executed.

   B. **Pick-off mechanics at third base**—The signal system and timing involved with pick-off plays at third base were previously detailed in the pick-off section of the Playbook. We will discuss briefly the mechanics for the pitcher in the pick-off plays available to him for the runner at third base. The pitcher and third baseman must always keep in mind the importance of not allowing a pick-off at third base to result in an overthrow, since this will practically always result in a run scoring.

      1. **Pick-off mechanics at third base (righthanded pitcher)**—From the stretch delivery, the pick-off mechanics at third base for the righthanded pitcher are exactly the same as they are for the lefthanded pitcher throwing to first base. Since the righthanded pitcher does not rely on this pick-off move to third base as much as the lefthanded does for the move to first base, it is not practical to expect all the righthanded pitchers on the staff to fine tune a deceptive move to third base. However, they must develop the pick-off move from the set position so that they might have a legitimate opportunity to retire a runner who might be taking a large primary lead with an aggressive secondary lead off third base. They must be sure to step in the general direction of third base when making their throw to the base, similar to the restriction that is placed upon the lefthanded pitcher's throw to first base from the stretch delivery. The pitcher does not have to throw to third base if there is no play on the runner. The key to a successful pick-off move to third base is the length of time the runner can be deceived to think that the pitcher is going to deliver the ball to the plate. The righthanded pitcher should review the mechanics for the pick-off at first base that were presented to the lefthanded pitcher.

      2. **Pick-off mechanics at third base (lefthanded pitcher)**—With baserunners at second and third base, the lefthanded pitcher should check the status of the runner at second base by looking over his left shoulder. He would then check the runner at third base by looking over his right shoulder. By looking over the left shoulder in this situation, it will also allow the pitcher the opportunity to check the runner at second base which will allow him to be in a position to respond to a possible pick-off play on that runner at second base. This will also enable the pitcher to see the third baseman if there is a timed pick-off play involved around the third baseman's break toward third base. With a runner at third base only, with the pitcher at the set position, he can check the runner over the right shoulder. A timed pick-off throw from the pitcher to the third baseman is not highly recommended due to the fact it is practically a blind side throw and it is very difficult for the pitcher to react to the movement of the third baseman. If the runner is observed taking a large primary lead, then a timed pick-off play can be set-up with the third baseman, with the pitcher picking up the third baseman out of the corner of his eye.

THE PITCHER AS A FIELDER

   Once the pitch leaves the pitcher's hand, the pitcher can no longer consider himself a pitcher. He is now a fielder until the ball is cleanly caught by the catcher. Many pitchers leave the distinct impression that they feel their job is completed when they throw the pitch to the plate. The pitcher who takes tremendous pride in his fielding responsibility can save many a ball game for himself and his team.

   It is the responsibillity of the coach to make certain that his pitching staff knows how to deal with every type of defensive situation that they might face in the course of a game. In the fundamental drill series and situation plays that were previously detailed in the Playbook, the pitching staff can be drilled in these basic defensive responsibilities. The following are the areas of fielding responsibilities and mechanics that the pitchers must be drilled on so that they can provide the team with a capable fifth infielder:

1. **Fielding position on the follow through**—To be a consistent fielder, the pitcher must finish with his follow through in a squared position to the batter so that he might be ready to respond defensively to a batted ball. If his delivery to the plate causes him to fall off to either side of the mound, his defensive capabilities will be drastically diminished. The pivot foot should end up as near parallel to the stride foot as possible on his follow through, with the weight equally balanced on the balls of both feet. Once in this basic fielding position, he must anticipate that the batter will be hitting the ball back at him on each pitch. A good fielding pitcher who can knock down ground balls directly up the middle of the infield can allow his shortstop and second baseman to move a couple of steps away from second base, which will make the infield defense that much tighter.

2. Fielding the ground ball hit back to the mound—There is not an infielder around who would like to face the prospect of attempting to field a ground ball off an incline such as the pitcher is confronted with in the case of the mound. This is why the pitching staff needs to receive plenty of fungoed ground balls while positioned on the mound in their follow through stance. Since the pitcher is only about 55 feet away from the hitter on their follow through, they must be prepared to get their glove on the ball for two reasons: (1) to field the ball in order to make a play on a runner; and (2) to protect themselves from bodily injury. Knocking the ball down will generally give the pitcher the chance to retire a runner since the ball will reach the pitcher quicker than to any infielder. If they can cleanly field the "come-backer", they should have no problem getting an out somewhere. Thus, the pitcher must accept the challenge of keeping every ground ball back to him in front of his body. He must get his glove on the ball unless the hitter hits a "rocket". It is important that the pitcher look the ground ball into his glove, and then take his time exchanging the ball out of the glove to his throwing hand.

3. Throwing the ball from the mound to first base—If the play on the runner is to be at first base, the pitcher must allow the first baseman ample time to get set-up at the base. This is especially true when the pitcher fields a hard hit ground ball when the first baseman is playing well away from the base. If this is the case, the pitcher should shuffle step or crow hop toward first base as he waits to throw the ball to first base. Throwing from a stationary position on the mound can cause an inaccurate throw to first base. He should always throw the ball as soon as the first baseman is set on the base so that if the throw is off target, the first baseman has time to come off the base to field the ball and still return to the base for the force out. The pitcher should never play games with the runner heading for first base. The pitcher must be sure he gets his elbow up so that the ball does not tail on the first baseman on its way to first base. He should never aim the ball, for this is the main reason for inaccurate throws to first base. This is especially the case when the pitcher has plenty of time, and starts thinking about the throw. The ball should be thrown about three-quarters the normal speed of the pitcher's fast ball to the plate. Of course, if he boots the ball or there is an extremely fast runner heading for first base, he will have to deliver his best fast ball to the first baseman. As the pitcher steps and throws to first base, he wants the ball to be caught by the first baseman from the area of his chest to his shoulders.

4. Fielding bunts and slow rollers—The key to the success of a pitcher getting an out on a slowly hit or bunted ball is the quickness of the pitcher off the mound to the spot where the ball will be fielded. Once he gets to this spot, he must have his body under control so that he might field the ball and set his feet properly for a strong and accurate throw to a base. Another key to getting an out on this play is the pitcher's ability to keep his eyes on the ball throughout the fielding stage. Too many times a pitcher, in his rush to come up throwing, never sees the ball into his glove which may prompt a misplay on the ball. Any misplay or bobble on this type of play will result in the defense not getting an out. The pitchers must be cautioned to always field the ball first, and then worry about the throw to the respective base where the play will be made.

5. Balls to the first base side of the mound with a play at first base (righthanded pitcher)—On slow hit or bunted balls to the first base side of the mound, the righthanded pitcher should use his glove as a shovel, with his bare hand scooping the ball into the glove. Both hands should come up together toward the right shoulder as the pitcher plants his right foot for the throw to first base. The pitcher should never bare hand the ball unless it has stopped on the grass. This would be a do-or-die play at first base. There may be times that the righthanded pitcher will not have time to straighten up to throw the ball to first base. If that is the case, he needs to get his elbow up as high as possible when releasing the ball off balance so that his throw is more accurate and the first baseman can see the ball more clearly. He should attempt to throw the ball to the inside of first base so that the first baseman gets a good picture of the ball. The first baseman must always yell "inside-inside" anytime the pitcher or catcher fields a ball close to the first baseline. The closer the pitcher is to the first baseman at the time of the throw, the higher the throw should be to the first baseman so that he can see the ball that much easier. Of course, the closer the pitcher is to the first baseman the softer the throw as well. If fielding a ball close to the first baseman, the pitcher needs to be sure to give him a clear view of the ball as he tosses it underhand to him (pull the glove out of the way). If the righthanded pitcher has time and he is a good distance away from first base when he fields the ball, then he should step toward first base to add velocity and accuracy to his throw.

6. Balls to the first base side of the mound with a play at first base (lefthanded pitcher)—The closer the ball is to the first baseline, the tougher the play will be for the lefthanded pitcher. This is due to the fact of the nature of the angle of the throw to first base and the full pivot necessary for the pitcher to execute a throw to the first baseman covering the bag. The lefthanded pitcher must overrun the ball slightly, spin on his left foot, and make the throw to first base by stepping in the direction of the throw with his right foot. All the other rules for making this play would be the same as they were described for the righthanded pitcher.

7. Communication on ball rolling near either baseline—Good judgment by the pitcher is necessary in dealing with bunts or slow rollers down either baseline. He must make the quick decision on whether to field the ball or let it roll in the hope that it will roll foul. The catcher should be in a position to help the pitcher in making this decision since he has a better angle on the movement of the ball in relation to the baseline. The catcher can yell out "field it" when he recommends that the pitcher field the ball in hopes of retiring the runner at first base. "Let it go" should indicate his desire to have the pitcher let the ball roll hoping that it will roll into foul territory. Anytime there is no chance of retiring the runner at first base, the ball should not be touched if there is any chance that the ball might roll into foul territory. "Hit it" is the communication that should be used by the catcher to have the pitcher touch the ball if it clearly is in foul territory in order to prevent the ball from rolling back into fair territory. The same communication can be used by the catcher in dealing with the first baseman and third baseman when they are fielding the ball near their respective baseline.

8. **Communication on balls to the first base side of the mound**—In addition to being aggressive off the mound on a slow hit or bunted ball, the pitcher must also be an aggressive communicator. Ideally, the pitcher wants to field every ball on the first base side of the mound so that his first baseman can remain at first base to field the throw from the pitcher. This means that the pitcher must let the first baseman know as soon as he reads that he can make the play on the ball. This would be communicated by a loud "I've got it". This command will allow the first baseman to remain or return to first base preparing himself for the throw to the base by the pitcher. If the first baseman sees that the pitcher will be unable to make the play on the ball, and he does not hear any command by the pitcher, he must aggressively go after the ball. The first baseman should also yell "I've got it" so that the pitcher might break toward first base for the throw from the first baseman. If both the pitcher and the first baseman call for the ball at about the same time, the pitcher should have priority on the ball since he has a better throwing angle to first base than the first baseman will have with his back to the base. Whenever the first baseman and the pitcher both break for the slow hit or bunted ball on the first base side of the mound, the second baseman will be responsible for covering first base for the throw to the base. With a lefthanded pitcher going to the first baseline for a ball, the first baseman will want to be a little more aggressive in calling for and fielding the ball. With a righthanded pitcher going toward the first baseline, he will not be as aggressive since the righthanded pitcher will have a much easier play on this type of ball than the lefthander. Anytime the catcher calls for the ball, he would have priority over both the first baseman and the pitcher since he will be moving toward first base as he fields the ball. Bunt communication was detailed in the bunt defense section in an earlier part of the Playbook.

9. **Balls in front of the mound with a play at first base (righthanded pitcher)**—The righthanded pitcher must break down as he approaches this ball aggressively communicating to the catcher that he will make the play by yelling "I've got it". The catcher will have priority over him if both were to yell for the ball. After he looks the ball into his glove, he will take a shuffle step toward first base with his right foot, and then step and throw with his left foot. The pitcher should never throw this ball flat-footed due to the distance the throw must travel to first base. As in all throws that involve a little distance, the arm should be up and the body in proper throwing position. This will insure better accuracy and velocity for the throw. The ball fielded in front of the mound by the pitcher should never involve a do-or-die play on the pitcher's part unless the pitcher was slow getting off the mound and the bunt was perfectly placed. If that is the case, hopefully the catcher can make the play. If not, it is better that no throw be made unless the pitcher is a great athlete and can make an across the body throw toward first base. Anytime the ball is booted by the pitcher, he should always pick it up with his bare hand rather than with his glove or his hand and glove together. Once the ball is in his hand, he will have to rush the throw to first base. He should just step in the direction of first base with his left foot hoping to get off as strong and accurate throw as his arm will allow him to make.

10. **Balls in front of the mound with a play at first base (lefthanded pitcher)**—The lefthanded pitcher will have to make a full glove side pivot toward first base in order to make an accurate and strong throw. The pitcher who has quick feet will have no major problem in accomplishing this type of pivot. Even though this pivot takes a little more time than if the pitcher was to pivot to his throwing side, it puts him in a much better position to throw to first base. If the ball is a little on the first base side in front of the mound, he can pivot to his throwing side. Anytime this is done, he must be sure that he steps directly toward first base with his right foot concentrating on getting his elbow up so that the ball will not sail on him to first base. The catcher should take the bunted ball in front of the mound near the plate with a lefthanded pitcher on the mound whenever possible.

11. **Balls to the third base side of the mound with a play at first base (righthanded pitcher)**—The bunted or slow hit ball to the third base side of the mound is a difficult play for the pitcher due to the fact that his momentum is moving away from the direction where the throw must be made (first base). In addition, he has a long throw to make to retire the runner at first base. The righthanded pitcher must field the ball cleanly making sure that he does not rush through the fielding of the ball and the transfer of the ball to his throwing hand. Once the ball is fielded, he must shuffle step toward first base to establish momentum for the long throw to first base. If the pitcher does not shuffle step (throws flat footed) he may get rid of the ball a little quicker, but the velocity and accuracy of the throw will be affected. Thus, whenever possible the pitcher should take the extra step to establish proper body balance and momentum for this long throw to first base. This is especially true the closer the ball is fielded toward the third baseline.

12. Balls to the third base side of the mound with a play at first base (lefthanded pitcher)—This is an extremely tough play for the lefthanded pitcher due to the fact that he not only has a long throw to make to first base, but he will have to make a full glove side pivot in order to make a strong and accurate throw to the first baseman. He must field the ball on his glove side with his right side already opened up slightly. The tendency will be for the lefthanded pitcher to rush through the fielding stage knowing that he will have a tough play to get the runner at first base. He must fully concentrate on looking the ball into the glove, and then with quick feet, pivot clockwise (glove side) stepping toward first base with his right foot. If time allows, he may shuffle step toward first base to establish more velocity and accuracy on his throw. Due to the fact that this is a very tough play for the lefthanded pitcher, the third baseman and catcher must take this ball away from the pitcher whenever possible.

13. Communication on balls to the third base side of the mound—As was the case with the slow hit or bunted ball on the first base side of the mound, the pitcher must be an aggressive communicator on the ball to the third base side of the mound. This means that the pitcher must let the third baseman and catcher know as soon as he reads that he can make the play on the ball by yelling loudly "I've got it". This is especially crucial with baserunners at first and second base when the third baseman is attempting to hold his ground near the base for the possible play at the base by the pitcher or catcher once the ball has been fielded. The quicker the pitcher can let the third baseman know that he can make the play, the easier it will be for the third baseman to return to third base preparing himself for the throw to the base by the pitcher. If the third baseman sees that the pitcher will be unable to make the play on the ball, or he does not hear any command by the pitcher, he must aggressively go after the ball in hopes of getting the out at first base. The third baseman should also yell "I've got it" so that the pitcher will not interfere with his making the play on the ball. If both the pitcher and third baseman call for the ball, the third baseman should have priority. The third baseman should also have priority over the catcher if both were to call for the ball. Of course, the catcher will have priority over the pitcher. Bunt communication was detailed in the bunt defense section of the Playbook.

14. Throwing the ball from the mound to second base—Before throwing the ball to the plate with a runner at first base and less than two outs, the pitcher should know whether the shortstop or the second baseman will be covering second base on a ball hit right back to him on the mound. With baserunners at first and second base with less than two outs, the pitcher should always throw the ball to second base unless the ball takes him to the first base or third base side of the mound. Many times a pitcher will throw the "come-backer" in this situation to the third baseman at third base forcing the third baseman to make a tough pivot at his base followed by a long throw across the diamond to try to complete the double play. With the bases loaded and less than two outs, the pitcher should always throw the ball to the catcher at the plate if he fields the ball near the mound area. At no time should a pitcher throw the ball off-balance to second base. If he is forced to his right or left to field the ball, he should throw the ball to the base that he is moving toward to insure getting at least one out. If the pitcher throws the ball to second base from the area of the mound, he will pivot after fielding the ball and step in the direction of second base before making the throw to the base. Since the throw is not a long throw, there should be no reason for the pitcher to have to shuffle step toward the base prior to releasing the ball. If he fields the ball in front of the mound, and finds his weight on his heels after pivoting toward second base, he may want to shuffle step prior to throwing the ball to insure a strong and accurate throw to second base. If the shortstop is covering the base, the pitcher should lead him slightly with the ball arriving at the shortstop side of the base at about chest height. If the second baseman is covering the base, the pitcher should throw the ball directly over the base. If the middle infielder covering second base is delayed in getting to the base on the hard ground ball back to the pitcher, the pitcher should shuffle step or crow hop toward second base as he waits to release the ball. He should never remain stationary on the mound waiting for the infielder to reach the base for this can cause an inaccurate throw to the base as the pitcher would throw flat footed. The pitcher must be sure that his arm is up when releasing the ball so that he might better get off a stronger and more accurate throw to second base. Since there is always a chance for the double play, the ball must be thrown with good velocity providing the pivotman with a chance to get the out at first base as well. However, the pitcher can never afford to rush his throw, and subsequently find that his throw is off the mark and no out is made at any base. If the catcher has called for the throw to be made to second base, and the pitcher boots the ball, he must quickly pick up the ball with his bare hand and make the play at first base hoping to retire the batter-runner.

15. Balls in front of the mound or near the baselines with a throw to second base—The mechanics of this play are basically the same for the righthanded and lefthanded pitcher. They both will have to make a full pivot after they field the ball in order to get off a strong and accurate throw to second base. The direction of the ball in relation to the baseline will determine the difficulty of the pivot for the pitcher. For example, the ball near the first baseline will call for a little easier pivot for a play at second base for the right handed pitcher than for the lefthanded pitcher. Vice versa, the ball down the third baseline will call for an easier pivot for the lefthanded pitcher in contrast with the pivot the righthanded pitcher will have to make. The catcher should assume the responsibility of directing the fielder of a slow hit or bunted ball as to which base the ball should be thrown. This communication was discussed in detail earlier in the bunt defense section of the Playbook. With a runner at first base and less than two outs, the pitcher has got to anticipate whether or not he will have a play on the runner advancing to second base as he approaches the ball. If the pitcher must go a great distance from the mound to field the ball, he can safely assume that the only play the catcher will call is to first base. In most cases, he should be thinking second base as he approaches the ball, so that he is not shocked when the catcher starts yelling "two-two". The pitcher should always field the ball on his glove side along with having his body slightly opened to the glove side so that the body does not have as far to pivot once the ball is cleanly fielded. By dropping back the foot on the glove side slightly as the ball is fielded, he is now in a better position to pivot toward second base. Once the ball is cleanly fielded, the pitcher must shuffle step quickly in the direction of second base as his throwing arm prepares to release the ball. The shuffle step is necessary due to the length of the throw that must be made to second base. Pitchers with extremely strong arms might not need the benefit of the shuffle step toward second base. They would merely pivot and bend low to push off the back leg as they step toward second base. The chance for the double play on a ball that takes the pitcher well off the mound is minimal. However, there is always the chance for the force out at second base. Late in the game, the catcher may wish to gamble on the lead runner and the pitcher must be prepared to get off a strong and accurate throw to the shortstop or second baseman on the bag. If the pitcher observes as he prepares to throw to second base that he will not have a play at the base, then he must quickly shift his feet so that he can step and throw the ball to first base.

16. **Balls in front of the mound or near the baselines with a throw to third base (righthanded pitcher)**—Anytime the pitcher is instructed by the catcher to throw the ball to third base ("three-three") on a slow hit or bunted ball, the situation is generally critical. If the attempt on the runner at third base is unsuccessful, it will put a runner at third base without the benefit of an out recorded. The righthanded pitcher is at a disadvantage on any throw to third base from in front of the mound or near a baseline since he will have to make a complete pivot before releasing the ball. The chances for a double play via third base on this type of ball is practically impossible, so the pitcher's full concentration must be on getting the force out at third base. Communication on the bunted ball is crucial to getting the out at third base, especially on the bunted ball to the third base side of the mound. This communication was detailed in the bunt defense section of the Playbook. If the ball takes the righthanded pitcher directly toward third base, he can merely underhand or flip the ball to the third baseman covering the base. If the ball takes him toward the third baseline, he might be able to pivot to his throwing side after fielding the ball if he feels that this is the only method to make the play at third base. Anytime he pivots to his throwing side, he must be sure to step as much as possible in the direction of third base. This requires quick feet on the part of the righthanded pitcher. He must also attempt to get his throwing arm up as much as he can to insure a more accurate throw to third base. This will also provide the third baseman with a clearer view of the ball as it leaves the pitcher's hand. On any other type of slow hit or bunted ball, the righthanded pitcher must make the full glove side pivot toward third base prior to releasing the ball. He should field the ball on his glove side, pivot quickly so that he pushes off his right foot and steps with his left foot in the direction of his throw to third base. If he fields the ball near the first baseline and is instructed by the catcher to make the throw to third base, he might have to shuffle step prior to his release of the ball to insure more velocity to his throw. Most of the time, the ball near the first baseline will not allow for a play at third base, unless the pitcher is very quick to the ball and the runner going from second to third base is very slow. All throws to third base for the force out should be thrown chest high to the third baseman. If the pitcher recognizes the fact that he will not have a play at third base, then he must quickly glove side pivot to set his feet for the play at first base on the batter-runner. The same holds true if he boots the ball when his intentions were to make the throw to third base.

17. **Balls in front of the mound or near the baselines with a throw to third base (lefthanded pitcher)**—The lefthanded pitcher has a distinct advantage over the righthanded pitcher in making the throw to third base after fielding the ball. A ball fielded to the third base side of the mound will require practically no pivot at all as the pitcher shovels the ball into his glove. The ball fielded on the first base side of the mound will require the lefthander to glove side pivot after fielding the ball on his glove hand side. If the pitcher needs to insure additional velocity on his throw to third base, he would shuffle step toward the base as he prepares to release the ball. The shuffle step should not be necessary for any ball fielded in front of the mound or to the third base side due to the short distance of the throw.

18. **Plays at the plate on a ground ball**—On any ground ball fielded by the pitcher with a play at the plate, he must be sure that he makes an accurate throw. He can not afford to rush this throw or make an off-balance throw, unless it is a do-or-die play with the tying or winning run attempting to score from third base. A poor throw to the plate will cause a run to score with no out recorded on the play. If the bases are loaded, the pitcher should throw the ball chest high to the catcher right over the plate. This will allow the catcher an easy ball to handle on the force out at the plate, along with his pivot toward first base to make the play on the batter-runner. The pitcher must step and throw with his arm up to insure the accuracy of his throw to the catcher. The closer he is to the catcher when he releases the ball, the softer the throw must be in order to allow the catcher ample time to pick up the flight of the ball. If the pitcher is moving toward the plate as he fields the ball, he can underhand flip the ball to the catcher. If the play at the plate is going to involve a tag play on the catcher's part, the pitcher will want to throw the ball at the catcher's left knee as he positions himself near the plate for the tag play.

344

19. **Faking the throw to first base on a ball with no play at any base**—There will be times when the pitcher will field a slow hit or bunted ball that will not allow him the opportunity to get an out at any base. With runners on base, the pitcher must fake the throw to first base in hopes that it might cause a runner at another base to take a wide turn anticipating the pitcher's throw to first base. Thus, once he fakes the throw to first base, he must quickly pivot in the direction of third base or second base with the thought in mind of making a throw to that base if the runner happens to be taking an aggressive turn.

20. **Faking the catch of a bunted ball**—With a runner at first base and less than two outs, the pitcher may be able to get a double play on a ball that is bunted to him in the air. Generally, the runner at first base will not break toward second base when he sees the ball in the air. If the pitcher catches the ball before it hits the ground, he must assume immediately that he will have a play at first base doubling up the runner off the base. With an intelligent runner at first base, this should not be the case. If the pitcher allows the ball to hit the ground, he will have a better chance to get the double play no matter how intelligent the runner at first base might be. Once the ball hits the ground, the pitcher should immediately field it and throw the ball to the first baseman at first base for the force out on the batter-runner. Hopefully, the runner at first base would not be advancing toward second base when he sees the bunted ball in the air with the pitcher in a position to make the catch. Once the first baseman receives the ball from the pitcher, he will touch first base for the force out on the batter-runner. He would then throw the ball to the shortstop at second base in hopes of retiring the runner who started out at first base. The shortstop would have to tag the runner coming from first base since the force out was eliminated when the first baseman touched first base retiring the batter-runner. The catcher might assist the pitcher in making the decision on whether to catch the ball in the air or allow it to hit the ground. If the catcher sees that the runner at first base has moved well away from first base on the play, he can yell "catch". The pitcher would then catch the ball in the air and throw the ball to the first baseman for the double play attempt. If the catcher sees the runner at first base reacting properly to the bunted ball in the air (stopping near his secondary lead), he can yell "let it hit" to the pitcher. The pitcher would then allow the ball to hit the ground. He would then field the ball properly and make a quick and accurate throw to the first baseman at first base. The first baseman would then complete the double play attempt with his throw to the shortstop at second base.

21. **Covering first base on a ball hit to the right side of the infield**—One of the most common defensive plays that directly involves the pitcher is those balls hit to the right side of the infield when he is responsible for covering first base. Of course, the quicker the pitcher can get to first base, the easier the play will be for him and the fielder who will be throwing the ball to him for the attempted play on the batter-runner. The pitcher can never afford to assume that the first baseman will be able to get back to first base to receive the throw from the second baseman. Once the first baseman starts movement to his right in hopes of fielding the ground ball, he is going to have a very tough play getting back to first base to receive the throw from the second baseman. This is especially true if the first baseman is playing off the base at the time of the pitch. Thus, the pitcher must break for first base on every ground ball hit to his left. Anytime the pitcher is moving toward first base on this play, and he sees that the first baseman is retreating to the base to field the throw from the second baseman, the pitcher must allow the first baseman to make the play. However, if he sees that the first baseman is going to have a difficult time getting back to first base, he should yell "I've got it" to the first baseman. This should prompt the first baseman to allow the pitcher to field the ball at the base from the second baseman. The same holds true on a ground ball hit to the first baseman with a runner at first base with less than two outs. If the first baseman throws the ball to the shortstop for the front end of an attempted double play, he will then break for first base for the return throw from the shortstop. If the pitcher sees that this will be a difficult play for the first baseman, he should yell "I've got it", and take responsibility of the bag for the throw from the shortstop.

22. **Footwork at first base receiving a throw from the first baseman or second baseman**—There are two methods that the pitcher can use in covering first base when receiving a throw from the first baseman or the second baseman in hopes of retiring the batter-runner:

A. **Angling into the base**—On a ball hit to the first baseman or second baseman that will be fielded by either one behind the baseline between first and second base, the pitcher should angle into the base to make the play. The pitcher will break off the mound full speed to a point adjacent to the first baseline approximately 10-12 feet from first base. He should be on the inside of the baseline at this point to avoid being run over by the batter-runner who will be running right down the line toward first base. Once he reaches this point he will stay on the inside running parallel to the line itself. At this time he will be preparing himself to catch the ball that will be thrown to him from the first baseman or the second baseman. He should do this by chopping his steps and slowing down to the point that he has his body under control to catch the thrown ball. Hopefully, the fielder will throw him the ball chest high or higher leading him in such a way that he can catch the ball about two steps before he touches the bag. If so, he will be in a position to watch the ball into his glove and then concentrate his attention on making proper contact with first base. The pitcher can not afford to catch the ball and then cross the bag into the path of the runner. He should attempt to hit the inside of first base with his right foot, and then get his body back under control so that he might be able to respond if a play develops at another base or home plate. If for some reason the pitcher gets to the bag ahead of the throw, he must stop at the bag and assume the responsibility of a first baseman. This happens generally as a result of the fielder booting the ball. The pitcher must be sure that he positions his feet so that they are not on top of the base, but at the same time, his feet must be in a position to contact the inner part of the base as he fields the throw. Most errors occur on this play when the pitcher takes his eyes off the ball in his attempt to touch first base. This is why it is so important that the first baseman or the second baseman lead the pitcher so that he can catch the ball about two steps away from the base.

B. **Going directly toward the base**—There will be balls hit to the right side of the infield that will necessitate the pitcher going directly to first base rather than angling into the bag as previously detailed. Anytime the first baseman will be fielding the ball in front of the baseline between first and second base, the pitcher should go directly to the base to prepare for the throw from the first baseman. This would also be the case if the ball gets by the first baseman and the second baseman would be fielding the ball in front of the baseline. The pitcher should also go directly to the bag at first base on the first-second-first double play ball. The reason for the pitcher going directly to the base is that there is no need for him to angle down the baseline due to the direction the ball will be coming to him at first base. It would also make for a very difficult play for the pitcher attempting to catch the ball coming toward him from behind his angle of approach to the base. He must break full speed directly toward first base in these types of plays. As he approaches the base he should start chopping his steps so that he can slow down in time to properly position himself to receive the throw from the fielder. He will now assume the responsibility of a first baseman as he positions his feet and body to receive the throw from either the first baseman, second baseman, or shortstop (3-6-1 double play). It would certainly not hurt the pitching staff to be aware of the shifting and stretching techniques used by the first baseman in receiving throws at first base. This information can be found in the infield section of the Playbook.

23. **Covering home plate on a pass ball or wild pitch**—Whenever there is a runner at third base and a pitched ball gets by the catcher, the pitcher must break full speed for the plate. This is also the case in those situations where the catcher is going after a fly ball that takes him away from the area of home plate with a runner tagging up at third base. As the pitcher gets near the plate, he should start slowing down by chopping his steps. He will want to position himself for the tag play at the plate so that he provides the runner with the outside half of the plate to slide into so that there is little chance for the pitcher to be involved in a collision with the runner. By straddling the inside half of the plate, he will be able to protect himself along with having a good opportunity to make a clean tag on the runner. As in all tag plays, he must look the ball into his glove and then make the tag. In this position, the pitcher will have to backhand the ball if the throw is coming to home plate from the first base side of the plate. The tag should be made, if at all possible, with the runner sliding into the back of the pitcher's glove so that there is little chance for the ball to be kicked out of the glove. At all times, the pitcher must protect his throwing hand from getting tangled up with the spikes of the sliding runner.

In earlier sections of the Playbook, the pitcher's defensive responsibilities dealing with the following situations were detailed: fly ball communication and priority system; backing up third base and home plate; bunt defense plays; and first and third double steal plays.

PITCHING MECHANICS CONCENTRATION PROGRAM

The pitching mechanics concentration program was developed to introduce the basic concepts of proper pitching mechanics: rhythm; timing; balance; and control. By following this program a coach should be able to drill his entire pitching staff without tying up his catchers in about 35 minutes. Its purpose is to get pitchers to concentrate intensely on the perfect execution of the prescribed drills. Instead of going through the motions for a long period of time, the pitchers will perform purposefully for a defined period of time. This will definitely lead to the assimilation of the proper pitching form.

In order to attain the staff's maximum potential, it is suggested that this plan be used early in Spring training to develop the groove and touch so vital for success. Coaches should note that the Chair Drill, Stand-up Drill, and In-and-Out Drill should be introduced, and properly assimilated by the pitchers before this program could be put into effect.

For example, the drills should be introduced during the first workout, and then incorporated into the regular warmup routine. The pitchers would first do their stretching and flexibility exercises and then loosen up their arms from the chair. They would then use the Stand-up Drill to continue the loosening up process. In the Stand-up Drill they can work on their entire repertoire of pitches. Then, they would finish by throwing from the windup and set positions from the regulation distance.

The Pitching Mechanics Concentration Program is used during the early part of Spring training to get the pitching staff in the "groove" quickly without putting their arms under any major strain.

We would like to thank Dr. Charles Greene for his help in familiarizing us with the drills in this pitching program. The following is an explanation of the drills.

CHAIR DRILL

This drill emphasizes getting on the glove side. After releasing the ball, body momentum should drive the pitcher directly to home plate and towards the glove hand side.

Set a chair 30 to 40 feet away from home plate. Stand square to home plate with pivot foot (right foot for righthanded pitcher) on the chair by your side. You will be throwing to your partner who is down on one knee at the plate. Go through the basic mechanics of throwing the baseball to the plate concentrating on rotating the pivot heel on the chair upon release of the ball and following through with the throwing shoulder to the opposite knee. The pitcher will set the chair at a distance away from him so that he can maintain the proper body balance as he pivots and releases the ball to the plate.

STAND-UP DRILL

This drill develops balance and the "feel" of not rushing. Stand 40 to 50 feet away from home plate. Start with the left foot pointed at the catcher, with the right foot parallel to the rubber. The distance between the pivot and striding foot should be your correct length of stride. The length of the stride is correct when the center of gravity (belly button area) is directly over the base of support (bent stride knee) upon release of the ball. The execution is the same as the chair drill. Rotate the pivot heel outward but keep it in front of the rubber. After releasing the ball, body momentum should drive the pitcher directly to home plate and towards the glove hand side.

IN-AND-OUT DRILL

The pitcher in this drill deliberately throws pitches outside the strike zone, alternating left and right of the strike zone, but never in the strike zone. The pitcher should get the feel of how to bring the ball from one side of the strike zone to the other.

INSTRUCTIONS TO PITCHERS

1. Will be working in pairs. Pick a partner. Lefthanders work together if possible.

2. Each pitcher will have a ball.

3. A pitcher will execute a drill while his partner catches on one knee.

347

4. Catchers—if you miss a throw from your partner, quickly throw him your ball.

5. On command, switch with partner at 1/2 speed, and assume a "ready position".

6. Concentrate. You will be drilling for only 1.5 minutes at a time. Working at normal speed, you will throw about 15 pitches. You will get what you put into the execution of these drills. Remember, "practice does not make perfect; **perfect** practice makes perfect".

7. In a 35 minute session, you will drill for 13.5 minutes, throwing between 150 to 165 pitches.

8. Make sure that you do all your stretching and flexibility exercises before the drills.

35 MINUTE MECHANICS CONCENTRATION PROGRAM

Chair Drill

1. **Fast balls**—Concentrate on: hip and front shoulder explosion, and releasing the ball as you rotate your pivot heel outward on the chair. This develops the correct upper body timing needed to deliver the ball at your maximum velocity......1.5 minutes.

2. **Curve balls**—Concentrate on: a quick, fluid, fast ball type arm action. Palm faces ear as the arm moves into the up position and elbow leads. Impart a 12-6 spin on the ball. Overemphasize your follow through. Finish with the chest over the knee......1.5 minutes.

Stand-up Drill

1. **Fast balls**—Concentrate on: proper arm action for the fast ball. Palm of ball-hand down as it comes out of the glove. Loose figure eight motion gets the arm down and up. 100% effort with forearm and wrist down and across to opposite knee. Feel the ball coming off the end of your fingertips. Impart a tight spin. Low strikes.......1.5 minutes. In-and-out......1.5 minutes.

2. **Curve balls**—Concentrate on: distinguishing between the feel of the strike and the strikeout curve ball. Strike curve balls......1.5 minutes. Strikeout curve balls......1.5 minutes. Strikeout curve balls break low and away from the plate; strike curve balls break to the middle of the plate.

3. **Sliders**—Concentrate on: achieving a bullet-like spin on the ball by holding it slightly off center and throwing it like a fast ball with a "yank" of the middle finger upon release. Best break is achieved if pitched low and away......1.5 minutes. (Note: if you don't throw a slider, then alternate fast balls and strike curve balls).

Pitching from the Set Position (at 60'6" and 3/4 hand speed)

Establish rhythm from the set position. Mesh the "gears" of the upper and lower body. Concentrate on: not leaning towards home plate until the hands break. Immediately after planting the front foot, expode the back hip forcefully toward the plate, and release the ball.....1.5 minutes. (Note: if you have proper rhythm, throwing at 3/4 speed should be an almost effortless, smooth progression of movements).

Control Contest from the Windup Position (at 60'6" and 3/4 hand speed)

Warmup tosses—3 fast balls and 3 curve balls. Best out of ten. Alternating fast ball/curve ball. Loser: add 20 situps to the regular 50 at the end of practice. Winner: see that the extra situps are done by a loser......1.5 minutes. (Note: in case of a tie, the pitcher who threw the last loses).

Drill Time Breakdown

Chair Drill
- Fast balls . . . . .1.5 minutes
- Curve balls . . . . .1.5 minutes

Stand-up Drill
- Fast balls . . . . .Low strikes . . . . .1.5 minutes
- In-and-out . . . . .1.5 minutes
- Curve balls . . . . .Strike curves . . . . .1.5 minutes
- Strikeout curves . . . . .1.5 minutes
- Sliders or alternating fast balls/curve balls . . . . .1.5 minutes

Pitching For Rhythm (set position)
- 3/4 speed fast balls . . . . .1.5 minutes

Control Contest (windup position)
- Best of ten throws. Alternate fast balls/curveballs . . . . .1.5 minutes

Time Data

Total drill minutes per pitcher . . . . .13.5 minutes
Total drill time . . . . .27.0 minutes
Time allowed for switching . . . . 5.0 minutes
Maximum average switching time . . . . .18.7 seconds
Total drill execution time (maximum) . . . . .35.0 minutes

RECOVERING FROM GAME DAY PITCHING

The baseball coach needs to set up a program for his starting pitchers for those days that they will not be throwing in an actual game situation. The purpose of this program should be structured around the following goals: (1) minimize soreness following pitching; (2) minimize range of motion soreness/stiffness following pitching; (3) aid in the recovery time; and (4) aid in the prevention of arm related injuries.

1. **Post-game recovery**

    A. Immediately following the last pitch in the game (unless experiencing pain)—15 to 20 cool down pitches in the bullpen—Throwing 1/2 to 3/4's speed.

    B. Training room—ice, elevation, compression

    C. Training room

        1. Medi-ball program—2 sets of 10 repetitions

            a. Tricep extension

            b. Shoulder circles

        2. Hang from a bar—2 sets of 30 seconds—relax

        3. Stick stretching—3 sets, 10-12 seconds each

            a. extension and bend

            b. behind head (down)

            c. behind head (up)

        4. Shower—good warm shower—extend and massage the arm.

2. **Day one after start**

    A. Prior to practice

        1. **Light** Nautilus or weight work with concentration on:

            a. full range of motion

            b. light weights with 20 repetitions—press; overhead pull, double chest, military, lower back

        2. Hang from a bar—2 sets of 30 seconds—relax

    B. At practice

        1. Maximum running day

        2. Body stretch

        3. Stick stretch

        4. Medi-ball routine

350

     5. Long toss lightly

  C. Training room—ice if needed

3. **Day two after start**

  A. Good running with some sprints involved

  B. Body stretch

  C. Stick stretch

  D. Medi-ball program

  E. Throw to catcher in bullpen with concentration on mechanics and follow through (8-10 minutes)

4. **Day three after start**

  A. Taper-off on running

  B. Body stretch

  C. Stick stretch

  D. Medi-ball program

  E. Throw to catcher in bullpen with some velocity although mostly 3/4 speed—work on basic pitches

  F. Ice, elevation, compression

5. **Day four (game day) if in three day between start program**

  A. Run a couple of foul poles to get body heat worked up

  B. Body stretch

  C. Medi-ball program

  D. Stick stretch

  E. Warmup for game

If a pitcher is pitching with four days rest between starts he should take the day off from throwing before the start. This depends entirely on the pitcher and his recovery time. If throwing with three days rest between starts, some pitchers might not want to throw the day prior to the game. The coach and the pitcher must coordinate the throwing program so that the pitcher is at his maximum on game day.

The pitcher needs to allow himself plenty of time to warmup for the game. The final four minutes of bullpen work should be done with a hitter at the plate. He should pitch in game situations—first half from the stretch, second half from the windup. He should allow himself a couple of minutes to return to the dugout, towel off, get a drink of water and mentally prepare himself to take the mound.

RELIEF PITCHING

The relief pitcher is a very important part of the pitching staff since more and more baseball teams are going to the bullpen earlier than ever before. The better teams have a good bullpen corps that they have confidence in due to the fact that they would like to have a fresh pitcher with confidence on the mound in crucial situations.

Pitching depth is always a troublesome area for coaches at all levels. Relief pitching can be an answer in saving the wear and tear of your number one and number two arms throughout the season. Relief pitchers are indeed specialists in baseball today. If that be the case, the coach needs to spend more time coaching his pitchers on what relief pitching is all about.

Many times coaches will call on one of their starting pitchers to relief in a game, and he finds out quickly that the boy does not know how to relieve. This may sound foolish, but it is a fact. Starting pitchers will pitch like starting pitchers many times, not as relief pitchers.

It is important that a coach discuss the art of relief pitching with his entire staff so that when they are called on in this role they have an awareness of what this task is all about.

1. Characteristics of the relief pitcher

A. A coach would like all of his pitchers to be competitors, but the reliever must be exceptional. He must enjoy being put into crucial situations. Another trait of a good reliever is one who has a positive lackadaisical attitude whereby nothing bothers him and he loves the pressure. He must want to have the ball in the tough situation.

B. He might not be the pitcher with the best 'stuff'' on your staff, but he has one pitch that he can always get over. He challenges the hitters with his best pitch not trying to be too fine with the pitch. He is one who can control the momentum and tempo of the game.

C. He must display self-confidence whenever he takes the mound. A coach would like for a relief pitcher to be saying to himself, "this is the situation . . . here I am . . I'm coming right at you . . . let's see what happens". His confidence must radiate to his teammates as he struts to the mound.

2. Type of relief pitchers

A. **Gimmick type**—This type of pitcher is one who has an unusual style of throwing. He might be a sidewinder or have an unorthodox motion in his delivery. He might be one who uses the psyche method to initimidate batters by mannerisms he uses between pitches.

B. **One pitch saver**—This type of relief pitcher relies on his one pitch whenever in doubt or in a crucial situation. It might be a fork ball, a split finger fast ball, a screwball, etc.

C. **Flame thrower type**—These are the gentlemen who rare back and let the "seed" fly. They attempt to throw the ball right through the bats.

3. Approach to relief pitching

A. **Mental**—The relief pitcher has a role to fill for the team, whether it be as a long reliever or as a short reliever. He must start preparing for this role by preparing first his mind. When everyone else is getting all excited about a play or a big hit, the relief pitcher must keep his emotions under control. During the course of the game he must classify the hitters he might be facing by making mental notes to himself as he watches the other pitchers work the hitters.

B. **Game**—The relief pitcher must challenge hitters throughout his stint on the mound, especially in a close game. Walks are even more detrimental to a relief pitcher than the starting pitcher. A relief pitcher can not pitch too fine. He must think strikes and throw strikes. He must breed confidence in his teammates, and this starts with his own self-confidence. He must know the score, outs, innings and the importance of the man at the plate. One run games need total concentration with mound intelligence.

4. Warmup thoughts

A. The relief pitcher must stretch and run early keeping himself loose throughout the game. He cannot spend an excessive amount of time having to get his body loose when called on to relieve. Between innings he might even want to jog down to the dugout and back.

B. The relief pitcher must anticipate the move of the coach. In this way he is not surprised when he is called on to get loose. If time allows, the pitcher should go through a complete stretching program. If little time is available a few simple stretching exercises should be all that it takes before he is ready to throw. He must know exactly where his glove is and have two good baseballs available in his glove. He must know who is the bullpen catcher so that there is no delay in getting the first pitch off in the bullpen.

C. It must be emphasized to all the relievers that time is important and good organization eliminates wasteful time. When starting to throw, throw quickly making the catcher back up as you get loose. The pitcher should always throw from the pitching rubber. There are times when the pitcher will want the catcher to back up beyond home plate for a few longer, stretching throws. This sequence should only be 10-15 throws and only take up to 2-3 minutes of time.

D. When the arm is loose, have the catcher down and work location. Increase velocity as you throw. Stay with the fast ball before moving to the breaking stuff. If time permits, mix up your pitches. When the coach calls for time and starts walking to the mound, you still should have time for 5-7 pitches. The greatest percentage of the time a reliever will be throwing from the stretch, so spend at least three quarters of the time throwing from the set position.

5. Work load

A. A big problem with relief pitchers is their work load. When the starters put together a string of complete games, relief pitchers have trouble getting enough work. A couple of days off will not hurt, but if the string of complete games becomes lengthly the relief pitcher must stay and pitch a couple of innings in the bullpen after the game. They should throw a designed number of pitches. It is best to throw the number and ratio of pitches that you throw in an average relief appearance.

B. Another problem can be too much work. It is easily recognized if the relief pitcher appears in game after game and a day off is necessary. However, many times a coach will have his relief man up four or five times during the course of one game. This presents the biggest problem because many times the reliever will tire himself and become less effective when called upon to appear in the game. In this case, the relief pitcher must keep himself loose and discipline himself not to throw too much. If he loosens early he can just toss to keep himself ready. By a pre-determined signal (such as a coach walking to the mound instead of jogging), he can still have time to throw between 7-9 pitches with velocity before he is called on to enter the game. This can be tough on the relief pitcher and coaches should avoid getting a man up and down four or five times a game if at all possible.

6. Situations that relief pitchers face

A. **Ground ball needed**—The double play will kill a rally. Good relief pitchers have a knack for throwing the ground ball when it is in order. A reliever must recognize the situation and pitch accordingly. He must answer, "what pitch best produces ground balls for me?" Mentally, all his pitches must be down in the strike zone. Stay with the sinking fast ball or the breaking ball down. Avoid change-ups. Think double play/ground ball.

B. **Strikeout or pop-up needed**—With the winning or tying run in scoring position the reliever must be at his best. It is even tougher with the winning or tying run at third base with less than two outs. The relief pitcher must go with his best stuff to get ahead in the count. The chances for the ground ball sneaking through is greatly increased with the infield in on the grass. The pitcher must challenge the hitter. He cannot be afraid to throw the ball up and in. He must have the confidence to throw the breaking ball down even if behind in the count. Avoid change-ups. The main objective is to go right at the hitter with your best stuff. Get ahead of the count and throw your best strikeout pitch.

C. **Strikes to bring the "W" home**—As mentioned earlier, the most important object is to think strikes and throw strikes. Walks let the opposition back into the game and must be avoided. With errorless defense it takes three singles to score one run. Use this information to your advantage. If a home run threat is at the plate and you are up by two or more runs, continue right at him. Continue to "pitch" but don't be too fine. If he hits the home run, you're still up by one run. Make it easy on yourself and throw strikes. The term "smells the victory" describes the pitcher near the end of the game who gets tougher and tougher.

D. **Pitch around philosophy**—There may be times when a team can just not get one of the opposing team's hitters out. In a crucial situation a team does not want this super hitter to be the one who beats them. If the winning run is in scoring position with first base open, a coach might consider pitching around this hitter. In pitching terminology, you would want the pitcher to make this batter hit his pitch or chase the bad ball. Breaking balls off the plate are good pitches, especially with the aggressive hitter at the plate. The most important thought is to keep everything out of his strong hitting zones. Basically, you are giving him absolutely nothing to hit.

7. Dugout to bullpen signals

A. In order to communicate between the dugout and the bullpen a system of signals should be devised. They should be standardized so that there is uniformity. This eliminates wasteful time and communication problems. If the bullpen is open, the pitcher(s) and catcher(s) should be protected by another player.

B. Hand signals are useful and can be easily implemented. The head coach should remain in one spot in the dugout so that those in the bullpen know exactly where he is at all times. The coach should use either his right or left arm depending on who he wants up in the bullpen. He should verbally call the relief pitcher's number or signal it with his hand. If he wants two pitchers up both arm signals would be used.

C. Depending on the situation in the game, the coach should use signals telling the reliever how to work:

1. With his arm he uses the "rainbow" arc which tells the pitcher to toss easy meaning he thinks the starter is tiring and he wants him to start getting loose.

2. "Arm roll" is a circular motion which tells the reliever to hurry and be ready as quickly as possible for the pitcher on the mound is about finished.

3. "Arm roll with his cap off" tells the reliever that he wants him when he is ready. The pitcher should return this signal by raising his fingers to let him know how many minutes he needs. If the reliever needs more time and the coach is ready to make the move, he should use a pre-determined signal to an infielder or the catcher to call time and talk to the pitcher.

When the reliever is ready he should return his signal by taking his cap off. If there is a coach in the bullpen these signs can all be flashed by the coach while the pitcher continues to throw.

4. If the coach wants the reliever to sit down he can cut his fingers across the throat. This tells the relief pitcher that he can stop throwing.

CATCHING

The fundamentals of catching are quite complex, and the achievement of a high degree of excellence demands that a catcher master numerous mechanical skills. The coach needs a fine athlete behind the plate due to the complexity of the position. He must also have a catcher who has the attributes of a leader, with a "take charge" personality. The catcher is the only player on the team with the entire field in front of him, and he will be called upon in numerous occasions to issue commands on various plays that develop during the course of the game. We will break down the basic fundamentals of catching so that the coach can provide this important member of the team with the expertise necessary for him to assume this all important responsibility.

GIVING SIGNALS TO THE PITCHER

A receiver's ability to communicate with his pitchers is a very important role for the catcher. The basic communication that exists between the catcher and the pitcher during the game takes form through the signals relayed by the catcher to the pitcher. The methods used by the catcher in relaying these signals are vital to the successful communication that is needed.

1. **Receiver's stance for giving signals**—The stance for giving the signals must be one that is comfortable, and from which the signals are clearly visable to the pitcher, shortstop and second baseman. At the same time, the signals must be hidden from the hitter and the first and third base coaches. The weight of the catcher's body should be distributed equally over the balls of the feet. The feet should be close together in a position where the heels can almost click together. He should assume a stance that will keep his rear end low, with his left knee pointing in the direction of the shortstop, and his right knee at the area of the second baseman. He cannot allow his knees to spread open any more than this for purposes of keeping the signals disguised from the opposition. The upper trunk of his body should be erect, presenting a larger image to the pitcher along with making it easier for him to see the signals. The receiver's head should be facing the pitcher as he is giving the signals to see whether or not the pitcher has accepted the signal or shook him off.

2. **Position of glove arm and hand**—His left forearm should be resting comfortably on the left thigh so that his wrist is approximately at the top of his left knee. The glove should rest gently along the front of the knee with the pocket facing the other knee or slightly turned in to help further conceal the finger signs from the third base coach.

3. **Position of the right hand and fingers in giving signals**—The right hand should be placed directly in front of the cup area. His right wrist should rest comfortably on top of his inner thigh. If the finger method is used in giving the signals, the fingers should extend down and slightly out toward the pitcher. It is also essential that the catcher keep his right arm and elbow as still as possible when flashing signs as excessive movement on a certain sign can give the pitch away to an observant base coach.

4. **Methods of giving signals for pitch selection**—It is recommended that the coaching staff standardize the method of giving signals for all the catchers and pitchers on the team. This will help prevent any unnecessary confusion between the members of the pitching staff and the catchers on the club when signs are flashed. It will also help alleviate the problem of a catcher getting crossed-up on a pitch. If the catcher calls for one pitch and then receives another one, it could result in a runner advancing a base or an injury to the catcher. There are three methods of giving signals: (1) finger method; (2) hand method; and (3) outside method.

A. **Finger method**—This is the most common type of signal system used by the catcher in giving signals to the pitcher. The index finger, indicating one, is generally the signal for the fast ball. The index and middle finger down, indicating two, is generally the signal for the curve ball. If the pitcher throws a slider rather than the curve ball, then the slider would be the two pitch. If he throws both a curve ball and a slider, then the two signal would call for the curve ball and the three signal would indicate the slider should be thrown. When flashing the three signal, the catcher should use his middle finger, ring finger and little finger. This is much easier for the catcher, since it allows him to hold down the index finger with his thumb rather than having to hold down the little finger with the thumb. If the pitcher happens to throw a fourth pitch, all four fingers will be dropped. If four fingers are to be used, it is best that the fingers are wiggled so there is no confusion in the pitcher's mind whether there are three or four fingers down. The catcher needs to be sure that the fingers are well apart when they are dropped making it much easier for the pitcher, shortstop and second baseman to pick up the sign. It is also very important that the fingers extend outward slightly rather than keeping them pointing straight down into the crotch. If the catcher wants the pitcher to throw a change-up, he can either flash the one signal (index finger) and wiggle the finger, or he can open and close the fingers of his hand two or three times. If the pitcher happens to throw a change-up off his curve ball, then he would flash the two signal (index and middle finger) wiggling the two fingers while they are in the down position. If more than one sign will be flashed (a baserunner at second base), then the finger signs must come down and back up rhythmically so that the signs can be easily readable. The pitchout sign can be a clenched fist by the catcher.

B. **Hand method**—This is a signal system that might be used in the lower levels of baseball, or when playing a night game on a field with poor lights. It can also be used when the pitcher's vision is not up to par. The whole hand with the fingers close together and directed downward would indicate the fast ball to be thrown. If the catcher clenches his fist in the area of the crotch, he is calling for the breaking pitch. If he positions the hand to the right inside part of the thigh with the fingers touching the thigh, it would call for the pitcher's third pitch. The catcher must be sure in using the hand method that he move his right forearm a little further down the thigh then he would position the forearm with the finger method of flashing signs. Otherwise an observant base coach might be able to see the movement of the forearm as the catcher's hand moves from the crotch area to the right thigh.

C. **Outside method**—The outside method of giving signals from the catcher is not recomended, but might have to be used if the pitcher is having a very difficult time seeing the finger or hand signs. This method involves the catcher touching a part of his body or catching equipment indicating the pitch to be thrown. The catcher should still give signals in the crotch area just as normal to make the opposition think that the pitcher is receiving finger signs, and then thinking that the other signs are location signs. After the decoy sign in the crotch area is given, the catcher would touch three or four parts of his body or equipment. Touching the mask might be the sign for the fast ball; the chest protector the curve ball; the right knee the slider; and the left knee the change-up. The catcher and pitcher would pre-arrange that whatever the catcher touches first, second or third indicates the pitch to be thrown. This can change from inning to inning if it is believed that the sequence is picked up by the opposition.

5. **Signals with a runner at second base**—Whenever there is a runner at second base, it is necessary for the catcher to go through a series of signals instead of just one signal that can be used at all other times. Otherwise, there is a good chance that the runner at second base might be able to signal the hitter what pitch is going to be delivered. This is normally done by the runner at second base touching a part of his body above the waist for the fast ball, and a part of his body below the waist for the breaking pitch. It is important for the catcher to remind the pitcher that signals will change when a runner reaches second base by saying to the pitcher "runner at second base". The pitcher should recognize this fact when he sees a series of signals flashed by the catcher when normally only one signal is provided, but the communication is still recommended. The series of signals should never be less than three signs nor more than five signs. There are teams that actually require the pitcher to add or subtract the finger signs to arrive at the pitch called for. Other teams might use an indicator sign followed by the pitch sign, or require the pitcher to count the number of signs flashed (number of fingers down mean nothing). These types of decoy signs should really not be necessary for it just serves to possibly confuse the pitcher, taking a lot of his concentration away from the task at hand. The second sign flashed, when there is a runner at second base, can be the actual sign as pre-arranged before the season even begins between all the pitchers and catchers. If the catcher or someone in the dugout observes the runner at second base flashing signs to the hitter, the catcher can call timeout and arrange with the pitcher to go with another sign in the sequence.

6. **Other types of signals**—Other than the signals for the basic pitch to be thrown, there are a few other signals that the catcher can flash to the pitcher:

A. **Pitchout**—The basic method for signaling a pitchout is with the catcher using a closed hand or fist. Since the fast ball will always be thrown for the pitchout, the catcher should not have to flash the fast ball sign followed by the pitchout sign.

B. **Knockdown pitch**—One of the more common signals for the knockdown pitch is for the catcher to have his thumb up while the fingers remain closed. The catcher should not snap his thumb up in such a way that a clicking noise is made for this could serve to warn the hitter. The pitcher and catcher should not try to hit the batter, but in some instances they must attempt to get him back off the plate for various reasons. All knockdown pitches should be thrown well up and in, never at the head or behind the head. The knockdown pitch should not be used in the lower levels of baseball due to the pitcher's inability to control his pitches and the batter's slower reaction time. The knockdown pitch is always a fast ball so there is no need to flash the fast ball sign prior to the knockdown pitch sign.

C. **Shakeoff sign**—There must be a signal esablished whereby the pitcher can shakeoff the sign that the catcher has called for. This can be a sign whereby the pitcher shakes his head back and forth, or glove wipes an area of the body. When this occurs, the catcher will flash another sign unless the original sign was flashed to him by the coach. If the catcher flashes a sign to the pitcher and then he changes his mind on the sign, he should have a sign to let the pitcher know that he has changed his mind. This could be done by wiping the throwing hand across the chest followed by his flashing the new sign.

D. **False shakeoff sign**—False shakeoff signs need to be established for both the pitcher and the catcher in order for the batter to think that the pitcher has initiated another sign than the one originally called for by the catcher. This can be done by the pitcher either shaking his head or glove wiping an area of the body. When this occurs, the catcher gives him the original sign again. The catcher may originate the false shakeoff sign by flashing the pitch sign followed by shaking his head. The pitcher would then respond with his false shakeoff sign and then throw the pitch that was called by the catcher.

7. **Location signs**—There will be times when the catcher will want to let the pitcher know the location that he would like to have the pitch thrown to. After giving the signal for the type of pitch, he would signal where the pitch should be thrown. There are numerous ways that this can be done after the pitch sign has been flashed. An example of a location sign system for a righthanded batter at the plate would be:

A. **Low and outside corner of the plate**—The catcher pats the inner part of his right thigh one time followed by a motion down with the fingers extended toward the pitcher. If he just wants the ball to be thrown to the outside corner, he would tap one time the inner part of his right thigh.

B. **Low and inside corner of the plate**—The catcher pats the inner part of his left thigh one time followed by a motion down with the fingers extended toward the pitcher. If he just wants the ball to be thrown to the inside corner, he would tap one time the inner part of his left thigh.

C. **High and outside corner of the plate**—The catcher pats the inner part of his right thigh one time followed by his touching one time his right shoulder.

D. **High and inside corner of the plate**—The catcher pats the inner part of his left thigh one time followed by his touching one time his left shoulder.

E. **Throw ball outside the strike zone.**—With a 0-2 or 1-2 count on the batter, and the catcher wants the pitcher to be sure that he does not give the hitter a good pitch to hit, he should provide him with a sign that would indicate the ball should be thrown a couple of inches outside the strike zone. This can be done by touching the right or left knee depending on whether he wishes the ball to go inside or outside the strike zone. Thus if the catcher wishes to throw a fast ball, down and away from the righthanded hitter a little outside the strike zone he would signal the following: flash the one signal for the fast ball; tap one time the inner part of his right thigh followed by a motion down with the fingers extended toward the pitcher; and touching the right knee indicating the pitch outside the strike zone.

F. **Shaking off the location sign**—If the pitcher likes the call of the pitch by the catcher but does not like the location, he can simply wipe down his jersey with his glove indicating he wants a new location sign. If he doesn't like the pitch call, he can simply shake his head.

8. **Catcher calling game via signals**—In the pitching section of the Playbook, we detailed for both the pitcher and the catcher the various items that must be taken into consideration before determining the type of pitch and the location of the pitch to be thrown. Please refer to this section for information in regard to this all important aspect of pitching to hitters.

BASIC STANCE BEHIND THE PLATE

It is very important for the catcher to assume a stance after the signal has been flashed that is both comfortable and mobile. The catcher will have two basic stances, one with no runners on base and the other with a runner(s) on base. The following are the basic mechanics of the catcher's stance noting the differences in the two stances:

1. **Feet**—The receiver's feet should be spread comfortably slightly more than shoulder width apart. His right foot should be one to two inches behind his left foot. With a runner on base in a possible steal or bunt situation, the right foot should be a couple of more inches back behind the left foot. The left foot should be pointed outward slightly in the direction of the pitcher, while the right foot should be pointed in the direction of the second baseman. This receiving stance with the feet should provide balance and stability, as well as being comfortable for the catcher. With no runners on base, the body weight can rest over the entire foot with and toward the inside of the foot. With men on base, a little more weight should be moved forward toward the balls of the feet. The catcher can never afford to have the weight on the toes or heels irregardless of whether there is a runner on base or not.

2. **Weight distribution**—Some catchers get into a very low crouch position behind the plate or even get down on one knee with no runners on base. They do this in order to give the pitcher a lower target. This should be frowned upon since it places

the catcher in a position that will not allow him to react quickly to a bunted ball or a pop-up. It will also expose the thigh of the knee on the ground to a foul ball. The weight of the catcher's body should be equally distributed on both legs so that he can move quickly to either the right or the left on a ball well outside the strike zone.

3. **Buttocks and back**—The positioning of the buttocks and back of the catcher will determine to a large degree how low the catcher will be able to get in his stance, but at the same time have the ability to move left or right on bad pitches. It is important for the catcher to stay low, not only for purposes of giving the pitcher a better target, but also to give the plate umpire a better view of the pitch. Staying low will also enable the catcher to better block low pitches since it is much easier and quicker to come up than to go down. The catcher's back should be somewhat extended but not rounded to a point where the catcher looks like he is slouching over. This will make it difficult for him to keep his arms semi-extended away from the upper part of the body. By keeping the weight forward on the balls of the feet, the buttocks should be kept up easily. With a runner on base in a stealing or bunting situation, the buttocks should be a little higher. This will enable the catcher to have more mobility forward to either throw the ball to a base or to come out in front of the plate to possibly make the play on a bunted ball. This raising of the buttocks should not be such that it hinders the plate umpire from seeing the low pitch.

4. **Glove arm, elbow and wrist**—The glove arm must be semi-extended in front of the body. If the arm is fully extended, the arm, elbow and wrist will become tense and stiffen. It will also take away from the ability of the catcher to receive the pitch with soft hands. By semi-extending the arm at the elbow, all the parts of the arm will be relaxed and ready to assist the hand in giving with the force of the ball into the glove. The elbow should be held slightly outward. If the elbow is held in toward the body, it will practically lock the catcher's glove hand preventing him from properly receiving and framing the various types of pitches he is required to cleanly receive. At no time should the elbow be placed inside the left knee. This would severely restrict the movement of the glove to handle and frame pitches properly. The wrist should be in a relaxed position, and like the arm and elbow, not overly extended toward the pitcher.

5. **Glove hand**—Since the pitcher must concentrate on a fixed target, the catcher should give him one that is easily visable and stationary. He must be sure that he does not move his glove target until the ball leaves the pitcher's hand. In giving the target, the glove should be held so that the little finger is pointed at a 45° angle to the pitcher. In this way the glove can be raised upward and lowered with a minimum of effort and movement, and still give the pitcher a good target to throw to. More information on glove positioning will be found later in the framing section. The glove hand should be placed in the glove so that a portion of the heel is exposed outside the glove. Both the heel and palm of the hand should not be pressed firmly against the glove pocket thereby having very little contact with the inside of the glove. Jamming the fingers completely into the glove should be avoided, because movement of the wrist will be hindered. The more relaxed and loosely the hand is held in the glove, the more wrist action there will be to move the glove quickly.

6. **Head and eyes**—The catcher's head should never be directly behind and peeking out and over the glove. Instead, the receiver should extend his neck and have complete visibility of the pitch. Extending or arching of the back will help the head clear the glove so that visibility will be better. The catcher must be conditioned never to jerk or flinch his head to the side or up in the air. In addition to being a bad habit, the catcher leaves himself open to serious injury to his throat or head.

7. **Bare hand**—An excellent procedure to help avoid hand and finger injuries is to not expose the bare hand too quickly on any pitch. This is especially true on the pitch that is down the middle to the outside corner of the plate when a righthanded batter is hitting, or a pitch to the inside corner of the plate with a lefthanded hitter. With no runners on base, it is best to place the bare hand right behind the right knee until after the ball hits the glove. The fingers of the right hand should never point toward the pitcher as serious damage can be done to the tips of the fingers if a ball was to be fouled back into the fingers. The fingers should also be extremely relaxed so that if a ball was to hit the fingers there is some give involved in the blow. With a runner on base, the hand should be placed directly behind the webbing of the glove. The thumb should be under the fingers so that the catcher can roll the ball into the fingers when having to make a quick throw to a base. All catchers should be encouraged to receive the pitched ball with two hands with a runner(s) on base. Receiving one handed with a hinged glove hinders quick release of the ball when throwing and also encourage backhanding and reaching out to receive the ball. Thus, it makes for a very lazy catcher.

8. **Positioning behind the plate**—The catcher should position himself with the midline of his body a few inches off to the right of the center of the plate and close enough to the hitter so that his arm, if extended, will touch the batter's rear shoulder. This positioning will provide him with the best basis for framing the pitch. This position puts him closer to second base and to a bunt, facilitates the handling of low pitches, enables the receiver to catch more pitches in the strike zone, and gives the plate umpire a better look at the ball. The catcher may move himself to the inside or outside corner of the plate for presenting a full body and glove target for the pitcher. A good rule to follow is that the catcher never lets the midline of his body line up outside

the strike zone. It will not tip the pitch away too much if done subtly before the signal is flashed. If the curve ball sign is given, the catcher might move up a couple of inches toward the plate to be in a better position to catch the low pitch a little closer to the plate and strike zone. However, the catcher must guard against tipping the pitches away by his movement behind the plate after the sign has been given to the pitcher.

RECEIVING THE BALL

The actual receiving of the pitched ball is the "heart and soul" of catching. Thus, much practice time must be spent with the catchers on their actual mechanics of receiving the pitch. With good receiving technique, the catcher will not only assist the pitcher in getting strikes called by the plate umpire, but it will also assist in the coordination of his movements in throwing the ball. The following are the basic fundamentals and mechanics for receiving the pitched ball:

1. **Catching the strike**—One of the prerequisites of a good receiver is to be able to catch every strike in the strike zone, and make the borderline pitch appear to the plate umpire as a strike. This necessitates catching the ball firmly with the arms and hands away from the body, and meeting the ball as close to home plate and the strike zone as possible. When the catcher meets the ball with a firm and relaxed glove away from his body, he is in a much better position to receive the pitch in the strike zone. One of the biggest faults in receiving is when a receiver catches the ball after it has gone through the strike zone, or catches the ball in such a way that the impetus of the ball into the glove carries the glove further away from the plate and strike zone. Catching the ball too close to the body often gives the impression to the umpire that the ball was received out of the strike zone. It also makes for a more difficult catch for the receiver, along with hindering the fluid movements that are necessary for the catcher to receive the ball and get it out of the glove quickly when throwing. At the same time, the catcher cannot get into the bad habit of reaching out for the ball. He must achieve the happy medium of letting the ball come to him, and at the same time catching it with a semi-extended glove hand. Reaching or stabbing at the ball will result in a far greater frequency of passed balls. It also promotes a damaging habit of reaching for corner pitches, and this can do nothing but push them out of the strike zone, creating a ball where a strike existed in the mind of the umpire.

2. **Holding the pitch**—A more effective method of assuring the pitcher a strike when he throws one is not only to meet the ball in the strike zone, but to hold it there for the umpire to see. This style is preferable when no possibility of a steal exists. If the pitch is well out of the strike zone, the catcher does not want to pull the pitch into the strike zone. This will only serve to upset the plate umpire, and could prompt him to give the close pitch to the hitter rather than the pitcher. The plate umpire has got to have a clear picture of the ball as it enters the glove, and movements of the glove right after the pitch is received only serves to make his job of calling pitches that much more difficult.

3. **Framing the pitch**—The excellent receiver will provide his pitching staff with numerous called strikes on pitches that could have gone either way in the mind of the umpire. This is due to the fact that the catcher positions himself in a way that the umpire always has a clear picture of the ball as it enters his glove. In addition, the excellent receiver has developed the fine art of framing the pitch within the strike zone. Framing the pitch basically involves keeping the borderline pitch within the confines of the strike zone. The mechanics of framing the pitched ball involve the following:

A. **Target glove position for proper framing**—When giving the glove target to the pitcher, the catcher must also concern himself with positioning the glove so that he can quickly move the glove for purposes of framing the pitch. It is recommended that the glove be held so that the little finger is pointed at about a 45° angle to the pitcher, with the elbow at about the same angle away from the body. This should be the target position of the glove when the target given to the pitcher is from the middle of the plate to the inside corner of the plate for the righthanded hitter (outside corner for the lefthanded hitter). If the catcher is going to provide a glove target to the pitcher on the outside part of the plate for the righthanded hitter (inside corner for the lefthanded hitter), then he would have the elbow and forearm of the glove hand practically parallel to the ground with the fingers of the glove pointing outward. This is not an ideal position for the glove for purposes of framing pitches that might be thrown to the inside part of the plate. This is the reason why it is recommended for the catcher to move his body a little to the outside part of the plate so that he might give his target to the pitcher with the little finger at about a 45° angle to the pitcher. This would also allow him to drop his elbow to about a 45° angle from the body. The catcher cannot afford to ever give his glove target on the outside part of the plate with his glove elbow pointed toward the ground near the midline of the body. This would make it practically impossible for the catcher to move his glove in a manner that will enable him to frame the ball properly.

B. **Framing the low pitch**—The low pitch is the pitch that the pitcher and catcher have to have for a strike in order for the pitcher to be effective. If the catcher takes this pitch away from the pitcher due to poor framing mechanics, the pitcher will have to locate the ball a little higher in the strike zone. This would be advantageous for the hitter. Once the receiver is able to distinguish that the pitch will be low he must roll his hands, extending his fingers downward. Rolling the hands involves turning the glove hand smoothly but quickly to the left, and the bare hand to the right so that the receiver catches the ball palm up rather than struggling to receive it down toward the ground. The good receiver will catch a low ball from underneath. Many low pitches are called balls because the catcher receives the pitch down rather than up. A subtle knee manipulation up can also make the ball appear a little higher in the strike zone on the low pitch. The toughest pitch to frame for the catcher is the low outside pitch to the righthanded hitter (low inside pitch to the lefthanded hitter). The catcher cannot afford to roll his glove to the left before he reads where the pitch is going. Once the low pitch passes the midline of the catcher's body to his bare hand side, he cannot catch the ball properly with the palm of the glove hand up. The best technique for getting a strike is merely to rotate the glove toward the plate, meeting the low outside pitch with the glove fingers down. The catcher should try to catch the outside lower part of the ball. However, if it looks like the pitch will break well below the strike area (breaking pitch), then he must rotate the glove with the thumb pointing upward. The breaking pitch moving toward the low outside corner of the plate will have to be caught in this manner so that there is no chance for the ball to skip off the glove, as might happen if the receiver tried to catch the ball with his fingers on the glove hand up.

C. **Framing the high pitch**—With the catcher giving his glove target to the pitcher with his little finger at a 45° angle to the pitcher, the receiver should have no problem framing the high pitch whether the ball is inside and high, or outside and high. Hopefully, with good framing technique the borderline high pitch might be called a strike by the plate umpire. As mentioned previously in framing the low pitch, the catcher must catch the ball from underneath. In contrast, the receiver must catch the high pitch from above. In further contrast, the low pitch should be received out and up, while the high pitch should be received deep and down. For the plate umpire's benefit, the catcher must avoid any movement of the body up in receiving the high pitch unless he must do so to prevent the ball from getting past his glove. A subtle knee manipulation down on the high pitch might be the deciding factor in getting the pitch called a strike. Catching the high pitch from above requires that the glove be a little higher than the ball initially so that the palm is angled toward the ball. As the ball makes contact with the glove, the wrist movement will bring the glove slightly downward so that the face of the glove is practically parallel to the ground. If the high pitch is caught with the fingers of the glove pointing straight up, it might take the pitch away from the pitcher as well as possibly the ball pushing the fingers back resulting in a ball getting past the catcher. If the glove is positioned so that the fingers are in front of the palm, the ball if dropped will drop in front of the receiver.

D. **Framing the pitch on the corners**—The catcher must give the plate umpire the impression that every pitch near the outside or inside corner of the plate was caught within the confines of the strike zone. In order for the pitcher to have a better chance for success, he has got to have the benefit of the doubt on the close pitches near the corners of the plate. Understanding that the black border surrounding the plate is in fact part of the plate, and that any portion of the ball that touches the extended black of the plate should be called a strike, the importance of framing the corner pitches properly takes on more meaning.

1. **Inside corner (righthanded hitter); outside corner (lefthanded hitter)**—This pitch should be the easiest pitch for the catcher to frame since the ball will be approaching the plate on the glove side of the receiver. The palm of the glove hand should initially be somewhat facing the ball, and as the ball contacts the glove the wrist should turn slightly toward the plate so that the palm is facing the plate. Thus, the ball would be caught from outside-in.

2. **Outside corner (righthanded hitter); inside corner (lefthanded hitter)**—The ball away from the glove hand side is more difficult to catch and frame properly. The glove action is more complex and involves the rotation of the glove so that the palm of the glove hand is around the ball and facing the outside of the ball. The thumb of the glove hand is rotated downward with the left forearm near parallel to the ground as the ball makes contact with the glove. As this is the hardest corner to frame, the advantage of setting up the stance slightly to the right of the middle of the plate becomes obvious. As most good pitchers will work the outside corner more than the inside corner, it is important to consider this advantage.

SHIFTING TECHNIQUES

There are three types of shifting techniques that the catcher can use when receiving a pitch out of the strike zone that will not hit the ground: (1) sway shift; (2) single step shift; and (3) shuffle shift.

1. **Sway shift**—The sway shift maneuver involves the catcher staying in the receiving position when the pitch is to the immediate right or left of the plate. Instead of lifting up or stepping out to receive the pitch, the receiver should receive the ball by moving his hips, legs, and arms but not his feet in a swaying motion in the direction of the pitch. The receiver should be able to stay in front of the ball while using the sway maneuver as well as receiving the pitch properly without blocking the umpire's view of the ball. This shift should give the umpire the impression that the pitch is very close to the corner of the plate.

The catcher must keep his arms and hands away from the body upon reception of the pitch. It should be emphasized to the catchers that movement on the obvious strike should be kept to a bare minimum.

2. **Single step shift**—The single step shift to the right or left of the plate involves the catcher staying in the receiving position even though the receiver must take one step to either side to receive the pitch. The procedure is to keep the body in front of the ball by taking one step inside or outside to receive the pitch. This is not a substitute for the sway shift, but is used when the ball is too far outside or inside to sway. The single step shift involves moving the leg on the side of the pitch in the direction of the ball by supporting the weight of the body with the opposite leg, and pushing off in the direction of the ball. A catcher can never afford to get lazy behind the plate and start reaching for these types of pitches.

3. **Shuffle shift**—The shuffle shift is used when the pitch is too far outside or inside to use the sway shift or single step shift effectively. The pitch is so far away from the plate that there is no chance of it being called a strike. Thus, the receiver can either stay down or lift up to complete his shift to get in front of the ball. The catcher must concern himself with getting to the ball and stopping it so that it does not go to the backstop. The procedure for the shuffle shift is for the catcher to first take a full step with either foot depending upon the direction of the ball. This is followed by the opposite leg pushing off the ground thereby developing the momentum to shuffle the feet and transfer the weight to shift in front of the ball. The receiver must always anticipate that a pitch will be wildly thrown so that he is ready to react quickly. There is no reason for a ball to go to the backstop when the ball was within easy reach of the catcher's glove. This is true moreso with a wild pitcher on the mound since the catcher should be anticipating a ball thrown well away from the strike zone.

HANDLING THE BALL IN THE DIRT

The catcher who handles the ball in the dirt well is a great asset to his pitcher and his team. If he is weak in handling these types of pitches, he will be a definite liability. If a catcher is a good athlete, is aggressive, and possesses good mobility he should be able to prevent most low pitches in the dirt from getting past him. The pitcher who likes to keep his breaking pitch low certainly will be more effective when he has confidence in the catcher's ability to handle this pitch. The following are some general guidelines for the catcher to follow in handling low pitches in the dirt:

1. The catcher must completely understand that with runners on base the low pitch in the dirt must be blocked, not caught. When he sees that the ball is going to be in the dirt, he must tell himself that he is going to get in front of the ball and keep the ball in front of his body. He must take tremendous pride in his ability to react properly to this pitch in the dirt.

2. The receiver must anticipate on every pitch that the ball will be thrown wildly so that he is not surprised when he sees the poorly pitched ball. Often times you will see passed balls occur more frequently when a pitcher with good control is throwing. This is due to the fact that this type of pitcher will literally "put the catcher to sleep" behind the plate as he expects every pitch to be close to the strike zone. With a "wild buck" throwing, the catcher is prepared for the wild pitch. Thus, his movements are quicker due to the fact that he was mentally prepared for the wild pitch.

3. The catcher must also come to the realization that no one in his right mind would instinctively throw his body in front of an object thrown at 80 plus miles per hour. Thus, for a catcher to achieve any degree of success in handling low pitches in the dirt, he must face these types of pitches repeatedly in practice sessions duplicating as much as possible game conditions.

4. The catcher must recognize the fact that certain types of pitches in the dirt react differently depending on the rotation of the pitched ball. The righthanded pitcher's breaking pitch will bounce to the catcher's left (opposite the rotation of the ball). Thus, on a righthander's breaking pitch to the catcher's right, the receiver should stay to the inside of the ball rather than rounding the ball with his hips and shoulders. A good rule to follow is for the catcher to play the ball off his right shoulder, allowing for the ball to "back up" once it hits the ground. Of course, the reverse is true when the lefthanded pitcher's breaking ball hits the dirt, so that catcher will play the ball off his left shoulder. The tightness of the spin and the velocity of the ball will definitely affect the movement of the ball off the dirt.

5. The catcher can prepare for errant breaking pitches by putting more weight on the foot away from the anticipated break. The receiver can also gain an advantage by a slight adjustment in his stance behind the plate. For example, the slider is generally thrown to a specific half of the plate (into a lefthanded hitter and down and away to the righthanded hitter-righthanded pitcher). The catcher can gain a half step on any pitch that might go into the dirt by sliding inside or outside knowing where the pitcher is intending the pitch to go. If the catcher knows his pitching staff well, he should be in a better position to know what to expect out of each pitcher in various situations.

361

6. The actual mechanics for blocking balls in the dirt are easily understood by most catchers. Performing the skill with a high degree of proficiency might be another matter. This is the reason why the low ball blocking drills that are described in the catching drill section later in this chapter are very important for the catcher's skill development in this all important aspect of receiving. The following are the basic mechanics for blocking balls in the dirt.:

A. **Balls directly in front of the catcher**—This should be the easiest pitch for the catcher to block since there is no lateral movement involved in keeping the ball in front. However, the lazy catcher will have a difficult time blocking this pitch because too often he does not wish to go to his knees when he might be able to glove the ball in front of him. With men on base, the catcher must go to his knees on any pitch in front of him that will be in the dirt. In blocking the pitch directly in front, the catcher goes to his knees quickly providing as wide a base with his knees as possible. He can increase his speed to the knees by concentrating on kicking his heels out and up as soon as he reads the ball will be in the dirt. At the same time as he starts going to his knees, he must quickly get his glove and bare hand in a position so that the ball cannot get under him between the legs. Once the catcher is able to distinguish that the pitch will be in the dirt, he must immediately begin rolling his hands. When blocking the ball he must also shift his weight forward. This will shorten the hop of the ball in the dirt and reduce the danger of the ball getting by him. The standard rule to follow is to block the high bounce with the body, and the low bounce with the glove. Anytime the catcher can reach out and catch the low pitch in the air or on the short-hop, he must do so with a runner on first or second base. This is another advantage of being set up close to the hitter with arms semi-extended. The receiver must place his glove and bare hand with thumbs out between his legs. This prevents him from being struck on the elbow or side of the fingers causing injury or an inproper deflection of the ball. The catcher can keep the ball from running up his chest or over his head by rolling his shoulders forward to "cup" the ball. The shoulders must be parallel to the pitching rubber so that if the ball hits the body there will be no angle for the ball to get to the side. This is especially true when the pitch is just a few inches outside or inside of the plate, and the catcher decides to go down on both knees to block the ball. The catcher's chin must be tucked into his chest to prevent the ball from deflecting off his throat, and to further assist in keeping the ball in front of him. Again, it is very important for the catcher to remember that he is blocking the ball and not trying to catch it.

B. **Balls to the catcher's right or left**—There are two ways that a catcher can attempt to block a pitch thrown wide of the plate. He can go down on both knees as described in (A), or he can step to the ball with the foot nearest the ball. If the catcher is going to block the pitch going to both knees, he must be sure that his body is angled so that the ball will not deflect off him and roll away from the inside of the diamond. This is practically impossible to accomplish with a pitch well away from the plate when the catcher goes to both knees. In most cases, the two knee drop is effective on the pitches in the dirt a few inches outside or inside of the plate. If the catcher reads that the pitch is going to hit the dirt well outside of the plate, he will have to step to the ball in order to have any chance of blocking the ball. On the ball to his right, the catcher should step out and slightly forward toward the ball with his right foot. He can not raise up his body to do so due to the fact that it would take away his lateral quickness along with forcing him to have to come back down again in order to block the ball. As the right foot moves out and forward to the ball, the catcher's left knee moves toward the right foot. His left knee would hit the ground with his glove and bare hand on the ground between the left knee and right foot. The right arm must be inside the right leg. The procedure would be reversed on a pitch thrown in the dirt to the catcher's left. He would step out and forward to the ball with his left foot. His right knee would hit the ground with his glove and bare hand on the ground between the left foot and the right knee. The left arm must be inside the left leg. Hopefully, all balls that deflect off the catcher will end up in front of his body keeping all runners on base from advancing.

THROWING

The catcher who possesses a strong and accurate arm with a quick release will endure himself always to a coaching staff and his teammates. Once a catcher "guns" down a member of the opposing team trying to steal a base, it will generally take the "heart" out of the opposing team's running game. With proper mechanics, a catcher who is not gifted with a strong arm can develop his throwing skills to the level that he can have some success in throwing runners out on steal attempts. A great throwing arm is often wasted if a boy has poor mechanics causing him to take too long in releasing the ball, or his throws have great velocity but are seldom accurate to the target. The following are the basic mechanics for the catcher in throwing the ball to a base for the purpose of retiring a runner on a steal attempt:

1. **Grip**—The grip in throwing is very important to all players, but especially so for the catcher. The grip, to a large degree, will determine the accuracy and speed of the throw. The proper grip will give the ball the proper rotation which in turn will make the throw carry better, and will be easier for the infielder to handle. As the catcher brings the glove and throwing arm back to "cock the gun", he must grip the ball with the index and middle finger across the seams. The index and middle finger should be spread slightly with the thumb tucked underneath and centering the index and middle finger. The thumb should be bent at

the first joint underneath the ball. The ring and little finger should rest along the outer side of the ball, but should not interfere with the actual release of the ball. If these two fingers touch the ball with any pressure, the catcher might not be able to get the proper rotation and the ball will die out and probably fade to the right side of the intended target. The grip should be firm, but not tight. If the catcher is gripping the ball properly, the coach should be able to take the ball out of his hand with little force, but with some resistance. The grip should allow the catcher to release the ball with a six-to-twelve rotation. This means that the ball will leave the hand off the index and middle finger as they apply pressure from on top of the ball.

2. **Bringing the arm back**—The use of two hands when receiving the ball will assist the receiver in not only catching the ball, but will allow him time to get the proper grip on the ball as he brings the glove and throwing arm back to prepare for the actual throw. The ball and the glove should be brought back to the throwing position via a straight route. The catcher can not afford to stop this motion at any point since time is of utmost importance if the catcher hopes to get off a quick throw. This is a rhythmical skill that can only be developed with constant practice. The speed in which the catcher brings the throwing arm and glove back will determine to a large degree the release time in his getting rid of the ball. The wrist should be cocked straight back with the elbow bent at about a 90° angle. The catcher can not afford to drop his arm reaching back for something extra, since this will seriously slow down his release time. It is important that the glove hand goes back all the way to the throwing side shoulder as this will not only help the catcher in getting the proper grip, but will also help close the front shoulder in a proper throwing position.

3. **Throwing the ball**—Catchers should attempt to throw the ball overhand whenever possible to insure that the ball is thrown accurately with the proper six-to-twelve rotation. This type of rotation on the ball will prevent the ball from fading on its way to the intended target. The only exception is when a quick release might be necessary after the catcher fields a bunt and the sidearm throw is the only way he can release the ball quickly. Catchers used to be instructed to release the ball from the area of the right ear, but this type of arm action causes short-arming of the throw. This will not allow the catcher to achieve the necessary velocity on the throw, especially for the long throw to second base. As mentioned previously, the catcher can not afford to reach back to gain a full range of motion in his throwing arm. Thus, he must find that happy medium between a short-arm type of throw and a full range of motion overhand throw. The arm must be brought through quickly, snapping the wrist down as the ball leaves the hand. If the catcher was to allow his wrist to turn to the right or left as the ball leaves his hand, it would cause the ball to slide or sail. The glove arm must aid the throwing arm as it starts forward on the throw. If the glove arm elbow is allowed to go above the lead shoulder, it will cause the back shoulder to drop causing the catcher to throw the ball "uphill". The receiver must keep his glove arm parallel to the ground as the right arm starts forward. As the right arm is about to release the ball, the catcher's left shoulder should be pointing directly at the intended target. The left elbow and glove should then be pulled down to allow the right side to stay on top of the ball. If the left elbow and glove are allowed to rotate parallel to the ground as the ball is about to be released, it would cause the catcher's throwing arm to drop. The catcher's right elbow must be as high as his shoulder and his hand on top of the ball for a significant degree of power to be achieved. A dropping elbow will drop the hand down which would direct the major force upward rather than toward the target. The catcher must reach out as he throws to the intended target making sure that he completes the throw with a full follow through. Usually, when the ball is released too soon, the throw will be high. When the ball is released too late due to the ball being held too tight or too long, the throw will be low and probably in the dirt. One of the principal causes of a slow release is the natural tendency for the catcher to raise his body to an erect position, and even to lean slightly backward to assure a strong throw. This must be avoided in order for the catcher to throw properly. Catchers who throw well do so with their knees bent, tail down, and chin well forward of their belt buckle. Thus, a six-foot catcher should throw with the top of his head between four and a half and five feet above the ground. Staying low will also aid the catcher in not running forward and causing his body to be out in front of his arm.

4. **Footwork**—The footwork involved in receiving and throwing the ball properly consists of limiting the number of steps taken along with providing the body with the necessary momentum for getting off a strong and accurate throw. The catcher with quick feet will be able to get the throw off much quicker than one who has slow feet since the feet have got to be set before the throw can be released. Essential footwork involves pivoting and pushing off the right foot, and striding in the direction of the target with the left foot. There are three basic methods of footwork involved in throwing the ball to second base: (1) step-catch-and-throw; (2) jump pivot; and (3) rock and fire.

A. **Step-catch-and-throw method**—This method utilizes the use of the right foot going into the pitch enabling the receiver to get momentum going into the throw before the ball actually reaches the glove. This method is preferred for a receiver who might not have very much arm strength, and needs to establish maximum body momentum into his throw in order to reach the intended target. For the pitch down the middle, the catcher would take a short step (six to eight inches) with his right foot into the pitch. The right toe should be pointed out so the foot is actually perpendicular to second base so that the hips can turn and pivot properly. He would then throw with his left foot stepping in the direction of second base. If the ball is to the right, he would take a step sideways (and somewhat forward) with the right foot and then throw with the left foot stepping toward second base. If the pitch is low and to the right, he would stay low to receive the ball with his right foot going toward the ball. As he strides toward second base with his left foot he would have to straighten up slightly to gain accuracy and velocity in the throw. For a pitch to the left of the catcher, he would step out and forward with his left foot. He would then swing the right foot behind the left and step with the left foot in the direction of the throw. Since this type of footwork on the ball to the left of the plate is somewhat time consuming, the catcher must understand that this pitch must be one that can not be handled easily with the right foot moving forward. If the pitch is just a little away from the left of the plate, he should glove the ball with his right foot moving toward second base, pulling the ball to his throwing side quickly. Timing is very important with the step method of throwing and it needs to be practiced daily. A catcher can not afford to start moving into the pitch only to find that he is not in a position to catch the ball. Any type of reaching for the ball will cause the body balance to be poor. The head plays a very significant role in this method:

1. The head position can help keep the catcher from throwing across his body. This is done by the catcher keeping his head outside the ball as it is received. It is then possible to get the body weight behind the ball in a direct line with the target. For example, if the head were inside the ball on a pitch to the catcher's right, his momentum forward would probably take him toward right center field and the throw to second base would then have to be made across his body. This would greatly diminish the power and accuracy of the throw.

2. The correct technique would be as follows: on a pitch to his right, the catcher's right foot should step toward the ball and his head should move to the right of the ball. Now his weight will have shifted so that only a slight pivot on the right foot is necessary for the throw to be made with a single step. For a pitch to his left, the catcher's left foot should step toward the ball. He would step back on his right foot with his head to the left of the ball as he receives it. In this way, as he steps forward on his left foot for the throw he will have his full body weight behind the throw.

B. **Jump-pivot method**—The jump pivot method is perhaps the most popular method used since it provides the catcher a quick route of attaining the proper throwing position. This method requires a catcher to have quick feet and good control of his body balance. The jump-pivot method should only be used on balls that are around the strike zone and do not require any lateral stepping movement. Any ball that forces the catcher to step laterally will automatically force him to use the step-catch-and-throw method. If the ball is going to be caught within the strike zone or close to it, the catcher may use the jump-pivot. As he receives the ball, he should quickly move both feet a quarter of a turn clockwise. When he has completed the jump-pivot, his right foot will be approximately under where his buttocks were prior to the jump. His left foot will land approximately under where his glove target was given. Upon completion of the jump-pivot, the catcher's body will momentarily be facing the first base dugout as though he were going to receive a pitch from that area. His body will still be low to the ground at this time. He will then take a short stride forward toward second base and transfer his weight to the stride foot as he releases the ball.

C. **Rock and fire method**—If the catcher possesses a strong arm, the rock and fire method might be one that the coach might allow the catcher to use in throwing the ball to second base. This method requires the least amount of movement which will aid in the accuracy of the throw. The techniques are relatively simple. If the catcher must step to the ball laterally, he then would use the step-catch-and-throw method. If he does not need to make a lateral step, he then simply catches the ball, slightly rocks his weight back to his right foot and then transfers the weight over his left foot as it strides forward and he releases the ball. It is important that the weight be transferred back as this will aid in achieving necessary momentum forward. There is a general tendency for catchers to transfer the weight forward too early which will cause the body to be too far ahead of the arm. This will hinder not only the velocity of the throw but also the accuracy.

4. **Throwing to third base on steal attempts**—While throws to third base are considerably shorter for the catcher than throws to second base, difficulties arise in two areas which are normally not involved with the throw to second base. First, the runner will normally have a larger lead and better jump to third base than he would from second base. This is due to the fact that there is not a positioned player holding him on at second base as there would be at first base. In addition, the pitchers pick-off move to second base takes longer than it does to first base. The second area of difficulty arises if the batter is a righthanded hitter. A large percentage of bases stolen at third base occur when a righthanded hitter is at the plate. The obvious reason is that the hitter becomes somewhat of an obstacle to the catcher's throw to third base.

A. **Footwork with lefthanded batter at the plate**—The catcher may use either the rock and fire method of throwing or simply take a short crow-hop in throwing the ball to third base. Most catchers will use the rock and fire method as the distance is much shorter to third base than to second base. If lateral steps are needed in the throw, the catcher must be sure to step laterally in the direction the ball is going to. If the ball goes to his right, he simply takes a step with his right foot being sure he

364

moves far enough so that his head is on the right side of the ball. When he catches the ball, his weight will be over his right foot and he then simply rocks and fires the ball to third base. If the ball is to his left, he simply steps out with his left foot, and upon catching the ball, he brings his right foot under his body and strides and throws to third base. If the catcher elects to use the crow-hop method to gain a little more momentum, he will simply take a short step or hop (6 to 8 inches) with his right foot toward third base and then stride and throw.

  B. **Footwork with righthanded batter at the plate**—With a righthanded batter, much will depend on the location of the batter in the batter's box. The problem that arises is that the catcher needs to make his throw to third base either in front of the batter or behind him. Throwing over the batter will not only obstruct the catcher's vision but will generally lead to poor, high throws. The general rule to follow is that if the ball forces the catcher to step to his right, he should attempt to not only step right with his right foot but also should try to step slightly forward. This will put him in a position to throw in front of the batter. On balls that require the catcher to step left with his left foot, the catcher should step back slightly as he is making this lateral step, and then bring his right foot back behind him and throw the ball to third base as he strides in that direction behind the batter. With balls that are received within the strike zone or in close proximity, the catcher will need to make a judgement as to whether to throw in front of the batter or behind him. Much of this will be determined by the batter's location in the box. In most cases, it is easier to throw from behind the batter. Whichever method the catcher chooses, he must take a step either slightly forward or slightly backward with his right foot. He then strides toward his target and throws the ball. The batter will normally be leaning forward either because he swung at the ball or as a reaction to the catcher's throw. This will aid in throwing behind the batter.

PICK-OFF THROWS

  In the pick-off section of the Playbook the various pick-off plays from the catcher to the infielders were detailed. The catcher should use the same throwing techniques for pick-off throws as previously described. The receiver must always be alert for a baserunner who gets too far off a base in his secondary lead. He can not be afraid to throw, but he should not be throwing to a base just to be throwing. Every throw to a base by the catcher must have a purpose. If a catcher is constantly throwing to bases, the opposing runners will become very alert and will probably not get careless. It is important to stress the fact that the catcher must step directly in the direction of his throw with his elbow up as he releases the ball.

CALLING PLAYS

  In previous sections of the Playbook, the catcher's responsibilities for calling plays were detailed. This is in regard to his making decisions for the fielder of the bunted ball as to which base to throw the ball, and his communication on cut-off and relay throws. The catcher must always be thinking in advance about all possible situations that might arise. He must call the play quickly, decisively and loudly. He can not be afraid of making a mistake in judgment. It is better to make a mistake on a decision than to make no decision at all, or to be indecisive about a decision.

FORCE PLAYS AT THE PLATE

  There are two types of force play situations at home plate that a catcher can be confronted with: (1) a force play with no chance of a double play; and (2) a force play with a chance of a double play at first base.

1. **Force play with no chance of a double play**—This will generally result from the infielder or pitcher having a very difficult play on a ground ball due to the velocity and the angle of the ball to the fielder. It could also result from the runner at third base getting a great jump on the pitch making the play at home plate close. In this situation, the catcher has no intention of throwing the ball to first base to complete a double play. When the ball is hit to the left side of the infield or back to the pitcher, the catcher should position himself so that his body is facing directly toward the fielder of the ball with his right foot located at the middle front to the right corner of the plate. This will enable the catcher to be clearly out of the runner's way as he slides into the plate. If the ball is hit to the right side of the infield, the catcher should again face the fielder of the ball moving his right foot more towards and on the right corner of the plate. He again is allowing the runner as much of home plate as possible so that he is not involved in a collision. He should provide a clear target for the thrower by holding both hands in the air a little above his head. The catcher must then assume the same responsibilities as a first baseman making the force play at first base. He must be sure that he does not stretch out until the ball is in the air, and he can determine the path of the ball. If he stretches out too soon, he might find that the path of the ball is such that he will have a very difficult time catching the ball properly while maintaining foot contact with the plate. The catcher must always be alert for a bad throw and be ready to adjust his footwork to make the catch and the putout. If the throw is going to be wide of the plate, his only concern then would be to catch the ball. If he still has time to come back to the plate for the force out, he should do so. Once he catches the ball with his

foot in contact with the plate, he should step to the inside of the diamond to prevent any possible contact with his foot by the sliding runner. If there are runners at other bases, he should always fake the throw to first base in hopes that a runner might take a wide turn at second or third base.

2. **Force play with a chance of a double play at first base**—When the catcher reads that there will be a chance of a double play at first base, he will position himself about one to two feet directly behind home plate facing the fielder throwing the ball to the plate for the force out. He should provide a clear target for the thrower by holding both hands in the air a little above his head. If the catcher sees that the fielder of the ball has misplayed the ground ball, he must immediately jump to the inside of home plate and assume the position as described in the force play with no chance of a double play. If there is the chance of a double play at first base, the catcher remains behind the plate until the ball leaves the fielder's hand. Once the ball is thrown, the catcher moves forward toward the ball by stepping with his left foot and transferring his weight in that direction. As he develops the momentum in this weight transfer, his right foot drags across home plate. As his right foot drags across the plate, he would then jump pivot quickly toward first base. This would put him in a position well inside the diamond so there was no chance of contact with the runner coming into home plate. He would now step and throw from inside the diamond to the first baseman hoping to complete the double play. The catcher must be sure that on a low throw that he does not rise up as he catches the ball coming across the plate, for this would make it very difficult for the catcher to receive the ball properly. The timing should be such that the left food lands inside the diamond as the ball hits the glove. If the catcher reads that the throw from the fielder will be wide of the plate, he must forget the double play and attempt to make the catch of the ball. If time allows, he can come back to touch the plate for the force out on the runner from third base attempting to score.

TAG PLAYS AT THE PLATE

There is probably not a more exciting play in the game of baseball than the catcher making the tag on a runner sliding into home plate in his attempt to score a run. It is important that the coach spend time with his catchers on the mechanics of making a tag on a runner. This is so that the catchers not only have a better chance of retiring runners at the plate, but even more important, to prevent them from being severely injured via an unnecessary collision with a runner. There will be times that a collision will be unavoidable, but in most cases they can occur with neither the catcher or the runner being injured on the play. The following are guidelines and mechanics for the catcher in regard to the tag play at home plate:

1. **Decoying the runner**—On a ball hit to the left side of the field, the ball will be coming to the plate from behind the runner. This provides an excellent opportunity for the catcher to decoy the runner in thinking that there will not be a play made on him at the plate. In order to decoy the runner into slowing up while he awaits the throw, the catcher must relax and act as nonchalant as possible. He should never yell to the cut-off man to let the ball go through. He would only yell if he wants the ball cut-off and thrown to the plate. Once the ball is near the plate he can then position himself to make the catch and tag on the runner.

2. **Using the cut-off man**—The quicker the cut-off man can get the ball to the catcher, the better the chance for retiring the runner at the plate. The catcher must get his cut-off man into position with as few words and direction as possible. He should have the cut-off man cut any ball that will take him more than two steps away from the plate when there will be a close play at the plate. If it looks like the ball will arrive well before the runner, he might allow the ball to be a little wider than two steps before having the ball cut-off. If the ball is dying or sailing on it's way to the plate, he should always have the ball cut-off by the first baseman or third baseman. In addition to watching the flight of the ball, the receiver should look at the runner rounding third base and heading home out of the corner of his eye. In this way, he will have a better idea of what decision he will want to make in regard to having the ball cut-off or not.

3. **Positioning at the plate to receive the throw**—The catcher must position himself at the plate awaiting the throw so that he has command of the plate, and at the same time allowing the runner with the back part of the plate to slide into. The catcher is not allowed to block the plate without having the ball in his possession. He should position his left heel on the middle front portion of the plate while awaiting the throw. The left toe should be pointing slightly toward third base for two reasons: (1) it will enable the catcher to shift into the tag much easier; and (2) it will not expose the side of the knee in case the runner was to slide into the left leg of the receiver awaiting the throw.

4. **Catching the ball**—A catcher will have a tendency, as all fielders do, to attempt to make a tag on a sliding runner as quickly as possible. Many times this will cause the catcher to misplay the ball since his glove is moving toward the runner before it is cleanly received in the glove. The ball must be caught before the tag can begin. The catcher must always start his glove on the ground and work up when the ball is bouncing into the plate area. This way the ball will not get under the glove. The catcher must catch the ball and squeeze it in his right hand against the pocket of his catcher's mitt.

5. **Movement into the tag**—When the receiver has the ball firmly squeezed in his right hand against the pocket of his catcher's mitt, he should move his left foot to the left corner of the plate or further forward if he has time. His chest should now be resting against his left thigh. The left leg will now be facing toward the runner to serve as protection against the runner's spikes and legs as contact is made. His weight will be transferred forward over his left leg while dropping to his right knee to provide stabilization while the tag is applied.

6. **Making the tag**—The catcher makes the tag by pushing the ball and back side of the mitt against the lowest portion of the runner's leg. The receiver's weight should start to transfer further forward rather than backward as he applies the tag. It is important that the catcher apply the tag with the back of the glove so that there is no chance for the runner to make contact with the exposed ball. It is also important that the catcher continue to hold the ball tightly as the tag is applied so that there is little chance that the ball will come out of the hand as a result of the tag on the runner. Perhaps more than at any other base, backdoor slides and hook slides are used often in slides at home plate. The catcher should be sure to always "stay home" and not get caught reaching out to make the tag. He should remember that the slider must eventually come to home plate.

7. **Follow through on the tag**—Once the tag has been applied, the catcher should follow through with help from the momentum he generated due to his transferring his weight forward. He should follow through by swinging his arms toward the throwing side as he rises up and shifts his attention to the playing field in case another play might develop at a base.

8. **Collision at the plate**—If a collision results at the plate, the catcher should roll forward to absorb the blow over a greater portion of his body. He should never challenge the runner when blocking the plate and give him the opportunity to jar the ball loose or knock him backwards. If the catcher happens to be knocked backward on the play, he must continue to keep the ball and glove together making sure that he does not lose his tight grip on the ball.

9. **Fielding a difficult throw and applying the tag**—The tag play at the plate is made much easier for the catcher when the ball is fielded in the air or on an easy bounce while he holds his left heel on the middle front portion of the plate. However, there will be many times that this is not possible for the throw coming to the plate will be such that he will have to leave the plate to catch the ball. He should leave the plate if he reads that by doing so he will be able to catch the ball in the air or on a short-hop. He can not afford to get in-between-hopped as this will make a very difficult play for the catcher. If he moves inside the diamond to catch the ball, he will then have to shift his weight back toward the plate in hopes of making a tag on the runner sliding into the plate. He should shift his weight to his left leg as he pushes off that leg and dives at the runner. If the receiver feels that he has enough time to tag the runner by diving directly at him rather than going to the plate, then he should do so. If this can not be done, he must dive directly toward the plate. Whenever the catcher must dive at the runner or at the plate, he must hold the ball firmly in his right hand inside the glove and use the glove as a shield as the tag is applied. Whenever possible, he should tag the runner at his foot or lower portion of his leg. If he tags the runner higher than the foot or lower leg, he could very easily be making the tag higher on the leg while the runner's foot or lower leg has already crossed the plate. If any contact is made the catcher should roll with the impact distributing the blow over a greater body area. Again, the catcher should always be ready to look for another play after the tag is applied.

10. **Fielding the ball up the third baseline**—There will be times that the catcher will receive the ball up the third baseline and have to make a tag on the runner attempting to score. Once the receiver has caught the ball and is waiting for the runner, he should never challenge him, but should position himself inside the third baseline. Since the runner is moving rapidly and the catcher is in a stationary position, the catcher will take the brunt of the force if a collision was to occur. This could result in the ball being jarred loose from the catcher's grip, and also cause serious injury to the receiver. If the catcher finds himself in the basepath with a runner coming right at him, he must lower his body as quickly as possible to minimize the blow, and then roll with the "punch". If he catches the ball inside the baseline, he should stride with his left foot toward the runner, transferring most of his weight in that direction. Again, he should grip the ball tightly in the right hand against the pocket of the mitt. His right hand presses against the pocket as the back of the glove provides both a shield and protection for the ball. He should attempt to make the tag from the waist to the top of the shoulder of the runner. He must avoid the runner's swinging arms or legs. If the catcher must go into foul territory to catch the ball up the third baseline, he must react in about the same way as he would if he were making the tag inside the baseline. He would transfer most of his weight to his left foot as he grips the ball firmly against his catcher's mitt. Then he would push the back of his glove against the runner.

CATCHING POP-UPS

The good receiver wants to catch every pop-up within his fly ball territory. At the same time the catcher must understand that many times the first baseman or third baseman might have a better angle on the ball, and should be allowed the opportunity to make the play. The better the catcher is at fielding pop-ups, the less chance that he will be interfered with by another fielder. As all fielders should do, whenever he wants to catch the pop-up himself he must let everyone in the immediate vicinity know of his intentions by calling for the ball loudly. Please refer to an earlier section of the Playbook where fly ball communication and priority system was detailed. There are numerous guidelines and mechanics that the catcher must know and work on in order to be able to master the catching of pop-ups:

1. **Finding the ball**—The catcher who happens to close his eyes on the batter's swing will lose sight of the starting upward flight of the ball. Thus, the catcher must keep his eyes open, for the location of the pitch and the type of hitter at the plate will be major factors in the direction the ball will be hit in the air. Generally, a righthanded hitter will foul an outside pitch to the catcher's right and an inside pitch to his left. The opposite applies in the case of a lefthanded hitter. As soon as the ball is hit in the air, the catcher should turn quickly, and at the same time, remove his mask holding it in his right hand. He should scan the sky slowly, for if he was to frantically look for the ball from side to side it makes it practically impossible for him to pick up. This is especially true when there is a high sky, or at dusk when the ball will be very difficult to see.

2. **Getting rid of the mask**—As soon as the catcher finds the ball in the sky, he should make sure that the mask will not interfere at all with his movement to the ball. When the direction of the ball is known, he should toss the mask a good distance in the opposite direction. If he sees that he will have to run a great distance to catch the ball, he should drop the mask immediately as he takes off full speed for the ball. The catcher can not afford to drop the mask to the ground, only to find that the ball coming down forces him back to the area where the mask is on the ground. This could cause a serious injury to the catcher if he was to trip over the mask, along with losing the chance of making the catch.

3. **Moving toward the ball**—If the catcher has a great distance to travel to make the play on the ball in the air, he must be sure that he runs on the balls of his feet. He already is tremendously handicapped by the equipment he has on, and can not afford to be running on his heels causing his head and eyes to lose sight of the ball as it starts it's downward flight. There are several things that will enter into the fielding of the pop fly in regard to it's movement in flight due to the elements and the spin on the ball:

    A. **Ball park**—If the game is being played in an enclosed ball park, the ball will rotate farther when it gets up over the top of the stands. The reason for this is that the wind is blocked off partially by the enclosed park, and when the ball gets higher than the stands, the wind will suddenly carry the ball.

    B. **Wind**—It stands to reason that the wind factor must be taken into consideration by the catcher as he moves toward the ball. Hopefully, if the wind is blowing straight out to center field, the first baseman and third baseman can make the play on the fly ball that is hit straight up in the air off the bat. At any rate, the catcher must follow the rule of always catching a ball moving into the wind and not with the wind.

    C. **Sun**—The sun may play a major part in fielding pop-ups. The catcher must be in a position to shade his eyes from the sun by shielding the sun with either his glove or bare hand as it starts it's downward flight. The first baseman and third baseman should catch any pop-up that they can reach when they see the catcher fighting the sun as he attempts to catch the ball.

    D. **Rotation of the ball**—In almost all cases, the ball will rotate toward the infield as it starts it's downward flight. The amount of rotation will depend on how hard and high the ball was hit, as well as the angle that the ball and bat have when they meet.

4. **Catching the ball**—Prior to each inning, the catcher must check all the conditions that might affect a pop-up so that he will be in a better position to react properly to the ball in the air. On the ball that will take the catcher into fair territory, he must get to a position where he thinks the ball will land as quick as possible and then turn his back to the infield. By turning his back to the infield, he will be in a better position to catch the ball as it rotates toward the infield on it's downward flight. If he does not turn his back to the infield, he will have to catch the ball as it comes from behind his head. On all balls hit directly over the plate, or in foul territory behind the catcher he must keep his back to the infield. With his back to the infield, the catcher should position himself so that the ball in it's downward flight looks as though it will fall about three feet in front of him. When the ball is approaching the catcher, he should then line the ball up with his nose. Most errors on pop-ups are made when the catcher does not take into consideration the rotation of the ball, and then finds that the ball will end up behind him. It is much easier to move forward at the last instant for the ball then to have to move backward. Thus, the catcher should be on the balls of his feet when the ball hits the glove. He should catch every pop-up with two hands attempting to catch the ball at eye level. The glove should have the inside (palm) facing up with the fingers pointed behind the catcher, very similar to the way an infielder or outfielder catches a fly ball. He can not afford to reach for the ball, for this will take away from the soft hands needed to catch the ball properly. He must let the ball come down into the glove. The coach must give his catchers a lot of pop-up practice by

hitting balls with the fungo into the air. Thrown baseballs or machine balls are not recommended since they do not get the backspin on the ball that causes the "infield drift".

FIELDING BUNTS

One of the most important plays that a catcher is called upon to make is fielding the bunted ball. In addition, the receiver will be making the decision on where the bunted ball is to be thrown if another player fields the ball. This was discussed in detail in the bunt defense section of the Playbook. The following are the basic fundamentals for fielding and throwing the bunted ball for the catcher:

1. **Moving to the ball**—When a ball is bunted in the catcher's area, he should start for it quickly. The quicker the catcher can get to the area of the ball the more time he can take in properly fielding the ball. If a catcher is slow out of the catcher's box on a bunted ball, he will not only have to rush through the fielding phase but also through the throwing phase. As he moves out for the bunt, he should flip off his mask in the opposite direction to which he is going. As the catcher nears the ball, he must start slowing down to get his body under control. This is best done by lowering his center of gravity, widening his base and taking short choppy steps.

2. **Fielding the ball**—Whenever possible, the catcher should attempt to field the bunted ball with his chest right over the ball. If the ball is still rolling, he must use his glove to stop the ball. He would then use his bare hand to scoop or shovel the ball into the glove. If the ball has stopped, he should pick the ball up (chest over ball) with his bare hand. He must be sure that he has a good grip on the ball before he rises up for the throw. The same holds true for watching the ball while it is being shoveled into his mitt. Trying to catch a glimpse of the batter-runner while in the act of scooping the ball leads to unwarranted hurry, since the runner, who is moving faster than the ball, creates a distorted image of speed in the mind of the catcher. The catcher must be sure to bend the knees to get to the ball, scooping the ball while bending at the waist will cause problems.

3. **Bunted ball down third baseline**—If the ball is bunted down the third baseline and the throw is to first base, he should field the ball with his body to the right of the ball and his back toward first base. On a rolling ball, he should place his left foot as close to the ball as possible, so that he has plenty of space to field the ball as it rolls to his right. If the ball has stopped rolling, he should place his right foot close to the ball, making a turn to his left on his right foot and then step out with his left foot as he throws the ball to first base. This method of fielding a ball down the third baseline helps the catcher maintain his balance in comparison with the method whereby the catcher fields the ball from the left side of the ball. If there is a possible throw to second or third base, the catcher should keep the ball in front of him.

4. **Bunted ball down the first baseline**—If the ball is bunted down the first baseline and the throw is to be made to first base, the catcher should approach the ball from the left side. If the throw is to be made to second base or third base he should go straight to the ball. In fielding the bunt, he should place the glove in front of the ball and scoop it into the glove with the throwing hand. He should do this while in a crouched position. After the ball has been fielded and the play is to be made on the batter-runner at first base, he should rise up and step in the direction of first base as he releases the ball. If the ball is fielded close to the first baseline, he should move into the infield a couple of steps before throwing the ball to first base to be sure that the runner does not interfere with his throw. If he has no time to do so, he should attempt to throw the ball to the inside of first base. Hopefully, the first baseman or second baseman will be set up inside on the base so that there is no danger of the ball hitting the batter-runner as he runs to first base.

5. **Bunted balls down baselines**—Bunted balls along either baseline should be permitted to roll whenever the batter-runner can not be thrown out at first base. If the ball rolls foul, it should be immediately touched, so it will not roll fair. If another base is occupied, the catcher must be alert that the baserunner does not advance an extra base if the ball does not roll foul. The catcher should be in the best position to help the pitcher, first baseman or third baseman make the decision on whether to field the bunted ball or let it roll whenever the ball is rolling close to the baseline. The catcher should yell out "field it" when he recommends that the fielder field the ball in hopes of retiring the runner at first base. "Let it go" should be the communication from the catcher to the fielder if he feels that the ball will roll foul and there is no play on the runner. "Hit it" is the communication that should be used by the catcher to instruct the fielder to touch the ball if it is clearly in foul territory in order to prevent the ball from rolling back into fair ground.

6. **Making the throw to a base**—Whenever possible, the catcher must be sure that he steps in the direction of his throw after he has fielded the bunted ball. He should also attempt to get his elbow up as he releases the ball so that the ball does not die or sail on him as it heads to the intended target. It is also important that the catcher gives the man covering the bag time to set-up whenever possible. If the catcher has the ball and the player is not ready for the throw, the catcher should continue to crow-hop toward his target to insure proper rhythm in his throw. The only exception to these rules would be on a "do-or-die"

play where the catcher is off-balance when fielding the bunted ball and must make the throw to a base with no time to set his feet for the throw. Coincidental with fielding bunts is the catcher's responsibility for covering third base on bunts handled by the third baseman with a runner on first base who is heading for second base and may continue to an uncovered third base.

PITCHOUTS

There will be times in the game when the catcher will want the pitcher to throw him a pitchout so that the batter can not make contact with the ball if the runner on base breaks for the forward base on a steal attempt. The pitchout can be called by the catcher or by the coach flashing a signal to the catcher. Hopefully, the catcher will be receiving a pitch that will be 8 to 12 inches off the plate around chest high. The pitchout mechanics for the catcher would be:

1. **Righthanded hitter**—The catcher should assume a target position toward the outside of the plate. Upon release of the ball by the pitcher, he should quickly bring his left foot to his right foot and then step out with his right foot. He should remain in a bent-knee low position always anticipating a poorly thrown low pitch. His right foot should bring his body far enough over so his head is on the right side of the ball. He then will stride forward with his left foot toward second base and release the ball.

2. **Lefthanded hitter**—Again, the catcher should assume a target toward the outside of the plate. Upon release of the ball by the pitcher, he should quickly bring his right foot to his left foot and then step out with his left foot. He should remain in a bent-knee low position always anticipating a poorly thrown low pitch. As he receives the pitch, he should bring his right foot back behind his left foot and then stride with his left foot toward second base and release the ball.

INTENTIONAL WALKS

There are two paramount concerns when intentionally walking a hitter. The first is that the pitch is not close enough for the batter to reach and hit the ball. The second is that the pitch must be catchable. The obvious problem arises in that the catcher can not set-up outside his catcher's box. Thus, there is a rather invisable target that the pitcher must attempt to hit.

The catcher should stand up and reach straight out with his right hand for a rather simulated target for the pitcher with a righthanded hitter at the plate. With a lefthanded hitter, he will reach straight out with his glove hand. Upon release of the ball the catcher will quickly bend his knees and move his left foot to his right foot, and then move his right foot directly out to receive the ball. This is with a righthanded hitter at the plate. The opposite will hold true for the lefthanded hitter. He would move his right foot to his left foot, and then step out with his left foot.

DRILLS FOR THE CATCHERS

The following are some of the better drills that the coach might use in helping further develop the skill level of the catchers on his team:

1. **No Hands Drill**

Purpose—Develops skills in blocking balls in the dirt correctly. It is used primarily for receivers who try to use their gloves to catch balls which should be blocked.

Technique—Catcher places his hands behind his back and shifts to block the ball in the dirt, keepng his head down and his shoulders rounded. The catcher must concentrate on keeping the ball in front of him. Use rag balls or tennis balls in this drill.

2. **Soft Hands Drill**

Purpose—To force relaxation of hands which aids in developing the soft hands necessary in receiving properly.

Technique—Throw tennis balls at the receiver from 30-35 feet away. Catcher needs only to wear a mask, since the balls should not be in the dirt.

3. **Quick Hands Drill**

Purpose—Designed to improve speed of the catcher's hands by using a pitching machine to throw baseballs from a short distance.

370

Technique—Catcher in full gear is positioned 40-45 feet from pitching machine. The ball is thrown hard and the catcher attempts to frame each pitch correctly. The machine should be adjusted to simulate high, low, inside, and outside pitches.

4. Quick Feet Drill

Purpose—Designed to improve the speed of the catcher's feet on balls to the inside and outside. These should be pitches that require more than a sway shift. A pitching machine is used in this drill.

Technique—Catcher in full gear is positioned 40-45 feet from the pitching machine. The ball is thrown hard and the catcher takes a jab step to the left or right attempting to get the middle of his body in front of the pitch.

5. Sway and Frame Drill

Purpose—Teaches the techniques of catching the outside of the ball on inside and outside corner pitches.

Technique—Use a pitching machine. The catcher is in full gear. Adjust the machine so that the ball is located slightly outside of the catcher's shoulders requiring a sway shift to catch it correctly. This is also a good drill for isolating the receiving technique for high and low pitches.

6. Glove Roll Drill

Purpose—Teaches the technique of rolling the glove to place the glove in the bent position to react to the ball.

Technique—The catcher with full gear starts with his glove in target position. As the ball is released, the catcher should move his glove one-quarter turn to the left so that the glove is perpendicular to the ground. His glove is now half way between a palms-up catch and a fingers-up catch. From this position, the receiver can best make a decision. By practicing frequently, this can become a learned reaction.

7. Two Knee Drill

Purpose—To emphasize throwing the ball overhand.

Technique—Catchers pair off. They get down on both knees and play catch. This practically forces the catchers to throw with the proper overhand motion.

8. One Knee Drill

Purpose—To develop arm strength and power on the catcher's throws to second base.

Technique—Catcher positions himself on his left knee behind home plate and attempts to make the throw to second base. If necessary, the second baseman or shortstop can position himself between the mound and second base when receiving the throws.

9. Blocking Drill

Purpose—Developing proper techniques on blocking wild pitches thrown to the left, right, and in front of home plate.

Technique—Using live pitching or pitching machine from 60 feet, the catchers with full equipment will block balls in the dirt in front of home plate as well as to the left and right of home plate. Arms should be padded with knee pads or football arm pads.

10. Foul Ball Drill

Purpose—Teaches the catchers the proper technique of fielding fly foul balls.

Technique—This drill can use a pitching machine that will throw pop-ups or a coach with a fungo. The catchers will wear masks and catch pop fouls using proper techniques.

11. **Shadow Drill**

   Purpose—To improve the catcher's ability to frame pitches and sway shift on pitches slightly outside the width of the catcher's shoulders.

   Technique—Coach positions himself in front of the catcher and uses a ball on a stick to simulate pitches up and down, in and out. The coach checks each catcher as he sways and frames pitches.

12. **Footwork Warmup Drill**

   Purpose—Catcher uses the same footwork that he normally would use in a game in making throws to second base.

   Technique—Two catchers get 70-75 feet apart and throw to each other playing "hard catch", excuting proper footwork and emphasizing quick release on throws.

INFIELD PLAY

A baseball team would like to consider every ground ball hit to an infielder as a "sure out". This can only be achieved by a lot of hard work in practice sessions, plenty of concentration on the part of all the infielders, along with an abundance of natural talent.

The mark of a good infield coach is one who can take the talent available, and develop that talent so that each infielder gets the maximum out of his ability. Playing the infield requires great athletic skill, but skills can be developed. We will detail in this section the basic fundamentals of infield play that must be developed in order to establish the consistency necessary to make the routine play on a regular basis.

We will begin this infield section with some guidelines that a coach can use in placing his infield candidates at their respective positions.

PLACEMENT OF THE INFIELDERS

The following guidelines should be used by the coach in placing his infield candidates at their respective positions:

1. First base

The ideal first baseman should have good size and be one of the stronger hitters on the team, especially in the power category. It would be nice to have a boy who is quite tall at this position, but most coaches would rather have a boy with good hands and agility at this spot even if he is not that tall. More balls are thrown in the dirt or wide of the base than there are balls thrown over the head of a first baseman. We would generally prefer a lefthanded thrower at first base due to the three plays that he can make a little easier and quicker than the righthanded first baseman: (1) pick-off play at first base from the pitcher or catcher since his glove hand is on the second base side of the base; (2) the 3-6-3 double play; and (3) the throw to second base and third base on the bunted ball to the right side of the infield. Arm strength should not be a major factor in selecting the first baseman, for a team can sacrifice a little arm strength at this position.

2. Second base

It is very important that the boy assigned to play second base be a very consistent infielder with good quick feet, good hands, and an accurate arm with a quick release. If the arm is a little short, he can still be a positive addition to the infield if he has a quick throwing release. If the second baseman's arm is very weak, it might necessitate the coach cheating his shortstop a little more up the middle to prevent the second baseman from having to field too many ground balls behind second base with the long throw to first base. It will also necessitate the shortstop having to be the front man on the tandem relay whenever there is a question as to which one will go out for the throw from the outfielder. The second baseman should have good range, and he must have the skill to knock down every ball hit hard at him or to his left.

3. Shortstop

This position should be assigned to your best athlete (righthanded). He should have the strongest arm in the infield and also possess great range with quick reactions. The shortstop should be a "take-charge" guy and one who has great leadership skills. He should be your most consistent glove man, for the ball will touch his glove more than any other defensive player other than the catcher, the pitcher, and the first baseman. The coach can sacrifice some offense at this position if he has a young man who can play this position well.

4. Third base

The third baseman, along with the first baseman, must be one of your better hitters on the team. This is not to mean that defense is not important at the corners of the infield, but you can sacrifice a little defense at these two positions for offensive threats. Such is not the case with the shortstop and second baseman. The third baseman must have the ability to field the ball coming in and making an accurate and strong throw while on the move. He should have the ability to knock the hard shots down, and come up throwing.

BASIC INFIELD POSITIONING

There are numerous factors that the infielders must take into consideration when they determine where they will position themselves before each pitch is thrown:

1. **Type of pitcher throwing**—Basic positioning in the infield will depend quite a bit on the type of pitcher throwing along with the manner in which the particular batter is being pitched to. For example, if the pitcher throwing has an above average fast ball, the infielders should shade a little to the opposite field side. Vice-versa, if the pitcher throwing relies on off-speed and breaking pitches, then the infielders should adjust accordingly by shading to the pull side of the field.

2. **Type of pitch being thrown**—The shortstop and second baseman should read the catcher's pitch and location sign to the pitcher. With this information they should be in a better position to follow the ball from the pitcher's hand and react to the batted ball. For instance, if there is a righthanded hitter at the plate and the second baseman observes that a breaking pitch is going to be thrown to the outside part of the plate he can move a couple of steps over to his left. The middle infielders cannot afford to possibly give away pitches with their movement, so any movement must be subtle. Many infielders will just make an adjustment in their weight distribution, rather than making any movement in one direction. The coach may want his shortstop and second baseman to flash the pitch signs to the outfielders so that they might also make adjustments on each pitch. This is not recommended, since it takes too much concentration away from the infielder's basic responsibilities in regard to what he will be doing with the batted ball in various situations. The shortstop might want to establish a verbal sign with the third baseman when he reads that a change-up will be thrown with a righthanded hitter at the plate. The same would hold true for the second baseman alerting the first baseman of a change-up being thrown with a lefthanded hitter at the plate. This will allow the corner men to follow the flight of the ball better from the pitcher's hand and be alert for a hard smash in their direction.

3. **Type of hitter at the plate**—It is very important that the infielders make adjustments in their positioning depending on the type of hitter at the plate. They must take into consideration: the hitter's baserunning speed; and whether he is a pull hitter, opposite field hitter, or a spray hitter. As mentioned previously, adjustments must also be made in light of how the pitcher is pitching the particular hitter.

4. **Ability of the adjacent infielder**—The adjacent infielder should have an affect on where each infielder plays to take advantage of the adjacent infielder's strengths and weaknesses in going to his left or right. For example, if the third baseman has great lateral movement to his left, this will allow the shortstop to move a few steps to his left. We would prefer that the infielders squeeze the middle of the infield whenever possible unless there is a strict pull hitter or opposite field hitter at the plate. Squeezing the middle of the infield takes a lot of pressure off the shortstop and second baseman from having to make too many plays to their right, and trying to make the tough throw to first base to get the out on the batter-runner. This is especially adaptable when the shortstop and/or the second baseman possess less than average arms. In this way, the third baseman can help the shortstop on the ball in the hole, and the shortstop can then help the second baseman on the balls up the middle. Of course, if the corner men are required to guard the line late in the game the middle infielders would have to play accordingly. Also, if there is a drag bunt threat at the plate the third baseman would have to move toward the line a little more than normal.

5. **Arm strength**—It is very important that an infielder never position himself in the infield at such a depth that he cannot make a relatively easy throw on a routine ground ball. It does an infielder little good to be in a position to field a ball in the hole, and then find that he is not able to throw the batter-runner out at first base. Of course, the stronger the infielder's arm, the deeper in the infield he can play.

6. **Ability to go right and left**—The ability or inability to range right or left will be a prime consideration as to where the infielder positions himself in conjunction with the range capabilities of the adjacent infielder(s). Very few infielders can go equally well in both directions. For example, if a third baseman goes to his left very well but does not go to his right well, he would have to position himself a little closer to the line.

7. **Infield texture and the condition of the infield**—On a poor infield (rocks, poor grading, loose dirt, high grass, etc.) an infielder must play shallower than if the infield was in good condition. This is especially true if the grass and dirt are wet due to rain prior to the game.

8. **Coverage at a base**—Each infielder must also determine his positioning in the infield in conjunction with any possible base coverage responsibilities he would have as result of a steal attempt, hit and run possibility, force out opportunity, bunt coverage, or pick-off play.

9. **Movement by the count**—In a previous section of the Playbook, the infielders' responsibilities in regard to movement with the count was discussed. This movement with the count will play a major factor in the infielder's positioning on each pitch.

10. **Situation in the game**—The score, the number of outs, runners on base, etc., will play a major factor in the position each infielder will assume at the time of the pitch. Some examples would be: (1) the last two innings of the game when the tying or winning run is at the plate, the first baseman and third baseman would protect the lines to prevent the ground ball or line drive from getting past them down the line for a possible double putting a runner in scoring position; (2) when ahead in the score, the infielders would generally play a little deeper to insure outs on ground balls with runners on base to prevent the big inning; (3) when ahead in the score, the shortstop and second baseman do not have to cheat up the middle as much with a runner at first base since the steal or hit and run potential will be less, especially if well ahead in the score; (4) the first baseman would not have to hold the baserunner at first base on the bag when ahead in the score, especially when well ahead in the score and a lefthanded hitter is at the plate; (5) with a baserunner at third base and less than two outs, the score and the inning will dictate where the infielders position themselves depthwise; and (6) with two outs and an important run at second base, the infielders would play deep in order to keep the ground ball in the infield.

THE READY POSITION

Just as batting stances differ greatly from hitter to hitter, the same holds true for infielders in their ready position stance. However, as in hitting there are basic fundamentals that an infielder must have in order, to achieve the optimum ready position. One of the most important factors involved in successful infield play is the mental frame of mind of the infielder. Each infielder must pretend in his mind, while assuming the ready position, that the batter at the plate is a fungo hitter. He must pretend that this hitter at the plate is attempting to hit a ground ball to him on every pitch. In this way, the infielder will not be surprised when the ball leaves the hitter's bat and is heading in his direction. The infielder has got to play this little game in his mind on every pitch even though there will be times when the ball is never hit in his direction. The second he fails to perceive the hitter as a fungo hitter, and the ball is hit to him, he will have a tendency to rock back on his heels. This will certainly put the infielder at a distinct disadvantage in moving quickly toward the ball. It takes a disciplined player to play this game with the hitters on every pitch. He has got to want and expect the ball to be hit in his direction on every pitch. The following are the basic mechanics of the ready position:

1. As the pitcher is looking to the catcher for his sign and then begins his delivery to the plate, the infielder can either have his hands on his knees or be in an upright position moving toward the fielding position as the ball reaches the plate. We prefer to have the infielder in the hands on knee position prior to the ball reaching the plate. This is due to the fact that it proves to be a more comfortable position for most infielders and allows them to relax their body in anticipation of quick movement to the batted ball.

2. The knees should be slightly flexed with the degree of flex depending on the infielder's size and body build. The feet should be slightly outside the shoulders with the feet being a little farther apart for the taller infielder. The weight should be on the inside of the balls of the feet once the hands drop into the fielding position so that lateral movement can be obtained that much easier. The toes should be turned out slightly to prevent any knock-knee type of ready position which retards lateral quickness. The entire body should be very relaxed in the ready position. The glove hand and bare hand rest comfortably on the flexed knees while the eyes follow the ball toward the plate.

3. Just as the ball is about to reach the plate, the infielder drops both his glove hand and bare hand off his knees. This will force the infielder to move his weight more onto the balls of the feet to prevent any chance of his weight shifting back onto the heels as the ball leaves the hitter's bat. If done properly, the infielder will achieve the sensation of moving toward the hitter. It is highly recommended that the infielder allow this sensation to take the form of slight movement toward the hitter in the way of bounce steps. These bounce steps should be such that the infielder's weight continues over the inside of the balls of the feet. Many infielders feel that the bounce steps forward allow them the opportunity to get a much quicker jump on the ball than to react from a stationary position as the hands drop from the knees. The same holds true if the infielder's ready position goes from the upright position to the down position. The steps should be no more than two to three inches forward so that the infielder will end up with the toes practically parallel as the ball reaches the plate. Infielders who wish to bounce step forward need to drop their hands from their knees slightly earlier than the infielder who just drops his hands from the ready position. If the infielder reads the slow curve ball or change-up is thrown, he can continue the bounce steps forward so that he is not caught flat footed as the ball reaches the plate.

4. As the ball reaches the plate, the glove and bare hand should be open. The glove should be out in front forcing the

upper part of the body down to achieve an optimum balance position for quick lateral movement to the ball. The arms should end up slightly outside of the legs as the glove and bare hand open toward the plate. The glove and bare hand should end up about two to three inches below the knees. The closer the glove and bare hand are to the ground the less quickness the infielder will have. The first baseman and third baseman can drop their hands a little closer to the ground since they must be prepared for the ball getting to them a little quicker than it would to the shortstop or second baseman. At this point, the infielder should be ready to move quickly to the ball or be in a position to hold his ground on a sharply hit ball right at him.

FIELDING GROUND BALLS

Once the ball is hit, the infielder must respond in the right direction and at the proper angle as quickly as possible. To help the infielders determine how quickly they must get to the ball and at what angle, the coach might use the production rating system to grade ground balls. The grading of ground balls follows the grading system detailed in an earlier section of the Playbook. This grading of ground balls allows the infielder to judge the proper approach, the proper angle, and whether or not he will have a chance for a force out at a forward base or will only be able to make a play on the batter-runner at first base.

For review of the production rating system, the following are the guidelines for determining the type of ground ball hit to the infielder:

1. **4 ground ball**—The 4 ground ball is a slow roller or a ball not hit well enough to be considered a routine ground ball. On a 4 ground ball, the infielder must charge the ball quickly. The infielder should not be concerned with establishing angles to the ball unless it is a hard 4 type ground ball. The throw will generally have to be rushed, and all plays in the infield with runners on base will have to be made to the base the ball takes the infielder. There are no double play possibilities on a true 4 ground ball.

2. **5 ground ball**—The 5 ground ball is the routine ball hit on the ground to an infielder. A double play can be made on most 5 type ground balls as long as the infielder does not have to go a great distance to field the ball, and he is not playing too deep in the infield. The lead runner should be retired on most 5 ground balls. The approach to the 5 ground ball should be quick, but should not force the infielder to rush through the act of fielding the ball unless the infielder is playing deep or there is a quick runner going down the line. On most 5's, the infielder (not the first baseman) should be in a position to round the ball in order to gain momentum on his throw to first base.

3. **6 ground ball**—On a true 6 ground ball, the infielder has plenty of time to field the ball and throw out the lead runner since a 6 ground ball is a very well hit ball. If the infielder can go three or four steps to his right or left and field the ball, then it is not a true 6 ground ball. The double play is always in order on this type of ball.

As the coach hits the infielders ground balls in practice sessions he can help the infielders grade the balls so that they completely understand what type of approach and angle they should take on each ball. The grading of ground balls also is important when teaching the infielders where to go on ground balls fielded with runners at first and third base and less than two outs. The basic rules for force plays can be found in an earlier section of the Playbook. As we continue through the infield section we will refer to the nature of the ball hit by this production grading system.

The following are the basic fundamentals that need to be developed for an infielder to field a ground ball properly.

1. **Approach to the ball**—One of the biggest problems that a coach will have with his infielders is to teach them to be aggressive in their approach to the ball, but at the same time be in a position to field the ball under control. The coach must convince his infielders that the only way they can make the routine play on the ground ball is to get to the ball quickly, and then fight to get under control during the actual fielding process. If an infielder does not go full speed initially to the 4 or 5 type ball he will run into two major problems: (1) he will stand a greater chance of having the ball play him, which will increase the chances of being in-between-hopped; and (2) he will have to rush through the fielding and throwing phase of retiring a runner on the play. The consistency of properly charging a ground ball and fielding it under control can only be achieved with a lot of ground ball work in practice sessions. It is highly recommended that the coach stress to his infielders that whenever they are taking ground balls in these practice sessions that they go "game speed" simulating game conditions. This means that they might only want to take 10-12 ground balls at a time, and then rest. Otherwise, if they take too many ground balls at a time they will start sitting back on the ball due to fatigue. Everytime an infielder takes a ground ball he must take the proper approach and angle to the ball so that what he does in these practice sessions will carry over into the game itself. The proper approach to the ball will depend entirely on the nature of the ball and the direction that the throw will have to be made. On a 4 or 5 type ground ball, the infielder must break full speed from his ready position so that he will have adequate time to field the ball

properly. Too many infielders break for the ground ball from the ready position carrying their glove as though they are about to field the ball. They must pump both arms as they run in order to establish the necessary quickness to the ball. Only when they are breaking down to actually field the ball will the glove and bare hand open up to the ball. In a later section we will discuss the angle approach to various types of ground balls.

2. **Glove down**—Once the infielder properly approaches the ball, half the battle is over and now the glove must complete the task. Many infielders get the label of having "bad hands", but actually with a little more work in proper glove technique they can establish their hands to the point that they can develop "good hands". If the glove does not start from the down position near the ground there is little chance that an infielder can develop "soft hands". The infielders should be instructed that the glove should never leave the ground until the ball takes its last hop. This is due to the fact that a ball cannot take a bad hop while off the ground. It is much easier and quicker to move the glove up than it is to move it down. This glove on the ground technique should even be done on 5 or 6 type ground balls that take on the appearance of a big hop. This is so that the infielder gets into a consistent habit of keeping his glove on or near the ground. In addition, what might appear to be a big hop to the infielder might not be the case as the ball hits the ground. Any error on a ground ball should be made from the glove on up, never with a ball getting under the glove. When a 6 type ground ball is hit at an infielder he must fight to get the glove in the down position so that he can better knock the ball down. By just keeping the sharply hit ball in front of him, he will have a good chance of retiring a runner. All infielder's gloves should be covered with dirt stains on the back indicating that the glove has been in contact with dirt on practically every play.

3. **Glove out in front of the body**—As the infielder sets himself for the ground ball with his glove on or near the ground, his glove and bare hand should be well out in front of his body. This is one of the toughest skills to teach young infielders, for most of them will have a natural tendency to position their glove and bare hand too close to their body. How far out in front the hands should be will vary from infielder to infielder, but a good guideline would be that the glove heel and bare hand should be at least two to three inches in front of the forehead as the infielder gets into the proper fielding position with his upper body. When the hands are positioned out in front of the body in this manner, the infielder should be able to easily see the ball into his glove. It will also force the upper body over the balls of the feet which will give the infielder the optimum balance position for properly fielding the ball. Another plus for the hands being out in front of the body is that it will enable the infielder to make quick adjustments with his hands if the ball was to take a bad hop. If the hands are too close to the body it is practically impossible for the hands to adjust to any unnatural type of hop off the ground. From this out in front position of the glove and throwing hand, the infielder will be able to give into the body with his hands as the ball enters the glove.

4. **Glove angle to the ball and body**—Another common fault of young infielders is that they become careless in their glove angle to the ball in relationship with the body. Many infielders will end up fielding the side of the ball rather than presenting the glove to the ball in such a way that the fingers of the glove meet the ball direct with the path of the ball. If an infielder fields the side of the ball with his glove, the ball can easily enter the glove at an improper angle causing the ball to roll off the side of the heel of the glove. This occurs often when an infielder approaches the ground ball with his hands flying off to the side of his body forcing his glove hand to come in from the side of the ball. This problem of improper glove angle must be eliminated very quickly, for otherwise an infielder will experience a great deal of difficulty in developing the proper glove action. The approach the glove takes to the ball and the movement of the glove to the body on contact with the ball is of utmost importance in "sure-hand" fielding of ground balls. In order to position the glove so that the entire center of the pocket is facing the ball, the infielder will have to keep his glove side elbow in direct line with the path of the ball. If the elbow is positioned at an angle away from the path of the ball, it will automatically force the glove to position itself at the same angle. By rolling ground balls to the infielders, the coach can easily check the angle of the glove along with the angle of the glove side elbow as the ball enters the glove. The bare hand and bare hand side elbow should be at a slight angle to the ball as it enters the glove. This is especially true when the infielder gets into the good habit of fielding ground balls on his glove side. The more the infielder fields the ball to his bare hand side with his glove, the more the bare hand side elbow must be in toward the midline of the body. There are two other mistakes an infielder can make in regard to his glove angle: (1) heel of glove too perpendicular to the ground; or (2) heel too flat to the ground. If the heel of the glove is too perpendicular to the ground, it would restrict the fielding surface of the glove to the ball as it enters the glove causing a ball to easily be misplayed. If the heel is too flat to the ground then the infielder will find that the ball can easily roll off the heel of the glove. This is the reason why an infielder might have a lot of ground balls roll up his arm after they leave the glove. Each infielder must find the happy medium of his glove angle to the ball so that the fingers of the glove allow the ball to enter the pocket area, and then the heel of the glove keeps the ball in the pocket area. An infielder can not afford to get into the bad habit of "glove flipping". This occurs when an infielder approaches the ball with the back of the glove facing the ball, and then at the last instance, he flips the glove over exposing the pocket of the glove to the ball. This will cause the fielder to constantly have problems with bad hops and retards the ability of the infielder to make glove adjustments to the ball as it is about to enter the glove. The glove surface must be fully exposed to the ball as soon as the infielder positions himself to field the ball.

5. **Fielding on the glove side**—It is extremely important that the infielder get into the good habit of fielding the ground ball on the glove side of the body whenever possible. Whenever a coach teaches an infielder to field the ball at the midline of the body, he will find that the infielder will have a natural inclination to field the ball slightly on his throwing side. Fielding of the ball on the glove side means that the glove should be positioned anywhere from the midline of the body to the glove side foot. He should never attempt to field a ground ball on the outside of his glove foot unless he is moving laterally for the ball and cannot make the play with the glove in front of the body. The ideal position of the glove for most infielders when contact is made with the ball is about two to three inches on the glove side of the midline of the body. There are four reasons for fielding the ground ball on the glove side whenever possible:

A. It will help to soften the hands of the infielder. When an infielder fields the ball on the throwing side of the midline of his body, he will have to straighten out the elbow and wrist in order for the glove to reach the ball. The more he fields the ball on the throwing side, the straighter the elbow and wrist will become when contact is made with the ball. By fielding the ball on the glove side, it will enable the infielder to have a slight bend in his elbow and wrist as the ball makes contact with the glove. This is important in fielding the ground ball with soft hands. Anytime the glove side elbow and wrist are straight or locked when the ball is fielded, the infielder will find that his glove hand is rigid when contact is made with the ground ball.

B. Any unexpected bad hops can be reached much easier with the ball being fielded on the glove side of the body. This is due to the fact that the range of the glove to the right and left is increased. If the glove was positioned on the throwing side of the body, the infielder's movement of the glove is severely restricted if the ball was to take a bad hop well to the throwing side of the body.

C. If the ball is misplayed by the infielder when fielding the ball on the glove side there is a greater chance for the ball to hit the ground in front of him, which will enable him to replay the ball and make the throw to the appropriate base. If he attempts to field the ball on the throwing side of the midline of the body and the ball is misplayed, more than likely the ball will hit the ground in a direction away from where the throw needs to be made. For example, if a shortstop boots a ball on his left side (glove side) and the ball hits the ground, it will generally fall in the direction of first base. If he fields the same ball on his right side (throwing side) and the ball hits the ground, it will generally fall in a direction away from first base.

D. By fielding the ball on the glove side it will also allow the infielder the opportunity to get a better grip on the ball as he brings the glove and ball into his body. When fielding off the throwing side, the ball exchange is generally much quicker from glove to hand, and this could cause an improper grip on the ball. There is no question that the infielder will be able to release the ball a little quicker when fielding the ground ball on the throwing side, but all the other advantages of fielding on the glove side outweigh this one advantage. Many times infielders attempt to release the ball too quickly at the expense of an accurate and strong throw. We would rather sacrifice a little quickness on release, for fielding the ball properly and making a strong accurate throw to the intended target.

6. **Eye contact with the ball**—If the infielder is in proper fielding position, he should be fielding the routine ground ball in front of the glove hand eye. As in all athletic skills involved with moving objects, it is very important that both eyes see the object being played. This certainly holds true for fielding a ground ball. Following the ball all the way into the glove with both eyes will also force the upper part of the infielder's body to be in a better mechanical position for fielding the ball. If the eyes are taken off the ball as it enters the "fielding zone" of the glove, the head and shoulders will not remain in the proper position to allow the glove to make good contact with the ball. Anytime a part of the infielder's upper body moves up prior to the ball entering the glove, you will find that the infielder's ability to glove the ball properly is severely hindered. Also, any infielder who has a tendency to take his eyes off the ball is generally rocking back on his heels due to the fact that his head and upper body are forced back over the heels. "Looking the ball into the glove" with the eyes will also enable the infielder to bring the ball and glove into the body that much easier.

7. **Wide base**—The only way all of the previous skills can be accomplished is to have the feet spread well enough apart to enable the glove to be down and out in front of the body. Generally, the taller the infielder the wider his feet should be to achieve the optimum balanced fielding position. How wide the feet need to be spread apart when fielding the ball depends on the size of the fielder, the nature of the ground ball hit to him, and his ability to get the glove out in front of the body. This wide base of support should force the weight onto the balls of the feet allowing the infielder a better chance to make the proper adjustments with his glove. As a general rule, the tougher and harder the ball is to field, the wider the feet must be to force the glove and body down into the proper fielding position. If an infielder has a narrow base with his feet when in the act of fielding the ground ball, he will find that he will have a very difficult task in getting his glove out far enough in front of his body. He will also find that his glove elbow will be locked as he fields the ball since he will have to reach for the ball with his glove since the

narrow base will not allow the glove to be positioned on the ground properly. The wider the feet are the less chance that a ball will get under the glove of the infielder. However, if he gets too wide with his feet it will not allow him to field the ball and then position his feet quickly for the throw. It is the responsibility of the coach to help the infielder determine how far apart his feet should be to properly field the ball, and then transfer his weight for the throw to the respective base where a play will be made.

8. **Rounded shoulders**—The glove position well out in front of the body cannot be obtained without the shoulders being rounded on contact with the ball. Rounded shoulders will also insure that the head will be down which means that eye contact during the fielding stage should be adequate. Anytime an infielder's shoulders are moving up prior to or on contact with the ball, the glove will also be moving away from the ground. Thus, the shoulders should remain rounded until the ball makes contact with the glove. Rounded shoulders will also keep the upper part of the body over the balls of the feet making it much easier for the infielder to make adjustments with his weight if he must make a last second move to the ball.

9. **Knees bent**—The degree the knees need to be bent depends primarily on the height of the fielder and the length of his legs. The taller the infielder or the longer his legs, the more the knees must be bent in order for him to be in the proper fielding position with his glove and bare hand. There is no way an infielder can be in proper fielding position without the knees being bent allowing the upper part of the body the opportunity to get down to the level necessary to adequately field the ball.

10. **Toes parallel**—Many infielders are taught that when the glove makes contact with the ground ball that the right foot (righthanded thrower) should be slightly behind the left foot. This positioning of the feet leads to fielding the ball on the throwing side and also insures that most balls misplayed off the body cannot be replayed due to the fact that the ball will not end up in front of the body when it hits the ground. The infielder should have his toes practically parallel when he fields the ball to help insure that he is fielding the ball on the glove side of his body. This also enables the infielder to keep his body in front of the ball so that if a misplay occurs, the ball can still be replayed in front of him. The more the right foot is placed behind the left foot the greater chance that a ball off the body will hit the ground in a direction away from the intended target.

11. **Bent elbow and wrist**—On the moment of impact with the ball, the elbow and wrist on the glove arm must be slightly bent so that the glove can be used in its proper fashion. Anytime the elbow and wrist are locked and rigid on impact, the infielder will have a tendency to field the ball with "hard hands". This is a common problem with young infielders who get the label of having "poor hands". This slight flexion of the elbow and wrist can only be achieved if the ball is fielded on the glove side and the upper part of the body is down and over the ball. The bent elbow and wrist on impact should not be encouraged so much that the infielder gets the tendency to pull the glove into the body before the ball actually makes contact with the glove. The timing involved is important in developing an infielder's "soft hands".

12. **Bringing the ball into the body**—When the ball enters the glove, the glove should then give with the ball to cushion it so that there is little chance for the ball to bounce out of the glove. The glove should bring the ball slightly into the body in the same direction that the ball entered the glove. Many times an infielder will field the ball, and just as the ball enters the glove, the glove hand moves to the body in a direction contrary to the direction the ball entered the glove. This could cause the ball to enter the glove in such a way that it exits the glove as the infielder brings the glove hand into the body and then up to the throwing position. Thus, the ball enters the glove and the infielder brings the glove into the left side of the body (if that is where the ball was fielded). At this time the bare hand should have a firm grip on the ball and then the glove and ball will quickly be moved toward the throwing shoulder. Many infielders in their rush to get rid of the ball will actually move the glove toward the throwing shoulder before the ball has firmly entered the glove and the bare hand has had an opportunity to get a good grip on the ball.

13. **Bare hand**—The bare hand must be positioned next to the glove so that it assists the infielder in securing the ball in the glove as the ball makes contact with the glove. It is preferred for the bare hand to be positioned in such a manner so that this movement of the bare hand into the glove is quick. Rather than positioning the bare hand flat on the ground as the ball makes contact with the glove, it is best for the hand to be angled slightly toward the glove. This will quicken the bare hand into the glove and will also provide the infielder with an opportunity to use the bare hand to trap a ball that might "kick" off the bare hand side of the glove. Many times balls roll out of a glove on the bare hand side of the glove and this is due to the fact that the infielder was slow in getting the bare hand on the ball or the hand was not positioned properly to prevent the ball from leaving the glove. As the bare hand secures the ball, the infielder will now have time to get the proper grip on the ball as he brings the glove and throwing hand back into the body and then up to the throwing side shoulder. Hopefully, the ball can be gripped across the seams on each throw since this is the grip that will provide the infielder with more velocity and accuracy on his throw. An infielder who fields the ball on his throwing side will often not allow himself enough time to get a proper grip on the ball since the ball will be in the glove a little less time than when he fields the ball on his glove side. As mentioned previously, one of the reasons for fielding balls on the glove side was to allow the infielder time to get a good grip on the ball.

14. **Fielding the ground ball right at the infielder**—The toughest ground ball for an infielder to field is the ball hit right at him for the following reasons: (1) it will tend to freeze the infielder since it is the toughest ball to read off the bat; (2) it is difficult to judge the hop since the ball is not coming to the infielder at an angle; (3) it is very difficult to judge the speed of the ball; and (4) the ball right at the infielder will generally cause the infielder to raise up as the ball is hit due to his inability to read the ball properly. The infielder must move forward toward any ground ball that he reads is hit directly at him to insure that he stays on the balls of his feet. Moving forward toward the ball will enable the infielder to make adjustments that he will not be able to make if he waits back on the ball until he reads the speed of the ball off the bat. By moving forward initially, it is much easier to stop whenever a proper hop is detected by the infielder. When the infielder sits back on the ball, it is practically impossible to generate the proper momentum forward if the infielder reads that he must make a move to the ball. The infielder who continually sits back on ground balls hit right at him is "letting the ball play him" rather than him playing the ball. The good infielder will field practically every ball at the top of the hop, on the down hop, or on the short hop. The infielder who consistently fields balls on in-between hops is not reading the ball properly. The infielder who is aggressive forward towards the ball hit right at him will be able to make the routine play moreso than the non-aggressive infielder who consistently sits back on the ball. A good rule for the infielder to follow is for him to move towards the ball whenever in doubt as to the nature of the ball that is hit right at him. If he reads a 6 type ground ball right at him, he must be sure to take at least one step forward to insure that he is on the balls of his feet. He must then widen his base and make sure that his glove is on the ground working the glove up from the ground as he reads the nature of the hop. He must knock down the 6 ground ball making sure that the ball stays in front of him if it rebounds off his glove or body. At no time can he allow his weight to transfer back over his heels, or have a narrow base with his feet since he will not be able to position his glove on the ground properly.

15. **Rounding the ball**—An infielder cannot afford to field the ground ball right at him or one that is slightly to his right side without rounding the ball slightly prior to fielding the ball. This would not be the case on a true 6 type ground ball since the ball will be in the area of the infielder too quick. On a 5 or a hard 4 type ground ball at the infielder or slightly to his right, the ball must be rounded in order to better read the speed and the hop of the ball. Rounding the ball will also enable the infielder to field the ball with his weight moving toward first base at the time of contact with the ball. Rounding the ball will also assist the infielder in fielding the ball on his glove side. It is more important for the third baseman and shortstop to round the ball than for the second baseman since they have a much longer throw to make to first base. The angle the infielder takes to round the ball cannot be so great that it takes away from his speed to the ball. Rounding the ball is just a gradual angling to the right side of the ball on the approach. This is especially important on the ground ball hit slightly to the right side of the infielder.

16. **Ground ball to the glove hand side**—One infield fundamental that will make or break an infielder is his ability to range to his right or left for a ground ball. The marks of a good infielder is one who can move laterally to the ground ball and still position himself properly to get into the proper fielding position. The coach can help an infielder increase his quickness to the ball with a lot of fundamental work in lateral movement, but the basic tools of quickness must still be there for an infielder to make a routine play of a ball to his right or left. The following are the basic fundamentals for an infielder in moving to his glove hand side to field a ground ball:

A. **The cross-over step**—The proper ready position at the time the ball meets the bat will be a big help in increasing the infielder's quickness laterally to the ball. The basic cross-over step must be used when the infielder must go a distance away from his ready position to field the ground ball. In the case of a ball hit to the glove hand side (righthanded thrower) it will necessitate the infielder to cross-over with his right foot in the direction of the angle he wishes to take on the ball. The cross-over step is so very important in achieving the proper momentum to the ball and establishing the proper angle taking into consideration the speed and direction the ball has taken off the bat. This cross-over step must be worked on daily in practice sessions so that the infielder has no wasted motion on the initial step, and he stays low enough with his body to achieve maximum acceleration very similar to the cross-over step used in stealing a base. Any false step taken with the foot nearest the ball must be eliminated for it will severely hinder the infielder's quickness to the ball. Carrying the body low during lateral movement should allow the glove to stay close to the ground so that the infielder does not have to reach down for the ball at the last second. Most misplays on balls to the left or right occur under the glove when the infielder does not carry his glove low enough while attempting to make the play on the ball. The head should not raise up on the cross-over step nor should the infielder push up off the ground on his initial step toward the ball. Any movement of the body up on the initial step will decrease the infielder's quickness to the ball. If the infielder is moving toward his left on the cross-over step, he must drive his right hand in the same direction as his right foot to assist in the acceleration of his movement to the ball. If a well hit ball is not hit a great distance from the infielder, he must keep his glove hand palm open to the ball.

B. **Fielding the ball at the best angle with the best hop**—On a 4 or 5 type ground ball, the infielder must quickly determine the proper angle he must take to the ball and still get the best possible hop so that he does not make contact with the ball on a hop that makes for a very difficult play. Most young infielders lack the aggressiveness forward toward the ground ball to their left or right. They then find themselves sitting back on the ball only to find that they will have the ball play them rather than them playing the ball. As mentioned previously, it is always best to establish momentum toward the ball whenever in doubt about the nature of the ground ball. In this way, the infielder can always slow down to field the ball on the best hop. Once the infielder slows down or stops, and the ball is still a great distance away from the glove, it is impossible to regenerate the momentum toward the ball. Of course, if there is a runner in scoring position at second base, the infielder must take a much deeper angle on the ball to prevent the runner from scoring on a ground ball that gets by the infielder.

C. **Carrying the glove**—If the infielder has to range a good distance to get to the ground ball, he must pump his arms as he runs to the ball just as he would in a sprint. Many infielders get into the bad habit of running to the ball without the benefit of the arms pumping to increase their quickness to the ball. These infielders run to the ball with their glove open to the ball too early hindering their ability to get to the ball as quickly as they could with the use of good pumping action with their arms. If the ball is just a few strides away from the infielder, then he must open the glove to the ball to insure that he does not have to flip the glove over at the last instance to field the ball. The infielder must travel low with the glove at knee level or lower whenever the ball is hit a few steps away from the infielder on a well hit ball.

D. **Fielding action**—A ball hit to the glove hand side should be the easiest ball for the infielder to handle since the angle of the ball will enable him to easily read the speed and nature of the ball. At the same time, the ball can be easily fielded on the glove hand side of the body unless the infielder was to overrun the ball. The infielder must always use two hands to field the ball on the glove hand side whenever possible using the proper fielding mechanics previously detailed. A lazy infielder will often time his movement to the ball on his glove hand side in such a manner that he fields the ball with only the glove hand extended. If the ball does take a bad hop, the ball will generally end up in the outfield. When two hands are used to field the ball on the glove hand side the infielder must still bring the glove and ball into his stomach and then quickly and smoothly bring the glove and throwing hand up to the throwing side shoulder for release of the ball to first base.

E. **Throwing the ball**—The natural tendency for the infielder fielding the ball on his glove hand side is to release the ball to first base while off-balance. If time allows and the momentum to the glove hand side is not too great, the infielder should always attempt to straighten up with his body, step in the direction of his throw, and get the elbow up as he releases the ball. The quickness of his release will be a little slower, but the velocity and accuracy on the throw should make up for the slower release time. Of course, if the infielder's momentum is too great to straighten up for the throw, then he will have to throw the ball three-quarters or lower in order to get the throw off to first base. Any time the infielder must throw off-balance dropping his arm on release, he must take this into consideration as he targets for the throw since the ball will tail on the way to the intended target. Whenever possible, the infielder should attempt to make the throw to first base off his right foot rather than throwing off his left foot which would not enable him to get off a more accurate and strong throw to first base.

17. **Ground ball to the throwing hand side**—The backhand play for the infielder can prove to be a very difficult play unless the proper mechanics are used. Infielders should not fear this play, for if done properly, they should be in a much better position to get off a strong throw. Many times an infielder will fight to get in front of the ball to his throwing side only to find that he will field the ball with his momentum going away from first base and he is not able to get off a strong throw. The only time the backhand play should be discouraged is when there is a baserunner at second base who would score if the ball gets by the infielder. On a smooth surface infield that is well maintained the infielder can backhand the ball much easier than he can on a poor surface. The following are the proper fundamentals for backhanding a ground ball and getting off a throw to the intended target.

A. **The cross-over step**—The fundamentally sound cross-over step with quick movement to the ball is essential if an infielder is to properly backhand the ball hit to his throwing side. The infielder must become adept at cutting the ball off at the sharpest angle possible in order to field the ball quickly along with shortening the distance of the throw to the target. The cross-over fundamentals would be the same for the backhand play as they were for the play made to the glove hand side. Of course, the infielder would have to cross-over with his left foot (righthanded infielder). The glove must be carried low if the ball is hit sharply close to the infielder so that there is no chance that the ball gets under the glove. The infielder must also read the nature of the ball hit in order to field the ball on the best hop that he can get, since the backhand play is much more difficult than the play made to the glove hand side.

B. **Positioning of the body**—Once the infielder reads that his best play on the ground ball will be the backhand play, he must get his body under control. There is little chance for success in backhanding the ball without some degree of body balance as the ball nears the glove. The infielder must bend at both the waist and the knees as he extends the glove so that the upper part of his body enables him to achieve practically a full extension of his glove on the ground as he prepares to field the ball. He must be sure to keep both eyes on the ball with a steady head.

C. **Glove action**—The ball should be fielded about six to ten inches in front of the glove hand side foot with the elbow of the glove arm slightly bent. One of the biggest faults infielders have on backhand plays is that they often make contact with the ball too close to the body. This does not allow them to properly see the ball into their glove along with providing a very poor feeling for the ball as it enters the glove. At the same time the infielder cannot afford to reach for the ball since this will cause his center of gravity to fall well over the lead foot further complicating the difficulty in keeping the body under control. The good backhander will be able to time his approach to the ball so that the glove is in a proper position to make contact with the ball as the feet are set. The glove must be opened fully to the ball by turning the left elbow up and out. The infielder needs to spread the palm of his hand in the glove to widen the glove pocket exposing the entire pocket of the glove to the ball. Many infielders have found success on the backhand play by moving the glove slightly into the ball as it nears the glove. They find that this slight movement of the glove to the ball allows the ball to stay in the glove better than having the ball enter the glove while the glove is in a stationary position. In addition, this technique with the glove starts to square the shoulders around to the target and further insures that the glove is out in front of the body. It is not wise to move the glove to the ball if the infielder is fielding a hard hit ball, especially one that will short hop the fielder. As soon as the ball is firmly in the glove, the infielder must bring the glove up quickly to the throwing side shoulder where the bare hand grips the ball for the throw to the intended target.

D. **Planting the foot**—The infielder's degree of momentum away from the intended target of his throw will dictate the type of footwork he must exercise in order to get off the throw. If the infielder needs to get off a relatively short throw (shortstop making force out at second base on a ball fielded on his throwing side) then an off-balance throw is much more practical than if he must make the throw from the hole to first base. Many infielders with strong arms feel more comfortable fielding the backhand ball with their right foot forward. When fielding the ball with the right foot forward on this play the infielder takes away from the benefit of taking the extra step with the right foot to use as his push-off leg for the throw. When fielding the ball with the left foot forward, the infielder must then take another step with his right foot in order to brace himself for the throwing action. Most infielders need this extra step to get their body under control and to allow them to push off the right leg to generate power into the throw to first base. This extra step will slow down the infielder's release of the ball, but it will enable him to get off a more powerful and accurate throw to the intended target. By bending low with the knees as the ball enters the glove, the infielder will be in a much better position to control his momentum away from the target. As the ball enters his glove, he must take the short extra step with his right foot in the direction that his momentum is taking him. If the step with the right foot has to be a large one due to the momentum of his body away from the target, the infielder would probably be better off just "eating" the ball since he would then have to get his feet back under him before he can release the ball. However, if the infielder fields a 6 to his backhand side and is forced to take a large step away from the target with his right foot, he still might have time to gather himself to make the throw on the batter-runner. If the infielder fields a 6 with his right foot forward to the backhand side it is always preferred to have him shuffle step toward his target to insure a strong and accurate throw. It takes an infielder with a super arm to throw the ball a great distance with something on it when he releases the ball without benefit of getting his right foot planted under him. If the right leg is under the right shoulder as he releases the ball he will get off a stronger throw than if the right leg is in front of the shoulder. Anytime an infielder backhands the ball and is going to throw planting the right foot, he will have to drop and drive with his right leg in order to get the proper push-off. If the infielder does not drop and drive with the right leg he will not be able to get off the type of throw necessary to throw out most runners. When an infielder fields the backhand ball with the left foot forward and he takes the short step with the right foot away from the target to brace himself and push-off, he must make every effort to turn the right toe in so that he gets the proper push-off the ground. His weight should be centered over the inside of his right foot as he opens up his hips and steps toward the target with his left foot.

E. **Throwing the ball**—As is the case with any long throw that a fielder must make, the infielder fielding the ball to his backhand side must attempt to throw the ball across the seams with a high elbow. He must step directly toward his target and attempt to release the ball with good six-to-twelve rotation.

18. **Fielding the slow rolling ground ball**—The slow hit ground ball has got to be fielded cleanly or there can be no play at any base, which makes it a play that has got to be made the first time around. The slow roller to the third baseman, shortstop, and second baseman has got to be accepted as a challenge for it is one of the toughest defensive plays to make in baseball. This is due to the fact that the infielder must aggressively charge the ball, field it cleanly off-balance, and still make a strong accurate throw to first base. The following are the proper fundamentals for fielding a slow hit ground ball:

A. **Approach to the ball**—One of the key fundamentals in making the play on a slow rolling ground ball is for the infielder to get to the ball as quickly as possible, yet still getting his body under control so he might field the ball cleanly and get off a decent throw. The infielder must aggressively charge the ball, for if he does not get to the ball quick enough, he will have to rush through the fielding and throwing phase. If he must run some distance to get to the ball he must pump his arms as he would in sprinting. Many infielders charge slow rolling ground balls with their glove hand not pumping the arms properly since they have their glove open to the ball even though they are not close to being in a position to field the ball. As the infielder nears the area where the ball will be fielded, he must start slowing down by shortening his steps and lowering his center of gravity by bending at both the waist and the knees. Through a lot of practice in fielding these types of ground balls, the infielder should become somewhat proficient in judging the timing involved in when to start slowing down to field the ball. If he slows down too soon it will hinder his time in delivering the ball to the intended target. If he slows down too late his body momentum will not allow him to field the ball cleanly due to poor body control. As to how quickly to come into the ball and whether or not to throw off-balance will depend on: where the ball is fielded; the speed of the runner; the infielder's ability to throw off balance; the speed of the ball; and whether or not a bad off-balance throw could allow a runner to score. Whenever possible, infielders should set up to throw, but there will be times he must make the "do-or-die" play on the ball. If time allows, the infielder should attempt to round off the ball a little to achieve a better angle into the ball. If time does not allow him to round the ball, he will have to approch the ball straight on.

B. **Fielding the ball that is rolling**—As the infielder nears the ball he must concentrate on fielding the ball with two hands in front of the body. Some infielders attempt to field the ball with just their glove hand but this can lead to an improper exchange between the glove hand with the ball and the bare hand. An infielder should never attempt to bare hand the ball unless it has stopped on the grass or it is just about to come to a stop as it rolls on a smooth grass surface. Since the second baseman has a very short throw to make generally after fielding the slow roller, it is recommended that he field the ball about four to six inches on the inside front of his left foot as it lands. For the shortstop or third baseman who will have to make a much longer throw to first base, it is recommended that they field the ball about four to six inches on the inside front of the right foot as it lands. The infielder cannot afford to get caught in-between steps meaning he is fielding the ball without either foot being on the ground in front as the ball enters the glove. If so, his body balance will be thrown off, and it will make for a very difficult ball to field cleanly. The palm of the glove must be completely open to the ball with the bare hand gripping the ball as the ball enters the pocket of the glove.

C. **Throwing the ball**—If fielding the ball with the left foot forward, the infielder must then release the ball as the right foot hits the ground. This is why this type of fielding mechanic should only be used by the second baseman who fields the slow rolling ground ball near first base since he does not have a long throw to make. The second baseman must concentrate on giving the first baseman a throw that he can easily see since the release point will be difficult for the first baseman to pick up. The closer the second baseman is to the first baseman at the bag, the higher and more arc the throw must have so the first baseman can easily catch the ball. Preferably, the ball should be caught by the first baseman from shoulder level to a foot above his head. If the ball is thrown lower than the first baseman's shoulders it will make for a very difficult play for the first baseman. When an infielder fields a slow rolling ground ball well away from first base, he will generally have to field the ball with the right foot forward. He would then quickly bring his hands to the waist just inside the throwing hand hip as the glove leg (left) moves forward. At this time the body should rise up to raise the center of gravity which helps break the momentum along with allowing for a better throwing position for the arm. The hands would break as the throwing foot (right) starts forward. As the throwing hand foot lands, the glove is "thrown" to the glove hand (left) shoulder. The head and belt buckle would then face the target as much as possible and the infielder will throw the ball off the throwing hand (right) leg. The throwing arm must be parallel or better to the ground to provide more power and accuracy to the throw. The ball should be thrown to the outfield side of the base to allow for some natural tail on the ball since the ball will be released in a manner that will cause the ball to move into the first baseman. After throwing the ball, the infielder should continue running in the same direction as when he fielded the ball to avoid cutting off momentum too early. If the infielder fields the ball with his left foot forward and will be throwing the ball when the right foot lands, he will not have time to get the arm up parallel to the ground. This means that the release point will be somewhat lower, and this is the reason why this type of footwork should only be done by the second baseman fielding the ball close to first base. A coach may find that some infielders can throw equally well on this type of play throwing the ball off the left leg. If so, then he should be allowed to do so even though this will generally cause the ball to tail much more since the left hip will be closed to the target as the ball is released.

D. **Fielding the ball bare hand**—At no time should an infielder be encouraged to bare hand the slow roller unless he finds himself in a position that this is the only way he will be able to get off the throw on a "do-or-die" play. If he finds that he is well on the glove hand side of the ball, it might be the only way he can field the ball and get off a throw to first base. If the ball has stopped on the grass, or is rolling slowly about to come to a stop, then the infielder may bare hand the ball. If so, he must get himself under control as he nears the ball. He must bend at the waist and knees so that his throwing hand can easily get down to the level of the ball on the grass. The ball must be picked up with the fingers scooping the ball up rather than having the fingers facing the ground. By scooping the ball there is a greater chance for fielding the ball cleanly in the bare hand, along with having the hand in a much better position to release the ball for the throw to first base. Which foot should be out in front when the ball is fielded would be an individual matter since some infielders are adept on this type of play throwing off the left foot while others need to throw off the right foot. If the infielder bare hands the ball with the left foot forward, the ball should be released as the right foot hits the ground. If he fields the ball with his right foot forward, the ball should be released as the left foot hits the ground. The throwing arm must be parallel or better to the ground to provide more power and accuracy to the throw, even though this is very difficult to do on the "do-or-die" play with the fielder's body momentum moving forward to a large degree. As was the case with the two handed pickup, the throw must be made to the outfield side of first base to allow for some "tail" on the ball. Anytime there is a runner in scoring position, the infielder must be sure that his throw to first base is an accurate one since the ball that gets by the first baseman will result in a run scoring.

19. **Recovering a booted ball**—Infielders must have the ability to keep their composure when a ball is booted so that they might have a chance to make a second play on the ball and still get an out on the play. If the boot occurs from the glove or above there is a chance on a 5 or 6 type ground ball for the infielder to make a second play on the ball. Of course, if the ball gets under the glove there is no chance for the infielder to make any type of play on that particular ground ball. By fielding the ground ball out in front and on the glove side, an infielder will be able to keep most misplayed ground balls in front of him so that a second play might be able to be made on the ball. An infielder should never attempt to pick up the ball with only his glove for his chance of gloving the ball cleanly and exchanging the ball with his throwing hand is a difficult feat to master. It is best for the infielder to move quickly to the ball on the ground making sure that his chest is over the ball as he picks it up with both knees bent. The ball must be picked up on the first grasp, so it is important that the infielder keep his composure so that he does not have to go back down a second time to pick up a ball that he should have possessed the first time. In most cases, with a long throw involved, the infielder will have to quickly shuffle step toward his target in order to get off a strong and accurate throw after picking up the ball. If a short throw is involved, the infielder might be able to just throw the ball to the target without moving his feet (force out at second base).

THROWING THE BALL

Once the ground ball has been properly fielded, the next task for the infielder is for him to throw the ball to the intended target with some degree of velocity, accuracy and quickness. Many infielders run into problems when they sacrifice velocity and accuracy as they attempt to establish quickness in their release of the ball. For young infielders especially, it is highly recommended that they sacrifice quickness to gain velocity and accuracy in their throws after fielding a ground ball. The experienced infielder will gain quickness in his release and still maintain a high degree of velocity and accuracy as he matures as an infielder. It does little good for an infielder to get rid of the ball with great quickness only to find that his throws lack velocity and accuracy.

If an infielder has an average or poor throwing arm, then he should be encouraged to play shallow in the infield so that he can make the basic routine play on most ground balls. This is especially true for a third baseman or a shortstop. Generally, the stronger the arm the more depth an infielder can achieve in his ready position. The only way to build up arm strength is to throw, so the infielders must be encouraged to throw as much as possible in practice sessions. Ground ball work off the fungo bat is helpful, but unless the infielders are challenged to treat every ground ball like a game situation, they will never completely develop their total infield skills. When infielders are receiving balls off the fungo bat they should always field the ball as if there was a 4.0 runner going down the line. In this way, what they do in practice should carry over somewhat to the game. An infielder who sits back on the balls in practice and does not practice establishing his throwing skills, will have a very difficult time responding in a positive manner in the actual game. Each infielder should be encouraged to take at least 15 to 20 ground balls each practice session with throws to first base going full speed as he would in a game. Some of the fundamentals that need to be stressed to the infielders in regard to throwing follow:

1. Infielders should try to field the ball in the same part of the glove each time so that when the fingers of the bare hand go into the glove to extract the ball they can consistently find the "handle". There is little time to "fish" for the ball. All infielders should be encouraged to use a small glove so that they can get a better feeling for the glove along with being able to find the ball in the glove quickly.

2. The fingers and thumb of the bare hand should grab the ball as soon as the ball enters the glove. All four fingers and the thumb should have good control of the ball before the bare hand is extracted. By bringing the glove and bare hand into the body as the ball enters the glove, the infielder should have plenty of time to get a proper grip on the ball.

384

3. Infielders should be encouraged to grip the ball the same way each time as they pull the ball out of the glove. It is preferred that the ball be gripped across the seams with the ball out on the fingers. It is practically impossible to get off a strong and accurate throw if the ball is "choked" in the throwing hand. One of the major reasons for throwing errors is an improper grip on the ball along with throwing the ball at various arm slots.

4. The quickness the infielder can get the ball out of the glove and get the throwing arm up to the throwing position is of utmost importance. This necessitates a short arm angle out of the glove to achieve this quickness. An infielder who extends his elbow out while getting the throwing arm "cocked" will dramatically slow down his release time. The glove should be brought back to the throwing arm shoulder with the ball in order to provide the infielder ample time to grip the ball along with assisting in keeping the left shoulder closed.

5. Once the ball enters the glove and the bare hand has a firm grip on the ball, the infielder's feet must quickly prepare the infielder to get off the throw. What kind of footwork used by the infielder depends to a great degree on the arm strength of the fielder, where the ball has been fielded, the distance of the throw to be made, and the weight distribution of the fielder at the time he makes contact with the ball. An infielder certainly wants to eliminate any extra steps in throwing, but sometimes extra steps will be necessary in order to achieve a strong and accurate throw. An infielder with quick feet will find that he can release the ball quicker than the infielder with slow feet, since it is impossible to release the ball properly without the feet being planted.

6. The length of the stride and the degree of bend in the upper body as the ball is released will differ for each infielder. A coach will find that most bad throws are as a result of the infielder either overstriding or understriding, along with a poor arm slot or grip on the ball. When an infielder overstrides on his throw he will find that his upper body will not allow him to get on top of the ball as it is released causing the ball to be thrown high to the intended target. If he understrides, he will have a tendency to throw from a straight up position which will cause control problems in addition to taking away from the velocity of his throw. He must concentrate on stepping directly toward his target with his front foot.

7. As the infielder's arm is brought back out of the glove he must fully concentrate on the target of his throw, not on the runner. The arm arc should be such that the infielder does not short arm the ball, but at the same time he cannot afford to swing the arm down, back and through as a pitcher would do in achieving velocity. Once the arm starts forward, the elbow should straighten out as the arm comes past the ear so that upon release the infielder is achieving the maximum angle of acceleration of his throwing arm. A second baseman is the only infielder who can get away with being a "short armer", but there are plays that the second baseman must make where the short arm arc will take away from the velocity of his throw. The infielder can never afford to aim the ball to the intended target, no matter how much time he has to make the throw. He should attempt to throw the ball with the same velocity each and every time to establish the consistency necessary for proper throwing technique.

8. The infielder's follow through must be emphasized so that the infielder is not throwing from a straight up position which can easily cause the elbow to drop which leads to poor throwing mechanics. The infielder should sense the feeling that the ball is being released out in front of the body.

BASIC INFIELD PLAYS

In previous sections of the Playbook, we have presented other material involving infield play such as: (1) movement with the count; (2) infield communication; (3) fly ball communication; (4) rules for force plays; (5) cut-off mechanics and communication; (6) bunt defenses; (7) double steal defenses; and (8) pick-off plays. The following are other aspects of infield play not previously covered in detail:

1. **Fake throws**—Anytime an infielder, pitcher or catcher has no play at a base he should always fake the throw to that base whenever there is a runner advancing to another base. This is much better than just holding onto the baseball and not taking advantage of an over aggressive runner rounding another base. He must be sure that he has a tight grip on the ball before executing the fake so that there is no chance for the ball to slip out of his fingers. The better the fake, the better the chance for retiring a runner at another base. Some of the better times to execute the fake throw are:

A. Baserunners at first and second base and a ground ball is hit with a force at second base but no chance for the out at first base. The pivotman (either the shortstop or second baseman) should full arm fake the throw to first base. As soon as the fake is completed he should turn glove side and look to third base for a possible play on the runner rounding third base from second base.

B. Anytime a bunt is fielded with no play at first base, a full arm fake to first base is sometimes enough to cause a runner rounding third or second base to take that extra step. If so, the fielder may have a play on the runner rounding the base too far.

C. When a 4 type ground ball is hit and there is no chance for the out at first base, the infielder should always full arm fake the throw to first base and then check any other runner who might be rounding another base.

D. With a runner at second base, and the shortstop has to go in the hole to field a ground ball, there might be an excellent chance to throw behind the runner at second base after a full arm fake to first base. Of course, if the shortstop has a play at first base he should go ahead and throw the ball. Many runners will try to take off for third base on this play, and with a good fake, the shortstop may force the runner to take off before the ball leaves his hand.

2. **Decoy plays**—Anytime an infielder will be involved with a tag play at a base where the ball is coming to the base from an angle behind the runner, the decoy play should be performed by the infielder. If done properly, the baserunner might come into the base standing up or with a very non-aggressive slide. There are basically two ways that the decoy play can be done effectively: (1) the infielder positions himself two to three steps behind the base in line with the throw and moves into the base arriving just as the ball reaches the bag; or (2) the infielder positions himself astride the base or right next to the base simulating to the runner that there will be no play on him by standing erect, and then at the last second positioning himself to field the ball and make the tag on the runner. A good decoyer will have an excellent chance of retiring runners during the season on this type of play.

3. **Tandem relays**—In the fundamental drill series number two-drill number 5, the tandem relay play was presented as a practice drill. The following are the basic fundamentals of the tandem relay play for the infielders:

A. **Nature of the ball hit**—Anytime the ball is hit in the outfield in such a way that the hitter will have a sure double, both the shortstop and second baseman will move to their tandem relay positions. If there is any doubt that there might be a play on the batter-runner at second base, then the shortstop or second baseman must remain at the base depending on who has coverage of the base.

B. **Second base coverage on the tandem relay play**—In order to prevent the hitter from rounding second base too aggressively, the following assignments are made for the defense on the extra base hit:

1. Anytime the ball is hit over the center fielder's head or anywhere on the left field side of the field for a sure double, the right fielder will break full speed to cover second base. If the first baseman is already there, then the right fielder will back up any possible throw made at second base from a member of the tandem relay. If there was a runner at first base at the time of the pitch, the first baseman will be involved in cut-off position at the plate, so the right fielder will have full responsibility for second base.

2. Anytime the ball is hit directly over the right fielder's head or down the right field line, the center fielder will have second base coverage. If the first baseman is already there, then the center fielder will back up any possible throw made at second base.

The only time there will be no one covering second base on an extra base hit will be on a "gapper" between center field and right field since the left fielder will be backing up third base to allow the pitcher to back up the plate, and the first baseman will be in cut-off position at the plate if a runner was at first base at the time of the pitch.

C. **Shortstop and second baseman front and back man**—Generally, the coach would want his strongest arm as the front man on the tandem relay, which in most cases will be the shortstop. As a rule, the shortstop would be the front man on any ball hit over the center fielder's head to the left field line. The second baseman would be the front man on any ball hit to the right field side of the center fielder. If both the shortstop and second baseman both go out at the same time to be the front man, the shortstop will have priority over the second baseman.

D. **Distance of the front man from the outfielder**—The front man would want to give the outfielder somewhere between a 120 to 150 foot throw. The stronger the outfielder's arm, the further the front man can position himself. However, he should never be more than 150 feet away from the outfielder unless he has an unbelievably strong throwing arm. If the outfielder has a weak arm, the field is wet causing the ball to be slippery, or the warning track is muddy then this would cause the front man to move closer to the thrower.

E. **Front man's responsibilities**—The front man on the tandem relay must get to his proper position as quickly as possible so that he is in a stationary position when the outfielder picks up the ball for his throw. He should position himself as close as possible in line with the outfielder and third base with the following exception. Anytime the ball is hit near either foul line, the front man should position himself at a slight angle away from the line to allow the back man in the tandem the opportunity to get into the proper position. If the front man was to line himself on or near the foul line, the back man will just about have an impossible task to be in proper position behind him as the outfielder releases the ball. The angle the front man assumes away from the foul line should be no more than 20 degrees from the outfielder throwing and the line. With the ball hit down the right field line, this angle would just about place the front man in line with the right fielder and third baseman anyway. The front man should have both arms in the air as the outfielder picks up the ball so that there is no problem in him being easily seen by the outfielder. As the ball is in the air, the front man must begin to position himself for the throw to either third base or home plate. He will be listening for instructions from the third baseman and the back man as the decision is made as to which throw will be made, if any. Since the back man is so close to the front man, he will have the final decision as to which throw to be made, if a throw will have a chance for retiring a runner. "Three-three" is the communication from the third baseman and the back man that the throw should be made to third base. "Four-four" is the communication that the throw should be made to the plate. "Hold-hold" will inform the front man that there is no play at third base or the plate and the ball is to be run back into the infield area. If the throw from the outfielder is a strong one on the glove side, then the front man should begin moving in the direction of the intended target to cut down the distance of his throw to either third base or home place. The front man must always attempt to keep the ball on the glove side so that he will not have to turn to throw the ball to the intended target. At the same time, he can generate momentum into his throw by movement toward the target as the ball reaches his glove by keeping the ball on the glove side. If the throw from the outfielder is off target or is losing velocity, the front·man must go to the ball. If at anytime he finds that he will have a tough play to catch the ball, he must allow the ball to be fielded by the back man. This means that the front man should not leap for the ball or attempt to field the ball on a tough hop since the defense cannot afford to have the ball deflect off his glove. In throwing the ball to third base, the tandem relay members will not have a cut-off man. The first baseman will be in cut-off position on any throw made to the plate. He must be sure to step in the direction of his throw to gain velocity and accuracy on the long throw that has to be made.

F. **Back man's responsibilities**—Once the back man on the tandem relay sees that the hitter has a definite extra base hit, he must break full speed to a position about 30 feet behind the front man. Once he achieves this position, he has two basic responsibilities:

1. As the outfielder is picking up the ball, he should quickly turn his head toward the infield and make a decision where the play will be made. The third baseman and possibly the catcher will generally be yelling one of the commands previously mentioned, but the back man will be the one who must make the final decision as to what he wants the front man to do with the ball.

2. As soon as the outfielder starts his throwing motion, the back man's full attention goes to the ball in the air as he is yelling out the command to the front man. He must pretend that the front man is not there for purposes of making the catch of the ball thrown by the outfielder. He must position himself so that he does not have a tough play to make on the ball, and since he is further from the outfielder than the front man, he should have no problem being in a good position to make a clean catch on the ball. Unless the ball is thrown extremely high, the back man should never have a ball get past him or deflect off his glove. Once the back man fields the ball, he will then throw the ball to third base, home plate, or run the ball back to the infield area.

4. **Going back on fly balls**—In a previous section of the Playbook (Fly Ball Communication for All Fielders), the basic communication and priority system was detailed in regard to fielding fly balls. It is very important that time be spent in a few practice sessions teaching the infielders the proper mechanics for going back on fly balls. This will enable the infielders to feel more comfortable in moving back into the outfield to make a play on a fly ball, along with increasing their quickness to the ball. The following are the basic mechanics that need to be stressed by the coach in working with infielders in drills where they are fielding fly balls over their heads:

A. **Drifting on the fly ball**—There is nothing worse for an infielder to practice when going back on a fly ball than for him to start drifting on the ball. Drifting can cause serious communication and priority problems since other fielders are never sure whether or not the infielder drifting on the ball is going to be able to make the play. It is important that the coach stress the sound habit of going full speed on any fly ball that they have to turn on so that they can get themselves under control before the ball reaches the glove. In most cases, an outfielder is not going to bother an infielder if he is under the fly ball and calling loudly for it unless he sees that the infielder is struggling on the ball. If an outfielder sees the infielder backpeddling on the fly ball, then he should be instructed to take the ball, if he can reach it, since there is no assurance that the infielder is going to be able to make the catch. Another benefit to the infielder in not drifting on a fly ball is that he can make adjustments in his positioning if the sun or wind are going to be a factor to contend with as the ball starts downward. An addition, if there is a runner tagging up at a base, the runner can easily take advantage of an infielder catching a fly ball with his momentum going into the outfield. There will be balls hit in the air where the infielder will not have the time to get under the ball, but hopefully every ball that time allows him to get under he can do so with ease.

B. **Turning on the ball**—On any fly ball hit directly over the infielder's head, the infielder should turn glove side on the ball. This is due to the fact that it is much easier for him to make the play on a fly ball with him being on the glove side of the ball rather than having to reach across his body or head to make the catch. Of course, if the ball is hit over his head to the throwing hand side, he must turn in that direction. As with outfielders, it is recommended that the infielder know exactly which direction the ball has been hit before making any turn on the ball.

C. **Drop step going back**—As the ball hits the bat, the infielder should have his weight equally distributed over the balls of both feet. Once he reads the direction he will have to take on the fly ball hit over his head, he must drop step with the foot on the side of the turn. The angle of the initial drop step will depend entirely on the direction the ball has been hit. The first reaction of a lot of infielders when they read that a fly ball has been hit over their heads is to straighten up, which has a detrimental effect on their quickness to the ball. The infielder must stay low during the drop step in order to generate the proper momentum of the body in the direction he needs to travel. He must pump his arms aggressively in order to increase his quickness, making sure that he is running on the balls of his feet so that he does not jar his head as he runs. If the infielder runs on his heels he will find that his head will be jarred with each step making it that much more difficult for him to watch the ball.

D. **Path to the ball**—The infielder's path to the ball should be such that it places him in the general area where the ball will land as quick as possible. If the ball is hit quite high in the air, the infielder can afford to take his eyes off the ball as he runs to this area in order to insure that he is generating as much quickness as he can. However, once the ball starts downward the infielder must have eye contact with the ball so that he might be in a position to make any adjustments in his path as he follows the ball downward. If the infielder happens to turn the wrong way on the ball in his initial drop step, he must make the correction quickly by turning in the direction that he wishes to go without ever backpeddling on the ball. For example, if the shortstop turns glove side on a ball hit over his head by a lefthanded hitter and finds that the ball will be coming down on his bare hand side due to the flight path of the ball, he must turn as he moves toward the ball keeping his back toward the plate. He can not afford to turn with the front of his body facing the plate for this would cause for a very slow turn along with severely hindering his quickness to the ball after the turn is completed. This proper turn when the mistake is corrected will cause the infielder to lose sight of the ball for an instance, but this should not cause any major problem as long as the ball is hit high in the air. If the fly ball is not hit very high or far from the infielder, he can then turn to the ball without turning his back on the ball. If time allows, the infielder's path to the ball should place him three to four feet behind the area of the ground where the ball would land if not touched by the fielder. This positioning would force the infielder to be moving forward as he catches the ball with two hands in front of his head. Most errors made on fly balls occur when the infielder misjudges the ball and finds the ball coming down on the outfield side of his position. Since it is much easier to move forward at the last instance than to move backward, the infielder must position himself behind every fly ball that time allows him to get under.

E. **Catching the fly ball**—All fly balls must be fielded with two hands whenever possible. There will be times that this is not possible since the infielder will be moving to the ball with his back to the infield. In this case, he might have to attempt the catch only using his glove hand so that he is able to reach farther for the ball. Anytime the infielder will attempt to field the ball on the run with just his glove hand, he must position himself so that the glove hand is extended away from the body. If the glove hand makes contact with the ball too close to the body, it is very easy for the infielder to lose sight of the ball as it enters the glove. Fielding a fly ball directly over the infielder's head is a very difficult play, and all the infielder can attempt to do is to position himself to the side of the ball as it enters the glove so that he does not have to follow the ball into the glove from directly over his head. Hopefully, an outfielder will be able to call off the infielder whenever the infielder would have to make an over-the-head catch, but many times this is not possible since the outfielder might be playing the hitter quite deep in the outfield.

5. **Watching the runner(s) touch the base(s)**—The infielders must be held responsible for making sure that all the runners touch every base, along with the catcher making sure that each runner attempting to score makes contact with the plate. The first baseman should be responsible for the batter-runner touching first base on every extra base hit. The only exception would be when he is involved in going after a fly ball hit down the right field line. In this case the catcher should

watch the batter-runner touch first base. The first baseman should also be responsible for second base whenever an extra base hit forces the shortstop and second baseman out for the tandem relay. If there is a runner at first base when the extra base hit occurs, he must first watch the runner who started at first base touch second base, and then pick up the batter-runner as he touches first base. Anytime there is a runner at first base and a single to the outfield allows the runner at first to advance to third base, either the shortstop or second baseman is responsible to make sure the runner touches second base. This will generally be the responsibility of the second baseman since the shortstop will be involved in the cut-off position for a possible play by the outfielder to third base. The third baseman will be responsible for third base except when there is a runner at second base and the ball is hit to left field and he is now responsible for the cut-off play at the plate. In this case the shortstop must watch the runner touch third base. The players and coaches in the dugout must also get into the habit of watching the opposing runners touch the bases. The responsibility for making sure that a runner does not leave the base too soon on a tag up on a fly ball is also the responsibility of the player responsible for that base.

6. **Appealing a runner missing a base or leaving a base too soon on a tag up**—In appealing a runner missing a base, the following procedure must be followed:

A. If time has not been called by one of the umpires, then the ball should be thrown in to one of the infielders or the catcher (appealing home plate) and the base touched by the fielder with the ball. While touching the base, the fielder must notify the umpire involved in the decision which runner missed the base or tagged up too soon. If he fails to identify the proper runner to the umpire, the umpire can not make the proper call and will call the runner safe.

B. If time has been called prior to the fielder touching the base or the plate, the ball must be put back into play by the pitcher in order to make the proper appeal. The pitcher must go to the set position, step back off the pitching rubber and throw the ball to the base being appealed. The fielder would then catch the ball, touch the base and notify the umpire which runner is being appealed.

C. If the throw will be made from the pitcher to the first baseman to appeal the batter-runner missing first base, the second baseman should stand about 30 feet down the right field line (in fair territory) until the pitcher steps back off the rubber. He can then break to a position behind first base to back up the throw from the pitcher to the first baseman. If the appeal is being made from the pitcher to second base, either the shortstop or second baseman would back up the throw. If the appeal is being made at third base, the shortstop should stand about 30 feet down the left field line (in fair territory) until the pitcher steps back off the rubber. He can then break to a position behind third base to back up the throw from the pitcher to the third baseman.

7. **Faking ground balls**—Anytime a baserunner is stealing second base on a regular steal or hit and run, the shortstop must always fake that he is about to field a ground ball whenever the ball is hit in the air unless the shortstop is involved in an attempt to field the fly ball. If the second baseman is playing close to second base at the time of the pitch, he might be the one who fakes the ground ball if not involved in fielding the fly ball. If the runner does not look in toward the plate at the time the ball is hit, this faking by one of the middle infielders might cause him to continue full speed toward second base. This could allow the fielder of the fly ball to make a play at first base on the runner after the catch.

8. **Infield positioning during an intentional walk**—When an intentional walk is being issued to the batter, the infielders should assume their regular position in the infield in case the pitcher throws a pitch near the strike zone and the hitter attempts to make contact with the ball. If there are runners on base, which normally would be the case with an intentional walk, the infielder responsible for keeping that runner close to the base should position himself near the base. He still should be well enough away from the base so that he can make an attempt on a ball that might be hit in the area where he normally would position himself.

9. **Tag plays at the bases**—In perfecting the proper mechanics on making tag plays at the bases, the coach needs to present the following mechanics to his infielders:

A. **Movement to the base**—The infielder must get to the base where the tag play will occur as quick as possible in order to get set up properly at the base for the throw. An infielder can not be breaking directly for a base until the ball passes the hitter's bat. If he was to break for the base before the pitched ball reaches the hitter, he would make the defense very much susceptible if a ball was hit to the spot which he vacated in covering the base. The footwork on this movement to a base is crucial in order to insure that the infielder can still react to the batted ball. Infielders must be encouraged to cheat toward their base of coverage, especially in those situations where there is an above average runner on base in a stealing situation. The distance the infielder needs to cheat toward his base of coverage depends on the following: the infielder's speed and quickness to the base; the baserunner's speed and stealing ability; the texture of the infield dirt; the type of hitter at the plate; the type of pitcher throwing; and the catcher's arm strength and release time. The footwork necessary for steal coverage is especially important at second base since this is the base most commonly stolen, and a second baseman or shortstop breaking toward the base before the ball passes the hitter will expose a very large hole for the hitter to hit the ball through. The middle infielder covering second base must position himself so that he has the proper angle into the base once he reads that the ball will not be put in play by the hitter. It is not recommended that the middle infielder cheat so shallow toward second base that he cuts down on his ability to field a ground ball in the infield. Cheating too shallow toward second base will also force the infielder to break toward the base at a sharp angle, which will not allow him good vision of the ball as it leaves the catcher's hand. This will also make fielding a poor throw from the catcher that much more difficult due to the fact that the infielder does not have a good angle on the throw coming toward the base.

1. **Footwork for the shortstop and second baseman covering second base on a steal or hit and run**—The determination as to whether or not the shortstop or second baseman has the responsibility for second base on the steal or hit and run must be determined before the pitcher assumes the set position. They both need to be aware of the fact that if the second baseman has coverage at second base and the hitter squares around to bunt, then the shortstop must assume coverage of second base. This is due to the fact that the second baseman must break toward first base in case the first baseman moves forward toward the bunted ball. Of course, all infielders must be aware of the possibility of the fake bunt and slash by the hitter. For this reason, an infielder can never afford to be moving full speed toward a base until the ball is actually bunted. Once the middle infielder covering second base sees out of the corner of his eye that the baserunner is breaking towards second base, he must begin the proper footwork for his coverage. The first baseman must yell "there he goes" to further assist the middle infielder and catcher in knowing that the runner at first base is breaking toward second base. The recommended footwork for the shortstop and second baseman would be the following depending on which has coverage of the base. He must take four steps toward the plate as the ball is delivered to the plate by the pitcher. These four steps directly toward the plate would allow the middle infielder to be a little closer to second base, and still allow him to be in a position to react to the batted ball. He can not afford to be making any motion toward second base until the ball passes the batter. As soon as the second baseman reads that the runner is breaking toward second base, he would step: right-left-right-left toward the plate. If the shortstop has coverage at second base, he would step: left-right-left-right toward the plate. The timing should be such that just as the fourth step hits (left foot for the second baseman and right foot for the shortstop), the ball has reached the batter. As the final step takes place, the middle infielder's toes are parallel and his weight is on the balls of his feet, enabling him to move quickly in any direction as he reacts to the batted ball. If he happens to finish his footwork toward the plate before the ball reaches the hitter, he can take a little bounce step with both feet to insure that his weight remains on the balls of both feet. The steps taken by the shortstop or second baseman are short and choppy so that the middle infielder has his body in complete control at all times. If done properly, the distance traveled by the second baseman or shortstop is about nine to ten feet as the ball is delivered to the plate. This footwork takes a lot of practice in order to get the timing down so that the middle infielders feel comfortable reacting to the batted ball or breaking toward second base to field the throw by the catcher. Once the ball passes the hitter's bat, the middle infielder responsible for the base would use an explosive cross-over step in the direction of second base.

2. **Footwork for the third baseman covering third base on a steal or hit and run**—The nature of the third baseman's footwork would depend entirely on where he is positioned at the time of the pitch. If he is playing near the bag close to the baseline between second and third base, he would just break for third base after the ball passes the hitter. If he is playing well behind the baseline between second base and third base and well away from the bag itself, he would have to accomplish the same four step footwork as done by the shortstop and second baseman when they are responsible for covering second base. The third baseman should take his initial step with his right foot so that his left foot is the last to land (push-off foot for the cross-over step to third base). If he is playing in front of the baseline, he is going to have a very difficult time returning to third base properly without moving before the ball passes the hitter's bat. He will have to drop step with his right foot breaking for third base as the catcher sets up to throw. Due to the difficulty in returning to third base for the catcher's throw to third base, the third baseman must never allow himself to be too far in front of the baseline with a runner at second base in a stealing situation. The shortstop must yell "there he goes" to alert the third baseman any time the runner at second base breaks for third base on the pitch.

B. **Approach to the base**—The shortstop, second baseman and third baseman must concentrate on getting to the base as quickly as possible for two basic reasons: (1) the quicker they can get to the base, the more time they will have to set up properly to field the throw and make the tag on the runner; and (2) by being in the area of the base quickly, they will be in a much better position to field a poor throw from the catcher. As the infielder nears the base, he must start getting his body under control by shortening his steps and lowering his center of gravity. There is nothing anymore frustrating to a team then to see a catcher make a perfect throw to second base only to find that the infielder responsible for the base is either late covering the base, or the infielder mishandles the throw due to the fact that he was not under control as he attempted to field the ball. The explosive cross-over step by the infielder covering the base is crucial to his getting to the base in time to field the throw and make the tag on the sliding runner.

C. **Footwork at the base**—One of the biggest problems infielders have in covering a base to make the tag play is improper footwork at the base. It is recommended that the shortstop and second baseman hook their left foot on the ground on the back corner of second base, and have their right foot in front of the base as they field the throw from the catcher. The same type of footwork should be used at third base by the third baseman so that he has complete control over the back of third base (left field side of the bag). If the infielder positions himself in front of the base, he will field the ball in front of the base, and then have to bring the glove and ball back to the base to make the tag on the runner. The ball in the air will travel much faster than the glove can, so it is important that the infielder allow the ball to come to him rather than he go to the ball. Of course, if the infielder reads the throw from the catcher will be low, he will need to reach out with his glove to the ball in order to field the ball at the best angle. Most runners sliding into a base with a throw being made by the catcher will slide into the back of the base. This is the reason why the infielder should have control of the back part of the base with his left foot. By controlling the back part of the base, the infielder can easily reach out left or right for the ball thrown near the base, and have control of the base at the same time. If the infielder was to move both feet to the ball a little off target to the base, he would then have to move both feet back toward the base in order to have any chance on making the tag on the runner. If the infielder arrives at the base early enough, he will be in a position to read the type of throw he will be receiving from the catcher. If he reads that the throw is going to be in the air and near the base, he merely straddles the base as he awaits the ball. If he sees that the ball is a little off target, he can keep contact with the base with his left foot and step toward the ball with his right foot. If he sees that the ball will be quite wide of the base, he can move quickly toward the ball in order to prevent the ball from going into the outfield. In this case, he would vacate the base in order to keep the ball from getting past him giving up any chance on making the tag play on the runner. If the infielder sees that he is going to be able to field the ball on a short hop or big hop, he should be able to hold his left foot on the ground on the back corner of the base and still make the play on the ball. This only pertains to the shortstop and second baseman, for the third baseman must come off the base and keep any low throws in front of him to prevent the runner from scoring on a ball that he can not be assured of fielding cleanly. If the middle infielder reads that he is going to be in-between hopped on the throw from the catcher, he must jump in front of the base in his attempt to keep the ball from going into center field. If he fields the ball, he still might have a play on the runner sliding into second base. It is very important for the middle infielder to block all low throws coming to second base from the catcher when there is a runner at third base. Any bad throws quite wide of the base should be caught at the deepest angle by the infielder so that he will have a better chance of getting his glove on the ball. If the throw takes the infielder slightly into the path of the runner, he should attempt to field the ball in front of the baseline in hopes that he can catch the ball and still make a tag on the runner. However, if a run would score if the ball gets by the infielder, he should play it safe by taking the deep angle on the ball forgetting about making the tag. The footwork by the infielders on any pick-off throw by the catcher is the same as described for the steal.

D. **Making the tag on the runner**—Once the infielder is under control and set at the base, he must center his entire attention on catching the ball and making the tag on the runner. The ideal throw from the catcher would be one caught on the side of the base the tag will be made on, with the ball arriving somewhere between the knees and waist of the infielder. The infielder's knees should be bent on the perfect throw, so that he could easily touch the ground with his glove. If the knees are bent properly, he will not have to bend the knees much further to make the tag on the runner once the ball is caught. Nothing is accomplished when the infielder attempts to make a quick tag on the runner only to find that the ball was never caught properly. Thus, it is important that the infielder makes sure that he catches the ball first before moving the glove toward the area where the tag will be applied. As the ball is caught, both knees are quickly bent in order to get the glove to the area of the tag as fast as possible. The glove must be moved at the shortest angle to the tag position. If the ball arrives below the infielder's knees, he must be sure to reach out slightly for the ball so that he is not catching the ball directly in the path of the runner. Otherwise, there is a good chance the runner will hit the glove as the ball enters the glove which will make it practically impossible to hold onto the baseball. At no time should the ball be exposed to the runner sliding into the base. He should be tagged by the back of the glove which would prevent the ball from being kicked out of the glove by the runner. On all close plays it is recommended to use the sweep tag. This means that as the infielder catches the ball and moves the glove and ball down to the tag area, he will pull the glove away as the runner slides into the glove. This sweep tag should give the umpire the feeling that the tag was made in advance of the runner touching the base, and it also protects the hand and arm of the infielder from the baserunner's spikes if he is sliding feet first. On tag plays where the throw easily beats the runner, the infielder must hold the tag until the baserunner's feet or hand (head first slide) are a few inches from the glove. At this time the glove can be pulled away. Umpires should not expect an infielder to hold the tag when the throw easily beats the runner, and if the infielder pulls the glove out of the tag area right before contact with the runner, the out should be called. If the infielder sees that the runner is going to hook slide or head first slide to the outside or inside of the base, he must move the glove to the side of the base the runner is sliding. No matter how safe the runner might appear on a hook slide or head first slide to the inside or outside of the base, the infielder must stay with the tag. This is due to the fact that there is always a chance that on these types of slides the runner will overslide the base. The infielder can not move the runner off the base with his glove, but if he makes a hard tag on the runner, it may cause the runner's foot or hand to leave the base due to the momentum of the slide. At no time should the infielder ever reach for the runner when the ball is fielded, especially if the baserunner is coming into the base standing up. The infielder should just hold the glove on the side of the base allowing the runner to tag himself out as he comes into the base.

E. **Tag plays at second base on balls coming in from the outfield**—Balls coming in from the outfield to second base will cause the shortstop and second baseman to make adjustments in their footwork to better position themselves to make the proper tag on the runner coming in to the base from first base. On any ball being thrown from left center field to the right field line, the middle infielder should control the inside edge of second base (home plate side of the base) with his right foot. The left foot would be on the outfield side of the base in a direct line with the throw. On any ball hit from left center field to the left field line, the middle infielder would control the right field side of the base with his left foot. His right foot would be on the outfield side of the base in a direct line with the throw. If he reads a poor throw from the outfielder, he would have to vacate the base in order to keep the ball in front of him, in hopes that he can still field the ball and make a tag on the runner. Anytime an infielder is receiving a throw at a base that is going to take a tough hop, he must start his glove on the ground and work up with his glove. This is to prevent a ball from getting under his glove.

10. **Rundown plays**—Whenever a rundown takes place in the infield, the team on defense should get an out practically every time without any major difficulty. With a little practice and good timing, the rundown play should present little difficulty for the defense. The whole key to perfecting the rundown play is to prevent the play from taking more than one throw. If more than one throw is executed, the chance of an error is greatly increased. In addition, the more throws it takes to retire the runner in the rundown, the more chance for other runner(s) on base to advance. The following are the mechanics for the one throw rundown play:

A. **Setting the runner up for the rundown**—The nature of the rundown play will be dictated primarily by the status of the runner. It should make little difference in the rundown play as to which base to force the runner to make his move toward since one throw should be all it takes to get the out. When referring to a base we are also referring to the possibility that the rundown might take place between third base and the plate. Many coaches require the runner to be forced back to the previous base, but this is not necessary if the mechanics of the rundown play are executed properly. Once the runner is hung up, the fielder with the ball will dictate which direction the play will be made once the runner's status is determined. Anytime the fielder with the ball can make the tag on the runner without a throw, this is highly preferred. Many times a runner is stuck between bases with a fielder running right at him from inside the infield. If that occurs, the fielder should run right at the runner making the tag himself if the runner does not make a full effort in either direction. Many times the runner will freeze, and the fielder can make the tag himself.

B. **Runner breaks full speed to the forward or back base**—Many times the runner seeing that he is caught up between two bases, will just take off full speed for the forward or back base. This would not be the typical rundown play since the fielder with the ball will just have to throw the ball to the fielder covering the base the runner is heading toward. Hopefully, time will allow the thrower of the ball to take a step either inside or outside the baseline so he is not throwing the ball directly down the line. If he throws the ball directly down the baseline he will chance having the ball hit the runner, along with providing the receiver of the ball with a very poor view of the ball as it approaches him in the direct path of the runner. If the baserunner has already gotten a great jump toward the base, and the only play the fielder has is to throw the ball directly down the baseline, he should do so trying to keep the ball to the inside or outside of the base. When the receiver sees the runner heading full speed for him in the baseline, he will pick up the fielder who is going to throw him the ball, positioning himself either inside or outside the baseline. The decision on which side of the baseline to position himself will have to be dictated by the direction the thrower positions himself.

C. **Responsibility of the fielder with the ball**—The player who has the ball in his possession must force the runner hung up between bases to move toward the forward or back base at full speed. Of course, if he can make the play himself without throwing the ball then this is the best play to be made. Anytime a tag is made on a runner, the fielder should make the tag with the ball securely in his glove with the bare hand gripping the ball. This two handed tag should insure that the ball does not come out of the glove during the tag on the runner. In the conventional rundown, the fielder with the ball must start running full speed at the runner to force the runner to also run full speed toward the base (or the plate) that the play will be made. The fielder with the ball must quickly establish the angle of his approach on the run so that the receiver of his throw can set up on the inside or outside of the base. This is so that the throw will not hit the runner, along with allowing the receiver to have a clear view of the ball in the air. If the fielder with the ball finds himself starting at the runner in the baseline, he must quickly move to his throwing side as he begins his pursuit of the runner. If he finds himself on the other side of the baseline, he should stay on that side as he pursues the runner. The distance inside or outside of the baseline should be about two to three feet depending on where the runner establishes his actual path. The fielder with the ball must have his throwing arm up as he runs full speed at the runner. He should never fake the throw as he runs for this will only disrupt the timing of the play. When he does throw the ball on command from the receiving fielder, he does not need to reach back to throw the ball. It should be just a snap throw with the wrist to insure a more accurate and soft throw to the receiver. Since this throw will be made on the run, the snap throw must be practiced in rundown drills. The ball should be thrown to the receiver somewhere above the shoulders and no more than a foot above his head. A throw lower than the receiver's shoulders would make for a tough catch since the receiver will be catching the ball on the run, if the play is executed properly. The thrower will key the timing of his throw to the actions of the receiver which will be detailed later. Once the ball leaves the thrower's hand he now has two additional responsibilities: (1) to evade the base path of the runner so there is no chance that the runner can stop and backtrack on him, attempting to make contact with the fielder causing obstruction; and (2) to cover the forward or back base in case the runner evades the first tag and a play will need to be made on him with a second or third throw. Once the ball leaves the thrower's hand, he must veer out away from the return base path of the runner. If he is over one-half way down the baseline when he throws the ball, he should continue running toward the forward base. He would then be responsible for that base if the rundown is prolonged. If he is less than one-half way down the baseline when he throws the ball, he should turn quickly and cover the back base. Hopefully, additional fielders are available to cover the bases in case the thrower is late in covering his base of responsibility. If the rundown play is executed properly, the chance for more than one throw being made should be minimal.

D. **Responsibility of the fielder receiving the throw**—The first responsibility of the fielder receiving the throw is to prepare for a possible throw by the fielder with the ball if the runner was to break full speed toward his position. He must quickly get on the inside or outside of the base (or the plate) depending on which angle the thrower of the ball has positioned himself. If the runner is now breaking full speed toward him, the fielder with the ball will begin the one throw rundown play. The receiver must quickly move to the inside or outside of the base depending on which side of the baseline the fielder with the ball has established as his throwing side. The receiver must stay at the base as the fielder with the ball starts running full speed at the runner. This should start the runner moving full speed toward the receiver's stationary position. The receiving fielder would then determine when the fielder with the ball will throw the ball to him by executing the following three keys at the same time: (1) throwing both hands in the air about head high; (2) moving directly toward the thrower with an aggressive step forward; and (3) yelling loudly "now". If the timing on the play is proper, the baserunner running full speed would be allowed to "put the brakes on", get turned around, and start heading back in the other direction. The timing should be such that the runner will be tagged on the back as he attempts to evade the fielder with the ball who has built up a "head of steam" forward while receiving the ball. The receiver of the ball must determine when to "ask" for the ball taking into consideration: (1) the speed and baserunning ability of the runner; (2) the distance the runner is away from his stationary position at the base or the plate; and (3) his own speed. If he waits too long to come forward with his hands up yelling "now", the tag on the runner will have to be rushed. It makes for a very difficult play for the receiver to catch the ball and then have to quickly apply the tag. We would rather have the receiver call for the ball early than late so that the tag will always be made on the receiver's back rather than on the front of his body. If the receiver is aggressive forward as he receives the ball, he should be running full speed toward the runner after a few steps. The ball should be received above the shoulders, which would allow the receiver to not only field the ball much easier, but also to maintain his quickness toward the runner in the rundown. Thus, if the timing is good, the runner should have little chance to escape from the first throw. If the receiver of the ball has called for the ball too early and cannot "catch" the runner to make the tag, he will then become the thrower in the rundown and another fielder stationary at the base or plate will become the receiver of the ball. The same timing would then be executed hoping to retire the runner with one additional throw. Anytime the defense traps two runners at one base, they need to recognize the fact that the back runner is out, since the forward runner has "title" to the base. It is recommended that the front runner be tagged first in hopes that the front runner steps off the base thinking that he has been called out due to two runners being on a base at the same time.

11. **Angle throws in the infield**—Anytime throws are made in the infield with the baserunner advancing to the forward base or the plate, and the thrower's position in the infield would cause the ball to be thrown in line with the runner, a proper throwing angle by the thrower and fielder must be quickly established. There will be times that this is not possible due to the fact that the runner has a great jump on the play, forcing the thrower to make the best possible throw. He would then hope that the runner is not hit by the ball and the receiver has a clear view of the ball in flight. Anytime the thrower fields the ball outside or inside the baseline of the runner, the receiver must quickly execute the following two functions: (1) set up on the inside or

outside of the base or the plate with both his glove hand and bare hand held head high to provide a proper target for the thrower; and (2) yell either "inside" or "outside" depending on what side of the base he wants the ball to be thrown. If a fielder finds himself with the ball directly in the baseline of the runner, he should take one step to his throwing side if time allows. The receiver should quickly pick this up, moving to that side of the base while communicating either "inside" or "outside" to the thrower. The most common times this play occurs are: (1) bunts fielded down the first baseline; (2) dropped third strikes picked up by the catcher either foul or fair near the first baseline; (3) 3-6-3 double play attempts; (4) pick-offs at first and second base with the runner advancing toward the forward base; (5) pick-off at third base with the runner breaking for the plate; and (6) infielders fielding throws from the outfield in the baseline with a play at a forward base or the plate.

12. **Double plays in the infield**—The defense can certainly assist the pitcher whenever they can properly execute the double play. However, many innings are needlessly prolonged when an infielder in his attempt to get the double play, rushes through the fielding and throwing stage of the play. Thus, what could have been two outs many times just becomes one out or no outs, due to the carelessness of one or two members of the defense. The basic necessity whenever a double play type ground ball is hit (5 or 6 type ground ball) is that one sure out is always made. The mechanics necessary for a pivot man to make the double play cannot be achieved unless he has a decent throw to handle. Time must be spent with the infielders in practice sessions working on the proper throwing technique for double play throws to the pivot man from various angles of the infield. Once the ball is in the air to the pivot man, the next stage of the play involves around the pivot man's handling of the ball.

A. **Pivot man at second base**—The following progression steps are necessary in order for the pivot man on the double play to execute the "twin-killing": (1) catch the ball; (2) touch the base and pivot; (3) throw the ball to first base; and (4) get out of the way of the runner. If these four steps are not done in the proper sequence, the chances of completing the double play are minimal. One can imagine what would happen if a pivot man was to be concerned about executing step number 4 before step number 1 is even completed. The great pivot men follow the sequence down the line, but they accomplish all four steps so quickly that it looks like they are doing them all at about the same time.

1. **Catch the ball**—The only way the pivot man can progress to the next three steps in the double play attempt is to catch the ball. He should attempt to catch the ball in the same spot of the glove each time so that there is little chance that the pivot man would have to "double grab" for the ball as he executes the pivot. This is one of the reasons why it is important for the shortstop and second baseman to use small gloves. The pivot man must always assume that the fielder throwing him the ball is not going to give him a good throw at the base. In this way he will not be surprised if the path of the ball is such that he will have to make an adjustment in his pivoting footwork. One of the ways that he will be able to make an adjustment on a bad throw is by getting to the base under control before the ball leaves the hand of the fielder throwing him the ball. The only way that this can be done is for the infielder to "cheat" towards second base. He must also break toward the base as quickly as possible when he reads the ground ball will prompt a play at second base. As the pivot man gets within three or four steps of the base, he must shorten his steps so that he will be able to get to the base in complete control of his body. Anytime a 6 type ground ball is hit to an infielder who is going to throw the ball to the pivot man for the double play attempt, he must allow the pivot man a chance to get set up at the base before the ball arrives. This might necessitate a shuffle step in the direction of second base. The shortstop and second baseman must get to the base with their toes almost touching the bag, with their feet about shoulder width apart. The pivot man's knees must be slightly bent so that he can generate quickness to his left or right to field a poor throw. The knees bent position will also enable the pivot man to field a low throw much easier. His glove hand and bare hand should be held at chest height to provide a target for the thrower along with facilitating his quickness in catching and exchanging the ball to his throwing hand. His hips should be lined up directly toward the fielder throwing him the ball. He should achieve this ready position before the ball leaves the thrower's hand. The pivot man is now ready to execute the double play pivot as long as he has a decent throw to work with. If he reads that the throw will be in the dirt in front of the base, he must quickly jump in front of the bag and attempt to make the catch. He cannot afford to let the ball get by him under the glove. All throws to the left or right of the base should be fielded while holding one foot on the base, if possible. On a 6 type ground ball, the pivot man might have time to come off the base to catch the ball, and then return to the base for the force out on the runner. His main concern must always be on a ball thrown wide of the base to catch the ball, and then return to the base if time allows to retire the runner. If the pivot man reads that there is no chance for a double play, then he must jump in front of second base in a stance similar to the first baseman's position when receiving throws at first base. This generally occurs on 4 type ground balls, muffs on 5 or 6 type ground balls, or balls in the hole. The back heels of both feet should be in contact with the base as the infielder prepares to stretch out to receive the throw, if it will be a close play at second base on the runner attempting to advance from first base. He must be sure to never stretch out with either foot until the ball is in the air so that he can react to a poor throw. Once the fielder catches the ball and has touched the base with either foot for the force out, he must come off the base quickly to prevent being hit by the sliding

runner. Most pivot men want to receive the ball for the double play slightly on the glove side of the body about chest to shoulder heighth. Any ball thrown lower than the chest would make for a more difficult catch and ball exchange for the pivot man. Receiving the ball on the glove side of the body enables the middleman to glove the ball much easier with soft hands, along with providing him a little more time to exchange the ball from the glove to the throwing hand. If the shortstop or second baseman has to glove the ball on his throwing side it would make for a more difficult play due to the following reasons: (1) he would have to reach for the ball across his body; (2) reaching for the ball will cause his weight to shift away from first base where the throw will be made; (3) he will have a more difficult time looking the ball into his glove with both eyes; (4) it will not provide him enough time to properly exchange the ball from the glove to the throwing hand; and (5) it will delay his footwork on the pivot to complete the double play. Just as the ball makes contact with the glove, the pivot man's bare hand should be in the area of the ball so that the ball can be extracted from the glove as quick as possible. Young infielders will not be able to exchange the ball from the glove to the throwing hand as fast as experienced infielders, so they must be cautioned to take their time in the exchange process. Otherwise, they will chance having the ball drop out of their glove causing the runner sliding into second base to be safe. A good pivot man will have the ball in his bare hand with the proper grip just after the ball enters the pocket. This can only be achieved through constant practice and game experience. Keeping the knees slightly bent through the fielding stage of the pivot will keep the infielder's center of gravity low so that his hands can do the job with the body well under control. He is now ready to progress to the next step in the double play.

2. **Touch the base and pivot**—The experienced pivot man would actually be touching the base and beginning his pivot as he catches the ball. This would be when he has received a throw from the fielder to his liking. Caution must always be taken that the pivot does not begin until the middleman on the double play reads the nature of the throw. Too many times one sees an infielder rush through the pivot at second base only to find that the throw to him is wide of the base. Since his weight would already have shifted into the pivot, any ball thrown wide of his pivot position would be practically uncatchable. There are numerous ways that the shortstop and second baseman can touch the base and pivot for the throw to first base. The type of pivot used will depend on: the ability level of the pivot man; the type of throw he is receiving from the fielder of the ball; the nature of the ground ball handled by the fielder (speed and direction); and the status of the runner heading into second base. We will now detail some of the more common types of pivots used by shortstops and second basemen:

Second baseman pivots—We will assume that the second baseman has achieved the basic position for the beginning of the pivot as detailed in step number 1. This means that his body is facing directly in line with the throw so that he can react equally well to his right or left on a bad throw.

A. **Step over pivot**—The step over pivot can be used by the second baseman when he reads that he has some time to work with before the runner will be sliding into his position at second base. Once the ball is in the air, and the second baseman reads that the ball is coming over the base or slightly to the first base side of the base, he will merely step over the base with his right foot. The right foot should land on the ground just as the ball touches his glove. The heel of the right foot should land no further than two inches from the base to insure that he has his right foot under his body. If his right foot lands further than two inches away from the base, the second baseman's weight will be going too far toward third base. This will not enable him to push off the right foot in such a manner that he will be able to get off a strong throw to first base. If the second baseman reads that the throw will be slightly on the first base side of the base, he will step in the direction of the throw with his right foot. Thus, as the step-over foot lands on the ground (right foot), the ball is in the glove and the transfer of the ball from the glove to the throwing hand takes place. As this is occurring, the left foot will drag over the base so that the toe of the left foot makes slight contact with the base to achieve the force out. This should be the only contact made with the base on the pivot, for the right foot should not touch second base as the second baseman steps over the base as he catches the ball. As the left foot drags across the bag, the throwing arm should now be drawn back and then brought forward in a short arm arc. Both knees should be slightly bent at this time to allow the body's center of gravity to stay low to maximize the power of the body for the throw to first base. As the left foot comes over the base with the toe dragging on top of the base, the left side of the second baseman's body must open up toward first base to allow the left leg to swing open and plant the left foot in a direct line toward first base. The heel of the left foot should land about two inches on the inside of the baseline between first and second base. Thus, the heel of both feet should be parallel as the throwing arm comes forward to prevent the second baseman from having to throw across his body. If the left foot lands further on the inside of the baseline between first and second base he will have a most difficult time getting off a strong and accurate throw toward first base. As in all throws to first base, the toe of the left foot should be pointing directly toward first base as the throw is made to maximize the power in the throw, along with preventing the runner from sliding into the second baseman's left leg with the side of the knee exposed to the runner.

B. **Straddle pivot**—The straddle pivot can be used when the throw to second base will easily beat the runner to second base, and the second baseman does not have to worry about evading the runner until well after the ball is released to first base. The second baseman can either straddle the bag as he awaits the throw, or he can step into the straddle position as the ball is received. The straddle position should place the left foot about two to three inches away from the bag in a direct line with first base. The right foot would be about an inch away from the right side of second base so that the right foot is directly under the right shoulder. As the ball is received in the straddle position, the second baseman would kick the inside of the bag with his left foot. His weight would transfer to his right leg as the left foot hits the bag, and he would push off the right leg as the left foot steps directly toward first base. This type of pivot would be extremely dangerous if used with a runner sliding into the second baseman since the second baseman's left leg will be exposed to the runner at an improper angle.

C. **Direct step pivot**—The direct step pivot is another type of pivot that can be used when the ball arrives at second base well before the runner nears the base. The second baseman would place his right foot directly on the base as he catches the ball. His weight would transfer to the right leg as he pushes off the right foot for the throw to first base. His left foot would land in a direct line with first base as the ball is released with the toes of the left foot pointing directly at first base. The second baseman must wait to step on second base with his right foot until the ball is in the air so that he can react to a poor throw wide of the base to either side.

D. **First base side shuffle pivot**—When the second baseman reads that the ball has been thrown wide to the first base side of second base, his first obligation is to catch the ball. He must quickly take into account the position of the runner coming into second base so that he can take the proper angle to the ball. He certainly would not want to be catching the ball directly in the runner's baseline between first and second base when the runner is near the base. If the second baseman can catch the ball and hold onto second base with the right foot for the force out, this would be beneficial to the defense. Pivot men must be cautioned continuously that a base umpire will generally require the second baseman or shortstop to have contact with second base on a wild throw as the ball is caught. Most umpires will allow the pivot men to "cheat" when the ball is perfectly thrown over the base, and the middleman is attempting to pivot and get out of the way of the approaching runner. If the second baseman's left foot is positioned inside or outside the baseline between first and second base as the ball is caught, he can then execute the flip throw to second base without taking his right foot off the base. This is an extremely difficult type of throw especially when the left foot is on the infield side of the base line between first and second base since the second baseman will have to throw well across his body. Some second basemen become very proficient in flip throwing (throwing the ball to first base without the benefit of a step toward the base). Most second baseman need to take the extra step before throwing in order to get off a more accurate and strong throw to first base. With this being the case, the second basemen's right foot would leave second base as soon as the ball is caught. The right foot would quickly be moved to where the left foot was positioned on the catch, while the left foot takes the step directly toward first base. The right foot would then be the "push-off" foot for the throw. This is the basic shuffle step used quite frequently by infielders to set themselves for throws when they find themselves off-balance as they field the ball.

E. **Left field side rock and fire pivot**—If the second baseman reads that the throw from the fielder of the ball is wide of second base on the left field side, he must attempt to hold the bag with his left foot on the left field side of the base. He would then step toward the ball with his right foot. In order to insure the catch, he may have to vacate the bag with his left foot, returning to the base as the ball is caught. If time allows, he still might be able to get off a throw to first base for the attempted double play. He must never attempt to throw the ball to first base with his weight moving away from first base. Thus, he would attempt to transfer his weight back toward second base, touching the base with his left foot, and pushing off his right foot for the throw to first base. If on the catch his right foot is on the inside or outside of the base line extended between first and second base, he should step directly toward first base with his left foot as long as the force out has already been achieved. The throwing mechanics would be the basic rock and fire technique with the second baseman pushing off his right foot, and transferring his weight to his left foot as the throwing arm comes forward.

F. **Jump step pivot**—Whenever the runner coming into second base to break up the double play attempt is close to second base as the ball reaches the second baseman, the pivot man will need to execute a pivot to insure that he can clear the runner, and still get off a throw to first base. The jump step pivot will provide the second baseman the opportunity to execute the throw to first base from inside the base line. This will not insure that he will evade being hit by the sliding runner, but it will provide him the opportunity to at least clear the base line. As the ball is in the air to second base from the fielder of the ground ball, and the second baseman reads that the throw will be over the base or slightly to the first base side of the base, he will step on second base with his left foot as he catches the ball. He will then quickly step to the inside of the base with his right foot, planting the foot so that it is directly under his right shoulder. His left foot would then come off the base, and he would step with that foot in the direction of first base. This type of pivot should put him about a foot and a half inside the base line as he releases the ball. The feet must be moved quickly in this pivot in order to clear the runner, along with planting the feet as fast as possible to get off a strong and accurate throw to first base.

G. **Drag over pivot**—The drag over pivot is another type of pivot that can be used by the second baseman to clear himself from the sliding runner. This type of pivot will require the second baseman to take an extra step before releasing the ball to first base, but it will put him a little further inside the base line than the jump step pivot. As he reads the throw over the base or slightly to the first base side of the base, the pivot man would step over the base and to the ball with his left foot as the catch is made. As the left foot lands on the ground, he would drag over the base with his right foot achieving the force out. The left foot should be about a foot inside the base line as it lands. The right foot would then be quickly placed about 4-6 inches further inside the base line and will become the push off foot for the throw to first base. The second baseman would then step with his left foot toward first base to execute the throw.

H. **Drop step pivot**—On balls thrown slightly to the left field side of second base, the drop step pivot can be executed. It can also be used for throws directly over the bag so that the second baseman can change his pivot routine in order that the runners cannot always assume that he will be pivoting to the inside of the base line each time a double play is attempted. As the ball is in the air, the second baseman would place his left foot on the right field side of second base. He would catch the ball and then step back with his right foot about a foot away from the base. He would then take his left foot off the base, and step with the left foot towards first base while pushing off the right foot to provide power into the throw. The right foot can not be dropped back too far or else the second baseman's weight would be on his heels rather than on the balls of his feet. Some second baseman become very proficient in this type of pivot, and can even get off an extremely strong throw by stepping further back with the right foot than the one foot prescribed. If the throw is slightly to the left field side of second base, he must move his right foot back in line with the throw attempting to keep his right foot under his right shoulder. If the right foot is outside the right shoulder, the second baseman will have a very difficult time pushing off the right foot to achieve a strong throw to first base.

The coach who works with the second basemen should allow them the opportunity to experiment with the different types of pivots that can be used to complete the double play. After exposing them to the various pivots, the coach must assist each player in determining the two or three pivots that are best suited for his particular ability level. The pivots used must be instinctive on the second baseman's part. This will only be achieved with a lot of practice around the bag under game type conditions.

Shortstop pivots—The shortstop has a distinct advantage over the second baseman in pivoting on the double play, in that he will be receiving the throw with his momentum going toward the intended target (first base). He will also be in a better position to observe the runner's status as he attempts the pivot. As was the case for the second baseman, there are numerous ways in which the shortstop can pivot at second base to complete the double play. The shortstop's approach to the base is identical to the way the second baseman must get to the bag. He must be at the base and under control before the ball leaves the hand of the fielder throwing him the ball. The shortstop's first obligation is to catch the ball, so he can never start pivoting for the double play attempt until he can read the nature of the ball thrown to him at second base. The shortstop must line himself up directly toward the area where the ball is coming from so that he is in a position to move equally well to both his right and left. Generally, the shortstop will line himself up slightly on the right field side of second base when the ball is fielded outside the base line between first and second base. When the ball is fielded inside the base line, he would generally want to line himself up slightly on the infield side of second base. Most shortstops prefer to have the ball thrown from their chest to their shoulders on the side of the base that they are positioned.

A. **Basic footwork in catching the ball**—With the ball being thrown from outside the base line between first and second base, the shortstop should set up behind second base shading slightly to the right field side of the base. He should place the toe of his right foot about an inch away from the bag at the center. His left foot would be about a foot on the outside of the bag with the left toe pointing in the direction of the fielder throwing him the ball. If the ball is being thrown by the first baseman from outside the base line, the shortstop should shade a little more to the right field side of the bag. This will give the first baseman a better outside target away from the runner heading for second base. The same holds true for when the first baseman fields the ball inside the base line, whereby the shortstop would shade further inside for the benefit of the first baseman in making the throw. Both feet should be under the shoulders with the knees bent whenever awaiting the throw from the fielder of the ball. His glove and bare hand should be held at about chest height facing the fielder. As always, his first concern must be to catch the ball. He must be in a position to move quickly to his right or left as soon as he reads a poor throw wide of his basic position behind the bag. On any wide throw to the inside or outside, the shortstop must be able to shift, hoping that he can maintain contact with the base as the ball is caught. If the throw carries him to the outside, he would attempt to hold the corner of the bag with his right foot as he steps with the left foot to catch the ball. If he must shift to the inside on a wide throw in that direction, he would attempt to hold the inside corner of the base with his left foot, and step to the throw with his right foot. If necessary, he must come off the base to catch the ball, and then if time allows, return to the base for the force out.

B. **Outside drag pivot**—The outside drag pivot should be used on any ball thrown to the outside of the center of second base. This does not mean that the outside drag pivot can not be used on a ball thrown a little to the inside half of second base, but it would require the shortstop to reach across his body for the ball since he is set up on the outer half of the bag. If the shortstop waits until the ball is in the air to move to the ball with the lead foot, he can easily make an adjustment in his pivot depending on which side of the base the ball has been thrown. If he is receiving a throw to the outer half of the base, he would step toward the ball with his left foot attempting to catch the ball as the foot lands on the ground. This step forward with the left foot must be such that the shortstop has established good momentum into the throw, but it still provides him great control of his body to complete the pivot. If his left foot steps out too far on this lead step it will force his body momentum more toward right field than toward first base. There is no reason, except to catch a wide throw, for the shortstop's left foot to go any further than a foot and a half to the outside of the base line. His left foot should land at about a 45 degree angle from the direct line between second and first base, with his left toe pointing in the direction of first base. If the left toe is pointing out toward right field, it will cause his body momentum to go in that direction. By pointing the left toe toward first base, it will also assist the shortstop in closing his left shoulder to assist him in getting off a stronger and more accurate throw to first base. As the left foot is landing on the ground, the right foot is dragging the outside corner of the bag making contact with the bag with the inside of the big toe. At this time the ball has been caught and the shortstop is in the process of exchanging the ball from the glove to the throwing hand. The shortstop would then quickly execute a jump step pivot with the right foot as he is bringing his arm back to make the throw to first base. The right foot should land on the jump pivot at just about the same spot on the ground that the left foot landed when the ball was received. As the right foot is about to land on the ground, the shortstop's left foot would be stepping toward first base. The right foot would be the push-off foot for the throw to first base so that foot should land on the ground perpendicular to the base line. The quicker the shortstop's feet are in this drag step pivot the quicker he will be in getting off the throw to first base. This pivot properly executed should enable the shortstop to clear the base line, and at the same time, position himself for the throw to first base. It is important for the coach to stress to his shortstops that the outside drag pivot should be completed with their body under control with their feet set under them for the throw to complete the double play.

C. **Inside drag pivot**—The shortstop should be in a position at second base to react to a throw from outside the base line that will take him to the inside of the base. This is the reason why the shortstop can never be stepping with his left foot on the initial pivot until the ball is in the air. If he reads that the throw will be to the inside of second base, then he will step over the bag with his right foot toward the ball. He would then drag over the base with his left foot, touching the left field side of the base with the toes of the foot as he gets the force out. He would then step toward first base with the left foot as he makes the throw to first base. If he reads that the throw will be well to the inside of the base, he must quickly place his left foot on the third base side of the base stretching toward the ball with his right foot.

D. **Direct step pivot**—There will be times that the shortstop does not have to worry about the runner since the throw will be caught at the base well before the runner arrives in the area. In this case, he can catch the ball that is over the base with his right foot directly on the base, and then step with his left foot down the base line. This is not a recommended type of pivot due to the position in the base line that it leaves the shortstop, but it can be executed in those situations where time is not a major factor.

E. **Pivots on throws from the first baseman**—The type of pivot used by the shortstop on throws coming to second base from the first baseman will depend on the angle of the throw in relation to the base line. If the first baseman fields the ball directly in the base line, and proceeds to throw the ball right down the line, the shortstop is going to have a very difficult time picking up the ball due to the runner being in line with the throw. There are various types of pivots that the shortstop can use in fielding balls from the first baseman that are in the base line. If the ball is coming directly over the base, he should use the inside pivot since his glove can remain over the base a little longer than if he was to attempt an outside pivot. With the inside pivot, he would step to the inside of the base line with his right foot, and drag over the left field side of the base with his left foot, making sure that he catches the ball before his left foot drags the side of the base. His first obligation must be to catch the ball, even if the runner is about to make contact with the base. By staying slightly behind the base as the pivot begins, he should not be in a position to get hit by the runner unless the runner roll slides through the base. This would be an illegal type of slide by the runner. After stepping with his right foot, he would then step with his left foot toward first base putting him about a foot inside the base line. If the ball is moving toward the outer half of second base, he should touch the bag with his right foot (right field side of the base), stepping out with his left foot to clear the base line. He would then execute the jump pivot as described in the outside drag pivot. Another type of pivot that is used by shortstops when the ball is being thrown down the base line is where the shortstop catches the ball behind second base, stepping on the base as he throws to first base. In this pivot, the shortstop will position himself about a foot and a half behind second base in line with the first baseman's throw. As he catches the ball he steps on the bag and throws the ball to first base. If the ball is fielded inside the base line by the first baseman, the shortstop should be yelling "inside-inside". He would position himself so that his left toe is in contact with the back of second base on the left field side corner of the bag. If the throw comes to the inside of the base, he would step to the ball with his right foot at about a 45 degree angle from the base line ending up about a foot and a half inside the line. He would then drag with the left foot over the back corner of the base, and step with that foot in the direction of first base. If the throw from inside the diamond takes him to the outside of the base, he must quickly place his right foot on the right field side of the base and step with his left foot at about a 45 degree angle from the base line. He can either throw from that position, or he can jump pivot with his right foot, and then step and throw to first base with the left foot. He would jump pivot anytime the runner is going to be sliding directly into the base as he is pivoting. Otherwise, he might just step and throw with his right foot on the outer side of the base. If the first baseman fields the ball outside of the base line, the shortstop should be yelling "outside-outside" to the first baseman. He would position himself so that his right toe is in contact with the back of second base on the center field side corner of the bag. If the throw comes to the outside of the base, he would step with his left foot at a 45 degree angle from the base line. He would drag with the right foot over the back corner of the base, and then execute the jump pivot with his right foot.

F. **Pivots on throws from the pitcher or catcher**—The shortstop will generally be the pivot man on any balls fielded by the pitcher or catcher with a play at second base. The type of pivot he should execute will depend entirely on the direction the throw takes on its way to the base. If he catches the ball on the shortstop side of the base, he can merely step on the base with his left foot as he throws to first base. If the throw takes him to the first base side of second base, he should execute the outside drag pivot. If the throw takes him to the inside of the base, he would execute the inside drag pivot. Hopefully, the shortstop will be positioned at the base early enough that he can move toward the ball with either the right or left foot depending on whether the throw takes him to the outside or inside of the base.

G. **Pivots on throws from the third baseman**—With a lefthanded pull hitter at the plate, the shortstop might become the middleman on a double play type ground ball fielded by the third baseman. If so, he must get to the left field side of second base lining his hips up with the third baseman throwing the ball to second base. His left foot should be about three inches from the base with his left toe pointing at the third baseman. As the ball is in the air, and he reads that the ball is coming directly over the bag, he would step on the third base side of the bag with his left foot. He would step toward the ball with his right foot, catching the ball as his right foot lands. This should place him well inside the base line with his right foot. He would then step toward first base with his left foot. If he reads that the throw from the third baseman will arrive at the base on the first base side, he must quickly move his feet so that his right foot steps on second base on the right field side of the base so that he can reach out for the ball with his left foot. From this position, he can throw direct to first base, or he can execute the jump pivot in order to evade the sliding runner. If the ball takes him to the left field side of second base, he can easily catch the ball, and then step on the base with his left foot as he makes the throw to first base.

3. **Throwing the ball to first base**—Once the pivot man catches the ball and touches the base for the force out on the pivot, he now must concentrate his attention on throwing the ball to first base to complete the double play. One of the primary concerns in this facet of the double play is that the pivot man might need to sacrifice some quickness in releasing the ball in order to achieve a high degree of accuracy and velocity in his throw to first base. This is especially true for the inexperienced second baseman or shortstop. Many pivot men attempt to "quick release" the ball to first base, and subsequently, the ball thrown to first base has poor velocity and accuracy. If the

399

middle infielder can display a good degree of quickness in his release of the ball without losing accuracy and velocity in the throw to first base, he is now in "business". This takes a lot of practice in game situation drills as the infielder matures as a pivot man. The defense can ill afford to ever lose the "sure out" at second base when the shortstop or second baseman drops the ball trying to release the ball too quick as he pivots to throw the ball to first base. The pivot man must achieve a high degree of body balance while releasing the ball so that his body position enables his throwing arm to come forward at the proper angle. His left foot should be straight in line with his throw to first base if at all possible, so that he can achieve this proper balance for his throw to first base. It is also important that his throwing elbow be up as much as possible as he releases the ball to aid in achieving the velocity and accuracy desired. However, many middle infielders can become proficient in releasing the ball to first base with their elbow down slightly. The coach must assist each individual pivot man in determining his best arm slot on the double play throw. Of course, the arm slot many times will be dictated by the type of pivot used and the momentum of the infielder's body through the pivot. The short arm arc out of the glove is probably the most important skill in developing the quick release desired. If the shortstop or second baseman extracts the ball from the glove and his throwing hand drops down below the level of the glove, he will be wasting valuable time in getting rid of the ball. The throwing hand must get to the throwing position as the pivot is completed. As he pulls the ball out of the glove, his throwing hand must draw back and up as quick as possible. As the arm goes back, he can not afford to reach back for something extra on the throw. He also can not afford to "short arm" through the throwing motion whereby his elbow remains bent through the entire range of motion of the arm. Some infielders can achieve a lot of power in their throws with a "short arm" delivery, but in most cases they would be able to achieve more power in their throw by a semifull arm arc. The fingers must stay on top of the ball as the hand leaves the glove and the arm goes back to the throwing position. If the fingers get under the ball, it will slow down the infielder's quickness in getting the arm back, and it will also lead to dropping the elbow down on release. The extraction of the ball from the glove should be such that the fingers have complete control of the ball prior to the ball leaving the glove. The glove should be brought back with the throwing hand near the right shoulder to allow for a little more time to get the proper grip on the ball before the ball is extracted from the glove. If the ball is caught in the same area of the glove each time, and the infielder has his bare hand going into the glove as soon as the ball touches "leather", he should be able to get a good grip on the ball as he brings his throwing arm back to throw the ball to first base. The quickness of the infielder's release will also be affected by his ability to move his feet through the pivot. If he has slow feet on the pivot, his arm will have to wait until the feet are somewhat set on the ground upon the completion of the pivot. If he rushes his throwing arm before his feet are set, he will generally be making an off-balance throw to first base. The pivot man whose momentum takes him well to the infield side of the diamond during the pivot, with his feet not under him on the throw, will invariably drop his elbow on the throw to first base. There are many second basemen and shortstops who have been able to throw from "down-under" with great success, but this should only be done as a rule when the infielder's body is not in a position to make the "over-the-top" throw to first base. The "down-under" throw occurs quite a bit when the shortstop drag pivots to the right field side of second base, and releases the ball while his body's momentum is going out toward right field. If at all possible, he must get his feet under him so that his body momentum is heading toward first base to provide additional power and accuracy on his throw. It is also very important that the coach stress to his pivot men that they should not throw the ball to first base when there is no chance for getting the second out on the double play. Anytime the shortstop or second baseman gets the force out at second base, he should always full arm fake to first base if there was a runner at second base at the time of the pitch. Many times the runner will round third base too aggressively, and when he sees the pivot man's arm go forward toward first base, the runner might take some additional steps toward home plate. If that occurs, the middleman would spin glove side and throw the ball to the third baseman covering third base. In addition, if the second baseman or shortstop is definitely going to be hit by the sliding runner and the ball is still not in the "cocked" position yet, good judgment will dictate whether or not the throw should be completed. If there are runners in scoring position, and a wild throw to first base would allow the runner(s) to score, then the throw should not be made. In double play practice sessions, it is a good idea to time each ground ball hit so that the middlemen learn how much time it takes to complete a double play. Anytime the throw to first base on the double play is made under 4.3 seconds, the double play would generally be successful in retiring the majority of runners. This time is from the crack of the fungo bat, to the time the ball hits the glove of the first baseman.

4. **Getting out of the way of the runner**—The middle infielder on the double play must expect some contact occasionally from the runner coming into second base to break up the double play attempt. The rules now require the runner to be on the ground when making contact with the pivot man, and also, the runner must be sliding into the base itself. This is to prevent the standing or rolling "take out" slide, along with the slide that makes contact with the pivot man when he is positioned well inside or outside of the base line between first and second base. Most pivoting at second base is done somewhat close to the bag, which means that contact will be made with the shortstop or second baseman pivoting on the base in the following situations: (1) steal or hit and run is on and the fielder of the

ground ball attempts to get the out at second base; (2) slow rolling ground ball is thrown to second base; (3) a ball forces the fielder to range well to his right or left, and after fielding the ball he throws to second base; and (4) a ground ball is bobbled by the fielder of the ball, and after recovery decides to throw the ball to second base. The fear of getting hit by the sliding runner has caused many erratic throws to first base at all levels of baseball. The shortstop or second baseman who is always concerned about the sliding runner will have a poor success ratio in completing double plays. Getting out of the way of the runner can only take place once the ball is in the air to first base. If the middleman is getting out of the way of the runner while pivoting and throwing the ball, he will find that his throw to first base will not be one with a high success ratio. If the pivot man exercises a proper pivot, his chances of getting hit hard by the runner is minimal. If he does not execute a good pivot, his chance of getting hit by the runner in the situations presented will be high. Anytime the pivot man realizes that he has no play at first base, he must receive the ball in a force out position at second base. This means that he should have the heels of both feet in front or back of the base with his hips facing the area the ball is being thrown from. As the ball reaches the base, he will hit the base with the toe of one foot, and then come off the base as quick as possible. If he must stretch out to catch the ball he must be cautious not to stretch until the ball is in the air, so that he can make adjustments around the base if the ball is thrown wild. The pivot man does not want nor need to get tangled up with a sliding runner when he has no chance of getting the double play at first base. On those occasions when the double play is a possibility, then the pivot man must go through with his pivot. The second baseman and shortstop's pivot should place him at least a foot and a half inside or outside the base line if the runner will be sliding into second base at the time of the pivot. If the runner is well away from second base at the time the ball is received, the pivot man will not need to make the inside or outside pivot. Once the ball leaves his hand, then he must concern himself with evading the runner so that he does not chance an injury. This can easily be done by pushing off to the inside or outside of the runner's sliding position. If the runner is right on top of the pivot man, he can jump in the air off his stride leg. If contact cannot be avoided with the baserunner, the second baseman or shortstop must be sure that his stride leg is facing the baserunner so that his ankle, knee and hip are not hit from the side. This could cause a serious injury to the pivot man if a joint was hit at an improper angle. Upon contact, the infielder should give with the sliding runner in order to cushion any blow to the body.

B. Feeds for the pivot man—The infielder, pitcher or catcher throwing the ball to the pivot man at second base can make the pivot man's job that much easier on the double play pivot by giving him the ball as quick as possible, and as accurately as possible. Most pivot men like to have the ball thrown from their chest to their head on the first base side corner of second base. It is important that the infielders spend enough time in practice sessions on feeds to the pivot men at second base so that they become aware of how the pivot men like to have the ball thrown to second base for their type of pivot. The quicker and more accurate the feeder throw to the middleman on the double play, the better the chance for the "twin-killing". This is the reason why it is so important that the infielder's position themselves at double play depth, and then take an aggressive approach to the ground ball. The more aggressive the infielder is toward the ground ball, the deeper he can position himself in regard to depth. The following five double play feeds will now be presented: 5-4; 5-6; 6-4; 4-6; and 3-6.

1. **5-4 feed**—The third baseman should always attempt to keep his elbow up on his throws to second base in order to prevent the ball from sailing or sinking on its way to the second baseman. Any movement on the ball makes the pivot man's job that much tougher as he attempts to make his pivot at second base. A third baseman with a strong arm should not have to take a shuffle step toward second base on his feeder throw if he fields the ball right at him or slightly to his left. If the third baseman needs the shuffle step in order to get off a strong and accurate throw to second base, then this would certainly be preferred over a throw that loses velocity and accuracy on its way to the base. The shuffle step will take a little longer time, but sometimes this is preferred if the throw will be stronger and more accurate. If the third baseman must go to his right to field the ball, then he would have to shuffle step in order to throw the ball to second base with something on the throw. This will also hold true if he has to come in on the ball. If the ball takes him well to his left, it might necessitate a three-quarters throw to the second baseman due to the fact that an off-balance throw will be required. The main consideration must always be accuracy, to insure that an out is always made at second base. It does little good to rush through the fielding and throwing stage only to find that the ball is misplayed, or the throw is one that can not be handled by the second baseman.

2. **5-6 feed**—There will be times that the second baseman will need to swing well to the right field side of the diamond when there is a lefthanded pull hitter at the plate. With this being the case, he would have an almost impossible task of getting to second base for a double play feed from the third baseman on the ball hit right at him, or slightly to his left. Since the shortstop will be playing the lefthanded pull hitter to the pull side, he will be in a much better position to be the pivot man on a ball hit to the third baseman. The second baseman must still break for second base on any ball hit to the left side of the infield in case the ball takes the shortstop to his right, which would

necessitate the second baseman being the pivot man at second base. In this case, the chance for a double play would be slim so the force out at second base is all that might be obtained. If the third baseman fields the ball, the shortstop will move toward second base full speed positioning himself at the base in accordance with the mechanics previously discussed on the 5-6-3 double play attempt. The third baseman must give the shortstop the ball right over the base so that the shortstop can properly pivot for the throw to first base. If both the shortstop and second baseman break for second base, the second baseman would have priority over the shortstop. As mentioned in the infield communication section of the Playbook, the shortstop, second baseman and third baseman must communicate that the shortstop will be covering on this play by the communication of: "five-six-three".

    3. **6-4 feed**—Since the shortstop's feed throw to the second baseman will generally be from a short distance, accuracy is a very important consideration. The second baseman will not have as much time to react to a wild throw from the shortstop as he would from the third baseman. The second baseman must also be able to see the ball clearly as it leaves the shortstop's hand in order for him to read the ball prior to the pivot. This is why it is so important that the shortstop never drop his arm slot to the point that the ball is leaving his hand at a position where the second baseman can not pick up the ball easily. The shortstop should not have to straighten up to make the throw to second base since the distance of the throw is minimal. If his momentum is taking him toward second base, he must flip the ball underhanded to the second baseman. He should also flip the ball to the second baseman any time the distance to the base is such that an overhand throw would take too much time and make for a very difficult ball for the second baseman to pick up out of the hand. If the ball must be flipped underhand to the second baseman, the shortstop should step with his left foot toward the base as the ball is released. This will assist in establishing an accurate flip along with giving the second baseman the ability to time his pivot with the forward step toward the base. Whenever the ball must be flipped underhanded, the shortstop must be sure that he keeps his glove down as his flip hand presents the ball to the second baseman. If the glove comes up with the flip hand, it will interfere with the ability of the second baseman to see the ball leave his hand. The closer the shortstop is to the second baseman at the point of the underhand flip, the higher the arc and softer the flip must be to the second baseman. The shortstop should allow his momentum to continue on toward second base as he flips the ball to insure more accuracy and velocity on his flip. This is especially true if the shortstop decides to underhand flip the ball to the second baseman from a great distance. If the shortstop has to go behind second base to field the ball, this would necessitate his backhand flipping the ball if he can not get in front of the ball for the regular straight flip. In the backhand flip, the shortstop would release the ball with an inward turn of the wrist, making sure that the ball arcs on its way to the second baseman, aiming for the flip to be at eye level to the second sacker. There is generally no chance for a double play anytime the shortstop must go behind second base to field the ball unless he was playing the hitter close to second base at the time of the pitch. If the ground ball to the shortstop will be fielded in front of his body, his first concern must be to be aggressive to the ball. He must field the ground ball with the same basic mechanics he would use if throwing the ball to first base. So many times one sees an infielder rush through the fielding stage of a double play type ground ball, only to find that he boots the ball due to his not following proper fielding mechanics. The shortstop must be quick to the ball; slow down during the fielding of the ball; and be quick in getting the ball back to the throwing position. Once the ball is in his glove, the shortstop should open his left foot slightly toward second base. This would be just a pivot on the heel of the left foot to enable the shortstop to better open his left side to the second baseman. This will also enable the shortstop to get his elbow up a little higher on release. At the same time, he should pivot on the toe of the right foot to further assist in opening his left side toward second base. If he keeps his left foot closed and does not execute a pivot on his right toe, he will have a tendency to drop his arm making it very difficult for the second baseman to clearly see the ball leave his hand. He should not have to raise up when delivering the ball, unless he fields the ball a long way from second base. The closer the shortstop fields the ball toward the baseline between second and third base, the more he will have to open his front side while releasing the ball to second base. The pivoting can not begin until the ball is securely in the glove of the shortstop. If done before the ball is fielded, the chance for an error on the play will be greatly increased. If the shortstop has to range to his right to field the ball, he must attempt to cut the angle on the ball as much as possible. If he drifts deep on the ball, the chances of completing the double play will be minimal. If the shortstop is playing a hitter well away from second base and the ball takes him further to his right away from the base, it might necessitate his striding toward second base with his left foot once the ball has been fielded. This is to insure a more strong and accurate throw to the base. If the shortstop has to backhand the ball, he should attempt to do so with his right foot forward so that he can just pivot on the right foot while making the throw to second base. If he has his left foot forward as he backhands the ball, he will have to either jump pivot or take an additional step with his right foot away from second base in order to throw the ball to the second baseman. On all throws to second base, the shortstop must drop his glove as he throws so that the second baseman will have no problem seeing the ball released.

4. **4-6 feed**—The second baseman has a much tougher play than the shortstop on the double play feed due to the fact that the second baseman must throw the ball at an unnatural angle to the shortstop at second base on most of the 4-6 feeds. The most important aspect of this type of feed is for the second baseman to be aggressive to the ball, and then take his time as he fields the ball and pivots for the throw to second base. Too many times second basemen rush through the fielding stage, since they have to get off a quick feed to the shortstop in order to complete the double play. When they start pivoting too early, they chance not fielding the ball cleanly, and end up not getting a single out on the play. The 4-6-3 double play is a difficult one to complete unless the second baseman receives a 5 or 6 type ground ball to work with, so time taken during the fielding stage will be time well worth taking on the second baseman's part. There are various types of pivots that can be used by the second baseman when feeding the ball to the shortstop at second base. The type of pivot used would depend on the speed of the ball, the nature of the hop received, the direction the ball takes the second baseman, and the distance and angle of the feed to the shortstop at the base. On a ground ball hit directly at the second baseman, or a few steps to his right or left, the knee drop pivot is preferred (5 or 6 type ground ball). Once the ball is cleanly fielded, the second baseman would quickly drop to his left knee as he rotates on his left toe. This would allow the knee to hit the ground at about the area where the ball was fielded, if the ball was fielded near the midline of the body. At the same time, the second baseman would rotate on the heel of his right foot so that the right toe is pointing toward second base as the arm goes back for the throw. This type of pivot will enable the upper body to turn toward the target. The throwing arm must be brought back quickly with a short arm arc as the pivot takes place, and with the elbow up at shoulder height, the ball is thrown to the shortstop at second base. If the ball is fielded behind the baseline between first and second base, the shortstop would generally want the ball thrown to the right field side of second base at chest to shoulder height. Another type of pivot similar to the knee drop pivot is where the second baseman pivots as described above, but his knee does not touch the ground during the pivot. He would pivot so that his left knee is about a foot above the ground as his body rotates to the right. The advantage of the knee drop pivot over the jump pivot is that it generally forces the second baseman to hold a little longer in the fielding stage. The jump pivot can also be executed when the second baseman fields the ground ball a distance away from second base that will not enable him to underhand flip the ball to the shortstop. The degree of the turn on the jump pivot would be dictated by the angle of the throw the second baseman would have to make to the shortstop at the base. Once the ball is fielded, the second baseman would jump pivot as he brings his arm back to throwing position. The pivot should enable him to have his left foot pointing in the direction of his throw, with his right foot ending up near where the left foot was at the time the pivot occurred. If he does not make the complete pivot with both feet, it can cause the second baseman to drop his arm making it that much more difficult to get off an accurate throw to the shortstop. The more he drops his arm, the tougher it is for the shortstop to pick up the ball as it leaves his hand. If the second baseman fields the ball well behind the baseline between first and second base, the degree of the turn on the pivot is greatly reduced. The closer he is to the baseline at the time he fields the ball, the more he must turn in order to make the proper throw. If the second baseman is moving toward second base at the time the ball is fielded, the underhand flip is recommended. When flipping the ball underhand, the second baseman must be sure that he presents the ball to the shortstop so that he can easily see the ball throughout the flip. The closer the second baseman is to the shortstop at the base, the higher the arc must be in the flip. The glove must be pulled down at the time of the flip so that the ball is not partially obstructed by the glove. The second baseman should step toward the shortstop with his right foot as he flips the ball to insure better accuracy on his feed to the shortstop. If the second baseman is moving toward the baseline near the bag, or is inside the baseline at the time the ball is fielded, he should execute the reverse flip of the ball to the shortstop. This flip is done with a counter clockwise flip of the wrist so that the ball leaves the hand with the back of the hand facing the second baseman. The ball must be released with a full extension of the arm toward the target. This type of flip takes a lot of practice, but when executed properly, is the best feed to the shortstop when the angle to second base does not allow the second baseman to execute the underhand flip. If at all possible, the second baseman should attempt to tag the runner heading toward second base. If the runner was to stop prior to reaching his position, he should run at the runner a couple of steps. If he can not make the tag after these two or three steps toward the runner, he should throw the ball immediately to the first baseman to retire the batter-runner. This should enable the first baseman to have a play at second base on the runner, with the shortstop applying the tag since the force was eliminated with the out at first base. If the second baseman has to range well to his left to field the ground ball, he can either jump pivot or execute a glove slide turn in getting a throw off to the shortstop at second base. The glove side turn should be done when the second baseman's momentum to his left will not enable him to jump pivot. In the glove side turn, he must field the ball with his left foot forward (toward the right field line). He would then take a short step with his right foot in the direction of his momentum, planting and pivoting on the right foot as he turns glove side toward second base. He must be sure that he bends the right leg as he pivots so that he can break his momentum away from second base. This will also enable him to get off a stronger and more accurate throw to second base. If time allows, he must step directly toward second base with his left foot as he throws. If his momentum is carrying him away from second base

as he pivots, he may have to make an off-balance throw to second base with a three-quarters or lower arm slot. The second baseman should get the out at first base anytime his momentum carries him well away from second base, rather than chancing a most difficulty play at second base. If the ball carries the second baseman behind second base, he may have to backhand the ball. If so, he can either underhand flip the ball, or if his momentum is carrying him well past the base, he may have to flip the ball to the shortstop from down under. The shortstop should be facing the second baseman as he prepares to receive the feed. On all tough throws or flips to the shortstop for the force out, the second baseman must forget about the double play. This will allow him to center all his attention on getting the force out at second base.

5. **3-6 feed**—The 3-6-3 or 3-6-1 double play is by far the toughest double play to complete, and also leads to the most errors made per chance of any double play. This is due to the fact that the first baseman has a long throw to make to second base, the runner many times is in the throwing path of the ball, the shortstop must rush his throw to first base to have any chance for a double play, and the righthanded first baseman has a tough pivot to make in order to get a throw off to second base. For all these reasons, a coach must impress upon those involved in this play to make sure that the force out at second base is made without any consideration for a double play. Once the force out is made, then they can center their attention on getting the out on the batter-runner at first base. The major concern in the first baseman's mind must be to field the ball cleanly before beginning the pivot for the throw to second base. This is especially true for the righthanded first baseman who many times feels that he must rush through the fielding of the ball due to the nature of his pivot toward second base, and the long throw that must be made to the shortstop. The lefthanded first baseman has a much easier time getting the ball to the shortstop, since he will have very little pivoting to be done, unless he fields the ground ball with his momentum carrying him toward the first baseline. The first baseman must get the out at first base anytime he fields the ground ball within two steps from first base, or his momentum is carrying him toward the base with a very difficult throw to make to the shortstop at second base. If the ball is a 5 or 6 type ground ball, he should still have a chance of getting the runner at second base after retiring the batter-runner at first base. The first baseman must always yell "tag" as he delivers the ball to the shortstop so he is aware of the fact that he must make the tag on the runner, since the force has been nullified due to the batter-runner being called out at first base. This will generally necessitate a throw right down the baseline between first and second base. If at all possible, the lefthanded first baseman should throw the ball to the inside of second base, and the righthanded first baseman to the outside of the base. If time allows, he should step to the inside or outside of the baseline prior to throwing the ball. Any ball hit well away from first base, the first baseman must quickly decide on whether to throw the ball to the shortstop at second base, or get the batter-runner with a throw to the pitcher covering first base. This decision depends on a number of things: (1) speed and direction of the ground ball; (2) where the ball was fielded; (3) first baseman's arm strength; (4) speed of the runner heading toward second base, and the speed of the batter-runner; (5) score of the game; and (6) number of outs. The type of pivot used in throwing the ball to second base would be different for the righthanded and lefthanded first baseman.

A. **Righthanded first basemen**—If the first baseman fields the ball in the baseline between first and second base, or inside the baseline, he should generally execute the glove side pivot turn when throwing the ball to the shortstop at second base. With this type of pivot, he is in a better position to get off a more accurate and strong throw to second base. If he was to jump pivot once he fielded the ball, it would require a full jump pivot in order to step with his left foot in the direction of second base. This would also lead to a tendency on the first baseman's part to drop his arm which would seriously affect the accuracy and power of his throw to second base. The glove turn pivot has to be completed when the ball takes the first baseman toward the line in order that he can stop his momentum by planting and pivoting on the right foot. The glove side pivot would require the righthanded first baseman to complete his pivot before he releases the ball. As he turns glove side, the first baseman must plant his right foot in order that he might push-off the foot for a better throw to second base. He would then step directly toward second base with his left foot as he releases the ball. Of course, the quicker the glove side turn, the quicker the ball will be released. Caution must always be taken that the turn not begin until the ball is clearly fielded. If the first baseman fields the ball behind the baseline, he should execute the jump pivot after the ball has been fielded. The jump pivot is executed the same as was described for the second baseman, but it is important that the first baseman achieve the full turn of his body due to the distance of his throw to second base. This means that as the ball is released, his left foot must be pointing directly toward his target at second base. He must also be sure that he keeps his elbow up as he releases the ball so that the ball does not "sail" on him on the way to the shortstop. If the ball takes the first baseman toward second base behind the baseline, it will probably necessitate an overhand flip of the ball to the shortstop at the bag.

B. **Lefthanded first baseman**—The lefthanded first baseman's pivot on his throw to second base for the force out is basically the same whether he fields the ball in front of the baseline or behind the baseline. The only difference being that he would have to open up his right side a little more when fielding the ball in front of the baseline in order to step in the direction of second base with his right foot on the throw. If the first baseman possesses a strong arm, he should be able to throw the ball to the shortstop at second base without having to shuffle step toward the base. If the ground ball takes him toward the first baseline, he may have to shuffle step due to the fact that his momentum has carried him away from the intended target of his throw. As in all throws involving some distance, it is important that the lefthanded first baseman raise up to make the throw after fielding the ball. This is to insure that he will be able to get his throwing elbow up, enabling him to get off a more powerful and accurate throw to the shortstop. If the ground ball carries the lefthanded first baseman toward second base, it might necessitate an overhand flip of the ball to the shortstop at the bag.

Once the first baseman has released the ball to the shortstop at second base, he must now concern himself with returning to first base in order to be in a position to receive the return throw from the shortstop. If the first baseman fields the ball well away from first base, or his momentum is taking him toward second base as he releases the ball to the shortstop, the pitcher will be responsible for fielding the return throw from the shortstop. If both the first baseman and the pitcher are both moving toward the base, the pitcher should have priority over the first baseman due to the fact that he will have a much better angle into first base. However, if the first baseman can return to the bag in plenty of time, he must call the pitcher off by yelling "I've got it". This communication would also be used by the pitcher if he sees that he and the first baseman are both moving toward first base for the throw by the shortstop. Once the ball is released by the first baseman to the shortstop, he must concern himself in getting back to first base as quickly as possible. In most cases, this will necessitate his running to first base with his back to second base. Once he gets to the base, he would then turn and face second base, and ready himself to catch the throw from the shortstop for the attempted double play. The first baseman can not afford to be back peddling toward first base as this would slow down his quickness to the base, along with making it very difficult for him to find the base with his feet to make the catch and touch the bag at the same time. There is no reason why a first baseman would have to run a great distance to return to first base since the pitcher would be covering the bag. This is why it is so important that a first baseman does not start moving toward first base as he is releasing the ball to the shortstop. His first obligation after fielding the ground ball is getting off a good throw to the shortstop.

13. **First basemen play around the bag**—One of the primary responsibilities of the first baseman is to receive throws from the infielders, the pitcher and the catcher. Not only must he be responsible for fielding the throw, but he also must be responsible for making contact with the bag so that the batter-runner can be retired. There are basic fundamentals that must be mastered by the first baseman in his basic footwork around the bag so that he can be in a proper position to make the catch and touch the bag.

A. **Setting up at the base**—It certainly stands to reason that the quicker the first baseman can get to first base, the more time he will have to set himself to catch the ball and make the tag of the base. There will be times that the first baseman is required to position himself well away from first base in order to properly defense the batter. When well away from first base, he will have to sprint to the base in order to provide himself enough time to turn, face the thrower, and react to any possible throw that might be heading toward his position at the base. Once he arrives at the base, he must quickly turn and face in the direction of the throw. Once he has found the base, he should place his heels about three inches away from the base itself, with both toes pointing in the direction of the throw. His feet should be base width apart so that he can move to either his right or left quickly, or jump in the air to attempt to catch a throw that might be above his head. At no time can he afford to stretch for the throw until the ball is in the air. If he stretches before he can properly read the flight of the ball, it will severely restrict his mobility in moving to both his right and left. It would also cause him to have a most difficult time catching the ball that is thrown above his head since his stretch will prohibit him from jumping up to glove the ball. If the throw is coming from an area near the first baseline, he will have to position himself either inside or outside of the base informing the thrower of the ball this fact by the command of either "inside" or "outside".

B. **Receiving throws**—The first baseman should learn all he possibly can about the fielders who will be throwing balls to first base in game situations. This will certainly be helpful to him as he sets up at the base and reacts to the throw. Information he should be aware of would involve: whether the fielder has a strong or weak arm; whether the fielder's throws have a tendency to take off or sink; how his throws react when the fielder has to throw the ball to first base off-balance; and the fielder's accuracy on his throws. If at all possible, every throw to first base should be caught with two hands out in front of the body. There will be times that this will not be possible due to the fact that the first baseman might have to stretch to catch the ball. The first baseman must follow the ball with his eyes directly into the glove so that there is little chance that the ball is misplayed. Following the ball with his eyes into his glove is especially important on the balls fielded near the ground. The first baseman must keep the palm of the glove up on all throws below the waist, and the palm of the glove down on all throws fielded above the waist. Throws in the dirt should be fielded as close as possible to the point of contact with the ground. This might necessitate his going out to the ball on the stretch in order to field the ball in the dirt on the short hop. If the ball in the dirt can not be fielded on the short hop, the first baseman must attempt to block the ball with his body or glove. This is especially important if there is a runner or runners on base who would score if the ball was to get past the first baseman. On all tough plays on balls in the dirt, the first baseman must start his glove on the ground, and then work up to insure that the ball does not get under the glove. He can not afford to slap at the ball in the dirt with his glove, since this would make it that much more difficult to catch the ball cleanly. After stretching for the ball in the dirt, he must expose the pocket of the glove to the ball. On contact with the ball, he should give slightly with the glove in toward the body, making sure that any movement toward the body does not take place until the ball has entered the glove. Otherwise, the first baseman will not allow the ball to enter the glove properly. If the first baseman must jump in the air to catch a high throw, he can use the bag to his advantage by springing off the bag. This could only be done if the first baseman can detect the high throw quick enough, since his heels will be a few inches in front of the base in his basic positioning. He should try to come down on the infield side of the base so that the runner has the center and back of the base to run through. Balls thrown to the inside or outside of the base may require the first baseman to leave the base. His primary responsibility is to catch the ball, and then if time allows, to attempt the tag on the runner or return to the base for the touch. If the throw takes him to the inside of first base (home plate side), he can attempt to tag the runner coming down the line after the catch. This will be a sweep tag using just the glove to make the tag. If time allows, the first baseman should tag the runner with both hands.

C. **Footwork for the force out**—Proper footwork is essential for successful first base play in getting the force out. Of course, the footwork is different for the righthanded and lefthanded first baseman. As mentioned previously, the first baseman must first line himself up directly facing the fielder of the ball so that he can react to any type of throw that might be made to first base. Throws directly at the base for the righthanded first baseman should cause him to tag the second base side of first base with his right foot, stretching to the ball with his left foot (glove side foot). The same would be true for the lefthanded first baseman, except that he would touch the base with his left foot, and stretch to the ball with his right foot (glove side foot). For balls thrown to the right or left of first base, the first baseman should just shift his tag foot to either the outside or inside of the base as he stretches for the ball. Some first baseman have quick enough feet and good instincts that allow them to shift for a ball thrown to their non-glove side by shifting their glove side foot to the corner of the base closest to the ball, and then stretching out with their non-glove side foot. For example, a righthanded first baseman sees the ball is coming toward the base on the right field side. Instead of touching the base with his right foot, he would shift his feet in order to touch the right field side of the base with his left foot, and stretch out to the ball with his right foot. This is done so that he does not have to backhand the ball. Since the first baseman can reach out further for the ball using the cross-over step and he does not have to change his footwork on the base, it is preferred that he use the cross-over step and backhand the ball. If he reads a low throw in the dirt to his non-glove side, then he could shift his feet so that his glove foot is on the base in order to keep his body in front of the ball. On a throw from the home plate area, the first baseman should place his left foot on the second base side of the base and reach out for the ball with his right foot. If the throw will be coming from the foul line side of first base, he should step across the base into foul territory. He would then place his right foot on the foul line side of first base and stretch out for the ball with his left foot.

D. **Holding a baserunner at first base**—In the signal section of the Playbook, the various signs that might be used by the coach to the first baseman was discussed in regard to positioning on or near first base with a runner at first base. When the first baseman is holding a runner at first base while positioned on the base, he must not only position himself for a possible pick-off attempt by the pitcher, but must be able to move quickly to the inside of the base to prepare for a batted ball that might be hit in his direction. In holding a runner on, the first baseman should face the pitcher with his right foot along the home plate side of the base with the toes of his right foot even with the corner of the base. His left foot should be on or near the baseline so that his body is facing directly toward the pitcher. His glove should be extended out toward the pitcher at about waist height, with his throwing hand resting comfortably on the knee. He must be in a position that he can move equally well to both his right and left if the throw from the pitcher was thrown wide of the base. If the pitcher attempts to pick-off the runner at first base, the first baseman must catch the ball and then quickly drop the glove down to the second base side of first base. He can not afford to go after the runner who does not slide, since it might allow the runner to get back to first base under the tag. He should allow the runner to slide into his glove positioned in front of the base. The lefthanded first baseman has the decided advantage in making this tag at first base since his glove is on the side of the tag, making for a quicker tag than the righthanded first baseman can perform. If the runner coming back into the base feet first or head first slides to the right field side of first base to evade the tag, the first baseman needs to move his glove to that side of the base. He must always stay with the tag in this situation in hopes that the baserunner might come off the base after his initial contact with the base.

E. **Movement off the base after the pitch**—When the pitcher delivers the ball to the plate, the first baseman must quickly position himself inside the diamond to prepare to field a ball that is hit in his direction. If a lefthander has an exceptionally good move to first base, the first baseman will have to hold a little longer so that he is never moving inside the diamond when the pitcher attempts a pick-off at the base. The depth and distance that the first baseman assumes off the base will depend on the hitter and the situation in the game. The movement away from first base would be initiated with a cross-over step with the left foot. If more distance is needed away from the base, he would then shuffle step after the cross-over step. The first baseman must have his body completely under control as the ball reaches the hitter, with his weight on the balls of both feet. If the catcher attempts a pick-off at first base, the first baseman would quickly cross-over with his right foot back to the inside corner of first base. A shuffle step after the cross-over step should put him in position at the corner of the base to make the catch and tag. If the first baseman is playing behind the runner at first base, he can move in any direction after the ball is thrown to the plate. For example, if the first baseman is playing a little behind the runner at first base with a lefthanded pull hitter at the plate, he would want to take a couple of steps backward as the ball is delivered. Again, any movement by the first baseman while the ball if heading toward the plate must allow him to be completely under control once the ball reaches the plate.

F. **Feeds to the pitcher at first base**—The coach needs to stress to his first basemen that they do not have to look "pretty" many times fielding ground balls. Their main responsibility is to knock the ball down and keep the ball in front of them so that they can still get the out at first base via the pitcher covering the base. Once the task of fielding the ground ball has been achieved, the first baseman must then make the decision as to whether he will get the out himself, or use the pitcher moving toward first base. Whenever possible, the first baseman must make the play himself to eliminate the chance of a misplay on the feed to the pitcher. If the pitcher will be needed in order to get the out, the first baseman must concern himself with giving the pitcher the proper feed. The feed must allow the pitcher to catch the ball two to three steps from first base so that the pitcher can catch the ball on the run, and then concentrate his attention on touching first base. This is not always possible when the first baseman boots the ball, or fields a slow ground ball, or has to range wide to his left or right to make the play on the ground ball. Whenever throwing the ball to the pitcher covering first base, the first baseman must attempt to give him the ball at shoulder height. This will make for a much easier catch for the pitcher covering the base than if the ball was thrown lower than his shoulders. Anytime the first baseman fields the ground ball near the base and can not make the play on the batter-runner himself, he will have to underhand flip the ball to the pitcher covering. The righthanded first baseman should step with the left foot when making this underhand flip, and the left-handed first baseman should step with his right foot. He must also concern himself with making sure that he drops the glove as he underhand flips so that the pitcher has a clear view of the ball as it leaves the first baseman's hand. If the first baseman is some distance away from first base when he fields the ball, he should then proceed with a normal throwing motion. He must be sure that he allows the pitcher a clear view of the ball as it leaves his hand, so any sidearm or three-quarter action of the throwing arm should be discouraged.

All other responsibilities of the first baseman have been discussed in other areas of the Playbook.

407

OUTFIELD PLAY

In many baseball programs, at all levels of competition, the most neglected area of coaching is working with the outfielders in better refining their skills. Many times a coach will place a young man in the outfield without adequately preparing him to cope with all the fundamentals of outfield play, and all the situations that he might be confronted with as an outfielder. It is not only important that an outfielder be made aware of all the basic mechanics necessary to play the outfield, but that he fully understands the means and methods available to take advantage of his own individual strengths and weaknesses.

PLACEMENT OF THE OUTFIELDERS

The following guidelines should be used by the coach in placing his outfield candidates at their respective positions:

1. **Left fielder**—The left fielder should preferably be a right-handed thrower so that he can better cover and release the ball that is hit down the left field line. A lefthanded left fielder will have a difficult time holding a runner to a single on any ball hit down the line. However, this is not the most important concern in placing an outfielder in left field. Since the left fielder will only have one long throw to make (to the plate), the left fielder should be the fielder with the weakest arm. Due to the fact that the majority of hitters are righthanded, he will have less problems on balls that slice away from him than the right fielder. Thus, the weakest of the three outfielders should be placed in left field.

2. **Center fielder**—The center fielder should be the quickest outfielder due to the fact that he will have more area of the outfield to cover than either the left fielder or right fielder. He must be the most instinctive outfielder in reacting to the batted ball, along with being the most aggressive one of the outfielders. With the numerous back up responsibilities he will have, along with patrolling the largest area of the outfield, the center fielder should be the team's all around best defensive outfielder. A team can sacrifice a little offensive production when they can place a young man in center field who can run the ball down. A coach can sacrifice a powerful arm for an accurate one in his center fielder, but he can never sacrifice speed and the ability to get the jump on the ball.

3. **Right fielder**—The right fielder should preferably be a left-handed thrower so that he can better cover and release the ball that is hit down the right field line. However, the strength of his throwing arm has got to be the most important consideration in placing a young man in right field. Since he will have two long throws to make (third base and the plate), it necessitates having the outfielder with the strongest throwing arm in right field. The right fielder should be an experienced outfielder due to the nature of the balls hit to his position, mainly the line drives hit by righthanded hitters that will have a tendency to slice toward the right field line. Being that right field is the sun field in most baseball parks, the right fielder must have the ability to handle the obstacle that the sun might present in fielding a fly ball.

BASIC OUTFIELD POSITIONING

1. **Ability of the adjacent outfielder(s)**—There is no reason for outfielders to position themselves an equal distance apart from each other when they all have various strengths and weaknesses in regard to going after a ball hit in the outfield. For example, the center fielder should always shade toward the side of the slower outfielder. Another example would be the case where the center fielder has great speed, which would allow the left fielder and right fielder to shade a little closer to their respective foul line.

2. **Wind factor**—When the wind is going to be a factor affecting the flight path of the ball, the outfielders must shade a few steps in the direction of the wind as they position themselves for each hitter. The distance away from their normal position would be affected by the intensity of the wind. It also must be understood that the baseball will carry farther in light dry air, and carry less in heavy damp air.

3. **Position of the fences**—The distance of the outfield fence should play a big part in the basic positioning of the outfielders for each hitter. The closer the fence, the shallower the outfielder can play. The farther the fence, the deeper the outfielder must play. The same holds true to a lesser degree in regard to the fence distance away from the foul line. If the fence is very close to the foul line it will enable the right fielder or left fielder to play a few steps further away from the line then if the fence was quite a distance away from the line.

4. **Speed of the infielders**—If the infielder in front of the outfielder has great speed, and can go back extremely well on a fly ball, this will enable the outfielder to position himself a few steps deeper. Likewise, if the infielder in front of the outfielder

has poor speed, and has proven that he has a difficult time going back on fly balls, the outfielder would have to position himself a few steps shallower.

5. **Pitcher's ability**—If the pitcher on the mound is a power pitcher with an excellent fast ball, it will usually cause batters to hit the ball late. If he is a breaking ball pitcher with very little velocity on his fast ball, the tendency would be for most hitters to pull his pitches. If a pitcher is wild, it is best to shade all hitters a little deeper, especially if the pitcher is wild high. If a pitcher is tiring late in a game, it is best that the outfielders shade a little deeper.

6. **Batter's ability**—Each outfielder must quickly assess each individual batter's hitting ability in order to properly position himself for that particular batter. The coaches can assist the outfielders in evaluating the opposing hitters by watching them hit in batting practice or through the use of scouting cards which chart each ball hit in previous games. Any positioning in the outfield acknowledges the batter's strength areas and where he is most likely to hit the ball hard.

7. **The count on the batter**—In a previous section of the Playbook, defensive movement with the count was detailed for the outfielders. Movement with the count for the outfielders must be standard for all three fielders so that gaps are not created in the outfield when only one or two outfielders move with the count.

8. **Runners on base**—Before each pitch, the outfielders must know how many men are on base, where they are, how fast they are, and what effect will be on the status of the game if they score. The batter-runner would also be considered as a baserunner. This information would better allow the outfielder to make the proper throw, anticipate steals, pick-off plays and bunts.

9. **The inning and the score**—Each outfielder must discipline himself to continually know the inning, the score, and late in the game what runner(s) represent the tying or winning runs. This information will often dictate how deep the outfield must play.

10. **The number of outs**—Since most hitters will go after the long ball with two outs and no runners on base, the outfield should shade a little deeper in this situation. With two outs and a runner at first base, the outfield should shade a little deeper to get better angles on balls down the line or in the gap to prevent the runner at first base from scoring. Runners will run differently according to the number of outs, and this needs to be taken into consideration also. Thus, the number of outs will help dictate depth in the outfield.

11. **Outfielder's own ability**—This is one of the primary concerns when an outfielder positions himself in the outfield. His arm strength, ability to go left and right, ability to come in on the ball, ability to go back on the ball, are all taken into consideration by the outfielder in deciding where to position the hitter at the plate.

READY POSITION

Between pitches is the time when the outfielders must do their mental homework so that they are better able to anticipate all situations that they may be confronted with if they were to field the ball in the outfield. The following are the basic mechanics for the outfielder in preparing himself to react to the batted ball:

1. **Pitcher in the windup or set**—As the pitcher starts his windup, or has reached the set position in the stretch delivery, the outfielder must assume a relaxed ready position. A proper ready position would be a well balanced stance that will allow the outfielder to move forward, backward, and laterally with the quickest possible acceleration. The feet should be spread about shoulder width apart with the toes parallel to each other. Since it is practically impossible to accelerate quickly off a stiff leg, it is very important that the outfielder's knees be moderately bent. The upper body is bent in a semi-crouch, with the entire body as loose as possible. It is most important that the outfielder be loose and free of tension in the ready position, for the more tension there is in the body, the slower the start will be to the ball. Many outfielders like to place their hands on their knees as they await the ball to reach the plate, so that they are in a relaxed position with the entire body. Other outfielders feel like they can relax better and get a quicker jump on the ball with their arms dangling from the side as the pitcher gets ready to deliver the ball to the plate.

2. **Pitcher releases the ball**—As the pitch is made, the outfielder must rock forward onto the balls of his feet. This will enable the outfielder to get a much better jump on the ball then if he was flat footed at the time the ball reached the hitter. Even though the outfielder is a long way from the plate, he should be able to see what type of pitch has been thrown. If the outfielder has his hands on his knees as the pitcher delivers the ball to the plate, he will need to drop his hands as the ball reaches the batter. This will force his weight to be over the balls of his feet.

MOVEMENT TO THE BALL

From the ready position, the outfielder must be able to react to the ball the instant it leaves the hitter's bat. This is very difficult to teach, although with much practice and concentration an outfielder can improve his ability to react properly to the batted ball. A fungoed baseball is no substitute for a batted ball in improving the effectiveness of an outfielder in getting a jump on the ball. This is why it is so important in batting practice sessions for each outfielder to work for 10-15 minutes in the outfield reacting to the batted ball as in a game situation. After a few minutes rest, he can give it another good 10-15 minutes of concentrated effort. It is also very important that the outfielder pretend that the hitter at the plate in an actual game has a fungo bat, and is hitting every ball that is pitched in his direction in the outfield. In this way he is never shocked to find that a ball has been hit to him which should improve his reaction time considerably. The following are basic fundamentals for moving to the ball in the outfield:

1. **Eliminating the false step**—Many experienced outfielders are adept at moving from the ready position before the ball arrives at the plate. This is especially true for the center fielder since he can better follow the pitch to the plate, moreso than the left fielder and right fielder. Balls hit to the right or left of the outfielder are much easier to pick up and get a jump on since the angle of the ball off the bat provides the outfielder with a clear sight line on the ball. The line drives and balls hit right at the outfielder are the toughest to get a jump on because the outfielder does not have a side view of the ball. A line drive may sink, rise, or sail and it is very difficult to tell how hard the ball is hit initially off the bat. Since the outfielder can not afford to take a false step backward or forward, he must wait a split second before moving to the ball until he has a good "read" on the ball. This is why the outfielder must be a good concentrator, so that he can hold his ground until he knows exactly the route he must take to the ball. With the use of aluminum bats at all levels of amateur baseball, it is practically impossible for the outfielder to get a good "read" on the ball by the sound that the bat makes when contact with the ball has occured. Thus, anytime an outfielder is in doubt on the status of the ball, he must hold his ground until he can pick up the flight path of the ball.

2. **Initial step toward the ball**—As in all athletic skills requiring quickness, the initial step toward the ball is all important for the outfielder in achieving quickness to the ball. The outfielder must be in a relaxed position with his entire body as the ball leaves the hitter's bat. If his body is under any degree of tension, it will seriously affect his quickness in his initial movement to the ball. The first step must be a hard driving step if the ball requires the outfielder to exercise quickness to the ball. On any ball hit to the left or right of the outfielder, it will necessitate an explosive cross-over step. On balls hit to his left, he must make his first step crossing over with his right foot while pivoting and driving off his left foot. On balls hit to his right, the outfielder must make his first step crossing over with the left foot while pivoting and pushing off his right foot. On the cross-over step, the outfielder must keep his body low, raising up gradually as he accelerates toward the ball. The first steps must be hard driving steps accompanied by vigorous arm action. On balls hit over the head of the outfielder, he must pivot on both feet in the direction of the turn. He must drop back with the foot nearest the ball at the angle he wishes to travel in pursuit of the ball. If the ball is hit directly over his head, the outfielder should turn glove side on the ball. This would make for an easier catch for the outfielder since he will be able to catch the ball on his glove side. If he turns to the non-glove side on the ball hit directly over his head, it would necessitate his having to reach across his body to glove the ball making for a very difficult type of catch.

3. **Movement to the ball**—Whenever possible, the outfielder must position himself as quickly as possible where the fly ball will land, or where he can field the ground ball at the best possible angle to where the throw will be made in the infield. This means that the outfielder must practice sound running fundamentals as he sprints to the ball. The basic running fundamentals that were presented in an earlier section of the Playbook would certainly apply to the outfielder moving toward the ball. Getting to the fly ball or ground ball as quickly as possible has obvious benefits: (1) it is the key to cutting down a runner(s) opportunity to take the extra base; (2) allows the outfielder to get into proper throwing position; (3) helps eliminate communication problems between other fielders in the area of the ball; and (4) provides the outfielder the chance to make the tough play. The outfielder must also take good angles on fly balls or ground balls so that he can cut the ball off at the best possible angle. Many times we see an outfielder cutting the angle too sharply on a ball only to see the ball get by him due to the improper angle. As the outfielder moves to the ball he must take into consideration: wind conditions; sun factor; his speed; quickness of the grass (ground ball); and the movement of the ball in flight.

CATCHING FLY BALLS AND LINE DRIVES

One of the keys to successful outfield play is the ability of the outfielder to not only get to a fly ball or line drive quickly, but to make the catch positioned properly to make a strong and accurate throw to a base or the plate. A lazy outfielder with good speed can be a detriment to the outfield defense due to the fact that he will often take poor angles on balls, or is guilty of drifting on balls hit in his direction. The following are the basic fundamentals for catching various types of fly balls and line drives:

410

1. **Catching the routine fly ball**—An outfielder should attempt to catch every fly ball with two hands, unless it becomes necessary to catch the ball with one hand due to the nature of the catch. Using two hands will insure a better chance of making the catch, and will also enable the outfielder to have his throwing hand on the ball just after the catch is made. On routine fly balls, the outfielder should catch the ball a little above his eyes with both arms away from his body for free movement of the arms and hands. His hands should be relaxed and should give slightly to soften the impact as the ball enters the glove. He should look the ball into the glove no matter how routine the catch might appear to be. He can never afford to be looking into the infield as the ball approaches his glove. The ball should be caught with the fingers up when he is catching the ball at chest high or higher. On balls caught from the waist down, the fingers should be down. Basket type of catches should be avoided because this type of catch has obvious fielding and throwing deficiencies.

2. **Catching line drives**—Balls hit hard down the lines are usually much tougher to field than those hit to center field due to the fact that they will break more sharply in flight. The left fielder and right fielder must be aware that a pulled line drive down the line can break toward the line just as opposite field line drives do. The line drive hit right at the outfielder are very tough to "read" off the bat, so the outfielder must hold his ground before making any move back or forward on the ball. The outfielder must guard against breaking toward a line drive in front of him without being absolutely sure of his angle and approach to the ball. A line drive that gets by an outfielder will easily roll all the way to the fence, and does not allow time for adjacent outfielders to back up the play. The experienced outfielder knows when he can afford to gamble on catching the line drive, or when he must play conservative making sure that the ball does not get by him.

3. **Shoestring catches**—If the outfielder is moving forward on a low line drive, he will have two alternatives: (1) he can hold up and catch the ball on a long hop; or (2) he can continue running full speed forward for a possible shoestring catch. If he decides to go for the ball in the air, he must lower his body as he comes in for the ball to get his eyes as much in line with the ball as possible. This will also allow his glove to get down to the level of the ball. If he decides to hold up on the ball, he must quickly shorten his steps, and try to get his body under complete control. He must get his glove down in front of the ball, and if he has to, knock the ball down with his body. If the outfielder must leave his feet for the attempt on the sinking line drive, he should use a bent leg slide to assist in keeping the ball in front of him. Whenever catching a sinking line drive it is important that the outfielder reach slightly for the ball, whether fielding it on the dive or slide, or when attempting to field the ball while keeping his feet. If he does dive for the ball while extending his body, he must catch the ball and then roll so that there is less chance for an injury. In addition, the roll will have less of a jarring affect on the glove in hopes that the outfielder will be able to maintain control of the ball. Most dive plays occur on short fly balls in front of the outfielder. These dives should be encouraged on these types of fly balls since they will not go very far behind the outfielder if the ball is uncatchable. Many times low line drives or short fly balls take unusual bounces due to the spin on the ball. An outfielder must always approach balls that fall in front of him cautiously so that the ball can not skip or hop away from him.

4. **Catching balls hit over the head**—To be a good outfielder, a young man must be able to go back on a fly ball. He must be able to do this with quickness, and when he gets his glove on the ball, he must be able to make the catch practically every time. The shallower an outfielder can play, the better he will help the team's defense. If he is unable to go back well on balls hit over his head, he will have to shade practically every batter deep allowing balls to drop in front of him for base hits. The experienced outfielder can turn his back on balls hit over his head, checking on the flight path of the ball with one or two quick glances over his shoulder. Inexperienced outfielders must watch the ball during the entire flight path due to the fact that they do not have the ability or experience to pick up the ball in flight after taking their eyes off the ball. One can certainly run quicker when not having to look over the shoulder constantly for the ball. Of course, if the ball is hit deep to the right or left of the fielder, he should be able to run to the ball without losing sight of the ball. With constant practice and game experience, an outfielder should be able to turn his back completely on the ball hit directly over his head once he knows exactly the direction his path must be to the ball. The ball hit quite high in the air over the outfielders head should prove no major problem in turning his back to the infield after picking up the flight path of the ball. Of course, if the ball is more of a line drive over the outfielder's head, he will have to maintain eye contact with the ball as he turns and races for the ball. The outfielder must make every attempt to keep his body on the side of the ball that will allow him to catch the ball without having to attempt a backhand catch. This is why it is so important for an outfielder to turn to his glove side on any ball hit directly over his head. If the outfielder finds that he has turned the wrong way as he is running toward the ball, or the ball starts hooking or slicing on him, he will have to make the proper adjustment as he continues running to the area where he suspects the ball will land. He should execute this turn with his back to the infield by turning from glove side to throwing side, or vice-versa. This means that for a split second he will lose sight of the ball. This should present no problem as long as the ball is not coming down near the outfielder at the time of the adjustment turn. The outfielder should never turn on the ball that is still high in the air by turning so that the front of his body faces toward the infield. This is acceptable if the ball is coming down in the area of the outfielder and he can not afford to lose sight of the ball. If he turns on the ball with his front side facing the infield, with still some distance involved for him to get to the area where the ball will be landing, it will cause him to backpeddle on the ball. Backpeddling is the slowest way to move toward a ball hit over the outfielder's head. It also causes serious body balance problems, forcing many times the outfielder

to make the catch on his heels. Whenever possible, the outfielder must get a few steps behind where the ball will land so that he can come forward to catch the ball. Catching the ball while rocking back on his heels is not practicing good outfield mechanics. It is also very important that the outfielder attempt to square up his body with the ball that he has had to go back on, if at all possible. This will make for a much easier catch, along with providing him with the opportunity to move into the ball and get off a strong and accurate throw to his target. If the outfielder is on the run for the ball hit over his head in any direction, he must attempt to make the catch with two hands if possible. He also must concern himself with making sure that the glove is well away from the body when the ball makes contact with the glove. It makes for a very difficult catch when an outfielder runs to the ball only to find that the ball is coming down very close to his body. The play must be timed so that he will have to reach out slightly for the ball, so that he can see the ball as it enters the glove.

FLY BALL COMMUNICATION

In a previous section of the Playbook a detailed presentation of a communication and priority system for fly balls was presented. Thus, there is no need to repeat this information in this section on outfield play, but there are a couple of points not mentioned in that section that pertains specifically for outfielders.

1. **Inside-outside routes**—If all three outfielders use the proper communication and priority system there should be no problem in regard to who will be attempting the catch of the fly ball or line drive in most cases. Proper communication can prevent the frightening defensive collisions that sometimes occur in baseball games. The primary collision area is in the gaps where the center fielder and one of the wing outfielders are both going aggressively for a fly ball or line drive in the gap. Of course, the center fielder has priority over the left fielder or right fielder if both were to call for the ball in right center field or left center field. In order to build confidence and aggressiveness in the outfielders as they sprint to the ball, it is important that an inside-outside route be run so that there is no chance for a collision between the two outfielders as they both make an attempt to catch the ball. The center fielder should always take the inside route on all balls hit in the gap when either the left fielder or right fielder are moving toward the ball also. This means that the center fielder would be fielding the ball low (below the waist). The left fielder or right fielder should take the outside route when converging with the center fielder. This means that he will be fielding the ball high (shoulder or above). This inside-outside route would produce a gap between the two outfielders that would enable both of them to make the catch until one of them might call for the ball at the last second. The distance between the two outfielders would depend on the trajectory of the ball in flight. This inside-outside routine can be worked on in the fundamental drill series previously presented in an earlier section of the Playbook.

2. **Moving toward the infield on short fly balls**—It is important that the outfielder be aggressive as he moves toward the infield to make a possible play on a fly ball in front on him. He must attempt to catch any ball that an infielder in front of him is not positioned under and calling for the ball. This is especially true with a runner or runners tagging up and possibly advancing if the infielder catches the ball while moving away from the infield. The outfielder should always stay on his feet whenever possible in catching the ball in front of him since the infielder should hit the ground if a collision might occur. This would prevent any head on collision between the two fielders. If the outfielder must leave his feet to catch the ball, he must be sure that the infielder is not in the area where he will be diving. The aggressive outfielder can make an infielder's job much easier in going back on fly balls so that the infielder does not have to make the over-the-head catch on the ball. The outfielder can not afford to call for the ball until he is sure he can make the catch, for when he does call for the ball, the infielder will give ground to allow him the chance to make the catch.

PLAYING THE SUN

The majority of baseball fields are laid out with the sun facing the right fielder in the late afternoon. Occasionally the left fielder or center fielder will have to battle the sun also. All outfielders must get used to wearing flip down sunglasses in practice sessions so that they do not have to learn how to use them when an actual game is played. The sunglasses should not be flipped down until the flight path of the ball has been ascertained by the outfielder. Once he acknowledges the fact that the sun will be a problem and he knows the flight path of the ball, he can quickly flip the glasses down to eliminate much of the glare from the sun. Even if sunglasses are used, the bare hand or glove hand might be needed to shade the sun on extremely bright days. If sunglasses are not used, then either hand will have to be used to shade the sun or else there is a good chance the ball will be misplayed if it was to pass anywhere close to the sun in its downward flight. The outfielder should shade the sun with the hand on the side the sun is on. The glove hand is better suited for shading the sun due to the size of the glove, so this hand should be used whenever possible. If the bare hand is being used to shade the sun, the hand must be held close to the eyes in order to properly screen out much of the sun's glare. If the sun is low, the outfielder may have to shade his eyes from the moment the pitcher delivers the ball to the batter. On high fly balls that pass through the sun while still well away from the outfielder, his vision can be temporarily impaired when he follows the ball through the sun. If so, the outfielder should cast his eyes down briefly, to restore his vision. He can then pick up the ball in its downward flight. Another procedure used by experienced outfielders in battling the sun on fly balls and line drives is to position himself as he awaits the ball so that he is not looking directly into the sun. Thus, he would angle his body away from the sun as he follows the ball into his glove. Anytime an outfielder has lost sight of the ball due to the sun, he must immediately yell out "I can't see it". This will allow another outfielder or an infielder to continue moving to the area where the ball will land to make the possible catch. Outfielders must concentrate extra hard when battling the sun on a line drive or fly ball, but they should treat this situation as a challenge to make a tough catch.

PLAYING THE FENCES

When playing fly balls near the fences in the outfield or in foul territory, the outfielder's main responsibility is to race to the fence as fast as possible. This will eliminate his moving back toward the outfield fence on a high fly ball, and then having to backpeddle the last few steps while not sure when he will hit the fence. This backpeddling will cause many balls to be misplayed, and sometimes the ball will be actually caught by the outfielder to only be dropped when he hits the fence with his back. If he races to the fence on these high fly balls, he can then concentrate all his attention on catching the ball without fearing a collision with the fence during or after the catch. If the ball is hit extremely hard, the outfielder will not have enough time to reach the fence first. In this case, he should attempt to catch the ball while running sideways so that he will at least hit the fence with the side of his body, and not head first. This is especially important when playing on a field that might have a concrete wall for the outfield barrier. Many baseball fields have a warning track so that when the outfielder runs from the grass onto the warning track he will know how far away he is from the fence. The outfielder should always know how the ball will rebound from the fence or wall, so that if a ball can not be caught, he can then turn on the ball and ready himself for the expected rebound. The back up outfielder should also be in a position to assist the outfielder if the ball was to rebound off the fence past him onto the grass. If the outfielder is at the fence or wall and he will have to jump for the ball, he should turn his body sideways. He can jump much higher in this position than if he was to attempt to jump for the ball with his back to the fence or the wall. If possible, he should jump sideways in such a way that his bare hand is facing the barrier so that he might use his bare hand to brace himself as he jumps up and his body hits the fence or wall. Fielding a fly ball at the fence in foul territory will necessitate the same basic mechanics as when the outfielder is approaching the fence or wall behind him. He must get to the fence as fast as possible, and then work away from the fence to catch the ball. Any time a foul ball is hit to an outfielder in foul territory with a crucial run on third base with less than two outs, he must allow the ball to hit the ground if he has little chance of throwing the runner out at the plate after the catch. In most situations, a crucial run would be the tying or winning run in the last two innings of a game. If there is doubt in the outfielder's mind that the ball will drop in foul territory, he must always make the catch.

BACK UP RESPONSIBILITIES

In the situation section of the Playbook, the outfielder's positioning on various types of situations that may occur in a game were diagramed and discussed. The following would be some additional coaching points that need to be stressed to the outfielders in regard to their back up responsibilities:

1. An outfielder should know the back up responsibilities for all three outfield positions so that he will be ready to properly play each position if called upon in a game. Cutting down extra bases on defense wins baseball games, and it is important for outfielders to back up all thrown balls to bases, along with balls hit to the adjacent outfielder.

2. The outfielder must know all the bunt defense, pick-off, and double steal defense signs so that he is ready to move to his proper back up position as soon as the play develops. At no time can an outfielder be moving to a back up position until the ball passes the batter.

3. The outfielder must run to a point in line with the hit or thrown ball if possible, and then close the distance down. He can not afford to get too close in his back up positioning, so that he is unable to glove a ball that gets past the player he is backing up.

4. The outfielder can never assume a play will be made by another fielder no matter how easy of a play it appears to be. He must charge all ground balls hit to infielders until the play has been made. He must be alert for rebounds off other outfielders or off fences.

5. Outfielders must be prepared to break toward the infield to cover a base when a rundown play begins. If the bases are adequately covered, he must assume a back up position for any possible overthrow during the rundown.

FIELDING GROUND BALLS

The majority of errors made by outfielders occur on ground balls. This is the reason why it is so important that the coach spend adequate time working with his outfielders on the proper mechanics of fielding ground balls. The experienced outfielder will consistently charge all ground balls so that he can slow down, getting his body under control during the fielding stage. Like infielders, the outfielders must attempt to field all ground balls on the big hop or short hop, so that they do not get in-between hopped or allow the ball to play them. Taking proper angles on ground balls is just as important as taking good angles on fly balls and line drives so that the outfielder can keep the ground ball in front of him whenever possible. It would be advisable for the coach to require his outfielders to read all he can in regard to infield ground ball mechanics. He should also allow the outfielders the opportunity to field ground balls during batting practice sessions. There are various types of ground balls that need to be fielded taking into consideration: the speed and angle of the ball hit; the ability level of the outfielder; the position of the runner(s) on the bases; and the situation in the game.

1. **Blocking the ground ball**—The outfielder must block all hard hit ground balls so that there is little chance for the ball to get past him. If the hard hit ground ball gets past him, the back up outfielder will not be in a position to field the ball, unless the ball was hit in the gap between left center and right center field. It is most important to block the ground ball in the following situations: (1) there are no runners on base; (2) when playing on a rough outfield surface; (3) it is not a gambling situation; and (4) the throw after fielding the ball will not result in a possible putout. Since the aggressive batter-runner could attempt to stretch a single into a double when he observes an outfielder playing the ground ball conservatively, the outfielder must be sure that he is aggressive toward the ball. By being aggressive toward the ball, it will allow him more time to get set up to adequately block the ball. There are two basic ways that a hard hit ground ball can be blocked by the outfielder:

A. **Dropping to one knee**—As the hard hit ground ball nears the outfielder, he would drop to the knee on his throwing side. He would then attempt to field the ball with two hands, making sure the ball is fielded in front of the body. As soon as the ball is fielded, he would rise up to throw the ball into the infield.

B. **Heels together squat**—As the outfielder prepares himself to block the hard hit ground ball, he would squat with his heels together with his arms and hands between his knees. This is a preferred method over the one knee drop since the outfielder is in a much better position to block the ball with his body, and is also in a better position to come up throwing once the ball has been fielded.

2. **Fielding ground balls infield style**—The outfielder should field all ground balls infield style whenever a possible play might have to be made in the infield. If he sees that he is going to have to field a tough hop on a rough surface, he could always block the ball with the one knee drop or the heel together squat. Fielding the ground ball infield style basically revolves around the same basic mechanics used by infielders in fielding ground balls. Thus, we would refer the reader to the infield section of the Playbook for a complete review of these mechanics practiced by infielders. It is important that the outfielders understand that this style of fielding ground balls is only used when the ball is not hit that hard, and there is no baserunner attempting to advance to a forward base or the plate in a crucial situation in the game.

3. **The one-handed do-or-die pick-up**—This style of fielding ground balls should only be used by the outfielder in those situations when the winning run is in a position to score in the last two innings of a game, or when the defensive team is behind in the score in the late innings. Some outfielders are very proficient in this style of fielding ground balls that they can be encouraged to exercise this fielding technique at other times in the game. Good judgment by the outfielder must take into consideration: the quality of the outfield surface; the nature of the ground ball; the angle of his approach to the ball; the speed of the runner; and the probability of throwing the runner out. If in doubt about the ability to field the ball cleanly with the one-handed pick-up, the outfielder should field the ball infield style. There are numerous reasons why the one-handed do-or-die pick-up should not be used unless absolutely necessary:

A. There is a greater chance that the ball can get by the outfielder since the ball will be fielded slightly outside the body.

B. If the outfielder is too aggressive in his approach to the ball, he could easily be off-balance when he comes in contact with the ball increasing the chances of an error.

C. Due to the forward momentum of the outfielder's body in this method of fielding ground balls, it will take longer for him to recover and retrieve the ball if it gets past him.

414

D. Unless the outfielder practices good fielding and throwing mechanics, it is very difficult for him to get off a strong and accurate throw.

In this method of fielding ground balls, the ball is fielded slightly outside and in front of the foot on the glove side. Preferably, the ball is fielded just as the foot lands on the ground. Both knees must be bent as the ball is fielded to allow the upper part of the body to bend over allowing the glove to reach the ground with ease. The outfielder must be extremely aggressive to the ball so that he is able to slow down during the actual fielding stage, in order to glove the ball under some degree of control. The body must then be quickly adjusted to the throwing position. If the outfielder was to take several steps to get into throwing position, the advantage of the one-handed do-or-die method is wasted. The ball is fielded as the glove side foot lands, and then the outfielder should take a step toward the target with his throwing side foot. He would then crow-hop off the throwing side foot which should place his body in the proper position to get off his throw. If the ball has stopped on the grass, it is safer and quicker to bare hand the ball rather than attempting to pick it up with the glove. When bare handing the ball, it should be scooped up from underneath with the fingers to insure a better chance of picking the ball up cleanly.

4. **Fielding the ground ball in the gap or down the line**—The outfielder must always take into consideration the condition of the grass and playing field when breaking toward any ground ball so that he can take the proper angle on the ball. This is especially true for those balls hit in the gap or down the line. If the outfield grass is wet, the ball will generally stay low and will have a tendency to "take off" on the outfielder. If the grass is high, the ball will slow down quickly and the outfielder must get to the ball as fast as possible to prevent any baserunner from taking the extra base. If the outfield grass is cut short and the ground is hard, bouncing ground balls will have a tendency to pick up speed as they hit the ground. When two outfielders are in a position to field a ground ball in the gap, the outfielder in the best position to make a throw should field the ball. For example, if a righthanded center fielder and a righthanded right fielder both have a chance to field the ball in the right center field gap, the right fielder should field the ball since the ball would be fielded on his throwing side. Anytime an outfielder fields a ground ball in the gap or down the line and finds himself off balance when coming in contact with the ball, he should regain his balance before crow-hopping toward the intended target of his throw. The inside-outside route that is run by the outfielders on fly balls and line drives in the gap, should also be run on ground balls (center fielder takes the inside route and the left fielder or right fielder takes the outside route). If the ball happens to get by the outfielders and rolls to the fence or wall, the outfielder with the ball on his throwing side should field the ball, if possible. He must quickly get to the ball with his body under control, so that when he attempts to pick the ball up, he gets a firm grip on the ball the first time. Otherwise, he will have to go back down to try to pick the ball up again, which is valuable time lost. He should pick the ball up with his chest over the ball whenever possible. His body should be sideways in line with the relay man. Once the ball has been picked up, he should execute the crow-hop to initiate the proper momentum on his throw to the relay man. Anytime the outfielder's momentum when fielding the ground ball in the gap or down the line is taking him away from where the throw must be made, he must get himself under control before executing the throw. If he fields the ball on his throwing side, he would then gather himself and crow-hop step toward the target. If he fields the ball on his glove side, he would have to execute a glove side turn. After he turns toward his target, he would crow-hop in order to establish the proper momentum for a strong and accurate throw.

THROWING THE BALL

One of the prime prerequisites for being a fine outfielder is the ability to throw the ball with accuracy, power and quickness. It does little good for an outfielder to have a strong throwing arm only to have him throw wildly to his target practically every time a throw is made. It also does little good for the outfielder with a strong arm to have to take one or two additional steps to get off this strong throw. Thus, the experienced outfielder is one who can put his throwing all together so that he is getting the maximum out of his throwing ability. The following are the basic fundamentals for throwing the ball from the outfield:

1. **Positioning for the catch and throw**—An outfielder who constantly drifts on the ball will always be in poor position to get off a strong throw to his intended target. This is due to the fact that he will not have his body moving in the direction of the throw once the catch is made on either a fly ball or a ground ball. The experienced outfielder knows the direction to which the ball will be thrown prior to contact with the ball so that he can get his body going in that direction as he fields the ball. On fly balls, the outfielder should start behind the contact area and start forward under control in the direction of his throw. When this is properly done, it will prevent the outfielder from having to take additional steps after the catch to generate body momentum into the throw. On fly balls, the ball should be caught with two hands on his throwing side so there is no time wasted getting the ball to the throwing side once the ball has been caught. Generally, four to five steps before catching the ball is all that is necessary to get the proper momentum into the throw. The same holds true for the ground ball which must be thrown into the infield with quickness, accuracy and power. The outfielder needs to get to the place of contact with the ground

ball as fast as possible in order to position himself, not only to catch the ball, but to be in a position to get off the good throw to the infield area. All baseball coaches have seen young outfielders with exceptional arms catching a fly ball or ground ball and then having to take three to four steps to get rid of the ball. As a rule, for every step taken by the outfielder in releasing the ball that has been caught, the runner(s) is taking two steps.

   2. **Footwork and body mechanics during the catch and throw**—There are two basic methods of footwork that can be used by the outfielder in throwing the ball after making the catch of the fly ball, or after fielding the ground ball: (1) the crow-hop method; and (2) the jump step method.

      A. **The crow-hop method**—If properly done, the crow-hop method of throwing will enable the outfielder to generate momentum into his throw without taking any extra steps prior to releasing the ball. We will describe the crow-hop method for a righthanded outfielder. The footwork would of course be the same for the lefthanded outfielder.

         1. **Fly ball**—If the outfielder is under control as he moves into the fly ball, he would catch the ball as his pivot foot lands (right foot). His body should be squared up with the ball as he makes the catch slightly on the throwing side of his body. The right foot should land on the ground slightly out in front of his right shoulder with the toes of the right foot pointing outward at about a 30 degree angle from the direction of the throw. The right knee should bend slightly as the right foot lands on the ground and the ball enters the glove. As the outfielder begins the crow-hop step off his right foot, the stride leg (left leg) should pull him straight ahead and slightly off the ground. As the outfielder crow-hops off his right foot toward the target, the left side of his body should close in order to allow the outfielder to ''gather'' himself for the throw. This should bring the body to a good balanced throwing position, allowing the weight to get behind the throw itself. When the right foot lands on the crow-hop it is now the pivot foot for the actual throw. Thus, the right foot must be facing at about a 90 degree angle from the intended target when the crow-hop step is completed. The distance and height of the crow-hop step is an individual matter for the outfielder, taking into consideration the amount of momentum he has generated into the throw. The average height off the ground would be about three inches, and the average distance of the crow-hop to the target is about two to three feet. As the pivot foot lands on the crow-hop, the right knee should now be bent far enough that the outfielder can get a maximum push off his right leg. In the meantime, the stride leg swings around to stride directly toward the target so that his hips and shoulders end up facing the target. The stride leg must be bent at the knee as the throwing arm moves forward. The stride leg should act as a brake against the explosive drive off the right pivot leg. If the outfielder overstrides with his left foot, he will have poor balance, along with the tendency to rush with his body causing the throw to be high with little velocity. Poor balance and rushing will also cause the outfielder to drop his arm slot in order for the arm to catch up with his body. This is very similar to the problem a pitcher has when he rushes with his body in delivering the ball to the plate. In order to maximize throwing power, the outfielder should not open up his front side until the arm starts forward. The hips and shoulders should be close to parallel to the ground throughout the throw. The front hip and shoulder may be slightly above the back hip and shoulder as the pivot leg bends under the body weight. On balls caught to either side, where the outfielder can not get in position to throw properly, he must quickly get himself under control. Once under control, he should then crow-hop off his right foot in the direction of his throw. The same would hold true for balls caught over the outfielder's head. An outfielder can never afford to make a long throw flat footed no matter how off-balance he might be as he catches the ball. The extra step he would take in the crow-hop will provide the power and accuracy in the throw that he would not achieve if he threw the ball without benefit of the crow-hop step.

         2. **Ground ball**—The crow-hop method of throwing should be used no matter what type of style used in fielding the ground ball: (1) blocking; (2) infield style; or (3) one-handed do-or-die pick-up. In the blocking and infield style of fielding ground balls, the outfielder would take a step toward his target with his right foot (righthanded outfielder) after fielding the ball. He would then crow-hop off his right foot following the same basic mechanics as was described when crow-hopping after catching a fly ball. On the do-or-die pick-up, the outfielder should make every attempt to field the ball when his stride foot (left foot) lands. He would then step toward his target with his pivot foot (right foot), followed by the crow-hop step with his right foot. If he fields the do-or-die ball one-handed when his right foot hits the ground he will have to: take a step toward his target with his left foot; follow with a step with his right foot; and then crow-hop off his right foot as he prepares to release the ball. This extra step would have to be taken in order to allow the outfielder to get his body under control. It would be practically impossible for him to execute the crow-hop step without the benefit of the extra step if he fields the do-or-die ball initially off his right foot. Thus, it is very important that the outfielder attempt to field the ground ball when his stride foot (left foot) lands so he can eliminate having to take this extra step. If the outfielder does not have his body under some degree of control after fielding the ground ball in the do-or-die method, he will have a tendency to rush through the crow-hop. This could cause severe body balance problems in getting off a strong and accurate throw to the target.

B. **The jump step method**—Many outfielders use the jump step method of footwork in getting off throws that require a long distance. It is not advisable for an outfielder to throw with the crow-hop method along with the jump step method. He must make a decision as to which method he will use so that he can better refine his skills in that method. Otherwise, the outfielder might combine both methods in getting off the throw which can easily lead to extra steps and poor body balance. We will describe the jump step method for a righthanded outfielder.

1. **Fly ball**—If the outfielder is using the jump step method of footwork in throwing the ball after making the catch of the fly ball, he should attempt to catch the ball as his left foot (stride foot) hits the ground. If he fields the ball as his right foot (pivot foot) hits the ground, it will necessitate his taking an extra step in order to properly execute the jump step. Even though the outfielder will be catching the ball with his left foot forward, he still must catch the ball with two hands slightly on the throwing side of his body. His body should be squared up with the target of his throw, and his body momentum at the time of the catch should be moving toward the target. The left foot should land on the ground slightly out in front of his left shoulder with the toes pointing in the direction of the throw. The left knee should bend slightly as the left foot lands on the ground and the ball enters the glove. The outfielder would then jump towards the target off his stride foot (left foot) to continue forward momentum. The jump off the left foot should only be a few inches high, or just enough to get his body turned sideways to the target and getting his pivot foot (right foot) directly under his body. This will transfer all of the outfielder's weight directly over his right foot. The higher the ball is fielded, the lower the jump should be. If the outfielder happens to field the ball low, he will have to jump a little higher. As the outfielder jumps, the left side of his body should close in order for him to be able to open the left side as the throwing arm comes forward. If he does not close his left side on the jump, he will be throwing with just his arm without the benefit of the additional power which can be generated with the proper use of his body. When the right foot lands on the jump step, it now becomes the pivot foot. The pivot foot should land with the toes at about a 75 degree angle from a direct line with the target. This will further assist in getting the front side of the body closed to initiate proper body momentum toward the target as the throwing arm comes forward. The right knee should be bent far enough that the outfielder can get a maximum push off his right leg. In the meantime, the stride leg swings around to stride directly toward the target so that his hips and shoulders end up facing the target. The stride leg must be bent at the knee as the throwing arm comes forward. As was previously mentioned with the crow-hop method of throwing, the outfielder can not afford to overstride with his left foot. The basic mechanics of the throw in regard to the use of the hips and shoulders are identical with that mentioned in the crow-hop method. The outfielder can use the jump step method after fielding a fly ball or line drive that he catches going laterally or over his head. Once under control, he would just lead with his left foot, execute the jump step, and step toward his target with the stride foot (left foot).

2. **Ground ball**—As was the case with the crow-hop method of throwing, the jump step method can be used no matter what type of style is being used in fielding the ground ball. In the blocking and infield style of fielding ground balls, the outfielder would take a short step with the left foot toward the target followed by the jump to the right pivot foot. Some outfielders with strong throwing arms would not have to take the step with the left foot in the infield style of fielding ground balls. However, when a long throw is involved the outfielder would generally have to take this initial step forward with the left foot in order to initiate the proper body momentum. If no step with the left foot is made, the outfielder would just jump off both feet onto the right pivot foot after fielding the ground ball infield style. If fielding the ground ball with the right knee on the ground (blocking the ball), the outfielder would jump to the right foot off the left foot after the initial step forward by the left foot. When fielding the ball one-handed do-or-die style, the outfielder can execute the jump step method better if he fields the ball with the right foot forward. If fielding with the right foot forward, once the ball has been gloved, the outfielder would step toward the target with his left foot followed by the jump off the left foot to the right pivot foot. If he fields the ball with the left foot forward, the righthanded outfielder would have to take an extra step in executing the pivot. Once the left foot hits the ground and the ground ball is fielded, he would have to take a step with his right foot to regain his balance. He would then step with his left foot toward the target, executing the jump off the left foot to the right pivot foot. If the outfielder has his body under control during the fielding stage of the do-or-die play, he might be able to jump step off the left foot after fielding the ball without having to take the extra step with his right foot. However, in most do-or-die plays the outfielder's forward momentum is such that it would be very difficult to regain his balance quick enough to jump step off the left foot after fielding the ball. It will also make it very difficult for the outfielder to accomplish a full arm swing back to throwing position in such a short period of time.

3. **Gripping the ball**—As soon as the ball is fielded, the outfielder must quickly concern himself with getting a firm grip on the ball before the ball and throwing hand leave the glove. The ball should be gripped across the seams whenever possible. It should not be gripped too tightly since a tight grip will lock the wrist and cause loss of velocity and carry on the throw. The ball should be gripped out on the fingers so that it is not gripped too deeply in the hand. As the ball is released, the

417

index and middle finger should be directly on top of the ball. These two fingers must pull down as the wrist snaps forward in order to increase velocity and carry by effecting the backward spin on the ball. If the outfielder was to grip the ball along the seams, he will generally find that the ball will sail or slide on him which will take away from the ball's ability to achieve the necessary carry for the long throw required. The ball should leave the hand with a six-to-twelve rotation.

4. **Throwing motion**—The outfielder must have a long arm action out of the glove and through the throwing motion since most throws he will be required to make involve his achieving some degree of velocity. Accuracy is also an important aspect of the throw for the outfielder, and this can be achieved with concentration along with proper throwing mechanics. The throwing arm must be brought back out of the glove in a downward arc in order to achieve the long arm arc necessary to achieve velocity on the throw. The elbow should come back first followed by the forearm in one continuous motion. As the arm swings down and back, the body should still be closed preparing to open up as the arm starts forward. As the arm starts forward, the elbow should lead the way making sure that the elbow stays even or above the level of the throwing arm shoulder. This is to insure that the outfielder does not drop his arm during the throwing motion which would cause the ball to leave the hand at an improper angle. The elbow should lead in an explosive arm action, followed by the whipping forward of the forearm and wrist in a loose and relaxed manner. It is important that the arm action is straight toward the target. At the same time that the arm starts forward, the hips and upper body should open up quickly from the sideways position to a position facing the target. The outfielder must be sure that the glove side shoulder is pointing straight at the target as the throwing arm comes forward. If his hips and upper body open up before the arm starts forward, it would cause the outfielder to push the ball through the throwing motion rather than whipping the arm toward the target. The glove arm should assist the outfielder in getting on top of the ball by being pulled down and into the body as the front side opens up on the throw. The outfielder's head and eyes should be on the target throughout the throwing motion until the ball leaves his hand. The outfielder's throwing motion should be completed with a smooth follow through of the throwing arm so that the throwing arm ends up outside of the stride side knee.

5. **Throwing principles**—It does little good for an outfielder to have a strong and accurate arm if he does not consistently make the proper throws following sound throwing principles. The good outfielder will take into consideration all the factors he is confronted with as he decides on where to make the throw after he fields the ground ball or fly ball. This can only be done if he concentrates on what he will be doing with the different types of balls hit in his direction prior to the ball being delivered to the plate. He must consider that every ball pitched will be hit to him so that his thought patterns are already energized, and he is prepared to not only field the ball, but to make the proper throw once the ball has been fielded. There are numerous factors and principles that the outfielder must consider before making his throw, taking into primary consideration the strength and accuracy of his throwing arm:

A. **Throwing to a cut-off man**—The cut-off man can be the outfielder's best friend if he uses him properly. If his throw is such that the cut-off man can not properly catch the ball, then the outfielder has made a cardinal sin that can endanger the chance of retiring the lead runner along with allowing other runners on base to advance an additional base. The outfielder should aim all throws to the cut-off man's knees. In this way, if the ball is a little off the mark high, the cut-off man might still be able to make the catch. If the ball is a little low of the cut-off man's knees, he can still handle the ball. Any ball that sails over the cut-off man's head can prove disastrous for the defensive team. With concentration and proper mechanics there is never any reason for an outfielder to throw a ball over his cut-off man.

B. **Making short throws to second and third base**—Anytime there is a play to be made on a runner advancing to second or third base and the outfielder is fairly close to either base, he must attempt to throw the ball in the air to the player covering the respective base. The outfielder can not afford to short-hop or in-between hop the infielder attempting to catch the ball and make the tag on the runner attempting to advance. He should aim his throw directly over the base at waist height of the infielder.

C. **Making long throws to the bases or the plate**—Anytime the outfielder is called upon to make a long throw to a base or the plate, he should have a cut-off man to throw through. The outfielder should attempt on these long throws to have the ball bounce one time prior to reaching the infielder or the catcher at the respective base or the plate.

D. **Determining where to throw the ball**—The intelligent outfielder will take all factors into consideration before he releases the ball when he has various throwing options available to him once he fields the ground ball or fly ball. The following would be some of the basic principles involved in this decision, taking into consideration the strength and accuracy of his arm:

1. Late in the game, the outfielder must attempt to keep the tying or winning run off second and third base even

at the expense of **possibly** getting the out on the lead runner. This is especially true in keeping the batter-runner off second base with less than two outs. This will allow the defense to have a double play possibility.

2. When deciding on whether or not to try for the lead runner at the expense of another runner(s), the outfielder should gauge his success in regard to his making an average throw. Even the best outfielders do not make great throws all the time.

3. One of the main guides an outfielder should use in deciding on whether to go for the lead runner is where the baserunner is in relation to the base when the outfielder has control of the ball. If the outfielder fields the ball at medium depth in the outfield, he should be able to make a solid play on the lead runner in the following instances (taking always into consideration the runner's speed): On a runner attempting to score, if the outfielder fields the ball and the baserunner is two or more steps past third base, the outfielder should make no play on this runner unless he is the winning run late in the game. On a runner rounding second base, the outfielder would generally have a play at third base if the runner is four strides or less past second base when the outfielder fields the ball. It might be just two strides past the base for the right fielder depending on his arm, the situation in the game and the runner's speed.

4. Using the production rating system for grading the velocity of ground balls off the bat, the outfielder can determine his chances of retiring the lead runner. A complete discussion of the production rating system can be found in an earlier section of the Playbook. On a 6 type ground ball right at the outfielder, or just a few steps to his left or right, he should have a play on the lead runner. On a 5 type ground ball right at the outfielder, he should have a play on the lead runner if the ball is hit directly at him and he takes an aggressive approach to the ball. If the outfielder is charging the ball, he can take a look at the lead runner and still have time to readjust and throw the ball to second base. The more the 5 type ground ball takes the outfielder away from the direct line of his throw on the lead runner, the less chance for success in making the play. On a 4 type ground ball, there is generally no chance for a play on the lead runner unless the runner held up to make sure that the ball got through the infield (runner at second base with less than two outs and a ground ball is hit in front of him). These are all general rules that can only be applied while taking into consideration the total situation of the game, and the ability level of the outfielder and the runner(s).

5. The outfielder should never throw behind a runner unless the runner has stopped near the base the outfielder is throwing to, or he is returning to the base he last touched. An intelligent runner can easily deceive the outfielder into thinking that a play behind him has some chance for success. Once the ball leaves the outfielder's hand, the runner would then take off for the forward base or the plate which would necessitate two quick and accurate throws to retire him.

GAME ADMINISTRATION

Along with preparing his baseball team for competition, the baseball coach must also concern himself with various details and procedures in regard to the administration of the home games played on his field. Hopefully, he will have the availability of people on the athletic staff or faculty to assist him in handling these administrative areas. If not, he will have to secure the assistance of others in the community such as parents, booster club members, or fans of the program.

Some of the game administration responsibilities that need to be handled are: (1) paying the umpires; (2) pre-game field maintenance; (3) staffing of the concession stand; (4) staffing of the ticket sellers and ticket takers; (5) ball shaggers and bat handlers; (6) scoreboard operator; (7) official scorer; (8) public address announcer; (9) program sellers; and (9) flag tender.

One of the primary ingredients for a successful baseball program is the manner in which the organization and administration of the home games are handled. If a home game is administered properly, all the players, umpires, game workers and fans will enjoy the game that much more. This takes a lot of pre-season planning and work by the head coach so that when the season begins he can spend most of his time concentrating on the coaching of his team.

Later in the Playbook information pertaining to the following game administration areas are detailed: (1) public address announcer's responsibilities; (2) official scorer's responsibilities; (3) umpire coordination on game days; (4) manager's responsibilities; and (5) administration of a baseball tournament.

We will now deal with areas of game administration that the head baseball coach must be directly responsible for.

PRE-GAME SCHEDULE

Well in advance of the scheduled home game, the baseball coach should send to the head coach of the visiting team the pre-game practice schedule. This should provide the visiting team coach with all the information he will need in regard to the time schedule for batting practice and outfield-infield practice. On the next page is an example of the pre-game practice schedule for games starting at various times of the day and night.

NAME OF SCHOOL

PREGAME PRACTICE SCHEDULE

GAME TIMES

	1:00		1:30
Visitors Batting Practice	11:15-11:50		11:45-12:20
Home Batting Practice	11:50-12:25		12:20-12:55
Visitors Infield Drill	12:25-12:35		12:55- 1:05
Home Infield Drill	12:35-12:45		1:05- 1:15
Field Maintenance	12:45- 1:00		1:15- 1:30
National Anthem	1:00		1:30

	2:00	2:30	3:00
Visitors Batting Practice	12:15-12:50	12:45- 1:20	1:15- 1:50
Home Batting Practice	12:50- 1:25	1:20- 1:55	1:50- 2:25
Visitors Infield Drill	1:25- 1:35	1:55- 2:05	2:25- 2:35
Home Infield Drill	1:35- 1:45	2:05- 2:15	2:35- 2:45
Field Maintenance	1:45- 2:00	2:15- 2:30	2:45- 3:00
National Anthem	2:00	2:30	3:00

	6:00		7:30
Visitors Batting Practice	4:15- 4:50		5:45- 6:20
Home Batting Practice	4:50- 5:25		6:20- 6.55
Visitors Infield Drill	5:25- 5:35		6:55- 7:05
Home Infield Drill	5:35- 5:45		7:05- 7:15
Field Maintenance	5:45- 6:00		7:15- 7:30
National Anthem	6:00		7:30

Visitors may hit up to their designated time and will not be restricted to only thirty-five minutes unless field maintenance is needed prior to the visitor's batting practice time.

Both teams will hit on the main field.

Name of home team coach

Office phone number

Home phone number

It is recommended that music be played while both teams are taking batting practice and outfield-infield practice before the game. The music can be administered by the public address announcer or by one of the managers. The pre-game practice schedule should operate on a strict time schedule so that the field maintenance crew has at least 15 minutes to prepare the field for the game.

Once the home team has completed their batting practice, all the screens and cages need to be quickly removed from the field so that there is no delay in the visiting team taking their outfield-infield practice. A sample screen and cage crew sheet can be found on the next page. This sheet should be posted in the locker room and in the dugout so that every team member knows exactly what his responsibility is for the entire season.

After the home team has completed their outfield-infield practice, there should be about a 15 minute break for the following to get accomplished:

1. Field maintenance.

2. Paying of umpires if done at game site.

3. Pre-game running programs.

4. Starting pitchers getting warmed up in the bullpens.

5. Public address announcer giving the starting lineups.

6. Umpires, coaches and captains meeting at home plate to exchange lineup cards and go over the ground rules.

7. Introduction of the starting lineup by the public address announcer of the home team by defensive positions.

8. Playing of the national anthem.

1. **Field maintenance**—This is an area that causes great concern for many head coaches due to the fact that many times there are not enough maintenance people available to handle this important responsibility prior to the game. If that is the case, then the coach will have to rely on members of his team to take care of the field maintenance. They can be assisted by the managers and coaches. If the coach uses a corp of bat girls in his program, they may even be asked to assume this responsibility. The following is the basic field maintenance necessary prior to a game:

A. Dragging of the infield.

B. Raking of the baselines and areas around the bases.

C. Raking, tamping and watering the mound area.

D. Raking, tamping and watering the plate area.

E. Watering of the infield dirt if necessary due to dry conditions.

F. Putting out new bases or sweeping off the bases that were used in pre-game practice.

G. Putting down the batter's box at home plate.

H. Sweeping off the pitcher's rubber and home plate.

SCREEN AND CAGE CREW

As soon as the last cut is taken in pre-game batting practice, the below players are assigned to quickly remove their respective screens, cages, ball box and rugs.

First Half of the Season		**Second Half of the Season** (April 17th game)	
Back up screen	Bartley Cliburn Loe	**Back up screen**	Taylor Susce McDonald
First base screen	Hardwick Kurtz Pruser	**First base screen**	Johnson Reagan Pruser
Pitcher's screen	Mundie Reagan Wilson	**Pitcher's screen**	Mundie Kurtz Hardwick
Ball box and rug	Susce Taylor	**Ball box and rug**	Cliburn Bartley
Batting cage	Kelley Kocol Lowther Paslay Pavlou Winkler Castoria Conner Smith	**Batting cage**	Dixon Hannah Klipstein Schlosser Torres Weisheim White Galloway Sterling
Back up for anyone absent	Purnell	**Back up for anyone absent**	Purnell

TARP CREW

As soon as the home plate umpire stops the game due to a rain delay, the following players are responsible to immediately secure the tarps for the areas below:

Home plate tarp and blocks

Hitters

Mound tarp and blocks

Pitchers

When the home plate umpire asks that the tarps be removed, the above players will be responsible to immediately remove the tarps and secure them.

2. **Paying of umpires**—This responsibility should be handled in the manner in which the athletic administration policy manual sets forth. If the umpires are to be paid prior to the game, the head coach or an assigned individual should take care of this responsibility at that time. In a later section of the Playbook, more detailed information can be found regarding the coach's responsibility to the umpires who work his baseball games.

3. **Pre-game running program**—Prior to every game, practically every player on the team should be involved in a pre-game running program. This should be done at this time for two reasons: (1) it serves the purpose of getting the entire team loosened up for the game itself; and (2) it serves as a conditioning program for those days that games are being played. Some teams have their squad run after the game, but this can be a negative situation especially after a tough loss. The pre-game running program should be started immediately after both teams have completed their outfield-infield practice. The pre-game running should take no longer than ten minutes, which gives the players in the starting lineup a chance to get back in the dugout and relax for about five minutes before the start of the game. On the following page is a sample pre-game running schedule. This schedule should be posted in the locker room and in the dugout.

4. **Starting pitchers getting warmed up in the bullpen**—After outfield-infield practice for both teams is completed, the starting pitchers for both teams should begin warming up in their respective bullpens. If the home team pitcher needs longer than 15 minutes to get warmed up, he should begin throwing while outfield-infield practice is still going on. If all the catchers are participating in the outfield-infield drill, then one of the coaches or a manager can start catching the pitcher until the assigned bullpen catcher is available. The starting pitcher for the home team should have time prior to the starting time of the game to return to the dugout, towel off, get a drink of water and prepare himself to take the mound when the team is introduced defensively.

5. **Public address announcer giving the starting line-ups**—As the umpires, coaches and captains move out to the area of home plate to exchange lineup cards and go over the ground rules, the public address announcer should announce the starting lineups for both teams. A complete script for the public address announcer can be found in a later section of the Playbook.

6. **Pre-game meeting at home plate**—Approximately five minutes before the scheduled starting time of the game, the coaches, umpires and captains should be in the area of home plate to exchange lineup cards and go over the ground rules. Each coach should have at least three copies of their lineup card available at that time. He will present two copies to the home plate umpire, who will inspect both of them to be sure that they are identical. He would then give one copy to the coach of the opposing team, and keep one copy for himself. The third lineup card should be kept by the coach. It is recommended that the coach prepare four copies of his lineup card so that he can post one of them in the dugout for the player's benefit. There are numerous types of lineup cards available from many sources, but it is best to secure lineup cards that have a carbon backing so that when one card is prepared they all are identical. This also saves valuable time for the coach responsible for completing the card. On this page you should find an example of a lineup card commonly used in baseball today.

OFFICIAL BATTING ORDER

CLUB _TEAM A_   DATE _4/26/82_

	ORIGINAL	POS.	CHANGE
1	WAGNER	4	B
			C
2	JONES	7	B
			C
3	BUCKLEY	9	B
			C
4	SMITH	DH	B
			C
5	GRADY	6	B
			C
6	BUTLER	2	B
			C
7	FERRIS	5	B
			C
8	MILLER	8	B
			C
9	ROSS	3	B
			C
	LEE	1	D
			E

PRE-GAME RUNNING SCHEDULE

The following pre-game running schedule will be completed as soon as both teams have finished their outfield-infield practice. Run at least one-half speed to the starting point and back to the dugout area.

Pre-game running for pitchers

Designated long reliever(s) . . . . .4 - 7/8's speed foul poles
Designated short reliever(s) . . . . .7 - 7/8's speed foul poles
Starting rotation pitchers

    Day after a start . . . . .15 - 7/8's speed foul poles
    2nd day after a start . . . . .15 - 7/8's speed foul poles
    3rd day after a start . . . . .12 - 7/8's speed foul poles
    4th day after a start . . . . .12 - 7/8's speed foul poles

All other pitchers not in the starting rotation and not designated as long reliever(s) or short reliever(s) for this game will run 12-7/8's speed foul poles. Those pitchers assigned to run 12 or 15 foul poles can begin running them while the teams are taking outfield-infield practice.

Pre-game running for hitters

The only one excused from the pre-game running for hitters is the catcher assigned to catch the starting pitcher in the bullpen. Hitters will run from the left field foul line when we are in the third base dugout and the right field foul line when we are in the first base dugout. The foul line is considered your secondary lead spot, so your left foot is on the line using the cross-over step stealing mechanics. You will run a 90 foot stealing sprint.

Players in the starting lineup . . . . .4 - 3/4's speed stealing sprints
                                                                                                                                                          4 - full speed stealing sprints
Players not in starting lineup . . . . .4 - 3/4's speed stealing sprints
                                                                                                                                                          7 - full speed stealing sprints

---

This type of lineup card allows the coach to list his substitutes as they enter the game on the actual card. A better type of card for the coach to keep track of his substitutes and available personnel can be found on page 426. If he desires, the coach can have the printing department on campus make numerous copies of this card on cardboard making enough to last the entire season.

After the lineup cards have been inspected by the home plate umpire and returned to the respective coaches of each team, the ground rules for the field should be detailed. If the home plate umpire has worked games on the field before, he should be responsible to cover these ground rules. If not, hopefully the base umpire can cover them. If neither umpire has worked on the field prior to the game, then the home team head coach must be responsible to go over these rules for his particular field.

7. **Public address announcer giving starting lineup of the home team by defensive positions**—At the completion of the meeting at home plate, the home team coach should return to his dugout and check to be sure that his starting team is ready to take the field. Once they are ready, he should cue the public address announcer to introduce the players by their defensive positions. The manner in which this might be done can be found in the public address announcer's script found later in the Playbook.

8. **Playing of the National Anthem**—Once all of the players have assumed their defensive positions, the national anthem should be played over the public address system. The flag can either be up on the pole, or it can be elevated up the pole as the

BASEBALL LINE-UP CARD

UNI. #	POS.	BATTING ORDER	#	SUBSTITUTES	INNING	POS.	UNI. #
			1				
			2				
			3				
			4				
			5				
			6				
			7				
			8				
			9				
			P				

USED	POS.	PINCH HITTERS AVAILABLE	BATS R	L

USED	PITCHERS AVAILABLE	THROWS R	L

USED	PINCH RUNNERS

426

National Anthem is being played. As this is a time of respect for our country and flag, it is recommended that each player and coach stand at attention with their feet together and their hat over their heart. Players and coaches in the dugout should come out in front of the dugout and assume the same position. Upon the completion of the Anthem, the game should begin after the pitcher throws his designated number of warmup pitches to the catcher.

GAME ADMINISTRATION - POLICIES

The head coach should meet with his team prior to the opening of the season to go over policies and procedures that will be followed by the team in regard to game administration. The following would be a list of items that need to be covered so that there is no confusion on a player's part in regard to what is expected of him during the course of a game.

1. Following time schedule for pre-game practice. Manner in which one may receive an excuse for being late or missing a game. Time schedule for the starting pitcher.

2. Grooming standards for the season in the way of appearance and how to wear the game uniform properly.

3. Discuss pre-game batting practice procedure; outfield-infield practice procedure; removal of screens and cage procedure; introduction of starting lineup by defensive positions procedure; pre-game running procedure; and the manner in which they will stand for the National Anthem.

4. Discuss the manner in which the team will go on and off the field, return to the dugout after outs are made; and what is expected of them as hitters when the ball is put into play.

5. Communication requirements when dealing with the bat handlers, and how the bat and helmet is given to them when returning to the dugout.

6. Discuss what is expected of them when in the dugout and bullpen. Set up ground rules for who is allowed in the bullpen.

7. Discuss what needs to be done as soon as the other team makes the third out in regard to the infielders and outfielders stretching their arms between innings. Who is responsible for the ball that will be thrown? How will the ball get back to the dugout?

8. Responsibilities in regard to the placement of their gloves, hats and sunglasses in the dugout so that they can receive these items quickly when they make the last out on the bases. Who is responsible to bring them out?

9. Go over the ground rules for the home field.

10. Discuss the manner in which the relief pitcher and bullpen catcher leave the dugout area to get down to the bullpen and the signs used from the dugout to the bullpen.

11. Discuss policies in regard to: eating on the field; talking with spectators before, during and after the game; communication with the umpires; communication with members of the other team; and communication with members of your own team.

12. Discuss how substitutions will be made and who is responsible for notifying the substitute of the change.

13. Complete discussion of game conduct in regard to: safety of teammates; safety of opposing players; arguments with umpires; second guessing coaches; handling adversity; and general game attitude expected by the coaching staff.

14. Manner in which you handle yourself after a win or loss.

GAME ADMINISTRATION SHEET

A game administration sheet needs to be posted in the locker room and in the dugout for each game so that every coach and player knows exactly what time schedule will be followed and who is responsible for all the various game administration details. On the following page is a sample game administration sheet.

GAME ADMINISTRATION SHEET

DATE:___April 17th_____

OPPONENT:___Smith High School_____

TIME ON FIELD:___1:45_____

TIME FOR BATTING PRACTICE:___1:50 - 2:25_____ (35) MINUTES

BATTING PRACTICE PITCHERS:	Welsh	(20) MINUTES
	Southard	(15) MINUTES
BATTING PRACTICE CATCHERS:	Loe	(20) MINUTES
	Wendtland	(15) MINUTES
BACK UP MEN BEHIND SECOND:	Mundie	(20) MINUTES
	Susce	(15) MINUTES
FUNGO ON FIRST BASE SIDE:	Smith	(20) MINUTES
	Herzog	(15) MINUTES
FUNGO ON THIRD BASE SIDE:	Carter	(20) MINUTES
	Hartley	(15) MINUTES
FIRST BASEMAN AT BASE:	Castoria	(10) MINUTES
	Parker	(25) MINUTES

SCREEN AND CAGE CREW:___Number 2_____

OUTFIELD-INFIELD PRACTICE FUNGO HITTER:___Polk_____

TIME OF OUTFIELD-INFIELD PRACTICE:___2:35 - 2:45_____

GAME TIME:___3:00 (One nine inning game)_____

STARTING PITCHER:___Morlock_____

LONG RELIEVER(S):___Borders_____
                   ___Clark_____

SHORT RELIEVER(S):___Hardwick_____
                    ___Winter_____

FIRST BASE COACH:___Osborne_____

THIRD BASE COACH:___Johnson_____

PITCHER'S CHART:___Smith_____

MOST VALUABLE PLAYER CHART:___Purnell_____

SCOUTING CARD:___Baldner_____

PITCHER PATTERN CHART:___Nelson_____

BASERUNNING CHART:___Sumner_____

BULLPEN CATCHERS:___Weaver_____
                   ___Porter_____

428

This game administration sheet contains all the information that the team will need in regard to the pre-game schedule. It also contains information in regard to game responsibilities for the players and coaches. Some of these responsibilities include the keeping of various charts during the course of the game.

GAME CHARTS

Later in the Playbook will be found a description of a Most Valuable Player system that can be incorporated into a baseball program at any level. This is one of the charts that must be kept during the course of each game. There are numerous other charts that can be kept and we will examine some of the more common charts at this time.

A word of caution in regard to keeping game charts needs to be mentioned. Some teams have their club keeping every type of chart imaginable only to find that the charts are never put to good use during the game. They are also very seldom used for evaluating performance after the game. It is highly recommended that only a few charts be kept during the game so that they might be better incorporated into game strategy and post-game evaluation of performance. We will now examine a few of the more common types of game charts.

1. **Pitching charts**—There are numerous types of pitching charts that can be used to chart the pitchers for your team. One can find a chart that will list everything imaginable, but it becomes somewhat complicated to keep and more complicated to evaluate. On pages 430-431 can be found a very simple type of pitching chart. This chart should be kept by the pitcher who will be the starting pitcher for the next game, especially if this pitcher will be facing the team that he is charting.

The charter works the chart the same as if he was keeping a scorebook with the major difference being that he is also concerned with charting every pitch that is thrown. The person keeping the pitching chart would write the pitcher's name, the date, and the name of the opponent in the top left hand corner of the chart. He will need a red pencil and a regular pencil since he will be charting the pitcher throwing from the stretch (red pencil) and from the windup (regular pencil). The name of each batter on the opposing team is placed in the box on the left. He will also record the player's uniform number, and whether he bats right; left; or is a switch hitter. As each batter takes his turn at bat, the charter indicates the type of pitch that was thrown in the box of either the ball or strike line (1 - fast ball; 2 - curve ball; 3 - slider; 4 - change-up; and 5 - speciality pitch). Next to the number of the pitch, the charter can indicate when a strike is thrown and what the batter did with the pitch. For instance; 1C is a fast ball called strike; 2S is a curve ball that the batter swung at and missed; and 3F is a slider that the batter fouled off.

In order for the coach and pitcher to easily evaluate the pitching chart upon the completion of the game, the charter needs to record the balls and strikes in sequence in the boxes. For instance, if the first two pitches thrown were curve balls that were balls, it would be recorded as it is on the pitching chart to the first hitter (Smith). The third pitch was a fast ball that Smith swung at and missed (1S). With the count 2-1, Smith took a fast ball for a called strike. With the count 2-2, he took a fast ball for a ball making the count 3-2. On the 3-2 pitch he hit a curve ball for a fly ball to right field for the first out. The second hitter is Jones, who is a switch hitter. He fouled off the first fast ball, took a curve ball and a fast ball for a ball. With the count of 2-1, he swung and missed at a curve ball. He then hit a fast ball to left field that was well hit. The charter may be asked by the coach to describe the location of the pitch hit, which in the case of Jones, was a high fast ball.

If a batter swings and misses or hits a pitch it is always recorded as a strike even though the pitch might not have been in the strike zone. Some coaches deem it important to chart the pitchers from the stretch and from the windup, and this can be done quite easily through the use of the different colored pencils. The charter must be sure to make lineup changes for the opponents just as he would do if keeping a scorebook. Upon completion of the game, this pitching chart would be used by the coaching staff to: (1) better evaluate what pitches are getting opponent hitters out, and what pitches the individual hitters on the other team are having success with; and (2) evaluation of the pitching performance of the pitcher(s) throwing in that particular game. Thus, a scouting report on the opponent hitters can be developed in regard to how they will be pitched too and defensed in future games. After the coaches have reviewed this pitching chart, it should be handed over to the pitcher who was charted for his evaluation of his performance. The pitching summary chart on page 432 is the form this pitcher can use to properly evaluate his pitching performance. The pitcher should present this pitching summary chart to the pitching coach the next day properly filled out so that the pitcher and the pitching coach can discuss and evaluate his game performance on the mound. The pitcher's summary chart is designed to evaluate the pitcher's control on all his pitches, along with determining if the pitcher was throwing in any set pattern. It will also help the pitcher to determine the types of pitches he is getting his strikeouts with, along with those he is giving up his hits on. On the bottom of the pitcher's summary chart, he should answer in one or two sentences each of the five questions. In answering these questions, he will provide himself the opportunity to fully evaluate his pitching performance. The coach should sit down with the pitcher at this time and together they can come up with some suggestions for improvement.

Pitcher **JOHNSON**

Date **4/27**

Opponent **JONES HIGH SCHOOL**

Red — Stretch

Pencil — Windup

KEY:

——————▶ Well hit—fly ball or line drive

— · — · — Average—fly ball or line drive

- - - -▶ Well hit ground ball

- - - - Average hit ground ball

⌒ Pop fly

1 — Fast Ball
2 — Curve Ball
3 — Slider
4 — Change
5 — Other

 # 12 B RIGHT

SMITH

F-9
⌒ ⓪

B	2	2		1	
S			15 1C	2	

 # 7 B SWITCH

JONES

1B
HIGH PITCH

B		2	1	
S	1F		2S	1

 # B

 # B

 # B

 # B

 # B

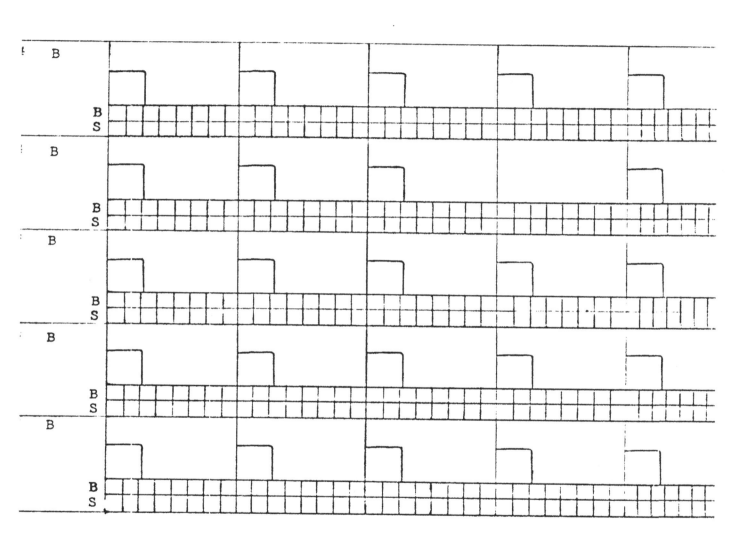

PITCHER'S SUMMARY CHART

DATE_____   PITCHER_____

TYPE OF PITCH	NUMBER OF STRIKES	NUMBER OF BALLS	PITCH USED FOR 1ST PITCH	PITCH USED FOR K	PITCH USED FOR BASEHIT	PITCH USED FOR 2 — 0	PITCH USED FOR 3 — 1	PITCH USED FOR 3 — 2
FASTBALL								
CURVE								
SLIDER								
CHANGE								
OTHER								

1. What was your best pitch?

2. If you had control problems, which pitch and where?

3. Were you pitching by any set pattern?

4. Which pitch was hit the hardest?

5. Comment on your ideas for improvement.

---

2. **Pitcher pattern chart**—The pitcher pattern chart that can be found on the next page should be kept by one of the coaches in the dugout. If a coach is not available to keep this chart then one of the more reliable players or a manager must be responsible for keeping it during the course of the game. This chart serves two useful purposes: (1) it evaluates the pitching pattern of the pitcher on the opposing team to see if he is falling into a set pattern with his pitches; and (2) it provides the coach with a scouting report on this pitcher that he can go over with his team the next time they face this particular pitcher.

The charter will put the name of the team playing, the name of the pitcher throwing, the date of the game, and his name as the charter in the spaces indicated on the top of the chart. He will also indicate whether the pitcher is righthanded or lefthanded next to the pitcher's name. Once the game begins, the charter will chart every pitch that is thrown by this pitcher using the symbols on the bottom of the chart. He will put the symbol in the column that the ball-strike count was at the time of the pitch. As soon as the charter observes any set pattern the pitcher and catcher have fallen into in regard to their pitch selection, he will make the players in the dugout aware of this information. For instance, he may quickly find out that the pitcher is throwing a fast ball on every 2-0 count. This should alert the hitters to look for the fast ball on the 2-0 count. The charter should not provide the dugout with this type of information until about the third or fourth inning so that the pitcher's pitching pattern is firmly established. Many pitchers throw differently early in the game than they do late in the game, so this is the reason why the chart is divided into the first three innings, the middle three innings, and the last three innings. The charter will use a new chart for each pitcher that enters the game for the opposing team.

432

PITCHER PATTERN CHART

CHARTER_____

TEAM_____PITCHER_____THROWS_____DATE_____

	FIRST PITCH	SECOND PITCH 1-0	0-1	1-1 COUNT	AHEAD IN COUNT 0-2	1-2	2-2	BEHIND IN COUNT 1-0	2-1	2-0	3-0	3-1	3-2 COUNT	STRIKEOUT PITCH
FIRST THREE INNINGS														
MIDDLE THREE INNINGS														
LAST THREE INNINGS														

COMMENTS_____

BEST PITCH_____

HOW DOES HE HOLD RUNNERS_____

TIP OFF ANY PITCHERS_____

KEY: FAST BALL — 1   CURVE BALL — 2   CHANGE — 3   SLIDER — 4   OTHER — 5

STRIKE — ○   WELL HIT — □   WILD PITCH — △

The next time the team faces this pitcher, the coach can refer to this chart to properly provide his hitters with information on what they might expect from this pitcher. The person keeping the pitcher pattern chart should also indicate on the comments line on the bottom of the chart anything about the pitcher that the team needs to be aware of when they face him again. This information would include the pitcher's pitching style, arm slot, unusual pitching delivery and any other information that would be helpful to the club. For instance, he might put down on the comments line that this pitcher likes to work extremely quick with no runners on base, and has an extremely high leg kick. The charter should indicate in the space provided what the pitcher's best pitch is and how he holds runners on base. If the pitcher happens to be tipping off his pitches in any manner, this information needs to be noted as well. Many times a team does not face a particular pitcher that often so this information on each pitcher will certainly be helpful in refreshing everyone's memory.

3. **Baserunning chart**—The baserunning chart on the following page should also be kept by one of the coaches if at all possible. This is not a time consuming chart to keep since the charter just needs to keep track of what the pitcher does from the stretch position with runners at either first or second base. This information can be used in the actual game that is being played, along with future games when the team is facing the same pitcher. After completing the information on top of the chart, the charter will concern himself with a close observation of the pitcher when the first baserunner reaches first or second base.

BASERUNNING CHART

DATE_____TEAM_____

PITCHER_____#_____CHARTER_____

A. MAN ON FIRST BASE

1. NUMBER OF LOOKS:

ONE	TWO	THREE

2. PICK-OFF ATTEMPTS

MOVE ONTO RUBBER	GOING UP	GOING DOWN	SET

* INDICATES GOOD MOVE

B. MAN ON SECOND BASE

1. NUMBER OF LOOKS:

ONE	TWO	THREE

2. PICK-OFF ATTEMPTS

MOVE ONTO RUBBER	GOING UP	GOING DOWN	SET

* INDICATES GOOD MOVE

C. SPECIAL PICKS/COMMENTS:

D. PITCHER DELIVERY TIME TO HOME PLATE:

E. CATCHER DELIVERY TIME TO SECOND BASE:

434

The charter should also have a stopwatch in his hand to time the pitcher's delivery time to the plate on both the fast ball and the breaking pitch. As soon as the pitcher makes his first movement from the stretch, he should start the watch and then stop it as soon as the ball hits the catcher's glove. This information can be used by the head coach to determine how long it takes for the pitcher to deliver both his fast ball and breaking pitch to the plate. For instance, if the pitcher's time to the plate is 1.9 seconds (a slow delivery time), then there should be no reason why the team cannot steal some bases during the time this pitcher is on the mound. That is as long as the catcher does not have a "cannon" for an arm. If the pitcher's time to home plate is 1.4 seconds on his fast ball (a fast delivery time) then it will be difficult to steal second base unless the catcher has a below average arm. Thus, the offensive game strategy can be affected with the time of the pitcher's delivery to the plate from the set position.

It is further helpful to the head coach if the charter can get an accurate time on the catcher's throw to second base. As soon as the ball hits the catcher's glove, he will start the watch and then stop the watch as soon as the ball touches the glove of the shortstop or second baseman covering second base on the steal attempt. If the time is 2.0 seconds or lower, it means that the catcher has an above average arm. Thus, if the pitcher's delivery time to the plate happens to be a great time of 1.4 seconds, and the catcher's delivery time to second base is a super 1.9 seconds, then stealing second base is going to be a very difficult task. If the pitcher's delivery time to the plate happens to be a 1.9, and the catcher's delivery time to second base is a 2.3, then stealing should be quite easy while this pitcher and catcher are in the lineup. The pitcher's delivery time to the plate on the breaking pitch is very important so that the coach flashing the offensive signs has an idea how long it is taking this pitch to get to the plate. This is so he might be in a better position to steal second base with his runner at first base when the percentages call for a breaking pitch.

The charter needs to indicate in the number of looks at first base column how many times the pitcher looks over to first base and the types of pick-offs attempted at that base. Many pitchers only throw to first base on a pick-off attempt from only one of the designated four spots in the stretch delivery. This information is certainly helpful for that particular game and for any future games that this pitcher is throwing. The charter has the same responsibility for the pitcher holding the runner on at second base. He needs to chart the number of looks and the number and type of pick-off attempts made at that base during the time this pitcher is on the mound. Once a pitcher establishes himself as a "one-looker" at second base, then the one-looker steal can be attempted from second base on occasions. The charter also needs to note any special type of pick-off play attempted by the pitcher during the game at any base. This will provide the coaching staff with information that they can provide their team when this pitcher might be faced again later in the season. A separate chart will be kept on every pitcher faced in the game.

4. **Scouting card**—As with the previous charts already discussed in this section, there are numerous types of scouting cards that can be used by the coaching staff to chart the opposition hitters and baserunners. An example of a scouting card that can be used is found on the next page. These scouting cards can be made up by your printing office on campus. The coach can purchase a small two or three ring notebook to keep the cards in during the game so that they are protected from the elements and make it easier for the coach keeping the scouting cards to keep them in the proper batting order sequence. As with the other charts previously discussed, the scouting card will be most helpful to the coaching staff for the game being played and for future reference when this same team is an opponent in the future. The basic purpose of this card is to evaluate every hitter on the opponent's team in regard to his hitting tendencies at the plate. The coach keeping the scouting card would also have access to the pitcher's chart during and after the game to evaluate what type of pitches the individual hitter is making good contact with, and what type of pitches the hitter is having little success with. The coach keeping the scouting card might even wish to keep his own pitcher's chart whereby he can chart every pitch thrown to each hitter. This might be a little difficult to do along with keeping the scouting card.

The coach will make a separate card on each hitter on the opposing team. The hitter's name is placed in the top right hand corner of the card along with the other pertinent information called for below the hitter's name. The speed of the hitter can be evaluated upon the completion of the game by grading him on a one to three scale. One being an above average runner, two being an average runner, and three being a below average runner. The dates of the game that this hitter was evaluated should be placed on the line on top of the card. This particular card could be used for as many as six games. After six games, a new card should be made since a scouting card fills up quite quickly especially in the hitting spray area section.

It is recommended that a different color pencil be used for each game so that the coach can note the production for each game and making it easier to match with the type of pitcher his team was throwing that day. Upon completion of the first game, the information on the top left corner of the card should be completed. This information details the type of stance, stride, hand position, and bat speed of the hitter for future reference.

Each time a particular hitter strikes out, it should be noted on the card the type of pitch he struck out on and the location of the pitch. If the runner steals, the count he stole on should be recorded. The same holds true for the count if a hitter attempts a drag bunt. Hitters and baserunners get into set patterns on steals and drag bunt attempts and this information can be of great use to the coaching staff in future games. Any hit and run attempts should also be noted on the runner and the hitter's card in regard to the ball-strike count on the batter.

The symbols in the lower right corner of the scouting card are used by the coach to keep track of the type of balls hit and where the balls were hit. These symbols would be placed on the playing field outline that is in the center of the card. Next to each symbol, the coach may wish to note the type of pitch hit, the location of the pitch in the strike zone and the ball-strike count on that particular pitch. The coach keeping this card will find various ways that he can make notes on the card that he can use for future reference.

From all this information, the coaching staff should be able to come up with a scouting report on each hitter on the opposing team. Of course, the more games that the hitter can be evaluated the more reliable the scouting report will become. On the bottom of the card, the coach may begin formulating a type of pitching plan on this particular hitter and a hitting spray area tendency to better position his defense. Whenever a team is played numerous times during the course of a season, the coaching staff should be able to develop a fairly accurate scouting report on each hitter. This is certainly helpful to the pitching staff and the defense as they prepare to pitch and defense the individual hitter.

SCOUTING CARD

GAME DATES: #1 _____ #2 _____ #3 _____ #4 _____ #5 _____ #6 _____   NAME: _____

STANCE: OPEN _____ CLOSED: _____

BATS: RIGHT ___ LEFT ____ SWITCH ____

STRIDE: AWAY _____ IN: _____ LENGTH OF STRIDE _____

POSITION IN ORDER: ____

CHOKE ON BAT: (HOW MUCH) _____

SPEED: GRADE 1-2-3 ____

HANDS: HIGH _____ LOW _____ AVERAGE _____

UNIFORM NUMBER ____

CROUCH: STRAIGHT UP _____ SLIGHT _____ BENT _____

BAT: QUICK _____ SLOW _____

K'S - PITCH

1. _____
2. _____
3. _____
4. _____
5. _____
6. _____
7. _____

Key

→ DEEP FLYBALL OR LINE DRIVE

⌃ AVERAGE FLYBALL OR LINE DRIVE

--→ WELL HIT GROUND BALL

---- AVERAGE HIT GROUND BALL

⌒ FLYBALL-POPUP

SB - PITCH NUMBER

1. _____   3. _____
2. _____   4. _____

BUNTS (DRAG) PITCH NUMBER

1. _____   3. _____
2. _____   4. _____

HOW TO PITCH: _____

_____

_____

_____

HOW TO PLAY DEFENSIVELY: _____

_____

_____

PUBLIC ADDRESS ANNOUNCER AND SCRIPT

An excellent public address announcer at a baseball game can be a positive part of the game and reflect favorably on the baseball program of the home team. At the same time, a poor public address announcer can easily be a negative part of the game and reflect poorly on the home team's baseball program.

We have all attended baseball games where the public address announcer does a very professional job of presenting the information that the spectators can use in enjoying the game. Then we have all been at a ballpark where the public address announcer gets carried away to the point where he is literally giving a play-by-play description of what is taking place on the field. Thus, it is the responsibility of the baseball coach to not only secure a public address announcer for his home games, but to make sure that the announcer knows exactly what his responsibilities are behind the microphone.

It is beneficial to secure a person who has a nice speaking voice that is pleasant to the ear. It is also very helpful that the announcer have an appreciation for the game of baseball whereby he or she understands the timing involved in presenting the proper information. A good speaker system certainly adds a touch of class to the atmosphere in the ballpark, and makes the announcer's job that much easier.

The following is a public address announcer's job description along with a script that can be used in performing his or her responsibilities. The baseball coach needs to review this script with a new announcer so that he or she is completely aware of these responsibilities.

Responsibilities

1. Be at the field at least 45 minutes prior to the scheduled time of the game. This should give you adequate time to set up the speaker system and obtain the starting lineups from both teams. If music is to be played while both teams are taking batting practice then someone needs to set up the speaker system and play the music prior to your arrival.

2. Be sure that the National Anthem is available and the speaker system is operating properly.

3. Make sure that all announcements made during the course of the game reflect positive on the baseball program. You are not to reflect favoritism in your presentation although your delivery certainly can assist in promoting excitement in the stands.

4. Upon the completion of the game, make sure that the speaker system is stored properly in a secure place.

Public Address Script

1. Five minutes before game time, the coaches will exchange lineup cards and go over the ground rules at home plate. At this time, you will announce the starting lineup.

"Good (afternoon) (evening) ladies and gentlemen, and welcome to _____ Field, home of the (year) (name of the team) baseball team. This (afternoon's) (evening's) game features the (nickname of home team) versus the (nickname of visiting school) of (name of school)."

"And now for the starting lineups: first, for the visiting (name of school and nickname) with a season's record of _____ wins and _____ losses."

"Leading off and playing _____ # ____, (first and last name)
Batting 2nd and playing _____ # ___, _____
Batting 3rd and playing _____ # ___, _____
Batting 4th and playing _____ # ___, _____
Batting 5th and playing _____ # ___, _____
Batting 6th and playing _____ # ___, _____
Batting 7th and playing _____ # ___, _____
Batting 8th and playing _____ # ___, _____
Batting 9th and playing _____ # ___, _____

"And pitching with a season's record of _____ wins and _____ losses is (first and last name)."

"The head coach for the (name of school) is (first and last name). He is assisted by: first and last name of all assistant coaches."

"And now for the (year) (name of school) (nickname of school), with a season's record of _____ wins and _____ losses."

"Leading off and playing _____ # ____, (first and last name)
Batting 2nd and playing _____ # ____, _____
Batting 3rd and playing _____ # ____, _____
Batting 4th and playing _____ # ____, _____
Batting 5th and playing _____ # ____, _____
Batting 6th and playing _____ # ____, _____
Batting 7th and playing _____ # ____, _____
Batting 8th and playing _____ # ____, _____
Batting 9th and playing _____ # ____, _____

"And pitching with a season's record of _____ wins and _____ losses is (first and last name)."

"The head coach for the (nickname of school) is (first and last name). He is assisted by: first and last names of all assistant coaches."

2. As the head coach gets back to the dugout and he indicates that his team is ready to take the field, then begin introducing the players by their defensive positions (first and last name and position). Introduce in the following order: right fielder; center fielder; left fielder; first baseman; second baseman; shortstop; third baseman; catcher and pitcher.

3. Just as the pitcher reaches the mound announce: "Ladies and gentlemen, would you please rise for the playing and singing of our National Anthem". Play the National Anthem over the speaker system.

4. As the pitcher begins his warmup pitches to the catcher announce: "The battery for (name of school); catching number _____, (first and last name); and pitching number _____, (first and last name)".

5. After introducing the battery for the home team, introduce the umpires: "The umpires for (today's) (tonight's) game: behind the plate, (first and last name); and on the bases, (first and last name)".

6. In the bottom of the first inning, as the visiting team's pitcher begins his warmup pitches to the catcher announce: The battery for (name of school); catching number _____, (first and last name); and pitching number _____, (first and last name)".

7. Just prior to each batter stepping into the batter's box announce: "Number _____, (position), (first and last name)".

8. At the end of each inning, announce the runs scored, hits, and errors for that inning. Do not announce the score unless there is no scoreboard on the field. "For (name of school), _____ runs, _____ hits, and _____ errors."

9. At least three times during the game, announce the next three home games and dates of any road trips that the home team will be taking within the week. Remind them on what radio station the games can be heard while the team is on the road.

10. At the end of the game, give the final score and invite the fans to the next game.

MANAGER(S) RESPONSIBILITIES - GAME DAY

It is quite helpful to the manager(s) for the baseball team to know exactly what their responsibilities are to the team on game days. The manager(s) can be an invaluable part of the game administration. We have listed a sample selection of responsibilities for the manager(s) on game days.

1. Make sure that the game administration sheet is posted in the locker room, in the dugout and on the batting cage. An example of a game administration sheet will be found later in this section.

2. Make sure that the lineup card is posted in the dugout, and one has been given to the official scorer.

3. Make sure that all the equipment that might be needed for pre-game practice and the game itself is on the field at least 15 minutes before the scheduled time of pre-game practice.

4. One manager will be designated as the time coordinator for the pre-game batting practice. He must have a stop watch and remain in the batting cage area throughout the entire batting practice time.

5. Upon completion of the game, make sure that all equipment is put away properly.

6. Coordinate with the trainer any liquid refreshment needed on the field.

7. Make sure that the visiting team has six towels in their dugout. Upon completion of the game, make sure that you receive back all six towels.

8. Will be responsible for the visiting team locker room. Make sure that the manager for the visiting team has a key to their locker room and enough towels for their squad's use after the game. Make sure that the key is returned along with the number of towels provided them once they leave the locker room.

9. Make sure that the umpires are provided towels for their use in showering after the game if they are dressing in one of the locker rooms.

10. Prepare the baseballs for the game. Rub up at least six baseballs for the beginning of the game and present them to the home plate umpire. Make sure that the visiting team is provided one game ball for their starting pitcher to use in warming up in the bullpen. Make sure that the visiting team pitcher brings the ball with him to the mound.

11. During the game you are responsible for seeing that the baseballs which are returned to the dugout get out to the home plate umpire between innings, and/or at any time the umpire runs out of baseballs.

12. Coordinate your efforts during the game with the bat girls so that all bats and helmets are properly in place and removed from the area of home plate once the play has ended for that batter. All baseballs hit to the backstop must be retrieved by either the bat girls or one of the managers.

13. Secure ball shaggers for each of the home games. Give each of the ball shaggers a new baseball after the game if they gave you a good effort.

14. Make sure that at game time all the charts for the game are in the proper hands of those responsible for the charts. Assignments for the charts can be found on the game administration sheet.

ESTABLISHING PROFESSIONAL RAPPORT WITH UMPIRES

Baseball coaches are generally negligent in establishing professional rapport with individual umpires and the association of which these umpires are members. This negligence can cause serious problems that could be alleviated quite easily if each would better understand the objectives and attitudes inherent in their respective positions.

Coaches are often critical of the umpiring profession for many reasons, with the number one reason probably being that umpires are established by the rules of baseball as the sole position of authority once the game begins. This position of authority is the same for the good as well as the bad umpire. Thus, this creates a feeling of subjugation on the part of the coaches.

Many baseball coaches defeat the real purpose of inter-scholastic competition when they display an attitude of intolerance with a man assigned to make judgement calls. This intolerance on the part of the coaches is easily passed onto the players which can create an antagonistic attitude toward the umpire from the entire team jeopardizing his effectiveness in handling the game itself.

It should be apparent to baseball coaches that there are many advantages in creating proper rapport with the umpires assigned to their games. The most important advantage being that umpires come in contact with many players, coaches, parents, press people and fans. If the umpire is impressed with the type of baseball program you conduct at your school, he will publicize this fact. This will certainly be advantageous for public relations in the community. If he is unimpressed with the way the coach handles his team and their relationship with the umpiring crew, this will also be publicized in a rather negative manner, thus hurting the public relations of the baseball program. Proper rapport with the umpires will also serve to upgrade the games being played on your field, establishing that professional aura to the game itself.

It is the intent of this section of the Playbook to present some of the means and methods available to a baseball coach whereby he can foster a better working relationship with the individual umpire and the association of umpires that he deals directly with during the course of a season. The first would be those items dealing with the umpiring association in the community:

1. The baseball coach should attend as many of the association meetings as possible, as long as this is acceptable to the umpires. This is especially true when they conduct seminars or umpiring clinics in the community.

2. The coach should make himself available to speak to the association of umpires at one of their meetings concerning what a baseball coach expects out of an umpire, or any other subject that would be of interest to the association.

3. He can offer his playing facility and team for any on-the-field umpiring clinic that the association might wish to conduct. He might offer the association the opportunity for them to evaluate their young umpires in inter-squad games that are played on his baseball field.

4. The coach can assist the association of umpires in the field of public relations by helping them coordinate their efforts with those of the local baseball coaches association. He can assist them in publicizing the efforts of the umpires in improving the quality of the baseball programs in the community.

5. He might assist the association in the recruitment and selection of competent umpires in the community.

The coach should be able to offer the umpires working his home games with the best possible working conditions. He can do this by:

1. Providing adequate dressing and showering facilities. These facilities should be separate from both teams and made available for use both before and after the game.

2. Providing adequate security for this dressing facility and provide security for the umpires when entering and leaving the playing field.

3. Providing the umpires with an adequate supply of rubbed up baseballs before the game and assigning a manager to keep the plate umpire supplied with these balls during the course of the game.

4. Making sure that there is a bathandler at each of the games to retrieve the bats in the area of the plate so that the umpire does not have to concern himself with the bats.

5. Making sure that the umpires working the game are provided liquid refreshment at times during the game.

The baseball coach should handle all administrative matters in regard to the umpires in an efficient and professional manner. This can be done by:

1. Sending to each of the umpires assigned to his games a complete home schedule along with the dates and time of contest for each game the individual umpire is assigned.

2. The coach must be sure that a check or cash is available for the umpire prior to the contest.

3. At the completion of the season, a thank you letter should be sent to all the umpires that worked his home games. In addition, a letter should be sent to the umpiring association thanking them for their assistance in providing umpires for his games.

The baseball coach's on-the-field relationship with the umpires should be based on the following principles:

1. The coach should always treat the umpires with respect in accordance with their responsibility as the chief administrators for the game. This respect should carry over during any argument or disagreement that might take place during the course of the contest.

2. If at all possible, all on-the-field communication between the coach and the umpires should take place between innings rather than voicing constant displeasure while the game is in progress. Judgment calls should not be challenged unless the umpire was out of position or has not been consistent in his calls. Arguments on judgement calls should be kept to a minimum.

3. The coach should never allow any of his players to argue with an umpire. The players should be instructed to treat the umpires with respect and to address them as they would the coach.

4. The coach should handle any situation in which a fan gets too carried away in voicing his displeasure in the performance level of an umpire. This will help prevent any minor problem from turning into a major problem.

These are just some of the ways that a baseball coach can foster a better professional relationship with the local umpires and the association to which they belong. The umpire can be one of your best professional friends, and one of the better supporters of your baseball program if you treat him with respect and assist him in making his very difficult job that much easier.

PLAYER EVALUATION

In this section we will present a player evaluation system whereby all the players and coaches are provided the opportunity to evaluate every player on the team. This system can be used to trim the roster, along with determining which players will be in the starting lineup and pitching rotation for the regular season.

We feel that at the high school and college level, athletes are very much aware of the ability level of their teammates and because of this we want them to express themselves, along with all the coaches, in the evaluation process. This evaluation is done not only to provide the means for a democratic evaluation, but we as coaches should want to know what our players' opinions are on each player at their respective position.

The following are the guidelines that can be used by a coach in the proper selection and evaluation of the personnel on his team:

1. A baseball coach has an obligation to each individual player to do everything within his power to evaluate his performance as a potential team member and as a contributing factor to the success of the team. Any coach who does not use sound evaluative criteria in the selection and evaluation of his personnel can do severe harm not only to the players involved, but to the other team members, and his entire program.

2. Baseball ability is not cut and dried like a sport where a participant is racing the clock. This means that there are subjective evaluative criteria involved in the selection of baseball personnel.

3. It is to be understood that the more qualified coaches one has on his coaching staff, the better the job of evaluation that will take place.

4. Better evaluation will be in effect when a baseball coach uses objective criteria as much as his program will allow.

5. Each player should be completely familiarized with the means and methods used in evaluation; evaluation in terms of their fate as a member of the team, and also in terms of the amount of playing time they could expect to receive during the course of the season.

6. As the various evaluations take place, the players should be able to see the results and feel free to discuss the evaluation with any of the coaches involved.

7. The evaluative method should also entail the evaluation of the players of themselves and each individual member of the team.

8. The baseball coach needs to do a good job of evaluating his personnel and at the same time achieve those necessary objectives in preparing his team for the regular season.

9. It must be the goal of the baseball coach to insure that every boy who is cut from the program feels as though he was evaluated fairly and that his lack of success on the field was due to his inability to perform the necessary skills which would enable him to be a contributing member of the team.

The player evaluation can be done as many times as the head coach deems fit. It is recommended that it be done at least two times in the pre-season program. Chart Number 1 is an example of the evaluation form that the players and coaches can use in ranking the members of the team. Prior to handing out the evaluation form, the coach needs to explain to the entire team the reasoning behind allowing them an opportunity to evaluate each other, and also explain what criteria they should use in making their judgments.

It is recommended that they do not rank themselves until the final evaluation takes place right before the opening of the regular season. On the evaluation form, they put their name on it so that the coaches know how each of them ranked the team position by position. This is very helpful to the coaches, especially when they can see how each of the catchers evaluated the members of the pitching staff; and vice-versa, what catcher each of the pitchers has the most confidence in behind the plate.

442

PLAYER AND COACH EVALUATION FORM

Instructions — Place your name in the space below. You are to rank each pitcher and non-pitcher using the criteria that we discussed. Do not include yourself in this evaluation:

Name:_____

Pitchers	**Rank**
1. Beck	1. _____
2. Gerdes	2. _____
3. Gibson	3. _____
4. Griggs	4. _____
5. Kruppa	5. _____
6. Manos	6. _____
7. Morris	7. _____
8. Read	8. _____
9. Vandersluys	9. _____

Hitters	**Rank**
1. Butler	1. _____
2. Buchar	2. _____
3. Cash	3. _____
4. Chauncey	4. _____
5. Garcia	5. _____
6. Ivins	6. _____
7. Miller	7. _____
8. Moore	8. _____
9. Morrison	9. _____
10. Person	10. _____
11. Pietsch	11. _____
12. Prosser	12. _____
13. Ryan	13. _____
14. Salter	14. _____
15. Toth	15. _____
16. Weicht	16. _____

This evaluation is not designed to be a sociogram, but the coaching staff can determine if there might be some problem with a certain individual as a result of the way he was evaluated by the team. Players must be told to not use this evaluation as a personality contest, but base their evaluation of each player on his individual worth to the team. This would be based on their observation of him over past seasons, or during the pre-season program.

We sincerely feel that if this evaluation is presented properly to the team, the coach will find the players will not generally base their evaluation on any criteria other than the individual player's ability to help the team. Occasionally, you might find an evaluation that does not conform to the rest of the team, but this will invariably happen whenever any type of evaluation of personnel takes place. Sometimes you will find a player who just has poor evaluative judgment, but this is extremely rare, especially at the college level.

The players and coaches should be given a full day to complete and turn in their evaluation. They should be instructed to complete their evaluation without consulting with any member of the team, outside the coaching staff.

Chart Number 2 shows how the results are listed for the players and coaches information. These results should not be posted for anyone outside the club to see. In this evaluation the six coaches are assigned a number so the members of the team do not know how each of the coaches evaluated each player. On the final evaluation prior to the season, the head coach should be noted so that each player knows how he stands in the eyes of the person who must make the final decision in regard to the lineup.

If the team has quite a few players out for the team, the coach can make the evaluation out so that the players are evaluated position by position. In addition, he can then have them ranked all together under the hitter category. This will allow each position player to see how he is evaluated against the other players at his position, and then see how he stands with the other hitters as a whole.

In the player rankings, the players are listed by their overall ranking. The point total next to their ranking reflects the totals of the rankings. For instance. Vandersluys was ranked the number one pitcher with a 37 point total. Thus, if one player voted him number two on the staff, another player voted him number one, and another player had him number three, his cumulative point total for those three votes is six.

Chart Number 2

Pitchers Evaluation by Coaches

| Pitchers | Ranking | Coaches | | | | | | Total Points |
		#1	#2	#3	#4	#5	#6	
Vandersluys	1	1	1	1	1	1	1	6
Gibson	2	2	2	2	2	2	2	12
Gerdes	3	4	4	3	3	4	3	21
Beck	4	3	3	4	5	3	4	22
Kruppa	5	5	6	5	4	5	5	30
Griggs	6	6	5	6	6	6	7	36
Manos	7	7	7	7	7	7	6	41
Morris	8	9	8	8	8	9	8	50
Read	9	8	9	9	9	8	9	52

Hitters Evaluation by Coaches

| Hitters | Ranking | Coaches | | | | | | Total Points |
		#1	#2	#3	#4	#5	#6	
Morrison	1	1	3	1	1	1	3	10
Pietsch	2	3	2	2	2	3	1	13
Person	3	2	1	3	4	2	2	14
Cash	4	4	4	4	3	4	4	23
Butler	5	5	5	5	7	5	6	33
Salter	6	8	7	7	5	6	5	38
Weicht	7	9	9	6	6	10	7	47
Moore	8	7	6	8	10	9	9	49
Garcia	9	6	10	10	9	8	8	51
Chauncey	10	10	8	9	8	7	10	52
Toth	11	12	12	11	12	11	11	69
Ivins	12	11	11	12	13	13	14	74
Ryan	13	14	13	13	11	14	12	77
Buchar	14	13	16	14	14	12	13	82
Prosser	15	16	14	15	15	15	16	91
Miller	16	15	15	16	16	16	15	93

Pitchers Evaluation by Players

Pitchers	Ranking	Points
Vandersluys	1	37
Gibson	2	51
Beck	3	95
Gerdes	4	104
Griggs	5	138
Kruppa	6	161
Manos	7	176
Read	8	197
Morris	9	206

Hitters Evaluation by Players

Hitters	Ranking	Points
Pietsch	1	49
Morrison	2	67
Person	3	76
Cash	4	80
Butler	5	139
Moore	6	167
Salter	7	198
Chauncey	8	207
Weicht	9	243
Garcia	10	258
Ivins	11	279
Toth	12	303
Ryan	13	327
Buchar	14	362
Miller	15	381
Prosser	16	403

On Chart Number 3, the coach would then provide the players with an evaluation comparison so they can see the differences, if any, between the players and the coaches in regard to the evaluation. We believe the coach will find that the coaches and players evaluation will be very similar. This reinforces for both the players and the coaches that the evaluation process in regard to player ability can be achieved and standardized by numerous parties taking part in the evaluation. If there happens to be a wide variance between the player and coaches evaluation of one or two players, then it behooves the coaching staff to try to analyze where the problem might be. The more evaluations completed, the closer the results between the players and coaches, as a rule.

The players must be aware of the fact that the results of the evaluation are similar to that of a report card one receives for classroom work. It is an indication of his ranking at that time with others on the baseball team. As with report cards, a player might be very disappointed or pleased with his evaluation. We feel it is important that a player knows how he stands on the team at all times. This evaluation comparison provides the players with not only his evaluation by the coaching staff, but by the other players as well. In the final player evaluation, each player should be allowed to place himself in the evaluation as to where he thinks he belongs compared with other players at his particular position. This is the opportunity for the player to express to the coaching staff how he evaluates himself.

Chart Number 3

Evaluation Comparison

Pitchers	Players	Coaches
Vandersluys	1	1
Gibson	2	2
Beck	3	4
Gerdes	4	3
Griggs	5	6
Kruppa	6	5
Manos	7	7
Read	8	9
Morris	9	8

Hitters	Players	Coaches
Pietsch	1	2
Morrison	2	1
Person	3	3
Cash	4	4
Butler	5	5
Moore	6	8
Salter	7	6
Chauncey	8	10
Weicht	9	7
Garcia	10	9
Ivins	11	12
Toth	12	11
Ryan	13	13
Buchar	14	14
Miller	15	16
Prosser	16	15

On the final evaluation prior to the regular season, the coach might ask all the players and coaches to name their starting lineup for the first game. Chart Number 4 would be an example of how this information can be provided to the players and coaches. The players may place themselves in the starting lineup if they deem themselves worthy.

Chart Number 4

Starting Lineup by the Coaches

Six coaches voting. ( ) means the most popular spot indicated in the lineup, thus this is the consensus. One number in ( ) means four or more coaches indicated this spot in the lineup.

Player	Righthanded Pitcher	Lefthanded Pitcher
Butler	6 (1 & 2)	6 (7 & 8)
Buchar	0	0
Cash	6 (5 & 6)	6 (5)
Chauncey	6 (1 & 7)	4 (7 & 8)
Garcia	6 (9)	5 (1)
Ivins	0	0
Miller	0	0
Moore	0	6 (6)
Morrison	6 (4)	6 (4)
Person	6 (3)	6 (3)
Pietsch	6 (2)	6 (1 & 2)
Prosser	0	0
Ryan	0	0
Salter	6 (8)	6 (8 & 9)
Toth	0	1 (9)
Weicht	6 (6 & 7)	1 (6)

Starting Lineup by the Players

26 players voting. ( ) means the most popular spot indicated in the lineup, thus this is the consensus. One number in ( ) means that over 75% of the players indicated this lineup spot.

Player	Righthanded Pitcher	Lefthanded Pitcher
Butler	26 (1 & 2)	26 (1 & 2)
Buchar	0	1 (8)
Cash	26 (5)	26 (5)
Chauncey	26 (1 & 6)	21 (8 & 7)
Garcia	20 (8 & 9)	22 (8 & 1)
Ivins	3 (2 & 6 & 8)	1 (8)
Miller	0	0
Moore	8 (6 & 9)	23 (6 & 7)
Morrison	26 (4)	26 (4)
Person	23 (2 & 3)	26 (2 & 3)
Pietsch	26 (3)	26 (3 & 5)
Prosser	0	0
Ryan	0	1 (8)
Salter	26 (8 & 9)	25 (7 & 8)
Toth	2 (7)	2 (1 & 7)
Weicht	16 (7 & 8)	2 (7 & 9)

MOST VALUABLE PLAYER CHART

The following most valuable player chart can be used by the baseball coach to determine the most valuable hitter and most valuable pitcher on the baseball team. It is a system whereby plus points are awarded to a player when he contributes in some way to the success of the team, and minus points are given to a player when he does something that hinders the success of the team.

It is important that the same coach or manager keep this chart for every game so that consistency is maintained throughout the season. The head coach can assist the person keeping the chart in determining those subjective performance points, such as: heads up baserunning; and outstanding defensive play.

Each week the cumulative totals for the team should be posted in the locker room for all the players to observe. At the completion of the season a plaque or trophy can be awarded to the most valuable hitter and most valuable pitcher.

MOST VALUABLE PLAYER CHART

OPPONENT: _____ DATE: _____ ADMINISTRATOR: _____

OFFENSIVE	PLUS PTS.	PLAYERS NUMBER
EACH R.B.I.	3	
BASEHIT (1 PT. EA. BASE)	1	
REACHING BASE OTHER THAN BY HIT OR FIELDERS CHOICE	1	
RUN SCORED	1	
STEAL	1	
SACRIFICE BUNT OR FLY	2	
BREAKING UP DOUBLE PLAY	1	
ADVANCE RUNNER TO THIRD	1	
HEADS UP BASERUNNING	2	
GAME WINNING HIT	4	

DEFENSIVE	PLUS PTS.	
DOUBLE PLAYS (ASSIST ONLY)	1	
PICKOFF PLAY (ASSIST ONLY)	1	
CATCHER THROWING OUT RUNNER	1	
OUTSTANDING DEFENSIVE PLAY	2	
OUTFIELDER MAKING ASSIST	2	

PITCHING	PLUS PTS.	PLAYERS NUMBER
VICTORY	6	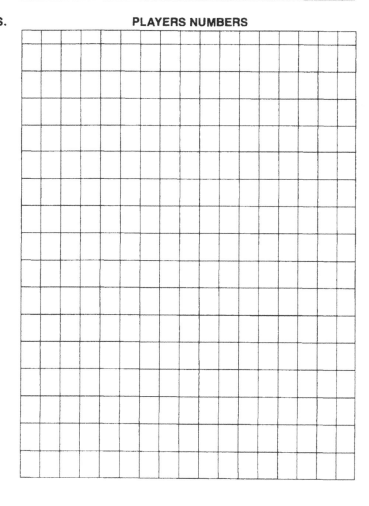
NO ER IN COMPLETE GAME	6	
ONE ER IN COMPLETE GAME	5	
NO MORE THAN 3 ER IN CG	4	
EACH STRIKEOUT	1	
FEWER THAN 12 PITCHES IN AND INNING	1	
NO WALKS IN AN INNING	1	
COMPLETE GAME	6	
SAVE-FACE TYING OR WINNING RUN IN RELIEF	6	
PLUS POINTS TOTALS		

	MINUS PTS.	PLAYERS NUMBERS
CALLED THIRD STRIKE	2	
MISSED SIGNAL	9	
ERROR	2	
PASSED BALL	1	
WILD PITCH	1	
SWINGING STRIKEOUT	1	
BASE ON BALLS (PITCHER)	1	
WALK FIRST BATTER IN INNING	3	
HIT BATSMAN	1	
GIVING UP MORE THAN 4 ER	1	
FAILURE TO SLIDE	3	
PICKED OFF BASE	3	
PICKED OFF THIRDBASE	6	
GENERAL MENTAL MISTAKE	2	
MINUS POINT TOTALS		
GAME TOTALS		

448

AWARDING LETTERS IN BASEBALL

The baseball coach needs to set down criteria for his team in awarding varsity letters. The following is a sample criteria used in awarding letters in the sport of baseball:

A student-athlete representing (name of school) in the baseball program shall fulfill the following basic obligations before he may be considered for an athletic letter award.

1. Conduct himself in a manner which reflects credit on his school and the baseball program.

2. Return all equipment issued to him by the school.

Only athletes who have actually earned letter awards shall be entitled to wear a sweater or jacket which has a letter indicating he is a letterman. Only students who remain squad members for the entire season shall be considered for awards. Injuries may be an exception.

Requirements for earning an intercollegiate athletic award in baseball are:

1. Catchers, infielders and outfielders must play in a minimum of one-third of all games played.

2. Pitchers must meet one of the following criteria: (1) receive credit for winning three games; (2) receive credit for winning one game and pitching a minimum of 16 complete innings; or (3) pitch a minimum of 23 complete innings.

In addition to meeting the minimum participation requirements, an athlete must be recommended by the coach and athletic director, who have the right to take into consideration: general conduct; loyalty; sportsmanship; and overall contributions to the squad.

The coach may recommend that an award be granted to a student having fewer than the minimum participation requirements in cases involving injuries, weather, and loyal service. A player making normal progress toward an award at the time of an athletic injury should receive special consideration by the coach as should a senior squad member who has been a loyal squad member.

TREATMENT OF MINOR BASEBALL INJURIES

Hopefully, the baseball coach has a baseball trainer in his athletic department who can be responsible for treating any minor baseball injuries that might occur. If not, then the baseball coach must take on this additional responsibility.

In this section of the Playbook, we wish to present some basic information that can serve as a guideline for the coach in treating these minor injuries. It is by no means a strict outline for these injuries, but merely a suggested plan of action that the coach might follow. In athletics there is very little difference in the injuries that occur in the various sports. The significant difference lies in the manner in which these injuries occur.

The most successful program in athletic training is one of injury prevention rather than treatment alone. Care must be taken to eliminate conditions which might result in injuries to athletes. The coach should check the practice areas to remove hazards in or on the field of play (holes, broken glass, unpadded equipment, etc.). He should also eliminate drills which result in an abnormal number of injuries. Most important in the prevention of these injuries is a gradual goal-oriented conditioning program for a team. Emphasis on flexibility and strength will benefit the team not only in pre-season drills, but throughout the entire season.

The following are some of the more common baseball injuries and the proper treatment methods that need to be practiced.

ABRASIONS

Because of the appearance of many abrasions, they are more commonly referred to as "strawberries". These abrasions are usually the result of sliding or falling on a rough surface.

With proper instruction in the mechanics of sliding, many of these abrasions can be eliminated. It is also suggested that the athletes wear a pair of gym shorts or cut-off thermal underwear beneath their practice and game pants. These shorts protect the most vulnerable areas of the skin from severe abrasions.

If these abrasions occur, the following treatment may be taken:

1. Wash the wound thoroughly with soap and water or an antiseptic scrub. Take great care to insure that all dirt and foreign bodies have been removed from the wound.

2. Apply ice to the area to help control bleeding, reduce soreness, and eliminate some of the discomfort.

3. Apply an antiseptic solution and allow the preparation time to dry.

4. Apply an antibiotic ointment and a sterile dressing (non-adhering) to the abrasion.

5. Keep the wound clean and apply an antiseptic preparation or antibiotic ointment daily. You may want to expose the wound to the air to allow it to dry. You should cover the wound when clothing might come in contact with the area to prevent it from sticking to the material. Keep the wound padded when participation is anticipated.

ANKLE INJURIES

In baseball, it is impractical to protectively strap or tape all of your players. This practice is common in football and basketball where the danger of ankle injuries or sprains is more evident. However, if a player has had a history of ankle injuries, ankle strapping should be considered.

When an ankle injury occurs, immediate treatment should consist of the following:

1. Complete evaluation of the injury to insure that there has not been a break.

2. Ice application followed by applying a compression bandage to the area.

3. Elevate the ankle while the athlete is laying down or is seated.

4. Immobilize the joint if in doubt while a physician is summoned. Consult a physician for x-rays and other diagnostic tests.

With minor ankle injuries, the use of ice baths and exercise has proved quite useful. The athlete is instructed to place his ankle in a tub of ice water. Immerse the ankle to a point above the injury. When the ankle is numb, walk around normally until feeling returns. Make certain that the athlete walks as normal as possible. Repeat the ice bath and exercise at least three to five times per treatment. This type of treatment will quickly eliminate soreness, stiffness, and remove swelling from the joint.

Once swelling and pain have subsided, make certain that the ankle is rehabilitated to lessen the chance of reinjury. Riding a bicycle, toe raises, and range of motion exercises with light weights will aid in recovery. A small heel lift placed in the shoe may help the athlete walk around with less discomfort until he is fully recovered.

ATHLETE'S FOOT

Athlete's foot discomfort is not confined to the realm of athletics but can plague anyone in any walk of life. It is a fungal infection that attacks dead tissue in moist, dark environments such as the skin between toes. Athlete's foot is quite painful and, in severe cases, it can hamper athletic performance.

Athlete's foot can be prevented and may even be cured by following the steps suggested below:

1. Wear clogs in the shower and drying areas.

2. Pay special attention to dry thoroughly between the toes. Dust between the toes and feet daily with an antifungal powder.

3. Wear clean socks daily (cotton preferably).

4. Take every opportunity to expose the bare feet to the air.

5. If athlete's foot persists, consult a physician.

BLISTERS

There are two possible treatments for blisters. Choose the method which is the most desirable for your particular situation. It should be noted that some parts of the body might dictate the way in which the blisters are treated.

1. The first method is one in which the top layer of skin is actually cut away once the fluid has been drained. Cleanse the area thoroughly and apply ice to soothe the burning sensation. After the area is numb, apply a benzoin solution to toughen the exposed layer of skin. Once this solution has dried, apply an antibiotic ointment and a sterile dressing. The next day allow the blister to be exposed to the air. A pad with lubricant to reduce friction will aid the athlete while he participates in workouts.

2. The second method involves draining the blister by cutting a small hole in the blister to allow the fluid to escape. The hole should be large enough to allow the fluid to drain without closing over to accumulate more fluid, but small enough to allow the top layer of the blister to protect the underlying skin. Clean the area with soap and water and apply ice to soothe the discomfort. Benzoin applied through the opening in the blister will toughen the new skin. Apply an antibiotic ointment and sterile dressing to the blister, and pad it during strenuous activity. When the underlying skin is able to withstand the pressure of activity, the top of the blister may be cut away.

Blisters to the hands may be prevented by wearing batting gloves to cut down on friction. The best prevention for blisters to the feet is shoes that fit properly. Check socks to insure that there is no pressure points caused by folds in the material to result in blisters. Skin tougheners, foot powders, and skin lubricants are also beneficial in reducing blisters.

CONTUSIONS

A contusion (bruise) is the result of a blow to a muscle or other soft tissue anywhere on the body. This is often a very painful and incapacitating injury that can take anywhere from several days to several weeks to regain full function. Immediate treatment may mean a reduced recovery period. The following procedure is recommended:

1. Examination to determine the extent of the injury.

2. Ice application.

3. Compression bandage starting below the blow and continuing above the site of the injury.

4. Stretching the affected area to reduce soreness and stiffness.

5. For the next couple of days, maintain ice applications, stretching through the full range of motion, and a pressure bandage.

6. Progress to moist heat applications and gentle massage of the area. Pad the area to prevent further injury while participating in strenuous activities. If pain and discomfort persist, consult a physician.

DENTAL INJURIES

Although baseball is not a typical contact sport, dental injuries do arise from time to time. They usually occur as a result of collisions involving two or more participants, being hit by a pitch, or merely in the process of fielding a ground ball that has taken an unexpected bad hop.

The most serious of these injuries is a loose tooth or one that has actually been knocked free of its socket. The proper immediate action given to these injuries could help decrease their severity or even the permanent loss of the affected tooth.

The following procedure is recommended for the treatment of this type of injury:

1. Check the mouth to locate the injured tooth. If the tooth is missing, check the playing surface where the injury occurred and pick up the tooth. Handle it by its crown only.

2. Rinse the mouth out with cool water or a very mild mouthwash to remove unwanted debris and blood.

3. If the tooth is still in the mouth, try to gently place it back in its original position. Do not force it. If the tooth was knocked out completely, try to place it back in its socket or if you prefer, place it in a glass of clean water or even still, in the participant's mouth next to his cheek.

4. Notify a dentist of the existing situation and take the athlete to him immediately. Time is of the essence.

Other dental injuries such as a chipped tooth should be seen by a dentist immediately. Also encourage your athletes to follow a regular program of dental hygiene.

EYE INJURIES

The most common baseball eye injuries are those involving dirt or lime in the player's eyes. This problem can be solved by either irrigating the eye with cool water or a specially prepared solution. If this is not readily available, try pulling the upper lid over the lower lid. You may need to repeat this several times. If the irritation continues, consult a physician immediately.

In some injuries, the eye may actually be bruised or even scratched. This injury should not be taken lightly, and a physician should examine the athlete immediately.

It is necessary for a trainer and a coach to know whether his athletes wear contact lenses and if they are hard or soft lenses. If players use contact lenses, it is advisable that a small mirror and the proper solutions be carried with the team's equipment.

452

FINGER INJURIES

The most common injury in athletics is to the fingers. They are constantly subjected to injury regardless of the sport or the participant's position on a team.

Proper fielding mechanics will help eliminate many of these finger injuries in baseball. Protecting the hands while sliding is also of considerable importance. The slider must keep the fingers together as well as keeping them in the air when sliding whenever possible.

Make sure that when an injury occurs and there is some doubt whether a fracture is involved, a physician be allowed to examine the hand. Ice applications are recommended as immediate treatment in these cases. Later, moist heat applications, parafin wax baths, and taping may allow the athlete to continue participation.

KNEE INJURIES

Injuries to the knee resulting from a blow to the area or an exaggerated twisting motion may be more serious than they might first appear to an untrained individual. Knee injuries should be examined by the team physician immediately, preferably within twenty to thirty minutes after the injury. If a physician is not readily available, apply ice and a compression bandage, immobilize the knee and transport the athlete to an alerted physician.

With minor knee injuries, routine treatment with ice applications and later heat applications are advisable. Pad the knee with either commercially available items or make a pad by using foam rubber and an elastic bandage to secure it in place.

Knee injuries might be prevented or at least their severity reduced with a good conditioning program. The knee gains its strength from the quadricep, hamstring, and lower leg muscle groups. It is important that the legs are not neglected in any weight program.

MUSCLE STRAINS

The incidence of muscular strains or pulls can be greatly reduced by instituting a good conditioning and flexibility program. Stretching before participating in strenuous physical activity is essential.

There are other possible causes of muscular strains such as muscular imbalance, mineral imbalance, etc. If an athlete suffers from an abnormal number of these injuries in a season, a physician should be consulted to further evaluate the situation.

Muscle pulls may be treated in the following manner:

1. Ice applications for the first couple of days. Heat applications may be started after swelling and internal bleeding have subsided.

2. Compression to the area provided by an elastic bandage.

3. Gentle stretching to reduce stiffness and soreness.

4. Gentle massage to the affected muscle group. Rest is very important.

Muscle pulls can vary in severity. A minor strain may heal sufficiently in several days whereas a more severe injury with a large number of muscle fibers torn may require several weeks to regain normal function. During this period of recovery, it is also recommended that the athlete not neglect his condition. He must also work on gradual progressive resistence exercises to regain strength in the injured muscle. All too often, treatment is given while rehabilitation and conditioning are postponed. Rehabilitation and treatment must be given simultaneously in order for quick, yet complete recovery to occur.

SHOULDER, ARM, AND ELBOW INJURIES (MINOR)

These are common ailments where a ballistic movement such as throwing a baseball is involved. Throwing is a violent motion which places a great deal of stress not only on the musculature of the arm and elbow, but also on the connective tissues that surround these joints.

453

Pitchers seem to experience the greatest percentage of injuries to the shoulder, arm and elbow. This is not to say a catcher, infielder, or an outfielder cannot experience the same injury and discomfort.

In most cases, shoulder, arm, and elbow injuries can be attributed to a flaw in the individual's throwing mechanics. It is important to learn to throw properly from the very beginning of a player's career. Injuries as a result of overuse and poor mechanics at an early age can hamper an athlete through his entire baseball life.

Routine soreness and discomfort from throwing can be treated easily and quickly by the athlete himself. Here again, prevention is just as important as treating the throwing arm. Before throwing and during a workout, the following may prove helpful:

1. Moist heat applications (hydrocolator, whirlpool, etc.) and gentle massage.

2. Routine stretching exercises for the shoulder, arm, elbow and back.

3. Wear clothing that will retain body heat such as an undershirt with long sleeves.

4. Begin by gradually tossing and slowly increasing the throwing distance.

5. While throwing, alternate pitches. Throw a few fast balls, then some curve balls, etc.

6. At the end of the workout, gradually cool down by tossing at a shorter distance.

7. Stretch again after the workout is completed.

Once back in the dressing room, the shoulder, arm, and elbow should be iced. This treatment can be accomplished by immersing the arm and elbow in an ice bath for approximately fifteen minutes, applying ice packs, or even massaging the arm with an ice cup. After completing the ice application, elevate the arm above the head and massage the arm down towards the heart with a massage lotion.

A combination of rest, ice applications, massage, and stretching with a light weight on the day after a workout would provide ideal treatment for a pitcher. This procedure will help relieve soreness and decrease the recovery period between pitching appearances. Persistent discomfort indicates the need for a doctor's examination.

SPIKE WOUNDS

Cuts from spikes are often more severe than they first may appear to the trainer or coach. They are usually deeper than most cuts and in most cases, are similar to puncture wounds.

When an injury of this type occurs, it is necessary to thoroughly examine the area for a possible injury to blood vessels, tendons, ligaments and bone. If any of these are involved or if it becomes apparent that sutures are needed, a physician should be summoned to further examine the wound.

Minor spike wounds can be treated by thoroughly irrigating the wound with soap and water or an antiseptic scrub. Bleeding can be controlled by applying gentle pressure or an ice application. Apply an antibiotic ointment and a sterile dressing to the wound. Change the dressing daily and check for possible signs of infection. Protect the wound on occasions when strenuous activity is anticipated.

STRETCHING

Stretching cannot be over emphasized in preventing and treating athletic injuries. Stretching yields flexibility which not only reduces the incidence of strains and sprains, but also can improve athletic performance. Pitchers need not be the only players to participate in stretching exercises. Every athlete can benefit from a rigid and well planned stretching program.

Flexibility is developed gradually. Stretching exercises should be slow and deliberate. Avoid bouncing and abnormal forced stretching by a teammate. These practices may cause injury rather than flexibility.

Stretching exercises should be done on a daily basis, both before and after workouts. Stretching after workouts often helps combat soreness encountered after strenuous activity.

TAPING AND STRAPPING TECHNIQUES

In the space available in this Playbook, there is very little taping that can be discussed or better yet, illustrated. There are several excellent books on athletic training and taping which are available on the market today. These books go into much detail on certain injuries and actually diagram several taping techniques for each type of injury.

STRENGTH AND FLEXIBILITY PROGRAM

It is the feeling of most baseball coaches that the stronger and more flexible a baseball player can become, the better able he is to improve his skill level. This section of the Playbook will deal with the various aspects of weight training and flexibility that can be used in an off-season program or can be done in conjunction with the regular fall or spring program. Much depends on the equipment and facilities available to the baseball coach when he starts planning what type of program he wishes to develop. With proper facilities, time and supervision, a strength and flexibility program can prove valuable to the individual baseball player.

STRENGTH PROGRAM

The purpose of a strength program is to assist the baseball player in increasing his strength and endurance by overloading the muscles involved. Strength is achieved by overload, endurance by increasing the number of repetitions or sets of a given weight. The exercises described in this program are designed for a proper balance between strength and endurance, as well as overall body development. The coach should not interest his players in how much weight they can lift, but interest them in how much weight they can lift a greater number of times.

Weight training is a supplement to total body fitness and will serve to strengthen muscles that otherwise would not receive attention in regular exercises, running, and general sports activity. In no case should an athlete work with weights more often than every other day. There should be a recovery day between workouts. On alternate days, running and other conditioning activities can be done.

The coach must make sure that his players concentrate on going through a full range of motion when they are lifting weights so that they maintain full flexibility. This is the reason for not allowing them to bulk lift whereby they attempt to see how much weight can be lifted at the expense of repetition. It is also important for the players to concentrate on their breathing when lifting weights. They should always inhale upon exertion and exhale upon relaxation.

The weight program should be accomplished in the following manner:

1. **Arms, shoulders, upper back and chest**—Start with a weight that you can handle at least 10 times but not more than 15 times. If you cannot handle this weight at least 10 times, it is too heavy. If you can handle the weight 15 times, it is too light. The records of weight and repetition should be kept daily on a chart in order to evaluate progress and record information that can be evaluated by the coach supervising the weight training program. At each workout try to increase one repetition until you have reached 15 again, and then keep repeating the process.

2. **Legs and lower back**—The same procedure as outlined for the arms, shoulders, upper back and chest should be used with the exception that from 14 to 18 repetitions should be used instead of 10 to 15, and the weight increase should be from 10 to 20 pounds.

3. **Stalemate or sticking point**—If a stalemate is reached, extra weight should be added (5 to 10 pounds for the upper body and 15 to 20 pounds for the lower body) and fewer repetitions used for several days. Then you should go back to the weight and repetitions you were using prior to the stalemate. A stalemate may also be broken by increasing the number of sets of an exercise that you are doing. Before lifting, make sure that you do a good job of warming up for it is very easy to pull or strain a muscle when you begin lifting weights if you have not done a good job of stretching.

4. **Other exercises in conjunction with weight training program**—Along with the weight training program, other exercise programs should be performed to supplement the weight workouts:

A. **Running**—Running should be done daily for speed and leg strength. Endurance running combined with a weight training program may take away from each other. Sprint work and short distance work will strengthen the lower part of the body and may add quickness to your baserunning.

B. **Pullups**—These are highly recommended for all non-pitchers to help strengthen the arms and upper body. Work yourself to a peak so that you can do at least 18 pullups.

456

C. **Fingertip pushups**—These should be done sometime during your workout and can also be done before going to bed at night. Should work yourself up to 30 fingertip pushups.

D. **Ball squeeze**—If you need to strengthen your forearms and wrists, buy a rubber ball and squeeze it while you are watching television.

E. **Weighted bat**—If you can get ahold of a weighted bat, swing it at least 100 times a day. Keep in mind that it should not be so heavy as to cause you to swing differently than you normally would.

F. **Situps**—Should be done daily to improve and strengthen the stomach and abdominal area. Should be able to do at least 100 a day.

G. **Flexibility exercises**—These types of exercises can be used for warmup prior to the weight training workout or they can be used on off days. A further discussion of flexibility exercises follow in this section.

H. **Handball and paddleball**—These two types of activities are highly recommended for conditioning, endurance, and eye-hand coordination. They are excellent non-weight training day activities.

I. **Free weight workout program**—The following are the types of free weight exercises that should be incorporated into a workout program:

1. **Two hand press**—Standing position with feet comfortably spread, grasp the barbell with palms out and hands at shoulder width with the barbell held at chest. Raise barbell above the head until the arms are fully extended. Lower weight slowly to the chest and repeat. Stand erect and keep back straight. Do not arch the back when it becomes difficult to achieve another repetition.

2. **Biceps curl**—Standing position with feet comfortably spread, grasp the barbell with palms out and hands shoulder width apart, weight held at thighs. Flex the elbows and raise the barbell to shoulders, lower slowly to full arm extension and repeat. Do not allow the elbows to dig into the sides. Keep arms away from the body. Do not arch the back when it becomes difficult to achieve another repetition.

3. **Bench press**—Lying on the back on a bench, partner places the barbell across the chest. Grasp the barbell with palms down and hands spread very wide. Raise the barbell to full arms extension, lower slowly to the chest and repeat. Do not bounce weight on chest.

4. **Bent over rowing**—Standing position with feet comfortably spread, bend at the waist and grasp the barbell with palms in and hands spread wide. Bring the barbell to the chest as far as possible, lower slowly to full arm extension and repeat. Keep the back straight with the head up throughout the exercise. Move the elbows straight up and down. Do not allow the barbell to touch the floor.

5. **Bent arm pullover**—Lying on the back on a bench, grasp the barbell with palms up and hands four to six inches apart, weight above the head with elbows bent. Slowly lower the weight behind the head and then bring the weight to the chest, return to the overhead position and repeat. Keep the elbows bent throughout the exercise.

6. **Pull to chin**—Standing position with feet comfortably spread, grasp the bar with both hands, approximately four to six inches apart, palms down and arms extended downward. Standing erect flex the elbows and bring the barbell up until it touches the chin as you maintain the erect position. Lower the barbell by extending the elbows and come to rest at the ready position with the elbows fully extended and the barbell resting by the thigh.

7. **Three-quarter squats**—Standing position with feet flat on floor and spread well apart. Grasp the barbell with palms forward and hands spread wide, padded barbell held behind the neck across the shoulders. Squat to a three-quarter knee bend. Return to standing position and repeat. Keep the back straight and the head up throughout the exercise. Never do a full squat or deep knee bend.

8. **Reverse curl**—Standing position with feet comfortably spread, grasp the barbell with palms down and hands shoulder width apart, weight held at the thighs. Flex the elbows and raise the barbell to shoulders, lower slowly to full arm extension and repeat. Stand erect with back straight. Do not allow the elbows to dig into the sides. Keep arms away from the body. Do not arch the back when it becomes difficult to achieve another repetition.

If the baseball team has access to Nautilus or other non-free weight mechanical devices, they should be incorporated into the strength program. It is quite important that any weight lifting strength program be well supervised to insure that all the players are getting the maximum out of their workout under ideal conditions. If the athletes are well supervised and understand that safety is an important aspect of their workout, injuries should never be a problem.

FLEXIBILITY PROGRAM

It is a proven fact that athletes will incur more tendon, ligament, and muscle damage if they have poor flexibility. As an athlete increases his flexibility, he will also expand his range of motion. In baseball, the range of motion of a player's total muscle movement has proven to be an important ingredient in the success of an athlete. It has even been used as a measuring guide as a prediction of advanced baseball potential. Flexibility will help to prevent unnecessary injuries and will also aid in an injured player's recovery due to the initial condition of the muscle prior to the injury. It is important that each player realize this is a developmental program. We want to improve their flexibility and not simply maintain what they have. There is little doubt that these following flexibility exercises, if done properly and faithfully throughout the entire off-season, will bring the players to the start of the season with: (1) a body which is stronger; (2) a body which will be less prone to injury; and (3) a body with much more range of motion.

The following are the instructions that should be given the players in regard to the flexibility program:

1. The following flexibility exercises should be done a minimum of three times per week. If time permits, it will be advantageous to you to do these exercises every day. This is particularly true if you have poor flexibility or find that your body muscles are prone to painful strains and severe pulls.

2. Prior to stretching, jog to the track and run a 440 with a good 85% sprint during the last 60 yards. Do not neglect this preliminary part of the workout as it is needed to properly flood the muscles with blood by opening the millions of tiny capillaries. Your muscles will respond much better and more safely under these conditions. If it is too cold outside, then run in the gymnasium.

3. All flexibility exercises will be done with a partner. Your partner should be someone who is about the same height and weight as you are.

4. There are two phases to each of these exercises:

A. The first is the contraction or strength phase which demands a total effort by the performer being stretched. This is done for a slow ten-count against resistance.

B. The second is the relaxation phase where the muscles are actually stretched. It is mandatory that the performer concentrate on relaxing that muscle or group of muscles which he can feel resisting the stretch. The performer being stretched stands the slight discomfort as long as possible and indicates to his partner when he has had enough. Upon hearing this declaration, the man doing the stretching then ceases all movement and maintains his position for about two more counts. He then slowly lets the performer being stretched return to a more normal position. In other words, he does not simply and quickly release the stretch position when the performer indicates he has had enough. You stretch by going slow and steady and return by going slow and steady. There are no jerking, bobbing or sudden movements used. It is important that the man doing the stretching be alert to his partner's commands so that he does not go too far or move too fast. Visiting with a neighbor or "horseplay" can provide some unnecessary soreness or even an injury to the muscles involved.

5. Each exercise should be done twice in succession.

6. The exercises must be done in the following order:

Single Leg Up
Butterfly
Diamond
Lint Picker
Gastroc
Snake
Scissors
Endo

458

SINGLE LEG UP

Contraction Phase—total push downward on "B'''s shoulder.

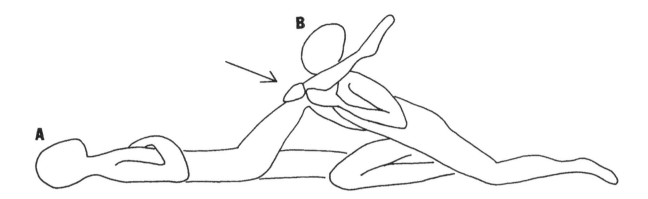

Relaxation Phase—Object: Touch foot to ground beside ear—one hand holds the knee on the ground, keeping it from bending. Opposite hand pushes up and toward the head being certain to circumscribe as big an arc as possible for a total stretch.

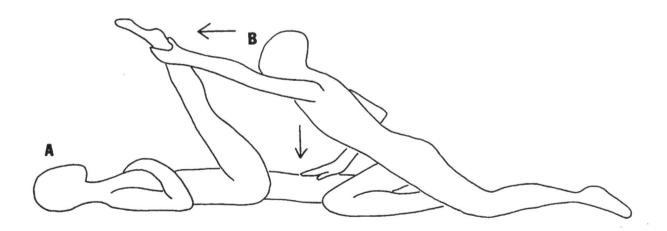

BUTTERFLY

Contraction Phase—The position of "B" is not shown, but should be clear since "B" must resist the upward push of "A"'s knees.

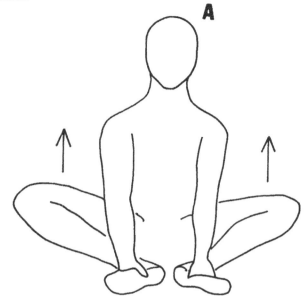

"B" pushes gently downward very slowly on the inside of the knees as indicated by arrows.

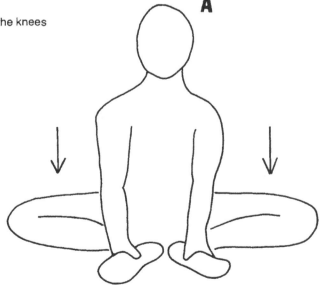

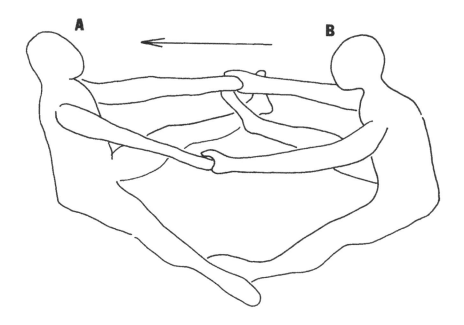

DIAMOND

Contraction Phase—"A" tries to pull "B" toward him using muscles of lower back. Strive to push buttocks down through deck. Do not simply lean back at hips with torso.

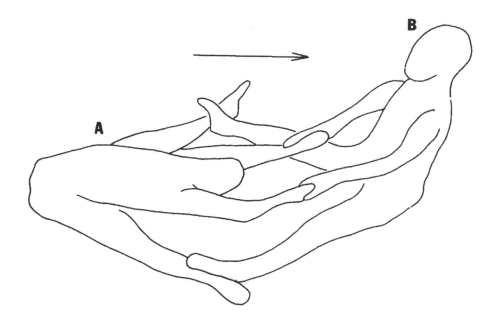

DIAMOND

Relaxation Phase—Object: To touch stomach to the ground. "B" pulls "A" using a horizontal motion. "B" pulls toward himself, not down. Pressure can be increased by "B" using his legs.

LINT PICKER

Contraction Phase—"A" tries to push back by using muscles of the lower back. "B" resists total effort by "A".

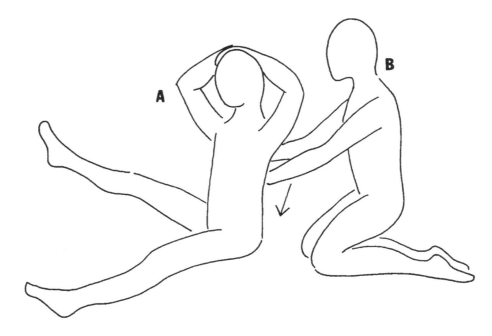

LINT PICKER

Relaxation Phase—Object: Touch the navel to the ground. "B" pushes "A" forward horizontally, not downward. "A" reaches forward with hands to assist movement.

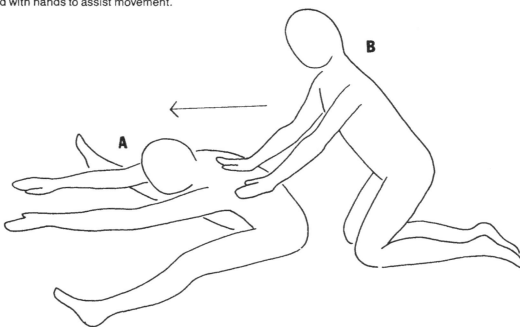

462

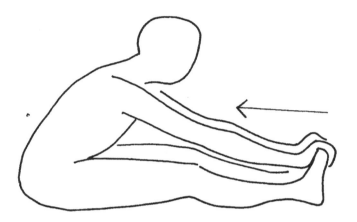

GASTROC

Object: Lift heels as high as possible. A player may execute the stretch by himself if he can grasp his own toes with his knees straight.

GASTROC

Contraction Phase—"B" resists "A" as he tries to point his toes.

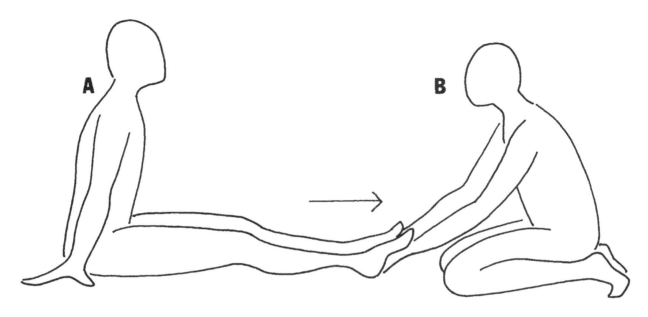

GASTROC—Relaxation Phase

"B" pushes on "A"'s toes causing heels to break contact with the ground. (Knees must be kept flat on ground.)

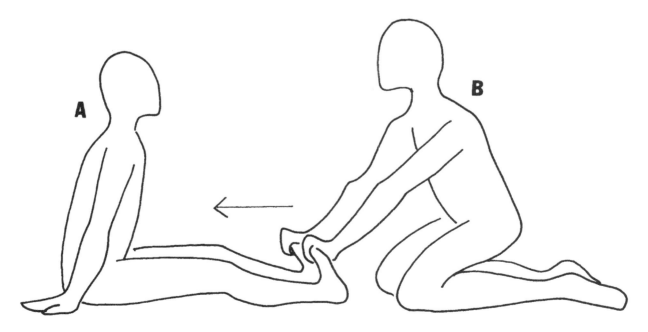

WRAP AROUND SNAKE

Contraction Phase—"B"'s arms go in front of "A"'s arms and behind his shoulders where palms are placed flat against shoulder blades. "B" resists "A"'s efforts to bring elbows together in front of his face.

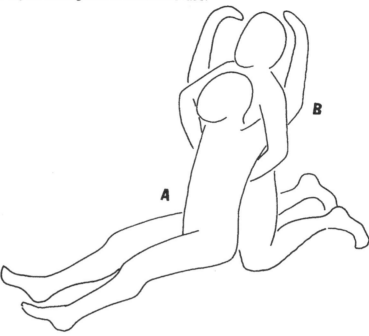

WRAP AROUND SNAKE

Relaxation Phase—"B" pushes up on "A"'s shoulder blades with palms and clamps "A"'s wrists and arms tightly to his body under the arm pits. "B" might have to squat down slightly to increase pulling angle. Do not push knees into "A"'s back!

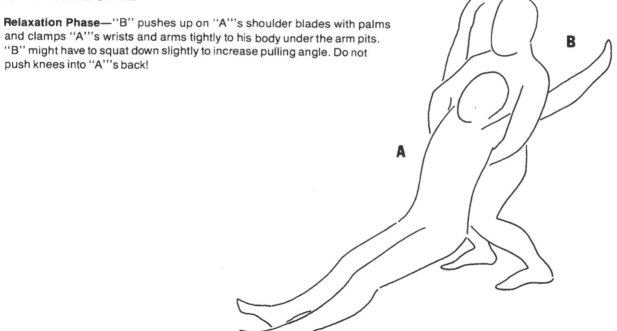

SCISSORS

Contraction Phase—"A" tries to bring feet together through ground. Emphasize total leg contraction.

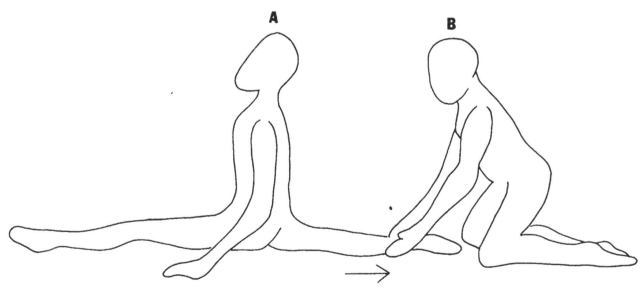

SCISSORS

Relaxation Phase—Object: Touch buttock of front leg flat with both legs straight. "B" simply lifts up rear foot so it will slide across ground. Review correct procedure for getting out of the split position.

466

ENDO

Contraction Phase—"B" holds up on "A"'s hands as "A" pushes down as hard as possible. Use all muscles of body.

ENDO—Relaxation Phase Object: Touch hands to the ground. "B" pulls on arms and circumscribes as big an arc as possible. There is no definite attempt to push arms downward. This occurs only when extension of arms at shoulders is completed and the natural arc dictates a downward path.

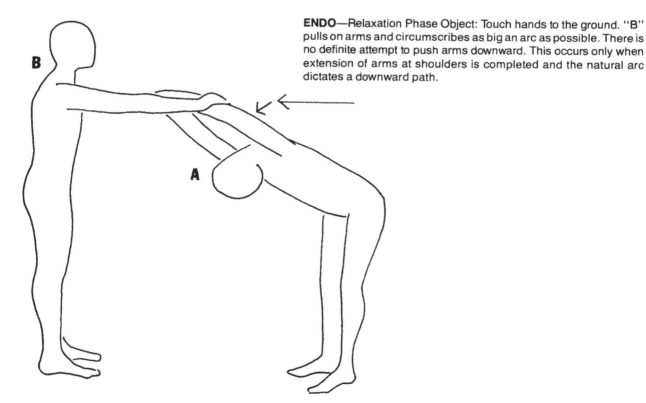

COACH-ATHLETE COMMUNICATION SYSTEMS

One of the most satisfying experiences a coach or athlete can have is to be a member of a team that gets along well and works together efficiently as a cohesive unit. Although many coaches seem to agree that cohesion or team harmony is an important aspect of successful sport performance, the question arises: "How does a coach go about creating a cohesive team?"

First of all, a coach must realize that individual differences exist among team members that come into your program. The athletes vary in ethnic background; they each have unique personality dispositions; they each have unique abilities to contribute to the overall productivity of the team; and they each have a variety of needs and incentives that are longed to be satisfied. Thus, a coach is like a catalyst in some type of chemical mixture. The successful coach is one who can make the chemistry of the team gel, that is, enhance the potential that lies within each individual athlete while at the same time getting the unit to gel in a synchronized coordinated manner.

In addition to developing an athlete's level of skill, the coach needs to instill pride, confidence, and a sense of personal identity within their athletes so that they may become better people in the way they define themselves both on and off the baseball field. A coach should be firm but affectionate, getting the athletes to gel within one's organizational system, yet sensitive enough to let the players know that their roles are valued and their efforts appreciated.

Before discussing ways to improve team morale, let's identify a few reasons why morale in the team may be poor:

1. The team may have poorly defined goals and roles resulting in a program that reflects aimless behavior.

2. The communication system between coach and athletes may be poor or rigid.

3. The group may be composed largely of individuals who fail to identify with each other's struggles and accomplishments.

4. Leadership and responsibility may be concentrated in too few hands. Thus, there may be no hierarchy of status in the group so that younger and newer members of the team have no one to look up to for leadership and admiration.

5. There may be too much emphasis on skill development with few or no socializing activities to induce interpersonal relationships.

6. The team may be divided into small groups which only identify with those within their group.

Developing Team Harmony

1. The coach needs to emphasize the importance of pride in the group, its sources and consequences for the team. Pride is associated with self satisfaction that comes with achieving goals. You as a coach should think of creative ways to develop pride within subunits (i.e., pitchers and catchers, infielders, outfielders, etc.). Give each unit goals and incentives to shoot for. This will enhance pride, determination and consistency in performance.

2. Clearly understood goals and objectives will facilitate team productivity, intensity of performance, as well as solidify the chemistry within the team. Groups unite behind common goals, so it is important to get athletes to think in terms of the values, goals and operating procedures the team is striving to accomplish. To have a truly cohesive group, each individual must be willing to place the welfare of the team ahead of one's personal goals. Therefore, individual goals should be kept in proper perspective with team goals.

3. Shared expectations of appropriate behavior. This refers to the norms or rules that govern your team. They should be conducive to the goals the group is striving to attain.

4. Make sure that each team member understands that his contribution to the team is valued. Each player's role on the team should be clearly defined and the importance of his contribution to the team emphasized at all times. A coach should use various means to underscore the fact that winning or losing is a product of team effort. Increasing the perceived significance of an athlete's contribution to a team will heighten one's sense of personal competence and self worth. Similarly, teammates must have mutual respect for the feelings, opinions, and capabilities of each other. Roles may change as the team evolves

into more maturing situations. Therefore, players must have faith and confidence in their ability to contribute when called upon.

5. Recognize those individuals who excel within their designated roles and who contribute to group goals. This is the goal you desire as a coach. You want your athletes to excel within their designated roles, to work with a sense of collective confidence and mutual effort.

Developing Coach-Athlete Communication

The following ideas represent ways for enhancing coach-athlete communication:

1. The foundation for effective communication skills is trust and mutual respect. Open communication channels among coaches and athletes lends depth, creativity, and rationality for the analyzation of task related and interpersonal skills. Athletes want to be involved in certain decisions that affect them directly. The coaching staff should create an atmosphere whereupon players have the right and freedom to express their ideas in a democratic way.

2. Individuals come to your baseball program with a variety of ideas, feelings, and solutions to draw upon. By utilizing a participative management style of leadership, coaches can get input from players in a responsible way so that they can collectively turn their resources into meaningful action. Morale and productivity will improve when individuals are given responsibility and a chance to express themselves in goal setting and decision making policies.

3. It is important to get the athlete's ego involved rather than just task involved. By using the resources of group members to solve both task relevant and interpersonal problems, a coach shows respect for the judgment and individuality of one's players which in turn reflects trust, belongingness and attraction to the team.

4. Involving the entire group in goal setting activities results in a form of psychological contracting which leaves group members with an increased commitment to team goals and a greater awareness of the degree of effort and discipline required to reach team goals. Furthermore, if goals and strategies are clear, individuals will coordinate their efforts with maximum efficiency, and begin to monitor their behavior and that of their teammates in a very consistent way.

5. Through the guidance of the coach, teams should set both long and short term goals. Whereas long term goals provide incentives, direction, and evaluation of progress, the attainment of short term goals reinforces intrinsic feelings of pride, confidence and personal accomplishment. The coach's biggest task is to make sure the goals and plans that have been made through group consensus are realistic, attainable and challenging. The coach cannot be afraid to change goals that are found to be unrealistically difficult. Once goals have been set, consideration should be given toward what obstacles might prevent the fulfillment of these goals and how these obstacles might be overcome by the team.

6. Periodic team meetings should be held during the season to allow both positive and negative feelings to be expressed in an open, honest, and constructive manner. A mature group can resolve its internal conflicts, mobilize its resources and take intelligent action only if it has a means for consensually validating its own experience. Team meetings could revolve around a variety of topics:

    A. Developing realistic expectations for the team.

    B. Redefining goals that may have been set too high or too low.

    C. Learning from mistakes or losses.

    D. Providing an outlet for the expression of positive or negative feelings.

7. The coach needs to stay in touch with the interpersonal grapevine. Individuals who possess high interpersonal prestige and status within the group should be utilized as communication links so that coaches can stay in contact with the interpersonal grapevine or prevailing attitudes and feelings that exist within the group's atmosphere.

8. If the coach wishes to inspire confidence in people, he should not solely focus on failure. Rather, reflect upon achievements that have already been gained, then point out how the mistake can be corrected. A few words of encouragement and a little pat on the back will go a long way.

469

9. Coaches and athletes must learn to keep competition in the proper perspective. Winning means more than just beating one's opponent. It means personal improvement and striving to do one's best. The focus should be on long term motivation, teaching athletes how to bounce back when things get tough.

Baseball teams consist of people who reciprocally affect one another in both task related and interpersonal situations. A good coach is firm but affectionate, getting athletes to gel within one's organization system, yet sensitive enough to let the players know that their efforts are appreciated. Cohesion is facilitated in groups that have common goals, compatible roles, a system of communication that enhances goal achievement, and mutual respect for the opinions, capabilities, and feelings of others.

PSYCHOLOGICAL CONSIDERATIONS IN COACHING BASEBALL

Athletes and coaches seem to agree that psychological factors influence sport performance. They further agree that sports is a medium which can provide numerous opportunities to stretch forth the limits of human potential. However, the greatest barriers that athletes confront in their pursuit of excellence are psychological barriers that they impose upon themselves.

It seems the best, most consistent athletes are the ones that can control their emotions effectively, fine tune their focus of concentration, and bounce back from setbacks in an emotionally mature way. Personal excellence is largely a matter of believing in one's capabilities and performing with a sense of desire, determination and personal maturity.

The purpose of this section of the Playbook is to present a variety of psychological skills that will assist in maximizing athletic performance and facilitate personal growth.

ANXIETY, AROUSAL AND COMPETITION

Anxiety and arousal are natural components of competitive athletics and have a direct effect on an athlete's attentional processes. Anxiety may be broken down into two major components: (1) a worry component (concern over performance); and (2) an emotional component (physiological arousal).

1. **Worry component**—When an athlete's mind is disturbed by anxiety or self doubt, the expression of one's potential becomes hindered which often leads to mental mistakes. This leads to overtrying. Overtrying is usually expressed in terms of tightness. Inevitably, there is an involuntary tightening of the muscles which interferes with the flow and execution of an appropriate athletic response. The response is triggered by self doubt and is magnified in those situations we think matter the most. This inner dialogue can only serve to worry or distract the athlete from optimum performance.

What is needed is not a self-doubting, worried mind, but an alert, concentrated, well focused mind. Relaxation and concentration are inter-related. The athlete's mind should be calm, but focused. The athlete should want his body relaxed, but ready. Relaxed concentration is a learned art which must be practiced to be perfected just as any physical skill in baseball.

The following is a list of typical anxiety provoking situations that might arise during a baseball game, with the appropriate response by the athlete suggested:

A. **Situation**—The athlete is trying to live up to the expectations of significant others in his life.

Response—Compete to better yourself. Remember that success is basically a piece of mind which is the direct result of self satisfaction. In knowing that you did your very best is all the self satisfaction you should need.

B. **Situation**—An infielder makes an error in a crucial situation.

Response—No member of the team should ever get down on another member of the team as long as he is giving his very best to perform a skill. Pick each other up by giving words of encouragement. Remember that nobody feels any worse than the person who made the crucial error.

C. **Situation**—The athlete is at bat and the game is on the line.

Response—Before entering the batter's box, the batter should take a deep breath and visualize himself hitting the ball hard somewhere. Attempt to be at your best mentally when the best is needed.

D. **Situation**—A pitcher has just gotten himself into a pitching jam with the bases loaded and the game on the line.

Response—The pitcher needs to step off the rubber and take a deep breath for relaxation. He must visualize himself delivering the ball to the proper location. He should then step back on the rubber, tune into the catcher's target and physically replay what his mind has already told his body.

The following stress management techniques represent an effective means for reducing anxiety and keeping it at a manageable level:

A. **Visualization or mental imagery**—If actions can be thought out ahead of time, an athlete will tend to make fewer mistakes during task execution. Visualization, or mental rehearsal, is an exercise in positive thinking.

B. **Application of visualization**—The applying of visualization to sport is simple. Just develop a very clear picture of yourself performing optimally and then imagine how it feels. When the experience is real for you, take the image and feeling and convert it into physical practice. A pitcher may aid his power of concentration by visualizing a pitch arriving at its proper location before actually throwing the ball. As for hitting, instead of thinking about making an out, a hitter should visualize himself getting a clean base hit before entering the batter's box. Thus, "pre-programming" is necessary to reduce the need for thinking while performing the task. It is important that the athlete feel fully involved in the behavior being rehearsed rather than "standing outside" oneself and merely "watching" oneself perform.

Visualization or mental imagery gives the athlete a chance to deal with the problem or event in their mind before confronting with it during competition. This process seems to be one way of focusing full attention on the task at hand. For some athletes it serves as a last minute reminder of the pattern they wish to reproduce; for others, it takes their mind off any thoughts of worry or self doubt, reaffirming a last second feeling of confidence.

2. **Emotional component**—This is the application of providing oneself with positive self statements during stressful situations. Emotional control refers to an athlete's ability to manage their own level of stress, anxiety, tension or nervousness. How athletes perceive competitive situations and what they say to themselves about the competitive environment determines, in part, their level of arousal or emotion experienced.

Learning to control arousal, to manage stress, is indeed a skill. Frequently, athlete's thinking patterns are based on implicit but irrational beliefs that there are catastrophic consequences in failing to live up to their own or others' expectations. Many times an athlete's response to stress is not directly triggered by environmental situations, but rather by what they tell themselves about the situation and their ability to cope with it. The more times the athlete allows himself to feel depressed, the less productive he will tend to be in performing a skill.

The best way to reduce unwanted and unproductive anxiety is to challenge and change irrational negative thinking. Essentially, athletes should be taught to replace negative self statements with positive self statements in order to strengthen one's ability to cope with a variety of stressful situations. These coping self statements are concerned with four aspects of stress situations:

A. **Preparing for a stressor**—The athlete analyzes the situation: "What is it I have to do?" He then gives himself positive self statements: "Don't worry, worrying won't help anything". "Be ready with no negative thoughts". "Think rationally and believe in the ability I possess".

B. **Confronting the stressor**—The athlete confronts the situation: "Time for a few deep breaths for relaxation. Feel comfortable, relaxed and at ease". "If the unexpected occurs, don't get bent out of shape, just roll with the punches". "I can meet the challenge". "Stay relevant, confident, I will succeed".

D. **Coping with the feeling of being overwhelmed at critical moments**—"If arousal comes, just pause, keep focused on what it is I have to do". "If my muscles begin to feel tight, relax, take a few deep breaths and slow things down".

D. **Reinforce oneself for displaying appropriate skills**—"I knew I could do it". "I handled things pretty well".

The practice of replacing anxiety producing negative thoughts with more appropriate positive self statements, places at the athlete's disposal an effective means for reducing anxiety and keeping it at a manageable level. This technique is particularly useful for pitchers who get themselves into a tight jam or hitters who come to bat in crucial situations.

A relaxed athlete is a confident athlete and the sooner baseball players comprehend this fact, the better they will perform.

472

MOTIVATION, GOAL SETTING, AND SELF CONFIDENCE

Motivation is a drive within an individual that arouses, directs and energizes a ballplayer's goal directed behavior. Motivation should be conceptulized along two basic dimensions: (1) **direction**—the goal one is working toward; and (2) **intensity**—how hard one is trying to reach one's intended goal.

Goals provide direction and evaluation of progress and represent a motivational factor that guides behavior and gives it its purposeful character. Thus, goals provide standards to inspire an athlete to do his best.

The ability to set specific goals and pursue them in a systematic way separate those who want to excel from those that actually do excel. The question arises: "How can we use goals to build self confidence within our athletes?" Goals should be challenging, yet realistic and attainable. A series of short term goals which relate to long term goals can be established, with specific target dates for achievement. For instance:

Long Range Goals	Short Range Goals
1. To have a winning season	1. Win one game at a time. Keep to the game plan and minimize physical and mental mistakes.
2. To reach the playoffs.	2. Strive to win two games in a row on the road. Play at least .600 ball at home.
3. Desire to hit .300.	3. Strive to hit the ball hard consistently every time up.
4. Lower my ERA.	4. Try to pitch a shutout or give up only one earned run each game.
5. Strive for excellence and reach potential.	5. Strive for consistency and learn from mistakes every day.

Satisfaction and feelings of pride are associated with the attainment of long range goals. While long range goals act as an incentive or guide for action, the attainment of previously set short term goals creates a growing sense of confidence, personal accomplishment and self satisfaction within an athlete. Therefore, if athletes can set subgoals just far enough ahead as to require continuous improvement and effort, but not unrealistically far ahead as to be unreachable, then the corresponding success will build confidence in one's capabilities.

The urge to do one's best, to excel, is a part of a constant urge for self improvement. Pride, poise, perseverence and patience are key attributes associated with successful performance. Worthwhile things come from hard work and careful planning. Therefore, concentrate on your objective and be determined to reach your goal.

BASEBALL TOURNAMENT GUIDELINES

Many times a baseball coach is called upon to host and conduct a baseball tournament at his school. This section of the Playbook should provide some valuable information for a coach that is assigned this responsibility.

We will deal with all matters pertaining to the host coach's involvement in organizing a tournament so that he might be in a better position to conduct a "first class" baseball tournament. We are very much aware that each school has its own special abilities and resources, and so it is not our intention to dictate exactly how the many sundry areas of concern should be expedited. If these guidelines can provide a baseball coach and his respective tournament committee valuable information that will assist them in the organization and administration of their tournament, then our objective has been attained.

Often most coaches, along with their institution, do not have much advance notice that they will serve as hosts for a tournament. In light of this, it behooves all coaches to have in their possession information on tournament organization. Once your institution has been selected as the host institution, the head baseball coach must then be concerned not only with properly preparing his team for tournament play, but also to indirectly be responsible for the tournament itself. Coaches may receive some assistance from championship handbooks that might be available through their state or national association. Each association responsible for tournament play may also send a representative from their organization to oversee the conduct of the tournament, but it is generally not his responsibility to handle various tournament matters that do not involve his jurisdiction.

Throughout these tournament guidelines we will refer the coach to his association handbook, if available. The handbook should contain information pertinent to the rules and regulations of the association's national or state office.

SELECTION OF A TOURNAMENT COMMITTEE

The selection of the tournament committee can offer the coach a valuable means to delegate many of the responsibilities of the tournament to others who have the expertise and knowledge to handle the various assignments.

It is suggested that the chairman of the tournament committee be one who the baseball coach and athletic director feel has the ability and experience to run a tournament of this magnitude. It is highly recommended that the chairman be an administrator on campus, and preferably, an administrator within the athletic department. It should also be a person who has been involved somewhat in the baseball program at the respective institution.

Once the tournament chairman has been chosen, the head baseball coach should assist him in selecting individuals to be responsible for the various sub-committees. These individuals should also be ones who have had direct involvement in the baseball program. It is very important that all committee members have the time available to properly assist the chariman to insure that their area of responsibility is well defined, and the task accomplished. It is recommended that the following sub-committees be established under the tournament chairman:

1. Ticket Sales
2. Security and Parking
3. Programs
4. Field Maintenance
5. Banquet
6. Hospitality
7. Press, Radio and Television
8. Housing
9. Finances
10. Medical
11. Transportation
12. Protest
13. Practice and Game Organization

Each of the sub-committee chariman would then pick qualified individuals to assist him or her in performing the task at hand. In some cases, one person might be able to handle the responsibility alone. Each sub-committee chairman who picks committee members should do so with the approval of the tournament chairman.

We will now break down each of these sub-committees detailing exact areas of responsibility and the means and methods that they might use in achieving their goals.

TICKET SALES COMMITTEE

In order to insure that your tournament is successful financially, the ticket sales committee is a very important part of the tournament picture. The chairmanship of this committee should be assigned to someone in the athletic ticket office who has dealt with the sales and distribution of tickets for athletic contests on campus.

Each association that oversees the tournament may have minimum and maximum ticket prices established in their handbook for tournament tickets. The handbook might also have restrictions on complimentary tickets and the number of competitor's passes that might be available. The chairman of this committee should be familiar with these policies before establishing ticket prices on a per game basis, or for the entire tournament.

The ticket prices may be scaled according to seat location. It is highly recommended that a tournament ticket be available to the general public and student body at a somewhat reduced rate than if someone would pay to attend all the games under a separate admission. Two tournament passes might be made available to; (1) General public; and (2) Students of the competing institutions. If reduced ticket prices are made available to students of the competing institutions, then these tickets should only be sold to those students who have in their possession the proper student identification card issued by the school.

It is the responsibility of the ticket committee to have printed the various tickets that will be sold at the ticket office and/or at the game itself. Thus, the following types of tickets need to be printed:

1. Reserved game tickets and reserved tournament pass.

2. General admission game tickets and general admission tournament pass.

3. Student game tickets and student tournament pass for students of all participating institutions.

4. Competitor, tournament official, and press passes.

The number of tickets printed should be determined by the chairman of the ticket committee based on his or her estimation on the maximum number of spectators that might be expected for all games. A reserve supply of ticket stubs should be available in case of an unexpected large turnout for one game, or for the entire tournament.

In order to prevent the passing of tickets from inside the stadium to those outside who then might use the same ticket to enter, it is recommended that each ticket be punched in a manner that identifies exactly the game that the ticket was used when they entered the gate area.

To insure a good gate for all tournament games it is important for the ticket committee to properly promote the sale of tickets. This can be done through the normal media channels available to the athletic department. This means that there needs to be close communication between the chairman of the ticket committee and the chairman of the press committee.

Information needs to be distributed throughout the area on ticket prices, along with where these tickets may be purchased. This can be done through the use of press releases that would be prepared by the sports information office of the host institution. Tournament passes should be pushed so that a generous amount of income might be derived before the tournament begins in case the host institution happens to be eliminated in the early rounds.

It is very important that the number of ticket sellers and ticket takers be kept to a minimum in order to assist in keeping down the cost of administering the tournament. However, it must be a prime concern of the ticket committee that there be easy access to the ticket distribution points and that stadium entrances are not burdened by extremely long lines. The sale of tournament tickets will alleviate much of this congestion.

All entrances to the stadium itself must be controlled with the assistance of the security committee.

SECURITY AND PARKING COMMITTEE

There are four areas that this committee must deal with:

1. Parking and security in the parking lot(s).
2. Security in the gate areas.
3. Traffic control.
4. Security in the stadium itself.

It is highly recommended that the chairman of this committee be someone in the security division of the campus security department so that he or she has access to the personnel that have actual experience in all four of the above areas. Hopefully, the cost of the security force can be kept down to a minimum. However, it is important that these four areas of concern are adequately covered.

1. **Parking and security in the parking lots.** The parking lots that will be used by the fans need to be patrolled so that easy access in and out of these areas are assured. If not, you can expect some immediate problems when cars can not exit the lot due to improperly parked vehicles. At least one police officer needs to be assigned the task of circulating throughout these parking areas during the game(s) so that the security of the cars are assured.

2. **Security in the gate area.** All entrances and exits to the stadium proper need to be secured at least two hours before game time so that the ticket sellers and ticket takers have little problem in managing their respective gates. At the conclusion of the game, all gates must be opened so that the exodus of the fans is smooth and orderly.

3. **Traffic control.** It is recommended that security officers be assigned to congested areas of entrance and exits so that all vehicles can enter and exit the stadium parking areas without any major problems or danger.

4. **Security in the stadium itself.** It is to be expected in any athletic contest that there will be many partisan fans who are very much interested in showing their support for their team. The security force in the stadium itself must be adequate to insure that the game proceeds without any interference from those interested spectators in the stands.

It is practically impossible to control vocal abuse upon the visiting players, coaches and umpires during the course of the game. However, this vocal support should never reach the point where it takes away from the game itself. It is advisable to assign at least one security officer near the dugout of the team playing the host institution's team. It should be his or her responsibility to control any flagrant abusive language heaped upon the players and coaches during the course of the contest. After one warning, any violator(s) should be asked to leave the stadium.

The throwing of objects onto the field should be dealt with by immediate expulsion from the stadium. The public address announcer can be of assistance in politely asking the complete cooperation of the fans in this regard. All areas of the field where spectators can obstruct play should be patrolled so that all players have the assurance that they will be protected from any thrown objects and that they will not be interfered with while competing in the contest.

Upon completion of the game, it is wise to prohibit anyone from coming onto the field of play unless they have field passes (media, etc.). At least one security officer should be assigned to the umpires to escort them both on and off the playing field.

Alcoholic beverages should not be available at the site of the tournament. This will assist in alleviating a major problem in fan misconduct.

PROGRAM COMMITTEE

The normal lack of advance notice one has concerning their institution serving as the host institution makes it quite difficult to put together a quality game program. However, some attempt needs to be made to provide a game program for the fans who attend the tournament games.

The program committee chairman should be one who has had some experience in putting together game programs for athletic contests. This person should be very familiar with the operation of the sports information department at the university, and could actually be a staff member out of this department. The program committee chairman and the press committee chairman should work closely together in producing the information that will be provided within the program itself.

476

The amount of time available to put the program together will determine how much advertisement can be solicited to subsidize the printing. The advertisement should be solicited by the members of the program committee. The cost for advertisement space and location of the ads within the program must be established quickly so that the members of the committee can readily contact prospective advertisers. Hopefully, enough advertising dollars can be sold to completely offset the printing cost of the program itself. Sales of the programs at the game can then provide additional revenue for the tournament.

It is recommended that the number of programs printed and the price to be charged for the program be established by the program committee chairman with the approval of the tournament director. The price should be based upon the size and quality of the program itself. The programs should be available for purchase at all entrances to the stadium and can even be sold throughout the stadium.

It is recommended that the following information be provided in the program, if possible:

1. Complete rosters of the participating teams including: full names, year in school athletically; position(s) played; uniform number; height; weight; hometown.

2. A message from the institution president, principal or athletic director welcoming the fans and participants.

3. An attractive cover with the names of all participating schools clearly depicted.

4. Final regular season statistics including game by game results.

5. Team picture, if possible

6. Information about the institution including: Conference affiliation, if any; nickname; school colors; enrollment; city and state institution resides in; athletic director.

7. Head coach and record.

8. Information about stadium; history, etc.

9. Listing of the chairmen of the tournament sub-committees.

10. Scorecard.

If time does not allow the committee to put together an extensive program of this type, then at least a small program needs to be prepared with the following minimum information provided:

1. Complete team rosters.

2. Scorecard

3. Cover with the names of all participating schools clearly depicted.

Host institutions are admonished to devote approximately the same amount of space in the program to each of the competing teams.

Each team should be provided enough complimentary copies of the game program for their entire party so that every member of the squad can have a souvenir of the tournament.

FIELD MAINTENANCE COMMITTEE

This committee's basic concern is to insure that the game field and any practice fields used are in the best possible condition for the duration of the tournament.

It is advisable to assign the chairmanship of this committee to the person who has been involved in the maintenance and upkeep of the athletic fields on campus. The reason being that he will have direct access to the personnel and equipment necessary to properly maintain and prepare the fields being used.

Some of the items that this committee needs to deal with are:

1. They must have the game field properly prepared for each of the tournament games making sure that the playing field meets all the rules and regulations of tournament play under the association guidelines.

2. They must monitor weather conditions at all times in order to prepare for any adverse weather moving into the area so that precautions might be taken to keep the field somewhat covered. It is certainly helpful to have a full infield tarp available in case of rain. However, if one is not available then it is important to have tarps to cover the mound and home plate area. It is further advised that there be readily available some dry dirt or drying compound to help eliminate moisture from the playing field.

3. They must properly maintain any practice fields that might be used during the tournament.

4. They must have enough personnel on hand to clean up the stadium and dugouts after each game.

5. They should assist in the moving of batting cages and protective screens on and off the field prior to the game.

6. Someone should always be on hand during the actual game in case of an emergency, such as a base breaking, etc.

As in all areas of concern, it is important that costs be kept down to a minimum.

BANQUET COMMITTEE

A baseball tournament is always enhanced by a banquet honoring the participating teams along with team officials, and the tournament committee. This affair should be put in the hands of a chairman who has great organizational ability and has had prior experience in organizing banquets of this size and scope.

The banquet should take place the night prior to the opening round of games to insure that all teams and officials are present. The conclusion of the banquet provides the time and opportunity for the general tournament meeting that should precede the first game of the tournament. The assigned member of the association responsible for the tournament can meet with the coaches and officials of the competing teams, the umpires and other officials directly responsible for the games themselves.

The chairman of the banquet committee can organize the committee in such a way that all necessary arrangements are made as expeditiously as possible. Areas of concern for this committee would be:

1. The site of the banquet should be reasonably accessible to all the competing teams. It would be ideal if an adequate size banquet hall is available on campus. The amount of space needed and the number of meals served will depend entirely on the number of invited guests and the number of tickets sold.

2. In consultation with the tournament chairman, a guest list must be prepared so that those people invited to the banquet are properly notified and supplied a ticket. It is highly recommended that this guest list be kept down to the following:

   A. Competing team members, coaches, trainers and managers.

   B. Athletic officials of competing teams.

   C. Visiting administrative officials from competing teams (example—President, Vice-President, Principal, etc.)

   D. Tournament umpires.

   E. Association games committee representative.

   F. Chairman of all tournament committees.

478

G. Administrative officials of the host institution.

3. Banquet tickets need to be printed and distributed to the invited guests. Sales of banquet tickets to the general public must be handled by this committee by offering opportunities for purchase of these tickets prior to the banquet itself. In order to provide an accurate count to the dining hall staff, all tickets for the banquet must be purchased in advance. Thus, it is not advisable to sell banquet tickets at the door.

4. The price of the banquet ticket to the general public should be enough to cover the actual cost of the dinner. Any additional surcharge attached to this ticket price can help offset the cost of the meal for the invited guests.

5. It is recommended that a multi-line buffet dinner be arranged so that the serving of the meal does not take an exorbitant amount of time.

6. All teams and their officials should be seated together to assist the head coach in the introductions. Tables should be set up perpendicular to the head table.

7. The head table should be elevated if possible and contain the following people:

A. Head coaches of the competing teams.

B. Association games committee representative.

C. Tournament director—Master of Ceremonies.

D. Athletic director or his representative of the host institution.

E. Chief administrative officer of the host institution or his representative.

F. Host city chief administrative officer or his representative.

G. Guest speaker, if any.

8. Upon completion of the dinner, a short program should take place. It is suggested that all segments of the program be kept short so that the entire speaking segment of the banquet not take much longer than 30 minutes. Welcoming addresses should be delivered by: the chief administrative officer of the host institution or his representative; the athletic director of the host institution or his representative; host city chief administrative officer or his representative; tournament chairman. The tournament chairman can assign himself the task of being the master of ceremonies for the banquet. Each of the head coaches of the competing teams should be given the opportunity to introduce each of his players, coaches, trainers, managers and any officials of the school in attendance. It behooves the master of ceremonies to caution the coaches to keep the introductions short and to the point.

9. A guest speaker could be invited to deliver a short message, but this is certainly not necessary. If a guest speaker is used, he should be one who has had experience in delivering short, humerous and inspirational messages.

10. Dress for the banquet should be informal.

11. The time of the banquet should be no later in the evening than 7:00 PM. This will allow the post-banquet meeting to start and end at a reasonable hour. Since each team will be allowed the opportunity to practice in the afternoon of the banquet, a starting time earlier than this might prove a hardship to the team practicing late in the afternoon.

12. Any decorations for the banquet facility should be appropriate to the occasion.

13. A representative of the city hosting the tournament might be able to secure an inexpensive gift for all tournament participants as a momento of their visit, but this is certainly not necessary.

HOSPITALITY COMMITTEE

The host institution, along with the host community, should attempt to provide as much hospitality as possible for the competing teams during their short stay in the area. This hospitality should not be an expense to the tournament itself outside those areas allowed by the association's championships handbook.

The chairman of this committee could be someone from the host institution, or it can be a civic leader in the community. Some of the functions that this committee can perform would be :

1. Assisting the chairman of the transportation committee to obtain complimentary dealer cars for the head coaches of the visiting schools, along with the association's baseball committee representative.

2. Assisting the chairman of the press committee in setting up and staffing fulltime the hospitality room which could be in the stadium itself, or in an adjacent building. This hospitality room would be for: members of the press, radio and television; coaches and officials of the competing teams; tournament committee members; and umpires. Refreshments need to be served from about one hour before each game to one hour after the completion of the game.

3. Each of the visiting teams should be greeted when they arrive at their hotel by the chairman of the hospitality committee, and a representative of the committee who will serve as the liaison person for that team for the duration of the tournament. This person will be available to help answer any questions for team officials along with providing them with the necessary information pertinent to the tournament itself and the activities involved with the tournament. Most of this information should be in writing so that most questions can be answered via this information sheet provided them once they arrive. The liaison person should provide the head coach with his home and office phone number so that he can be reached if a problem arises.

4. It would be a nice gesture to have a small get-together with the wives of the visiting team coaches and officials. This could take place the afternoon of the practice sessions in the hospitality room.

5. The hospitality committee should also be responsible for making sure the umpire's dressing room is open prior to the game, locked during the game, and reopened upon the completion of the contest so that the umpires might shower and dress.

6. Due to the fact that the duration of the tournament is generally short, it is not advisable to arrange for any entertainment for the teams involved. However, if weather conditions are such that teams can not compete on a given day it would be proper for the hospitality committee to attempt to arrange for some type of entertainment. As an example, a movie theatre in town might allow all the team members to attend a movie at no charge, or at least for a reduced rate. Tours of the area or other entertainment might be less practical but something that can be looked into if significant delays in the weather occur.

7. If possible, some small souvenir of the tournament could be presented to each team member and official. This could be something out of the city hall or the local chamber of commerce office, and could be presented by an official of the city or chamber at the banquet.

8. In coordination with the program committee, it is important that every team member and official receive a complimentary copy of the game program. This can be done at the banquet.

9. Assistance can be provided the team managers in getting the team laundry done by providing them transportation if no laundry facilities are within easy walking distance of team headquarters.

PRESS, RADIO AND TELEVISION COMMITTEE

The chairmanship of this committee should be assigned to the sports information director, or his assistant, within the athletic department of the host institution. His expertise in this area will allow him the opportunity to handle this assignment without any major difficulty.

It is the responsibility of this committee to disseminate the information to the media concerning the tournament. Of course, this includes pre-tournament information along with the results of each game. The association responsible for your tournament may have specific requirements in regard to the handling of the press, radio and television media. Make sure that the chairman of this committee reviews the association's championship handbook for this information.

The chairman of this committee will need full cooperation from the sports information directors of the competing institutions in providing publicity and program materials at the earliest possible moment.

As soon as a team is selected or has qualified to compete in a baseball tournament, the sports information director of the institution should forward to the chairman of this committee the following information: brochures, rosters (including name, position, numbers on both sets of uniforms, height, weight, age, number of varsity letters won, which way each player bats and throws, class in school and home town); season's record including scores of all games in the order in which they were played; complete up-to-date statistics on each player and team totals, to include all games prior to the tournament competition; assortment of head and posed action shots of individual players and head coach; and a team picture and a brief summary of the team's season.

The sports information director of the host institution will provide the sports information directors of the competing teams with a listing of the news outlets to which publicity materials are to be directed and shall indicate how each visiting director may assist in the promotion of the tournament.

Some of the other particulars that this committee should deal with are:

1. Should be responsible that the radio and television hookups are carried out by the telephone company or other agencies that are contracted to prepare the area for these media type agents. Consult with the association responsible for this tournament in regard to the rules and regulations pertaining to radio and television rights. Other areas of concern that the association rules and regulations will deal with in this area are:

   A. Establishment of a priority system for space in the press area for radio and television stations.

   B. Signing of radio and television agreements for those stations wishing to broadcast or televise tournament games.

   C. Rights fee for broadcasting or televising tournament games.

   D. Requests for film rights for tournament games.

   E. Geographical restrictions for transmitting tournament games.

   F. Advertisement restrictions on broadcasts and telecasts.

   G. Television news rules and regulations.

   H. Films and videotape rules and regulations.

2. The establishment of press credentials will be handled by the press committee following the guidelines set forth in the association's championships handbook. Areas of concern that the association rules and regulations will deal with in this area are:

   A. Priority system for seating members of the working press.

   B. Issuing press credentials for other types of media outlets.

It is the responsibility of the press committee to have prepared media passes for those issued proper press credentials. These passes should be presented at the gate and also entering the press box area.

3. The press committee is responsible for setting up an area where the coach and members of the competing teams can meet with the press upon the completion of the contest. This post-game interview set-up should follow the rules and regulations dictated in the association's championship handbook.

4. In accordance with the needs of the media, the press committee needs to be sure that the items needed for the press to properly file their stories are available (adequate number of phones, telecopier outlets, etc.)

5. The official box score needs to be picked up from the official scorer and mass produced for all members of the press, radio and television media. Official box score forms should be available through the association's national office.

6. If possible, each team's sports information director or his representative needs to provide the media with a copy of their baseball press guide, along with any tournament publication that their office has specifically prepared for the tournament.

7. The pre-tournament publicity needs to be extensive enough that the general public is very much aware of the tournament brackets, time of games, and ticket locations, etc. The amount of pre-tournament publicity can have an affect on the number of tickets sold.

8. Members of the media could be asked by the chairman of the press committee to assist in selecting the All-Tournament team and the Most Valuable Player. It should be mandatory that any member of the media involved in this selection be in attendance at all the tournament games.

HOUSING COMMITTEE

Once the teams competing in the tournament are known, the chairman of the housing committee needs to contact the head coach of each competing school in regard to the available housing accommodations in the immediate area. The chairman of this committee should be someone on the athletic department staff who has had experience in dealing with housing arrangements.

The chairman of this committee should assist the coaches in making their housing reservations. At the time of the call to the head coach of each team the chairman of the housing committee needs to have the following information for him:

1. Availability of hotels in the immediate area.

2. Cost per person per room for: two to a room; three to a room; four to a room. Availability of cots for each room. Whether the hotel offers a complimentary room for the head coach.

3. Distance that each hotel is from the game field and the practice fields.

4. Availability of additional rooms for parents and fans of the competing team.

5. Restaurant on the premise or within walking distance. Whether or not they serve team meals at the restaurant.

It would be helpful to these coaches to have at least three motels available for them to choose from. If the games committee decides to assign the teams to various motels this must be done in such a manner that no team gets preferential treatment. If possible, each of the visiting teams should be housed in separate motels.

Once the chairman of the housing committee has provided the head coach with this information, he should allow the competing teams to make their own specific reservations.

If, for some reason, there are not enough hotels or motels in the area to accommodate the teams, dormitory space might be secured at the host institution.

It would be a nice gesture for the chairman of this committee, along with the liaison man assigned to the team, to meet the team as it arrives at the motel. If room reservations have already been noted at the front desk, then the keys can be picked up and given directly to the head coach as they arrive.

Another responsibility of this committee would be to make lodging reservations for the umpires and the member of the association assigned to oversee the tournament. If possible, the umpires and the games committee association member should be housed in a motel other than the ones the competing teams are in. Once the reservations have been made, each of these individuals need to be personally contacted and informed as to which motel they are assigned to, along with detailed directions to the motel.

FINANCE COMMITTEE

The chairman of the finance committee for the tournament should be someone in the athletic department business office of the host institution. It will be his or her responsibility to follow the procedures for handling their finances as detailed in the association's championship handbook.

The areas of concern that this committee must deal with in regard to their responsibility are:

1. Establishing a proposed budget projection on anticipated income and expenses in administering the event. Forms may be provided by the association's national office for this budget preparation.

2. Host institution's responsibility for all expenditures over the approved budget (association policy).

3. Association's responsibility for guaranteeing transportation costs and per diem allowance for teams (association policy).

4. Defining what comprises net receipts and game expenses using association policies as the guideline.

5. Establishing whether the team managers will meet all expenses through the tournament including transportation, and then be reimbursed after receipt of their expenses.

6. Distribution of net receipts after all tournament expenses have been paid in accordance with association policy.

7. Filing a detailed financial report to the association's national office along with participating team's athletic director and business officer.

MEDICAL COMMITTEE

The chairmanship of the medical committee should be placed in the hands of the head trainer of the host institution who can appoint the members of his committee from his staff, including any student trainers who might be available.

Generally, each team will bring a certified athletic trainer with them to a tournament, so the committee's basic function is to coordinate their efforts and offer them the facilities and equipment necessary for them to meet the medical needs of their athletes.

As soon as the teams competing in the tournament are known, it is important that the chairman of this committee call the head trainers at the other competing schools to disseminate the information they need to properly prepare for the tournament.

Areas of concern for this committee would be:

1. Each scheduled session, practice or game, should have the presence of a person qualified and delegated to render emergency care to a striken athlete, preferably a certified and/or licensed athletic trainer.

2. Planned access to a physician, preferably a team physician, by phone or nearby presence for prompt medical evaluation of the situation, if warranted.

3. Planned access to a medical facility, including a plan for communication and transportation between the athletic site and the medical facility for prompt medical services, if warranted.

4. A thorough understanding by all affected parties, including the leadership of the visiting teams, of the personnel and procedures involved.

Treatment hours at the host institution's athletic training room needs to be available to all the visiting trainers and their athletes. This training room must be staffed by a trainer of the host institution, and it is highly recommended that a trainer from each school accompany any of his athletes when they go to these treatment sessions. This training room must be open and properly staffed during all games as well.

The chairman of the medical committee should be aware of any type of insurance coverage provided by the association responsible for the tournament and be in a position to offer advice to the visiting trainer and his athletes if a question arises over medical coverage. Generally this type of coverage by an association is restricted to those student-athletes and institutional representatives who are not covered through their institutional insurance program.

TRANSPORTATION COMMITTEE

The chairman of the transportation committee should be someone who is quite familiar with the modes of transportation within the host institution's immediate area.

Team managers should make all their own transportation arrangements to and from the tournament site. However, the chairman of this committee can be of great help to the person assigned by each team to handle their transportation of personnel to and from the game site.

If a team arrives by bus, vans or cars then these vehicles will be available at all times to transport the team to and from their motel to the practice fields, game site, etc. If that is the case, then they will be adequately provided for.

Any team arriving by air must have adequate transportation from the airport to their motel. It must be taken into consideration when providing this transportation that there will be a large amount of baggage and team equipment to be transported also. Of course, transportation back to the airport upon the completion of that team's involvement in the tournament must also be arranged.

Those teams arriving by air need to have local transportation while competing in the tournament. The chairman of this committee can assist the person responsible for each team's transportation in obtaining whatever means and methods they wish to use in moving their team and equipment from place to place.

The transportation committee can assist those on the hospitality committee to secure complimentary cars for the head coaches of the competing teams along with the association games committee member.

This committee would also be responsible for transporting the umpires to and from their motel to the game site if they do not have their own transportation.

PROTEST COMMITTEE

For most tournaments a three-man protest committee should be assigned by the chairman of this committee. Since the association games committee representative will generally not be familiar with baseball people in the immediate area, the protest committee should be assigned by this committee chairman.

All three members of this committee must be in attendance at all the tournament games. This committee should have reserved seats located with a good view of the playing field. These members must have a solid baseball background so that any interpretation of the rules that might come up can be handled with some understanding of the association rules incorporated into the actual situation that is being protested.

Some suggestions on who might serve on the protest committee: (1) a former college baseball coach in the area; (2) a certified umpire in the area not involved on the umpiring crew for the tournament; (3) a college baseball coach in attendance at the tournament as a spectator; (4) any other knowledgeable baseball person who is in attendance that the chairman has confidence in to handle a protest situation.

Rules and regulations for handling a protest can be found in the association's championship handbook that would be available at the tournament site. It is very important that each member of the protest committee have an up-to-date rule book specifically for the association that the tournament is sponsored by.

PRACTICE AND GAME COMMITTEE

It is very important that any baseball tournament runs smoothly from beginning to end. The organization and administration of the practices, pre-game ceremonies and the game itself are areas that need to be put in the hands of a capable administrator. The chairmanship of this committee should be assigned to someone on the campus of the host institution who is very familiar with the operation of a baseball tournament. This could be an area where an assistant coach might be the responsible chairman.

484

There are numerous items that need to be dealt with in this area of practice and game administration:

1. Practice administration

Each of the competing teams must have the opportunity to practice on the tournament field prior to the first game, if possible. The day prior to the tournament provides this opportunity for the practice sessions.

In scheduling the practice sessions, it is always advisable for the team that has to travel the farthest to the tournament site be given the opportunity to practice last, and the team that has to travel the second farthest distance the next to last practice time, on down the line. If all teams are scheduled to check into their housing area the night before the practice day, then the best thing to do is to go by alphabetical order of the schools in awarding practice times.

It is advisable to set up a strict timetable for the practice sessions with all sessions running 1½ hours with a 15 minute break in between. This 15 minute break will give enough time for one team to get off the field, the other to get on and loosen up. It will also provide enough time for the maintenance crew to quickly prepare the field for the next practice session.

The only maintenance that needs to be provided between practice sessions are: drag the infield dirt area; rake and tamp the mound; rake and tamp the area around home plate; and if the infield is extremely dry, a very light spray of water on the infield dirt and baselines is recommended.

All protective screens should be on the field and available to the practicing teams. This includes: the batting cage at home plate; pitcher's protective screen; first baseman's protective screen; and a back up screen behind second base.

If drinking fountains are not available in the dugout, a water cooler and cups should be provided for each of the teams practicing. Three to five towels should be available for the practice sessions which would be returned upon the completion of the practice.

All spectators, media personnel, etc., should be required to be in the stands during these practice sessions. It is not professional for members of the other coaching staffs to be in attendance when other teams are practicing, so this should be discouraged.

All the head coaches need to be aware that they have only the designated practice time available to them. A member of the practice and game committee should be in attendance at all practice sessions to handle any problems that might come up in regard to practice time restrictions. Of course, a team does not have to use all their practice time allocated to their squad.

2. Tournament format

The association responsible for the tournament should have in their championship handbook the brackets for the tournament games. This information should be in the hands of the participating teams as soon as they become available.

3. Pre-Game practice administration

If the tournament format, as decided by the association games committee, establishes an afternoon and a night game, then it would be appropriate to allow batting practice on the game field. Otherwise, all pre-game batting practice sessions should be held on another field near the game site.

If batting practice is to be held at another field, it is advisable that some maintenance work be done so that the field is in decent shape for a practice session. It is important that there be at least a batting cage and a pitcher's protective screen at any practice area used.

There should be a member of the practice and games committee at any practice site being used so that no interference is encountered by other groups wishing to use the field. The field should be reserved for the tournament's use well in advance of the practice sessions.

If at anytime adverse weather conditions prohibit the use of a practice field or the main field, this decision should be made by the association games committee representative. He can prohibit batting practice as well as outfield-infield practice when he feels that such practice will have an adverse affect on the field itself and make it unplayable for the game.

A strict time schedule needs to be enforced so that no team is denied an equal chance for practice time, and the starting time of the game is not delayed. If teams are taking their pre-game batting practice at another field, then an adjustment in time needs to be made in regard to the distance necessary to travel back to the game field.

Below is a sample pre-game practice schedule for a game that begins at 1:00 PM with both teams taking their batting practice on the game field:

1:00 PM Game

Home Team Batting Practice	11:30 - 12:00 Noon
Visiting Team Batting Practice	12:00 - 12:30 p.m.
Home Team Outfield-Infield Practice	12:30 - 12:40 p.m.
Visiting Team Outfield-Infield Practice	12:40 - 12:50 p.m.
Field Maintenance and Pre-Game Meeting	12:50 - 1:00 p.m.
Gametime	1:00 p.m.

It is recommended that 30 minutes be allowed for batting practice and 10 minutes for each team's outfield-infield practice. If field maintenance will take longer than the 10 minutes as indicated in the above schedule, then it would push everything back 5 minutes. There should be no reason to need more than 15 minutes for field maintenance unless the game is delayed due to adverse weather conditions.

4. **Pre-Game Program**

It is very important that both head coaches of the two competing teams be kept informed on any type of pre-game program that will take place prior to the starting time of the game. This could include the following:

A. **Pre-game Meeting**—The exact time of the pre-game meeting with the coaches, umpires, and chairman of the games committee should be known to all participants. At this time the coaches would exchange lineup cards with each other through the umpire-in-chief (home plate umpire). The ground rules would be discussed at this time, even though a printed copy of the existing ground rules should already be in their hands (given to them at the pre-tournament meeting). A sample copy of a set of ground rules are below:

GROUND RULES

The stadium is completely enclosed, therefore, all live balls will remain in play.

Exceptions: The ball is dead if:

1. The ball goes through, over, under or sticks in the fence.

2. The ball goes into the dugout beyond the curbing or is interfered with by a spectator.

3. The ball goes into the stands or out of sight under the wood facing of the dugout.

4. The ball goes into netting or strikes a metal pole of the batting tunnel located behind first base.

5. Fielder catches fly ball and falls into batting tunnel—**rule**—ball is dead and baserunners are awarded one base.

6. The ball goes behind end of batting tunnel or behind the brick wall at end of third base stands.

7. The ball goes above the "break" in the grandstand screen.

Foul Poles—Light Towers—Scoreboard—Left Field Wire Fence:

1. A batted ball striking any of these objects is a home run.

2. A batted ball striking the foul line marker on fence is in play.

Bullpen (Behind Third Base):

1. A batted or thrown ball which goes into this area is alive and in play. Players must make ample room for defense to play the ball; if touched by a player the rule book prevails.

Dugouts

1. Ball is in play in front of dugouts unless it goes beyond the concrete curbing-striking facing or bat racks or equipment—rule book prevails.

Note: There will be no warmup games, catch, pepper, etc. permitted in the dugout, home plate, first and third base areas.

Lights

1. Lights will be turned on at the discretion of the umpire-in-chief.

B. **Introduction of lineups**—It is advisable that the first time each team plays in the tournament, that their entire squad be introduced and lined up on their respective foul lines. This should include all players, coaches, managers and trainers. The introductions should consist of: full name; year in school; and position. You can have the starting lineup introduced first. It is also advisable before the first game to introduce the association's game committee representative, the umpires, and the protest committee members. Before each game, the umpires need to be introduced designating which position they will be responsible for in that particular game.

C. **National Anthem**—The National Anthem should be played before each game unless there are two or more games on the same day. It can be played before each game of a day-night doubleheader at the discretion of the tournament chairman. After the first game, it should be played when the defensive team (home team) has taken their positions on the field. For the first game for each team it can be played while both teams are lined up on their respective foul line. The flag should be flying in a conspicuous place in the stadium.

D. **Throwing out first ball**—It is a nice gesture to have someone throw out the first ball for the first tournament game. This should be done after both teams have returned to their respective dugouts after the National Anthem. The decision on who will throw out the first ball should be made by the tournament chairman and his committee.

5. Game Administration

Below are the items of concern in regard to the actual administration of the game(s):

1. **Official Scorer**—An official scorer for each game should be appointed by the tournament director, and his duties are outlined in the association's official baseball rules book.

2. **Length of Game**—The association's championship handbook should contain the rules and regulations concerning the length of each game. It should also contain information pertaining to the status of those games that are not completed due to adverse weather conditions.

3. **Playing Rules**—The official rule book of the association responsible for the tournament should be used.

4. **Determination of Home Team**—The association's championship handbook should contain information as to how the home team is determined for the first game and all succeeding games. Information pertaining to uniform selection by the home and visiting team should also be contained in the handbook.

5. **Public Address Announcer**—The public address announcer should be someone who has had experience in handling this assignment at numerous baseball games so he can do a first class job of handling this important assignment.

6. **Scoreboard Operator**—Like the public address announcer, the scoreboard operator should be someone who is familiar with the operation of the scoreboard, and has extensive experience in operating it during the baseball season. It is advisable to caution both the public address announcer and the scoreboard operator (if there is a message center on the board) that at no time would they show partiality toward any team in performing their job.

7. **Baseballs**—The association responsible for the tournament will generally designate the baseball that will be used for the tournament and will often supply the amount of baseballs needed. If not, enough baseballs need to be available to handle the entire tournament. An extra supply of baseballs should be available in case of adverse weather conditions, since this would cause the use of more baseballs than originally planned.

8. **Water in Dugout**—If the dugouts do not have water fountains, then water coolers should be provided both teams with an adequate number of cups available.

9. **Ball Shaggers**—It is highly recommended that ball shaggers be secured to shag all the baseballs that leave the field of play. Any ball that leaves the field and goes into the stadium area should also be retrieved by these shaggers. It is helpful to have them wear some type of uniform that identifies them as ball shaggers so that they are not hassled by those who might have secured the baseball. The public address announcer should make a few announcements during the game that all baseballs going into the stands must be returned.

10. **Bathandlers**—If batboys or batgirls are to be used during the course of the tournament, it is quite important that they have prior experience in working baseball games so that there is no problem with their interfering with the game itself. They should be in some type of uniform also.

11. **Ballhandlers**—A ballboy or batgirl should be used at each game to keep an adequate number of tournament baseballs in the possession of the home plate umpire. All baseballs that enter the game must be rubbed up in such a manner that the umpire-in-chief approves the baseball before it enters the game. The ballhandler should be in some type of uniform also.

12. **Press Media on the Field**—Press photographers will want to come onto the field to get their pictures of the action. The media should stay in those designated areas outlined by the ground rules so that they do not interfere with the ball in play.

14. **Maintenance Crew**—At least one member of the maintenance crew needs to be in attendance throughout each game to be of assistance in case a base breaks or some maintenance problem arises.

15. **Electrician**—If the lights will be used during the course of the tournament they should be tested prior to the beginning of the first game. A capable electrician needs to be on call in case an emergency arises in regard to the use of the lights for competition.

SCORING BASEBALL GAMES

The baseball coach has an abundance of administrative matters that he must be responsible for in regard to the playing of his games both at home and on the road. One of these responsibilities is the securing of a competent official scorer for his home games, along with someone who might be of assistance to him in keeping up-to-date statistics for his team.

If no one is available outside of the baseball team, then he will have to assign this responsibility to a manager or one of the players. As you can imagine, there are many baseball coaches who take on this responsibility themselves due to the fact that they are not able to secure a capable person to handle this very important task.

This section of the Playbook will provide some of the basic information on keeping a scorebook and statistics for a baseball team. In this way, the coach can use this information to train someone who might not have the experience necessary to handle this task.

SCORING THE GAME

Scoring a baseball game and making proper use of the resultant statistics are no harder than simple addition, multiplication, and division. In other words, a rookie scorer should not be intimidated by the scorebook or cumulative statistics that must be kept. A baseball coach should be able to teach someone the simple methods of scoring.

Interpretation may be another matter altogether. No pitcher and batter are ever going to see a play scored the same way, and it is logical that both would have a built-in bias. It is the official scorer's duty to decide such rulings, being as fair as he can be in determining when a batted ball is ruled a hit or an error, or deciding on the winning pitcher when the win can be given to anyone of two or three pitchers who throw in a game.

Before a coach selects a scorer or scorers for his team, he should look for the following attributes:

1. The official scorer should have some knowledge of the game of baseball. If not, then the coach is going to have a multitude of problems training this person.

2. He should have a fundamental grasp of basic arithmetic so that he can add, multiply or divide when these types of math procedures are called for in keeping up-to-date statistics.

3. The official scorer must be a reliable person and one who will attend every game, on time.

4. He should be one who will be able to back his decisions with a firm understanding of field conditions and the level of baseball being played. What might be an error in a major league game might not be an error in a high school game.

5. The scorer should be one who is neat in his script and appearance. A "class" program starts at the top and follows a smooth path right through to the statistician.

Scoring and statistics go hand-in-hand with all-conference recognition or possibly an all-state selection. Those legitimate .425 batting averages don't grow on trees, and honest statistics make the promoter's job that much easier in trying to influence the balloters about the ability of his player.

Scoring is a strong baseball tradition, but every scorer will have his own peculiarities or idiosyncrasies in marking down a play. The following will detail one system that is commonly used in scoring:

1. **Numbering system**—Basically, the scorer starts by looking at the position on a playing field as the numerals 1-9, and with the modern baseball heading of "dh" or 10 added when it comes to the lineup itself. Each position is designated with a number, and the numbers or playing spots should be denoted next to the player in the batting order to make for easier rendering of scoring plays, putouts, and assists. The number 1 is the person pitching; 2 stands for the catcher; 3 is the first baseman; 4 signifies the second baseman; 5 is the third baseman; 6 is the shortstop; 7 is the left fielder; 8 is the center fielder; 9 is the right fielder; and 10 is the designated hitter, if you wish.

2. **Completing the lineup**—After securing a copy of the lineup from both teams well in advance of the game, the scorer should enter the name and position of every player on both teams. He should not forget to include the pitchers at the end of the batting order. They can be credited with a fielding chance (putout, assist, or error) at any time during the game. The scorer should also put down in the scorebook the uniform number of each player to the left of his name. This aids in the solution of many protests about batters hitting out of order and gives the scorer a cross-check of the order of hitters in a given inning or of any changes in the field. A crucial reminder for the scorer is that he should never call to a coach or player when a batter hits out of turn. The coach or player of the opposing team is required to lodge the official protest. Once the names, positions, and numbers are neatly entered in the scorebook, the scorer is set for action.

3. **Shorthand annotations for a player who reaches base**—The scorer must know and be able to refer to the shorthand annotations for a player who reaches base. One of the easier ways that this can be done is listed below:

   1B or a (—) one-base hit (single)

   2B or a (=) two-base hit (double)

   3B or a (≡) three-base hit (triple)

   HR or a (≣) home run

The slashes denote the number of bases a player took without an error on the hit. Some scorers will even put a vertical line | with these slashes representing the number of bases reached on the hit, e.g., †, ╥, ╪, ╪.

4. **Denoting other ways to reach base without a hit**—There are numerous other ways that a batter can reach base without benefit of a hit. These ways would be noted:

   HBP or **HP**—Means hit by pitcher or hit by a pitched ball.

   BB or **W**—Signifies a base-on-balls, or in simpler terms, a walk.

   E—Means an error with a number after it to designate the guilty party. For example, E3 represents an error by the first baseman.

   FC—Means a fielder's choice. There will be more on this later, but basically, it represents a play where another runner ahead of the batter is forced out or ruled safe when the batter could have been retired on a play without the runner on base. An example of a fielder's choice would be on a ground ball hit to the shortstop, a flip from the shortstop (6) to the second baseman (4) for one out and then a late throw to first base (3). The runner is credited first base on a fielder's choice (FC).

   INT—Means interference by a defensive player on the batter. This usually results when the tip of the bat hits the catcher's mitt. The runner is awarded first base on an E2 and he is not credited with an official time at bat.

5. **Denoting cases where a runner does not reach base but a runner on base advances**—Situations that cause the batter not to reach base, but a runner or runners on base advance are noted:

   SAC—Means a sacrifice bunt where the batter sacrifices himself to advance a runner or runners on base. No official time at bat is credited when a runner is properly advanced by the bunted ball.

   SF—This shows a sacrifice fly where a runner scores on a fly ball which is caught by the opposition. A time at bat is not recorded for the hitter, and he receives a run-batted-in (RBI) on the play. A batter does not receive credit for a sacrifice fly if the fly ball moves a runner from one base to the forward base. Only if he allows a runner to score on the fly ball. A batter would also not receive credit for a sacrifice fly if the catcher makes an error on the throw to the plate allowing the runner to score. If the out would have been made if the catcher caught the ball, it would be recorded as an E2.

   PB—This is the scorer's symbol for a passed ball. On this play the catcher is adjudged to have let a ball get by him that could have been stopped with an average effort, and a baserunner advances on the play. In the case of a "catchable" third strike which gets by the catcher, the pitcher is credited with a strikeout, and the runner reaches first base on a passed ball. No error is charged to the catcher.

WP—This is the scorer's symbol for a wild pitch. The pitcher is charged with a wild pitch when a legal pitch is such that the catcher can not catch or control it with an ordinary effort, so that the batter reaches first base or any runner advances one or more bases. Scorers from the major leagues to the sandlots will tell you that when in doubt, rule the play a wild pitch. Almost any ball that hits the dirt before it gets to the catcher's mitt should be judged as a wild pitch. Judging between a wild pitch and a passed ball is essential since runs are determined to be earned or unearned by advancement on the base paths through wild pitches or passed balls.

BK—Signifies a balk when a pitcher is judged guilty of a balk by one of the umpires. This advances all runners when they are on base. If there are no runners on base, then the batter is awarded a ball in the count after the balk.

6. Other scoring symbols

K—This is the symbol that denotes a strikeout. Many have asked, "why not mark this with a strikeout sign such as SO?" Well, the only answer is that K is a baseball scoring tradition. Some scorers will mark a backwards K to denote a batter taking a called third strike while others will mark it down as K-c. For a swinging third strike, some make the notation K-s in the scorebook.

DP—This is the symbol for a double play. A double play is credited to one or more fielders when two offensive players are put out between the time a pitch is delivered and the time the ball next becomes dead or is next in possession of the pitcher in his pitching position. When an error or misplay occurs between the time one player is put out and the time a second player is put out, a double play is not credited. Also credit a double play if an appeal play after the ball is in possession of the pitcher results in an additional putout. A triple play meeting the above criteria can be recorded in the scorebook as **TP**.

RBI—This is the symbol for a run batted in. A run batted in is credited to the batter when a runner scores because of: a base hit (including batter scoring on a home run); a sacrifice bunt or sacrifice fly; any putout; a forced advance such as a base on balls or batter being hit by a pitch, or an error, provided there are less than two outs and the action is such that the runner on third base would have scored even if there had been no error. Scorer's judgment must determine whether a run batted in shall be credited for a run that scores when a fielder holds the ball or throws to the wrong base. Ordinarily, if the runner keeps going, credit a run batted in; if the runner stops and takes off again when he notices the misplay, credit the run as scored on a fielder's choice. It is not a run batted in if there is a double play from a force or one in which the batter is or should have been put out at first base.

F—This is another scoring notation which can be used to designate a ball which is caught on the fly. Thus, a pop-up to the second baseman would be an F-4. On a ball hit hard at the second baseman some scorers will score the unassisted putout as L-4 (lineout) or LD-4 (line drive caught by the second baseman).

U—This is the symbol when a player makes an unassisted putout on a ground ball or tags out a runner unassisted after a grounder. If the third baseman makes an unassisted putout at third base on a ground ball where the runner at second base was forced to advance, it would be scored U-5. Some scorers write the player's position down and circle the number, e.g. ⑤ to denote an unassisted putout.

SB—This is the symbol for a stolen base. A stolen base shall be credited to the baserunner whenever he advances a base unaided (such as by a base hit, fielder's choice, putout, error, balk, base on balls, wild pitch or passed ball). A stolen base shall be credited when a runner starts for the next base before the pitcher completes his delivery of the ball to the home plate area and the pitch results in what would otherwise be scored a passed ball or a wild pitch. There are other points to be noted for the scorer's benefit when dealing with a stolen base:

A. Where any runner is thrown out on an attempted double or triple steal, no runner shall be credited with a stolen base.

B. If a baserunner is tagged out while oversliding a base, he shall not be credited with a stolen base.

C. No stolen base shall be credited to a runner whose advance is the result of the opposing team's indifference to his advance.

E—This is the scorer's symbol for an error. An error is charged against any fielder (pitchers included) for each misplay that prolongs the time of bat of the batter or the life of a baserunner or permits a runner to advance one or more bases. The following are some rulings in regard to an error that an official scorer needs to understand:

A. Slow handling of the ball that does not involve mechanical misplay shall not be construed as an error.

B. It is not necessary that the fielder touch the ball to be charged with an error. If a ground ball goes through a fielder's legs or a pop fly ball falls untouched and in the scorer's judgment the fielder could have handled the ball with ordinary effort, an error should be charged.

C Mental mistakes or misjudgments are not to be scored as errors unless specifically covered in the rules.

D. An error shall be charged against any fielder when he catches a thrown ball or a ground ball in time to put out any runner on a force play and fails to tag the base or the runner, including a batter-runner on a play at first base.

E. An error shall be charged against any fielder whose throw takes an unnatural bounce, touches a base or the pitcher's rubber, or touches a runner, a fielder or an umpire thereby permitting any runner to advance. The scorer must apply this rule even when it appears to be an injustice to a fielder whose throw was accurate. Every base advanced by a runner must be accounted for.

F. Charge only one error on any wild throw, regardless of the number of bases advanced by runners.

G. An error shall be charged against any fielder whose failure to stop, or try to stop, an accurately thrown ball permits a runner to advance, providing there was occasion for the throw. If, in the scorer's judgment, there was no occasion for the throw, an error shall be charged to the fielder who threw the ball.

H. No error is charged to the catcher for a wild throw in an attempt to prevent a stolen base unless the baserunner advances an extra base because of a wild throw.

I. No player is charged with an error for a poor throw in an attempt to complete a double play unless the throw is so wild that it permits a runner to advance an additional base. However, if a player drops a thrown ball when by holding it he would have completed a double play, it is an error.

J. A fielder is not charged with an error for accurately throwing to a base whose baseman fails to stop or tries to stop the ball, provided there was good reason for such a throw. If the runner advances because of the throw, the error is charged to the baseman or fielder who should have covered that base.

K. If a fielder drops a fly ball or fumbles a ground ball, but recovers the ball in time to force a runner, he is not charged with an error.

L. No error shall be charged against any fielder who permits a foul fly ball to drop safely with a runner at third base and less than two outs if, in the judgment of the official scorer, the fielder deliberately allows the ball to fall in order to prevent the runner on third from scoring after a catch.

M. An error shall be charged to a fielder who commits interference that entitles a batter or runner to advance one or more bases beyond the base he would have reached had the interference not occurred.

7. Other scoring terms

A. **Fielder's choice**—As mentioned earlier, the symbol for the fielder's choice is FC. The term is used by official scorers to account for the following situations (the batter shall be charged with an official time at bat but no hit in all such situations):

1. When a batter-runner advances one or more bases while a fielder who handles a fair hit attempts to put out a preceding runner.

492

2. When a runner advances (other than by a stolen base or error) while a fielder is attempting to put another runner out.

3. When a runner advances solely because of the defensive team's indifference (undefended steal).

4. When a batter apparently hits safely and a runner who is forced to advance by reason of the batter becoming a runner fails to touch the first base to which he is advancing and is called out on appeal.

B. **Putout**—A putout is credited to a fielder who catches a batted ball in flight, tags out a runner or puts out a runner by holding the ball while touching a base to which a runner is forced to advance or return. When a batter strikes out, a putout is credited to the catcher, unless the catcher fails to field the pitch cleanly and must put the batter-runner out at first base. Exceptions to the putout rule are:

1. When a batter is called out for an illegally batted ball, for a foul third strike bunt, for being hit by his own batted ball, for interference with the catcher or for failing to bat in his proper turn, the putout shall be credited to the catcher.

2. When a batter is declared out on an infield fly that is not caught, the putout is credited to the fielder who is nearest the ball at the time.

3. When a baserunner is out because of being hit by a fairly batted ball, the putout shall be credited to the fielder nearest the ball at the time.

4. When a runner is called out for running out of the baseline to avoid being tagged, the putout shall be credited to the fielder whom the runner avoided.

5. When a runner is called out for passing another runner, the putout shall be credited to the fielder nearest the point of passing.

6. When a runner is called out for running the bases in reverse order, the putout shall be credited to the fielder covering the base he left in starting his reverse run.

7. When a runner is called out for interfering with a fielder, the putout shall be credited to the fielder with whom the runner interfered, unless the fielder was in the act of throwing the ball when the interference occurred. In that case, the putout shall be credited to the fielder for whom the throw was intended; the fielder whose throw was interfered with shall be credited with an assist.

8. When a batter-runner is called out because of interference by a preceding runner, the putout shall be credited to the first baseman. If the fielder interfered with was in the act of throwing the ball, he shall be credited with an assist. In no case can he be credited with more than one assist on any one play.

C. **Assist**—An assist is credited to a fielder when he handles or effectively deflects the ball during action that is connected with a putout or he handles the ball prior to an error that prevents what would have been a putout. If several fielders handle the ball or one fielder handles it more than once during a play, only one assist is credited to each of the fielders. The pitcher is not credited with an assist on a strikeout or when after a pitch the catcher tags out or throws out a runner. A play that follows a misplay (whether or not it is an error) is a new play, and the fielder making any misplay shall not be credited with an assist unless he takes part in the new play.

D. **Base hit**—A base hit is credited to a batter when he advanced to first base safely in the following situations:

1. Because of his fair hit (rather than because of a fielder's error). It is not a base hit if any runner is out on a force play caused by the batter advancing toward first base or would have been forced out except for a fielding error.

2. Because a runner is declared out for being hit by a batted ball or an umpire is hit by a batted ball prior to a fielder having an opportunity to field the ball.

3. When a fielder attempts to put out a preceding runner but is unsuccessful although there is no fielding error, and the official scorer believes the batter-runner would have reached first base with perfect fielding.

4. When a batter reaches first base safely on a fair ball hit with such force or so slowly, that any fielder attempting to make a play has no opportunity to do so. A hit shall be scored even if the fielder deflects the ball from or cuts off another fielder who could have put out a runner.

5. When a batter reaches first base safely on a fair ball that takes an unnatural bounce so that a fielder can not handle it with ordinary effort, or that touches the pitcher's rubber or any base (including home plate) before being touched by a fielder and bounces so that a fielder can not handle it with ordinary effort.

6. It is not a base hit when a runner is called out for having been touched by an infield fly.

7. In applying the rules to a base hit, always give the batter the benefit of the doubt. A safe course to follow is to score a hit when exceptionally good fielding fails to result in a putout.

E. **Extra-base hit**—A base hit for extra bases is credited to the batter when it is the sole reason for his safe arrival at a base beyond first. Any fair batted ball that in flight clears an outfield fense it is a home run. Other rules in regard to an extra base hit are:

1. When, with one or more runners on base, the batter advances more than one base on a safe hit and the defensive team makes an attempt to put out a preceding runner, the scorer shall determine whether the batter made a legitimate two-base hit or three-base hit, or whether he advanced beyond first base on the fielder's choice. For example, do not credit the batter with a three-base hit when a preceding runner is put out at the plate, or would have been out but for an error. Do not credit the batter with a two-base hit when a preceding runner trying to advance from first base is put out at third base, or would have been out but for an error.

2. If a batter overslides second or third base and is tagged out trying to return, he shall be credited with the last base he touched.

F. **Substitute batter**—When a batter leaves the game with two strikes on him, and a substitute batter strikes out, charge the strikeout to the first batter. If a substitute batter completes the turn at bat in any other manner, including a base on balls, charge the action to the substitute batter.

G. **Batting record**—Each player's batting record shall include:

1. In columns 1, 2, 3 and 4 in the box score, the number of times he batted, the runs he scored, the base hits he made and the runs batted in he was credited with. The batter is charged an official time at bat whenever he completes his turn, unless he has been awarded first base in those situations where he is not credited with a time at bat. In columns 5 and 6, the number of bases on balls and strikeouts credited to the batter shall be recorded.

Note—An official time at bat shall not be charged against a player when he hits a sacrifice bunt or sacrifice fly, is awarded a base on balls, is hit by a pitched ball or is awarded first base because of interference or obstruction.

2. In the summary, the number of extra base hits, sacrifice hits, sacrifice fly balls and stolen bases are noted.

H. **Fielding record**—Each player's fielding record should include:

1. In columns 7 and 8 of the box score, the number of times he assisted a teammate in putting out a runner.

2. In the summary, the number of errors and passed balls he committed.

I. **Pitching record**—Each pitcher's record shall include in the summary: number of innings pitched, base hits, runs, earned runs, base on balls, strikeouts, hit batters, wild pitches and balks.

Note—In computing innings pitched, count each putout as one-third of an inning. If a starting pitcher is replaced with one out in the sixth inning, credit the pitcher with five and one-third innings. If a starting pitcher is replaced with no outs in the sixth inning, credit that pitcher with five innings, and make the notation that he faced a specific number of batters in the sixth. If a relief pitcher retires two batters and is replaced, credit that pitcher with two-thirds of an inning pitched.

A sample official NCAA baseball box score is on the next page so that the scorer can easily see how information on game totals are placed in the box score.

J. **Earned run**—An earned run shall be charged against a pitcher when a runner scores because of a safe hit, sacrifice hit, sacrifice fly, stolen base, putout, fielder's choice, base on balls, hit batter, balk or wild pitch (even when the wild pitch is a third strike), provided that in each case it is before the defensive team has had an opportunity to make a third putout. In determining earned runs, the scorer shall reconstruct the inning as if there were no errors or passed balls. Give the pitcher the benefit of the doubt in determining the advancement of runners, had the defensive team been errorless. Other factors in determining an earned run are:

1. No earned run shall be charged to a relief pitcher if the runner was on base when the relief pitcher entered the game. Likewise, if a batter has more balls than strikes, unless the count is one ball, no strikes, when a relief pitcher enters the game and the batter receives a base on balls, charge the action to the preceding pitcher. Any other action of the batter shall be charged to the relief pitcher.

2. No run shall be earned when scored by a runner whose life is prolonged by an error, if such runner would have been put out by errorless play.

3. An error by a pitcher is treated exactly the same as an error by any other fielder in computing earned runs.

4. When pitchers are changed during an inning, the relief pitcher shall not be charged with any run (earned or unearned) scored by a runner who reaches base on a fielder's choice that puts out a runner left on base by a preceding pitcher. The intent of this rule is to charge each pitcher with the numbers of runners he put on base, rather than with the individual runners.

5. When pitchers are changed during an inning, a relief pitcher shall not have the benefit of errors made earlier in the inning. Thus, he will be charged with earned runs for which he is totally responsible.

K. **Winning and losing pitcher**—Some of the guidelines for the scorer to follow in determining the game's winning and losing pitcher are:

1. For all games of eight or more innings, a starting pitcher must pitch at least five complete innings to receive credit as the winning pitcher. For all games of fewer than eight innings, the starting pitcher must pitch at least four innings to get credit for the win. Additionally, the winning pitcher's team must be in the lead when he is replaced and must remain in the lead for the rest of the game.

2. If the starting pitcher does not pitch enough innings, the win is credited to a relief pitcher in the following manner:

a. The winning relief pitcher shall be the one who is the pitcher of record when his team goes ahead and remains ahead throughout the remainder of the game. No pitcher may receive credit for a victory if the opposing team ties the score or goes ahead after he has left the game. Whenever the score is tied, the game becomes a new contest insofar as the winning and losing pitchers are concerned.

b. If a relief pitcher conforms to the above regulations as in (a), but pitches briefly and ineffectively, the scorer should not credit him with the win. If a succeeding relief pitcher pitches effectively and helps maintain the lead, the scorer should award the win to that succeeding pitcher.

c. By prearrangement, if three or more pitchers are to be used, the pitcher of record shall be considered the winning pitcher.

OFFICIAL NCAA BASEBALL BOX SCORE

Date __5-7-77__ Time __1 p.m.__ Stadium __Smith Field__ City __Hometown, California__

State	AB	R	H	RBI	BB	SO	PO	A	Tech	AB	R	H	RBI	BB	SO	PO	A
12 Adair,cf	5	0	0	0	1	0	5	0	18 Henderson,cf	5	0	1	0	0	0	5	0
4 Caldwell,ss	5	1	2	1	1	0	0	5	30 Peters,rf	5	1	3	0	0	0	3	0
7 Murray,dh	5	1	1	1	0	0	0	0	17 Beck,ss	4	0	2	0	1	0	3	3
19 Irvine,lf	5	1	3	1	1	0	2	0	20 Robinson,3b	4	1	0	0	1	0	0	3
25 Simons,1b	5	2	3	2	0	0	7	1	5 Long,c	4	1	1	2	0	0	1	0
21 Grant,3b	5	1	1	0	0	0	1	3	24 Dean,2b	3	0	2	1	1	0	3	2
2 Quarles,rf	3	3	2	0	2	1	1	0	14 Taylor,1b	2	0	0	0	0	0	11	0
29 Kessler,2b	5	1	2	3	0	0	8	3	1 Evans,ph-lf	1	0	0	0	0	0	0	0
3 Elston,c	4	0	2	2	0	0	2	0	6 Nolan,lf-1b	1	0	0	0	3	0	1	1
18 O'Conner,p	0	0	0	0	0	0	1	1	25 Foley,dh	2	0	0	0	0	1	0	0
27 Ujdur,p	0	0	0	0	0	0	0	0	12 Young,p-dh	2	0	0	0	0	1	0	1
									19 Jackson,p	0	0	0	0	0	0	0	1
									11 Vasquez,p	0	0	0	0	0	0	0	0
									28 Ziegler,p	0	0	0	0	0	0	0	0
TOTALS	42	10	16	10	5	1	27	13	TOTALS	33	3	9	3	6	2	27	11

SCORE BY INNINGS

													R	H	E
State	0	3	2	0	0	2	0	3	0			—	10	16	0
Tech	0	0	0	0	0	0	0	3	0			—	3	9	3

E— Beck, Dean, Nolan

DP— State--2   LEFT— State--12   Tech--11

2B— Quarles, Kessler, Long, Dean   3B—

HR— Simons   SB— Irvine

SH— Murray   SF— Elston

State	IP	H	R	ER	BB	SO	Tech	IP	H	R	ER	BB	SO
O'Conner	6	3	0	0	4	1	Jackson	2.1	6	5	5	3	0
Ujdur	3	6	3	3	2	1	Vasquez	2.2	8	2	2	0	0
							Young	3.0	2	3	3	2	1
							Ziegler	1.0	0	0	0	0	0

WINNER— O'Conner   LOSER— Jackson   SAVE—

WP— Young   PB— Elston   BK— Vasquez

HBP — Taylor (by Ujdur)

U— Smith, Jones, Brown, White   T— 2:32   A— 12,172

SAMPLE OFFICIAL NCAA BOX SCORE

d. When a batter or runner is substituted for a pitcher, all runs scored by his team during that inning are to his credit in determining the pitcher of record.

e. The starting pitcher shall be charged with the loss if he is replaced at any time while his team is behind and remains behind for the remainder of the game. Similarly, any relief pitcher who is the pitcher of record when the opposing team assumes the lead and never relinquishes it is charged with the loss.

f. The pitcher of record shall be the one who is in the game at the time the winning team gains the lead, provided that the lead is never relinquished, or the one who is charged with the runs by which the opposing team takes the lead, provided that the lead is never relinquished.

g. To receive credit for a shutout, the pitcher must pitch the entire game or enter the game with no outs in the first inning and pitch the rest of the game without any runs scoring.

L. **Saves**—If a relief pitcher meets all of the following conditions, the official scorer should credit that pitcher with a save:

1. He is the finishing pitcher in a game won by his team.

2. He is not credited with the win.

3. He meets one of the following conditions:

a. He enters the game with a lead of not more than three runs and pitches at least one inning.

b. He enters the game with the potential tying run on base, at bat or on deck.

c. He pitches effectively for at least three innings. No more than one save may be credited in each game.

DETERMINING PERCENTAGES

The following procedures should be used to determine various percentages:

1. **Won-lost percentage**—To determine won-lost percentage, divide the total number of games played into the number of games won.

2. **Batting averages**—To determine batting averages, divide the number of official times at bat into the number of base hits.

3. **Fielding averages**—To determine fielding averages, divide the total chances (putouts, assists and errors) into the total putouts and assists.

4. **Earned run averages**—To determine earned run averages, multiply the earned runs allowed by nine and then divide by the number of innings pitched.

5. **Slugging percentage**—To determine slugging percentage, divide the number of official times at bat into the number of total bases.

In all cases where the remaining decimal is one-half or more, round to the next whole number.

CUMULATIVE PERFORMANCE RECORDS

1. **Hitting streak**—A consecutive hitting streak shall not be terminated if the plate appearance results in a base on balls, hit batsman, defensive interference or a sacrifice bunt. A sacrifice fly shall terminate the streak.

2. **Consecutive game hitting streak**—A consecutive game hitting streak shall not be terminated if all the player's plate appearances (one or more) result in a base on balls, hit batsman, defensive interference or sacrifice bunt. The streak shall terminate if the player has a sacrifice fly and no hit.

3. **Consecutive game playing streak**—A consecutive game playing streak shall be extended if the player plays one-half inning on defense, or if he completes a time at bat by reaching base or being put out. A pinch-running appearance only shall not extend the streak. If a player is ejected from a game by an umpire before he can comply with the requirements of this rule, his streak shall continue.

4. For the purpose of this rule, all performances in the completion of a suspended game shall be considered as occurring on the original date of the game.

KEEPING THE SCOREBOOK

Now that we have dealt with the rules of scoring and the use of symbols in keeping score, it is important that the official scorer understand how to keep the actual scorebook during the course of the game. Three different types of scorebooks will be presented so that the scorer understands the scoring methods used in each variation.

Chart A on the next page is the first example of a scorebook. This is more of a do-it-yourself version than some of the scorebooks which number each position and allow scorers to chart the balls and strikes in boxes found in each hitter's scoring block.

In the scorer's scorebook, the cross signs to denote hits are omitted. Instead, the scorer has substituted the number of the position where the hit occurs. For example, McDonald (number 26—third baseman), hit a single in the hole towards shortstop in the second inning. This is shown by placing a "6" in the quadrant between home and first. Some scorers will even go to the extra trouble of bringing blue or green felt-tip pens to mark the hits. This would enable the scorer to better follow the hits and errors which would be marked with a different color pen.

Let's take one inning and follow it through from the first to the last hitter. The third inning would be a good one since there was scoring, an error, and a couple of interesting plays afield.

In that frame, McCullough led off with a single to left field (a 7 appears in the quadrant between home and first), and then he advanced to second base on a fielder's choice when Smith grounded out to the shortstop (6-3). Kelley, the leadoff man, singled McCullough to third base with an infield single to short, and then stole second base to put runners at second and third base. McCann walked (BB) to load the bases, and if he had been purposefully issued a walk, it would have been scored "IBB" for intentional walk.

With the bases loaded, Aldrich hit a two-run single to left, and McCullough and Kelley scored on the hit. McCann advanced all the way to third on the single and scored on an E7 when the left fielder bobbled Aldrich's single. Aldrich meanwhile, moved to second on the same bobble, but only one error could be charged to the left fielder on that play.

Still with one out, Bender popped up to the first baseman (F-3) and then Pavlou hit a grounder toward the first baseman who flipped the ball to the covering pitcher (3-1) for the putout. That summarized the inning (at the bottom of the sheet) with three Team A runs, three hits, one Team B error, and one man (Aldrich) left on base when the inning ended. Two of the runs were earned.

For point of clarification, one might notice the scorer's use of hash marks to denote the headings across the right side of the page. These make for quick addition of the totals in a boxscore after the game and could be termed a "crutch" for cross-checking the scorecard. In the long run though, one can make intermittent "spot checks" of his or her work such as adding the putouts to make sure that the team has 21 (three per inning) through seven innings. Much sleep has been lost over a missed putout occasionally when a good cross-check would alleviate much of the headaches.

Glancing over the scoresheet and down the far right side of the page, one can see two denotations which have not been discussed. In the seventh and eighth innings, one will notice the wavy lines before the boxes in which McCann (seventh) and Smith (eighth) came to the plate. These denote changes in Team B's pitchers, and the two hurlers' names are placed below the pitching-changes' line. This helps to decide responsibility for runs in a game.

CHART A

TEAM A vs. TEAM B AT SMITH FIELD DATE 4/26

PLAYER	Pos. & no.	1	2	3	4	5	6	7	8	9	10	11	12	AB	R	BB	BI	SB	SO	SH	PO	A	E
2 Mike Kelley	8													4	2	1	1				3		
21 Howie McCann	4													4	1	0	1	1			2	2	2
22 Russ Aldrich	2													4	0	1	1				4		
29 Del Bender	dh													3	1	1							
5 Larry Pavlou	7													5	0	2			1		2	1	
26 John McDonald	5													5	1	3					1	1	1
19 Bob Kocol	9													5	0	1	1				3		
35 Tom McCullough	3													3	1	2			1	1	2	1	1
11 Tim Weisheim (R-8)	3													0	0	0			1		1		
18 Mike Smith	6													4	0	0					5	1	1
23 Mike Darby (1-2)	1																				1	0	0
12 Josh Reagan (P-7)	1																				0	0	0
TOTALS	R	0	0	3	3	0	1	2	0	0				39	6	11	3	5	4	1	1	27	10	1
	H	0	1	3	0	0	2	2	0	2													
	E	0	0	1	0	1	0	0	0	0													
	LOB	0	1	1	9	1	1	1	2	2				16									

2 base hits: McDonald

3 base hits: —

Home runs: Bender (7)

Double plays: —

Bases on balls, off: Dar.-1

Struck out by: Rea.-11

Innings pitch by: Dar.-6⅔ Rea.- 2⅓

Earned runs off: Dar.- 3⅓

Opponents' hits off: Dar.- Rea.-11

Wild pitches: —

Balks: —

Passed balls: —

Score: Krupca (2)

Winning pitcher: Darby (2-2)

Losing pitcher: Greenwith (3-)

Umpires: Paul Andrejcak, Bill Mize

Scorer: Crotz

Time of game: 2:18

499

Chart B on the next page is another example of a scorebook that can be used. The number of outs are put inside the scoring circle. The circles are filled in to denote runs scored, and the hits are designated as follows: (1) single—one line to the right of the circle with the field or position to where the ball was hit placed under the line; (2) double—a perpendicular line extending over the top of the circle, with the field to which it is hit being indicated by a number; (3) triple—a three-sided, unfinished square which extends into the left portion of the box next to the circle (see Kelley's square in the second inning); and (4) home run—a full square is drawn around the blackened circle.

Just to sample an inning of work, let's take the fifth frame.

Dixon led off with a single to left field before Castoria flied out to right field. Weisheim hit a slow roller in front of the second baseman for an infield single as Dixon advanced to second. Lowther hit a one-RBI double to score Dixon as Weisheim advanced to third. Weisheim then came home on a wild pitch. After Lowther's double, Schroll entered the game to pitch (indicated by wavy line), and he retired Conner 1-3 (groundout from Scroll to the first baseman). Kelley then singled in Lowther before Hannah (a pinch hitter as denoted by B-5 = batted in the fifth inning) grounded out to third base (5-3). While Hannah was at the plate, Kelley stole second base. That gave Team A the totals of three runs on four hits with no errors, and one man left on base.

Chart C on page 502 is the final example of a scorebook that can be used by the scorer. In this scorebook, the line method is used in scoring hits. Inning number six will give us a good inning to work with.

Castoria, the third baseman, leads off with a home run (completed box) over the left field fence. The scorer has also indicated the estimated distance of the home run (360 feet). Then Weisheim flies out to left field (F-7), Conner reaches first base on an error by the opposing third baseman, steals second base, and scores on Kelley's single (notice that an RBI is hash-marked in under Kelley's RBI column to avoid later confusion). In between, Pavlou grounds out to the first baseman, who makes the putout unassisted (3-U). Kelley steals second base after singling to center field, but Schlosser ends the rally by grounding out to the second baseman.

OTHER STATISTICAL INFORMATION

A scorer can get caught up in the statistical end of baseball to the point that he or she can keep so many categories of statistics that it becomes a very time consuming process. For instance: a scorer might keep each player's batting average for day games versus night games; batting average versus righthanded and lefthanded pitchers; batting average with runners in scoring position, etc.

If time allows, a scorer should provide his team with as many statistics as the coach deems necessary for the press releases that will be sent out during the course of the season. Cumulative baseball statistics are invaluable. How many times have you read in a newspaper, heard on radio, or watched a film report on television concerning a player who won 15 games in 21 starts as a pitcher, or a hitter was hitting .425 for a last-place team. From full-season statistics come post-season honors. The importance of keeping statistics up-to-date on every player can not be stressed too much. Professional scouts, summer amateur league coaches, college recruiters, the media all utilize these figures as much as time for a hitter from home plate to first base, throwing arm, or velocity of the pitcher's fast ball in evaluating a player.

The scorer must be cautioned to never fabricate statistics. The unfortunate occurrence every year in baseball at all levels happens when an overly-anxious statistician changes a sure error into a base hit during a road game, or several road games, "padding" a batting average of a hitter.

The scorer might want to keep statistics such as: game winning hits for each player on the team; runs scored by the team by innings; on base average for each player; and saves by each pitcher. Thus, there are many statistics and records that must be kept by the scorer-statistician if he wishes to do a "first class" job.

CHART B

	TEAM A	Pos.	1	2	3	4	5	6	7	8	9	10	A.B.	R.	H.	S.H.	P.O.	A.	E.
2	Mike Kelley	8											IIII	I	I	III	III		
20	Dale Hannah (B-5)	4											II 2		0		I	I	I
4	Randy Schlosser	4											I		0		I	I	I
19	Bob Kocol	9											III	I	II				
23	Terry Loe (B-6)	2															THH II 7		
26	John McDonald	2											III 3		0		II		
16	Scott Galloway (B-6) dh	5													0				
30	Rick Dixon dh	5											III 3	III 3	III 3				
3	Pete Torres (F-6)	5												I					
35	Bruce Castoria	5											III 3	III I	II 2				
11	Tim Weisheim	3											IIII	II	III		IIII		
30	Dave Lowther	7												II	I		II	I	
15	Dave Klipstein (F-7)	6																	
6	Boyd Conner	6											III 3		0		II 2	II 2	
18	Ken Kurtz (1-0)	1											I		0		I	I	
	Total		0 I	5 +	1 3	0 0	3 +	2 1									21	6	2

Two-Base Hits Weisheim, Wongetter, Lowther Three-Base Hits Kelley
Left on Bases AU- MS- Home Runs Earned Runs Kur-1
Wild Pitches Bec-1, Schroll-1 Kurz-1 Passed Balls Double Plays Hanah-Comer-Weisheim Hit by Pitcher
Total Bases AU- MS- Brown-Keady-O Finn Balks
First on Balls, off Kur-III off Bec-11 Intr-1 Schr-11 Struck Out, by Kur-THH THH
SB-Kelley by Schr-11

HARDWICK

CHART C

HOME __Team A__ SITE _Smith Field_ SCORER _Carter_ ATTEN. _6,467_ TIME _2:00_

No.	NAME	Pos.	1	2	3	4	5	6	7	8	9	10	11	12	AB	R	H	RBI	2B	3B	HR	BB	SO	PO	A	E
2	Mike Kelley	8	5-3				2-4								2	0	1	1				1	1	1	1	
4	Randy Schlosser	4	3-U		K		F-9	4-3							4	0	0					1	1	4	2	
19	Bob Kocol	9	6-3		K										3	1	1		1				1	1		
26	John McDonald	2		F-3		8									3	1	2	1			1			8		
26	Rick Dixon	dh		4-3			K								2	0	0					1	1			
35	Bruce Castoria	5		F-8											3	1	2	2					1	4	1	
3	Pete Torres (F-7)	5						F-7							3	0	0									
11	Tim Weisheim	3				6-3 1-4																				
6	Boyd Conner	6				F-2									2	1	0					1	1	1	1	
5	Larry Paulou	7				5-3		3-U							2	0	0					1	2		1	
15	Ken Kurtz (3-0)	1													2	0	0							1		
	TOTALS														24	4	6	4	1	0	1	4	3	21	7	2

	1	2	3	4	5	6		7 8 9
Runs	0	0	0	1	2	2		6 4 9
Hits	0	0	0	1	2	2		5 1 3
Errors	0	0	0	1	0	1		2
Left on Base	0	0	3	2	1	1		7

PITCHERS	IP	H	R	ER	BB	SO
Kurtz (W,4-0)	7	4	1	1	1	6

cs-1
SB— Conner-II, Kelley
DP— McDonald-Schlosser; Kurtz-Conner-Schlosser-Weisheim
SH— _____ SF— _____ HBP— Kelley (by Calhoun)
BK— _____ PB— _____
WP— Kurtz
WINNER — Kurtz   LOSER — Smith   Save —

PROOF

AB			PO	
BB			R	
HBP			LOB	
SAC				
INT				
This Figure			Must Equal	

MAINTENANCE OF BASEBALL FIELDS

So this is your first year to coach baseball and you find out that this entails being your own groundskeeper. When do you start maintaining your field? What type of mower should you buy? What kind of fertilizer should you use? What herbicide will kill those weeds on your field? These are but a few of the questions that you must ask yourself before you develop a total maintenance program for your field. Literally dozens of other questions must be answered before you can have a first rate field. In fact a 12-month maintenance program should be developed before you start ever maintaining your field. A professional turf manager or other turf specialist should be consulted for technical advice.

There are two broad areas that should be considered in your maintenance program: (1) turfgrass maintenance and (2) non-turf grass maintenance—i.e., skinned area of infield. Turfgrass maintenance will be discussed first followed by a discussion of non-turf areas.

TURFGRASS MAINTENANCE

1. Turfgrass selection for baseball fields

There are two basic types of grasses used on baseball fields in the United States: warm season grasses and cool season grasses. Warm season grasses grow best at temperatures between 80°F and 95°F and thus are used in the Southeastern and Southwestern portions of the United States. Examples of warm season grasses are bermudagrass and zoysiagrass. Cool season grasses on the other hand grow best at temperatures between 60°F and 75°F. Obviously, these grasses are grown in the northern portions of the country. The bluegrass and fescues are examples of cool season grasses. Cool season grasses are also used for overseeding warm season grass fields in the fall for winter and spring play. Figure 1 on the next page shows the regions of the United States in which warm season and cool season grasses are usually grown. In some cases both types of grasses are grown in the transition zone.

A. Warm season grasses

1. **Bermudagrass**—Bermudagrasses are the most commonly used warm season grasses for baseball fields in the South. Bermudagrasses lend themselves for use on sports fields because of their vigorous growth habits, excellent wear tolerance, and superior recuperative potential. Common bermudagrass is the most widely used bermudagrass because it can be easily established from seed. Common bermudagrass seed is readily available from most nursery or agricultural centers. Various turf-type bermudagrass cultivars are available; however, they must be established vegetatively as pugs, plugs, or sod. In general these cultivars form a vigorous and aggressive turf with high shoot density. Tifway bermudagrass is the most widely used turf type bermudagrass cultivar in the Southeast. This popularity is based on its ready availability from commercial distributors and excellent turf characteristics.

Other turf-type bermudagrass cultivars are briefly described in Table 1.

Table 1—Brief description of turf-type bermudagrass cultivars used for baseball fields.

Cultivar	Turf Description and Use
Tifway	Dark green color with high shoot density; medium fine texture; stiff leaf blades; vigorous growth rate; good wear and salt tolerance; excellent herbicide tolerance; susceptible to smog injury; resistant to mole crickets, sod webworms, and bermudagrass mite.
Tiflawn	Medium dark green color with moderate shoot density; leaf blades grow more perpendicular to shoot and tends to form a canopy of leaves; excellent wear tolerance and vigor; once dominant turf-type cultivar prior to release of Tifway bermudagrass.

503

Santa Ana	Dark blue-green color with medium high shoot density; medium leaf texture; excellent salt, wear, and smog tolerance; poor cold hardiness; resistant to bermudagrass mite; used on West Coast.
Midiron	Bright to dark green color with medium density; medium coarse texture; vigorous growth rate; good wear tolerance; **excellent** cold hardiness; used in upper South.
U-3	Dark grayish green color with medium high shoot density; medium fine texture; excellent drought and wear tolerance; used in upper South because of its excellent cold hardiness.
Turfcote	Medium dark green color with medium shoot density; medium texture; stiff leaf blades; good wear and salt tolerance; good cold tolerance; developed for sports fields, but has not lived up to expectations.

2. **Zoysiagrass**—Zoysiagrass is used mostly in the upper South because of its cold hardiness. Zoysiagrass produces a dense, low growing turf that is resistant to weed invasion. The leaves and stems are very stiff and results in mowing difficulties. Zoysiagrass has very slow establishment and recuperative rates because of its slow growth rate. It is susceptible to rust diseases. Meyer zoysiagrass is the most popular zoysiagrass for athletic fields.

B. **Cool season grasses**

1. **Kentucky bluegrass**—This is the most widely used cool season grass for baseball fields. It forms a dense rhizome and root system that has good wear resistance. The normal seeding rate for Kentucky bluegrass is one to two pounds per 1000 square feet. Some of the cultivars used for athletic fields are: Merion; Park; Adelphi; Baron; and Bonnieblue. Blends of two or more cultivars are often used to give added protection against disease.

2. **Perennial ryegrass**—This type of grass is occasionally used on baseball fields in the Southern portion of the cool humid regions of the country. Also, it is used for overseeding fields in the Southern United States. Perennial ryegrass is also used some in mixtures with Kentucky bluegrass. Some of the cultivars available are: Manhatten; NK-100; Pennfine; and Pelo.

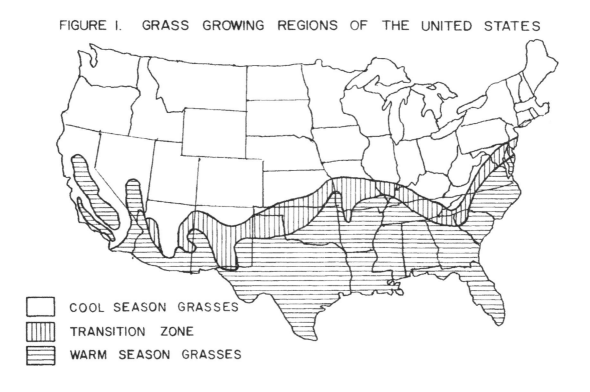

FIGURE I. GRASS GROWING REGIONS OF THE UNITED STATES

COOL SEASON GRASSES
TRANSITION ZONE
WARM SEASON GRASSES

3. **Red fescue**—Is used sometimes with Kentucky bluegrass in mixtures on baseball fields. It is very seldom used alone because of its weak rhizome system and slow recuperative rate. Dawson, Jamestown, and Ruby are some of the cultivars that are available.

4. **Tall fescue**—Is used some in the transitional zone between the cool humid region and the warm humid regions. It is generally lower in quality but can withstand intensive traffic. Kentucky bluegrass is sometimes used with tall fescue to increase the quality of the turf. Kentucky 31 is the most widely used tall fescue cultivar.

2. Mowing requirements

A. **Mowing frequency**—A general rule of thumb is to remove no more than one-third of the leaf tissue at any one time. For example, if you are maintaining your field at one inch in height, the grass should be mowed before it reaches one and one-half inches in height. This may mean a mowing frequency of one to three times each week during the most active growing season. Mowing frequency will vary depending on the grass species used, amount of rainfall or irrigation, fertilization and time of year.

B. **Mowing height**—Ths mowing height of the turf will depend upon the wishes of the coach and what type of team he has. For example, if he has a slow team, he may want the grass cut a little taller to slow the ball down more. The recommended mowing height for bermudagrass and zoysiagrass is three-quarter to one and one-half inches, with one inch being the most commonly used height. Kentucky bluegrass should be mowed at one to one and one-half inches in height, while tall fescue should be mowed at one and one-half to two inches. Fields overseeded with ryegrass are normally maintained at three-quarter to one and one-half inches in height.

C. **Mowing equipment**—What type of mower should be used? There are two types of mowers available that can be used. First there is the reel type and secondly there is the rotary type. The reel type mower gives a better quality cut and is normally used on the higher maintenance sports fields. Reel mowers are manufactured in a variety of sizes ranging from single to multi-reel units. Triplex reel mowers vary in cutting width from 76 to 84 inches. The rotary mower does not give as good a cut as a reel mower, but is much more versatile. It can be used on rougher terrain and for cutting much taller grass and weeds than a reel mower. The rotary mower does not require as much special maintenance, such as adjusting and grinding reels as the reel mower. A small push-type rotary mower is used to mow small areas. A nylone cord type trimmer can be a tremendous help in trimming around fences, poles, and other vertical obstructions.

3. Fertilization

Fertilization is second only to mowing in importance in turf management. A poor fertilization program usually means a thin, weak, weed infested turf. A good fertilization program is more than just going out and applying fertilizer once or twice a year. It should be well planned and carried out on a predetermined schedule. First let us look at the sources of plant nutrients.

A. **Nitrogen fertilizers**—Grasses require more nitrogen than any other nutrient. As a general rule the bermudagrasses require the most nitrogen followed by zoysiagrasses. The cool season grasses usually require less than one-half as much nitrogen as the warm season grasses.

1. **Ammonium nitrate**—Ammonium nitrate contains 34% nitrogen and is usually the cheapest source of nitrogen available. It is an inorganic nitrogen fertilizer that is water soluble, which means it is immediately available to the grass. Normally, ammonium nitrate must be watered in after applying to avoid burning the turf. For this reason not more than one pound of nitrogen per 1000 square feet should be applied at one time.

2. **Sodium nitrate**—Sodium nitrate contains 16% nitrogen and is also an inorganic nitrogen fertilizer. It is readily available to the plant and should be watered in after applying if possible.

3. **Ammonium sulfate**—Ammonium sulfate is also an inorganic nitrogen and contains 20% nitrogen. It also should be watered in after applying if possible.

4. **Urea**—Urea is an organic fertilizer which contains 45% nitrogen. Urea is water soluble and is readily available to plants. No more than one pouhd nitrogen per 1000 square feet should be applied at one time to avoid burning the turf.

5. **Ureaformaldehyde**—Ureaformaldehyde or ureaform as it is often called is an organic nitrogen fertilizer that is

505

water insoluble and not readily available to the plant. The nitrogen is released slowly over a long period of time and will not burn the turf if used in reasonable quantities. Ureaform contains 38% nitrogen and is one of the most expensive sources of nitrogen available.

6. **IBDU**—IBDU (isobutylidine diurea) contains 31% nitrogen and is an organic nitrogen source. It is released over a long period of time by hydrolysis and is not greatly effected by changes in temperature or bacterial action. IBDU may be applied at high rates without injuring the turf. As with all insoluble sources of nitrogen, IBDU is expensive when compared to soluble sources of nitrogen.

7. **Activated sewage sludge**—Activated sewage sludge is produced and marketed by the City of Milwaukee, Wisconsin, as Milorganite, and the City of Houston, Texas, as Hu-actinite. Activated sewage sludge usually contains 6% nitrogen, 3% phosphorus and significant amounts of micronutrients such as copper, zinc, manganese, molydenum, and boron. Activated sewage sludge has been known to reduce the incidence of disease of turfgrasses. Some of the characteristics of activated sewage sludge are: (1) has low nitrogen content; (2) high cost per pound of nitrogen; (3) little or no danger of burning turf; (4) resistance to leaching; and (5) long residual period of 4-8 weeks.

B. **Phosphorus fertilizers**—Although turfgrasses require less phosphorus than nitrogen, it is none the less vital to the plant. Phosphorus promotes the root growth of grasses; therefore, it is especially important during the establishment of the turf. Normally, phosphorus is applied in the spring or fall.

1. **Superphosphate**—Superphosphate contains 20% phosphoric acid (P_2O_5) and is the most important source of phosphorus for turf fertilization.

2. **Trebel superphosphate**—Trebel superphosphate contains 45% phosphoric acid (P_2O_5) and is widely used for turf fertilization.

3. **Basic slag**—Basic slag is a product of the steel industry and usually contains 10-12% phosphoric acid (P_2O_5). It also contains a small amount of magnesium and manganese.

C. **Potassium fertilizers**—Turfgrasses use more potassium than any other nutrients with the exception of nitrogen. High potassium levels increase the cold and heat hardiness of grasses. High potassium levels also decrease the incidence of several diseases including brown patch and dollar spot.

1. **Muriate of potash** (potassium chloride)—Muriate of potash contains 60% K_2O and is probably the most widely used of any potassium fertilizer on turf. It is water soluble and readily available to the plant.

2. **Potassium nitrate**—Potassium nitrate as the name implies is also a nitrogen source. It contains 44% K_2O and 13% nitrogen and is highly water soluble.

3. **Potassium sulfate**—Potassium sulfate usually contains 48% K_2O and a significant amount of sulfur which may be of great benefit to the turf if there is a sulfur deficiency.

D. **Other essential nutrient fertilizers**—There are 10 essential nutrient fertilizers that are used less frequently than the nitrogen, phosphorus, and potassium fertilizers that we have discussed. These secondary elements are: calcium; magnesium; sulfur; iron; manganese; zinc; copper; molybdenum; boron; and chlorine. These 10 elements are applied much less frequently because turfgrasses only require small amounts of them and because many soils contain enough of the nutrients to meet the requirements of the grass plants. If a secondary or micro nutrient deficiency is suspected, a specialty fertilizer can be applied that contains all of these nutrients.

E. **Mixed fertilizers**—Mixed fertilizers contain two or more nutrients, usually nitrogen, phosphorus, or potassium. The formation of these fertilizers may vary from simply bulk mixing of the nutrients to a more complexed process requiring strict control of temperature and chemicals. In some cases, mixed fertilizers which contain nitrogen, phosphorus and potassium also contain calcium, magnesium and sulfur that may not be indicated on the label. Most athletic turf is fertilized with a mixed fertilizer at least one time a growing season. Examples of mixed fertilizers are: 8-8-8; 13-13-13; 8-24-24; and 0-20-20.

F. **Calculating fertilizer rates**—Most fertilizer recommendations are expressed as so many pounds of nitrogen (N), phosphoric acid (P_2O_5), or potash (K_2O) per 1000 square feet. To obtain the number of pounds of fertilizer that should be applied, divide the number of pounds of fertilizer needed by the percent of the fertilizer source used. For example, if one pound of nitrogen per 1000 square feet of ammonium nitrate is recommended, how many pounds of ammonium nitrate should be applied? Since ammonium nitrate contains 34% nitrogen, you divide 34% into 1.0 pound which will give you approximately three pounds. You would apply three pounds of ammonium nitrate per 1000 square feet.

Example 1.

> Assume: Need two pounds nitrogen per 1000 square feet. Use ureaformaldehyde (38%)

$$\frac{rate}{\%} = \frac{2}{38} = 5.26 \text{ pounds per 1000 square feet.}$$

Example 2.

> Assume: Need four pounds phosphorus (P_2O_5) per 1000 square feet. Use 0-20-20.

$$\frac{rate}{\%} = \frac{4}{.20} = 20 \text{ pounds per 1000 square feet.}$$

Example 3.

> Assume: Need three pounds potassium (K_2O) per 1000 square feet. Use muriate of potash (60%)

$$\frac{rate}{\%} = \frac{3}{.60} = 5 \text{ pounds per 1000 square feet.}$$

Most turf fertilization recommendations are given in terms of the amount required per 1000 square feet. These rates can be converted into acre rates by multiplying the amount recommended for 1000 square feet by 43. Note: there are 43,560 square feet in an acre.

G. **Soil reaction—pH**—Soil reaction is the degree of acidity or alkalinity of a soil and is expressed as a pH value. Soils with pH values below 7 are considered acid or "sour", while soils with pH values above 7 are considered alkaline or "sweet". Soil reaction has many effects on turfgrass growth such as the availability of other plant nutrients, root growth, and microorganisms. Most soils pH values range from 4.5 to 8.5. Turfgrasses have different pH requirements but most grow best in the pH range of 6 to 7.

1. **Liming**—Lime is usually the material added to acid soils to increase their pH. Agriculture limestone and hydrated lime are the two most widely used liming materials on athletic turf. Agriculture limestone can be one of two types: calcium carbonate (calcitic limestone) or magnesium carbonate (dolomitic limestone). There are two types of hydrated lime: calcium hydroxide and magnesium carbonate. They rank second only to the limestones as the most commonly used sources of liming materials. Hydrated lime has about 20 to 30 percent more neutralizing ability than calcium carbonate. The amount of lime required to raise the soil pH to a certain level depends on soil acidity and soil texture and should be determined by a soil test.

2. **Correcting alkaline soil conditions**—A decline in turfgrass vigor may occur if the soil pH is above 7.5. This condition is usually the result of a deficiency of one or several of the micronutrients such as zinc, copper, or iron. To correct alkaline soil conditions, that is to lower the pH, sulfur may be applied to the soil. The amount of sulfur to apply to the soil should be determined by a soil test.

H. **Soil testing**—Baseball fields should be soil tested every two or three years to determine pH, phosphorus, and potassium levels. Some laboratories also have tests for calcium, magnesium, and a few micronutrients. All land grant universities either have or can recommend a nearby soil testing laboratory. It is important to obtain a representative sample of soil for the laboratory. Normally, the standard sampling procedure involves taking 12-15 one inch diameter soil cores at random from the field as shown in Figure 2. The infield may be sampled separately if desired. The core sample should be two to four inches in depth depending upon the recommendation of the particular soil testing laboratory being used. One to two pints of soil is usually required for analysis. Soil sample boxes and sampling instructions are available from most soil testing laboratories.

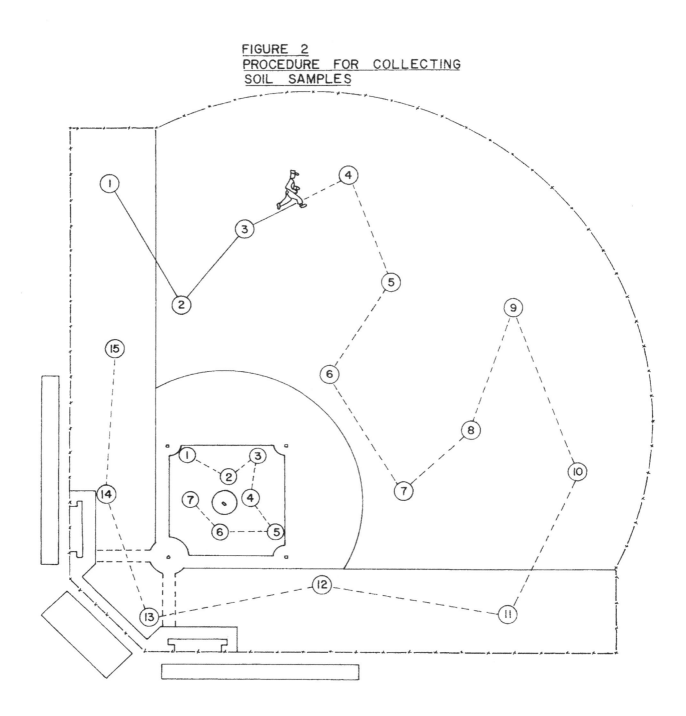

FIGURE 2
PROCEDURE FOR COLLECTING
SOIL SAMPLES

508

I. **Fertilization programs**—Proper turfgrass fertilization begins with a soil test to determine pH, phosphorus, and potassium levels. A complete fertilizer should be applied at least once and sometimes twice a year along with enough lime to maintain proper pH. Tables 2-5 are sample fertilization programs for bermudagrass and zoysiagrass fields. Tables 6 and 7 are sample fertilization programs for bluegrass fields. Please note that these are only examples and should not be interpreted as recommendations.

J. **Fertilizer application equipment**—There are two basic types of fertilizer spreaders, the rotary type and the drop type. Both types are available in various sizes ranging from small push units to large tractor mounted or drawn units. The rotary type spreader covers a wider area and is more widely used than the drop type spreader. Problems of skips or overlaps are minimized with the rotary spreader. The drop type spreader gives very uniform distribution, but covers a limited area. Overlapping and skipped areas are the major disadvantages of this unit.

4. Weed control

The best form of weed control is a strong healthy turf. Weak, thin turf is an invitation for weeds to invade your field. To prevent weeds from becoming a problem, you should: (1) mow properly; (2) have an adequate fertilization program; (3) have a good insect and disease program; and (4) water properly. When weeds are a problem, they must be controlled with the use of herbicides.

A. **Warm season turf weed control**—Weeds in southern turfgrasses occur in both summer and winter and are of two general types: grassy weeds and broadleaf weeds.

1. **Summer grassy weeds**—This includes such grasses as crabgrass, dallisgrass, and goosegrass. These weeds may be controlled with one of the arsonates herbicides, MSMA or DSMA. Two or three applications applied at seven to ten day intervals in the month of May or when day temperatures reach the mid 80's will be necessary for complete control. As with all herbicides, the recommended rate on the label should be used, mixed with enough water to provide sufficient coverage. Normally, 20-25 gallons of water per acre will give sufficient coverage.

2. **Winter broadleaf weeds**—This includes such weeds as henbit, chickweed, clovers, dandelion, wild onion and wild garlic. These weeds may be controlled with the recommended rate of 2,4-D + MCPP, 2,4-D + dicamba or 2,4-D + MCPP + dicamba. Applications can be made in November and March.

3. **Summer broadleaf weeds**—These as a group are difficult to control and require multiple applications of 2,4-D + MCPP, 2,4-D + dicamba, or 2,4-D + MCPP and dicamba. Weeds in this group include ground ivy, Florida betony, knotweed, spurge, and pennywort.

4. **Annual bluegrass**—This is the number one grassy weed in southern turf. This little pesty weed may be controlled with pre-emergence herbicides such as bensulide (Betasan), benefin (Triflan), or DCPA (Dathal). If these pre-emergence herbicides are to be used on an overseeded field, they must be applied 60-90 days prior to overseeding to avoid injury to the overseeded grass. The herbicide, pronamide (Kerb), will give both pre-emergence and post-emergence control of annual bluegrass. It may be applied from November to April. It should be noted that pronamide can not be applied to overseeded turf. Another method of controlling annual bluegrass is with a non-selective herbicide such as paraquat or cacodylic acid. These herbicides must be applied during the dormant season, usually January or February to prevent injury to the bermudagrass.

B. **Cool season turf weed control**—Weeds in cool season turf are generally divided into two broad groups: broadleaf weeds and grassy weeds.

1. **Broadleaf weeds**—This includes such weeds as henbit, plantians, dandelion, chickweed, knotweed, wild onion, and wild garlic to name a few. Most of these broadleaf weeds can be controlled with a 2,4-D + MCPP or 2,4-D + dicamba herbicide combination. Trees and shrubs are readily injured by these herbicides and should be protected.

2. **Grassy weeds**—Crabgrass, timothy, orchard, bromegrass, and annual bluegrass are examples of grassy weeds in cool season turfs. Crabgrass can be controlled with a pre-emergence herbicide such as bensulide (Betasan), benefin (Triflan), or DCPA (Dathal) applied in the spring. MSMA or DSMA used as a post-emergence herbicide will also control crabgrass. The non-selective herbicides paraquat and cacodylic acid may be used to remove timothy, brome, and orchard grasses. Care should be taken not to apply these herbicides on desirable turf.

Table 2. Sample fertilization program for Bermudagrass, Zoysiagrass Baseball Field using 100% soluble nitrogen.

Date	Source	N	P$_2$O$_5$	K$_2$O	Rate 1000 sq. ft.
Mar. 15 to Apr. 15	13-13-13*	1.3	1.3	1.3	10
May 15-20	Ammonium Nitrate	1.0	0	0	3
June 15-20	Ammonium Nitrate	1.0	0	0	3
July 15-20	Ammonium Nitrate	1.0	0	0	3
August 15-20	Ammonium Nitrate	1.0	0	0	3
Sept. 15-20	Ammonium Nitrate	1.0	0	0	3
Oct. 1-15	8-24-24	.8	2.4	2.4	10
		7.1	3.7	3.7	

*Actual analysis should be based on soil test.

Table 3. Sample fertilization program for overseeded Bermudagrass, Zoysiagrass Baseball Field using 100% soluble N (nitrogen).

Date	Source	N	P$_2$O$_5$	K$_2$O	Rate 1000 sq. ft.
Mar. 15 to Apr. 15	13-13-13*	1.3	1.3	1.3	10
May 15-20	Ammonium Nitrate	1.0	0	0	3
June 15-20	Ammonium Nitrate	1.0	0	0	3
July 15-20	Ammonium Nitrate	1.0	0	0	3
August 15-20	Ammonium Nitrate	1.0	0	0	3
Sept. 15-20	Ammonium Nitrate	1.0	0	0	3
Oct. 1-15	8-24-24	8	2.4	2.4	10
Dec. 1-5	Ammonium Nitrate	1.0	0	0	3
Jan. 15-20	Ammonium Nitrate	1.0	0	0	3
March 1-5	Ammonium Nitrate	1.0	0	0	3
		10.1	3.7	3.7	

*Actual analysis should be based on soil test.

Table 4. Sample fertilization program for Bermudagrass, Zoysiagrass Baseball Field using slow release nitrogen.

Date	Source	N	P$_2$O$_5$	K$_2$O	Rate 1000 sq. ft.
April 1 to 15	16-4-8*	1.6	.4	.8	10
May 15-20	Ureaform	2.0	0	0	5
July 1-5	Ureaform	2.0	0	0	5
August 15-20	Ureaform	1.5	0	0	4
October 1-5	8-24-24	.8	2.4	2.4	10
		7.9	2.8	3.2	

*Actual analysis should be based on soil test.

510

Table 5. Sample fertilization program for overseeded Bermudagrass, Zoysiagrass Baseball Field using slow release nitrogen.

Date	Source	N	P_2O_5	K_2O	Rate 1000 sq. ft.
April 1-15	16-4-8*	1.6	.4	.8	10
May 15-20	Ureaform	2.0	0	0	5
July 1-5	Ureaform	2.0	0	0	5
August 15-20	Ureaform	1.5	0	0	4
October 1-5	8-24-24	.8	2.4	2.4	10
December 1-5	Ureaform	1.5	0	0	2.6
February 1-5	Ureaform	1.5	0	0	2.6
		10.9	2.8	3.2	

*Actual analysis should be based on soil test.

Table 6. Sample fertilization program for Kentucky Bluegrass Baseball Field using 100% soluble nitrogen.

Date	Source	N	P_2O_5	K_2O	Rate 1000 sq. ft.
March 15 - April 15	13-13-13*	1.3	1.3	1.3	10
May 15-20	Ammonium Nitrate	1.0	0	0	3
June 15-20	Ammonium Nitrate	1.0	0	0	3
Sept. 15-20	13-13-13	1.3	1.3	1.3	10
Oct. 15-20	Ammonium Nitrate	1.0	0	0	3
		5.6	2.6	2.6	

*Actual analysis should be based on soil test.

Table 7. Sample fertilization program for Kentucky Bluegrass Baseball Field using slow release nitrogen.

Date	Source	N	P_2O_5	K_2O	Rate 1000 sq. ft.
March 15 - April 15	16-4-8*	1.6	.4	.8	10
May 15-20	Ureaform	2.0	.0	.0	5
September 15-20	Ureaform	2.0	.0	.0	5
October 15-20	8-24-24	.8	2.4	2.4	10
		6.4	2.8	3.2	

*Actual analysis should be based on soil test.

5. Sprayer equipment

Small hand sprayers with a capacity of one to three gallons may be used in certain cases such as applying non-selective herbicide to the skinned area of the infield. These sprayers are simple and economical.

Low pressure boom type sprayers with fan type nozzles are best suited for applying herbicides. Various length booms with interchangeable nozzles are available.

Herbicides or other pesticides should never be applied without first calibrating the sprayer that is to be used. It is best to calibrate the sprayer each time pesticides are to be applied to your field. High rates of pesticides are not only environmentally dangerous, but can cause disastrous results to your field. There are many different methods of calibrating sprayers. We will describe one of the easiest and most fool proof methods.

A. Adjust tractor speed, pressure, and spray tip size according to manufacturer's recommendations. A safe speed between 2.5 and 4.5 m.p.h. should be chosen. Most sprayers operate best at 25 to 50 psi pressure.

B. Measure off one acre (43,560 square feet) of the field.

C. Fill the sprayer tank with water. Spray the acre selected with water. Mark throttle and pressure settings. Remember the gear that was used.

D. Measure the amount of water required to fill the tank. This is the number of gallons of water applied per acre.

E. Add correct amount of pesticide to the tank.

F. Remember to use the same throttle, pressure, and gear settings as was used in calibrating.

6. Insect control

Insects may cause significant injury to baseball fields. The extent of the injury depends on environmental conditions and insect populations. It is important that the injurious insects be identified before insecticides are applied. If you are not sure of the identity of the insect, then a turf specialist or entomologist should be consulted.

A. **Sod webworms**—These are a major insect pest in warm season grasses and can also be a problem in cool season grasses. Sod webworms are the larvae of lawn moths. They are about three-quarter inches long when mature and are light brown to greenish in color. These insects feed in small round patches on the leaves and stems of the grass plant. They feed only at night. During the day they live in a silk web below the soil surface—hence, the name sod webworm.

B. **Armyworms**—These are also larvae of moths. They are about one and one-half inches long when mature or about twice as long as sod webworms. Usually armyworms are green with black stripes down each side of the body and one stripe down the middle of the back with an inverted V on their heads. They feed only during the day. Large populations of armyworms may devour all the leaves of the grass, leaving large circular bare areas.

Control of sod webworms and armyworms—The field should be mowed and watered prior to applying insecticides if possible. Insecticides are more effective if applied two to three hours before darkness when the pests are more active. Some of the insecticides which are effective in controlling sod webworms and armyworms are: (1) 25% diazinon EC; (2) 50% carbaryl (Sevin) WP; (3) 22.4% Dursban EC; and (4) 60% taxaphene EC, and zectran EC. See label on insecticide container for recommended rate. Apply insecticides in 50-100 gallons of water per acre.

C. **Grubs**—These insects may damage both cool season and warm season grasses. They are the larval stage of a large number of beetles (May, June, Japanese, etc.). Heavy infestation of grubs damage grasses by feeding on the roots, thus turning the grasses brown and eventually killing the grass. Large populations of grubs will result in entire areas of turf being destroyed.

Control of grubs—Insecticides for control of grubs should be applied in the spring or fall. Turf should be watered after the insecticide has been applied in order to wash the material down into the roots of the grass. Because of the location of the grubs, control may require one month or longer. Some of the recommended insecticides for grub control are: (1) 25% diazinon EC; and (2) 40.5% Dylox L.S. Apply 100 to 150 gallons of water per acre. Check label on insecticide container for recommended rate.

D. **Mole crickets**—These insects occasionally cause damage to grasses, especially bermudagrass. Newly seeded or sprigged areas are usually hardest hit. The mole cricket has modified shovel like front legs that enables them to make burrows in the turf. They feed on the young roots of the grass. Considerable damage may be done to the turf area if these insects are not controlled.

7. Disease control

Turfgrass diseases are the most difficult of the turf pests to identify. If the identity of the disease is not known, a turf specialist or plant pathologist should be consulted. The best disease control procedure is a good fertility program and sound cultural practices.

A. **Dollar spot**—This disease will attack most all turfgrasses, but is especially severe on bermudagrass, Kentucky bluegrass, and the fine leaf fescues. This disease occurs in small round spots about the size of a silver dollar. The spots may merge to form large irregular areas. The diseased turf is usually straw colored. The disease may spread until large areas have been destroyed.

Control of dollar spot—Adequate nitrogen fertilization will help to control the disease. The fungicides Benemyl (Benlate), Daconil, and Dyrene are recommended for control of dollar spot. Use the recommended rate on the label with 100-150 gallons of water per acre.

B. **Helminthisporium leaf spot or melting out**—Melting out is the common name given to a number of helminthisporium diseases that attack a number of turfgrasses including Kentucky bluegrass, red fescue, tall fescue, annual ryegrass, perennial ryegrass, and bermudagrass. The symptoms of this disease are small circular to elongated spots on the leaves. These spots first appear as water soaked areas and later become dark colored. The center of the spot becomes brown or straw colored as the spot enlarges. The upper part of the leaf dies if the spot extends across the entire leaf. The infection may spread to the stems and crowns of the plant. This results in a thinning or "melting out" of the turf in small, irregular areas.

Control of melting out—The use of resistant turfgrass varieties may be the best means of control. For example, Merion Kentucky bluegrass is highly resistant to melting out. A turfgrass specialist in your area should be consulted for assistance in selecting a resistant variety for your needs. Unfortunately, it is not possible to use resistant varieties in many cases; therefore, the disease must be treated with fungicides. Thiram, Daconil, and Captan have been found to be effective in controlling melting out. These fungicides should be applied at the recommended rate on the label with 150-200 gallons of water per acre.

C. **Pythium blight**—This is a disease found primarily on cool season grasses but has been known to occur on bermudagrass. It is especially a problem on fields overseeded with ryegrass in the South. It appears as spots ranging in diameter from less than one inch to several inches. A cottony growth of mycelium can usually be seen on the infected plants early in the morning. The plants then take on a dark, water soaked, greasy appearance and die within hours. The spread of the disease is very rapid covering large irregular areas.

Control of pythium blight—Since adequate moisture is necessary for growth of the pythium fungus, avoid overwatering during warm weather. Overseeded fields should be seeded as late as possible in the fall to avoid favorable conditions for pythium growth. Pythium blight is difficult to control with fungicides. However, the materials terrazole and chloroneb have been found to be effective in the control of this disease. Apply the recommended rate on label in 150-200 gallons of water per acre every seven days as needed.

D. **Fairy ring**—All turfgrasses are susceptible to fairy ring. The first symptom of this fungus disease is a small circle of dark green grass. Later the circle enlarges and mushrooms may appear around the circle. The grass on the inside and outside of the circle may die. The circle may increase in size until it is several feet in diameter. The fungus that causes this disease lives on decaying organic matter such as logs and stumps which are buried in the soil. The dark green grass in the fairy ring is due to the breaking down of this organic matter resulting in the release of nitrogen.

Control of fairy ring—Eradication of this disease is almost impossible. There are no effective fungicides available for control of this disease. As the organic matter in the soil is used up, the fairy ring will disappear, but this may take several years. The dark green can be made less conspicuous by applying a nitrogen fertilizer.

E. **Nematodes**—All turfgrasses are susceptible to nematodes. Nematodes are microscopic animals that range in length from 1/10 to about 1/75 inch. These small eel worm-like animals feed on the roots of the grass causing a yellowing and thinning of the turf. The turf will not respond to fertilizer. The root system of the grass is also weakened thus causing the grass to be more susceptible to other diseases.

Control of nematodes—If nematodes are suspected on your field, have a nematode analysis made. Your local county or area extension specialist can assist you in taking a sample of soil for analysis. Both granular and liquid nematicides are available. Prior to applying the nematicide, the field should be irrigated to a depth of six to eight inches if possible. Preferably the temperature should be between 60 and 80 degrees fahrenheit at the time of application. Immediately after application the field should be irrigated with one-half to one inch of water to move the material into the root system of the grass. A foliar burn may result if this irrigation is not done. Remember, do not apply a nematicide without the advice of a specialist and after taking a nematode analysis.

F. **Spring dead spot**—This is a disease of well maintained bermudagrass turf. The disease is most severe in the northern half of the bermudagrass belt. In the early spring when bermudagrass begins regrowth, well defined circular dead areas are evident in the turf. These spots may vary in size from a very few inches to several feet in diameter.

Control of spring dead spot—At the present time the causal agent of this program is not known. The general control measures are: a well balanced fertility program; good cultural practices; and good thatch control. Also if a field has a history of spring dead spot, it is advisable to have a small nursery planted so that ample grass will be available for sprigging and resodding.

8. Cultivation practices

Turfgrass cultivation may be defined as tilling turf by mechanical methods without significantly disturbing the surface of the turf. Turf cultivation helps relieve soil compaction, improves air and water exchange in the soil, reduces water run off by increasing water penetration, and increases the penetration of fertilizers. This all adds up to a deeper and healthier root system. There are two basic types of cultivation methods used for baseball fields. These methods are aerification and vertical mowing.

A. **Aerification**—This can be done by three different methods: hollow tine; spoon tine; and slicing tine:

1. **Hollow tine**—The hollow tine removes soil cores and thus leaves a small hole in the sod ranging in size from 3/8 to 3/4 inch in diameter and three to four inches deep. On baseball fields these cores are usually broken up by dragging with a steel mat. There is very little damage to the surface of the turf with a hollow tine.

2. **Spoon tine**—The spoon or semi-open tine is used when more severe renovation of the soil surface is needed. The tine enters the soil in an arc and loosens more soil than the hollow tine.

3. **Slicing tine**—The slicing tine is a V-shaped knife, usually four to six inches long, that provides a deep, narrow groove in the soil. Very little or no damage is done to the sod surface since no soil is removed.

More aerifiers used on baseball fields are tractor mounted or tractor drawn units. Cool season grasses are normally aerified in the spring and fall while warm season grasses are aerified in the spring and summer. Usually fields should be aerified two to four times per year.

B. **Vertical mowing**—This is another form of cultivation that involves the use of rotating vertical knives or blades that cut into the sod and in some cases, down to the soil. Vertical mowing is commonly used to control thatch and in preparation for overseeding. Spring time is usually the best time to vertical mow when removing thatch. Materials deposited on the surface must be removed by sweeping or vacuuming after vertical mowing.

9. Topdressing

Topdressing is the applying of a thin layer of especially prepared soil mix or sand to a turf area. Masonry sand is used mostly for topdressing baseball fields. Topdressing is used for thatch control and leveling turf surfaces. Normally, a self-propelled topdressing machine is used to work the material into the turf. The rate of topdressing is usually 1/8 to 1/4 inches in depth or .40 or .77 cubic yards of material per 1000 square feet. The frequency of topdressing ranges from none to three to four times a year, depending on the amount of thatch present and if the playing surface is level. Usually only the infield and selected areas are topdressed due to the cost of the topdressing material and the amount of labor required to apply the material.

10. Thatch

Thatch is the layer of undecomposed stems and roots that lies between the soil surface and vegetative green portion of the grass. This thatch or mat as it is sometimes called creates many problems including: (1) increased disease and insect problems; (2) scalping; (3) dry spots; and (4) foot printing.

Thatch can be caused by: (1) high nitrogen fertilization; (2) infrequent mowing; (3) high mowing height; (4) low pH; and (5) fast growing turfgrass species.

Thatch may be controlled by aerification, vertical mowing, and topdressing. Proper mowing, moderate fertilization, and liming will also aid in eliminating thatch problems.

11. Irrigation and irrigation equipment

Baseball fields should be watered when the grass begins to wilt. As a general rule, it is best to irrigate in the early morning. This may not always be possible because of the heavy use of the field. In this case, the field would have to be watered at night. The field should be watered as far in advance of scheduled games and practices as possible to avoid soil compaction due to intense traffic. Irrigation frequency is determined by soil types and climate. For example, irrigating one time per week on a clay soil field in a cool humid climate may be adequate, but this may be inadequate on a sandy soil field in a hot, arid climate. If possible, the field should be watered long enough to permit wetting of the root zone, which is normally at least six to eight inches. Deep and infrequent watering encourages deep rooting and results in a stronger, healthier turf. Shallow, frequent watering results in a shallow root system, which of course results in a weak turf. Overwatering should be avoided also. This results in a loss of turfgrass vigor which becomes more subject to diseases, weeds, insects, and damage from traffic.

Irrigation equipment may vary from a three-quarter inch hose with a single sprinkler to a complex automatic irrigation system complete with pop-up rotary sprinkler heads and time clocks. Many managers use traveling sprinklers for irrigation. This unit is mounted on wheels, and is driven by water power. On some models the rate of travel may be adjusted.

There are two basic types of sprinkler irrigation systems: the manual system and the automatic system. The manual system involves the use of personnel to move quick coupler sprinkler heads and hoses. The initial cost of a manual system is lower than an automatic system, but the annual cost of operation is higher because of the labor required. An automatic system uses time clocks to remotely control pop-up sprinkler heads. With an automatic system, the manager may preset the system to irrigate as long and often as necessary with little or no labor required. Figure 3 on the next page shows the automatic irrigation system for Dudy Noble Field at Mississippi State University.

12. Overseeding baseball fields in the South

Many baseball fields in the Southeast and Southwest are overseeded with cool season grasses in the fall to provide a green turf and a better playing surface in the winter and spring during the baseball season. Procedures for overseeding are as follows:

A. Around September 15, apply to the field three to four pounds of phosphate and potash plus any lime that is needed. The phosphate and potash is usually supplied from 0-20-20 or 8-24-24 fertilizer, applied at the rate of 15-20 pounds per 1000 square feet.

B. Between October 1-15, lower mowing height to 5/8 to 7/8 inch and remove clippings with a sweeper or vacuum. It may also be necessary to vertical mow at this time. It is best to wait until fall practice is complete before beginning overseeding procedures if possible, but overseeding should be completed by November 15th, regardless.

FIGURE 3

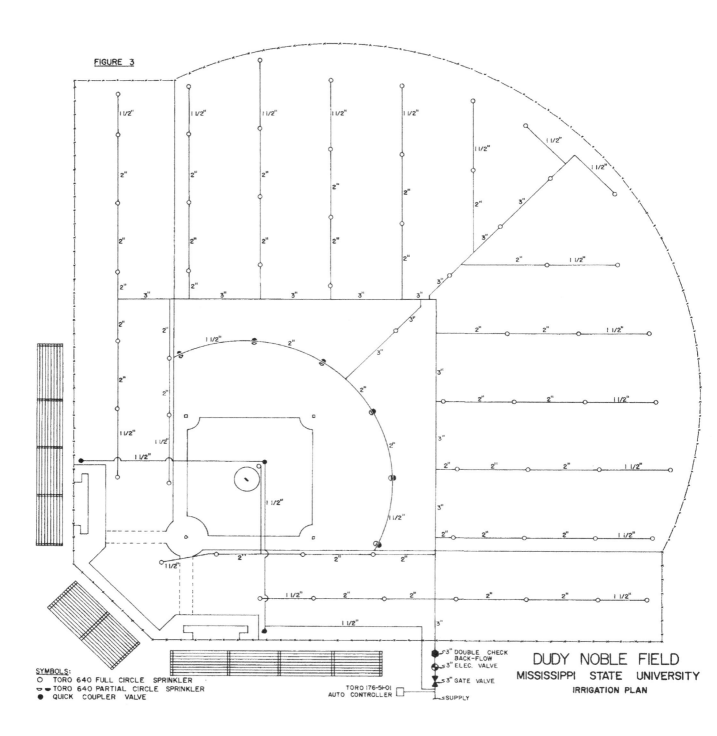

SYMBOLS:
○ TORO 640 FULL CIRCLE SPRINKLER
◡ ◡ TORO 640 PARTIAL CIRCLE SPRINKLER
● QUICK COUPLER VALVE

TORO 176-5I-OI
AUTO CONTROLLER

3" DOUBLE CHECK BACK-FLOW
3" ELEC. VALVE
3" GATE VALVE
SUPPLY

DUDY NOBLE FIELD
MISSISSIPPI STATE UNIVERSITY
IRRIGATION PLAN

C. Apply seed in three to four different directions with a rotary type spreader. In most cases, annual ryegrass or perennial ryegrass is best for overseeding baseball fields. These grasses should be seeded at the rate of 10-20 pounds per 1000 square feet. Annual ryegrass should be used only when your budget will not allow you to purchase perennial ryegrass. Annual ryegrass is susceptible to pythium blight, requires more nitrogen fertilization, is less cold tolerant, requires more frequent mowing, is more succulent which results in poor footing, and has less wear tolerance than perennial ryegrass. As you might expect, the major disadvantage of perennial ryegrass is the cost of the seed. It is four to five times more expensive than annual ryegrass seed. Some of the better turf-type perennial ryegrass cultivars are: Medalist 5; Derby; Manhattan; Pennfine; and Yorktown.

D. Topdress with 1/8 inch of topsoil or sand if possible. Normally, only the infield and selected high traffic areas are topdressed because of the amount of labor and topdressing material required. Topdressing results in a thicker, more uniform stand of overseeded grass.

E. Irrigate field two to three times each day until germination is complete. Irrigation is the key to a good stand of overseeded turf, especially on those fields planted late in the fall.

F. Mow at 1-1½ inches in height every 7-10 days as needed. Around February 1st, lower mowing height to ⅞-1 inch depending upon the wishes of the baseball coach.

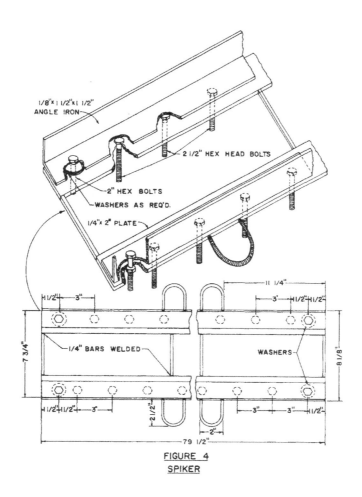

FIGURE 4
SPIKER

517

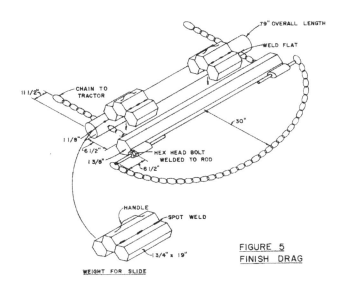

79" OVERALL LENGTH
WELD FLAT
CHAIN TO TRACTOR
II 1/2"
I I/8"
6 I/2"
I 3/8"
HEX HEAD BOLT WELDED TO ROD
6 I/2"
30"
HANDLE
SPOT WELD
I 3/4" x 19"
WEIGHT FOR SLIDE

FIGURE 5
FINISH DRAG

NON-TURFGRASS MAINTENANCE

1. Skinned area of the infield

Crushed brick is used in some areas of the country because it provides a good playing surface, is easy to maintain, and provides a good contrast in color with the green grass. Crushed brick requires a minimum amount of dragging and leveling.

Soil skinned areas are more commonly used and require more maintenance. A spiker (Figure 4) should be used when the surface dries out and becomes hard. A small tractor or turf vehicle is used to pull the spiker. A drag is used to do the finish leveling of the skinned area. Steel mats, chain link fence sections, sections of carpet, and various other devices have been used as drags on baseball infields. Figure 5 shows an example of the type of drag that might be used. Care should be taken not to drag soil onto the turf area so that a soil buildup or "lip" will not be created in the turf area adjacent to the skinned area. If a severe "lip" develops in the turf area, it may be removed by performing the following steps: (1) remove four to six feet of sod with a sod cutter; (2) remove excess soil with tractor and box scraper (remember to allow for thickness of sod); (3) till and level area; (4) replace sod; and (5) water sod each day by hand until grass has completely rooted.

2. Base paths

Base paths should be hand raked at the time of the dragging of the infield if possible. Be careful not to rake soil onto the turf area to avoid a soil buildup.

3. Pitcher's mound

Prior to practice or a game, the mound should be reworked by leveling with a rake and tamped with a hand tamper. Sprinkle on a small amount of water to make the area firm. Water may need to be added before tamping. If the mound is not firm enough a small amount of clay may need to be mixed with the soil.

4. Home plate area and bullpens

The batter's box, catcher's box, and bullpens should be maintained the same as the pitcher's mound.

5. Coaches' box and fungo circles

Coaches' boxes and fungo circles should be smoothed and leveled with a hand rake.

518

6. Warning track

Warning tracks should be maintained in somewhat the same manner as the infield. If the warning track is made of soil, then it should be spiked and dragged as needed. If it is made of crushed brick or cinders, then it will only need dragging and raking occasionally.

7. Marking the field

A. **Lines**—Care should be taken to make all lines neat and sharp. This adds to the appearance of the field. The infield baselines, home plate boxes, coaches' boxes, and fungo circles are usually lined with calcium carbonate (lime), which is sold under various trade names. There are several machines on the market that can be used to apply the calcium carbonate. The foul lines on the outfield grass can be painted with white paint or lined with calcium carbonate. The painted line is longer lasting and is better accepted by coaches, players and umpires. Special sprayers are available for applying the paint.

B. **Batter's box and catcher's box**—A frame similar to the one in Figure 6 should be used in marking off the batter's box and catcher's box. Calcium carbonate should be placed between the two frames by hand. Special care should be taken to make sure the frame is lined up correctly with home plate.

8. Covers for pitcher's mound and home plate area

Nylon or plastic covers should be used to cover the pitcher's mound and home plate area in the event of rain. These covers can be held in place by old tires, etc., or staked down at the corners with spikes. Covers for the entire field (160 feet by 160 feet) are available and provide the ultimate in protection against the elements. Care should be taken that the turf under the cover is not injured by heat build up. The cover should be removed as soon as possible to avoid injury to the turf.

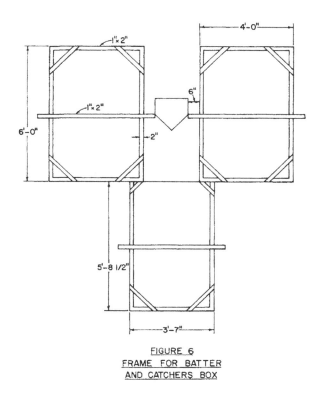

FIGURE 6
FRAME FOR BATTER
AND CATCHERS BOX

9. Pitcher's mound mat and home plate mat

A mat can provide protection for the pitcher's mound during batting practice. A five feet by ten feet piece of artificial turf, old carpet, or piece of plastic mat can be used for this purpose. It should be staked down at the corners with spikes.

Some coaches (managers) use a piece of artificial turf or nylon cover in front of the home plate area during batting practice to protect the turf area from abuse. This practice can be very beneficial especially in the winter and early spring. Care should be taken not to injure the turf by heat build up while it is under the mat.

10. Drying materials

For many years, calcinated clay has been the standard material used for drying infields. However, recently a new product made from ground corn cobs called Diamond Dry has been marketed and promises to be a superior product. It has a tremendous absorption ratio. It contains 100% organic matter; therefore, there can not be a harmful build up in the soil as with calcinated clay. Diamond Dry should be sprinkled over the wet areas, allowed to dry and then raked with a garden rake.

Made in United States
North Haven, CT
29 March 2024

50607867R10291